UGLY DUCKLING PRESSE :: DOSSIER

*Sixty Morning Talks*
Copyright © 2014 by Andy Fitch

ISBN 978-1-937027-20-9

Distributed to the trade by
SPD / Small Press Distribution
spdbooks.org

First Edition, First Printing
Printed and bound at McNaughton & Gunn
Designed by goodutopian
Some of these interviews were previously published
in *The Conversant*.

Ugly Duckling Presse
The Old American Can Factory
232 Third Street #E-303
Brooklyn, NY 11215

Funded in part by a grant from
the National Endowment for the Arts

NATIONAL
ENDOWMENT
FOR THE ARTS

uglyducklingpresse.org

# Andy Fitch
# SIXTY MORNING TALKS

With an Afterword by Amaranth Borsuk

## SIXTY MORNING TALKS
11


## AFTERWORD
Amaranth Borsuk
501


## INDEX OF INTERVIEWEES
504

For the interviewees and their publishers, for Anna Moschovakis, and for Maia Spotts—champ transcriber.

# SIXTY MORNING TALKS

INTERVIEW WITH AMARANTH BORSUK
Recorded on April 30, 2012
This interview focuses on Amaranth Borsuk and Brad Bouse's book *Between Page and Screen* (Siglio Press).

ANDY FITCH: Since it probably requires a new form of physical effort from most readers, can you first describe our experience encountering this book?

AMARANTH BORSUK: Sure. When you encounter the book, you find a square-shaped object with a patterned, red-white-and-black block printed at its center. When you open the book, you don't find printed poems, but only more black-and-white symbols. The only text you can read provides author names, mine and Brad Bouse's, and instructions to go to betweenpageandscreen.com, where you can "hold the words in your hands." When you arrive at the website and click on a link, you receive instructions to present one of these black-and-white markers to your webcam. When you do, a live image appears on the computer screen. You see your hands holding the open book, and, once one of those printed markers becomes visible to the webcam, a poem pops vertically off the page. This part resembles a pop-up book, but with text instead of shapes or images. This text stands vertically with respect to the plane of the page. As you turn the book's pages, the projected digital text also turns, so that it seems to hover above a page like a hologram. As you flip the book's pages, poems explode and their letters fly in all directions. And in between epistolary poems (consisting of love letters between P and S) you find concrete poems, anagrammatic or paragrammatic poems, each of which provides a different animation for how it disappears from view.

AF: This quick description could prompt the question, why make a book at all? Digital media already provide a substantial portion of innovative poetic projects. But did you want to make us just as conscious of the printed book as a technology—as a historically conditioned mode of textual interface? Is that part of why "P" sounds just as cagey as "S"? Do we encounter one techno-text talking to another? Does this project survey previous reading models as much as it anticipates future ones?

AB: Brad and I thought through those questions while conceptualizing the project. Our decision to produce a book came from wanting to meditate on the relationship between these two technologies, at a time when both play a huge role in our lives, as we read on both kinds of platforms and develop different capacities from each experience. By offering a physical book object, we meant to make readers conscious of the printed book as a technology. Even a traditional print book that you pull off your shelf has all these built-in cues (visual, lexical) that tell us the order in which to read things; how to hold the book relative to our body; the materials from which this book has been made and, therefore, the social value placed on it. Likewise, digital media, which can seem highly ephemeral, embody us as readers—through our interaction with screen texts, whether touch screens or computer screens connected to a mouse or track pad. All of these physiological/technological determinants embody and transform us as readers, and really dictate how we interact with texts. So *Between Page and Screen* reminds the reader of our relationships with both kinds of reading devices, here by putting an image of the reader on-screen the whole time. You never can escape this vision of yourself interacting with two types of texts. You see your hands, the book object, reflections of yourself (with words flying before your face), all further confirming the materiality of multiple kinds of reading.

AF: That helps to explain why Page and Screen could serve as partners in a love story, rather than Oedipal rivals in some conflict where one replaces the other. But I recall seeing my own reflection interposed between them, feeling like an interloper, a voyeur on the processes of meaning getting shaped. I never had a clear, fixed sense of my own identity in relation to the text.

AB: This aspect of the book did not occur to me until I first performed from it. The first time I gave a reading and found myself vocalizing both Page and Screen, reading their respective parts aloud, holding the book before me, encountering a projected image of my face—finally I realized the awkwardness of that situation. But yes, I feel that the reader's position should stay somewhat voyeuristic. In any epistolary work, you peek in on people's personal letters.

AF: I liked thinking about your title's "Between" as suggesting both some sort of policed division and some illicit correspondence between Page and Screen. But I also appreciated that between the page and the screen appeared blank space, an absence in which the reader must come forward to help construct meaning. I sensed some mirror-stage pun amid these refractive, triangulating constructions.

AB: Yeah, a mirror stage in which the moment of discovery on the reader's part requires not only recognizing the subject in the mirror, but recognizing, in fact, that one's movements get reversed by this mirror one confronts.

AF: That took a while to get used to. Then I wished I'd never gotten used to it because it had been fun.

AB: It does take time. I tend to forget because I've performed this work so often, and become somewhat choreographed in my behavior in the mirror. Though whenever I've watched somebody else interact for the first time with this book, there's that great moment when they want to see a poem more clearly, but instead push the image off-screen. Then they'll learn to play the role of intermediary. They learn to navigate that "between" space. This again demonstrates that our book, or all books, construct behavior and teach us ways of reading.

AF: As I got better at handling the book (placing it at an appropriate angle, manipulating projected letters, etcetera), I considered this project's fourth dimension—its projection into time. I realized extended concentration always had been my primary role in constructing literary meaning, and wondered if you had assigned me this consistent manual labor in order to prompt reflection on reading's temporal obligations.

AB: I like that. Would we call that a synecdoche—for the type of meaning-making labor in which readers constantly engage? Because certainly, as you say, this book's meaning takes shape in the reader. On a very literal level, in order for the text even to appear requires a reader's physical effort. So watching the time pass, watching these textual transformations, does alert you to your situated perspective.

AF: In terms of projecting oneself onto or between the interfaces: a deliberate alternation between Amaranth's text-emphasizing pages, and Brad's design-emphasizing pages, seemed to play out. But was this pure imaginary construct on my part? Did you both engage in unsuspected ways for every component of the compositional process?

AB: Yes, we did both engage throughout, but I find it intriguing that a reader might assume I wrote the parts that look like poems, while Brad designed the pages that seem more visual. In fact, his primary role was as programmer of the piece, and mine was as writer of its words. However, in any collaboration (at least collaborations I've worked on) those lines blur. First we sat down and brainstormed how we wanted this book to operate. In some cases, Brad challenged me to come up with better uses of 3D space for the concrete poems, and in some cases I challenged him to make possible a particular visual conceit. Poems changed based on these conversations—about, let's say, text that moves in a circular procession, around the head of a pin or something. A drawn latticework of words, like the fractal images in Christian Bok's *Crystallography*, doesn't necessarily get enhanced by 3D space. Gorgeous flat surfaces don't necessarily produce dynamic digital texts.

AF: Did you also develop some project-specific design elements as you went along? For example, you've described the disappearance of individual poems as always deliberate and distinct. Did you appreciate this component of textual meaning before you began? Or did you two discover it along the way?

AB: We discovered that along the way. We wanted to highlight ephemerality, so we'd intended to provide a moment of textual destruction between each page turn. But the decision to have the epistles animate out differently than the concrete poems (and then to have the concrete poems offer distinct, text-specific animations) arose as we saw what each screen looked like.

AF: A variety of temporalities exist as we move from page to page. Sometimes the reader sees a square, stable text. For others, words and phrases appear in spinning, prismatic, Ed Ruscha-style simplicity: "pale pawl peel pole." Sometimes letteristic, etymological clusters bounce around in patterns reminiscent of early Steve McCaffrey visual texts, or Brian Kim Stefans' *Dreamlife of Letters*. I wondered if, through these varied temporal experiences, you sought to establish something like the diversity we find in a dynamic collection of poems.

AB: That was on my mind—to show the different ways screen space can be used. A rich body of digital poetics already exists. So in addition to paying homage to concrete poets whose print-based projects had inspired me, I wanted to reference certain digital poets whose work remains quite influential. Pieces like our stock-ticker poem, which scrolls text so that it constantly enters and leaves, create the sense that there is always more text, off-screen, that you don't see, for which you must wait. People like Young-Hae Chang Heavy Industries, or Brian in *Dreamlife*, adopt this notion of restricting the reader's view to the screen space, manipulating the speed at which we read, manipulating our access to this text so that it can't arrive all at once.

AF: You've discussed the book's place in relation to contemporary digital poetics, and to concrete poetry. Can you provide a brief context for a book-arts tradition in which this project fits? And when I think of self-conscious book-arts traditions, I'll picture deliberately archaic practices, like Russian Futurists embracing peasant woodcuts, or William Morris patterning his aesthetic on historically resonant designs. Even the use of photographs more recently in projects by W.G. Sebald or Claudia Rankine or Juliana Spahr seems to draw on the increasingly outmoded status of that medium. So what are other precedents for your particular combination of self-conscious book-arts craftsmanship, and new technological possibilities?

AB: When Brad and I first conceptualized this book, we planned for it to be hand-bound and letterpress-printed. We didn't select hand-set type, which would be even more archaic than having photopolymer plates made. But the process did require me and my dear friend Genevieve Kaplan standing at a Vandercook proof press for several days, inking, turning, making things happen. The printing felt very physical, and we spent quite a bit of money on paper for the first edition. We wanted it to connect to a history of fine press printing, to construct this dialogue between the old and the new, the material and the ephemeral, blurring boundaries between them. So it took a while to realize that my weddedness to those physical (or historical) trappings was not necessarily integral to this project. Still I do feel that this first edition…I love having a limited-edition book on high-quality paper, so that the more you turn its pages, the more gray and ashy their edges become because of oils from your fingers.

AF: It's very delicate? Like a museum piece?

AB: Right. I even considered exhibiting it with a pair of white cotton gloves, which seems pretty standard when you visit archives, or even, in some cases, when you hold artists' books. But Brad kind of stared at me and said, well, do you want it to be this rare object, or to be more about getting people to interact and touch the pages and feel what a fine press book feels like, at the same time that they experience what a futuristic digital book looks like? Of course he was totally right.

AF: I got spooked, actually, when you mentioned white gloves. That does sound like the ghost of a text.

AB: It privileges the book object in a way that this project attempts not to, right? The project wants you to enjoy and interact with both media, and wants their conversation to provide a dialogue that you enter, rather than letting one form take precedence. When people asked us to autograph those limited-edition copies, we didn't, because we worried that would turn the object itself into the valued commodity. And now that this project's available in a trade edition, I think it remains an object, a beautifully designed book, but takes us in a more democratic direction.

AF: That democratic transformation comes across in the trade edition, especially because the book's font and design seem to offer some hybrid Bauhaus/De Stijl/Suprematist aesthetic—even in the squares that get scanned to activate digital text. Did you design those to this purpose? Or did the software require those blocky images?

AB: The software does require that particular blocky image. However, augmented reality can work with other kinds of images, too. We specifically chose to work with FLARToolKit, which relies on those square-shaped markers. I really liked those shapes because of their Bauhaus minimalism and cleanness. I like placing a square within a square, so that the book's shape mirrors the design's shape, with everything centered, concentric. Also each page's text has the same size, the same width, as those square markers, as though a virtual square held the words together. But your primary question had asked about historic precedents. I hope I don't sound like a broken record when I say that Dieter Roth's artist's books have been a big influence. He worked a lot with cutouts, and layering grids on top of one another to create different visual effects. His books construct a kind of temporal experience because of how things change as you turn the pages, as grids line up, as they overlap, as holes appear in different spots. For one project he bound together comic books then drilled holes through the pages. No, I think he drilled the holes before he'd bound them together, so that these holes sort of punctuate his book like Swiss cheese. It's very cool and very strange to read a book that isn't about the text at all—that's really about the visual shape of what text could be.

AF: With Dieter Roth, I always remember an installation of perhaps

100 televisions playing at MoMA, presenting him going about his daily business. Staggered loops simultaneously cycle through the different screens, creating an endless sense of delay. You could see this as a humanist monument to 20th-century technological advance (or surveillance), though what remains for me, from that show, is the static smell of all the old plugged-in televisions—as if I'd sniffed both the birth and death of a post-industrial revolution. Now, as you discuss your book, many projects seem both archaic and futuristic at the same time. Mimeograph work from the '60s seems both an homage to the typewriter, and a precursor to the Xerox.

AB: Another issue this brings up, in the case of, say, Russian Futurists creating their own artists' books (and certainly they take part in the tradition of a democratic distribution of the artist's book), revolves around the particular technologies at one's disposal. They had a letterpress, and they could create their own rubber stamps, and had access to all this discarded wallpaper, so they said let's make books using these techniques we have. When such technologies come into poets' hands, they're already, typically, somewhat behind the times in terms of what's available to industry. Still something about technology coming into writers' hands facilitates and motivates creating books as objects—taking control over this visual aspect of the work. You see that in mid-century poets' and novelists' use of the typewriter. You even see, in Apollinaire's calligrammes, that having access to a typewriter changes how he sees the page. The conclusion to this thought was something like: now that augmented reality provides a technology available outside the realms of large institutions (where you had to wear a helmet and enter an immersive location to experience a holographic interaction with language), now that we can access such interfaces through our mobile devices or laptops, this accessibility enables writers to create work for different technological platforms, and to draw on the idioms of those platforms.

AF: Well in terms of idiom: your sonic constructions remain striking throughout, with heavy emphasis on alliteration and assonance. Lines such as "a screen is a shield, but also a veil—it's sheer and can be shorn" seem to ask to be read aloud. So I'm curious: was silence the selected soundscape for any particular reason, or did the software you used not allow for audio?

AB: Sound definitely would have been possible. But we thought that the reader should play this role of textual performer. The language does call to be read aloud, and we hope some readers read it aloud. You'll find all these resonances—all the abundant alliteration, assonance, which I just can't keep myself from doing. Hearing also emphasizes a distinct voice for each of the characters. So this text definitely has an oral aspect, whether or not it gets vocalized. Even if aural in one's ear, rather than one's mouth, it remains ready, at any moment, to become spoken language.

AF: "Charcuterie" provides the most elaborate verbal text—a source of great pleasure as I sampled from its smorgasbord of language cuts. But the Apollinaire-esque page design, of course, adds to that satisfaction. You've basically already answered this, but does the book say something here about the corporality of text: print, digital, audio, relational?

AB: Definitely. We all know that the word "text" comes from a root related to the body. It surprised me, however, to learn that "screen" comes from an Indo-European word that also gives you "charcuterie," because their root means "to shine." "Charcuterie" relates to the cutting of meat using a shiny instrument. "Text" comes from a root that means "to weave" and also, as secondary meaning, "to shape with an axe." So "text," by definition, describes both creation and destruction. I loved how this carnality of "text" points to creation, generation, the slicing and dicing of language.

AF: One final, potentially dumb question that arose as we talked: what's it like to write a love story with your partner? I mean afterwards.

AB: Well, I can't say that my relationship with my partner influenced the writing of these poems, but I can say it did make for a wonderful collaborative experience, a process that felt generative and positive and rewarding. Brad's work inspires me. And though our relationship doesn't necessarily get reflected in this book's content, I guess the form marries our two fields, mine being language and his digital media. I like how the marriage of two minds gets mirrored in this book's creation.

## INTERVIEW WITH CHRIS SCHMIDT
Recorded on May 1, 2012
This interview focuses on Schmidt's chapbook *Thermae* (EOAGH).

ANDY FITCH: Could we start with waste, the focus of your current scholarly project and a subject that first appears in *Thermae*'s Baudelarian epigraph? Is *Thermae* an outlet—that's a pun in some ways—for your critical study? Did one emerge from the ruins of the other? Does one evolve out of the other? Do they both take on this role?

CHRIS SCHMIDT: They are related. One emerges from the cloaca of the other. Writing *Thermae*, which came after starting the critical text, helped explain to me why I'd landed on this topic of waste, what my transference to it was. *Thermae* connects its waste theme to issues of desire and sexual orientation—concerns that, because of my peculiar development, directed me to think through the idea of the archive. There's a figure named Sagat, a persona that organizes the poem's language, who is this French porn star. But he's almost a stand-in for (this makes the constellation sounds even more bizarre) my first erotic object, the '90s supermodel Linda Evangelista. Maybe they've become alter egos, anima and animus. The obsession with Linda calcified around the time I put a name to my desire. I had this obsession with her fashion photographs and collected all of her magazines, which now live in an archive in Berkeley, California, at a friend's house.

AF: Are these photos framed?

CS: I have a few framed objects, then expandable accordion files (those I kept in New York, alphabetically arranged). Like "A" for Atelier Versace or "V" for Vogue, a very big file. I'll hope that laugh you just gave gets transcribed.

AF: I'd been embarrassed to admit I didn't know who Sagat was.

CS: There's no reason you would.

AF: And I don't know if I'm dumb or straight or sheltered, but I don't know of Linda Evangelista.

CS: Do you know about Naomi Campbell?

AF: Yes.

CS: She's part of the trinity: Naomi Campbell, Christy Turlington, Linda Evangelista. Something about Linda's androgyny, I might say her hyper-mimetic quality in regards to glamour and femininity, attracted me. And for me to buy fashion magazines in the rural Midwest in 1997 truly was a transgressive act. Anyway, Linda seemed sort of a drag queen of a woman though androgynous at the same time, if that makes sense. She showed gender to be this glamorous masquerade of fashion, femininity. She sort of hystericized it. In the same way that Sagat, the porn star...his films don't interest me. I prefer the clips he makes for his blog. He's hyper-masculine, but will put on a pink spandex thong and do some Samantha Fox ultra-camp pantomime that blurs the line between masculine and feminine. The other notable thing, perhaps the first detail to notice, and this gets to his appeal, is he's bald, but has tattooed hair, kind of a blue-black helmet of hair tattooed onto his head. So again there's this hyper-mimetic quality. Instead of naturalizing his hair loss he gives the artifice of having hair. He camps the idea of disguising hair loss. I've been talking a while if you want to ask a question. -

AF: Could we address how thematics of waste play out in *Thermae*? Thermae asks, "Why think Sagat male merely because personaged. Consider persona Tiresian." I'd never thought through the relationship between your interest in waste and *The Waste Land*.

CS: The Tiresian reference, which happens once, presents a nod to this gender masquerade blurring boundaries between masculine and feminine. It calls them up as artificial. I should look at *The Waste Land* again. I feel that was an unconscious reference. But in terms of my critical project, the general thesis taken up: certain writers, among them Gertrude Stein, revalorize waste in a mode that's different from more traditional modernists like Pound and Eliot, who distain waste as symptom of cultural decline. Pound's "Cleaners' Manifesto" celebrates the ethos of modernist efficiency and technologization. I'm looking instead at Stein and writers who valorized waste, partly as a reaction to this totalitarian efficiency. Then the study carries through to more postmodern poets such as John Ashbery and, later, writers like Kenneth Goldsmith, who mine the waste products of logic and reason and history—history looked at from a Benjaminian perspective of things forgotten, the objects forgotten. So that's a long way of returning to how *Thermae* seemed different, just in that it directs me back to my personal relationship to waste. My original interest (what brought me to graduate school and writing) was figuring out why I collected those ephemeral magazines, then trying to make them into something more permanent, some archive of thwarted desire for this figure I did not desire per se, but who somehow emblematized my queer desire. Sexual identity comes into play in both projects as a kind of queer rooting through the archives.

AF: Could you discuss the relation between waste and collage? Though first I'm thinking of collecting and collage. I think of Wayne Koestenbaum theorizing mid-'50s queer collecting and collection. By contrast, if we use Eliot, Eliot represents this great anxiety, this fear in the face of the fragmentary culture he supposedly encounters. Yet there seems to be a separate, productive, happy assemblage mode taking place through collecting/collage, where those same fragments get playfully embraced rather than considered crumbling ruins of some totalizing edifice.

CS: Exactly.

AF: So how does that relate to waste?

CS: Poems in *Thermae*, for example, contain scenes where…ostensibly Sagat bears the traces of being a porn star. Some sexual identity places him in a bathhouse-type scenario. But then scenes shift so that he becomes a trash collector, scaling waste piles outside the city with his friend Socrates. Summarizing makes it sound embarrassing. Anyway, I've put some pictures in the chapbook since Tim Peterson published it on EOAGH, and there's one in which Sagat poses before this wall of supermodel images torn from magazines (I doubt they're his walls), and this captures the essence of his gender masquerade, which collages from an archive of ephemeral gender performances. Sagat and Linda draw on that gender archive in the way Andy Warhol describes an actor: they resemble walking tape-recorders, able to summon past performances at will. So they're sort of human collages. Or in terms of artists/writers focused on in *Waste Matters*, my critical study, James Schuyler's "Trash Book" exemplifies this. It's a poem, if I recall correctly, about the book he put together as a present for Joe Brainard.

AF: I think Schuyler's book contains stuff, objects. I think it's a Dieter Roth-style vitrine of physical mementos as well as concepts and texts.

CS: Right. The artists I look at tend to have a collage aesthetic, like Schuyler, Brainard, Ashbery, Warhol. One queer reading of this collage art argues that art-making correlates to constructing subjectivity out of a very robust consumer/media culture. This queer artist assembles codes in a more self-conscious way than a so-called normative subject might. In constructing personal identity, the queer artist becomes skilled collaging together some masculine, some feminine gestures (not that this needs to be binarized, or even gendered, but surfing semiotic codes of media culture, let's say). Stein's a bit more tricky. I don't think of her as a collagist. She's more addressing consumerism and consumption amid the production of her own sort of Taylorized factory system. But she does do cubistic things in her portraits or *Tender Buttons*, where she takes apart an object then collages it back together as shards of a carafe or broken plate, domestic objects she could have purchased at the Bon Marché.

AF: Her constructions of rhythmic or syntactical polyphony seem their own means of collage. And you've answered the question of waste and collage. It's easier than I thought. What's the word for slum in Rio?

CS: Favela.

AF: Favelas come up in the book and I'll just think of how, in general, one person's waste is another's collage? Is that the basic formulation?

CS: A certain relationship to otherness and, perhaps, queer history, develops as I work through this waste book. So a writer like John Ashbery might juxtapose discourses (or even Hart Crane, whom I don't write about, but someone I happen to be thinking of today, someone who puts together an almost Elizabethan rhetoric with very contemporary subject matter, such as modernization or Chaplin films). There's a sense of examining items considered trash, bits which have been discarded. Interesting that I mention favelas in the chapbook. I don't know how much we want to talk about class. I wrote this poem before I'd gone to Brazil. Perhaps some exoticization happens that might relate to an anterior text, one which also deals with colonialization and the "exotic" as a source of—hmm, overlooked value.

AF: Well another part of what interests me is there's never a wasted word in your writing. There's never a throwaway line. Everything seems recuperated for full potential value. I mean that in the best possible way.

CS: Thanks.

AF: So I'm curious what your relation is to work that includes "wasted" text.

CS: That's something people (even non-poets, looking at my first book) would say: there are fewer words than I've ever seen in a poem. Not that I write excessively short poems, just that there's something compressed about them. And in *Waste Matters*, one way I theorize poetry, or a kind of anti-absorptive poetic language, is that between excess and constraint there's a necessary tension, which I playfully term "waste management." I don't know if this is something I'd want to generalize to all poetry. But even in a work like Kenneth Goldsmith's *Soliloquy*, which provides a huge, long excess of words Goldsmith delivers into a tape recorder, some formal reduction happens, in that he recorded all his conversations but then cut out half—his interlocutors.

AF: In terms of this dialectical tension, one you find in Goldsmith, and going back to class: "the city," "the capital," "empire"—can you track the various geographical, cultural, semiotic registers in which *Thermae* situates these terms? Is each literal and allegorical at the same time?

CS: Yeah. I like the way you frame that question. I would say behind *Thermae* stand two books that are not poems. One is by Dianne Chisholm, called *Queer Constellations: Subcultural Space in the Wake of the City*. This is what Eve Sedgwick calls a fantasy book in that it's a book I own, possess, can place right in front of me, yet never have read.

AF: It gives a contact high.

CS: Sure. It's not particularly difficult, but becomes unreadable because the actual realization of it, even though it's topically so close to my interests, is so off from what I want to read. Still, in *Queer Constellations*, Chisholm considers other books, one of which is the second anterior text, or parent text, of *Thermae*, again embarrassing: Alan Hollinghurst's *The Swimming Pool Library*. Do you know that novel? You do?

AF: Students tell me to write something like it.

CS: That's funny. It's the first gay book I ever read. I bought it at a mall in Bismarck, North Dakota. But the book's set in London, and only nominally about swimming pools. The protagonist is ostensibly an architectural historian, though really just a flâneur, a dilettante who belongs to this club, this gay club that centers around this swimming pool. He remembers some swimming pool from childhood, where maybe he had his first gay experiences. But then he discovers, underneath London…the person he's considered writing a biography of, this Lord Nantwich, underneath Nantwich's house he finds this Roman pool with a frieze. Cavorting scenes on the side display sort of master/slave gay dramas. And the various swimming pools in this book provide what I might call a helixical model of queer history. Meaning, there'd been these queer moments in the past, yet how do they inform being queer in the present, when such moments have been erased or suppressed? Meaning we don't exactly have a queer history, since these scenes didn't get transmitted to a "next generation," since they got lost. So the tendency emerges to idealize those moments or sites where their remainders can be found and perhaps fondled, nostalgically. I don't know if that answers the question. "Sites" in *Thermae* are mediated spaces collaged together to create one singular city, or singular favela, or singular suburban dump where Sagat and Socrates cavort.

AF: Does something similar happen to poetic temporality? I'm just thinking of how, in *Thermae*, many lines could be extracted for aphoristic flare. I've got a couple written down: "Socrates arrives to the ruined scene late to edit, from his combines, lists. Knowledge wants to be held in scansion, life in looser array." But then, when I went back to the book, amid these dazzling nuggets, various narrative trajectories became legible. When I say narrative I don't mean plot—just the artful telling of something. I'm curious if Thermae deliberately develops new possibilities of narrative in this latter sense. You cite the choice between fractal and rhyme at one point. Is this a choice you take seriously?

CS: Well you could think of an aphorism as retrospective (reflecting back on experience), but also prescriptive (transmitting wisdom to some imagined future). In *Thermae*, time enters the sense of lateness, or "after." One thing I could say is the Hollinghurst book, which I keep dragging into this discussion, is set in post-empire Britain, and many Roman ruins appear. Then right in the middle we find journal excerpts recounting Britain's occupation of Africa, which might qualify as "late empire." I almost feel...not that it's embarrassing, but maybe the least digested part of my chapbook, perhaps the most trendy—we've probably both read lots about...

AF: Empire?

CS: Empire and capitalism et cetera. We don't need to name names. And that's all very relevant, but a bit of a reflex. But to take it seriously: waste provides a means of thinking through empire's end—its ruins—though also the success of empire. The way American globalism has been about importing materials from one place and consuming them here, then shipping the remainders, our waste, someplace else. I think of John Ashbery's *The Vermont Notebook,* which ostensibly...you'd assume it will celebrate pastoral Vermont. It ends up being about this sprawling, homogenous culture of consumerism that envelops America. It's basically placeless. Finally an interlude takes us to, I think Marco, Mexico (the global south), where whole islands, I picture them as fantasy islands, get built from trash, presumably American trash.

AF: Lots of tires.

CS: Tires, yeah. It's just one way of thinking about the American system plugging into what was an emerging globalism. That's maybe where favelas and my own travels come in—as life imitating art, I guess. As for the fractal versus rhyme question, I think that's great. I'll let the reader ponder that.

AF: Again on fractal versus rhyme: do you consider these lyrical passages as excerpts from a larger project? Do you prefer them remaining a coherent, self-sufficient chapbook? Do they only exist in relation to each other? Would they lose luster in some more totalized production?

CS: Let me put it this way: I'm very inspired by a Lisa Robertson essay from *Occasional Work and Seven Walks from the Office for Soft Architecture,* about scaffolding. We think of scaffolding as a skeleton, meaning unfinished or provisional. But Robertson's essay reverses that metaphor and says: actually, scaffolding is this incredibly febrile, hysterical skin that surfaces the city, and shows what it means to be a surface. And that a surface can be structural. In the same way artificial or anti-absorptive language, even with no narrative undergirding it—that artifice itself can be structural. This might speak to the question of what it means to write fractally rather than in more traditional rhyme, to reproduce structure virally. But then also what it means for a project to migrate other places and take on new shapes (still with the same underlying formulas of construction). So *Thermae* may disassemble and reassemble a new form later, but still possess its characteristic super-face. Does that make sense?

AF: This may be dumb. When you describe Lisa Robertson's conception of the scaffold and skin, it makes me curious about the relationship in your work between metaphoric and auditory association. "Stem…steam…stream" come up and could make for a corny allegorical system, but the constant pivot between allegorical and acoustic modes prevents that from happening. This creates a richer texture of reference than we'd find in most self-declared sound poetry.

CS: That make me think of *Tender Buttons*, or other Stein works. Not her most repetitive prose works, but those that show a bit more variation of approach. Joan Retallack says about Stein that there are those who want to read her just for sound sense, like Ulla Dydo or Charles Bernstein, and then those who want to decode her. But for me the pleasure of engaging Stein is how she throws us back and forth and confuses us from finding our way between these poles. That's why I could spend a whole life returning to Stein, even just to the same passages of *Tender Buttons*. They never will resolve and yet a matrix of meaning lurks behind them, beyond the sounds and the words, even though this matrix gets built from relations between the sounds. The contemporaneity of her work resides in its sound sense.

AF: Can we talk about small-scale developments? Can I cite a couple more of your lines: "carousing, carousel, narcotic, caretaking, crinoline, drowsing, dousing, dosing, drying." Or the section: "No hard globes to part. / No hard parts to pity. / No part hearts to market. / No blond parts to hearten. / No heart parts to batten." The auditory pleasures are immediate. But how do you characterize other modes of pleasure, other types of development at play here? Are they cognitive pleasures, affect? These passages trace both a litany and its opposite. But what would the opposite be? Desire and the fulfillment of desire? Or when I read "to feel the pain of delivery as a jeweled dowry"—that could have been this whole book.

cs: It's very gratifying to have you read. I don't know exactly what to say that would do more than annotate your points.

af: Did you want to describe the history of these constructions?

cs: Well for "carousing, carousel, narcotic, caretaking, crinoline, drowsing, dousing, dosing, drying"…obviously I keep referring to *Tender Buttons*. I'm writing about it now and read it aloud as part of a panel performance last week, so I keep returning. But the "Food" section starts with a list of what seem objects, different foods Stein plans to describe in this section. Though then occasionally something doesn't fit the grid she sets up. And the pleasure comes when Stein departs from this grid. Of course that's the excess or waste of poetry—the way it deviates from expectations for procedure or metrical scheme or whatever.

af: Something about the low-event horizon? Doesn't Ashbery address this in his Stein essay, "The Impossible"? Because a scene has stayed similar so long, the sudden break provides extravagant pleasure.

cs: We absolutely are thinking of the same idea. We're thinking of two different metaphors Ashbery uses in that same review. I remember a music metaphor, when he compares Stein's writing to a particularly dry passage among the strings, suddenly irrigated by the arrival of, let's say, the oboe.

af: Though I'm not saying your own lines are dry.

cs: In my other passage, there's perhaps something more sexual in the word play and reference inspiring it: "No hard globes to part. / No hard parts to pity. / No part hearts to market. / No blond parts to harden. / No heart parts to batten." Maybe a sexual act gave rise to this catalog of word play which then…

af: Is it like friction?

cs: More a substitution of parts. Not the whole body, but the plugging and jamming of body parts (words) into wrong structures, wrong holes. I'm leaping from the concrete to the theoretical, but there's something about pornography these lines describe—the poignance in bodies being objectified and atomized and marketed as commodities. Again, I'm less interested in the actual porn film than the pornographic star-system. That's why Sagat figures in the poem.

He fragments his own body, so his hard globes part and get pitied and marketed, which may be hardening but there's a certain vulnerability or sadness to that. And a sadness on the reader/viewer's part to participate in systematic commodification of a person. Someplace in there's "the global" we'd mentioned, the illusion of this "global" system that's actually very segregated.

AF: I love how, read together, those sequences seem tactile. But pictured as separate, stand-alone scenes they evoke the body you look at, the porn, pixilated.

CS: Words are objects, in a sense. You feel them as you say them. You feel them as you write them. But you never quite can possess a word. It's always not quite yours. I feel a desiring relationship to words because they're always going to leave, to go out into the market for somebody to buy and use better.

AF: I'm getting, from all you've said, a different understanding of these lines late in the text: "The open mind living the next / surface of empire. The blessing / taken further." This concept of empire as perhaps an ambivalent blessing. Can we close with you leading us into the final sentence?

CS: You want me to explicate it?

AF: Just to say something in response.

CS: "Are you looking at Russia more fully now that we have time?" It's sort of embarrassing. I think maybe the ghosted…there's kind of a Trojan Horse narrative, as one of those narrative shards you've mentioned. I imagine this line following an evocation of the Trojan Horse, also the erotic idea of the Trojan Horse.

AF: The Trojan Horse and sex were clear.

CS: All the men and spears inside. You can imagine all these bodies pushing out. And the Trojan Horse shows an obliviousness to the wages of empire. Here an "after the fall" expansion of time may be the real gift. Not consumption's frenzy but a moment of reparation, reflection. Also "having time" means considering what happens post-fall, looking to other nations, other empires, wondering which will rise or fall. Maybe there's the hint we're in this moment of cultural or national depression, in the sense of decline (I think also strong guilt). I'm no psychologist, but I feel guilt, guilt from having such high quality of living—relative. Then looking to other countries and seeing their emergence/re-emergence and feeling guilty and worried about the wages of this rise.

## INTERVIEW WITH ERIC BAUS
Recorded on May 2, 2012
This interview focuses on Baus's book *Scared Text* (Center for Literary Publishing).

ANDY FITCH: Can we discuss *Scared Text*'s cover, as a means of approaching less concrete concerns? You've called this cover image by Morin "appropriately gross," which it is, though not for reasons I expected. Each separate bug (a diverse array) gets highly individuated, picks up autonomous identity. Everybody looks better off on his/her own, yet yoked together to construct a digestible tableau—like a Balthus painting. Scale seems perfectly drafted for the isolated, individual being, but bizarrely distorted when placed side-by-side, with the beetle as big as a mouse it eats, or fucks? The overall composition feels self-contained, square, if also potentially part of a more expansive, cathartic scene. Then on the book's back, a blue beetle gets cloned in reverse, restructured. Does this help to describe what makes the cover "appropriately" gross? And, can I just add, the palate remains warm and earthy and cheerful.

ERIS BAUS: Your description resembles how I think about serial poems—focusing on relationships between different parts. As you spoke I stared at the cover and imagined each bug as its own paragraph. That makes a lot of sense. And the image's tone does seem important, since each book I've done contains a kind of world-building, like in science fiction or film. So the cover design lets you walk into the book's world. This includes discrete, unrelated beings placed beside each other so that you register strangeness, you know something strayed out of place but not so much that it looks random, or deliberate like a collage. The poems share this sensibility. I worked at the level of the word and sentence, looking at undertones, looking at implicit doubles. Still I didn't have much agency picking this cover. I suggested something I love and the publisher vetoed it and picked the perfect thing.

AF: Could I ask what you had in mind?

EB: I'd written brief entries for *Jacket2*, and my friend Noah Saterstrom's a painter whose work amazes me. He has let me use some images for free and they've always seemed appropriate.

AF: Do they look pink and furry? I wondered why I knew that name.

EB: I wanted to use a small drawing which shows this ghostly humanoid carrying a calf or cow on its back. The cow's legs sort of become the person's arms. Blending takes place between human and animal. I'd originally titled my book "Puma Mirage."

AF: Pumas do come up.

EB: Yeah, a lot. After the poem "Puma Mirage" a few echoes follow. Friends make fun of me for picking titles that seem hard to pronounce, or remember. That concerned the publisher. I thought, OK, I'll pick my battles—I'll just design some other weird title. So we agreed on *Scared Text*. All this negotiation with the press stayed helpful and interesting and was not alienating at all.

AF: I like how you consciously build worlds, as you've said, yet leave space for others to add their own editorial slant. Though it surprises me that anyone considers *Scared Text* an easy title.

EB: I know. It's phonetically difficult.

AF: "Sacred Text" seems the wraith-like complement.

EB: Totally. *Publisher's Weekly* reviewed it online as "Sacred Text," by someone who clearly had read the book, understood it. Of course that type of vowel slippage turns up often in my poems, creating double-take moments. And it still scares me that perhaps I stole this title from somebody, since it sounds so obvious. I thought, oh god, did I steal a John Yau title? I scoured my 25 John Yau books. Plus that sense of both the familiar and strange happening at once provides a good introduction to this work. When people call it "Sacred Text" I can't blame them.

AF: They do what you want them to do, not what you told them to do.

EB: Exactly. I've given readings from my first book, *The To Sound*, where people introduced it as "To the Sound." That second name got used for a blog I wrote because I'd realized, oh right, this makes way more sense.

AF: I approached *Scared Text* indirectly, with those allegorical questions about the cover, since you'll often refer to yourself as "thinking about" things ("thinking about" audio recordings, "thinking about" echoes), yet a reader might assume your book contains much less "thought" than one finds in a self-consciously didactic or reflective poet. Can you describe your mode of thinking in/through poetry? Does it make sense to distinguish, at least partially, between Wordsworthian thoughts in repose, and Constructivist thoughts in action, in production?

EB: I'd definitely identify more with the latter. For me, reading consists of an actual cognitive event that happens—not the seamless absorption of some text, but this ambient experience looking at the letters' shapes in a sort of abstract sense, while dealing with imagined sounds. I act in multiple ways and make various associations. We use shorthand to describe processes such as reading or thinking, which can make them seem quite linear, but I experience something more like a magnetic field of impressions bouncing off one another. So when I write, I don't pursue clarity of expression or try to capture a particular moment, as much as I pare down elements and put them into relation. Then I record their interactions. It feels more like recording, or live editing, than expression in the sense of having some coherent idea pour out. I have tremendous respect for poets who think like that, who can write like that. But writing for me comes from a bouncier, acoustic, echoey space. Thinking means something kinetic, building up the surface by prompting different exchanges.

AF: I love your bouncy, kinetic, acoustical thinking. But reading this particular book, I noted that the imagery you deploy ends up recalling Wordsworth more than Rodchenko. I can't imagine Constructivist art about beetles, ghosts, opals. *Scared Text* seems to thematize your long-standing interests in properties of mulching, bottom feeding, haunting, calcification—tracing some sort of correspondence between those images that do arise and the process-oriented project.

EB: That's right. I'm a recursive writer, thriving on bounciness, but also with much conscious revision. I guess the thinking, the reflection happens more through revising, the orchestrating of echoes across this book, rather than in any individual poem or utterance. Almost every sentence gets echoed or doubled or complicated some way. I've tried to create this vibrating space, but want it to feel fixed on the page with some certainty of voice. I love voice-overs in nature documentaries, for example, even as you deal with surprising content. David Attenborough will show something insane, but his voice suggests linearity. It interests me to track those two poles of watching phenomena unfold in unexpected ways, but pretending to possess a complete understanding.

AF: *Scared Text* now will seem all the scarier for me since I'll have that voice-over haunt the whole reading.

EB: Even with Charles and Ray Eames' films, you encounter these voice-overs all the time. Those stayed in my head for years, especially the Cold War authority of Charles Eames' voice. I mean no harsh critique of this voice, but appreciate the absurdity that pretends to know and put everything in its place.

AF: Well, in terms of faux linearity, what's the difference between work that aspires to pure sonic experience (if Hugo Ball does that, let's say) and a book which contains kings, oxen, characters named Minus and Iris? Does encountering those narrative snippets actually allow readers to absorb more sonic and cognitive variety? Do you agree with, I never know how to say…Kruchenykh? Do you know how to say that?

EB: I don't. I'm bad with pronunciation.

AF: But interested in sound? Still Kruchenykh told Roman Jakobson that Zaum is like mustard: you can't live on it alone. Similarly, does your book's image repertoire give our minds greater elasticity, allowing us to track myriad types of cognitive variation that occur throughout?

EB: I think that's true. My sense of sound poetry…at least revivals of that work, contemporary examples, tend to have more than sound driving them. I get a bit frustrated if the category "sound poetry" already has defined an experience for me. My brain begins to shut down listening to strict sound poetry. Though again, I don't mean this as a critique. I'm simply describing my own idiosyncratic processing of stuff. Readers really into sound poetry take much more from it. But for me, sound provides one pole to bounce off. On the other side you find elements of narrative that I use.

AF: More like Christian Bök's *Eunoia* has a narrative.

EB: Yes. I like spending eight seconds in a sound poem then four seconds in a weird Carla Harryman narrative space. Variation occurs, even if our critical vocabulary can't capture that complex experience. I'm sure when I listen to Hugo Ball, I perform small acts of narrativization or thematizing or projecting things, even as I just hear a bunch of "B" sounds.

AF: What functions do section breaks play in your book? Do they delimit a reader's experience, in order to make what happens within those confines all the more intense? And do separate sections play off each other? For example, "Scared Text" presents a very different pace than those nearby. Did you want to produce a tonic effect here? Did I just read faster when I found more words on the page? Do time-based media such as film and music inform your sense of proportion, dimension, volume?

EB: Definitely. Something like a film sequence or musical score lurks at the back of my head when I write. I think of a book in terms of momentum and pace and counterpointing. If I arranged *Scared Text* as one long section, or a collection of stand-alone poems, it soon could get monotonous or overwhelming in an unproductive way. I'd prefer to construct a discrete experience for each section, but with a bleed-through effect. Think of going to a natural history museum and approaching a diorama, and spending three minutes in its world, then moving on to the next display. You have distinct experiences, but your second experience shapes your ninth or tenth. You continue to absorb new scenes, without thinking this is the only piece ever to have existed. That type of afterimage remains important for me. Here, I wrote the poem "Scared Text" much earlier than some of the other sections. So it does present a much different pace. I'd wanted to write a longer, more dense and rich poem than I'd done before. A lot of what I do is spread out papers on the floor and try to see what could create an intense experience for the reader—what can engage but also keep moving. For me sound poetry tends to flatten out. Though that makes me seem like some advocate for moderation.

AF: To me you seem a stealth advocate for extremity.

EB: Thanks. I want that extremity to register. Some people have responded negatively to how I've discussed my writing before because they thought I'd written this crazy first book, then pulled back and become conservative. For my second book, *Tuned Doves,* I'm like, this stuff's still crazy. I'm not making quiet poems. I just want the quieter, more remote moments to feel as jarring or intense as the over-the-top sound moments. Basically my thinking here resembles Russian formalism—defamiliarizing experience in different ways.

AF: Though again it's weird: for Shklovsky's classic account of defamiliarization, he talks about Tolstoy.

EB: That's the funny part. I have a ton of Shklovsky books, and you read them and get all excited and then he mentions something so conventional. Or Reuven Tsur's book *What Makes Sound Patterns Expressive?* focuses a lot on Victor Hugo. When I read this type of criticism, I think of Bruce Andrews or somebody. It makes me feel I've appropriated Shklovsky's concepts in a way that could horrify him.

AF: Which sounds just fine. I have a question. You briefly mentioned the "discrete experience" of individual poems within this book. Of course we can distinguish these poems in terms of pacing, divergent formal structures. But discrete experience also could suggest disparities between individual readers. Here I think of Marjorie Perloff's statement that saturation produces difference. Returning to your image of the kid at the museum, roving from scene to scene: I love how this book provides for our highly variegated experience of each individual poem, but also prompts an awareness that each separate reader will have a discrete experience progressing through the work, since it stays sonically overwhelming, so different impressions stand out for different people. And no single reader could read the same book twice.

EB: I try to write so that you could read over and over and have different elements pop out, different types of kinetic experience.

AF: I also admire, in your discussions of poetry, how you stay very precise in terms of abstract technical or compositional or epistemic concerns. Nuance remains crucial—in order to delineate the complexities of any given instant. Does poetry provide distinct pleasure by offering you the opportunity to parse this way? Do you value giving readers something similar? Can you describe any broader cultural context in which the pursuit of discrete experience picks up communal or ethical or political implications?

EB: Sure. Discussions about a poetics of privacy or interiority can get misleading. For me, the ways that individual paragraphs echo or complicate each other might speak to broader social relationships. But I begin with very small units and build from there. When I think of a poet like Juliana Spahr (say, *This Connection of Everyone with Lungs*, or so much of her work I love), she seems to start from much larger questions, staring through the telescope. For whatever reason, I work best building up microscopic moments—punctuating each little stitch. Eventually this coalesces into something larger. Still I read so much that starts from the other direction, that pursues less abstract questions, that really moves outward. That's what I hope to explore right now. I guess I'm going to experiment with more intentionality in the future, but have no idea how that will work.

AF: And just to clarify: poets face far too many contexts in which people demand you graft your working process onto some big, broad, ethically legible scheme. So I very much value your work's micro-focus. For example, do you stretch logical possibility as you go through making micro-edits? You'll present this protagonist named Minus, an apparent non-entity, then "not-bodies" arise, and "the Ur-Mane," the "negative noon"—each one step removed from presence, depending upon a layered construction, upon the incremental stages that get laced throughout this text.

EB: That remains a really important part for me. I remember reading this Anselm Berrigan interview a decade ago, where he discussed showing all the seams in his poems. And I thought, as a writer, I'm the person who loves to hide the seams. I like to create these discrete, stitched-together landscapes, those bits of weird subjectivities like Minus, like the Ur-Mane. I'll push these Frankenstein entities, pretending they're more coherent than they are—rather than emphasizing their dissolution. I'm sure I just took Anselm out of context.

AF: Still it works. You hide the seams.

EB: Or I love when Tan Lin talks about (I never know how facetious he's being) wanting to make his textual surface as soothing and elevator-jazz as possible. I bet no one experiences his work that way. It's so intense and engaging on so many levels. Again that voice-over of certainty gets contradicted by your lived reading experience. Conversely, my work gestures toward narrative, toward coherence or connection, but literally does emerge from this pile of disconnected, fragmented bits sutured in an unruly way. My decisions take place on this microscopic level. That excites me. I can get lost in that. I get defeated by my intentionality so much, but find ways to continue and stay surprised as a writer and reader. I reread *Scared Text* when it came out and thought, what the hell did I do? I could talk about the first two books, but this one seems so processed, in a way that jacket copy can't explain. I wanted to frame a text which floats coherently for a while before people see it fall apart.

AF: I'd assume most interviews address bigger, broader topics. But could we look at some specific lines I love?

EB: I can say more about lines than I can about poems.

AF: Which seems part of this book's palimpsestic nature—even amid the smooth, carefully choreographed surface. How about, from "The Worm's First Film": "A still shows his core is a molting eel." The forward thrust of this phonically resonant, nonsensical sentence recalls "A is a kiss slow cheese," from Stein. Or "Sable arrested a fine comb," that Jack Spicer line Robin Blaser loves so much.

EB: I don't know if this type of context helps, but the poem came about through a bunch of people bringing objects into one room. Some offered plastic horses. I'd brought herbs from my acupuncturist, with different textures. I just drafted a bunch of notes, then my impulse to create a narrative arose from that. Though when I think of "A still shows his core is a molting eel"…I sense readers experience these lines as disembodied, directed by sound. But for me, a really straightforward imagistic event occurs that I can picture. I see a film still removed, resembling the process of an eel's molting. This line sounds like the voice-over for a nature film. I actually had an idea behind it in some ways.

AF: So it's almost paraphrasable.

EB: Yet a lot of the work isn't. I know some people experience a line like that as totally abstract. I'm not sure anyone looks at this the same way I do, but many crazy sonic moments come from—I strive to construct imaginable scenes. For some lines, even those filled with over-the-top sounds, hopefully you can picture them unfold in time and space. I'll see something like cinematic space. I'll see a molting eel, and sense the pleasure of watching this change from one state to another.

AF: And of course isolating individual sentences erases their context beside others. But how about, from "Glass Deer": "The sun a moth is in a strong clot of ether blinds its antlers."

EB: Sometimes I just try to outdo myself, seeing how much one can pack into a single sentence. A lot of synesthesia happens. Stein makes sense as a syntactical reference. But I consider Francis Ponge the patron saint of these poems. I steal much in terms of his voice of certainty. He's not so syntactically strange, yet you get to watch scenes unfold in space, and not just unusual scenes, but language itself and the material of words goes under the microscope. *Scared Text*'s sensibility seems to combine Stein's efforts to revive dead words and Ponge's pleasure of watching things unfold.

AF: Does the sentence pick up importance here, as something modular that stands out then fits back in?

EB: I struggle working with lineated forms. The doubling effect gets muddled. Or I can't tell how to begin or end. But my sense of the sentence…both micro- and macro-movements happen. I'll create sentences, then harvest them and try to get them talking to one another. Then I deal with one paragraph, one grouping at a time, move outwards from that. My sentences seem recursive or circular or fractal. Each sentence contains its certain logic, then the poem's specific logic echoes that, then the overall section presents a logic. I hope at least on an unconscious level people pick up this syntax of the book. I don't consider sentences as means to an end. I think of them as a space to hover in, in which to build a circus or landscape that can alter or mutate. Mutation seems a huge part of this book—not just echoes, but snipping off some piece and letting it grow strange in a different environment, then re-using it three or four poems later, and then having it echo eighteen pages later. Those thin strands connect everything.

AF: Along with clones arriving, and worms that can be split or sawed or abscessed, appears this subterranean lexicon of funk. I'll picture you spreading all your sheets on the floor, all these carefully groomed poems and sentences and paragraphs, and then I wonder: what's it like to have an "oud" emerge from this process?

EB: That I can speak to specifically. An oud is a Middle Eastern instrument like a gourd guitar. That showed up because "O-U-D," those letters, appear so often in words like "could" or "would." A lot of this book's lexicon comes from cutting away at existing vocabularies. I try to make a tool out of something abstract, or to physicalize, or materialize an idea. The Iris character, for example, used to be Isis, which first came from erasing a sentence and finding two of the word "is" beside each other. Though that had too much baggage. I didn't want people to read in terms of some specific mythology. So I changed it to a potential real name, while providing these other references to sight, to a flower. Trying to create objects and characters out of language seemed important—though people don't need to know this when they read it. You might pick up on faux names or parts of words happening. But for me: I like to keep a bit of curtain between the reader and writer. So many poets talk about making their work process transparent to the reader, with a kind of ethics attached to that, which I think is great. But I like the sneakiness of holding something back. A lot of these poems get cloned from my previous two books, too. "Negative Noon" provides this weird rewriting of the poem "The Continuous Corner" from *Tuned Doves*. I doubt readers ever would realize that. Still I appreciate these conversations that happen between individual sentences in a poem, between sections or between whole books, about repetition and difference, about variation and mutation. That's what makes it "scary."

## INTERVIEW WITH DANIELLE PAFUNDA
Recorded on May 3, 2012
This interview focuses on Pafunda's book *Manhater* (Dusie Press).

ANDY FITCH: Could we start with a brief comparison to your preceding book? I never know how to say, *Iatrogenic*?

DANIELLE PAFUNDA: *Iatrogenic*.

AF: OK. Sections of *Manhater* seem to invert gender dynamics that played out there. Iatrogenic's female-identified characters weren't passive, but manipulated certainly, altered, as the title implies, by exposure to others. Mommy V of *Manhater*, by contrast, is a stealth stalker with her own harem of "gakking," sperm-donating drones and victims. Did she emerge full-formed in her gush-sucking badness out of desires and concerns left over from previous projects? Does her predatorial prowess demonstrate you wanting to push Gurlesque tendencies in new directions?

DP: I would say, yes. I think *Iatrogenic*, and particularly the Mommy V of *Manhater*, are part of the same larger project for me—exploring various thrusts of feminist thought or theory, various approaches to the fact we live in the culture that produced us. If you're discontent with the patriarchy but you're its product, what do you do? So in *Iatrogenic* I'm sort of playing with Monique Wittig, in particular, her *Les Guérillères*, and other feminist writers who envision utopias of different sorts. Mine turns dystopic. It goes very badly. And so the question there would be, you quit this world, you build a new one, can you cease to be a product of your culture? How do power dynamics work without male or masculine figures? *Iatrogenic* explores how I felt those feminist utopian projects don't ever fully satisfy. In *Manhater* Mommy V still inhabits our world, and she's solo. She's not part of a collective...Hannah Arendt claims where there isn't power there will be violence (I'm paraphrasing clumsily). Out of that discussion one can ask why doesn't the women's movement become violent? Why don't women turn violent to seize or redistribute power? And it may be because women don't get seen as a discrete entity or group of any kind. We get projects like *S.C.U.M. Manifesto,* and they are real anomalies. What happens when that feminine figure coded as monster and mother and reproductive body turns to violence? *Manhater* explores what happens in this mode. So even though the books present two different agencies, their speakers work out similar problems.

AF: Two quick follow-ups. When you say these books are part of the same project, maybe this is dumb, but can you give a sense what you mean by project? Are they part of an ongoing series? And you describe Mommy V as "solo," as operating solo, yet she's a mother at the same time.

DP: [Laughs] Yeah.

AF: She leads a family.

DP: It seemed sort of obvious to me, yeah. Well, maybe I'll answer that one first. She's not solo. She has a brood. I just was playing with…there's a couple poems in there I'm really sweet on which felt dedicated to my second kid in some ways. But I really can't write that down since they seem horrible poems.

AF: Should we clarify for readers your second kid's the cutest boy within 200 miles?

DP: He's very cute and so far seems a boy. He seems to identify. He's my love. And there are moments when poems feel really tender, though I'm not sure that works clearly on the page. Mommy V does love her babies in this strange way. She's not human. She's post-human or vampire or something. So her system's a bit different than ours. And she doesn't have companions or partners. She has sort of her army, sort of her responsibility, her community, but it's not—maybe I'm psychologizing my speakers too much. She speaks to no one on an equal level. Also the poems provide experience of disability. They are about experiences of desire when desire fails. It's often about the isolation of a body in pain, or a body made monstrous by outside forces. That's how I think about her—pretty solitary. The other question, right, what kind of project. Maybe project's too solid a term. What drives me to write are various obsessions I have. My constant interest in how vectors of identity inform us, how it's impossible not to privilege the human, even when you try. What it means to be born into a body marked for a certain type of power or marginalization. I think about these all the time, and struggle with, and try to figure out how to navigate. So no matter what project I work on, I'm always interested—and this probably comes from Plath—in what happens when you attract the male gaze, pin it, then horrify or fill it with the abject? That's one basic thing in a lot of work I do. Investigations of power dynamics—and can you break them in the language out of which they're made?

AF: When you talk about provoking horror, and earlier when you said there's a relative lack of violence among women, am I right—maybe this is pedantic—but do you mean externalized violence? Or non-domesticated violence? Is that part of what Mommy V represents? Certainly there are violent female characters in literature. Medea comes to mind. But Mommy V seems different. She's a good mom.

DP: She is a good mom.

AF: The violence gets directed outwards.

DP: Yeah, and her violence…I don't know how personal it is. I don't know if she's personally invested in it. When I say there's a noticeable absence of violence among feminist movements, I mean in a very literal way. There aren't many bombings or murders or attacks or hostage-takings, for a variety of cultural and political reasons. And I'm not advocating those activities. But I'm saying it's curious. It's curious there's no global coup. That interests me. And I don't consider this a move away from Gurlesque tendencies. I think one thing the Gurlesque does is say, look, this work isn't meant to be edifying. It isn't here to show you an ethically superior way to discuss gender disparity, or moral ways to solve such problems. It's saying, often, here's a descriptive project and it might actually cause harm to describe these things. Or it might be violent to make this work, to make these kind of poems, but that's part of what's interesting. Of course violence on the page remains incredibly different from violence in real, lived experience. There's the difference between making a violent poem and committing an act of violence against another body. I think the Gurlesque project—and it gets a lot of flack for this—is not there to be in the right. It's there to investigate a power dynamic and ways we're complicit.

AF: Could we return to Mommy V for these reasons? Lorenzo Thomas appropriated the Dracula myth in part to depict the consequences of economic vampirism, and anxieties about miscegenation as these topics play out in tropes of blood or race. Your own Mommy V might, at first glance, seem the hero of a new feminist vampire epic, but she vamps in any number of contradictory ways. The interspecies implications come out clearly. Mommy V seems part black widow giving guys her "sure thing," a "favorite disease." She's part mousey homebody, resting under a cloth for an hour, still keeping her nose up, guarding her brood. She's part winged supermom whisking home to dish out "straws and spines." And part Miltonic feminized plague "alive with vermin, venison, pests." She can even play the histrionic femme fainting from headaches. Is it this shape-shifting that drew you to the vampire myth, or Dracula myth?

DP: I love teaching *Dracula*, when you get all the students in a room and talk about it, and try to piece together what Dracula is from this wild, contradictory set of characteristics. He becomes a lizard or wolf or man in a straw boater. This shape-shifting draws us into the vampire myth. But something really interesting about vampire mythology is that it's all about siring. Here we have a body, coded male, that gives birth on its own, right? This male vampire will bite somebody's neck, feed them blood, and suddenly you've got a new vampire. Its body morphs in ways that traditionally female bodies have. It performs tasks coded feminine. If we look at the evolutional of the Byronic vampire, up to the Edward Cullen kind of vampire, these are complicated developments in which he's simultaneously a grotesque body then a static, granite, beautiful, unaging body. In those mythologies the male body takes on aspects of the female body, appropriating them, while the female gets cut out of the process. I had gotten this grant to do vampire research, and bought all of the *Angel* series. At one point in *Angel,* a vampire, gets knocked up and has a baby and sacrifices herself for the baby to survive. And I was pregnant when watching this, freaky in all sorts of ways. But I became interested in how the sexiness of vampires (particularly the contemporary vampire) cuts out motherhood, which then gets reintroduced by shows like this. Or by Stephanie Meyer creating this really gruesome, out-of-hand book for the *Twilight* series. Bella's going to give birth to this monster baby that rips apart her placenta and almost kills her. In very strange ways these mythic, mutable vampire bodies connect with the mother-body, which always had been a site of the monstrous and grotesque. As I worked with Mommy V, I wondered, what if she controls this morphing? What woman will she choose to be? Which body will she wear? We both have some agency over this, as women, and lack a lot of agency in it. When we're talking about things like, even fashion or makeup, or how much control you have over the shape and size of your body, or what happens when another human might grow in there, there are ways in which we exercise agency; there are ways in which we reify a lot of things that harm us. Still sometimes you can use that agency to subvert a bit. And she's not supposed to be any more consistent than any of us. Sometimes she'll behave in ways that don't seem particularly feminist. Other times she's a badass feminist warrior.

AF: Along those lines, I'm interested in the more general fusion of serialized poem and narrative snags. Does grouping together a sequence of entries, none of which…it's not as though they'll speed up the plot, so much as they offer different vantages on Mommy V. Does this prioritize a polyvalent performance of roles and attributes, while stripping away identity-making, character-driven plot or catharsis?

DP: I believe I'd be a crap novelist. I love novels and a juicy story. I love narrative. I've been thinking about that a lot this week because we've got a Marjorie Perloff piece on conceptual poetry versus American hybrid kind of stuff. And Stephen Burt just reviewed all those conceptual anthologies. So I'll think about what happens when you're driven by both the conceptual and the lyrical, by narrative and voice and certain abstract, experimental parameters. But I'm not bound by the narrative constraints that often cause a project to go stale for me. I'm not fulfilling the same expectations and arc. Scenes don't have to be as stable. I don't have narrative relying on a stable voice, or stable figure. So I get to build the same architecture, a big architecture with a lot going on, but get to write just the parts that interest me. Or parts that contradict each other and might ruin another kind of project—though in this case get to be the substance of my project.

AF: The serial forms you adopt, do they correspond to cinematic or TV representations? Do those forms, movies or TV, fit particularly well for vampiric transformations?

DP: I think so. I do watch a lot of television. I love television. And that form can be really episodic. More than film, TV provides the opportunity to be self-contradictory. A later episode can contradict an early one. Something can shift. And of course since you've got multiple writers changing over time, you get that polyvocality there. Here it's just me making them. But if they contradict something from earlier, that's OK. Or it's better that way. That becomes kind of juicy. I also get to be very obsessive about the project, and to think about it from all different angles, and get to be occupied by it for a while, in very literal and figurative ways. I can do it until it's completely exhausted.

AF: I like this idea of being both episodic and evolving. Do subsequent sections of *Manhater* deliberately diversify the vampire/interspecies portfolio, as when the poetic-subject of "The Desire Spectrum Is Dead to Me Now" gets her wings pinned, butterfly-style, to a car steering column. Are you deliberately echoing the vampire motif? Could you talk about how different sections of the book cohere or deliberately don't cohere?

DP: I think they deliberately don't cohere. They are closely enough related and the mode in which the speaker functions is consistent enough, maybe even unrelenting enough, that it does feel all of a piece to me. But there's shifting. There's a very physical shift. The speaker of the illness poems and the "Desire Spectrum" poems, I can't tell. Maybe it's Mommy V, maybe not quite, maybe from a slightly alternate universe or space/time continuum. But it's similar enough to allow me to explore the nuances of power derived from abjection. Or dignity can be derived from abjection in one moment, but then in another moment is it more eradicating? Is abjection more shameful in other spaces? Again playing with some of that Plath performativity. Once you've got the male gaze fixed, is there some perverse power or perverse satisfaction performing abjection the audience is forced to witness, or doesn't get to respond to? And then in other pieces is it more shameful or pathetic? Can the speaker recover? Can the speaker continue to speak while getting pinned that way, under a steering column, amid a pretty subjugated situation?

AF: When you refer to the illness poems, I'm guessing that's the "In This Plate" section. You'd mentioned disabilities studies earlier. I'm curious how disability gets threaded in, especially by the affirmation of—it's the apparently grotesque body, but that basically just means any body. Just as Mommy V, when feeling good, grows "incautious with her bulk" and decides not to wash, the poetic-subject of the "In This Plate" section unwittingly has her "trauma dome come undone." Her "jolly worms seep out," as if the real vamping had been committed by the paranoid ego, trying to keep it all wrapped in a mummy cage. Are the plates…first, does that idea make sense?

DP: That did make sense.

AF: Are the plates…can you just describe this section? The concept of plate here interests me. Do the plates shift shapes like Mommy V? Do they have multiple existences as kitsch artifacts, imagistic records (like a photographic plate), cloning dishes, cannibalistic feasts? Is that all part of this plate section?

DP: Yes. That's the easy answer. Yes, that is so. They're inspired by the daguerreotype, that kind of plate, but in a *Blade Runner* technology kind of way. This future feels very retro. Plus I like the idea of tableaux that move slightly, or dioramas which feel a bit alive, when I want something more contained for a poem. The plates worked well for me because they brought in that idea of meat as cannibalism—but also image. The images would be on a plate. It could be this kind of silver ceramic plate, depicting a bit of movement, but we'd never get the full scene. And we'll always be aware that it's framed. And this was useful because one thing I haven't quite figured out is as somebody who turns to the grotesque a lot…it's an aesthetic strategy I really savor, only under the sign of disabilities studies it becomes tricky. I want to use the grotesque, and the feminine grotesque. I want to use them to horrify. Or I want to hurt the reader in certain ways. Or to see what happens when we glorify the abject. Though that doesn't always serve to humanize people whose bodies have been marked. So we've entered tricky terrain. I was having this conversation recently on *Montevidayo*, where I blog, and somebody asked, well, why do you privilege the human anyway? Why not dehumanize? Why privilege this weird illusion of self? My answer, as someone who works in postmodern modes, is sometimes it seems appropriate to question the human, or dehumanize, or embrace the monstrosity or the multivalent, multi-species situation. And then other times it does seem appropriate to privilege the human. It depends on the investigation and project. In this space where I'm working with both disability and feminist perspectives…I'm not really sure where I am with it. And here is where I like not always trying, or not often trying to edify. Because it's not my job to be unimpeachably ethical or good. I'm just playing with where the body that isn't coded "able" comes into contact with the body recognized as "female" or "feminine."

AF: In either of those cases, if you're privileging the body, it's hard to say if that's privileging the human or not. Again it seems to depend on context.

DP: I guess I'm privileging the feelings, or emotion, or the affect this body carries. If I'm privileging lived experience carried out by a body, I'm probably privileging the human. If I'm privileging the body itself, then we're talking fungus and protists, bacteria and all the good stuff Donna Haraway reminds us make up the body. My speakers and their bodies often face some form of unproductive friction. Or maybe productive friction. They don't always get along.

AF: I'd like to talk a bit about "The Desire Spectrum Is Dead to Me Now" section, how new vamping/vampiric possibilities play out. There's the vampirism of marriage in lines like "my very best friend, / which of these wilted corsages / would you stuff in your mouth // while we wait for the photographer / to unclasp and lead us away / from the pyrotechnic swan?" There's the vamping of chronic memory, trauma, and/or masturbation amid ruminations on the ex-dogs in your "crank case," the moments of "hand-built closet," and trips to a genital shack that houses "cocks I've found on men." Again, what can you tell us about how this section relates to its predecessors? About the post-sex posturing of this "jilt bazaar"?

DP: It's really helpful the way you're using the term "vamp." Because that is what happens: you write a book, it does this very specific, obvious thing, and you yourself don't come up with a word for it.

AF: Or you do at first but then worry about localized things.

DP: But I think literally saying the word "vamp" aloud, on its own, is helpful. Because that's the most unifying thread that appears. In the "Desire Spectrum" poems, one question they ask, or maybe one of the questions I was asking when I started writing them, was what do people like about desire? Why write poems about it? What's interesting or pleasant about it? I think (and maybe this is a little autobiographical because of health issues, because of my anxieties about germs and illness and that sort of thing) I think I respond to images of desire and sex a bit differently than other people. And these thoughts happened around swine-flu time. I got really freaked out because we had a new baby, who couldn't be immunized, and I just felt I didn't have a lot of control over our permeability or those pathogens. Then at some point while finding places not to touch doors on campus, and wondering if I could wear latex gloves or would it make me look weird, I saw a couple students in a very public space make out and my first thought was, why take your life in your hands? Why would you put your tongue in another human's mouth and risk this whole *Outbreak* monkey epidemic situation? Around this time I realized I'd really reframed my way of receiving and understanding physical affection between humans. At the same time, I'd go to readings and somebody would write about their lover or wanting a lover, and it was striking me so peculiar. And so I thought, what the heck's going on? And what should I do with desire in my own work? Desire and mortality, usually so closely tied in conventional or traditional poetry—I do have roots in that kind of lyric. Maybe I've lost track.

AF: It was how do vamping metaphors play out in many different ways in that section, in terms of marriage, trauma, memory, something like masturbation.

DP: It's funny because I was going to say, "that's the rub," right? There are these structures predefined for us that we're cultured by and move into, and we make our most intimate decisions based on something not very personal at all. In the sense that everything I write is, to some degree, autobiographical because I'm always informed by lived experience, I pull from experiences in mostly hetero relationships, or being a person who got married (I don't wear my ring, but did get married in a proper legal way to a person who identifies as a man).

AF: I've seen pictures.

DP: So you've got this tension between economic arrangements you've made and what you experience as love. Or the tension between desire, what you're told to desire, how your desire gets shaped to some degree by normative rules anyhow.

AF: Yes it's interesting when you ask why do people write about desire. And in terms of quasi-pornographic elements of Gurlesque writing, too, one other question is why write anything at all? Or read anything at all? That's where pornography makes sense as an emblematic means of communication, or seems the essential means of communication, suggesting speech is always just desire.

DP: I get that. And to come at it from the culturing and education I come at it from, yeah, it's about desire but often a particular type of desire. When we look at porn as a medium, it's there to construct a particular type of hetero, masculine desire in a lot of cases. And of course it's not a perfect system so it creates all kinds of unintended things, but what it often isn't there to produce or create or cater to is either queer or hetero feminine desires. So I think one thing the Gurlesque does is say, what happens when we are in this matrix (whatever our sexualities are, we're in the matrix of hetero desire), what does it mean to be both a tool and a figure in that space? And is there a way to move that discussion or decentralize the traditional desirer? Are there ways to create space for exploring different types of desire, in which the feminine is the agent of desire and other things get objectified—or not objectified? Can desire occur between subjects? All these great questions we ask all the time. Also, what does it mean when you start to get pleasure out of this system set up to oppress you? What does it mean to get your damage and your pleasure from the same place?

AF: Well, sometimes motherhood seems vampiric in this book, as

Mommy V muses on a "new treasure brewing in her gutter." And definitely childhood becomes vampiric, as Mommy V surveys the morning vomit while reflecting that her current little one will soon "have to fend, / have to fell his own hotlings." In either case, based on a lot you've said, this is a family affair. So is the real gross-out narrative simply that of bodies passing into other bodies? This goes back to siring to some extent.

DP: There are a lot of people writing really interesting pregnancy, childbirth, child-getting, and motherhood poems. And these are all different things. Pregnancy and motherhood are not the same, but get mixed up together. The fact that a human grows inside another human, that two bodies are made from the same body, that fetal cells detach from the fetus and lodge themselves in all these different places if you're a pregnant female body, then last for decades, and attach to other babies you have. There are all those very sci-fi facts that remain for now, very literally, sci. Watch the scientists try to make a narrative of that. They say, well, these cells give you cancer, yet also protect you from cancer. They make you love your baby more. They make rats smarter. But even in their well-trained, we-know-what-our-gender-roles are kind of way, scientists can't come up with a coherent narrative. And that experience of having a human come out of your body, rely on your body, be partially made of your body can be an amazing high. It can be really beautiful and wonderful. In literal ways it produces all sorts of high-making chemicals. At the same time it can be horrifying. It can feel out of control, in part because we don't have a lot of discourse that tends to it in really direct ways. We have all these euphemisms that don't cover it. These ways of writing about it that romanticize it or make it twee or whatever, when really you get weird impulses. When my older kid started losing her baby teeth, I had this weird desire to eat the baby teeth as those fell out. Which I didn't do because I thought that might poke a hole in my stomach. Though I definitely wanted to eat. And didn't feel…I don't want to take her back into my body. She's a separate person and has her own ecosystem going. But the teeth felt like mine. I made those. So I just put them in a box and try not to eat them. And particularly for nursing, a baby literally cannibalizes your body for its body. And your body will give up everything to make milk for it. So vampirism becomes pretty literal. They'll bite. You might bleed. They grow teeth. There are these old, maybe medieval myths about colostrum being devil's milk. That whole narrative of feeding and exchange. When female vampires occasionally do—I think they still call it siring—occasionally do make another vampire, they'll always feed them off the bosom. Dracula feeds Lucy from his bosom. It's a screwed up nursing scene.

## INTERVIEW WITH CATHERINE TAYLOR
Recorded on May 4, 2012
This interview focuses on Taylor's book *Apart* (Ugly Duckling Presse).

ANDY FITCH: In case the term seems fraught or unfamiliar to some readers, can you give a working definition of "reportage"? Your definition of reportage sounds more exciting than most. How does reportage relate to, or differ from, description, witness, testimony? Do you feel broadly invested in this mode of discourse? Did this particular project call it forth?

CATHERINE TAYLOR: For me, reportage first signifies some connection to histories of journalism. It suggests that the author has made a concerted effort to conduct research in a number of different modes, which might involve observation, archival investigations, interviews. This puts the investigator on equal terms with the writer—even if the end product, the finished piece, looks radically different from what you often find in a magazine or newspaper. Even if the writing seems experimental, it makes certain assumptions about documenting experience or facts or data. Of course the final written piece might manipulate those findings in a variety of ways, not necessarily fictionalizing facts, but using language that traditional journalistic forms reject.

AF: So in terms of if you provide a more exciting definition…

CT: I consider my definition much more boring.

AF: And did this particular project call forth a distinct mode of reportage?

CT: Absolutely. I do think of my work as part of a genre, called nonfiction. I do feel invested, vested in it. My connection to the field remains partially romantic. I have suspicions about my own romantic investment in the concept of reportage, but can't seem to give it up. I love projects that grow out of meticulous observation—research that touches upon ethnography or history, historiography. I guess I also would say that "reportage" means you've made a pretty serious time commitment. Not that invention doesn't take time also. But copious observation and ethnography and research take tremendous amounts of time. This often goes unacknowledged in contemporary nonfiction discussions, particularly those focused on the essay.

AF: Finally, in terms of "reportage": that word sounds like collage, montage. Do you know what the suffix does? I'm just dumb with French.

CT: I don't.

AF: Does reportage come from French writers?

CT: We should look that up. Why do we call it "reportage"?

AF: Or when you refer to histories of journalism, which of those histories most appeal to you?

CT: I first got engaged with narrative journalism through accounts of Vietnam. And modernist projects like *Let Us Now Praise Famous Men* fascinate me, despite their problematic representations of race. I even would include books like Reznikoff's *Testimony*, which does not offer official journalism, but adopts found texts from legal sources. I sense a connection to journalism, in trying to convey specific material conditions, something about people's lived experience. I guess with my first book, focusing on midwives...that finding some way to represent what felt crucial about their work reaffirmed for me this aspect of narrative journalism, despite the fact that my next book, *Apart*, became much more experimental linguistically. This reminds me of a passage in the book, right before archival excerpts that report killings and abductions and violence during South Africa's political unrest in the '70s and ''80s. Just prior to sharing those excerpts, I provide a brief meditation on visiting archives and trying to understand my place in relation to representational futility. There I realize that my own archival sources once functioned as reportage, once attempted to shape the world as events unfolded, but now sit on this shelf turned into a kind of history. Then it becomes clear that their role as reportage in fact persists, because history remains persistent. Those inequities hadn't disappeared, so these reports from forty years ago still can function as a kind of journalism for the present. And finally this section considers how archives can operate as a physical/social space—that the archivist always feels called upon to exit the archives, that studying journalism from the past puts pressure on a researcher to deal with his/her present. I'd constantly felt, while working in the archive, that I needed to leave and document life on the streets right now. Here again, in terms of your question about how reportage differs from witness or testimony, Shoshana Felman makes a great point when she says: "Testimony cannot be simply relayed, repeated, or reported by another without thereby losing its function as testimony." She's talking about Celan, whose disruption of "conscious meaning" allows his words to "enact" rather than merely report. Of course reportage can seem to lack this intimate engagement, to provide a second-hand telling without this same testimonial power. Though I would argue that often we only have access to testimony because of such secondhand reports. So the archivist's challenge becomes to perform this enacting that Felman calls for. Can you move your secondhand discussion of some testimonial piece into a zone where the reader feels its present enacted, in a vitalizing way, pushing us beyond passivity?

AF: Along those lines, could we discuss *Apart*'s architecture, its heterogeneous profusion of forms and textual parallelisms: of prose inquiry culminating in poetic flourish; of documentarian word and image; of transparent testimonial record and kaleidoscopic paratext; of lyric allusion and scholarly inquiry? Presumably this hybrid approach embodies your broader point that the telling of the collectivity remains inseparable from the telling of the individual, and vice versa. At the same time, you write that we can call "South Africa's legacy a narcotizing mix of electoral democracy, multi-culturalism, despair, inequity and material conditions unchanged, crimes unpunished, all the things to write, but not coming to the conclusion that reconciliation's hegemony must be interrogated, so that the sjambok of the past can still sting. No heliotrope here." Given your specific engagement with South Africa's post-apartheid legacy, given your abstracted inquiry into the potential for literary representations to prompt historical reflection and present action, given what you've just said now, I feel pointed back to *Apart*'s initial Wayne Koestenbaum epigraph—addressed to those "sick of mediation, of words that get in the way." I wonder if, as you put this motley/intricate book together, it seemed more or less mediated in the sense suggested by Wayne's epigraph. What had words gotten in the way of? And how do your parallel structures seek to evade this impediment?

CT: Hmm. Words got in the way, but maybe even more, familiar narrative structures got in the way of conveying both the complex histories I wanted to tell, and the impossibility of narrative closure for each of these "stories" I encountered. I would recognize that the archival information, the dialogues and events I absorbed did not contain complete stories, though I kept feeling trapped or pulled back into story mode. Perhaps I struggled most with how to step outside that, but without writing a text that disavowed narrative. Of course some books do this brilliantly. Some versions of my book tried to do that. But little nuggets of story kept appearing, because we always, in some way, form stories as part of our meaning-making process. I wanted to acknowledge and keep this present in the text, but still have every story fall apart. Just when the reader starts to get comfortable with my narrating voice as a guide, or comfortable with my position vis-à-vis race relations, or comfortable amid the contemporary South African setting, something new should make them uncomfortable. I want to return them to a place of discomfort or confusion or at least interruption. I hope to trace the knife edge of meaning and understanding and then realizing that a meaning we've made might be the wrong one. And then to ask: how could we tell it again?

AF: I hadn't thought of *Things Fall Apart*. I'm probably the last reader to get that allusion. Do you want to describe, in "Duffer's Drift" for example, the types of narrative split that occur, the types of mediation you evade, or construct?

CT: "Duffer's Drift" presents one text at the page's top, and a different text at the page's bottom, with a large white space in between. I'd started with a simple sense of the top text providing a white traveler's narrative, which dominates the bottom text's attempt to offer something more explanatory and less personal. The top text tells the story of me visiting a dance hall with my cousins, in a very white neighborhood, and in the middle of this community dance an intermission occurs where the band stops and a troupe for what is called a "Cape Colored coon show" comes on. My cousin cringes and tells me yes, this really is a coon show, but you don't understand. So when I went back and wrote the bottom piece, I researched the whole fascinating history of minstrel shows that traveled from the United States to

South Africa in the late 1800s—how they became a local tradition in colored townships around Cape Town, which continues to this day. I wanted to explore how the coon show remains an inevitably racist institution, though not necessarily racist in the way it first appeared to me. So my top narrative sounds moderately lyrical, and tries to sustain the moment of my confused encounter with this performance. The bottom half traces my research, yet never offers a complete account. Again, each evades narrative. Then somewhere in the essay's middle I start including images juxtaposed against the text. Some images develop a trope, if you will, of tents and shelters—photos of black South Africans forced to live in tents under apartheid. Other images show well-intentioned but naïve white students on U.S. campuses living in fake shanty towns (myself included), and then white South African soldiers, deeply involved in the oppressive regime, inhabiting their own military tents. Here I follow those juxtapositions with a quote from Jacques Rancière, who describes montage as having two different functions. One mode asks viewers to think about montage "revealing one world behind another: the far-off conflict behind home comforts." Yet Rancière also describes this second form of montage, of pulling unlike elements together, taking supposedly foreign elements and establishing a new sense of familiarity. Both of these montage movements happen at once, and become what he calls history. I like that idea. I kind of wish "Duffer's Drift" could run five volumes long, because I want to proliferate the juxtapositions and bring so much more into the text. But as always with archival work, you end up leaving so much out.

AF: Sure, basic questions of volume emerge through this dynamic contrast. Length limits could prompt anxiety on your part, but instead provide a constructivist means for creating new forms of readerly awareness. Perhaps this is a corny cliché, but the binary or tension between "truth and reconciliation" kept coming up for me. Have you just described something similar?

CT: Well the idea that a nation could stage events in which truths get told, and this telling of truths could allow for reconciliation, remains kind of an amazing one. It could sound amazingly naïve or amazingly utopian, but has become a real and tremendously powerful fact for many South Africans. Of course this bid for reconciliation failed to retain its utopian promise beyond that moment when the government broadcast it and sucked viewers into the spectacle of it. That spectacle had a cathartic impact on people, but without economic reparations or material shifts in citizens' lives to follow, they couldn't sustain this utopian space in any way. So definitely the truth and reconciliation dichotomy preoccupied my mind when I first got there. I first thought this book would focus on the Truth and Reconciliation Commission's work. I'd hoped to find moments of reconciliation I could recount. But that just wasn't my experience. The TRC's work felt incredibly distant. Nobody I spoke to seemed all that focused on reconciliation. People talked about poverty and redistribution of wealth. These quickly became far more important than the truth and reconciliation rhetoric that so dominated public discourse in the 90s.

AF: Again it interests me how testimony and something like rumination or critical reflection continually push against each other in *Apart*. In some abstract sense, truth and reconciliation seem to exist simultaneously within a piece like "Duffer's Drift."

CT: I certainly hope that happens. Facts and reflection hopefully become inseparable. "Duffer's Drift's" strict demarcations begin to collapse. Then maybe in the book's later prose-poem sections, similar tensions grow more tightly entwined. *Apart* opens on the topic of oscillation, of shifting back and forth, because I want the reader to feel continual oscillations between modes of discourse. Those increasingly rapid alternations might work even better in film than in a written text.

AF: Well, questions of address get foregrounded throughout, most obviously in the letters addressed to "A." This oscillation between the idiom of the journal-keeper and the idiom of the letter-writer intrigued me. From the opening Cape Town journals, you foreground scenarios in which a detached, dispassionate voice gets challenged, gets triangulated, pulled between self-consciousness and group-consciousness. The discursive register shuttles among self-identified black and colored and white South African voices. Perspectival shifts keep taking place. Then, amid all these shifting vectors, all of a sudden we read "You are writing a letter in your head," and encounter subsequent letters to "A" which offer this new mode of address, this tone both more intimate and more detached simultaneously. Can you discuss the role that those personalized/abstracted addresses to "A" play here? And please feel free, given what you've just said about cinematic possibilities, to bring in Chris Marker's film *Sans Soleil,* which ends with that memorable line "Will there be a last letter?"

CT: At first these letters felt heuristic for me. But I kept them because I did want that sense of intimacy you mentioned. The letters pretend, or attempt (but I want to say pretend rather than attempt) to provide some access to an intimacy with the narrator. They offer a quick glimpse of me in a relationship, separate from the history I seek to excavate, though critical to this research project. Trying to tell this one person what happened helped me keep going forward. And without that one person…I couldn't write a letter to the collectivity. Some writers can, or do, but I couldn't. Originally I didn't know whom I was writing the book for, or writing to, beyond myself and this one other person. Though I also think that something about the letters' erotic subtext….I can't tell how much this comes through, but an almost libidinal economy motivates the letter-writer, which gets tied to the personal relations and intimacies of her other stories. And of course, letters addressed to a specific other, then read by the reader, make this reader a voyeur. These letters both address and don't at all address the reader.

AF: That keeps the libidinal economy palpable for the reader, who again feels triangulated amid the exchange.

CT: And hopefully, if the reader becomes aware of this voyeuristic space, he/she can transfer that same awareness to other moments—to recognize the voyeuresque moment of the archives, or of overheard dialogues, or overheard encounters.

AF: To return to *Sans Soleil,* your letters themselves present Marker's film as a point of reference. And of course in *Sans Soleil* each letter begins with a female voice declaring, "He writes…" They imagine for us, or ask us to imagine, a respondent, presumably a letter-writer herself. Likewise, throughout *Apart*, I never have a definitive sense of a historical, autobiographical "I" coordinating the book. But then those letters seem to stage, to perform an identity, one specifically addressed to me, so calling forth this embodied subject on both sides—constructing a reader as much as a writer.

CT: That's why I preferred to use the word "pretend" just now. This book offers no real pretense that the letters come from or go to a particular person. But they do, as you say, provide some sense of a staged identity, both individual and collective.

AF: Here can we move a bit from the epistolary topic, the letters, to citation and transcription? Could you describe some types of research in which *Apart* engages? So many quotes arise—from Robert Sobukwe to Steve Biko to Frantz Fanon to Joan Didion to Walter Benn Michaels. Can you discuss how these citational practices relate to your own mode of reportage? If reportage typically offers facts on the ground, yours seems to suggest a much broader archival, scholarly, reflective process.

CT: I'm tempted to answer by turning to somebody else's work. Your question makes me think of Rachel Blau DuPlessis, her intensely scholastic notes to the long poem "Draft." I'll often end up reading that poem as footnote to the footnotes, as if the poem's linguistic explorations represent a response to her essay in footnotes. And I feel that my own work has some similarities, that citations form its base, that the citations represent a long-term engagement with particular texts and types of historical research—though again it didn't interest me to reproduce those histories in a comprehensive academic manner. Still citations truly undergird this text, even if they seem to present some fringe apparatus. They give little glimpses of that wall that stands behind everything else.

AF: Your book also responds explicitly to Gertrude Stein, Edmond Jabès, George Oppen, Robert Duncan, Robert Smithson. This particular grouping led me to wonder where you would position yourself amid attempts to distinguish between a political and an aesthetic avant-garde. What I mean is: Stein for one seems unlikely to appear in most accounts of South African history, yet ends up fitting perfectly here. Do you think of yourself as reclaiming political valences often ignored in the work of such figures?

CT: No. I don't think of myself as reclaiming something political in her work, though that might be there. Poets like Stein help me develop my own politics within my own aesthetics, but I don't seek to make some broader claim about her work in this way. I don't try to push that backwards onto Stein. *Apart* feels somewhat like a commonplace book, a glimpse into everything I'd read over the span in which I wrote this. Yet all those specific readings made perfect sense at the time. You know when you'll get in that space where everything you read seems connected? I think this impulse to connect probably just provides a way to listen in on the internal conversation you're already having—that the authors who appear in *Apart* are the ones who helped me think. People like Biko, or Ruth Leys (writing about shame), emerge in a much more focused way. Poets like Oppen offer more a general life raft. When I couldn't think about this project anymore, I could go read Oppen and feel buoyed for a bit. Referencing here often just means honoring those who provided a productive model. How can I keep going with incredibly difficult questions and problems about representation that seem endemic and perpetual? I can't get around them. I either have to walk away or keep trying. Those authors you mentioned helped me keep trying, because I'd watched them try something similar.

AF: Along such lines, in what ways can we consider *Apart* a broader attempt to write, ethically, from the perspective of privilege? You say somewhere that "the question of choice is always so buried by privilege." That "so" in "so buried" seemed perhaps the strongest editorializing in the whole book. And here the Gramsci epigraph stands out: "The starting point of critical elaboration is the consciousness of what one really is, and is 'knowing thyself' as a product of the historical process to date which has deposited in you an infinity of traces, without leaving an inventory. Therefore, it is imperative at the outset to compile such an inventory." The infinitudes of historical process and the traces that these leave inside us…does it remain an impossible task to extricate oneself from these types of privilege? Again, what negotiations between truth and reconciliation can guide us as we write from a perspective of privilege?

CT: Or as we try to figure out what that would even mean: what might it mean to write ethically from a position of privilege? What does it mean to be able to acknowledge privilege without dwelling too much on it? For me this goes back to the trope of oscillation. I need to acknowledge. I need to leave that trace. I need to make clear my subject position, though really this subject position seems not quite interesting, not what's at stake. So the aesthetic question becomes how long should I stay there and how quickly can I move off? When and where do I need to come back? How often could or should such examinations resurface in any text I write? Because I always write from a position of privilege. Or, to date, I've always written from some position of privilege. And perhaps, as writers, we all always write from a position of privilege. So how to keep those traces apparent without letting them take over the story?

## INTERVIEW WITH ANDREA REXILIUS
Recorded on May 7, 2012
This interview focuses on Rexilius' book *Half of What They Carried Flew Away* (Letter Machine Editions).

ANDY FITCH: I've got a couple design questions. The first came as soon as I glanced at your manuscript's title fading into gray by the time I'd reached its end—reminding me of digitized verbal art by someone like Jenny Holzer. Does this idea of kinetic text cued for the fleeting event, rather than the fixed, final object appeal to you?

ANDREA REXILIUS: I do think about text in a kinetic way, as communication based in tactile experience. I actually didn't design this book, but did make up the title, which suggests processes of erasure while keeping in place some sense of fixed, forward movement. This text's accumulation provides an active experience, an unstable act of pinning down language.

AF: Can you discuss the book's divisions into "residences"? Amid references to installation, performance, and relational art, not to mention Heideggerian conceptions of Logos as a dwelling, what additional connotations does "residence" acquire? What about Edmond Jabès' exiled, home-bound attachment to the printed page? What about Renee Gladman's installations? Or Gertrude Stein's meditations?

AR: Probably what resonates most there is Heidegger and Jabès. I return often to their ideas of language as a dwelling place or residence. And with these particular residences, I wanted the word "residence" to contain the idea of residue, residue as something gestural, which doesn't retain the initial object but maintains its trace, perhaps its shape. Then I wanted to address the idea of exile, like that kind of wandering through Jabès's *Book of Questions* (which has so many different sections housing their own discrete meditations, or series of concerns), so that each residence in my book also houses a specific concern, providing its secondary title: desire, water, territory. Amid these fleeting forms, something always morphs and becomes the next concern. No stable structure appears—only something that can be flown away.

AF: At first when I saw the word "residence," I'd thought of some stable, permanent dwelling (perhaps because I bought a house two days ago). But of course this word has particular connotations for poets, in the sense of a residency—some temporary, habitable place you might get booted from before too long. So I especially appreciated your interweaving of blank space, blank pages, sequential "crossings," all apparently designed to score or choreograph a more immersive durational experience for the reader. Do these blank passages contain intended affects, as they might in music, in terms of contextual meaning, tone, length of time one spends on them? Do you conceive of them as zones vacated of authorial control? Or do they have different functions in different instances? It always amazes me that this type of architectural scaffolding can get imposed upon a lump of prose long after most of the supposed writing has occurred, with the whole project then picking up an aura of organic inevitability, as if it always had been that way. So what was the actual assembly process here?

AR: I'll start with how the spaces got there, then circle back to what they do. Josh and Noah, Letter Machine's editors, suggested a lot of the spacing between sections, also where some crossings take place. Those we put in, and italicized. We thought of them as coming from a different voice, less me, or more me asking questions of the text. We'd wanted to signal some kind of vocal shift, or pronoun shift—to allow another voice to enter. But for the rest of this book's spacing: a durational prose project can get so bogged down with one thing after the next that those spaces serve as pauses to take a breath, to consider what you've just seen. I want blank space to become interactive, to provide a place where you can have your own moment to reflect or ask questions while still within the text.

AF: Could you describe a bit further how you three worked all of this out together, just since it sounds like a relatively harmonious, productive collaboration? What state was the manuscript in when Josh and Noah first saw it?

AR: In terms of written prose, it was pretty much in this final state. They read it and sent some notes—about commas, really small things. The centered text blocks now look a bit different. When writing, I'd just used a Word document and sprawled across the entire page. They had me clean that up. I already had revised this manuscript for a while before letting them consider it.

AF: Further design questions keep coming. But I feel I've already used metaphors of music, dance, architecture, performance, conceptual art, and I'd prefer to hear more from you about which media inform your modes of composition. Your book itself raises questions that obviously could be asked of its author. Can I pose a couple?

AR: Sure.

AF: These come from page 13: "How transparent is this genre? / Is it a conceptual event? / Is it a document of performance itself? / How might the degree of transparency map this object? / Is it a dog lapping up milk? / Is it informal?"

AR: Well, performance informs what I do quite a bit. I'll think of blank pages as a curtain closing, as a signal that some shift's taking place, that your palate should be cleansed before moving on to the next scene. Not just with this book, but with any of my writing, I think about and through performance—specifically conceptual events, not spaces of ideas necessarily, but more experience-based.

AF: Your book feels like that.

AR: For my MFA I went to the Art Institute of Chicago, because cross-genre classes interested me. Beyond just poetry or fiction workshops, you could take courses in performance or painting or sound. A lot of the poetry classes had image components, where you'd create a sculpture or film alongside a piece of writing. Professors encouraged interdisciplinary projects. Lin Hixson, who directs the performance group Goat Island, taught an influential (for me) performance art class. Goat Island does these fascinating performances based on everyday actions. They might look at the way a tree moves, or a dog moves, then translate that into human movement. They also combine film and text (not just their own text but texts from other writers) into beautiful multimedia performances based mainly in dance. So while taking Lin's class, I'd thought a lot about the body or through the body and how experience informs what and how we know things. When I would create performances, they came from a space that wasn't just about language, that wasn't about articulation. I wrote, but in a cyclical way. And later I'd see what those experiences gave me in terms of writing. I wouldn't literally translate them, but would track how bodily experience shaped my thoughts about the world. That duality always interests me. When I write I try to tap that unlanguaged experience even as I make something textual. Maybe I want a subconscious embedded in the consciousness.

AF: Just to clarify how performance shapes this book, am I right that *Half of What They Carried Flew Away* does not provide scores or scripts to be performed, but tries to operate in the way performance does?

AR: It's not meant to be performed, at least I hadn't thought of that. It's more about composition than actual performing. If I designed a performance based on the book, this would invoke parallel constructions rather than…

AF: Some literal reenactment.

AR: If that were even possible.

AF: Both sound fun. But your book opens with frequent, somewhat amorphous references to "they" (which reminded me of Juliana Spahr's frequent deployment of this pronoun), in a variety of first-, second-, third-person singular and plural contexts. Does your deployment of "they" deliberately produce, or just happen to suggest, a discourse of complicity—one that collapses distinctions between authorial testimony, readerly projection, abstracted narrative? Later in this book, "they" even picks up a more conventional, grammatically awkward usage, when "they" gets born as a baby girl.

AR: "They" helped me think through a couple of concerns. First, I wanted to experiment with writing something longer. Though I usually write long projects. I feel incapable of writing a single poem. I don't understand how to place one poem beside another, then turn that into a collection. I can't grasp how the "I" of one poem relates to the "I" of the next. Pronouns can become problematic for me. But "they" seems more relevant here than "I" does. And I wanted to experiment with not using an idea to generate work, but using a pronoun—as if writing a novel. I tried to trick myself into writing a novel. Of course, I knew it wouldn't be a novel. I began writing this poem, but wanted it to feel durational and progress in a somewhat linear way from the first residence to the second to the end of the book. Soon I had to ask myself: if this works like a novel, who will the characters be? Who will its pronouns be? I didn't really want characters, so "they" made sense. And I was in fact reading Juliana Spahr's *The Transformation*.

AF: Where she lives in Hawai'i, with her two partners.

AR: I'd read her book right before starting the project, and that seemed a brilliant way to solve this pronoun problem. Lots of questions already had arisen for me about "they" then Juliana Spahr provided this collective voicing, this displacement of an authoritative "I"—though still with a lyric echo. Those two seemed tied together. Or when I think about the lyric, I'll think of Cindy Sherman dressing up as other famous people and photographing herself. When I'm an "I" in poetry, it feels like Cindy Sherman in disguise: I'm here, but also distanced. I'm dressed up, performing, embodying someone else. It interests me how a pronoun could signal that, especially amid a lyric voice. Because I do think of this book's "they" as the lyric speaker. It still feels like lyric poetry, but calls attention to questions of embodied presence.

AF: In terms of the Cindy Sherman comparison, the multiplicity that you've described, can you discuss the function of this book's "crossings"? Do the crossings allow different personae or trajectories to intersect?

AR: Questions and answers show up at the crossings. Those two processes come together. Again, it's like Cindy Sherman posing simultaneously both as herself and as this other. At the crossings you can recognize that. Maybe this mimics an epiphany. Some opening happens, some dialogue instead of just statements.

AF: And given your desire to draft something like a novel, does prose's straightforward, cumulative delivery become crucial to the comparative, serialized experience? Prose seems more streamlined. We can absorb it fast, so we can place different units in relation to each other. Does that draw you to it?

AR: I do think it would be much more difficult (for me at least) to try something similar in lineated poetry. I prefer shaping blank space that parallels the prose blocks. This provides a lot more room on each individual page, between prose entries, even as each residence presents its own overall poem. Prose also helps maintain the trace of a plot, not that some very explicit plot happens, but situations arise through and across prose blocks in ways they couldn't in a more traditional poem.

AF: That definitely occurs on a macro level, in our comprehension of the book as a whole. But can we again look at a couple specific

*Interview with Andrea Rexilius*

sections? On page 41, for example, those lines: "The river remembers. Living resembles it. That spring is growing, composed of many songs. My windows and my doors are open. I can hear how it is turning into evening. It is comprehensible that they are becoming clearer. Separate spots here and there gather. Not even the smallest thing touches anymore." A paragraph like this, which comes to a resolution of content as much as it needs to, seems largely the product of compression, and editing for sound. Each sentence seems to feed into the next. Could you, in whatever way you want, describe the writing process of such lines, or the effect they have on you or you hope for them to have on readers?

AR: Especially in those first two lines, "The river remembers. Living resembles it," you can hear one word shift into another, more as a sonic progression than…I don't know.

AF: Narrative or something.

AR: Right. Still when I hear it, just under the surface I'll sense coherent meaning. I'm not sure how well I could articulate that. The line "My windows and my doors are open" suggests some idea of development, I suppose: spring growing, spaces opening, scenes turning, day becoming evening (but you hearing the turn to evening rather than seeing it). This all seems less about sight than emotion, as subterranean shifts resettle, then with that last line distinguishing itself, pulling apart to clarify the situation.

AF: Along analogous lines, certain words in this book accrue unanticipated additive meanings or tones. "Bone," for example, or "windmill" keeps popping up. Do such words deliberately get threaded throughout as an index of duration—giving a sense of time's passage, that we've returned to something then moved on again?

AR: Definitely. The windmill seemed this dualization of a crossing, both showing a cross and enacting that movement. The word "bone" I hadn't noticed repeating, but perhaps suggests something left behind.

AF: Well, given that this book starts with "they," I'm curious about the final page of text. That final page presents a series of I-driven statements, yet includes the line "I undertake not to represent, interpret, or symbolize, but to make maps and draw lines." Can you

63

discuss this final mapping of the "I"?

AR: As I wrote the book, I'd really tried not to...I tend, when drafting a project, to analyze where it's going. Here I didn't want to interpret while composing. But halfway through I couldn't help it. I couldn't hide the project from myself and started to wonder who "they" were—if "they" were ghosts or what. I was teaching this composition course about people whose voices didn't get heard during their lives, but who kept writing anyway. Then I realized: oh god, "they" are these people. So I grew more and more aware of who "they" were, and, as I became aware, tried to avoid adding too much interpretation. I wanted to stay out of this book a bit. Still, as I became more clear about "they," the "I" started to announce itself and become more present, like the director of the text. So that line you quote comes from me wanting not to speak for anyone else. I meant it to sound quite literal. I want this book to allow for experience to take place, but not for me to theorize who "they" or "I" are, or what that means in the world. Just inhabiting the "they" seemed enough—letting this text make a map, draw a line, which somebody else could look at, read, interpret, use.

### INTERVIEW WITH MATVEI YANKELEVICH
Recorded on May 8th
This interview focuses on Yankelevich book *Alpha Donut* (United Artists).

ANDY FITCH: You're the first poet I know to have a selected shorter works published. But why selected "works," not "poems"? Does "works" suggest something more constructivist, less lyrical? And to what extent have you stitched together a coherent book-length project out of these shorter works?

MATVEI YANKELEVICH: I call a few pieces "Poem," but it doesn't feel like a collection of poems. Many prose fragments come from a series called "Writing in the Margin." Then the book culls from another series and miscellaneous projects. I'd felt wary about assembling a collection. So I took this idea of the collection, of disparate parts, to its extreme—placing beside each other various rhythms and visual designs. The book doesn't cohere the way a conventional poetry collection might, with each section offering specific types of poems. I wanted to resist the process where you submit a manuscript for a contest or something and think about…people suggest a certain sequence will grab the reader from the start and announce a basic structure. This book runs counter to that. So "selected works" of course sounds ironic, though it also makes clear you won't find a book of self-contained lyrics. *Alpha Donut* coheres through typesetting, not content.

AF: *Alpha Donut*, A.D., sounds post-something.

MY: Nah. Not exactly. It refers back to a famous modernist volume (Anna Akhmatova's *Anno Domini*) from the early '20s. My grandfather also had those initials, and the book includes a little piece about my grandfather. I guess that A.D. part hints at being late—with my first poetic collection appearing when I'm almost 40. I really consider this my first book of poems, though I'd just described it as not a book of poems. My chapbooks feel like long poems. *Boris by the Sea* seems more a novel or fragmentary narrative.

AF: Shorter "works" popular in the U.S.—from somebody like Kafka, let's say—lean heavily on allegory, or some readers assume they lean heavily on allegory. I know this becomes a controversial topic with Kafka. But I also know that, for your Daniil Kharms volume, you argue against predominant Cold War depictions of Kharms as an allegorical critic of the U.S.S.R. What distinctive functions of a shorter work get overlooked by allegory-heavy interpretations?

MY: First, I'd hesitate to equate an allegorical reading with a political reading. My response to Kharms doesn't discount many possibilities for allegory. For instance, for his shorter works, I resisted describing them as "texts" since that sounds too closed, too finished somehow. So the Kharms book got subtitled *Selected Writings*. As for my own book, my friend Filip Marinovich first coaxed me into assembling a collection, though he suggested a title from one of the prose pieces: *In the Sunlight of Unemployment*. The book has much to do with employment or unemployment or work and leisure and an exhausted laziness, or anti-work. But finally this title seemed too ironic, kind of coy. My publisher Lewis Warsh didn't like it and never could remember it. Whenever he mentioned it, he'd change the title. Alpha Donuts, the physical place, is a coffee shop where I used to spend time, not really working, kind of listening to people, absorbing a foreign urban environment—one of my first New York neighborhoods. Alpha Donuts comes from a different time (before the end of the era of donut shops), though it still exists, surprisingly, since Queens doesn't change so fast as Brooklyn or Manhattan. Many customers seemed unemployed. I went when I was unemployed. I'd also go after working in the Queens public schools. Sometimes I'd stop in even after I moved to Brooklyn. I'd stop to have this weird, out-of-time/off-of-work experience. The book offers many short-attention-span pieces that happen amid the malaise of leisure or employment. For a while I tried titles that included "labor." Then I happened to pass this place while furiously searching for a final title. It dawned on me that with *Alpha Donut*...compared to Dunkin' Donuts, the singular "donut" seemed more interesting.

AF: The odd donut. The ugly duckling of donuts.

MY: Almost the suggestion of primary...of zero and a one, the first of something meaningless or banal, the number-one pastry. That phrase also spoke to labor and unemployment and life in this city—through some binary code of ones and zeroes.

AF: Yes, I've never known if the donut-shop era ended, or if I just moved on. But in terms of what you've said: does this aesthetic of idleness or laziness appeal to you in other writers? I think of Kenko, the Japanese author, his *Essays in Idleness,* or Pessoa's *Book of Disquiet,* or Robert Walser's and Peter Altenberg's feuilletons.

MY: Definitely all that stuff and Henri Michaux's drug writings, in some ways. I don't know the Japanese essayist you mentioned.

AF: Fourteenth century.

MY: Walser became important to me. This book spans twelve years of discontinuous projects, so the authors it responds to might seem all over the place. But that aesthetic you described appears in Kharms, in Walser. For me an important part of writing comes from the not-writing, the inabilities of writing. "Writing in the Margin" speaks to this subject.

AF: Could you talk about two of the book's series, both "Writing in the Margin" and "Bar Poems"? "Bar Poems" reminds me of Joe Wenderoth's *Letters to Wendy's,* but from the perspective of a communal "we"—perhaps the figment of a "we," the "we" of a bar, even an empty bar.

MY: Well, "Writing in the Margin" began in the late '90s, around my Alpha Donuts visits. Many parts remain unpublished. One chapbook appeared a decade ago. I wrote these fragments like marginal notes to a book that may or may not exist. I meant for them to seem secondary, sort of echoing your point about A.D. As for "Bar Poems," of the more than 100, I used maybe 25. I've written many different types of bar poems, then began working on them as a series in the late 2000s. Like the donut shop, the bar offers a space of non-working, but where you can think. It has a communal aspect. I wrote a few bar poems with other people, or often for other people—kind of as occasional poems. Some echo the pseudo-scholastic "Writing in the Margin," whereas others present a more boozy attitude.

AF: Depending upon the hour when you wrote them?

MY: I didn't always write them in bars, though back then you still could smoke in bars. I mostly stopped writing them once that changed. Bars no longer felt like spaces of leisure. They seem more like New York restaurants, where the staff is waiting for you to leave.

AF: Both series felt ongoing, potentially endless, perhaps much longer by now. Do you appreciate how, let's say, Robert Duncan's "Passages" or "Structure of Rime" get threaded through multiple volumes? And does your role as a translator of dead poets like Kharms (with his completed oeuvre, his completed life rather than the latest installment) shape your own perspective as a writer? Do you think, I'll just work on this ongoing series and maybe someday someone can put it together?

MY: Yeah, partly. I hope possibly to do stand-alone collections of "Writings in the Margin" and "Bar Poems." But when I've put them all together I again encounter this problem of book-length thematics, of overarching structure, which seems too monolithic to me. I don't mean to discount project-based work. But it interests me less to prove I can complete the project. That often feels like a false proof, a bad proof in math, as if we only can value finished projects. So, on one hand, I have groups or series published here and there that someday might add up to collections. At the same time, I doubt the necessity of doing that. I don't imagine a second selected shorter works—though if this book goes into a second edition it could change.

AF: Lytle Shaw has a new scholarly manuscript called *Fieldworks*, where he discusses Bernadette Mayer and Clark Coolidge in the mid to late '60s creating coherent, book-length projects considered radical at the time—because these broke from conventions of a poetic volume containing short, solitary lyrics. But you seem to have suggested that contemporary presses, or the way poetic contests work, have reversed this trend. Ugly Duckling itself has republished Mayer's terrific journal *0 TO 9*, and publishes many book-length projects.

MY: Sure, I've spoken without really referencing UDP, since my point of view on my own work stays separate. UDP often has mentioned in its mission statement that we seek out project-oriented works. I have endless admiration for such projects. And so far I've thought about my books not through a thematic but some kind of conceptual framework. I don't conceive of poems as perfected individual pieces. Still, for *Alpha Donut* I tried to take away any conceptual structure. Or take it in some other direction than what I do at UDP. Though of course project-oriented publishing remains quite marginal compared to collections of discrete lyrics, right? The majority of prizes and awards and broader literary recognition still go to poetic collections.

AF: Could an anti-structural book present its own cohesive structure? Robert Walser has a piece called "Combination Platter," and I'll wonder if *Alpha Donut* offers something similar, providing its own distinct arrangement.

MY: Yeah, often I find books too compartmentalized. Their combination platter feels rigid, with fixed dividers, like a TV dinner. I prefer the combination platter already picked through at a dinner party, whose pieces have shifted around. Yet I wouldn't have tried this with anybody's book but my own—to throw it all up in the air and think of how it lands as a rhythm. I wouldn't handle somebody else's work that way.

AF: How does this compositional process differ from *Boris by the Sea*? Both present a lightly thematized seriality, though with their sequence interrupting any progressive timeline. Boris will die, then he'll come back.

MY: In that sense they may seem similar. But *Boris* contains all these different endings to a single narrative or to different narratives that happen to the same character or at least to characters with the same name. I wanted fragments to exist without creating a whole, just as, with Kharms, you could have a collected works which doesn't add up, actually, as opposed to some modernist approaches which subsume the fragment—obscuring the fracture of the fabric. I wanted *Boris* to impede those moments where a narrative or chronology or theme might solidify. When my typeset proof came from *Boris'* publishers, they somehow formatted the text so that the end of one prose block got cut off. I almost asked them to correct this, then realized it looked great. You want to flip the page to see how or where this sentence continues. An accident cut out that part of the text which completed the text too well.

AF: Well, when I think of a defamiliarizing poetics, I first think of Language poetics. Though, as Eric Baus and I discussed last week, Shklovsky of course referred to Tolstoy. And in your own work I'll note what seems (again in comparison to classic Language poetics) a soft defamiliarization, one that tracks syntax just as carefully, yet allows for lighter touches. Both *Alpha Donut* and *Boris* provide a straightforward delivery, almost a narrative, as you say, but one that leads to enigmatic developments. I could give an example. Do you have the book near you?

MY: I'm a minute from the office, still walking, in the Can Factory now, not yet the office.

AF: You'd mentioned your grandfather. *Alpha Donut* contains the "After my Grandfather Died..." poem. At first this seems a straightforward allegory about "you" being unable to fit in your elders' shoes. Though then it ends: "My own father's feet are smaller than my own. I guess I'll never wear them." You'll never wear your father's feet? Those linguistic twists often happen here. On the next page, in "Notes to the Photographer," we encounter the line: "The tree trunk bare and gray against the full wall." What's a "full wall"?

MY: I love that question. I have no answer, just a curiosity, as you say, for little language glitches. I haven't fully articulated for myself this attraction to slightly derailing moments, since they tend to stay quiet and subtle. I'm not a very quick reader, and write slowly. I can't tell whether this causes classic defamiliarization, like Tolstoy's descriptions of the opera or something, because my prose doesn't take for granted that you know the place. It naively describes the world as though unknown to us. Whereas for Shklovsky, that familiar world now should feel fresh, in order to achieve literariness.

AF: Some sort of mimetic end gets reached.

MY: Give me one sec. I'm distracted. Sorry. Can you say that again?

AF: Well we could move on to...

MY: I'm kind of curious about it. I love Shklovsky and think his terms remain useful, and usefully misinterpreted by the Language school, which takes Russian formalism in an interesting direction before much of that work gets properly translated.

AF: I'd started thinking about defamiliarization as I looked at the prose passage "How to Use a Library." That's the first piece of yours I ever read, I think in *LIT* magazine 10 years ago. I always loved how, halfway through, the clause "if cat" appears—like in case you happen to be a cat. That brought me to the Shklovsky/Tolstoy comparison since Shklovsky's essay talks about Tolstoy writing from the perspective of a horse. But the more general question is: I too find Language readings of Shklovsky quite productive, yet I do wonder, following your work with Kharms, if you sense a wider defamiliarizing continuum (from Tolstoy to Futurists like Khlebnikov and Kruchenykh), a broader range in which forms of defamiliarization play out that depart both from Tolstoy's neo-realist and from Zaum's proto-Language poetics. Did Kharms give you some sense of other ways to go?

MY: Definitely, particularly in terms of narrative/non-narrative structure. Narrative stays important in Kharms, but primarily in terms of prose mechanics. So you could call it a much more allegorical style, not a mimetic style, yet a plot with physical movement in it. Strangely, this can seem much more formalist than the defamiliarization that Shklovsky imagines. Kharms of course pays careful attention to letters and spelling, or misspellings, and his focus on the letter level shapes my work. Also in distinction, as you said, to Language poetry, Kharms's prose delivery foregrounds a seeming directness, a seeming simplicity. Kharms's limitation or poverty of vocabulary remains really important to me, alongside his brevity and quick exhaustion of the text, rather than the New Sentence that could go on and on, or how Clark Coolidge can go on and on and on—with a kind of pleasure that to me gets too fascistic in some way.

AF: You've mentioned Kharms's interest in letters. In *Alpha Donut,* "letters" eventually evolve from being alphabetical notations (printed characters), to forms of correspondence. Or the word "call" will refer to naming something, then morph into making a phone call. Shifting degrees of intimacy recur throughout. I remember this from Boris as well. These short episodes seem to head one way though then turn out some other way, always kind of bittersweet. Do you value a melancholic/ironic tonal quality, and does that in part distinguish your work from Language poetics—that you remain less interested in circumventing or demystifying murky tonal convolutions than in embracing, probing, reinventing them?

MY: This gets hard to talk about, not because I don't want to, but because I don't know how exactly to discuss tonal shifts. I like what you'd said about shifts in intimacy. The Russian word for "letter," pis'mo [письмо], as in a letter you send, is also "writing" itself, as in écriture.

AF: Sort of like "belles lettres."

MY: Kharms explores this parallel, though not explicitly. Those minor shifts for me come perhaps more out of Kruchenykh's idea of sdvig [сдвиг], i.e. shift, a realignment or deformation rather than a defamiliarization—a slide, like a Derridean aporia. So defamiliarization derives from textual mimesis, whereas Zaum investigates textual textures themselves.

AF: I remember the lines, from your poem "A/M," "Proximity / of sky, despite its distance. Distance / of others in spite of proximity." I love those moody shifts throughout the book. They remind me of my favorite part in figure skating, which is just when the person starts skating backwards.

MY: Those sudden shifts in register that happen, in my own life, are what amaze me.

AF: You'll often throw in American colloquialisms, such as "ain't," and "come off it." But do song lyrics also get laced into this book? Like the phrase "between thought and expression" appears—the title of a Lou Reed collection. Or even for *Boris by the Sea*, I always hear Johnny Cash's line about "Georgia by the sea."

MY: Both in this book and in *Boris*, I'll always with some irony stay aware of my foreignness. So when I say "ain't" it sounds stupid, different, not really part of my lexicon. I'll deliberately borrow, provide a gimmick, pretend to be an American writer, specifically American, since for me that suggests so much problematic poetic and political history. I'll quote something, or echo some manner of expression, which nonetheless remains inaccessible to me. Even though I grew up in this country I feel a distance, a resistance to its language, as a bilingual speaker and bicultural person. Even within our small community, the difficulty of, say, pronouncing my name serves as a marker. So in terms of interjecting American speech, I do listen to a lot of American music, folk music. Sometimes I'll address this distance through that—partaking in the culture while keeping cognizant of my difference.

AF: Yeah, in terms of embodying an American writer, especially through colloquialisms such as "come off it," the poet that comes to mind for me is James Schuyler. Or now I'm remembering a Fabio Cleto lecture about the relationship between translation and camp—how each always offers a self-conscious performance of meaning, a more deliberate and deliberated communication. And in terms of such triangulations, I've got one last question. For your poem "In Memoriam Daniil Kharms" I couldn't get out of my mind Benozzo Gozzoli's late-Renaissance painting *The Beheading of John the Baptist*. Do you know that one?

MY: Yeah.

AF: Can you comment on the relationship?

MY: This relates to a whole genre, or motif, in art and literature, but specific to Kharms: my poem picks up on little references (veilings and unveilings) that occur in an important letter he wrote, and an amazing longer work, the play-poem "Lapa" ("The Paw"). This has a character named Amenhotep who also is at the same time the Nile River as well as a diagram. This diagram sort of maps out a person's headless body with its head on the side. That head also becomes a kind of creature but also a letter. Kharms doesn't refer directly to John the Baptist, but Amenhotep with his head torn off seems to prefigure that beheading. This figure's headlessness spatializes the body in a distinct way, foregrounding an aerial view, like of the city streets.

AF: And of course in the painting, as Salome does her Dance of Seven Veils, Gozzoli provides compartmentalized scenes, as does *Boris* or

*Alpha Donut*, with any number of discrete narrative snippets set beside each other, rather than any totalizing plot progression. Ok, we're way over time.

## INTERVIEW WITH LAURA WETHERINGTON
Recorded on May 19, 2012
This interview focuses on Wetherington's book *A Map Predetermined and Chance* (Fence).

ANDY FITCH: Perhaps because I respect your work on the audio journal textsound, reading *A Map Predetermined and Chance* lead to questions about sonic elements and music-related thematics. Your book may acknowledge that "this sentence does not rhyme," but its melopoetic touches, its deft assonance, syncopated prose rhythms and literal musical scores interrupted any quick assimilation of content. What are the autobiographical, literary, argumentative drives toward this diffusive focus on text as sonic performance?

LAURA WETHERINGTON: Developing textsound has influenced the work I do on the page, in that I think more about aleatory composition, randomness, Dada performance. I'll wonder, along the lines of anti-art, how could I make a poem sound the least poetic. Maybe you mean something else by "syncopated prose," but I'll hear a rhythm or rhyme in my head. Other times I'll move against that. I write freehand with a pen and paper. When I return to a draft, a poem will sound a certain way to my ear. I don't see words on the page so much as the voice in my head replays the tape. I've always struggled with how to map what I hear in my head. If I think of, you know, the "Nothing Funny About a Penis" poem—that didn't start as a musical score. It started out lineated. But I realized nobody would get it. So how could I turn the "ha ha ha ha ha" at the end, the "ha penis," into "happiness," in a way that made sense to people? Audiences have heard me give a live reading and said: oh god, we had no idea. Still I want to tell people something more than I want to write and have them read it. But because I'm so introverted, I make poems instead of hosting a TV show.

AF: Well this book definitely engages audio performance. Though what you've described sounds more like studio production, with an emphasis upon editing—shaping some equivalent to a live sensibility, perhaps, but through any number of behind-the-scenes decisions.

LW: Right "live" performance doesn't really exist in my poetry since so many revisions take place. I'll concentrate on where quick cuts come in or how to layer sections of static, replicating the mental disjunct that happens.

AF: As you describe this process, could we address "Dancing the Be-Hop"—a serial, polyphonic (sometimes purely phonic) project with excerpts apparently arranged out of sequence? Does "Dancing the Be-Hop" provide an ongoing aleatory performance? Should we expect to see more of it in the future? Has a particular seriality of music and sound, projects like Nathaniel Mackey's *Song of the Andoumboulou* and Robert Duncan's *Structure of Rime*, directed you toward this enterprise?

LW: I can't say, for now, that this current series suggests the start of some bigger broader project, but maybe it should. Aspects of the phrasal turns, the homophonic play, the rhythm or craziness probably show up in my new manuscript of fake translations. But that poem came from trying to wrap my mind around a friendship where the other person kind of had gone crazy, had a psychotic break, or some type of break. I hadn't known her very long. Then as she unraveled, I kept wondering who else has she been. Has everybody known her to be this way? Or has she now entered some different experience of the world? I sensed if her friends back home saw her they would do something. Though in a new friendship, what does one do?

AF: Again in terms of intimacy and its erotics, sexuality receives much thematic attention, often amid constellated concerns of time, measure, breath, orgasm. Does this intersection of music and sex point back toward your interest in embodied experience, whether on the page or at a reading or in sound files?

LW: I sort of want to change that "music" word to some other word. I like what you said about embodiment. Rhythm for me suggests less the playing of an instrument than how we use our bodies, live in our bodies, feel our bodies when we pay attention to them or don't pay attention. I've worked as a massage therapist and consider the body a complex system/series of interrelated rhythmic patterns and functions. And as a person with a female body, I'll think of how female bodies fit into literary history—about women as makers of literature versus women as objects of literary attention. You know, T.S. Eliot wrote about *The Waste Land* that Ezra Pound gave him a bunch of semen. There's this really, really male idea of genius. James Joyce expounds upon his own genius and maleness. So I think when a female body shows up here in terms of rhythm or orgasm or music, I'm pissed at those guys and responding to that.

AF: Assonance (a term hard to take seriously in this context) seems to suggest friction, rubbing—rather than the steady male orgasmic tap of metered rhyme. Similarly, your frequent repetitions of words, of phrasal clusters, establish a tactile pleasure in the turning of the verse line itself. Here I recall "The Open Glass of Water," with its emphatic return to "ocean," "impossible," "illevel," "vestment." Could you discuss these deployments of repetition in terms of thought or experiential patterns you wish to evoke?

LW: Perhaps the single-word repetitions, or the clustered repetitions, link to massage or hippie incantations, or mantras, or meditation. Or these repetitive sections could track how things sound in my head. Then I'll put it on the page and feel such relief to see the thing I'm hearing.

AF: What about Stein, Blake, Hopkins—anyone there of particular interest?

LW: Stein obviously, absolutely. Hopkins not so much. Who else did you say?

AF: William Blake, just in terms of the "ha ha happiness" stuff, which now makes me hear Devo's "Peek-A-Boo."

LW: I can see those links, though I wouldn't say reading Blake makes me rush to the page and write something. Here's a story instead of an answer: I spoke to Jared Stanley, who just has moved to Reno as well. We read each other's books. And he asked, where does your poetry's tone come from? And I said, what do you mean by the tone, I listened to a lot of Ani DiFranco in my 20s, it's that kind of fuck-you tone, maybe. And Jared said, that's not the tone. So I said, I don't know, Heather Christle? He was like, no. And I responded, OK, I don't know for me, how about you? And he said, Robert Duncan obviously, that's why I write poetry, still no one ever says my poems sound like Robert Duncan's. And I could say to Jared: of course

*Tender Buttons* or *The Autobiography of Alice B. Toklas* has done something inside me, but it's not as if I went from reading Stein to writing poems. I don't have a good answer here.

AF: That is a good answer. I also found interesting how sexuality often gets presented as a somewhat solitary, self-referential experience. You'll describe all orgasms as "just me clapping for myself on the inside." Or I have notes about one scene: "He undered her—pumped her chest like emergency rescue / until she was only the space in the middle of her brain." How does this alignment of the sexual and solitary relate to the pleasure and performance of poetry?

LW: Right. Of course that "clapping for myself on the inside" part presents a joke about the muscular contractions of female orgasms. This type of bravado again responds to Eliot or Joyce, as if to say: OK you guys, you claim this brilliance coming from your penis, I want you to know that every time I have an orgasm, that's me giving myself a standing ovation. Here I don't think of the line as solitary, but as communicating to other generations of poets. For the lines "he undered her…until she was only the space in the middle of her brain," I went through this phase, after Stephen Grant killed his wife in Michigan. I lived there, and watched the news and felt horrified like when I'd been in Berkeley and Scott Peterson killed his wife, Lacey Peterson. I started to think about how I don't understand what the word "love" means when some people say it. Or what does it mean to say, hey, let's see each other again? Does that imply, let's see each other then I'll put you in my trunk and dump you in a river? This seems an important topic because it happens a fucking lot. So for a while I couldn't stop thinking about what it means to love a person, then bring harm to her. So that poem actually describes a guy drowning his partner. And if you believe in some hippie massage techniques that I may believe in, the brain has these different ventricles. The ventricle in your brain's middle called, I think, the third ventricle, provides this hole where spinal fluid moves to and from—traveling up into your brain then back down to the bottom of your spine. Perhaps part of me thinks that hole is where a soul enters and leaves if we were to have one. I just imagined someone holding this woman underwater, until her soul exits her body through the hole in her brain. So once again, not solitary sex. Or maybe exactly that thing. The ultimate conclusion I've come to is that the more intimacy I share with another person (whether my mom or my sexual partner), I still don't really share their consciousness and they do not share mine. We can love each other and have completely different experiences of that.

AF: Sure, I think of Virginia Woolf on this topic, how we remain ultimately alone in our progression through life, even if alongside others. And here I'm curious about the directional pointers you provide throughout this book—what you expect us to take from them. I mean, for example, how long and unwieldy certain titles seem, even for the first poem, "In the Day I Dream in Future Tense: Past Sedative Plus Perfect." Does this deliberately disrupt our expectation for a lyric poem to yield compact, comportable, assimilable truths? Does it hint at the challenging mélange of tones and tactics to come? And of course, given that this first poem only runs eight lines, do you like the idea of directional pointers that don't necessarily lead us down the correct path, as much as there ever is one?

LW: Yeah, I hadn't thought about it quite that way, but it is kind of like: now that I have your attention, let me just talk and see how long I can keep this breath going. I do appreciate how that poem sets up an expectation then does something else. I prefer long titles because… perhaps it's the Charles Bukowski in me, the part that wants to say whatever, just to have a conversation. And I definitely like to include pointers, different types of indices, sometimes leading in the wrong direction.

AF: On this question of length, can we move toward your book's longest poem, "Visiting Normandy," which incorporates, according to the notes, accounts of D-Day from an oral history transcript of Lieutenant Carl H. Cartledge, University of New Orleans Eisenhower Center, June 14, 1988? Why this particular transcript? And what about your broader engagement with transcription? To what extent do "Visiting Normandy's" clean, descriptive lines suggest a strict documentarian text? Given the musicality of this book's previous sections, does deadpan delivery here take on its own distinctive sonic/rhythmic qualities?

LW: Maybe this last section feels like creative nonfiction which just happens to get included amid a book of poetry. Only that's not at all true, because I've made up parts and conflated and excised and attributed incorrectly. But this poem felt like it needed writing because when I think of my own identity…on the one hand I'm obviously a feminist and for the longest time felt non-violent. I attended a

Quaker high school and grew up wanting to help people, with kind of girly ideas. Then in my 20s I came to this understanding of myself as perhaps potentially violent. So part of me thinking about men killing their wives in my poems, or in the world, made that all seem not outside normal human behavior. It happens quite often. We all could be capable of it. So what does that mean for me, who thinks she's non-violent, yet in fact comes from a military family? All the men on my mom's side serve or served in the military, all the way back to the revolution. We've fought in every war this country has had. So when I think about these forms of violence, this family history, I think, oh you know what, if I had been a man, I probably would have joined the army, but instead I'm a woman, so a feminist. So I came to this new understanding of what my life means. My grandfather fought on D-Day. In 2004 I went with him to receive the Medal of Honor. Lieutenant Carl H. Cartledge is my grandfather. I've held onto his transcripts since I was about 10. They helped to shape this meditation on intergenerational violence. Because certainly now, in Normandy, buildings look different, but people know. They'll say, our city center used to look this way. The history here comes from listening. That poem came out of nonfictional, direct experience, though I did grapple a lot with how it sounded. I couldn't fully determine…it doesn't sound quite right in my mind. If the book had not been published, I'd still tinker with it. But at that point I just let it go.

AF: These intergenerational questions interest me again in how they relate to editing and a layered, studio-based performance. Your detached, descriptive, prose-like pacing will address (incongruously) quite confusing situations. As an airborne body plummets to Earth, you'll write: "He pushed his thumbs into the saddle / of the chute, sat down, and quickly unbuckled his leg straps, / preparing for water landing. He was working on his chest straps // when his show caught a small tree / and he smashed into the marsh."

LW: Maybe that disjointed relation between pacing and scene connects to your question about how titles point in one direction while their poems move another way. Some passages from Lieutenant Cartledge sound quite calm. Still they refer to D-Day, when half the soldiers dropping from planes won't make it, when others will kill people for the first time, with all that insane adrenaline—while the prose describes it kind of matter-of-fact.

AF: Does this matter-of-factness still contain musicality, desire, poetic pleasures?

LW: It's hard to answer in the affirmative about pleasure here. But certainly I do get drawn to the disjunct between a plain tone and dramatic events.

AF: Typography, format, design get emphasized throughout the book. Here the boxed texts resemble comic-strip thought balloons, or the gerrymandered erasure poetry of Tom Phillips' *A Humument*. Can you comment on those boxed texts? Did the occasional insertion of autobiographical snippets seem to call for this boxed approach? Does it reflect the intergenerational dynamics implicit in your real and imagined returns to Normandy?

LW: Right. Those boxes offer clarity. I wanted to separate two narratives, the present tense and super past tense, the lived situation and the transcribed text.

AF: The boxes worked well. I also love how you take up your own name with pride and gusto in poems such as "Weather Patterns." To quote from "The Encountered," how does it feel to have a name "made like clouds"? Or, more generally, could you discuss the pleasures of threading your signature into this most remorseless, erratic, unyielding of natural phenomena? I mean the weather (though sometimes I also heard "Wuthering").

LW: You know a "wether," as my name actually gets spelled, means a neutered sheep.

AF: Which maybe works, too.

LW: It seems quite cloud-like. But so how do I relate myself to the weather? I lived in Michigan five years, where it stayed so cloudy I just wanted to die.

AF: I know it.

LW: So weather remains important to my happiness. Sunshine seems essential. And after teaching in the New England Literature Program, during April and May, way up in Maine, living outdoors and hiking a lot, I sense why weather, or nature, the elements, always have been forces with which poetry must contend. We couldn't exist without the outside somehow making it into our poems.

AF: Cage brings the weather in, for example.

LW: Right. Because the whole idea of his *Lecture on The Weather* is to say no chaos really exists, that randomness happens amid a natural order. So when weather blows into my poems it comes this way—no matter how random they seem.

AF: I like that.

LW: The end.

## INTERVIEW WITH JENNY ZHANG
Recorded on May 20, 2012
This interview focuses on Zhang's book *Dear Jenny, We Are All Find* (Octopus).

ANDY FITCH: From this project's first line onward, we find prose formatting, often a prose pace, but also careful lineation accenting rhyme and sound play. Some sections contain blank spaces or slashes instead of punctuation. By page 20 in my manuscript copy, an "I" confesses "I lineated my prose to see if I could pass." What draws you, as a poet, toward apparently non-poetic forms?

JENNY ZHANG: Probably two things. I feel more intellectually secure with fiction. With poetry, I'm more the chubby kid making jokes about his chubbiness, or the clumsy person clowning around—preemptively pointing toward his own flaws and shortcomings and fears. And here I've tried to embrace as much as possible parts of me that don't seem poetic. I've cultivated what you could call rants or rambles. The rant as a written and spoken form remains dear to me, helping to establish space between storytelling and narrative.

AF: Rants and rambles make me think of Thomas Bernhard, Robert Walser, Eileen Myles, Rilke's *The Notebooks of Malte Laurids Brigge*, Pessoa's *Book of Disquiet*.

JZ: You've mentioned many of my favorite writers and books, which show that rants or fragments can make you bigger than you are, almost gigantic, even while they diminish you as a writer and speaker.

AF: Frank O'Hara also comes to mind. Lines turn in ways reminiscent of O'Hara. We could consider, from "Solecism," passages such as: "thus she was / the first woman with an eating disorder / the Victorians recoiled in horror, I swear / they strapped marrow against the nape / of someone very white and someone very savage." Then later, of course, appears the title "I write a million poems a day like Frank O Hara multiplied into fifty Frank O Haras." Has the world said enough about Frank O'Hara? Perhaps. But I sense you have something new and interesting to say about Frank O'Hara.

JZ: I don't know if I do. I've appointed him my poetic father. Certain poets seem like puzzles you can break down and master to form new links in your brain. But when I read Frank O'Hara, I just want to be the happy audience I am and have big, big feelings. Of course O'Hara's detractors find him small, careless, perhaps even thoughtless, and he is all those things, which makes me love his poems even more.

AF: As with O'Hara, I appreciate, in your work, never knowing the extent to which I've encountered an identity politics, or a camp performance of selfhood, or both. And the bragging about your own voluminousness stands out. What compels you to identify with volume, with productivity? Could you describe your relationship to the miniature, which can amplify identity, like you said, even as its compact nature continually calls forth the next installment?

JZ: I guess you could call me a voluminous writer. I write quickly, even carelessly, and haven't published many poems. I haven't had anybody read my poetry since I was 12, in middle school. When you first get drawn to poetry you write and write and write without the thought, however dim, that someone could call you out or expose you to be an idiot or fraud or whatever. I still inhabit that space. I remain enough of an ignoramus and dumb-dumb that I can write without worrying what it means to do that. For now poetry remains a preserve of pure joy and sometimes compulsion. Because I don't have to understand, I produce at great volumes and with great speed. But that won't last long.

AF: So the book celebrates this initiatory passage?

JZ: I think so.

AF: It does provide some sense of an "I"-driven debut. The first section contains countless references to siblings, parents, progeny. "The Kumiho Inside a Dumb Waiter" includes these lines: "My brother, when he was younger, fit inside a tire and we took it for a drive. Afterwards, he was a tire and in order to love him we polished him daily and remembered not to leave him out in the sun too long." Do you even have a brother? What various valences does "family" pick up in this collection?

JZ: I do have a brother. I have a mother and father. But the book's first section, "Motherlands," definitely addresses myth-making and the question of who gets to construct creation stories about a given culture. For me and many people, these kinds of creation myths came from the family unit, from the sense of your place amid a family and that family's place amid a larger family and a larger family. This point leads to the role that immigration and displacement have played in my development as a person and poet—the weird violence that exile and travel do to language and idioms and conversational expectations. Such topics forever will remain wrapped up with my family. They offered this understanding about where I come from and who I am, then brought this break in language where…I arrived in the U.S. as a semi-formed being, with no ability to express myself (suddenly, one day). That created obsessions which will stay forever mysterious to me. But the book also emphasizes love and becoming someone who can love and be worthy of being loved. For me this also always has to do with family. I grew up in a family so incredibly, suffocatingly loving that by the time I'd developed my own volition and ability to act, the number of sacrifices they had made for me had stacked up enormously. I never could love them back enough to free myself from that imprisonment. So ideas of family and love and how to be a person of value and worth in the world became another obsession.

AF: Often in this book's first section, the "I" identifies as a mother, potentially a cannibalistic mother.

JZ: I like that you call it cannibalistic. This "I" wants to…she doesn't really wish to become her own mother. Still one poem asks whether the "I" ever could be her own mother and be her own dream. Again this comes from guilt, from mounting waves of love and sacrifice, from being born already loved so much—perhaps unable to love back that much, or simply not wanting to. Of course this could seem an absurd burden, a great one to have. But that compulsion, that desire to ape being one's own mother and protector and giver of life, suggests a way to eclipse the impossible debt and gratitude.

AF: As you describe this I'll think of all poems being born in a potentially suffocating, over-loving environment. I just mean they demand interpersonal sacrifices to come into existence, and perhaps always must atone for this guilt, or try, or project themselves (like Rilke's and O'Hara's poems do) as being "needed by things." But I want to ask about identity. National and ethnic identity get paraded and endlessly permuted here, with references, in quick succession, to Chinese, Thai, Japanese, Korean relatives and affiliations—creating some kind of quasi-imperialist, quasi-Whitmanian or Nerudian pan-Asian panorama. Could you say anything about lines such as these from "The First Fancy Feast of Fancy": "my people put a pile of bricks / on an island and Korea was born / later, the Korean war was where / my grandfather's arms vanished / the false note of us / standing with streaming tears / in front of the Holocaust memorial / was played over loudspeakers / which hung like ripened fruit / in the backyards of every important person"?

JZ: Holy shit: I have so much to say. I don't know where to begin. Yes, a lot of the nation-building and references to colonialism, and this imperialistic tour around all of Asia, correspond to the powerlessness I feel as a person of color, an immigrant, an Asian-American woman, a Chinese-American woman. It's completely arbitrary that a Chinese person should identify with the term "Asian." And yet if you live in America long enough, you have no choice but to associate yourself with that word since others understand you this way. You can walk down the street and someone will speak Japanese to you since you look "Asian." So I've tried to play with how those countries and ethnicities and entire worlds get blurred and rendered meaningless (yet remain quite meaningful). Two years ago, as I drafted these poems, I found this World War II *Life* magazine article about how to tell a "Jap" from a Chinese person. It said Chinese people are our allies—we shouldn't throw rocks or hurl racial epithets at them, only at the Japanese. It contained this pseudo-scientific breakdown of how to tell who's Chinese, Japanese, or some other strange ethnicity of Asia. For me that article crystallized questions about coming from a culture deemed unworthy of being understood in all its nuance. My parents move through the world understood in a very vague way. They also go through their world hating Japanese people because of a history few people here know. So I feel this burden from knowing both how my parents get perceived, and what happens inside them. I can't tell if my parents sense others' perceptions, or sense my own internal state. Still I shoulder this responsibility, with feet firmly placed in both worlds, always explaining to people how they look to others, or what's really happening inside someone else. And the dearth of English-language narratives about the country I come from disturbs me. It embarrasses me to remember my mixed emotions reading Amy Tan's *The Joy Luck Club* in sixth grade. In part I thought, holy shit, I totally understand a lot of references, and many stories feel somewhat familiar in a broad, generalized, almost caricatured way. But I also thought, why the fuck does everyone cry all the time? Then I took this translation workshop at Iowa a couple years back, and felt struck by…that year's course focused on Chinese writers, and they brought 60 writers from all over the world and about 20 came from China or of Chinese origin. Every person they brought identified as a political refugee or dissident. And I just imagined, if the U.S. decided to send a delegation of its best writers abroad, that it wouldn't only chose writers calling to take down the government. Because that doesn't cover the full breadth or beauty of writing that exists in America. And it doesn't do so for any other country. And yet, since only select narratives get told, myths or stereotypes develop about a place. And the more limited that American conceptions become about my native country, the more I seem to identify with that country, even though in actual fact I barely identify at all with China. I lived there five years. I feel uncomfortable when I go. I don't feel at home linguistically, culturally, artistically. Still I have no choice but to claim it in those circumstances. I want to document all the violence that imperialism and colonialism have inflicted upon the Third World and the East. Yet I also want to discuss how my own country (China) has dealt out similar violence toward other countries, and all the multitudes of horribleness and bloodshed worth expressing and knowing and telling.

AF: I appreciated the deft way you'll approach though then upstage any easy racialized reading of a young Asian poet finding her voice. Here I think of lines like: "my name is the sound of three pots clanging / against a tin garbage can / my family is related to lao tze." You'll deliberately cultivate a certain stereotyped rhetoric if only to reject it. Even the line you mentioned earlier, "Can't I be my own dream?" seems both to resist an identity-based reading, and to echo Langston Hughes's question "What happens to a dream deferred?"

from his piece "Harlem"—which often serves as a classic example of the ethnic or race-specific protest poem.

JZ: Those different levels of interpretation and understanding and audience both interest and trouble me. Certain moments here require such depth, such intimacy with a specific immigrant experience, that I don't know how limited this makes them. Still I also sense that making each poem acceptable to some lowest common denominator would betray my own freedom and volition and ability to work within a distinct idiom.

AF: Could you discuss here the book's embrace of misspellings and idiomatic blunders—from its title to the exemplary line "I am quiet first and then the rapping is mispelle"? Beyond any obvious dramatization of a cross-cultural double-consciousness, you genuinely seem to enjoy such aberrant words and asyntactical phrasings, though never in a programmatic way. Sound often will predominate, in the more standardized English diction as well, such as "the impetigo of all the tornadoes and flies and tort laws," or "I wore fingerless nails / Walter Benjamin reflected like a bague / and my grandfather died in 1940." Can you describe the comfort and pleasure you'll find constructing such polyphonic lines, which again provide some sense of getting caught between two worlds while deflecting any reductive narrative?

JZ: I want to reclaim joy. I think the worst thing about learning a new language is how fucking dumb you sound for so long. You know you're not a fucking idiot, but can't express this to anyone. Even once you've learned a new language perfectly, awkward moments will plague you throughout your life if you can't use your native tongue. I remember, when I was 20 or some crazy age, for the first time saying "tunnel," like I need to get to the Holland "Ter-null," and sensing something weird had happened, yet not knowing what it was. Later I felt so ashamed. Then I lived in France last year and realized that my entire life I had based my self-esteem and personhood and identity on being a super clever wordsmith. Suddenly I became nothing more than a generalized nice person with no specific sense of humor, no specific personality. It felt like screaming into a box all the time—wanting to explain, no, I'm really funny, I can make you cry with words, I just don't know how to use these specific words yet. Of course I also realized that your most charming moments, as a language learner, come when you make mistakes. People laugh at how cute you sound mixing up the feminine and masculine forms of nouns or whatever. You know, you say "la chatte," which in French means "pussy," instead of le chat, which means cat. I just wanted to take some control over that. I wanted to refill this charming hole of shame with a sense of happiness and delight and say, I'm calling my cat my vagina purposefully at this point—no longer by accident. The same occurs in Chinese, as a Chinese-American, trying to take these mistakes and make them not mistakes, recognizing the power in that gesture, understanding that expressive language comes from such transformations, which evolve into words, into the broader English lexicon.

AF: Sure, Emerson calls all language fossil poetry (presuming every word initially derives from a creative act, with which we've lost contact). Was it in Paris that your own Celan-like compounds starting appearing, such as bloodturds and comefarts?

JZ: Yes, the "La France" section contains most of that stuff. Also at Iowa I read a lot of smutty French poets.

AF: Well as our level of discourse begins to descend, I can't help but note that many MFA applications, let's say, always seem to have been drafted the day after *The Vagina Monologues* left town. And there's plenty of pussy and cum and twat in this book—but did you have any particular female or male precedents for claiming your "diamond bunghole"? What about the anus's role in literature interests you?

JZ: The sad thing is I don't really respect Bataille's *Story of the Eye* or Artaud wanting to fuck the asshole of God—partially because much of Artaud's writing (and this might sound simplistic on my part) just seemed driven by mental illness and psychosis. I feel little emotional reaction to an articulation of someone's psychosis. And *Story of the Eye* disturbed me on two levels. First, I just disliked the writing. It's so bad, like a pulp novel, as if some idiot had written it. And then secondly, it made me uncomfortable but wasn't transgressive. It feels as transgressive as a kid shitting in the park then playing with his doo-doo, just very ordinary and puerile in this way I like, but only because I like puerile things, not because it's transformative. Shock, discomfort, transgression, innovation and profound discovery don't seem the same at all. And I should say, with Artaud, I went back a few years later and read his letters begging people to understand that he couldn't help but behave this way. I felt much compassion for that. I sensed, I'm the exact society that tormented and misunderstood him.

I had the same uncharitable thoughts. So I kept thinking of how easy it was to shock people in shallow ways, yet still couldn't help talking and writing about my twat all the time, since it affects me every day. Every day I tend to it. It's often sick. It's often physically ill and I just can't for a second get away from it. In France not a single day went by when I wasn't harassed or touched or groped or reached for by some random person on the street. For as much as I didn't want to think about womanhood or femininity, it was always fucking reaching for me, just as I'd said about one's ethnic or cultural identity—wanting to push beyond these but with everyone reminding you of them all the time. Gender probably snuck into every fucking poem because of that.

AF: The last line of your book reads "I nearly faint from the love I nearly was capable of." Does it end on an optimistic note for you?

JZ: Yes. This book is dedicated to my ex-boyfriend. I wrote the first two-thirds or so while we were together. During the second third it became increasingly clear we wouldn't last longer. But many of the final poems also are love poems: poems about not being a good enough person, about what I get from love, about desperately wanting to hold onto some love you think never could happen again to you. This last section concerns the horrificness of having a vagina and wanting and wanting and wanting all the time. Still it also addresses becoming OK with receiving and giving and searching out love again—romantic and familial and sisterly and all representations of love, all iterations.

## INTERVIEW WITH CHRIS VITIELLO
Recorded on May 21, 2012
This interview focuses on Vitiello's book *Obedience* (Ahsata Press).

ANDY FITCH: Can we start with you describing this book's basic structure? That could be physical, rhetorical or argumentative structure. It just seems important for us to do that.

CHRIS VITIELLO: I conceived *Obedience* abstractly before starting to write it. I already had fallen into a pattern of writing single-sentence aphorisms. I had written a bunch of poems that didn't stick that I called clarification poems, where I got into this structure of a sentence, then a line space, then a sentence, a line space. I liked how clean that felt. I'd needed some clarity in my life, so a tidy writing project (both to the eye and rhetorically) made sense. With *Obedience*, I decided to do one grammatically correct, conventional sentence and then a space, and then another and a space—but to limit the sentences to direct commands, factual statements, or assertions. This whole book, every line, offers one of three kinds of sentences. That became the basic premise. I'd already developed a sense of how cycling through many different topics and subject matters could come together. It would coalesce because of the consistent form. So I wrote for a good number of years. But as I moved towards really thinking of this as a completed book for the publisher to start typesetting, I started reading the whole project in its entirety, and found it felt kind of flat. I found that…I asked people about this, and they said they read the manuscript quickly. You know when with prose your eye just drops down the page, and sentences don't really register? Visually, formally, it had grown too consistent, so it went transparent. That's when I came up with…first I rejected other ideas for visually complicating the text. I basically wanted to slow down the reader. Then finally I realized I could write a variant of every line from the book, and each pair could face each other across the page spread. This brought linearity to the project, so you can read it backwards, forwards, across. That access to many different pathways keeps it interesting, prompting you to follow your own paths of curiosity.

AF: And then the upside-down element?

CV: I have to say: upside-down text attracts me. Otherwise, from a design standpoint, to place explicitly related lines across the page spread from each other, you have to justify from the center margin. Right-justified text looks bad. But glancing at words upside-down, I got excited about the idea of a backwards text. You can flip the book and find these two different covers. That provides a much more playful edge.

AF: You've raised many questions. First, I'm curious, when you describe a need for clarity in your life, if you note a similar pattern among many aphoristic writers. I'll think of Nietzsche, Wittgenstein, and what draws authors and readers to clean, precise statements. But more generally, in terms of what you've said: aphorisms often get presented as singular, self-sufficient entities. Your book provides prodigious aphoristic concision, but these individual statements on their own don't stand for much. Meaning accrues as one moves among them. So could you discuss both your relationship to the aphoristic tradition, and your present conflation of local details and overall, atmospheric arrangements?

CV: My biggest model is Wittgenstein. I love how you can pick up a Wittgenstein book and flip to the middle, and start from any part. Will you find an aphorism, a chunk of text discrete on its own? Not always. He does provide subset lines of inquiry and curiosity, which he'll follow then exhaust then return to on a higher level. But you can open Wittgenstein and read four pages and close the book with plenty to think about. I admire that aspect—that the text maintains a kind of independence from its author. Yet Wittgenstein also presents a logical progression I find pretty seductive. It's exciting to feel as though you've ferreted out something as you approach a conclusion. I appreciate this building of broader language possibilities through a series of discrete statements. Other models for me include Mei-mei Berssenbrugge, one of my favorite poets. I don't know if you can call her precisely an aphorist, but often her poems present that pattern of a discrete unit then a space then a discrete unit then a space.

AF: You could call her an incremental poet.

CV: For sure. Sometimes a line addresses a certain idea, then six lines later this idea returns from a different angle. I like how her poems seem to fall together and move toward a density, again as if you've built something. Your question's second part asked about…

AF: This accrual of meaning. I just wanted to probe the distinction between aphorisms as self-contained statements we can extract from any particular context, and aphorisms as inherently interconnected units—generating meanings through the movement among separate entries. I feel that your book examines this syntax of meaning-making.

CV: The three types of sentences this book offers track fundamental units of thought. Fact statements provide the syntax of "A is B." You recognize that as a truth statement—maybe not exactly true, but a statement that one could presume true. Assertions differ from truth statements by presenting more of a postulation, saying: I'm going to formulate an idea so that subsequently I can test it, and try to push it, try to find exceptions, try to treat it as a hypothesis and take some shots and see if it holds (of course Wittgenstein does that productively throughout his writing). And then direct commands always have excited me, as sentences that quite bare-facedly speak to the reader. The reader feels their prescriptive power. A sentence says, "Close this book right now," and you're holding the book, and you're like, I'm either going to obey or disobey that direct command. Sometimes, to continue reading means to disobey the text. I enjoy those kinds of problems. In terms of arranging these aphorisms: much of the time-consuming work for this book consisted of using scissors and a glue stick, cutting them out, rearranging them on the table, seeing how they held together, moving pieces up and down, building the poem often out of the middle of a given series. A few good runs of poems occur in *Obedience*, separated by those "GO ON" arrow pages.

AF: I'd wanted to ask about these indexical-seeming arrows, specifically in relation to your book's dedication to the word "this." I understand "this" as an indexical or relational term, tracing something present (physically, conceptually) to the beholder. No "this" exists without a beholder. Perhaps no "this" exists without an addressee as well. Did you feel drawn toward tracking overlapping modes of presence?

CV: To me, the word "this" and the arrow seem perfect opposites of each other. An arrow…you can't misinterpret an arrow. It points at a location or direction. Whereas "this" can cause utter confusion. Pronouns often play that role. But "this," in particular, remains one of these pronouns we use so very frequently with no antecedent. Or the antecedent becomes a kind of abstraction only called into being by the grace of that sentence, for the purpose of that sentence. "This" is a weird word that used to disturb me. Pronouns would upset me. I'd view a sentence, and sense some pronoun operating in its middle, which could have multiple antecedents, or no antecedent, and I'd almost have a reaction of stress. I became fascinated by that process over time. I really loved the tautology "This is this." One of the book's epigraphs comes from Robert De Niro's line in *The Deer Hunter,* where he holds up a bullet and says, "You see this? This is this. It's not something else." That knocked me out. I thought, here's one of the 20th century's great poems. It evoked so much about reference and language as constructions, as systems we've built to try to communicate with each other, to try to store meaning. Holes appear in those systems. Pronouns certainly provide such holes. They carry occasional, fleeting meanings then get used for a different purpose later. Pronouns are tools, not words.

AF: The *Deer Hunter* line gets echoed in your first sentence: "This is the first line of this and therefore is true." Those two "this," along with the "is" that kind of rhymes with them, demonstrate the pleasure or luxuriance you find in deploying pronominal shifters without specific context. And alongside this *Deer Hunter* epigraph comes one from Jabès, while, from the book's opposite direction, you open with Louise Bourgeois, Mary Burger. John Cage's exercises in measured simultaneity came to mind as I read your work. Vito Acconci's "Now read this, now read this" idiom seems to get echoed, as do Ed Ruscha's atmospheric word paintings and Lawrence Weiner's statement-based art. You cite the fact that human bodies regenerate themselves every seven years, and I recall a similar line from Hollis Frampton's film *Nostalgia*. Do any such points of reference seem pertinent to you? Can you expand (or narrow) the intellectual, artistic, philosophical discourse in which you see this book taking part?

CV: Well, some of those definitely. I'm a fan of Vito Acconci. But I also was a big *Scientific American* fan as a kid. My family had a subscription, and I'd always work my way through it. I became a Douglas Hofstadter fan. His book *Metamagical Themas* contains an amazing chapter on self-referential sentences. I love how you can create these classic "This sentence is false" unsolvable problems and paradoxes, even amid tiny, innocent-looking units of language. I love how you can break off language from points of reference and make it a linguistic exercise—which stays with me when I look at any manifestation of language, that it offers a total fabrication. Another important reference for me comes from Charles and Ray Eames' film *Powers of Ten*. I grew up in D.C.'s Virginia suburbs, and my parents would take me to museums on weekends. My parents would linger for a long time in the art museums, while I'd be saying, "Can we go now?" So they'd respond, "Go to the Air and Space Museum and meet usback here two hours later." So I'd walk to the Air and Space Museum and sit and watch *Powers of Ten* five consecutive times, consistently. That structure of stretching really, really far out from a point of reference (exponentially traveling away from it, then exponentially burrowing back into it), that sense of scale, particularly with mathematical increments, remains a crucial model for me. To float above a concept and try to see it as part of some network of ideas seems crucial. Often I, like most people, get stuck on a single fact, focusing on one piece of information, one datum. But I prefer to jump out to a broad scale and see huge networks of ideas and information. I think that, to return to your earlier question about how these aphorisms get arranged: I like that you can read something and six pages later read a related line, then flip back and note the variation. You'll start to find similarities. You start to track similar ideas and paths through a biological system, then a philosophical system. You start to follow relationships between the way an animal moves and the way weather moves. It excites me to make those connections. And *Powers of Ten* clued me in to the fact that making such connections might not require faculties of intelligence or deduction, but faculties of scale. It might depend upon your perspective. If you move far enough away, you might finally reach the appropriate scale for observing complex relationships.

AF: This makes me think of Rosalind Krauss's essay "Grids," in which she demonstrates that a grid painting can suggest a boxed-off structure, dividing the world into ever-smaller units, or the same grid painting could suggest one unit amid a universal coordinate system extending outward in every direction, kind of like a Cartesian grid. Grids channel both centripetal and centrifugal pressures and tensions. And the grid of your book's (or all books') machinery became clear when I first turned one of the pages. The first page spread had provided this balanced harmony of upside-down and right-side-up. But as I flipped the page, I just couldn't conceive of that structure maintaining itself. I expected the book would fall apart or something. Book-binding's implicit continuity never had seemed so exciting. Again, does that apprehension of short prose assertions and allover book-making, of local details and global processes, relate to the erotics of scale?

CV: I'm sure it does. Here it might be useful to introduce the word "iteration." I guess that when writing, I'll write from a point of not knowing something, but certainly suspecting there might be something to know. There might be a connection to draw. So, like Wittgenstein laying down an assertion then building momentum, I'll write a line then iterate that idea, develop a variant or extension, keep putting pressure on it as a poem accumulates. To me, that's the vertical push of the poem. It always has seemed counterintuitive that you start writing at the top of a page then drop down. If you want to construct, if you want to build relationships between units of writing, wouldn't you start at the bottom and let the lines climb up the page? Isn't verticality what you've tried to accomplish?

AF: I wonder if authors worry people would get tired that way.

CV: It sounds horrible to read—you're right. It sounds like headache material. But the horizontal impulse resides in the discrete aphorism, and the arrangement activates a vertical impulse. So right there you have your grid, with the vertical coming from the rhetorical construction, allowing an argument to accumulate and coalesce.

AF: One last question regarding your own grid-like structure: do you conceive of people flipping over this book to read its upside-down elements, or simply to read them upside-down? I found it surprisingly easy to read upside-down, except when you included a made-up word, or a word unfamiliar to me. Those were the words I couldn't read.

CV: The answer to your question is both. Of course, when you write something you get so familiar that it could be upside-down or reversed and you still could read it. But spinning this book around seems reasonable. At any point just flipping it…that hadn't occurred to me. That sounds like an entertaining way to progress through and discover patterns. I had to read back-and-forth in order to write it. Darting my eyes to the left-hand page and reading the upside-down text did not feel fun, just because it tested me to write another line for every existing line in the book. That became a difficult task.

AF: I'll often survey students and find that 98% of them visualize what they read. Reading for me provides more of an auditory experience, even a vocal experience. In terms of the echo-like quality of your second text haunting the first, I'm curious if you visualize scenes and/or hear a choral performance as you progress through this book.

CV: My first instinct is to say it's purely visual. Though I got a lot out of doing some readings from the manuscript early on, and finding a slow, methodical pace. So as I wrote the duplicate lines, I think I heard…maybe not hearing the sounds of lines, but hearing a performative echo, a performative second voice. I've experimented with recording an audio performance of one of these texts, while leaving spaces for the other text to get read aloud, so that you can combine two voices reading back-and-forth. And the voices take on two different personalities. It's almost like one voice tries to stay earnest and the other tries to undermine that. The second voice almost sounds a bit snide. This strange, unintentional personality emerges from the second set of lines' implied critique.

AF: That part of the project, those ever-shifting rhetorical vectors, reminded me of Carla Harryman's early dialogue-based works, which now makes me wonder about this book's relationship to post-structuralist, language-inflected poetics from the '70s and ''80s. Your text foregrounds the seeing of words, certainly, their materiality. Your interrogation of readerly projections develops not in terms of convoluted syntax, but in terms of self-referential pairings, as well as from the pronominal contingency of language and identity (the floating use of "you," for instance). So to what extent do you see your work consolidating and/or departing from insights offered by Language poetics?

CV: I don't think it really departs at all. I think I'm just trimming. With *Obedience*, I made a concerted effort to trim many different possibilities out of the project, so that I could write something that went somewhere. I decided to keep it formally very flat and consistent. I kept the sentences syntactically very normal, you know? I only wanted a couple brushes. I didn't need the whole set of brushes. That probably comes right down the line from a lot of Language poets. Ron Silliman remains a big writer for me. Carla Harryman as well. I love her writing. I went to Naropa for graduate school, where she came and presented a memory play—this unstaged dramatic reading of a memory play, which completely knocked me out. Let's take a stance and characterize it and write from that character. In a way that seems a simple form, not an easy form, but the simplicity becomes wonderful. You recognize it. It doesn't have to be explained. You just know it.

AF: So it offers a formal transparency, like Shaker furniture. You can sense how the work got put together. Or, at least, the work offers some sense of how it's put together—whether or not that's accurate.

CV: Yeah. I think *Obedience* instructs you in how to read it. It may not always seem transparent, but it never sounds ambiguous.

AF: You've described starting projects with no clear sense of how to accomplish them. Did this particular project require you to hone your knack for spare, hyper-minimalist, non-clunky sentences or entries? Did that spare syntax became all the more appealing as you put the finished diptych together? And for the imperative tone, which you've mentioned several times: does that seem the most streamlined tone one can take, in terms of using the fewest words? Your text doesn't even have to say "You should go on to the next entry." It just says "GO ON."

CV: Direct commands often lack crucial parts of speech. Just shouting a verb aloud can form the most basic sentence. But for the first part of your question: many sentences went through twenty or twenty-five versions. That became a bit unnerving. Even as I looked at galleys for this book, I found stray, inessential words and felt the need to take them out. I caught myself exaggerating or overstating all the time. That's quite—I don't want to say natural, but reflexive. You want to convey strong feeling, so you include the word "very," or some adjective that conveys a type of tone. But for *Obedience*, just from reading and rereading and rereading it, I've learned how to recognize…I don't know that it's a writing skill. It seems more a reading skill. I'd learned to recognize the inessential words and expressions. Two things I couldn't anticipate came out of this. First, I found that the actual words of a sentence, and its meaning, had a really loose relationship. I now have a firm idea of what each sentence means, and believe I could put down each sentence's meaning in at least five different sets of words. So the logical question becomes, what relationship between the words and meaning exists, if a different arrangement could mean the same thing? The second observation that this sanding-down of sentences produced: for a decent number of sentences I reached a tipping point when I would take it past a certain spareness, and its meaning would fall apart.

AF: You could tell?

CV: I would get this feeling. I'd think, I shouldn't put this sentence in the text; there's nothing left that needs to be retained. My next thought would be, well, I've worked on the sentence for a long time; it must have some value; I should keep it. Those emotional attachments made me suspicious of myself. Many sentences got removed from the text. Sometimes I'd try to find another spot for a sentence. Some sentences moved into the category or function of meaningless sentences for this book.

AF: It interests me that the most streamlined possible syntax can create these strange, topsy-turvy writer/reader relations. The more honed that the syntax becomes, the more it prompts epistemic questions about how a reader should respond. That tension clearly comes across. I'm in Japan right now, and we just had a class on high-context and low-context languages. It's fun to talk to you while that's happening. Now here's one last question. To return to Jabès, and Wittgenstein, I do sense either a mystical rhetoric at play in your book, or a playful, polyvalent reference to the mystical connotations of much aphoristic writing—in your commands to "Move without moving," in your incrementally engaging the impossible. We'll progress from a sentence that says "Stop reading," which still seems a possibility, to "Do not read this line," which seems impossible. Then throughout, your attention to reading's temporality remains compelling. You present an analogy to music, that with music what you hear blends with what you'd expected to hear, and those commingling temporalities create the experience. Of course it could provoke a stifling self-consciousness for some readers to think through their reading experience this way, but it also could call forth an ecstatic, open-ended bliss. So the question is: do you consider your interrogation of the reading experience both something like cold, hard, empirical science, and something like incantatory bliss? What is your own ideal experience as a reader?

cv: I think if you average mystical bliss and empirical reality, you get attention. Maintaining attention has inherent value, whether you maintain attention to a text or to events happening around you. Being able to pay careful attention seems a crucial part of being a good human being. Still the word "mystical" makes me nervous. I'm not a believer. I don't understand belief, and for that reason feel like a pretty solid empirical person. I guess with someone like Jabès and his *Book of Questions*, he presents many different disembodied rabbis who make these statements. You can't tell whether they converse with each other or not. And the rabbis never seem to repeat. It's not like a few rabbis talk back-and-forth. It's all different names throughout.

af: But always names. Not Rabbi 1, Rabbi 2.

cv: Exactly. And no name recurs in those rabbi lines. I like the idea of that space. These characters don't have bodies, but also kind of do. They have names, sentences placed in quotation marks, presumably spoken lines. But there's no setting, no action, no interaction. So their lines build a philosophical space. You as a reader must learn how to work in this space. You have to make decisions about the text. You notice a lack, or an ambiguity, and in order to continue you really do have to take a tack with it. It's like, OK, I'm going to read this as a conversation between a bunch of rabbis gathered for some reason, an occasion of some significance or they wouldn't have gathered. You start making a play of it. Or you could just disregard the names and quotation marks and read a series of statements in linear order. You could make that decision. Either way, the reading seems self-conscious. I don't find that disruptive. I just find that to be how one reads. I read a lot with my daughters. My younger daughter is turning six this summer and she's pretty good at decoding words she hadn't encountered before. She's willing to make a run at pretty much any text you put in front of her. It's cool to see. But she'll hit a word like…we read a book tonight where "certain" came up. And she knows that word and uses that word as a sound, but couldn't get enough of a decoding bite on the word to recall it when she read it. I think reading's like that for all of us. We can decode bigger chunks, say paragraphs or chapters. We hit it and try to break it down into parts we can recognize, then assemble those parts into a whole which perhaps we could understand. The fundamental parts might now be chapters, but the decoding remains terrifically self-conscious.

## INTERVIEW WITH JOEL CRAIG
Recorded on May 24, 2012
This interview focuses on Craig's book *The White House* (Green Lantern).

ANDY FITCH: From talking to you in the past, I know music metaphors come easily, that we could call the progression from poem to poem an arrangement, could consider it a macrocosm of the meticulous mix within any individual piece. I hope we get to all that. But first, *The White House* seemed to offer several basic types of poems—the long sequences of indented prose blocks, the testimonial projects suggesting unauthorized biographies or autobiographies, and then shorter, more emotive and/or opaque lyric flourishes. Variety abounds in how you put these types together, with distinctive uses of lineation, speech-based idioms, elliptical juxtapositions. So here's the question: did the different types appear over discrete spurts, during the many years that this book came together? Did you develop all three types simultaneously? Do you feel further drawn to working within or among those types?

JOEL CRAIG: That makes sense to describe three rough styles. I think of the indented pieces as travelogue poems, sometimes mixed with real elements of travel. When traveling I tend to concentrate on physical spaces I visit and people I meet, and therefore voices I hear. Then other poems get born more out of my past—the dense little jewels that reflect my love for surrealism. They can seem, as you say, kind of opaque and dark-humored. And the diffuse, biographical-style poems share with these first two types the fact that multiple voices make up their lyric "voice." Both the travelogue style and the biographical/monologue style I hope to keep expanding and exploring.

AF: On this topic of multiple voices, I recall a recent Danny's Reading Series event you put together, with Lewis Warsh, Dodie Bellamy and Kevin Killian. I hadn't realized before, but should have, how your work engages New Narrative. Could you discuss New Narrative's legacies and contemporary practices and what you hope to do alongside or in response to them?

JC: Could we define New Narrative first?

AF: Here I'm thinking of specific people like Dodie and Kevin and Bruce Boone and Chris Kraus, of prose with less a cumulative thrust than a perspectival diversity—though different from a "New Sentence" or collage-based focus on the textual surface. Not pure syntactical innovation. More affect. More performed intertextual inquiry. More embodied queerness. More rhetorical depth, but in an abstract way.

JC: I've thought of my book in relation to Lewis' work more than the others, but I can try to speak to what you've mentioned. All of that excites me. That voice of experience and immediate (yet evolving) emotive connection seems lacking in much recent poetry. Kali, my girlfriend, says when we go on a first date with someone we send our very best representative. Quite often I feel that poets send a representative who somehow isn't their best representative at all. Though Dodie and Kevin stand out as poets not afraid of the scatological, not afraid to share a scene we might consider off-putting but that can evoke an immediate relation, or can introduce an intimate or wide range of friends and acquaintances—whether or not we as readers actually know these people. That blend of voices attracts me.

AF: How does this blending relate to a poem's length? Could you discuss further what you've described as the evolution of an emotional connection?

JC: An immediate situation grabs us, with which we want to continue, which we sense could expand into an ocean of reflections or questions we want answered. Rudimentary levels of experience often open up my mind that way. All of our experience contains so much abstraction. So I love work that slows me down and gets me to reconsider these basic mysteries.

AF: One of your book's first poems, "Street Dad," presents what I called the indented-prose type, and produces a phenomenon I note throughout the book. I'll track discrete sentences, which I associate with prose, but also sense broader rhythmic movements reminiscent of Lewis Warsh's *The Origins of the World*.

JC: I read Lewis' book while writing "Street Dad" and "California Poem." I immediately wanted to steal the indented-prose structure, but also to aggravate it—to pay homage while making it my own.

AF: Could you describe how your form differs?

JC: First off, I had to learn how to write a long line to contain these sentences. Just by imitation I discovered that the indentations increased my comfort with longer lines. The stanzas allowed me to make jumps while maintaining a prose-like tone that could provide a calm or continuity. At least that's how I heard it. One key experience shaping my poetics is that I've spent years DJ-ing records, many different styles of music. I've learned not only how to put together an arrangement, but how to bring a room along with it. The long poems internalize this sense of when listeners might want to sustain something, or need a break—or what might seem to me a natural place to end, but I'm obligated to keep going since people came for a certain durational experience. Those considerations helped the different voices to emerge and the different pacings of the prose sentences and the poetic sweeps. I've strained against these tensions and pushed with them as well.

AF: So does a story exist in advance, behind your poems, which then gets split into different voices, different utterances, different sentences? Or does the overall narrative emerge and evolve bit-by-bit as pieces get placed and layered?

JC: Definitely the latter, though this might include kernels of lived or imagined experience. The impetus for "Street Dad" came from talking with a homeless man in San Francisco. We only had a short conversation, but he obviously struggled with some kind of mental illness, and had a massive story to tell which continued to morph as he went on, yet stayed engaging whether or not true. Initially I wanted to recreate his fusion of imagination and memory, but as I began to build the piece, of course my own memories of past conversations came in. I built up these multiple components and wrote and wrote—not thinking in terms of shaping a poem, just pushing the ideas. That all resembled creating a DJ set. You bring some specific raw materials which need to evolve decisively into their own arc as an experience unto themselves.

AF: Some poems here, such as "Rational Rational," emphasize anaphora—repeating lines that begin with "add" or "plus." An alternately light/heavy sense of accumulation takes place. Or "California Poem" offers "A clear vision of big cities as actors in their own right." You'll foreground these loose, aggregate sums (such as the Paterson-like city as actor), yet also provide cramped, more menacing references to pervasive new construction projects, or to the growing powers of "the state." Does *The White House*, more generally, track various means by which circumstances accumulate—staying vigilantly concerned with recording such processes, though uncertain what might turn out good or bad?

JC: Much of my personality seeps into the work. For that line about cities I bastardized a sentence from the book *Dead Cities*, by the California historian and social critic Mike Davis. Reading him got me thinking about the many ways we experience a heavily authored place like California—a state that presents quaint or glamorous versions of itself, even as less ideal realities occur. The military-industrial-complex money and the technology-complex money so vastly outweigh those comparatively puny figures Hollywood throws out. This suggests such a strong diversion that, to my mind, it can't seem anything but intentional. So after traveling I tried to sift through each experience and how it relates to diversionary habits in the lives of people I know. Not that they're dishonest, but they'll display one thing while something else happens in secret. Of course we all do this, and observe it in all people, depending how well we get to know them. Here I don't try to connect every dot, just to work through some, again as an exercise (to see what they reveal).

AF: Well often your lineation, indentation, visual structure complicates the forward march of a sentence.

JC: It will look like a hatchet sawed down the page.

AF: Does that hatchet scene again point toward a staccato musicality lurking within the utilitarian sentence? I wasn't an English major, and never really understood this term, but I read your poems and often felt my mind undergo a mental caesura.

JC: Oh wow. I work as a designer and, as I like to do in design, I found a simple concept then tried to aggravate it and stick with it and see what it forced out of me. My training in poetry, if you will, treats the line as the most important thing—that each line should provide a poem unto itself in some way. A poem's structural strength resides there, and so these hatchet marks provide a very jagged, rough and imperfect model. Still I spent much time reciting these poems aloud, editing to make them musically subtle. I wanted them to relax then expand and promote different types of physical movement. I want to provoke a physical reaction with each poem. So I thought, I'll present both a kind of uniformity and a visual challenge. This felt at times quite natural, and at other moments became such a pain in the ass. But the music helped resolve that.

AF: What about repetition in general—the repeated words such as "level" (which keeps appearing in "Street Dad"), or the repeated lines in "Instructions for Building a Paper House," or other phrases that circulate throughout the book? How does your work in design and in music shape these conspicuous structures?

JC: I've listened to much techno music, which I find similarly limiting yet expansive through its limitations. Basic constructs will form a kind of symphony out of rudimentary sound and sound designs. And from a design perspective: to brand something always requires repetition. Ideally, you direct a style of image so that someone can have a specific emotive response to what they see. Then when they see something else you did, they recall that previous experience and build upon it. Whether this really happens I don't know. But that logic from other parts of my life worked its way into these poems. A repeated line provides a launch pad, though each time this launch pad changes. I try to direct that process.

AF: Does your own experience as a reader elicit strong cognitive/bodily responses?

JC: I certainly remember, say in my 20s, reading John Ashbery's *Flow Chart,* how he could make music out of anything, and how potent and narcotic and formative that experience felt—although I don't read him much anymore.

AF: A long poem like *Flow Chart* returns us to questions of scale, of the part's relation to the whole—questions that play out in your short lyrics as well. You'll foreground a quick inversion of tone or perspective. "Chairs Missing" seems to present itself as an elegy or in memoriam, though then ends with this enigmatic, valedictory salute: "The wonder of the world is ever present. / Tell me when you get there."

JC: I love that kind of play. I'll find endless potential there. Of course this can become too studious and practiced to seem truly experimental, so I always try to tether those experiments to something real. I did write "Chairs Missing" in memoriam, to someone I could picture quite vividly. Still at the same time, given the sense of loss, the inability to resolve that relationship, I wanted to acknowledge this person's spirit. So that last line gestures at an opening.

AF: For "Structured Settlement," which I can quote in full ("I love the smell of sauerkraut / in the morning. It smells like sauerkraut / in the morning"), perhaps because I'm in Japan right now I appreciate the haiku-like equanimity, with everything riding on that ambiguous "it."

JC: Yeah I hope to keep experimenting with this form. I just had reviewed *Star in the Eye*, James Shea's book heavily rooted in haiku experience. Also, I ride my bicycle to work every day, and for four years had ridden past this sauerkraut factory. I wrote that poem in my head on the bike. I just figured, OK, it's a joke, but I need to put it down and acknowledge it as a poem. It's a joke because it riffs off a line from *Apocalypse Now*: "I love the smell of napalm in the morning…It smells like victory."

AF: Do you know the Basho poem "Even in Kyoto / hearing the cuckoo's cry / I long for Kyoto"?

JC: I don't. But that's beautiful.

AF: Your embrace of the passive voice also interests me, and stays quite prominent throughout the book. For one example: "So far it wasn't at all like my fantasy. The kitchen was comfortably large, / with a linoleum floor so old its original pattern / was lost in a general brown-ness." Here the passive voice allows you to shift quickly from one vantage to another, constructing a kind of big-tent present. But at the same time, many of your still-life descriptions hint at drama or action or revelation, such as: "Something was taking shape across the room. There was a sense / of gold somewhere in the red. The legs / of the red-painted kitchen table glowed, / and the room was alive with a soft light." Present moments seem to crystallize then dissolve throughout this book. Personal, embodied experience will drift toward more detached reveries or recollections or synesthesiac abstractions. Could you describe your poetic and/or personal relationship to the present?

JC: I guess I'm an observant person, but can get lost in the present—very much so. I tend to rely on detailed spatial impressions, especially when anxious. But I generally stay aware of what happens, or maybe hide from what happens, or maybe just contemplate what's happening. That passive voice can reflect a passive me, for sure. But I don't sense any specific poetic intent beyond loving those moments or feeling quite comfortable with them. The word "comfortable" often recurs in these poems. Perhaps such pauses in a poem force me to consider some kind of action. Because I know they often do in life. Now I'm contemplating, see?

AF: In terms of design and DJ-ing, ekphrasis and synesthesia, both very important to early-20th-century poetics, get reinvigorated in your book. Here the poem "Penguin" comes to mind, which deploys visions, rainbows and prisms in order to invoke the making of a Fleetwood Mac album—all from the perspective of an "I" that, in a final twist, becomes Stevie Nicks, not you. Do these studies of music, of simultaneity, also then become studies of the dynamic, refracted, ever-charged and ever-changing present? Does densely textured music offer some analogy for how you (or we) experience the present?

JC: Absolutely. Often we have to focus on specific tasks, even as so many points of view and contexts collide and overlap. That chaos fascinates me. To try to shape that simultaneity into something linear excites me. I doubt I'll ever find any single, over-arching purpose, so just to delve into waves of experience (as opposed to the static idea of an experience) motivates me.

AF: Most well-textured pop music presents no clear narrative throughline that we could paraphrase. Still a strong emotional identification occurs from nuanced moment to nuanced moment, which provides for a coherent passage of time. And your diffusive, sentence-based structures allow for something similar to happen. But to close on a more singular detail: "green" appears throughout the book, again often as a point or place of solace. Can we end with you discussing "green"?

JC: I most obviously mean nature in all forms, something I never get enough of and don't seek out enough, but which remains always on my mind. Though more generally, what does green as a representative color suggest? I hope to leave that open, so anybody can latch onto it however they prefer. I'd rather not define it that much. Pop music, for example, gets built out of regurgitated components subtly reshaped by the individual artist, yet still offering a familiar formula we know we can count on and relate to pretty efficiently. Perhaps we can think about "green" like that, as a chord or note or even a progression, a place to latch onto for the moment—providing imaginative expansiveness until the next change comes along.

### INTERVIEW WITH BRANDON SHIMODA
Recorded on May 25, 2012
This interview focuses on Shimoda's book *O Bon* (Litmus Press).

ANDY FITCH: In *O Bon*'s author statement (itself perhaps more poem than transparent autobiographical record) you mention, as poets often do, the desire to create a ritual space through or within the text. Yet your book, unlike many, points toward a quite specific ritual space, one associated with both the Obon holiday and Bon Odori dance. Can you provide some sense of how these particular cultural practices work their way into the idiom, thematics, and/or architecture of the book—especially in terms of its emphases upon honoring one's ancestors while enacting a dance or procession?

BRANDON SHIMODA: I'm still trying to figure that all out. This goes back to 1988, when I first experienced the Obon festival and dance as a 10-year-old, standing with my family on a bridge in Kyoto. A lot of this book comes from trying to piece together what happened on that beautiful and terrifying night. It felt like a million people stood on the bridge, which seemed to sway over the Kamo River. So I remember the festival, people dancing, and I carried those two scenes subconsciously until I started writing this book. First I'd begun thinking about my grandfather's life. I hoped to write something relatively simple and straightforward. Then as I started to…I don't know, maybe some rhythm from that night came back. I sensed the festival calling me back. Or I sensed that he, my grandfather, had returned in the form of that festival. This early writing raised basic questions like: what am I even doing? Why does it seem important to address this person's memory? How can I do so without feeling sick? But soon more of the festival's various aspects came back. A lot of this work involved just imagining it, while sifting through conflicts I had about the idea of ancestor worship. Also I'd lived in Oaxaca six months. I'd been there in November for their Festival of the Dead. That had an enormous impact. I probably overlaid that onto the Japan experience. I'd found all these ornate, baroque rituals happening down in Mexico, and wondered how they related to my own thoughts about death, as embodied by my grandfather. Still, ultimately, I don't know. This book seemed the first attempt at something I'm trying to articulate to myself, which remains difficult and hazy, as if I've constantly misunderstood my own ideas.

AF: I'm curious why your grandfather, specifically, prompted these reflections, From what I remember the Obon holiday has to do with ancestors, right? Does it welcome the spirits of ancestors?

BS: It's the time of year when they come back. Their family prepares food and participates in rites and rituals. I think it's actually, of course, for the families, for the living. As to your question of why this dude, my grandfather: that's my main frustration. I don't know. I'm working now on a simple and straightforward prose book about him. My other grandparents are still alive, but he passed away when I was 18. He'd had Alzheimer's for over two decades. Even when we spent time together, he'd always seemed a mythic figure. He was an artist, a photographer, and, at least for me as a kid, a brilliant storyteller. Although I didn't understand then that he wasn't telling stories. He just lived in another world. He'd transpose some other location with where we sat at the time, which I found fantastic. Then he passed away and all these serendipitous events started to happen. I was oblivious and irresponsible and didn't have much of a vision for life. But I started to write about him. The first piece I wrote, the first I ever published, was a story about him taking pictures. This became the focus of what became my poetry, to the extent that now it seems I'm creating ritual spaces for an exorcism. I love him, and remain fascinated with his life, but want to stop thinking about him this way (which has been this desperate love). So the book begins to formalize some of those ideas. When I think about the Bon Odori dance, the Obon festival, this book feels like the first notes of a song. As you listen to sounds of bells, the sound of the breeze, this book floats in. Though I don't yet know where it's going.

AF: Well I'd guess if we looked at the Obon festival itself, we couldn't really say where it's going, either, as this ritualistic enactment that both provokes and consumes memory. And if we think of the Obon as tracing concrete or tangible memory, our physical continuity with the past, what happens now when you return to this festival? Can you still access that night in 1988? Do you gain new perspectives each time on your grandfather? Or does it become an event in which to participate, but not the same immersion experience? Would it just provide a spectacle?

BS: I don't know. The experience I mentioned felt really terrifying. I thought I would die. I can return to that moment on the bridge, with so many people that if you fell you wouldn't fall—you'd remain standing, right over this ink black river. I remember pieces of white paper floating down the river. It was scary, and I lost my breath. I'm sure I cried. At a certain point the festival kind of shattered, or fractured and became something else. Of course many people attend for whom the Obon Festival is ceremonial, formal, a way for families to come together, as with any holiday. Japanese culture relates to death differently than here in the States. Those elements get tethered to responsibly, both within a familial and a ritual space. Though what I've obsessed about, contrary to ritual space, is burial space. I've tried to chase down a body so to speak, chase my grandfather's ashes to their burial space. The ritual space is what remains accessible. Descendents can congregate there. But the burial space provides a kind of last laugh for the deceased. They bury themselves, or have family bury them in some remote spot, unmarked, so that years later nobody can find them and they can live out their next incarnation in peace. I guess I've wanted to dig this guy up, and eke out a few more minutes before he has to go back. Still something happened in Japan last year.

First, for the final part of Obon, the Daimonji Festival, they light five fires on five mountains overlooking the city (each fire takes the shape of a character). So in 2011 we got to Kyoto and found Mount Daimonji. We decided to climb it, which is not too far. But the sun already had started dropping. We reached the top and looked down at this bridge I'd stood on as a 10-year-old. You could see the entire beautiful city down to the sea. Then we started descending and got lost. At this point the sky turned black.

AF: I just got lost dropping down a mountain in Kyoto on Sunday.

BS: Really? So it's darkness, night. We wandered through thick woods. And this is July, with huge firewood stacks covered in white cloth. These stacks had been prepared for the festival. The bonfires get absolutely enormous. So we're standing completely lost on the mountain slope, in this thick wood, and the sky goes black and we can't see anything. I say, oh, the trail's over there. And Lisa says, the trail's over here. We start to panic. We get really scared.

AF: The hills have those rustic, minimally marked trails (with hidden canyons).

BS: But we're not even on a trail. At a certain point I say, let's just move toward the lights of the city. But the city's lights look far away, with pitch-black forest between us. We get further lost and decide to climb back up the mountain to regroup, reassess. We arrive back on the mountaintop to find two young guys sitting, having a drink. And this mountain is steep. It's a chore just to lift your legs to climb this mountain. So we explain to the guys—we don't speak Japanese well—that we're lost. Clearly they don't seem concerned. They don't have flashlights. I don't know how they got there. They agree to lead us down. This takes about an hour. And we'd been way off. We'd gone in the complete opposite direction. Those two Kyoto University students saved our lives. Then they just take off on their bicycles. There's been a lot of that, where I go to cites or places I'd experienced before and get completely lost. It feels like finding a burial site, as if somebody forces me to ascend or descend into darkness, and they're laughing and having a great time at my expense. I've been pursuing absurd pilgrimages for which I feel ill-prepared and utterly irresponsible. That's part of the frustration.

AF: Can we consider the reader's role in this? On the topic of ritual spaces, for example, I'll often wonder, when encountering books that seek to construct ritualistic space, how does or could a reader help to construct that space? Should he or she passively observe the ritual? Should he or she identify with its participants? Would such supposed identification potentially produce reductive generalizations, in some cases primitivist stereotypes? But for your book I can ask a focused question. *O Bon* presents such elegantly rendered diction that it seems pitched specifically to an English-speaking audience. But that very audience seems unlikely to have any proper means for gauging how the book relates to Obon, or to Bon Odori, or even, one could argue, to the lived experiences of Hiroshima and Nagasaki bomb victims—which get evoked. So here's the question: does that dissonance between how adept your self-selecting audience can be at appreciating the project's intercultural registers feel problematic? Or do you deliberately stage and probe this tension?

BS: In no way to be disingenuous, but I imagine a reader's experience resembles my own, in that I come at this book with lots of holes in my understanding of what actually happens. Of course very specific things get referenced, as you said, such as the bombings of Hiroshima and Nagasaki, or the Bon Odori dance. But they're not the real thing. I don't know what they are. There's an energy I wish to transfer through the writing process, of having my own incomplete relationship to these topics, and aiming to form a fuller expression through the writing. What you asked in relation to subject matter: that's hard. Again, I should emphasize the really valuable experience (not to harp on this) of being young and encountering something decontextualized, in a foreign country, through a language not my own, at night, surrounded by thousands of strangers. That was formative. I feel that was a writerly moment. What I'll imagine recreating, in a book like this, is an analogous moment in which some other youthful presence can wander and sense a similar terror, and maybe that somehow can translate the experience across the ages. That sounds pretty grandiose. But to let that nighttime experience take over and let my body be contained in other people's bodies who have come before and made these poems possible…I don't know why I keep returning to that moment, but it could be in what I'm saying right now.

AF: It interests me that the Obon festival actually worked for you. That's what's supposed to happen, right? We're supposed to feel undone by such an event and gain access to something beyond our normal day-to-day experience. So I'm still curious how that process can be embodied for the reader. For example, *O Bon* often provides a flickering evocation of presence and absence as inseparable sites of inquiry. The book's opening statement, "When I close my eyes I think about the breakaway," seems to reflect this indeterminate status. This piece gets italicized, as if an epigraph, though then runs significantly longer. It offers the tone of a dream, an invocation, and elegy all at once. References to the Hiroshima bomb appear. But first a world of substance gets described, of creaturely human life contrasted to (or at least placed beside) the void of the impending bomb. That bomb itself only can come into existence by eclipsing this substantial world. Here again, a relationship between presence and absence first gets thematized then formally registered. There's this flash—and the flash could yield a subjective insight, a camera's objective record, or a destructive force unparalleled in human history. That ambiguous flash serves as hinge between the two worlds you describe. That's my single-minded summary of what occurs in *O Bon*'s first section. So how does this dualistic investigation of presence/absence play out through the rest of the book, and how does it relate to broader concerns that interest you in contemporary poetry?

BS: The flash is another event that…I have a set of obsessions or perhaps possessions, things I've been possessed with. That flash, of course, suggests all those topics you mentioned, and relates to a couple photographs of my grandfather which I have been possessed by for the last seven years. There's this one photo taken during the war, at a Department of Justice camp in western Montana, of him wearing a bra and a slip. I've written, I don't know, a hundred thousand words about this photograph (all garbage). I'm trying to reach the moment of this flash, and I've read so much about the flash of the bomb itself, the imprinted silhouettes on stone steps and walls. There's some equivalence, however difficult to make, between those two flashes. And in terms of a balance, or correspondence between presence and absence across this whole book: in one foundational way, I guess, *O Bon*'s a ghost story. The author's note begins with a ghost story. I'll need to think about that more.

AF: Do you want to do so now?

BS: Challenging that presence/absence dichotomy seems true and necessary, especially with poetry—poetry as a process through which we can engage speculative space in order to reevaluate or reimagine past events, or even present events (something overlooked in its own moment). I have the sense that nothing that happens happens completely. No true moment exists. When we try to deal with an historical event, this event itself remains incomplete. So poetry, for me, can enter a speculative or subterranean or ethereal space, can begin to understand what happened or what's happening. I'll need to think through the relation here between presence and absence. I wrote these poems at night in bed, with my glasses off, with nothing on my mind. I tried to force out any thoughts. I'd begun writing them in Missoula, Montana, where my imprisoned grandfather wore that bra. But I had no plan. I just wanted to sink into bed, to sink toward sleep, to hover at the edge of preconsciousness and see what would happen. What happened was I felt I'd started to translate his voice or his incomplete experience. For him, for any number of reasons, he didn't have full access to his voice. There seemed to be something even he didn't know, even he didn't have access to, in the same sense that, as we've discussed, we don't have full ownership over this moment. Then that translation experience would disappear and I couldn't recover it in any way.

AF: Many localized arrangements in the book seem to channel your grandfather's voice. Some suggest a choral or double-voiced lyric. Examples appear on pages 8 and 10, with their double columns, which could be read horizontally, vertically, simultaneously both ways. How do these diptych structures relate to recurring themes of history, ancestry, cannibalism even?

BS: Yeah, cannibalism. I would love to find instances of cannibalism in my ancestry.

AF: I mean reflection on ancestry as its own form of cannibalism.

BS: Just as a side note: I had this dream a couple weeks back of standing before a class, and a moment of silence occurred between topics, and I said aloud, when a woman eats another woman, is this the same as when a man eats a man?

AF: That's a good question.

BS: The students stared quizzically and I felt the need to give a disclaimer. I said, is that a really misogynistic question? Then I woke up. I don't know what it meant. Those poems you mentioned happen in relation to the Daimonji festival's five fires. That's why I use numbers. Some of the language, like page 12, I took from my grandfather's FBI file. How these voices relate, I don't know. In my first book a few pages contained just bunches of letters scattered across… there's no strict way to read them.

AF: This is the Flim Forum book?

BS: Yes, called *The Alps*. I wrote it at the same time as this one. That book addressed my parent's wedding. They got married in the Alps in 1972. Toward the book's end its words and letters start dissociating, scattered across the page. Then they regroup and the book closes. I came to poetry through drawing. I studied visual arts up until age 23. I still retain a desire to draw, but that muscle kind of vanished, or got parlayed into writing poetry, into picturing the Daimonji Festival and feeling myself (as a child) turning in a circle and regarding these bonfires burning on the hillside—how each represents a different idea, or a different aspect, or different emergence of some historical theme. Ultimately they all blur into one. All the fires become this cloud of hovering smoke. Into that cloud I insert my own communication with my grandfather, or records from his FBI file, or on page 8, which you mentioned, that language comes from the story of Hoichi the Earless, the blind monk who plays the history of the Dan-no-ura battle on his biwa. The movie *Kwaidan* which Kobayashi made…I think it's the first film in that series, beautiful. He's a monk, blind, and enters a cemetery every night to recreate this epic battle from the Samurai era's beginning. He basically sits alone but creates an entire world. He does so as a memorial. He reconstitutes the lives of his clan. That's something else with which I became obsessed, through the movie, from the great Lafcadio Hearn story.

AF: Can you keep describing how source texts get ingested into your book? You'd mentioned your grandfather's FBI file. You run a Tumblr site devoted to Hiroshima and Nagasaki bomb victims. You'll excerpt passages from Yasunari Kawabata's palm-of-the-hand stories, yet you've streamlined these and removed punctuation.

BS: I also did that on…there's something from the Kojiki or the Nihongi, where I not only cut punctuation but took away words and put in long dashes.

AF: If you could discuss the significance of such transformations as they'll get integrated into *O Bon*.

BS: I have this love for source material, as paper. This hopefully is a really short story. After I graduated high school I got a job cleaning houses in Connecticut. One house belonged to a *New Yorker* cartoonist. She'd illustrated for the *New Yorker* for decades. Her husband was a writer who published one book, but otherwise operates as sort of a house dad. I'd been assigned to clean their master bedroom, which included his office. She had this beautiful studio and he had this tiny cramped corner of the bedroom for eking out stories. But what I loved was that in his bedroom corner hung hundreds and hundreds of index cards and notes and pictures taped to the walls—story and character ideas, and sentences. I referred to that corner as the Paper Cockpit. To me this seemed so much cooler than anything he could have published. I read his book and liked it, but it lacked the energy of his Paper Cockpit. I thought, why can't we just exist in this space, surrounded by our notes and ideas and jottings? I worship that space. But then of course comes the other compulsion to turn all that stuff into a book.

AF: Do you mean why can't we exist for readers in that space? Or why can't we just comfortably remain by ourselves in that space?

BS: What was the first part?

AF: Why haven't we learned to communicate with readers while remaining in this cocoon-like space, never needing to extract ourselves from it? Or why can't we abandon the idea that something of greater value exists beyond this space?

BS: Well, certainly something of value exists beyond that space. Though I'll often wonder what it is I do, or any of us do. Where is that thing? Where is the creative moment and what happens on its other side? I spoke to a photographer here in Tucson who takes thousands of pictures each week. He said his true creative moment comes when shooting the photos, which sounds common, but I don't know at what point his audience enters that moment. Or back to the Paper Cockpit: I'm probably as much of a reader as this guy's ever had. I made his bed once a week for months and months, and tended to that space religiously. It was my favorite house and I didn't give a shit about the *New Yorker* cartoonist, despite the fact that I'd steal cartoons from her garbage can. I don't know. I think I constantly try to figure out, where is it and what is it? I do have a deep love for the object, and want to integrate diverse elements into the book. But sometimes

I want the book just to be composed completely of external elements, and to make that process visible, because that could be how I feel most myself as a poet. Then I'll start to write a poem, and feel I've done grave disservice to the moment.

AF: As you further describe the Paper Cockpit metaphor, I think of *O Bon*'s section, "The Inland Sea," which includes your parents' description of the day of your birth, and which ends with the line "I don't even remember when I first saw you." This seems to conclude a sequence of poetic reflexivity, in which you write the poem as the poem writes you. That reminds me of the Paper Cockpit moment, which embodies a threshold of thinking or speech. Could you connect "The Inland Sea" to the Paper Cockpit, or just address this concept of an inland sea? Is there an inland sea of introspection we need to cross as writers?

BS: It's funny. I didn't realize at the time, but I did the same thing with *The Alps*, in that I'd asked both my parents for the journals they kept in '72, when they got married. They'd traveled around Europe and got married in a small Swiss town. So this other book, this long poem, also ends with words from my mother's journal. I guess I'm basically saying I turn to my mom to finish all my writing. But for the Inland Sea—have you gone down there?

AF: We just went. Both Miyajima Island and Hiroshima.

BS: Miyajima, where wild deer roam? Did you climb to the top of Mount Misen? You get this pretty incomprehensible view of the Inland Sea. And that's only a small part, its southwestern edge.

AF: I remember oceans, plural, and mountain ranges in every direction extending to infinity.

BS: Right. And then closer down you spot oyster traps, or whatever those long white bone-things are. We went up there. I kept thinking about the inexpressible. I thought of the Inland Sea as a language I wish I had the capacity to speak. That doesn't mean necessarily the view. I don't know what it means. It came to my head as I stood up there. My grandfather was born...as you stand atop that mountain, if you look relatively east, you'll see the island on which he was born, in a small town called Oko, on Kurahashi Island. Though again, I don't know the where or why of this writing. I don't know what I'm after really. I can't reach even the surface of things I get carried away with. I constantly try to find, then quickly fall in love with these moments. There's Borges' story "The Aleph," with that amazing description of the moment in which everything can be seen and comprehended at once. I constantly look for such instances in a much smaller way. I can't even say I look for them. I'll partly write into and out of them, and feel consistently dissatisfied with the whole process, which could be a life problem, or mental problem. I don't know if that's a poetic problem, or a labor problem.

INTERVIEW WITH HOA NGUYEN
Recorded on May 29, 2012
This interview focuses on Nguyen's book *As Long as Tress Last* (Wave Books).

ANDY FITCH: Can we start with the title? *As Long As Trees Last* perhaps once signified a spacious, secure span of time. Now it suggests something more conditional, as if it could be so long as trees last.

HOA NGUYEN: Yeah, sure. The title can impart an open, hopeful sense, but also could provide more of a warning. That line comes from a poem. I like its monosyllabic percussiveness. I tend toward monosyllabic rhythms for their sense of pulse and urgency. Multisyllabic words tend to be more Latinate and more the language of administration. And there are a lot of trees in this manuscript, returning tree characters, not really—but as though they were.

AF: Your work long has offered these compressed, monosyllabic verbal clusters, which often track evanescent modes of experience. The line you just mentioned reads as follows: "Too fast / a bird that goes and sends a net // I hide or flee / who finds the fossil pieces // Beech-tree white // a candy for a hearth / as long as trees last." The rhythms and idioms seem recognizably your own. With this particular book, however, I sensed a more ominous undertone to that characteristic focus on speed and precision. "The Soul They Say," one of the concluding poems, quickly ends on the phrase "Worlds die," then gets followed by "Cassandra Poem." Has your attunement to the unstable, immediate moment taken on new significance here?

HN: Perhaps more poems contain multiple layers of critique (self-critique, critique of humans, critique of oppressive institutional structures). A couple pieces reference the war in Southeast Asia, in Vietnam, where I was born. And within both the U.S. and global landscapes, many events do cause concern. You've probably noticed I'm a poet who tends to write from a singular moment, rather than towards some sustained, book-length project. Patterns I construct have more to do with the environment in which I find myself, which includes poems that reference the tsunami and nuclear problems in Japan, or the earthquake in Haiti. I'm not saying life suddenly got worse, though the poems kept bringing me there.

AF: Writing the poems prompted these reflections?

HN: Yes, because I don't sit down and say, I'm going to write a poem about ecological disaster. Something just surfaces, part of the environment—partly from what I read, partly from dictation.

AF: As you describe your compositional process, I remember tiny moments of linguistic mutability. The poem "Intimate," for example, opens with the parenthetical "(intimate)." This seems to accentuate the multiplicity both of that word and of your poetics, which presume a great deal of intimacy with their subjects, yet also imply a more suggestive mode of inchoate intimations. So "Intimate" puns and plays on that word, pointing toward both the familiar and the never fully known. Or one poem's critique of U.S. citizens redirects its symmetrical scrutiny to "us" citizens.

HN: "US," it's called. I took that from a *Time* magazine. My lovely mother-in-law sent us a subscription. It arrives every week and I flip through to see its particular read on the world, which includes pictures, cultural things, and little blurb-like factoids. One of these stated that the United States contains more televisions than people. That appears in the poem, along with this mirroring device, as if the study had flipped itself.

AF: Again, with the mirrors and punning—perhaps it was just my mood while reading but this book seems to present a quite menacing sense of equivalence. Contamination creeps in. You'll describe breast milk that yields rocket fuel. Dangerous or false substitutions keep happening.

HN: You can find rocket fuel in lettuce, also.

AF: In Wyoming I think we've got a lot.

HN: I think articles I read about this focused on Wyoming.

AF: You've said your work tends to get organized around shorter units, and I definitely hear in it the elided idiom of Charles Olson, Lorine Niedecker, Larry Eigner, Alice Notley. But when I read "Exercise #3 from Colloquial Vietnamese," the abstracted concordances struck me, with all those lines hinging on "and," which brought a sense of dreamy duality.

HN: That's actually a found poem, in the way that found poems can become quite purposeful when they get re-purposed—especially here with the conditional phrasings. In terms of Alice Notley and Charles Olson: I'll take what they do, but try to make it super compressed.

AF: And they're already pretty compressed.

HN: I guess I'm picturing their longer projects. Alice Notley's bigger project has been about the epic for some time, and a kind of narrativity, too. That's part of what interests me regarding influence, and this might relate to your previous question about my poem which starts "(intimate)." I've taken from Olson, as many people have, his model of the poem as a transference of energy, a transmission on the page, a transmission to the reader through the mind and ear and the syllable, the heart, and the line's breath. I've tried hard to internalize what that could mean for me. I've learned a lot from Joanne Kyger, who has articulated so elegantly similar concerns with a kind of constellated energetics, with keen attention to how you breathe the sounds. Pound, whom I quote for this book's opening, says at one point about rhythm: "Rhythm is a form cut into TIME, as a design is determined SPACE." That suggests still another way for organizing one's relation to the music and language.

AF: Though your work tends toward shorter, discrete units rather than expansive plans or projects, I do often sense book-length continuity. Here it comes, I guess, from oscillations regarding fertility, in relation to menstrual flow and drought. I'm not looking for an allegory, but seemed to find this *Waste land/Fisher King* thing. There's the meeting at a dry river bed, which soon just becomes "the bed." There's even the phrase "grail jewels." Then the final poem, entitled "Swell," presents a worker bee buzzing and begs: "Please / just open the door / to the sun." I did sense a very compressed, very minimalist, but nonetheless book-length circulation of meaning.

HN: That's great. I think that happens with my method, which is just to keep writing while staying informed by your environment. Central Texas, where I lived for fourteen years, went through a cycle of drought. Meteorologists suggest this is a trend. And of course the zones of gardening there (officials decide which trees can get planted in a particular zone) have shifted and changed. I'd read a *New York Times* article about Chicago now planting completely different types of trees.

AF: I always quote that article. They now plant trees from Baton Rouge.

HN: During our drought even native trees grew distressed and started dying. Then this terrible uncontained fire blew through. So the book ends up tracking local environmental and global monetary disaster, with appropriated quotations like: "'It's simpler now to retire— / you just die in the office.'"

AF: Which is pretty common where I am in Japan, I think. But on drought, specifically the Texas drought, I felt, perhaps incorrectly, that droughts have appeared before in your work, with now a more pointed focus on a particular threatened prairie ecosystem.

HN: For the fourteen years I'd lived in Austin, this drought went deeper and deeper. The lakes continue dropping and dropping. So yes, my second book also included drought. It makes it so that you become very aware of your water usage and your neighbors' water usage. Watching someone soak the sidewalk and so forth, with sprinklers, gets maddening.

AF: Soon I'll head back to Wyoming, to a high plateau surrounded by brown dead trees because of pine beetles that survive the warm winters. I used to read about this on the *Times*' editorial page, while living in Brooklyn, but didn't have any concrete sense what it meant. So I'm curious about your ongoing engagement with the local. You and Dale have spoken eloquently in many contexts about attending to the local. But here, as you addressed local conditions with global implications, I wondered about your relation to your audience. Does your attention to a particular local have an informative purpose for distant readers? Does it stay attentive to its local situation as a model that others could apply to their own?

HN: I hope that poetry in general can expand one's attention or imagination about place and relation to place. I'm not sure I'm so much instructing. I've lived on the border between the Edwards Plateau and the Blackland Prairie, and gone through the ecosystem that way, in essay form. Then I attached poems to it, as a way to speak to my relationship to place. But in terms of audience, I would just hope my poems provoke some continuities of attention, I suppose.

AF: Well I'm intrigued by your cagey mode of political critique. As you said, many layers of critique appear.

HN: I like that you called them "cagey."

AF: The title "Rage Sonnet," for example, offers a potential oxymoron. And the book's first four poems address the BP oil spill, a poisonous "Operation Ranch Hand," unemployment, Agent Orange. Yet each remains characteristically spare, elliptical, collage-like from line to line, or within the line. So do you start with straightforward-seeming sentiments of outrage, though then wind up with something more polyvalent, more complex?

HN: I'm usually deeply engaged with another poet's work. For the Agent Orange poem you mentioned, I'd been reading Emily Dickinson. I think she appears one other time in that sequence. And when I enter this relationship with another poet, her strategies, I learn a lot. I'll write through those strategies as well. In this particular poem, I quote her. I'll absorb then try to discharge that same poetic energy. Her incredibly compressed lines have so much fire to them. I remember, once in class, someone saying Dickinson's words felt like knives and I thought, yeah, I want my language to pick up that kind of pointedness. That was the occasion for this poem.

AF: When you immerse yourself in a preceding poet's strategies, does that also somehow redirect energy to your own historical present?

HN: Yeah. I think partly what brought me to Dickinson was her writing during the worst part of the Civil War—yet pointing to the artifice that she's writing a poem. So for my "Rage Sonnet," I tried to place myself in a sonnet. I always appreciate poems that let me as the reader admit, hey, here we are, in a poem. That feels more honest somehow.

AF: On this question of artifice: your work often provides a compressed synthesis of mundane physical fact, yet takes on metaphorical intimations. One of my favorite lines from this book is, "Kind of day: beans on toast." You have these physical, sensual, suggestive spare lines, but then your collagist sense of how to juxtapose tone, idiom, subject-position remains just as striking. And those tendencies toward collaging seem to get thematized as well, in "So Obvious," for instance, when you say "I mix / these pieces seeing inside & / outside and cutting cutting / the cutting of two / the woman cut into two to make / the earth and the stars / two worlds that is one world." I'm used to modes of serial production that involve lots of repetition. Collaging together short, singular, discrete lyrics seems more difficult and, like her fascicles, more Dickinson-esque.

HN: Thanks.

AF: But do you end up discarding tons of material? Can you recycle it elsewhere? Have you honed processes for collecting and organizing and sifting through these short units?

HN: I just was thinking about that. When I mentioned Dickinson's fire—I'm trying to conjure that in my poems. I have to access that state or else the lines stay in my notebook. Of course on occasion a phrase or mood will totally change and enter some poem of the future. But generally speaking, as I write, it's very much an application of available forces. It feels almost architectural. Maybe that's too wooden. Maybe it's more like I have to put pieces together so that they can constellate a dynamo sense of themselves.

AF: I've thought a lot about Joe Brainard's approach to additive and subtractive construction. Those terms come from art criticism. For subtractive construction, this is like a corny formulation you hear in high school, that Dostoyevsky splits up the Russian soul into three distinct characters: Ivan is intellect; Dmitri is impulse, etcetera. But for additive construction, no original, overall meaning exists, which then gets parsed into smaller units. Global meanings only arise as local elements get placed beside each other.

HN: That reminds me of something Ted Berrigan discusses, that what he'd learned from painters (probably including Joe) was the compositional theory of push/pull.

AF: From Hans Hoffman.

HN: How do you lay down—though he meant in terms of language—how do you lay down pigment to construct dimensionality? Things bleed or pop out or have this texture, even though you only see two dimensions. Berrigan applied that to language. I thought that a smart way to talk about the energetics of a poem's different parts, which have to do with their sound and rhythm and form on the page. How do you arrange these compositional elements to produce their own gestalt, their own sense of being?

AF: On these questions of compositional strategy or architecture, architectonics—I'm assuming we could apply them to the collection as a whole.

HN: You mean the various poems placed together? Sure. I'm trying to remember how I did it. It felt kind of thematic, with departures and returns and moods. Often that includes a chronological component. I know the order in which I wrote them, and definitely didn't order them according to strict chronology, but did pay attention to…like I wouldn't want the seasons to switch back and forth within consecutive poems.

AF: Throughout your mom remains hovering nearby, sometimes as an invited guest, sometimes more a talisman, a symbol.

HN: We'd spent much time together over the course of my writing these poems, with her on extended visits. She lives in the D.C. area and would spend the winter wanting to be around family. Her health is a little compromised, and she's this amazing figure for me of endurance and strength and cunning and modernism. She was and is incredibly modern. She left home at 15 and joined a circus and became a motorcycle stunt-woman in Vietnam in the early 1960s. She did these amazing things contrary to what her position as a poor woman, born in 1942 in the Mekong Delta, should have been. So she does serve as a figure here. I like that word you used—a talismanic or sometimes symbolic figure, sometimes literal, sometimes offering incisive commentaries. She said something helpful when we saw images of Haiti, which reminded her of war destruction. There's much dream matter about her in the poems. I did a lot of dream work for this book.

AF: Will we ever hear more details about your mom's motorcycle stunt career?

HN: I keep hoping to write that project, to get funding for it. I need to visit Vietnam and do some research. I'd like to write both towards my mother's biography and towards the impossibility of this project—but with me in the project as a part of her. I've also thought about this in relation to the political, social, environmental aspects of the place where I was born and raised. We have these amazing photographs of her motorcycle stunt stuff, and people say, you need to write that book. I know.

AF: You're making me realize I had this diving-board failure dream last night. Do you want to discuss your dream work?

HN: I'm not sure what I would say.

AF: We could consider recurring dreamy motifs from the book, like Chinaberry. How and why did Chinaberry keep coming up?

HN: I developed a relationship to this tree. Our last residence in Austin stood on level with a Chinaberry. We had this deck that backed directly to the tree's crown. It is a feral Asian tree—considered a trash tree. When I first lived in Austin I had a negative relation to one. One at our first place fell over and got messy. Year later, when I lived so closely to this other Chinaberry, I was offered a different view, a close view where I could observe its cycles more carefully. Something shifted. Partly that had to do with like…OK, this was imported here. Communities actively introduced them in a lot of places that have low water, because they survive droughts. It's Asian, OK, and introduced to this environment, so it became this other symbol, too. And it still got stressed in the drought. It grew really droopy. But the berries that I used to consider nuisances, that used to drop on the car, now hung in clusters. Then fruit-loving birds, Cedar Waxwings, came during our last years there and swarmed on this eyelevel Chinaberry. They ate its fruits and got kind of got drunk from fermented fruit. Butterflies would come through when it flowered. And I didn't know Chinaberries had a delicate lavender fragrance until I'd moved this close to one. So the tree became a figure again in my writing environment, a figure in terms of its relationship to its environment, and became also me, and not me.

AF: Did you say one tree fell over?

HN: Our first place's backyard had an old Chinaberry with a vine wrapped around it. During one storm that all fell over. But I was like, good riddance. At the time I had a very different approach. In fact, I wasn't dealing with the tree at all. Then I realized I'd developed a relationship and Chinaberry references started surfacing, the way that happens: you look into the Chinaberry's history and other references happen.

AF: I like how all of this relates to your title, too, to all the different ways that trees last. You're definitely a poet attuned to your environment, both ecological and social. So anything you want to say about moving to Canada, how that has altered your relationship to physical, cultural, political landscapes?

HN: I can't yet say much. I'm still getting my bearings. We've been here less than a year, but it's interesting. I've started seeing differences articulate themselves in many different ways. It's really exciting to feel a part of one of Toronto's numerous poetry contexts. We've found great people. There's so much going on. I'm trying to become sensitive to this environment. We've already hosted a few readings and brought poets from the U.S. to pair with local poets. Bringing those two communities closer, getting them speaking to each other in an informal living space—our home—has been fun and generative.

## INTERVIEW WITH DALE SMITH
Recorded on May 30, 2012
This interview focuses on Smith's book *Poets Beyond the Barricade: Rhetoric, Citizenship, and Dissent after 1960* (University of Alabama Press).

ANDY FITCH: For people who know you best as a poet or advocate of poets, can you first reintroduce yourself as a critic, talk a bit about your rhetoric background, when you started and how it generally informs your life and work?

DALE SMITH: I did an MA at New College, a funky school. I went to study with poets and deepen my study of poetry. Then in the mid-90s Hoa and I moved from California to Austin. We published magazines and books, and hosted readings at our house. I delivered flowers, worked as a security guard, that kind of thing. As we had kids and needed more and more money I found myself teaching at a community college, but soon realized I could make as much in a PhD program as I could as an adjunct. And I could write critical prose quite easily. So I enrolled at the University of Texas, mostly because a professor named Jeffrey Walker was the only scholar of modernist poetry doing what interested me. His first book focused on Williams, Pound, Olson, and Hart Crane, yet he specializes in rhetoric—particularly, now, ancient rhetoric and poetics. At that time I had no idea what rhetoric was. Though Jeff did interesting things in his work I wanted to know more about. The rhetorical tradition emphasizes democracy and citizenship, going back to Athens, since that's what the rhetors, or orators, of Athens did by negotiating the civil society of their time. But Jeff went back and said actually this begins with poetry, with Homer and Hesiod and how they model rhetorical possibilities in poetry. This history of language uses going back to antiquity interested me—everything from ancient rhetoric to medieval, Renaissance, all the way up. I tried to situate what I saw happening in contemporary poetry amid that much larger tradition. Still, when poets ask about rhetoric...people understand linguistics and understand theory, though rhetoric in the States most often gets tied to composition, that kind of pedagogy, which represents an important but not exclusive aspect of rhetorical studies. The questions Jeff posed helped me understand a lot: does poetry do anything beyond the poem, beyond the poet, beyond the coterie, beyond institutional audiences? What relation does it have to popular audiences? The book I wound up finishing at the end of this long process asks similar questions: how does poetry place itself in the world? How does it respond to social or cultural situations?

AF: I've got substantial follow-ups. But you said you can write critical prose easily?

DS: Yeah. In part I came to poetry because you can't just write your own poetry—you've got to advocate in some way. My friends do translation, publishing, scholarly work. Years ago, I began writing book reviews for people. For whatever reason I could do this easily. I enjoyed advocating for certain types of poetry, and using critical prose to discuss broader cultural conditions. People had invited me to write pieces. I'd stumbled into it. In graduate school I learned to develop my perspective within a larger tradition of writing.

AF: This helped in your role as advocate? To have additional historical context?

DS: It did. I'd found myself, besides needing money, at a point where I was writing book reviews, had a book column, had my own journal *(Skanky Possum),* and did a lot of writing but felt something still missing. Studying the history of rhetoric and poetics helped open a larger conversation about what poetry does, what writing does, what writing instruction and public engagement can mean. What does it mean to be both a citizen and a poet—to participate in smaller communities? These questions provided a foundation for considering what writing does in specific situations for specific people.

AF: Since it might be a new concept for readers, can you provide a quick description of a rhetorical poetry? This phrase appears early in the book. Is all poetry inherently rhetorical if viewed from the appropriate perspective? Do you value certain self-conscious elements to the rhetoric found in particular historical eras, or specific individuals?

DS: Those are helpful questions, since "rhetoric" as a term remains contested, and various readers use it quite differently. I think about a rhetorical poetics as not aimed to the coterie, to the local community of initiates, but at some broader possible public. That audience could take many different forms. Allen Ginsburg and the Beats moved beyond their local community into a much larger popular community. Others, like the New York School, say Frank O'Hara writing in the '50s, spoke, at least initially, to a much smaller coterie of fellow poets. The poetry that most interests me, and that my book calls rhetorical poetry, aims at a public space. Of course people ask, what's public space? To some extent, public spaces describe imagined communities, imagined spaces. I look for moments when poetry reaches beyond in-group poetics, and enters the world in a distinct way, possibly to affect a wider public audience—like how Denise Levertov or Robert Duncan addressed the Vietnam War, or Kristin Prevallet and Anne Waldman respond to recent wars in Iraq or Afghanistan. The use of the poem matters most here.

AF: Does this necessarily relate to intention, to something thought through in advance, with anticipation of a potential audience and a strategy for reaching and engaging that audience? I ask because, while conducting these interviews, I've noticed how few of the poets claim some conscious intention for their work and its anticipated future. I'll find it hard even to pose such questions, since no conscious intentions guide most of my own writing. So in terms of the vocabulary you've presented, would these be instances of in-group insularity, which don't even recognize themselves as such?

DS: Here I think of how Duncan and Levertov addressed the Vietnam War. Their letters from 1967-69 rehearse various possibilities. They know where they come from as poets, reading Olson and Pound and Williams. But now they get confronted by a larger social or political conflict. How should they apply their poetic attention to this particular purpose? Levertov really wants to reinforce the peace movement's drive and urgency—to support it and help increase its numbers and make it an important social phenomenon. Duncan wants to reach a larger audience that could include even the opposition, the conservatives. So it's not just about transferring in-group desires to broader social situations, but shaping a poetry that can prompt people to reflect on the meaning of war, its terrors.

AF: Just to get a few more critical terms in place, could you define the epideictic mode? Could you place that in relation to deliberative and forensic modalities?

DS: Epideictic is just a fancy-ass word Aristotle used, along with forensic and deliberative modes of rhetoric, to describe familiar situations of language use. Forensic discourse happens in court. A jury assembles; somebody's dead; who did it; how do we prosecute the accused; how do we remedy this situation? Deliberative discourse takes place in a congress or parliament. People stand up, make speeches, try to decide should we go to war, should we not go to war? Deliberation demands considering different sides of something, making a conclusive decision. Whereas the epideictic, Aristotle says, encompasses a rhetoric of praise and blame. It's largely ceremonial. In my book, again following Jeff Walker and people like Sharon Crowley and recent work in rhetorical theory, I look at the epideictic as a space of belief and desire, as a rhetorical mode addressing ideology in some way, addressing people's beliefs. Of course, ideologies also get constructed and reinforced through language situations that are neither deliberative nor forensic. Car commercials reinforce certain expressions of masculinity—those kinds of things.

AF: Does Roland Barthes' *Mythologies* fit here as a point of reference, a study of how ideology reinforces desire and desire reinforces ideology?

DS: You could talk about semiotics and signs. Though in rhetorical studies, emphasis might get placed on the situational discourse, considering audience reception, not just the sign itself. Rhetoric also intersects with cultural studies, again in its emphasis on the larger discursive situation.

AF: When you describe the epideictic as a discourse of praise and blame, I'm curious as well how it relates to aesthetics, to aesthetic criticism, to a criticism of value.

DS: Literature and aesthetics clearly would fall into the realm of the epideictic. The epideictic has existed for a long time. This mode of descriptive discourse precedes even the idea of literature or aesthetics. Literature became institutionalized and first practiced fairly recently, really as an invention of the 18th century. The belletristic arguments of Hugh Blair or Adam Smith of the Scottish Enlightenment invent what becomes literature. They develop the taste and audience to appreciate the aesthetics that only a "literary genius" provides. This ties into developing the morals of a society changing and growing during the Enlightenment and just following. To me, aesthetics and literature seem recent inventions, carrying on what people called the epideictic in Aristotle's day, and later in Cicero's, or into the Middle Ages. So I look at poetry not just in terms of how it interfaces with literary institutions or aesthetic theory, but as something beyond those, outside those, pointing toward other types of public, social, cultural practices. That's where I see rhetoric and the epideictic differing from certain literary practices to which we've grown accustomed—at least in the English department, right?

AF: Could you here articulate the concept of scale shift that gets applied in your Charles Olson chapter? Something that stood out (in relation to questions of Olson's immediate political impact, versus the exemplary role he might provide for future poets' civic engagement) is that publishing in the *Gloucester Daily Times* doesn't seem a dramatic scale shift, in terms of quantity of readers. It still sounds relatively local. I'm not saying that's bad. But could you describe the concept of scale shift so to explain away this potential contradiction?

DS: Sure. A scale shift doesn't depend upon numbers for me, but types of audience. I take the term from Jules Boykoff, a poet and scholar of political science, someone interested in less literary types of audience formation. Boykoff uses the example of Martin Luther King. How does King go from leading a local Montgomery congregation, to addressing large national audiences? Such questions definitely involve size. But Olson moves from a focused literary coterie to a broader public discourse. This requires advocates, newspaper editors and publishers, interpreters that can make sense of Olson's project for other people. He advocates to preserve Gloucester's historical homes and buildings, its wetlands. Many of his projects, most of them, fail. But beyond those particular topics, Olson tapped a collective pain shared by the community through the recognition of fundamental economic changes coming to Gloucester. Olson shared his civic awareness with others. So this doesn't reflect an equation like "scale equals mass." It's more like scale equals some other possibility, some other modality, some terrain in which poetry does not limit its scope to those readers trained by English departments. Instead you find many institutions interfacing.

AF: As you describe Olson's public intervention, one which doesn't produce pronounced physical consequences, I wonder about the concept of the poet as witness (which gets thoroughly critiqued in the '70s and '80s)—this potentially elitist formulation of a sensitive poet suffering for others, providing a pseudo engagement that prompts further complacency. How do you respond both to traditional and more recent characterizations of the poet as witness?

DS: The poet as witness is not a realm that interests me. It doesn't seem a rhetorical concern. In order to make it rhetorical, it ultimately has to involve some kind of action. To witness just means that you observe or emotively respond to an event. For poets I discuss, what takes them beyond the level of witness is that they call forth some kind of action, or try to inspire some better possible outcome beyond the literary scene. They don't just pay tribute to the moment. Rhetorical studies emphasize dynamic forces, change. Of course this could take the form of propaedeutic, self-reflective writing, which expands local audiences' capacities to respond to future debates. I don't demand some deliberative discourse in which the poet stands up and provokes instantaneous action. I focus on addressing beliefs and desire, how our capacities to live in this world change over time—how, as we encounter new ideas, our feelings change. Those smaller confrontations might not force us to make decisions right then and there, but to open up and reflect and consider further outcomes down the road.

AF: One last question about Olson. His *Gloucester Daily Times* pieces most amazed me because they sound like Olson the poet, not some conventional op-ed columnist. I wondered what you would think of, let's say, a poet who becomes a speech writer. Or conceptual art projects from the '60s in which artists go work at factories, and intervene at the places where society gets engineered. Do these provide effective means of rhetorical engagement, or an entirely separate enterprise? Do you focus on Olson because he does remain a difficult poet even when writing for the newspaper?

DS: Yeah. He remains that poet. And if you remove the label of poet, and examine it in terms of performance, he publicly performs this masculine-constructed voice amid working-class Gloucester in the '50s and '60s. He appeals to his audience in a certain way, through a performance that only can happen because the editors and the publisher provide that space, and produce their own performances of editorializing—proclaiming Charles Olson the poet of Gloucester, this important figure. Olson desires to say something about a house scheduled for destruction, then comes in and it's just full-on Olson, right? He gets invited to write a weekly column and turns it down, basically arguing that it would interfere with his poetry life too much; he wants to get involved, but won't become this civic entity; he's very much his own engaged person as a poet. Still he valued that poetic/civic space as a modality of the possible. Olson saw Gloucester's basis of economic security eroding. He wanted to address the beliefs and desires of people there. He designed poetry that made readers reflect on these transformations, and placed it in very public venues.

AF: In terms of your previous comparison between Ginsberg and O'Hara, and how their cultivations of audience play out: you've suggested that a rhetorical poetics presumes some future trajectory of agency, one that extends beyond the writing or reading of the poem. Here I'm curious if you could discuss how scale shifts relate to poetic temporality—to questions of present versus future engagement. What I mean is, for example, Craig Dworkin's recent article "Seja Marginal" discusses the "long tail" of literary circulation. Over the long term, if you look at, let's say, Amazon sales, books that never became bestsellers can maintain some purchase on the future and end up constituting (if you add this whole conglomerate together) where most readers' attention really seems to lie. So could you describe how scale shifts play out in relation to an audience of contemporaries versus audiences of the future?

DS: Nobody read Blake in the late 18th century, right? But everybody reads him now. Clearly some kind of scale shift took place as critical advocates desired to institutionalize him. I'll think about that in terms of marketing. Malcolm Gladwell writes about this ad nauseum, how word-of-mouth marketing campaigns remain much more effective than any other approach. He gives the example of Hush Puppy shoes. In the '90s, Williamsburg hipsters started wearing Hush Puppies, and overnight Hush Puppy saw its sales shoot through the roof. Our access to the internet and Facebook and instantaneous news prepares us to participate in these dramatic shifts. Somebody's YouTube video goes viral and gets known overnight. Still, these are rare exceptions. Poetry tends to work slower, behind the scenes, through critical advocates, through conversations you have with people. Of course Facebook and similar media might allow for new ideas, books, modes of critical engagement to filter through more quickly than they did twenty years ago. But scale of quantity doesn't matter so much as the quality of dissemination. A really passionate connector will help to move a project in a certain direction, which remains much more useful than the *New York Times Book Review* for giving you the right audience—that long-term, self-sustaining audience you mentioned.

AF: Could we return to the Duncan/Levertov chapter? First, it may be helpful to distinguish between arguments of advantage and a rhetoric of suasion. But then, in the Duncan/Levertov chapter, you do such a persuasive job presenting this rhetoric of suasion (a model that seems to deny static critical binaries), that I wondered if no strict dichotomy had been there to begin with.

DS: For that particular chapter, the theories come out of Kenneth Burke, who was a friend of William Carlos Williams, though also remains a huge figure in rhetorical studies to this day. The rhetoric of advantage involves what we traditionally think of as rhetoric—where you try to get somebody to see your point of view and to act on it. A direct relation emerges between the speech used and some ultimate action. So Levertov wanted to persuade people to...she wanted to reinforce opposition to the war in Vietnam. Her poetry pretty much across the board does that (whether successfully or not remains a separate question). For Duncan I applied Burke's concept of a rhetoric of persuasion, or pure persuasion. Burke discusses this as an almost innate activity we can't keep ourselves from doing. Though for Duncan, this develops into a larger dialectical process. He doesn't seek to gain advantage over some person or specific group, but tries to reach out across a vast cultural terrain, to point toward certain poetical arguments or possibilities that others could see and reflect on, act on, perhaps. It's less a science than an art. The social scientist might say, well, where's the empirical outcome? How effective was it? Whereas Duncan hopes for subtle strategies to take root and transform, and move us down the road. Here I found it more interesting not to judge these two different modes of engagement, but to look at how they frame their arguments around particular public practices, to consider how these practices intersect or diverge or endure in different ways. It seems more useful to explore a situation in which poets want the same thing, but have a different sense of audience and practicalities around what poems can do. Does this start to answer the second part of your question?

AF: So your critical approach itself provides a rhetoric of suasion, in which you willfully recoup what remains beneficial from the argument of advantage, not dismissing or demonizing it, but putting it to the best pragmatic use.

DS: I consider these both valid models for what poetry can do. Levertov makes some fascinating moves. At the height of her disgust with the Vietnam War, she can sound a bit annoying as a poet. But Duncan can sound just as annoying. When he describes LBJ as a monster, you sense he can't maintain that strategy for long. Still Duncan does a better job, I think, of pushing beyond this impasse. Consider his famous statement, you know, that the poet's job isn't to oppose evil but to engage it. That seems a more interesting possibility, right? Though sometimes that position too needs to be opposed, and a more explicit stance should be taken. I appreciate and entertain both sides as providing compelling possibilities.

AF: Amid this Duncan/Levertov distinction, you develop quite interesting, somewhat related distinctions in how Poets Against War and Poetry Is Public Action contest the post-September 11th Bush era. It would be great if you could provide an analogous take on our current historical present. You completed this manuscript, for example, before the Occupy movement emerged. What forms of rhetorical poetry most intrigue you today?

DS: Sam Hamill's Poets Against War project interested me because most of it happened online. I'd wondered what does this particular community, the online public, bring, if anything? Hamill gets invited to the White House and turns it down, which creates a public situation. Lots of anti-war poems come in. That's great and all, but there's, what, thousands of poems nobody reads ever which didn't stop the war, and we see that. At the same time, Poetry Is Public Action occurs at a street level, pasting poems around New York City, performing public acts to draw attention to these poems. Again, this didn't stop anything. Scale-wise, and ideologically after 9-11, the country's mood was like, fuck it, let's go to war. The opposition couldn't achieve that much. Whereas now, amid Occupy, I think that the structural, economic transformation has grown so intense, which can produce a very different type of moment. This situation doesn't reflect an ideological problem exactly. It reflects structural problems about money, jobs, debt, student debt, exhausted resources. So our present rhetorical situation seems to demand persistence, and numbers. I just spoke with Linh Dinh, who, for his State of the Union blog, travels around the country, or around Philadelphia, taking photos of what he sees on the street—which make for compelling visual statements. They don't offer outright arguments. They don't provide a call to action necessarily. But they put a frame around certain people and situations. They document political and social realities we face, which seems crucial right now. We need a rhetoric that persistently acknowledges reality. Because our grasp on that reality remains up for debate by different institutions and disciplines and political machines. There's little confrontation or engagement beyond those venues, toward people on the street or outcast from institutions. I could go on about this. I hope that, as structural economic transformations continue, we'll see much more of this street-level focus. Again, the Vietnam War is not Afghanistan. Iraq War protestors did something different than Occupy. Each situation demands new communicative strategies.

AF: I'm going to read back one sentence from near your book's end: "One noticeable change in the present is that the formal obligations of poetry are beginning to give way to a more thoughtful understanding of the contexts in which forms contribute to arguments that can persuade public audiences on issues of social significance." So, given the broader structural changes you've mentioned, can you point to analogous structural changes taking place in poetic communities or poetic discourse?

DS: Yeah, yeah. I don't know. It depends on who you read. Poetry has so much happening, right? My ideal involves a kind of dumb earnestness in the face of reality. Linh does a good job with it, in terms of documenting the actual, what's real, what happens in the world. Roberto Tejada looks at the discursive international forces that shape individual identity, cultural identities. Poets who most interest me expand our capacities to deal with what's coming. Many poets across the globe do this. In America there's a bit more blindness. A couple of years ago I gave a talk at Naropa about the Duncan/Levertov debate, and mentioned structural economic changes and resource contraction. This poet from Mexico City came up afterwards and said, hey, you're the only American I've ever heard discuss this stuff. In America we rarely acknowledge that level of economic reality. It requires an attention that wasn't developed...or tools not given to us by English departments or by literature. So working outside institutions, or putting different institutional models together and then smashing them up I find really appealing right now. I can think of novels, films, the Mexican director Iñárritu, or Alfonso Cuarón, who did *Children of Men*—people working on global problems and issues, not giving us answers but helping us understand the questions we need to ask.

## INTERVIEW WITH SRIKANTH REDDY
Recorded on June 5, 2012
This interview focuses on Reddy's chapbook *Readings in World Literature* (Omnidawn Books).

ANDY FITCH: Appropriated text has become a familiar part of your poetic practice. In *Voyager*, this takes a form resembling erasure poetry. For *Readings in World Literature,* something closer to citational practice appears. As in Craig Dworkin's prose text *Dure,* citational processes arise amid an investigation at times whimsical, at times more grave, but consistently an investigation of pain, wounds, human frailty. Do these excerpted quotations in Readings take on the status of lacerations, scars (though those two themselves seem quite different)?

SRIKANTH REDDY: Well many people make a powerful case for those two phenomena, textuality and embodiment, being metaphors for each other. I don't know that that's the way my literary imagination works right now. But citation and quotation do interest me as practices arising out of a kind of woundedness. These wounds may be more psychic than physical or corporeal. So the speaker of this poem kind of shores up fragments against his ruins, though not ruins of the body so much as ruins of…an inwardness he tries to negotiate by consulting other works, as a means of reconstituting identity for himself. Probably you could connect this process to scarring, or lesions. But I have enough difficulty conveying a sense of my own embodiment as speaker, without treating the poem itself as embodied presence.

AF: Part of what I'd wondered with embodiment: insistent references to mortality occur throughout this work. I'd…did you just want to say something?

SR: I'd say the work I now do, and probably have done for a while, has been obsessed with mortality. The entry point into this mortal condition isn't so much textual as—let me think. Perhaps the best way to discuss this would be through my own encounter with mortality. Doctors diagnosed me with melanoma, a nasty cancer, three years ago, the same week I learned my wife was pregnant with our first child. Fortunately, we caught my condition early and things seem OK, but questions of mortality have remained continuous with my autobiography.

AF: Should we address the extent to which these *Readings* provide an autobiographical narrative?

SR: I think that the experience of illness can prompt one to identify one's work with one's physical presence in the world. For me, that process sublimated into more rarefied questions of what poetry is. I guess I'd hope to divorce my poems from bodily existence, since that gives them a better shot of enduring. Again, much interesting work does enact a convergence of textuality and physicality, but I'm perhaps too uncomfortable with my own body to do that.

AF: In terms of how this chapbook addresses mortality: awareness arrives not in some dramatic, transcendent finale, but in any number of chilly asides. I'm looking at, say section 30, lines such as: "They are not learning. I am not teaching. Hades, who tucks everybody into bed in the end, is escorting us, still breathing, to the shore of the River Akheron." Or section 32 ends: "What we deem reality is in fiction fact. What we deem fiction is in fact reality. And so on. I have never been good at dead languages. Even the living ones feel dead to me." Again, this concludes: "The only theory that makes any sense is the one where the protagonist never returns." Your quick, deadpan tone seems to call forth further reflection on the reader's part. So I'm especially curious about the interstitial passage's function as it relates to reflections on mortality. I'm thinking specifically of Nietzsche describing the philosopher's role as…the philosopher plunges into a pool of ice, something like that. The philosopher brings back that which only can be caught by a quick grasp. Or Emerson tells us "The glance reveals what the gaze obscures." Can you discuss here the roles of digression, juxtaposition, aphoristic concision—what these practices grant access to that we can't find or couldn't bear in longer forms?

SR: Longer forms can open space for aphorisms too, for flashes of insight. More and more I find that long work allows the poem to reflect a dailyness of experience, and provides context for the surreal or nightmarish encounter with mortality, or similarly overwhelming scenes of awareness. Maybe this strays off topic, but the notion of an underworld remains a helpful tool for keeping in mind the world of the dead, the dead's presence, directly underfoot. The underworld maps those vertical relations. It also provides for the possibility that our world increasingly resembles the underworld, or an underworld. And this brush with disaster (in the form of illness) confirmed an intuition that I, we, are in some respects "already dead." This feeling of being dead seems a pretty universal experience. One sometimes gets overtaken by the sense that mortality already has overtaken oneself. Keats mentions his posthumous existence while still alive. I consider these states of afterlife, or post-life, part of mortal experience. For me, encounters with those feelings provoke poetic utterance. So when you mention a digressive or interstitial turn to these moments, I'm gratified that you've tracked this in what I've written, but I would say, I guess, such moments seem omnipresent. That digressive turn, that sudden, dawning glance at posthumous life remains part of our everyday.

AF: Again here I appreciate the torqued perspective provided by aphorisms or digressions. As you broach this concept of the underworld or, presumably, overworld, two distinct vantages seem to gaze back upon each other, echoing various theorists' depictions of the choreographed aphorism. But when you mention situating shorter instances amid a longer form, I'm curious, in this particular project (which does offer any number of brilliant elliptical formulations), about the deliberate staging of translation, research, teaching. Could you discuss the role that the loosely embodied "I" plays in stitching together these very Auerbachian *Readings in World Literature?* Does the reader's potential identification with this "I" allow for an experience of duration lacking in any single episode, allusion, digression?

SR: Yeah, I want this speaker to appear as intimate and personal as possible. So I have no problem referring to this poem's speaker as myself. Of course, for many people this may seem a no-brainer, obvious, uncontroversial gesture to make. But after working on a series of erasure projects for seven years, to me that felt like a significant step. The second part of your question asks how this individual speaker engages the archives of knowledge, the scene of instruction into which many poets find ourselves parachuted as teachers. I'd wanted to address my own sense of unbelonging with regard to the field I work in every day—my feeling of preposterousness as I enter a classroom to teach a course on world literature to a diasporic group of students, who come from all over the world and often know much more about their various literary traditions than I possibly could. There's an abjection that one experiences if one teaches with any kind of reverence toward one's subject, since one ought to, on some level, feel hopelessly unqualified to teach even canonical books like *Moby Dick* or whatever. But I'll try as a teacher to convert this state of unknowing into a negative capability, one that can enhance my relation to other persons in the classroom. For this particular writing project, I hope to develop a much longer book, and to arrive at some kind of rapprochement with the necessary impossibility of teaching.

AF: Hmm. I like the parallel between how an individual fragment or digression exists within a greater body of work, and how that unbelonging or unknowing you've described (which could seem the abdication of your responsibilities as a teacher) actually takes place within a broader institutional context, one in which this position of unbelonging, when modeled for students, can pick up productive value.

SR: Right. Part of that involves acknowledging (not abdicating, but acknowledging) one's lack of qualification, one's democratic position on the same level as students. Teaching becomes an act of mutual exploration. Which is why, in that poem you quoted, when I say "They are not learning. I'm not teaching," I mean to suggest that something different than pedagogy happens in my best classroom moments. These don't offer a top-down model of transmitted knowledge, but rather a mutual voyaging that often feels digressive. Your use of that term seems appropriate. The digressive excursion probably provides the best model of how learning happens for myself and my students.

AF: Our recognition of mortality places us not only in an abject state, but one that's difficult to endure, maintain, extend. Here I'm curious about this chapbook's relationship to humor, about *Readings*' very funny attempts at a further redaction of Kafka, for example. Comedic instances occur throughout. Could you talk a bit about the role that humor plays within the pedagogical/anti-pedagogical depiction of your abjected professor protagonist?

SR: The comic turn has been a long time coming for me as a means of negotiating this abjection of mortality or illness, this unbelonging in relation to one's own profession, in relation to political history as it happens right now. More and more, I take consolation in a comic reading of those phenomena. And that was a difficult transition, because I'd always been inclined toward Vedic, or epic, or traditionally "ambitious" forms of addressing such problems. But as I enter my late-30s, and arrive at a certain kind of detente with regard to those ambitions, I find that a comic register best allows one to explore the absurdity of the human condition, and that the laughter generated can be productive—can allow one to carry on and feel pleasure. As a poet, I had felt myself increasingly dragged down by the undertow of all kinds of things, from our country's foreign policy, to my own personal experiences with mortality, to the pull of skepticism and negativity. Lately, however, the happiness and pleasure of laughing at those problems has made poetry once again a really alive place.

AF: On this topic of laughter as mode of engagement, I'm curious if you conceived of this chapbook specifically for the art exhibition cited in your acknowledgements page. And even if you didn't, your text seems the "call" for that "Call and Response" show. So the questions arise: did any particular content or approach seem appropriate for the "response"? Was affirmation in some more abstract sense called forth? I remember specific call-and-response episodes from the *Readings* themselves, such as in Section 7, when the "I" gets asked "Is it you?" and provides the perfect reply, "I think so." Or Section 10: "'Qu'est ceci?' Chen asked. 'Voici,' said the servant." More generally, how do implicit or explicit call-and-response processes play out in this chapbook's thematics?

SR: That makes me think of your own stuff. As a writer I myself remain far more uncomfortable with the give and take of call-and-response. I tend to curl up in my little study carrel, or wherever I can escape the rest of the world, and try to grind writing out of some place within. For me, any kind of call is cause for anxiety. But when this project came up in D.C., I appreciated it as an occasion just to say to myself: I need to start writing. This was the perfect kind of call, because I really didn't know what form the response would take, who would respond, or anything of the sort. I simply knew that a visual artist would produce something related to the poem. Then of course I was bowled over and delighted when I saw Job Bobby Benjamin's sculptural installation that arose in response to what I'd written. That piece responded only to the first seven or eight sections of the chapbook. That's all I had completed at the time. But what you ask goes even deeper into the nature of this poem, in that there are certain moments when the speaker gets called upon. Those begin as instances of extreme awkwardness for this speaker. I put the speaker in those situations again and again because I'd wanted to explore that kind of discomfort. Students call upon a teacher to account for himself, and he can't. I consider these scenes of self-recognition—where the speaker comes to learn something in his own classroom, because of this call or claim his students make upon him. I've learned a lot from that type of call-and-response of teaching, which seems a metaphor for many kinds of relations.

AF: That echoes questions this chapbook poses (and happily does not answer) regarding what is the proper content of "Readings in World Literature." Or actually, does the chapbook pose this question? Does it deliberately evade this question? Does it provide an indirect answer, as the dynamics of individual life, family life, gradually propel the narrative forward, even amid more labyrinthine intellectual and poetic reveries?

SR: That's the challenge of trying to continue with this book. I don't consider it finished by any means. Part of me wants to push through those questions and let the underworld in which the speaker finds himself fill with light and become a kind of paradise. Or at least purgatory, I hope. It's too easy, artistically, to wallow in a morass of uncertainty. And because this project runs parallels to my own experience, I would like to use it as a means of moving forward into more positive affective relations to my work and my mortality and all kinds of things. But much remains to be seen. New problems arise amid the effort to construct a forward-moving narrative, resolving such questions. Narrativity brings a whole other set of issues that complicate the writing of poetry.

AF: Certain lines seem to offer a Brechtian effect, foregrounding their constructed nature, perhaps pointing towards some higher realism beyond the immediate narrative purview of the poem. I'm thinking of how, after snappy dialogue in Section 19, we encounter the line, "The room had assumed the tenebrous gloom of a star chamber." Here I love the echoing vowels and anachronistic diction. Again, I don't use this word pejoratively, when I say "excess," but does that excessive assonance or detail or metaphoric heft—which interrupts our absorption of transparent narrative—does that, in some way, present its own drama (the narrative of narrativity amid time's mute, ceaseless progress, or something)?

SR: That sounds good. I kept in mind while writing this poem the possibility that the poem itself, or any piece of literature, can provide a text of the world, or can conceal the subtext of a more real world, a more real experience. At a certain point in this poem (which I've tried to make as life-like as possible), I wanted to acknowledge a still deeper reality beneath it. That relation between the "real real" and the "symbolic real" of this poem seemed quite similar to the relationship between our culture's sense of the empirical world and various cultures' notions of an underworld. Something always lurks beneath this text, beneath this poem, something that feels more bare, raw, unspeakably real. So these moments when the writing starts to sound more artificial or Brechtian, as you say, pointing to the overall artifice, become moments when I hope to affirm this underworld subtending the work. The poem's surface offers just one level of the many worlds you encounter. That's not new, of course. Percy Shelley thought that the perceived world is just a veil of appearances, behind which stands another world. I wanted to thematize that at certain points.

AF: Again the interstitial allows for complex, convoluted vantages. Also, as you've briefly mentioned, you include references to the U.S.

occupation of Iraq, Guantanamo Prison, oil spills. You'll provide that level of a political history happening within or alongside the personal narrative. But then here's another example of those loaded lines I described: "Sunk into the deep sea bed like a page awaiting translation, a wrecked tanker oxidizes below." These extravagant analogical sequences appear. Those pivots I find so interesting. And finally Borges surfaces in goggles and flippers. Was this inevitable from the start?

SR: Well you know, probably, and I'm not making any news as yet another poet obsessed with Borges and Kafka and Dante. Of course Borges, Kafka and Dante lived in entirely different places, historical periods, societies, but I think that a shared sense of the constructedness and fragility of reality circulates through all of their work. The everyday social tissue we subsist on constantly gets ruptured. Maybe this takes us back to the scar metaphor. That sense of fragility draws me.

AF: I didn't even ask—there really is a class "Readings in World Literature"? You taught such a course? But the broader question is: ultimately this chapbook does, to some extent, present what it advertises, right? Is there, to some extent, the implication that a dense or reflexive enough autobiographical work by a contemporary poet will provide a reading in world literature?

SR: Yeah. I don't know if I'll keep the title, but that is a class I taught at the university. I excerpt actual student evaluations from the course. Of course I had to dig deep to find those negative evaluations! But yes, that's real. I taught "The Epic of Gilgamesh" alongside epics from various ancient cultures. And while reading about encounters with the underworld, I felt that the protagonists of these poems (Gilgamesh, the Mahabharata, the Odyssey, etcetera) kind of touched bottom with a sense of my own mortality—because of where I was with my own illness, and the birth of my daughter, and all kinds of dramatic personal events. I've grown to feel that the more intimate and personal a poem becomes, the more it attracts me. Again, that might be a no-brainer to many people wiser than myself, but I've spent much time invested in a modernist, impersonal tradition of writing, so for me this seemed a revelation.

AF: With the figure of Borges still in mind, can we finish by discussing (and I'm glad we didn't start with this) your chapbook's status as poetry? I'm perfectly happy to grant, to acknowledge that status. But given the constructed scenes of inquiry, given your departing musings about dream and reality, what precludes us from considering this fiction or, in a more convoluted sense, nonfiction? What here does poetry distinctly provide?

SR: For me, what's important is that the imaginative writing has traction for readers. I don't profess a deep commitment to the lyric as the model for what confirms something as poetic, or to any number of prosodic or technical registers and indices for what marks something as a poem. I think I probably have a more (I don't know why he keeps coming up) Shelleyan notion of poetry as an imaginative faculty that subtends all kinds of different practices, from a basketball layup to a ballet performance. If such performances can arise out of the poetic faculty, then I have no problem categorizing Beckett, a Beckett play like *Acts Without Words*, as poetic. Or a Barthelme short story as being a poem. Similarly, I loosely consider this chapbook poetic—because I pay lots of attention just to syllables, basically, and that acute investment in language seems enough.


## INTERVIEW WITH EMILY PETTIT
Recorded on June 6, 2012
This interview focuses on Pettit's book *Goat in the Snow* (Birds, LLC).

ANDY FITCH: *Goat in the Snow* opens with two questions. Questions appear throughout. What appeals to you in the interrogative gesture?

EMILY PETTIT: Everything. My mind moves fastest when asking questions. That's part of moving forward through the world. It's a good way to find out stuff. I try to ask a lot of questions.

AF: I'll be curious how these questions relate to readers. Do they get addressed to particular people and perspectives? Do they call for a specific response? But first, in terms of reader relations: one could detect, in lines such as "I would do anything / for a different look from you," or in your book's overall quick, chipper delivery, a deep desire to accommodate the reader. Yet this accommodating tone also has, as in Robert Walser's writing, its perverse, insistent extremes, including the lines "I know you don't want an umbrella, but here's an / umbrella. And here's another umbrella. And another. / Another another." Similarly, your poems often gesture toward self-effacement, though also demonstrate conspicuous charm. Or shyness and modesty become sources of pride, as when you say "To be shy alone is to have an unusual fact." Could you describe the role that these contradictory principles (sadistic kindness, extravagant effacement, boastful shyness) play in your poetics?

EP: Can you say that again…sadistic what?

AF: Sadistic kindness.

EP: Oh wow.

AF: I don't mean that in a bad way. Your book seems playful.

EP: Alright.

AF: We could start with the umbrella and the umbrella and the umbrella. Kindness that goes too far, generosity that gets excessive.

EP: For me, I don't have that idea. It doesn't seem excessive. And yes, I talk about shyness quite a bit. I'm shy like many people are shy, and both in myself and others this manifests in all sorts of unusual ways. "To be shy alone is to have an unusual fact" suggests it's funny one could feel shy even sitting by yourself. I've witnessed and experienced shyness my whole life. It's all over the place and these poems.

AF: "To be shy alone is to have an unusual fact"—once you've told us that, you seem less shy. Once the poem addresses somebody you don't seem so alone, either. Those are the contradictions I'd meant.

EP: I feel shy but still have to go to work. I don't see that as a contradiction. I see it as a constant reality, humans dealing with contradictionary emotional and/or intellectual reactions to that.

AF: Anything about Walser you'd like to discuss? Are you still a big fan?

EP: I love Walser. Yes. I love him. Perhaps he was shy. Walser's writing often explores social anxiety and different situations in which shyness gets conquered or cannot be conquered. *The Robber* means the world to me. It often sounds quite bossy, which I also love.

AF: Yeah, this makes me think of *Jakob von Gunten*, where the protagonist adopts this bossy tone, though really just wants to be a butler. Again I'm curious, here in terms of persistent form: what mode of reader engagement do you seek to construct through your many "how to" poems? These don't offer the loose, baggy listings we'd find in a "things to do" poem. They don't answer questions of "why" since, as one poem says: "it is easy to say things. It is harder / to mean things. Build a pyramid. Have no / idea why." Overall, *Goat in the Snow*'s "I" seems more interested in grasping codes of conduct, in "Understanding conduct like understanding / a complex and lively bee." It seeks to maneuver in effective ways. Can you characterize the types of knowledge this "I" goes after? What makes a process-oriented inventory of operating systems safer than questions like "why" or "who"?

EP: Well, process interests me. Both processes of animate and inanimate things. I'm interested in recognizing that there is a process.

AF: Right. Though what makes questions of process different from explanations, from definitions, from questions about identity?

EP: Nothing.

AF: All of those seem just as relevant?

EP: Totally.

AF: And the feuilleton, the short newspaper-column form Walser often used. I'll wonder again…you give poems titles like "How to Hide and Stay Hidden." Or you'll mention wanting to disappear. Do the forms *Goat in the Snow* adopts assist in achieving these intentions or goals?

EP: While writing the book I became attracted to this idea that people respond to instruction. I remember reading a funny internet list of "how to" everything. Impossible things (behavioral, how to act appropriately). I thought, this is funny: the idea of contruction, processes, the grasping for an understanding of process.

AF: This "how to" form raises further interpersonal questions. You provide multiple references to telephones, to "a new kind of emergency," to resembling for consecutive days a "misguided fire truck." Those lines evoke the legacy of Frank O'Hara. Do you consider *Goat in the Snow*'s agile, off-the-cuff seeming negotiations between an "I" and a "you" your own form of personism? Do you explore similar reader/writer relations?

EP: Not consciously.

AF: Anything more about telephones?

EP: I'm often on the telephone. I talk on the telephone all the time. The telephone has played a huge part in my life. Telephones are everywhere! You cannot go anywhere, almost, without seeing people on telephones. And now getting on the telephone can mean all kinds of things, because telephones do more than make telephone calls. My interest in telephones comes from constant encounter with them, in the same way that weather occurs all the time, in the world and in my poems.

AF: Along with devices for establishing connection come processes of encountering limits. I'll sense a poetics of limits here. You've got the lines "These are my boat / shoes. I don't go on boats." Those stand out. Or starting a poem "This is no articulation of ethics." Or you'll close with a balancing act: "We stand holding a suspended pivoting pole with a bucket / on one end and a counterweight on the other." You'll posit restrictions: "To glide / through the air without propulsion, / in the way that a bird does without flapping // its wings or an airplane with its engine off." I'm curious about these articulations of what poems or their objects will not do, as well as how this relates to the short, compacted, prose-like sentences you construct.

EP: I see the line "These are my boat / shoes. I don't go on boats" as a potential contradiction or certainly confusing, but don't see it as anything else.

AF: Though why foreground this contradiction?

EP: I guess since people contradict themselves all the time. I do. That line is simply a reaction both to my own brain constantly contradicting itself, and to watching other brains contradict themselves.

AF: Alongside contradiction, what about the elaborate descriptions of balance? Again, with "We stand holding a suspended pivoting pole with a bucket / on one end and a counterweight on the other," does something about that depiction of balance, of carefully steering one's way through a situation, appeal to you?

EP: I don't know if "appeals" is the right word, but I'm often trying to balance things, both figuratively and literally. That's something people often do.

AF: With those emphases on contradiction, on balance, how about your short, modular sentences? Do you associate that syntax with this particular book? Can you see yourself adopting something similar in the future?

EP: The new book I'm writing does it too. I'm not doing it because I think I should. I'll do it because I can't seem to help myself. The line as a unit of meaning interests me, and the sentence as a unit of meaning, then how these work together and complicate each other.

AF: The phrase "permutation symmetry" appears. And I'll like how sentences feed off themselves, how one seems to thrust or split off from another. In "How to Control a Blackout," for example, we encounter the lines "I don't know what I want. What I mean / to say is, This here is a fuse box. / I mean to say, I know nothing about fuses. / Did I say fuses? I meant to say facts. / I need to get good at tracking. Track / my own thought back to a black horse." Whole poems will pivot from one sentence to the next. Is that part of what you like about short, spare syntax? Obviously we don't have to give it a fixed meaning, but could this be a good example of permutation symmetry?

EP: I think it could, though I hadn't thought of that before. These poems move in the way my mind leads itself, its general mode whether I write or not, which includes both related thoughts and other… I'll often say not quite what I mean. Quite often I'll encounter people saying things they don't mean.

AF: In terms of building poems one bit at a time, I'd noticed a recurring motif of ladders. I'm curious if ladders fit well amid the permutation symmetry. Ladders, like telephones, do they suggest forms of communication, or moving from one place to another?

EP: Well they do suggest moving from one place to another. They suggest all sorts of things. Different types of ladders appear throughout the book. So many items get repeated that…ladders, like telephones, appear because ladders exist everywhere. I see ladders all the time. I have a general interest in looking at them.

AF: And what about repetition itself? I'll think of a ladder as an object that develops incrementally or repeats itself as it gets somewhere. Are there unspeakable pleasures for you in such repetitions? Do you admire particular poets' use of repetition?

EP: I love repetition. Repetition is everything and everywhere. We are repetition, on a molecular level. Poets I admire, writers who use repetition? It seems harder to come up with a poet who doesn't use repetition.

AF: The line "Dump truck, dump truck, dump truck": to me, it echoes Stein. Stein repeating "cow" all the time. When Alice takes a shit, Stein calls it a "cow." Also an orgasm. The pleasure of "Dump truck, dump truck, dump truck" for me—it has those resonances. What about for you?

EP: It doesn't. It's literal. Dump truck as a literal dump truck. As an idea being repeated.

AF: Given these repeated objects, and the repeated constructions, I'm curious why you chose the singular title *Goat in the Snow*, rather than something pointing toward the persistent "how to" poems. Does *Goat in the Snow* better fit a self-conscious literary debut?

EP: Well it certainly wasn't about any idea of the book being a literary debut. *Goat in the Snow* suggests the spirit of this book in general, the whole book. I decided to title it *Goat in the Snow* during my junior year of college. I'd mentioned to my brother and his friend (Rory Jensen) standing at some party and wanting to be a fly on the wall, and Rory said, "Be a *Goat in the Snow*." And I said, "What?" And he repeated it. And I thought, I want to title my book that.

AF: With being a fly on the wall, or Goat in the Snow, could you describe your relationship to performance? Many of these poems seem to end with a surprising, conclusive/inconclusive line that would work well before an audience at a live reading. Do you write with that live audience in mind? Or as fly on the wall, *Goat in the Snow*, is this the farthest thing from what you'd like to think about?

EP: That is furthest from what I want to think about. Performance is very hard for me. I dislike being looked at, especially by groups of people who are listening to me. Of course if you want to share your work it's a good, important thing to do. But if I thought about it while writing, I imagine I never would write again.

AF: How's it going doing the readings right now?

EP: OK. Especially when I forget the fact that I'll be giving a reading.

## INTERVIEW WITH CARYL PAGEL
Recorded on June 7, 2012
This interview focuses on Pagel's book *Experiments I Should Like Tried at My Own Death* (Factory Hollow Press).

ANDY FITCH: Can we start with your table of contents? It hints at a musty, encyclopedic cabinet of curiosities which then get delivered out of sequence and in elliptical, lyric fashion. Apart from obvious pleasures of designing the table, how does it relate to a book-length conceptual framework?

CARYL PAGEL: You can decide if I should answer. I'm happy to, but this table's one of the major things that changed when *Experiments I Should Like Tried at My Own Death* went to print.

AF: Interesting.

CP: The finished book provides a more traditional table, though I still can speak to the former one.

AF: Please. Especially since your book already felt haunted.

CP: One main inspiration came from the formats of various antiquated texts I was reading. Or even Sebald: he's more recent but still includes these strange, horizontal summaries of what happens in the chapters. Though my own titles, as you've mentioned, didn't necessarily correspond with their supposed sections. They worked more like adjacent descriptions. Pulling out these descriptive clusters helped me to think about how titles work, and what associative phrases can do. Since this book tracks experiments with form, and becomes its own experiment as a book, I kept wondering, what is a table of contents' point? Is it purely organizational? Does is it just list the page something sits on? I played with the idea that perhaps instead of saying, "Levitations" comes on page 13, my table could preview material or ideas and create this sort of suspense or ghosting. In the end, we changed it. I can't remember why. I think potentially in order not to alienate readers, so that they'd more readily accept the general weirdness.

AF: Part of what interests me: I've read a lot lately about paratext, about multiple levels of meaning shaping our engagement with the text, meanings that typically don't get analyzed because considered background or secondary or non-authored. So I'd appreciated how your table functioned as paratext alongside, as you say, thematics of the paranormal. I like how, now that the table exists only while we discuss it, that makes it all the more "para."

CP: Right. Many parts of the book seem related, though might not do the exact same thing. The "Bodies" poems sound sort of like ghosts of encyclopedia entries or mythologies or fables that disintegrate and change throughout. I tried to find every opportunity for doing that when I'd started to think of this as a book.

AF: What did you read for this project? Did you read specifically for the project?

CP: Hmm. I did a lot of reading, although it was much looser than formal research. It was more that I fell in love with one set of materials which inspired many of the poems…and then various events that happened around the books also became source material. These books were the *Proceedings of the Society for Psychical Research.*

AF: Psychical?

CP: Yes. The poem "Table Talking" addresses this most directly. It mentions William James and the broader Society. But my interest began with strange experiences surrounding (this all sounds goofy when I discuss it) working in a building here in Iowa City, where I return to each summer. They took place in Seashore Hall, on campus, which is sort of famous for being haunted. It has a lot of vacancies. Hallways end and disappear. It's just this place I'd already thought a lot about by that particular point in my life, which was a couple of years ago, a time filled with ghosts and griefs and elegies. I already felt prone to the dark side, or what have you. My poems had moved in that direction. But one day I stumbled upon, in the Psychology Library—which always seemed empty and tucked in some hidden corner of this crazy building—their row of the *Proceedings of the Society for Psychical Research*. The library had collected maybe 20 volumes. More volumes exist, but they owned a bunch. And while I waited out a thunderstorm (I know, this whole story's very romantic) the books just fell on my head and I opened one and it opened this whole new imaginative world for me. My poems don't always address that in an obvious way. But I began to study the group of scientists who founded this Society in the late 1800s. William James is probably the most famous member. Sir Arthur Conan Doyle was one. A bunch of the scientists worked at Harvard. Some lived in London. Basically their idea was that we experience, or perhaps think we experience, or have heard about someone experiencing paranormal or psychic activity. We may or may not believe it. It may or may not be real. No known source exists for this apparitional or telepathic behavior. So the SPR addressed the paranormal, though they also studied coincidence or intuition or visions. They didn't laugh at that stuff. They performed scientific experiments. They developed methods of organization and fact-finding and compiled evidence. It wasn't necessarily: we want to prove ghosts exist. It was more: we plan to record all the ghost sightings we can and look for patterns. That approach to the unknown appealed to me. And the writing seemed amazing. *The Proceedings,* these volumes, were filled with experiments and testimonies, pages and pages of testimony from individuals seeing things, not knowing what they are. Or testimonies of mediums or clairvoyants or people who'd walked outside and been scared by a shadow. So when I refer to my research, I mean reading these volumes and just living with them. I checked them all out that day. I came home with a big old box. And the librarian, the work-study student laughed, because most volumes hadn't been checked out since 1931.

AF: That's often the case with books I check out.

CP: But I took these, then shortly thereafter the Psychology Library closed. I went back one day and it was gone.

AF: While you had the books?

CP: I still have the books. I renew them once a year though if I ever did return them—they've gone out of circulation. The university won't let me buy them, but also won't lend them to anyone else.

AF: I remember James' *Varieties of Religious Experience* and his *Principles of Psychology*, and am especially interested when you mention testimonials. Your book's saturation in a trancelike, lamps-about-to-burn-out, late-19th-century ambiance, does that tonal quality derive from the readings themselves? Did they evoke that mood in you? Did you deliberately construct it for elliptical narrative effect?

CP: Something happened with my mood. Just reading this stuff all the time, encountering a language more like testimony, trying to filter the unknown through my way of thinking—all that definitely influenced me. You can see this in the book's weird, antiquated turns of phrase. But more than just the language, it infected the spirit of the book, the desire to reconstruct enigmatic experiences at a later date, even those that still don't make sense. Like people devoted to describing dreams, trying to see how close language can get, which often is not very close.

AF: When you pose this question of how effectively description can grasp experience, the experience is one of reading, some sort of mood that reading brings on, right? It seems a particular form of experience, which is the spell the *Proceedings* produced.

CP: The spell of the books, yes, but then honestly how they transformed me. At least for one particular year, when I felt very open to paranormal experience. I still didn't believe in anything exactly, but tried to figure out if I could conduct my own psychic experiments. Or if I could pay attention the way some of these scientists paid attention. So the process definitely was based in my reading, but was not purely textual. At the time I'd moved into this supposedly haunted house. I was looking all over. Once you become obsessed with something you find it all over the place. That's one of the most powerful parts about reading—not just when language stays with you, but when it becomes physically and mentally transformative.

AF: Well your book could seem to present a vague narrative sequence. All I mean is from "Levitation," the opening poem, to "Spirit Cabinet," which is the final poem (and which, like many pieces in the book, starts and ends on the same word) forces of outward and inward motion remain at play. There will be out-of-body scenes, but also grounded introspection, which again raises questions of what role embodied experience performs here. What status does the "I" possess? This "I" often referred to in a clinical yet slightly abstracted, mystical, confessional tone.

CP: What I'd mentioned in terms of research, and also elegy and grief and more personal things, all of this revolves around—now it seems so obvious to say—the idea of the body, the "I" and the body. And how much the body has to do with this "I." And what happens when the body disappears or disintegrates or transforms. Where does the "I" go? Part of this manifests in a floaty "I." "Levitation" provides one example, where the body does things the mind can't process, hasn't seen, or couldn't see, or stays incapable of recognizing in some way. This body/mind split also manifests in the book's obsession with naming. Naming the body or the self or the self's identity—what does this process have to do with the "I"? Who is the labeler labeling? When the name changes, does the identity change? Where is the "I" when the mind goes someplace the body can't follow? The title, *Experiments I Should Like Tried at My Own Death*, refers most directly to…this story about William and Henry James. When William died he'd asked Henry and William's wife to visit mediums and see if they could communicate with him via an agreed upon word or name. For example, I would say: Andy, if there's life after death, if there's any place my mind or consciousness goes, I'll communicate that to you through the term "pineapple." This idea of designing an actual code between life and death fascinated me.

AF: Your epigraph from Inger Christensen refers to the solace of names. I'm calling you from Australia, Melbourne, remembering Bruce Chatwin's study of Aboriginal song lines, these elaborate songs memorized as the equivalent of dreaming, of haunting, mapping, of travel all at the same time—also the closest thing to property or possession. I'm curious if you could talk a bit about the solace you take in names and naming.

CP: As long as we're starting with that Christensen quote, have you read *Alphabet*?

AF: I haven't.

CP: It deals with what you're describing. Inger Christensen was a Danish writer who died a couple of years ago. She wrote this book, *Alphabet*, which employs the Fibonacci Sequence. I'm not sure if you remember the mathematical sequence that goes from 0 to 1 to 1 to 2 to 3 to 5, and traces the mathematical manifestation of spiraling. Through it Christensen organizes a way to talk about all spirals in nature, all the places this pattern repeats itself. And her project forms its own repeating patterns. So the first line of the book is "apricot trees exist, apricot trees exist." Then each section progresses through the alphabet, while following patterns found in nature. She lists very, very specific details, from the minutiae of chemicals and cellular phenomena to animals, flora, fauna, geography. And at first she's just listing. She is very much obsessed with the power/fallacy of names and I found myself thinking of that spiraling process as a way of creating a body, as counteracting the apparitional nature of a lot of my book, which builds off abstraction. Whether that's an index or encyclopedia or, as in "Herbarium," the idea that accumulated names can construct something bigger than their bodies. Because eventually *Alphabet* becomes huge and its lists get overwhelming. So Inger Christensen is an inspiration, and I return to her book over and over. I'm not sure if I can say exactly what that solace is, but it seems magical somehow. She recreates our entire world, our physical world, through this listing. And one of the most magical things (you should buy this book immediately—it changed my life) is how she goes in and out of the political and personal the further she gets. So when she gets to g's... she begins with natural things, but then has to bring in "guns exist" and "war exists" and all these manmade things. At first her repetitions feel deeply comforting, though as you read more you realize how haunting they are and how many parts of the natural world have disappeared or will disappear, or that we've ruined in some way. But after that come moments when love exists and a walk in the rain with your lover exists, and the book spirals back, as the whole project keeps spiraling, and will not allow you to wholly embrace the apocalyptic vision one feels at some points.

AF: You'd mentioned your "Herbarium." What about Dickinson, and Dickinson's herbarium? I mean we once would have thought Dickinson's herbarium consisted solely of the domestic. Now she's considered a poet with much greater scope. What's your relation to Dickinson's herbarium in writing this book? What is Dickinson's herbarium? I hadn't known she made one.

CP: It's a collection of plant life and things she found in her garden and the woods, with her notations, her labels. I can't explain why it captivated my imagination. This certainly has to do with spending much time with Dickinson's work, her rhythms and her "I," so that when I did discover her herbarium, after reading all of her letters for years, and her talking about all of these places, it did seem magical. In part because of how ordinary it is. There's nothing special about an herbarium. It's a somewhat strange thing to assemble. But she faithfully collected all this beautiful plant life. The book itself looks beautiful, first of all. Though then she would name the flora. She would label them, as anyone with an herbarium does, but not always correctly. Editors of her herbarium intervened and revised much of her naming. The headings I borrowed come from that. I was fascinated with these layers of lists or addendums or revisions, which the legacy of Dickinson always has to deal with.

AF: Dickinson often seems happy to adopt an out-of-body vantage, or to project herself as dying or already dead. This reminds me of, in your "Botched Bestiaries," how often "I" gets listed among the common names. This idea of not only constructing lists, but placing yourself in a modest object-position within that list, interests me. Could you describe the transcriptive, citational, collagist practices for the Beastiaries?

CP: That "I" thing's interesting because I'd never really associated this "I" amid the common names with my actual "I." I'd pictured more of an objective, universal "I." But now I see what you said.

AF: I like both of those.

CP: In terms of collaging: first our conversation has moved very much in the order that I wrote these pieces. I started with the more visionary psychical research poems, then went on to the naming, plant-based ones. And then the Botched Bestiary parts probably were most recent. So during the Botched Bestiary phase I'd thought about many of the issues we've discussed. For example acts of naming, and how identity can float. Also how research and collections and texts inform our sense of self and the knowledge that makes up consciousness. How do we know what we know? Here collaging provides a focused way to look at a whole bunch of sources at once, to put together all this information in one place. Plus I was reading, as I cite in the back of the book, *The Postmodern Animal* by Steve Baker, his study of how the body, specifically animal bodies, get represented in contemporary art. Pieces like Rauschenberg's *Monogram*. Much postmodern art, specifically sculpture and installation, deals with ruined bodies or surreal bodies, or moves into post-human conversations (all these hybrid bodies), foregrounding hybridity and messiness as one way of actually speaking to and about the body. So the Bestiaries started as a loose translation of what I saw happening in postmodern artwork. I was thinking, how could language pull these various parts together? That's why I used quotes, as hinges. I tried some more procedural processes. I looked at all these animal studies and gathered information, then pulled out the common names as a way of making this weird, imaginary mythology or history or definition of what the body is, what it has experienced, what it has seen.

AF: Still on this question of collaging and adjacency: as a Dickinson aficionado, can you give your theory of the dash, since you use them too? What does only the dash allow?

CP: That's a big question. Dickinson remains the master of the dash. She teaches everyone its strange, magical quality. It gives pause in a visual way, but seems more a dart or arrow, shooting ahead while creating space. There's a bit of contradiction in that symbol, which of course connects, however loosely, while also violently stabbing the separation.

AF: When you first said "dart," I'd thought you meant in terms of tailoring. I pictured Dickinson's fascicles stitched together. But I also like this violence of the dash. And what about blank space? Atmospherically, and in terms of content, how does blank space play out your book? What does it mean to have a blank space in your title? Or is there not? I thought I saw one in my PDF.

CP: The original had one. It didn't end up on the cover because of the design. But it makes sense to include blank space where bodies keep falling apart and coming back together and appearing apparitional. A lot of these spaces seemed rhythmically dramatic. Theatrical. Some just felt weird, probably alienating. I tried to keep both possibilities alive because I didn't want that space to be just visual or just controlled. Though most of the book deals with form in one way or another. There's a whole bunch of sonnets. The "Botched Bestiaries" have their own encyclopedic form. "Taxidermy," and some of the longer narrative pieces, were written in syllabics. There's the obsessiveness of trying out different forms (or in my mind experiments), in part to highlight the scientific/organizational modes of thought I'd developed reading. Still, if these poems didn't have spaces, or some of the other strange things happening, they would seem a lie. They would look too perfect. They would try to engage or produce the uncanny or paranormal without leaving gaps for mystery and enigma and apparition. I guess that's how it happened. This is all easy to discuss now that the book's finished. I'm not sure I knew while writing it.

### INTERVIEW WITH AMANDA NADELBERG
Recorded on June 8, 2012
This interview focuses on Nadelberg's book *Bright Brave Phenomena* (Coffee House Press).

ANDY FITCH: Could we first discuss the book-length structure? Certain poems seem to have sequels scattered throughout. "Me and the Bad Ass" gets followed, significantly later, by "Me and the Bad Ass, Part II," and III. Travel/dream narratives get interspersed amid shorter lyrics. Thematics of circulation continue to circulate. Does that help to stitch together the overall structure? Can you delineate its guiding principles?

AMANDA NADELBERG: When I started writing poems that eventually became the beginnings of this book, it seemed important to have no structure. My first book had been a project with very clear rules. I actually wrote a second manuscript between the first book and this one, based on yet another project. After that, a friend said, do the thing you're not comfortable doing and don't write a project. For a long time I interpreted that wonderful advice as don't write anything cohesive. I collected scraps of notes for poems. I kept little lines in a small box. Eventually I started dipping into this material to connect…not quite collaging, but it felt like quilting (and I'm not saying quilting because I'm a woman). But stitching older lines became an instinct, a practice while writing. I'd written a couple of the early poems before I began grad school, and then grad school's rigor and/or leisure allowed me to finish this book in a year and a half. Near the end I began to sense some wild but actual structure I hadn't intended—which felt really satisfying. I remember first seeing it when I laid out everything on the living room floor. There were the "Badass" poems and another group of poems visually structured in a specific way. Then I saw the longer poems with asterisks that are all related, both in form and because I wrote them while watching Éric Rohmer movies. So structures existed but they didn't feel deliberate. Looking back at that emotional timeframe, I now can detect a structure I hadn't even imagined, built up poem by poem.

AF: It's great that your attempt to write a book of discrete poems became its own project. Do you want to describe the project-oriented nature of your preceding book?

AN: For my first book, *Isa the Truck Named Isadore*…well, I should say that in college, I'd had a lot of trouble with titles. My relationship to them felt horrific. So after college, I was moving to Minnesota, driving across the country, shortcutting through Canada, when a truck passed by that read "Isadore Trucking." A lightning blip in my brain said, oh, go buy a dictionary of first names and those can become your titles—find names you want to name poems, then write that many poems. So I did, from September 2004 to March 2005. Some names related quite well to their poems' contents while some seemed more like untitled markers. But that's the structure.

AF: Isadore's a good name with which to start. It sounds very Gertrude Stein. Your relationship to titles had been horrific because you disliked them? Because you couldn't design them right?

AN: Yeah. I couldn't recognize one. I didn't know how to find them or what they sounded like, or I felt cocky in this act of imagining… you know, a title can intimidate by seeming self-important. Or the process of titling itself could seem that way. I rarely had trouble coming up with poems but yeah, putting that cap on felt phony.

AF: I wonder how this relates to being project-oriented, to having a diffuse, all-over consciousness spread across the work, rather than giving it a face and foregrounding how it ought to be read. Do specific books appeal to you for finding their overall structure through emergent process, rather than preemptive strategy? I'm thinking, in response to your phrase "emotional timeframe," of projects like Creeley's *Day Book* or some James Schuyler, who offers a book of the seasons—or his longer poems.

AN: I love both poets, but can't speak to those specific works standing out in my mind. Though I remember the first time I read Christine Hume's *Alaskaphrenia* I totally died in wonder of its structure-less structure. Visually all of those poems don't look the same, yet some emotional tenor keeps her book cohesive, related to itself, while never seeming overhanded.

AF: Éric Rohmer here interests me, too. "France" circulates through the book, as does Rohmer's attention to the weather and the seasons—both as generalized concepts and more specific manifestations. 1986 appears several times. Often these motifs hint at referential elements, potentially connected to your own life, though also at devices arranged for abstract musicality.

AN: In Iowa, Ben Estes introduced me to Rohmer's movies, which reminded me, backwardsly, of mumblecore movies and also aspects of Whit Stillman and Noah Baumbach and their films' awkward honesty. So I began to watch Rohmer movies by myself. After I watched *Claire's Knee* I wrote the poem called "Poem from *Claire's Knee*." Because I adored it, I rewatched the movie soon and found myself talking at the screen, and talking to myself, talking into the film. I didn't speak aloud (that's crazy!), but I wrote notes. Something about this felt productive. The poem "Another Interpretation" came from that. Suddenly I was writing a long poem that emerged through quick, almost immediate transference. I continued this method with several other films. I constructed each poem pretty much in one sitting, because I'd just pause the movie when I couldn't write fast enough, then resume watching. These poems were written in response to—what are they called?

AF: Did you watch his seasons cycle?

AN: I hadn't yet seen the seasons cycle. No, the "Six Moral Tales."

AF: Oh like *My Night with Maud*? All those?

AN: Yes, *My Night with Maud* and *La collectionneuse, Claire's Knee*. The world of those films made me think about France. But also watching those movies many times made France appear in other poems, unrelated to this particular series. Those French landscapes fit so well with the imagined scenery of the rest of this collection. Then during the book's making I also watched a lot of home videos, mostly from 1986 and 1987, from family trips (sometimes with the volume off while listening to music).

AF: I like the image of you speaking, silently, to Rohmer films. Watching Rohmer feels like reading to me, in part because of his serial projects. Typically, when you watch a single film, you have no control over its temporality. You've mentioned pausing certain scenes, but at the theater a film keeps pushing forward. Still I love how you can pick your way through somebody's interrelated corpus and follow your instincts and watch one film then another. And I'll note such serial tendencies in your own book. One literary device that appears almost incessantly, like Rohmer's repeated motifs, is analogy and, along with it, parataxis—placing two things side-by-side. So your poem "How Did This Happen," for example, contains two "likes" in its opening sentence. The next sentence starts with an elaborate "as" clause, then "like" and "as" keep appearing. Many poems here operate similarly. Even titles such as "Another Interpretation" or "Alternatives Considered" make me curious about this role of the comparative in your poetics.

AN: That's funny because I just was thinking today when I used the dictionary how I'll often spend more time with the thesaurus. And I wondered why my brain has such an easier time with a thesaurus than it does with definitions. So your question kind of answers that for me.

AF: The thesaurus pivot, or shift, appeals to you?

AN: It's almost like thesaurusland is one language and dictionaries are another, and I want to belong to the thesaurus. There's some kind of reading comprehension I get stuck on, with definitions, that doesn't happen with "this is like this is like this is like this." I love patterns and connection-making, like "red car, red car, red car on the street." Pattern-seeking feels natural and comfortable. "Like" and "as" provide a mode of explaining in which you always can keep piling on likeness. What's helpful to me about this way of thinking (I say so after the fact) is that amid all the wading through impossibility or failure or solutionless life, there's still the delicacy of placing two things beside each other and seeing how that goes. And another point related to the beginning of your question, when you said that watching Rohmer films resembles reading: I love watching movies with captions because it's so nice to be around people (the actors) but reading simultaneously. Also, I love to read with that kind of picture behind the reading, like a moving picture book for adults. In fact, the size of a subtitled line is often as long as lines in poems.

AF: Just quickly back to this problem of titles. They often seem to classify and define, and to interpret in advance of a poem. But now in terms of you laying things side-by-side, parallel bodies appear a lot. The final stanza of "Dear Fruit" provides an example: "What I found in the river / is the night we found each other. / Quiet, green he laid down, my / head hurt like the top of a train, / a dog shaking clouds out of the sky. / I wear a helmet so you don't hurt / me, I wear a helmet to keep a / heart. I am a small raincoat, you / are the weatherman. Fall down, / fall down. I mean the woods." With these bodies, the helmet, the raincoat, I'll picture a Balthus painting's figures overlapping on separate planes, not touching. Coupling in your book takes the form of parallax, with dreams not about having sex, but sex endlessly deferred. At the same time some longer poems do function as quasi-narratives. Those seem to move a plot along. So here's the question: how do narrative and parataxis blend in this book? The poem "Our Flowers are Called Waterflowers, and They Need a Lot of Water" seems strung together by non-sequiturs and shifts in modes of address. I'm curious if these longer poems, such as what I've called travel narratives, or the "story" about Henry and bears in Alaska, do these operate according to similar procedures as the shorter lyrics?

AN: Yeah, that's a good example. I think there was some of this smushing together in "Our Flowers." But not entirely. And no absolute rule exists for the shorter poems. For "Our Flowers" I remember someone saying it felt very disjointed. Then I remember other people making a connection between the mackerel and the river (where mackerel might go), and a bird being by the water and some sort of scene that happens. I don't identify this poem as nonsense. I think it tries to communicate something, and tries various ways until that something gets communicated, which might mean speaking in a slightly different manner.

AF: I'm thinking of traditional distinctions between poets whose syntax emulates visual art more than narrative (again placing things near or next to each other). Meaning can get structured through space, rather than through a causal chain of events.

AN: My parents will disagree when a friend says, I don't understand your daughter's poetry. My mom just described this the other day—something like, I'll look at it as I would an abstract painting, and you don't know what's going on, but get a feeling from it. My father's response is more, I don't know what it means, but I know she's trying to say something she means, or that I might be in that poem, even though I can't tell I'm in the poem. And I believe in an answer somewhere between them.

AF: This fluid crisscross seems crucial to your poetry, and often gets held together by a conspicuous, though not necessarily conclusive, last line. "You Are a Thieving Joy" ends "Something like an ocean lives in the grass." That last line takes on added heft. Can you describe the role last lines play in the book?

AN: Yes, and again, it's funny: near the end of writing this book I took a seminar about the ends of poems taught by Geoffrey G. O'Brien. We read Barbara Herrnstein Smith's *Poetic Closure*. I remember growing more conscious as a reader, though that didn't appear to translate to my work as a writer. Looking back, I do see certain familiar spaces almost like my landing gear for a certain kind of ending. When I've done some readings lately I'm like, oh, that poem ends the same way as this poem—I shouldn't read them together. Still it's interesting you pointed to "You Are a Thieving Joy," because that poem's end felt wrong and stayed slightly different for a very, very long time. Then at some point I cut half of the line in half and it felt finished. I guess around the same time that I began to recognize what a title sounded like, I started recognizing the ding-dong of a poem's last line. Sometimes I think they are interchangeable, or at least I'll wonder. I haven't yet made an Excel chart, but I mean, "you are a thieving joy" could end a poem. To some extent this book became a lesson in rearranging. For the "Powerage" poem's end (actually that whole last stanza), I'd been working on the poem for a year, on and off, and originally it ended "Watch me open this cheap beer with my teeth." Then a teacher pointed out that that stanza could be rearranged any number of ways. So I found myself printing the lines and cutting them out, rearranging them on my kitchen table until something felt right. But books don't come in that state. My lines don't come in a plastic baggy you get to rearrange on your kitchen table, but it would be interesting if they did. I'm open to that looseness, or muddled sense.

AF: I've wondered if you interact with public texts this way. I'll encounter a line like "Huffed against a fence post" and think, did Amanda just read the Huffington Post? Or AC/DC will pop up and I'll picture you at a deli buying bottled water.

AN: I do sometimes read the Huffington Post, but don't think…I don't remember where "Huffed against a fence post" came from. That just seems some sort of emotional image. And I don't mean emotional like I'm crying all the time. It just seemed a true idea. For AC/DC: around the time I wrote that poem, a friend saw me dancing and said, I bet you'd really like AC/DC.

AF: Suggesting a music to fit your dance?

AN: Yeah. It was a good time for listening to AC/DC and I like the kind of gross and bawdy, but also awesome anger in some of those songs. Those videos of Bon Scott and the younger brother, Angus Young, offer amazing feats of happy destruction. So I found myself listening to AC/DC, and liking what this did to my rhythms or durations of a sentence. "Me and the Badass" and "Powerage" are two of the book's earliest poems. Especially with "Powerage," once I'd finished it I knew...that poem made me realize I was doing something different, that a time was beginning in which I would write poems that could sit down at the table with this poem.

AF: Amid this AC/DC phase, mean people keep appearing—assholes and bitches. The "I" refers to having had a recent angry period. Do these playful gestures hint at autobiographical reference? Do they reflect a phase of lived experience, less in terms of events than tonality?

AN: I guess. Though there always have been mean people.

AF: Any reason why here they came up often?

AN: Perhaps the music's punchiness got me thinking about other kinds of punchiness, about assholes. But I'll also say: the autobiographical question interests me. I'm fascinated by the idea of the imaginary confessional. Because if confessional poetry (and I consider this true) became forbidden at a certain point, in certain communities, still there's something quite satisfying, reading-wise, in terms of peeking through the windows of confessional poetry. This book resembles a mess or stew of some truth but mostly fiction, which can nevertheless feel ordinary and daily and lifelike. That's what I admire about Rohmer movies. He'll use lines that, if you saw them in a script, might make you say, this doesn't belong in a beautiful movie—this is so ordinary. Or, this line costs five cents and every line of dialogue should cost five dollars. Something interests me in the mode or tonality of confessing (not in a religious sense) amid the context of make-believe or fiction. That's more important to me than writing a book of events that actually happened. I'm comfortable in the way you can hide or not hide yourself in something believable but not necessarily true.

AF: I appreciate the classic analogy between confessional poems and a window. I like how you're intermixing windows, paintings, film screens—how any of these could provide access to an interchangeable network.

AN: That's good. That's good.

## INTERVIEW WITH LEONARD SCHWARTZ
Recorded on June 9, 2012
This interview focuses on Schwartz's book *At Element* (Talisman House).

ANDY FITCH: Could we start with your title page, which identifies these works as "prose poems"? Perhaps I'm old fashioned, but the phrase "prose poems" makes me think of Max Jacob, James Tate, John Ashbery's *Three Poems*. Your long, serialized, Adorno-esque pieces feel more like essayistic meditations. Though can you outline a prose-poem tradition in which projects like "The Sleep Talkers" fit? Do Edmond Jabès and Francis Ponge count as prose poets?

LEONARD SCHWARTZ: *At Element* combines lineated poems and prose formats. The long prose poem "The Sleep Talkers" almost passes over into a kind of lyric philosophy or lyric essay, departing from Baudelairian or Rimbaudian prose poetry. I read a lot of Nathalie Stephens, the contemporary Canadian writer, while developing this piece. I even obliquely addressed parts to her. Jabès long has interested me, though I didn't read him much at the time. But Jabès constructs a textual form that allows him to think, specifically to engage in poetic thinking—which skirts oppositional binaries to plumb the richness of metaphor. And I do take Adorno quite seriously as a prose stylist, though *At Element* lacks the philosophical density or ambition one finds at the level of the proposition in Adorno.

AF: You've mentioned *At Element*'s heterogeneity. Formal cues highlight this fact, such as "The Impossible's" conspicuous fluctuations in line length, which seem to announce sometimes subtle, sometimes dramatic shifts in mood or epistemic register. And you've presented Jabès' poetics as a prompt to thinking. Could you describe how your own thought processes get shaped by or help to shape the poetic forms you construct?

LS: The book does foreground my ambition to create linguistic structures that can house or annunciate multiple modalities of thought: ranging from the philosophical to the associational to the dream and then, of course, to sleep—not sleep as state of dormancy or rest, but as a mode of thinking in and of itself. This does put pressure on poetic form, here suggested by the title…

AF: "The Impossible."

LS: Bataille's book by that name posits poetry's essential function as a process of thinking the impossible. He offers the terms Eros and Thanatos, the ego and death impulses, then tries to think through, or rather work through, their relationship. Likewise, my long poem "The Sudden" draws in any number of poems, written in different places, now housed amid an elastic yet unified structure. Too much fragmentation could produce homogeneity. Every piece would enact and evoke contextlessness. Too much continuity closes down a line of thinking, confines narrative, reduces everything to linear interpretation. So for me, poems like "The Sudden" and "The Impossible" foreground a structure sufficiently fragmented (so as to subdue the linear), yet sufficiently continuous (so to produce some broader context for the thoughts and emotions they present).

AF: Amid this tension between a fragmentary surface that could produce a flat rhetorical experience, and a continuous narrative that might suggest a predetermined or didactic or mechanistic readerly text, can you position your own poetics in relation to something like Language poetry? On a syntactical level, on an axis between the fragmentary and the continuous, where would you place *At Element*?

LS: I read much Gertrude Stein. A specific type of experimental formalism most intrigues me. Yet readers often say my work feels traditional, which may be a put down or compliment, depending who says it. *At Element*'s line-by-line continuity does demonstrate a commitment to phrasing, rather than syntactic dishevelment. The phrases of a Wallace Stevens poem appeal to me, and confirm the conservative (in a good or bad sense) role that philosophy can play in a poem. So I recognize the prison house language has to be, and sense the need for liberatory forms of grammar, yet when returning to my own poems often construct a thought process that demands somewhat regularized syntax.

AF: We could consider a couple lines, such as: "One hopes that one's writing destabilizes the static yet stabilizes the piece that was about to fall off and vanish into oblivion, letting that piece continue to exist in such a way as to be the fragment it was tending towards." Here Roland Barthes's self-placement at the rear guard of the avant-garde comes to mind. And I don't mean to pin your book on any fixed continuum, but am also curious about *At Element*'s prefatory emphasis upon Nature Poetry. First why does Nature Poetry get capitalized? But more generally, why situate this book within the fraught definitional context of nature poetry? Of course we could outline an elastic notion of ecopoetics, and find a place for *At Element*. But could you provide your own definition of Nature Poetry, then contextualize that within prevailing attempts to define nature poetry?

LS: Sure. I do mean to critique the notion of Nature Poetry as a fixed, distinct form. I've written pieces in *Jacket* and elsewhere characterizing conventional modes of nature poetry as nature porn—poems that fetishize the natural object, cleaving away historical and social context, excluding all such relations from this construct of "nature." Like in a *National Geographic* program on giraffes, you don't see sets and camera people. You don't see economic forces and governmental policies circumscribing the lives of giraffes. You receive a reified representation of nature. So my opening preface argues that a nature Poem might not resemble a Nature poem. It may function quite differently. Here even the title *At Element* plays with a certain topos, a form of psychogeography. This is the first book I've written that seems attached to the place I've lived the past nine years, the Pacific Northwest. In the Pacific Northwest, one too easily falls into a specific type of Nature Poem. It must include a heron, a pinecone. Yet as I look out my window, as we speak, Douglas firs really do surround me. While we've talked I've watched a hawk or eagle fly to my left. This immersive relationship to other species and ecologies has produced an imperative, a responsibility of address. Still I can't think of a more compromised literary choice than to write a typical nature poem, which converts a complex ecology into an easily consumable landscape. So "The Sudden" takes much from localized vocabularies specific to the Pacific Northwest, yet doesn't explicitly address questions of "nature" or eco-poetics. It enacts, I hope, a dialectic between desire and aggression—not just in an abstracted Freudian sense, but in a destructively physical sense.

AF: Amid this discursive ecological scene, could you contextualize the place or metaphor or trope of sleep? "The Sleep Talkers" sometimes presents sleep as the other, as animal. Could we place sleep within the context of interspecies relations? Should we consider ourselves coeval with sleep? Do Nature Poems address such questions?

LS: First "The Sleep Talkers" distinguishes between sleep and dream. Dream we know how to deal with aesthetically—in terms of narrative and image. Sleep remains more inaccessible, as inaccessible as the mind of a cat or raccoon. Yet we share sleep with many animal forms. Each night, when one goes to bed, one reaches back toward an emergent stage of the mammalian, perhaps even beyond animal development. Sleep has stayed relatively stable over hundreds of millions of years. And traditionally, as your Barthes quote suggests, the avant-garde steps backward in order to push forward. It probes what happened prior to rationality, in order to move past rationality. Here sleep remains an extraordinary resource, a means of accessing the archaic or primeval (if I can use a bit of Romantic language).

AF: Because I'm sitting in Sydney on the morning of the 10th, as you talk in Olympia on the evening of the 9th, I can't help but think of relationships between sleeping, dreaming, walking, mapping, singing—as such topics play out in (at least) white Australian conceptions of Aboriginal consciousness. *At Element*'s lyric "I" presents walking "nowhere" as a foundational form of reverie. Can you articulate an intuitive logic that links walking to sleep? And I don't mean to take your book too literally, but did some specific experiences inform its claim to have been written "in" your sleep?

LS: Like you, I have encountered these notions of Aboriginal dream time, and only can admire those concepts from a distance, perhaps producing my own projected equivalents—figuring out, in my stumbling way, what happens every night as I sleep. Then for walking: the lineage of the flâneur from Baudelaire and Benjamin first comes to mind. I didn't learn how to drive until age 39. I already spent so much time in reverie, walking around without paying attention, that driving seemed likely either to cut down my dream time or to cause a serious accident. Unfortunately, I did learn to drive nine years ago, and it did restrict my time for reverie, so perhaps I overcompensate now—writing for those hours I don't spend wandering. Driving recalls the problematics of the nature poem, because it makes the landscape static and deadens the observer. Whereas peripatetic perception needs to keep moving through some sort of scape in order for perception to happen, in order to avoid a falsely fixed and centralized point of view. For me walking, or even sitting in a train looking out the window, creates that sense of movement, motion, event, possibility of transformation, presence of the body as opposed to just the eye. I actually don't write while walking or sleeping. But these experiences produce their affects and after-images. Part of the flâneur's allure has to do with how his/her language likewise stays in motion.

AF: Again at the National Gallery of Victoria yesterday, looking at Aboriginal paintings, knowing I'd interview you, I thought about... or clusters of ideas came about Aboriginal consciousness—these prefabricated concepts housed in my head, filtering my more immediate thoughts. Here, thinking itself seemed a form of reverie, just as reading does. Thinking and reading suddenly seemed not that different from sleep. Language seemed a murky dream we drift in and out of. So the question is: could we consider not only writing, but also reading and thinking, as forms of sleep?

LS: Reading and sleep go hand-in-hand, or eyelid-to-eyelid, because the eye turns down, closes a bit, diminishes perception in order to focus on an apparent nothing. Some people fall asleep easiest by picking up a book, which I don't mean as criticism of that book. Sleep does enact a mode of thought. Any book leading one toward that state should get praised rather than castigated as boring. And I can't embrace existing notions of a collective unconscious, but I do consider sleep both the most highly individuated of actions (even if lying beside someone, your sleep constructs a kind of absolute distance), and a highly social act. Good sleep demands extreme social trust. Sleep makes most species most vulnerable to attack. So whether or not we take turns as sentry guard, sleep happens among others, and thanks to protection provided by others. Of course we could say the same about reading and writing—both highly individuated acts dependent on a particular social tissue, on the extreme permission granted by our shared language.

AF: To get back to that cozy prison house of language: we've described how metaphors of sleep play out, but could you also discuss the overall construction of "The Sleep Talkers"—by far this book's most expansive piece? Did any specific projects provide a model? At first Francis Ponge's *Soap* came to mind, in terms of celebrating an overlooked, everyday element. Then the elastic address to an amorphous "you" recalled Martin Buber. I heard Simone Weil's mystical idiom in the claims against speech and in favor of silence. Keats we know likes to sleep. There's Whitman's "The Sleepers." And these points of reference come just from the poem's opening sections (before the boulder, the paranoia, the depersonalized Oedipal conflict). But what other sleep texts does the "The Sleep Talkers" engage?

LS: Well, I first should thank the French poet Jacqueline Risset. Her book *Sleep's Powers* came as a revelation. That book collects short, witty, succinct essays tracking figures of sleep in her personal life and her reading. This instantly suggested sleep as a subject I'd been circling, that I needed to think about. Second, I definitely deploy Martin Buber's "I/you" structure, both to celebrate its prompt to poetic thinking and to probe the extent that this "I/you" comes up short. Paul Celan's poems famously baffled Buber. He couldn't respond when Celan kneeled before him, in effect asking for his blessing. Then, Emmanuel Levinas seems more phenomenologically sophisticated than Buber in some ways, especially his sense of language as a form of responsibility, of ethics—always addressed toward the "you." Proust, by way of Risset's suggestion, became important for the dialectic of total memory/total amnesia. Likewise Lydia Davis, who did a terrific translation of Proust, published a book of short stories entitled *Almost No Memory*. It struck me that Proust's great translator herself has almost no memory, or at least cultivates this self-image in her writing. I also should mention the Russian/Chuvash poet Gennadiy Aygi. He writes in Russian although he comes from Chuvashia, a minority place and language within Russia. His extended piece "Sleep and Dream" distinguishes between sleep poets and public poets—so that with someone like Mayakovsky, poetry's relation to revolution precipitates a public action, whereas in other cultural contexts poetry becomes a sleep action, functioning almost as silent communication. And lastly (this figures in terms of content as well as form) I consider Richard Wagner one of the great sleep artists. Many of the "The Sleep Talkers'" later sections explore dramatic situations from Wagner's Ring cycle. They take Wagner's narrative scenes and work through the metaphors involving sleep. Brünnhilde on her rock gets awoken by Siegfried. Or Erda, earth goddess, all-knowing at the start of the cycle, just wants to be left alone and go to sleep by its end. Fafner, a giant who transforms into a dragon once he acquires the dragon's treasure, goes to sleep with that treasure.

AF: Amid these Wagnerian references, "The Sleep Talkers" progress also seems to drift toward personal narrative, parable, extended literary allusion. You make broader references to "self-realization" or "the education system." I wondered if this expansive scope of "The Sleep Talkers" suggests a drive toward the all-encompassing modernist poems offered by Pound, Zukofsky, Williams, Blaser.

LS: Interesting. I do try to depict or formalize a conception of sleep that can liberate us from the stale analogy to death. And Wagnerian conceptions of the total work of art do lead us to Pound and Zukofsky and the notion of a totalizing poem, a poem that contains everything. Certainly that Poundian tradition running through Zukofsky and Olson attracts me. My poems tend to accrete or accumulate, moving towards a larger structure. Of course in terms of such processes of accumulation, Pound and Wagner likewise share the notion that all ages are contemporaneous.

AF: And just as history's purported progress can get folded into a continuous present, the supposedly static state of sleep moves, develops, changes. Along these lines, I noticed a similar Wagnerian architectonics shaping your overall book. *At Element* could seem to operate as a self-contained long poem, proceeding from "Flash Light" to "Knees and Toes" to "Top of the Morning To You," then finally returning to "Tabula Rasa." Does an overall trajectory get implied?

LS: I hope so. I like to think of this trajectory not necessarily building toward a climax, but shifting from impressionistic atmospherics to something less visual—more slumberous, tending toward music. That last piece, "Tabula Rasa," borrows its title not only from John Locke but from the Estonian composer…

AF: Arvo Pärt.

LS: His wonderful piece "Tabula Rasa" extends certain notes seemingly for hours, as if representing sleep by way of music. No one sits around and watches Andy Warhol's film *Sleep* for the full five hours, though we can talk and think about this terrific conceptual project. Whereas Pärt, in "Tabula Rasa," creates a sense of sleep as something pleasurable to listen to. That's the type of trajectory I hope to track.

AF: Amid *At Element*'s broad tonal range, could we pause for a second on "Welter," which seemed so tonally different from the rest? I should think through the word "welter" more clearly. At the moment, I can't even think of what it means. But can you discuss the motivations, procedures and/or historical experiences shaping this poem which offers, instead of personal confession, a slightly detached, displaced, Alice Toklas-style combination of inference, projection, juicy gossip? Does "Welter" have a particular intended audience, a particular point of provocation? Here my question remains haunted by a line from "The Sleep Talkers," about "that desperate, desperate impulse for more attention that ruins so many poets."

LS: That juxtaposition of "The Sleep Talkers" and "Welter" makes a lot of sense. I think of the "welter," as the social relations one enters into as a person, or even more specifically as a writer or poet. For each of that poem's sections I first wrote the names of eight to 10 poets at the top of a piece of paper, then tried to write one line for each person—based on the quick sensations people leave in our minds as we encounter and pass by them and overhear them and joust with them. This welter of conversation often takes place unconsciously, because one already has moved on. I wanted to probe this layer of quick conversation that happens now as technology takes us from one person to the next. So I started with the names of poets I admire or have learned from or have had conflict with, and tried to recreate that tapestry or thicket of social relations one engages in all the time (pre-reflectively). Though here again, I did want the piece to present a reading experience, not just a conceptual experience. Concepts and conceptual writers and artists interest me and produce great pleasure. But here I relaxed the methodology if someone held my attention for a couple additional lines. I followed no strict, definable form. I outlined a process then let things happen.

AF: Anything you want to add about the "desperate, desperate impulse for more attention"?

LS: I won't mention names, but do remember sitting beside a very fine poet at a Metropolitan Museum of Art event, and the fine poet wanted to machine gun everyone on stage, presumably because he wasn't up there. More generally, this terrible inattention that most of us acknowledge as part of being a poet can gnaw at someone and transform how he/she thinks, as I've noticed in elders and sensed somewhere inside myself. So "Welter" seeks to pay attention (even if anonymously) to some of our peers, acknowledging the richness of our overall conversation, of the infinite ways we attend to each other without even noticing it.

AF: On this topic of elders, you dedicate *At Element* to the memory of Robin Blaser. Jack Spicer has received much attention for the past decade or so. Poets and critics continue to find new ways of engaging Robert Duncan's still-expanding corpus. Blaser seems less well-integrated into contemporary poetics discourse. Could you tell a relatively ignorant reader why Blaser's work still needs to be read?

LS: This takes us back to questions of topos and the Pacific Northwest, because I think of Blaser as the great poet of Pacific Northwest topologies, ranging from his Berkeley Renaissance days up to his time teaching at Simon Fraser University in Vancouver. Certainly when I moved to this area I looked out for Robert Blaser. I brought him as a guest to Evergreen. I'd met him at a poetry festival in Portugal, where his performance overwhelmed me. Blaser's person presented a richness of voice, a richness of intelligence, a kind of imaginative grandeur—just as Blaser's writing contains a kind of maximalist poetics that I agree we have not fully acknowledged. Still, Blaser the man remained extremely generous and filled with vibrancy until the very end. I think of him as a kind of magisterial exemplum of what a poet might be. For Blaser, as I hope for *At Element*, poetry presents a positive, life-giving, attractive force, yet nonetheless stays conscious of all the ways this can get stymied or stopped—so that the job of poetic language becomes to sublimate, or celebrate, Eros on the sly.

## INTERVIEW WITH LYTLE SHAW
Recorded on June 11, 2012
This interview focuses on Shaw's book *Fieldworks: From Place to Site in Postwar Poetics* (University of Alabama Press).

ANDY FITCH: Could you give a quick genealogical account of prominent concepts and practices at play in postwar site-specific art—as these relate to the history of late-20th-century poetic experiment? Perhaps we first can consider "field," for example, as physical terrain, as social space, as point of interdisciplinary contact.

LYTLE SHAW: The most obvious terms appear in this book's title, which foregrounds a poetics of place in certain postwar literary projects and a turn toward site specificity in art. After publishing my

1999 book *Cable Factory 20*, which emulated site-specific work, I wanted to tell myself a history of site-specific art's relation to the poetics of place. But most work coming out of a poetics-of-place tradition embarrassed me—whereas Smithson, particularly his version of site specificity, fascinated me. Of course Williams and Olson didn't embarrass me, so much as how this poetic impulse got domesticated into a workshop mode by the late '70s. You no longer had to proceed reflexively. You could just represent yet another place through lyric form.

AF: So we've arrived at one discourse of poetic space—prioritizing physical location?

LS: Yeah. I don't attempt to cover every poetics of place. The book presents a diachronic series of case studies, making claims for self-reflexively rich explorations of place and site that occur at different moments. I hadn't anticipated, for example, such a stark distinction between the Williams/Olson models of place and what followed in the 1960s. Of course Williams and Olson themselves have many differences. Yet each dug into his respective town, Gloucester or Paterson, and dug out these alternate genealogies of American culture, American history. That physical "ground" of poetic place presented raw material for future social formations—formations that didn't exist yet in those towns. You couldn't find them in Gloucester or Paterson. Both Williams and Olson remained somewhat hostile to their next-door neighbors, the Marcia Nardis and Vincent Ferrinis hanging out and saying, hey, I do poetics of place—let's chat. Though then in the '60s, even as subsequent poets begin an intensive dialogue with Williams and Olson, this all starts to change. '60s poets prefer to point to actual, existing social formations—either excavated from past cultures, or created in the present. The poetics of place has to be embodied or grounded in an actual social formation as the demand for a coincidence of theory and practice increases. Disparate writers conceive of this embodiment in irreconcilably different ways, but they all move toward living out a poetics of place.

AF: For readers less familiar with applying terms such as "site" and "non-site" to poetry, could you distinguish here between place and site? Then as we consider the historical span from Williams and Olson to subsequent '60s projects, what new relations to language arise, or to the social contexts you've begun to outline, or to geographical/ecological space itself?

LS: Place often gets figured as some form of experiential unity, conflating an empirical location and a person's experience of that location (thereby containing and defining both). Site, by contrast, designates an expanse that hasn't come into fixed focus as the experiential property of a subject. It can be quite literal geographically, but a "site" also can designate a set of power relations or institutional relations that don't get contained within one discrete space. And then, just to clarify how I understand the development of these terms during the past decade: we haven't progressed in smooth linear fashion from prioritizing an experiential connection to place, to discovering a demystified relationship to site (an enlightened position from which we can exist as global or digital subjects, disabused of nostalgic connections to particular physical places). Instead, both place and site ultimately remain heuristic categories. I may identify more with a site-specific way of operating, yet I still need some sense of place in order to conceptualize writers' links to particular locations. So I wanted to put these two discourses into conversation, rather than presenting place as some fantasyland for dupes, and site as our critical, self-reflexive corrective.

AF: Just to return for one second to the more reductive historical model: the demystifying movement toward site in art coincides with a re-mystification of place in poetry. What forces shape these divergent trajectories?

LS: First let me follow through a bit on the historical trajectory of poetic place I began to outline. The familiar, dominant story claims that a series of self-reflexive poetries starting in the late 1960s (coming from the more critically minded wing of New American Poetry and then, of course, from Language writing) begins to position language as a certain kind of site. They begin to critique poetic identity and/or its relation to a particular location. They situate their poetics amid a discursive field of language. Almost all dissertations on Language poetics now start from this basis. But in *Fieldworks* I want to develop an alternate narrative, one that recognizes this rich and generative moment—yet doesn't present it as some kind of proscenium toward which all significant poetic trajectories must tend.

AF: And just to extend the parallel/divergent timelines your book posits, the dematerialization of the commodified art object, and the utopian potential people find in this gesture (along with subsequent critiques of that gesture), anticipate, paradoxically, the materialization of language in poetry—so that *Fieldworks* offers a corresponding critique of this utopian turn toward materiality. But I'm speaking in quite general terms. Could you draw out this specific historical analogy?

LS: Sure. Lucy Lippard documents the dematerialization of the art object in her fantastic book. The desire for this dematerialized object suggests that art has become too sellable. Artists try to escape these conditions of commodity exchange by pursuing purportedly non-aesthetic, "de-materialized" media, such as the photograph—still thought of in the late '60s and early '70s as neutral, informational, at least under certain non-art-photography circumstances. Though again, of course, any such gestures quickly can get recuperated by a commercial regime. The supposedly non-aesthetic and dematerialized moment of conceptualism produces its own style, its own preferred fonts even. So within art history, the art object's material status frequently becomes a charged topic, a domain where one generation or movement intervenes in relation to the recent past. But these interventions don't always tend toward dematerialization. For instance in the '30s, under the grip of social realism and related class-based critiques, pictorial art moves from the easel to the mural. The mural seems more materialist—larger, less personal, more public. And it doesn't present a discrete, sellable commodity. This shift puts new pressure on the easel-based painting as a quaint, exchangeable thing. In this case "materialization" provides the necessary corrective.

AF: And Abstract-Expressionist painting follows, I assume. But the logic you've outlined also reminds me of broader historical phenomena, such as the emergence of seriality—which prompts a change in our perception of art's material form, yet doesn't present a systematic dematerializing project. Like in Hal Foster's account, late-19th-century Monet exhibitions diffuse our focus beyond the individual canvas frame, and set up a perspectival, proto-installation scene, privileging the viewer's physical relation to the gallery space. Nonetheless, single paintings get bought, sold, dispersed.

LS: I consider that the great generative contradiction for serial work. I don't know the particular Monet series, but this happens throughout the 20th century in various ways, and then massively in minimalism. Meanwhile, on the writing side, the literary object seemed too easily consumable for opposite reasons—because it wasn't material enough. Your consumption of it produces no such friction or resistance, no blockage where you become aware of yourself as a meaning-making reader. Instead, narrative allows you to identify with some hypothetical story and project yourself into it and forget your status as a passive consumer. At least that's how Ron Silliman and other Language theorists frame it.

AF: Or Steve McCaffery claims that a descriptive lyric poetics likewise offers a transparent window onto a scene—one into which we project ourselves as readers.

LS: Description too often gets maligned, but sure. At that late-'60s/early-'70s moment, description faces the same pressure, the same need to roughen and defamiliarize and render something material so as to make it inconsumable. Those opposite trajectories (the dematerialization of art and the materialization of language) shape postwar art and poetry. Yet they come from the same impulses and happen simultaneously.

AF: And then in terms of these ongoing dialectics between the material and the dematerialized, between the parts and the whole, we can update the Monet reference by considering Warhol's Campbell's Soup Can show at the Ferus Gallery. Warhol catalogs all the different types of soup Campbell's produces. Yet from that comprehensive constellation, the audience gets invited to pick one of these cute, easily identifiable icons—and take it home as a solitary, self-contained product.

LS: Yeah. An increased tension arises between the imaginary unity and the sellable object.

AF: Given Warhol's mode of displaying that show, which Benjamin Buchloh describes, with each painting perched on a shelf, product-like—can we here begin to pivot toward questions of institutional critique? When I try to understand how small-press poetry has picked up the project of institutional critique, the analogies never line up for me. So first, to what extent does art-world institutional critique pose a specific challenge to the physical space of the supposedly transparent, natural, neutral art gallery? To what extent does institutional critique seek to subvert a more rarefied discourse of the author (or artist), with all of that discourse's accompanying reinforcements? I know I'm dumb for associating institutional critique with particular buildings. But what does get critiqued by institutional critique? How does "institution" get defined here? How can institutional critique then manifest in poetry? *Fieldworks* discusses, for instance, the dissolution of the individual poem in book-length conceptual projects by early Bernadette Mayer and Clark Coolidge. How does that particular form of institutional critique (with its sweeping departure from conventional modes of dissemination, of publication, of New Critical dissection) differ from the critique posed by Language's defamiliarizing syntax?

LS: I think your oscillation between the more concrete concept of the building as site of critique (as a literal "institution"), and the more abstract discourse of the author as site of critique, provides a good way to frame this history. In one narrative of institutional critique, minimalism gave people bodies.

AF: The audience.

LS: Right. No internal complexity exists inside the minimalist art object, no space for you to project yourself and vacate your body. So there you stand, a phenomenological subject in a room, in relation to this thing. Though then subsequent post-minimalist phases said, hmm, maybe this universalized phenomenological subject is an illusion? Maybe our race or gender or class status matters. Maybe we need to register these differences in our analysis of the gallery space and the institutions of art. So we encounter a continual turning of the screw of interpretation—an incremental attempt to foreground ever more specific sites. The performing body becomes one place where we see this process at work. Mierle Laderman Ukeles, for instance, does the "Hartford Wash" piece, where she washes the Wadsworth Athenaeum's floor. Not only does her action prompt our awareness of the loathsome toil necessary to maintain this supposedly neutral arena of perception (the museum), but such work now gets assigned to a body with a gender. The problem I find, less with Ukeles' than with Hans Haacke's early versions of institutional critique, is that they prioritize sociological analyses of the institution of art, without presenting any thorough analysis of the institution of sociology.

AF: Here the term "institution" gets complicated for me.

LS: Well "sociology," too, describes a disciplinary site where power struggles happen, where different methodologies come into play—and where all such positions should get critiqued. Sociology doesn't offer a neutral and magical window that suddenly reveals the politics of other disciplines, like art. We've inherited this story, for instance, that self-important art objects get replaced by altruistic, dialogic critiques and interviews—presuming that interviews just immediately embody some progressive politics.

AF: I'm guilty.

LS: I want a thorough analysis of the actual functioning of sociology more generally, and of interviews more specifically. The book I've just finished, which follows *Fieldworks*, called *Specimen Box*, tracks shifts in the discourse of institutional critique over the past several decades. It departs from this process of standing-back and sociologically negating some institution. It privileges practices that deliberately over-identify with institutions—absorbing their idioms of meaning making, forcing these (through imminent transformation) to say something they never could have said before.

AF: Could you contextualize this mode of absorptive intervention amid developments in Language poetry or conceptual poetry or appropriative poetics?

LS: Yes. It took a while to figure out an appropriate frame for Language writing. For me, when I think of the confluence between institutional critique and Language writing, Susan Howe (though not a perfect fit for either field) presents a compelling model, because she consistently engages actual archives. She produces not only a new reading of literary history, but a reading of the power dynamics that shape her access to such manuscripts—that allow her to produce that reading. Then in terms of conceptual poetry: again sometimes poets presume that appropriation by itself embodies a specific politics. I'd prefer to think about post-conceptualism, though that term hasn't stuck.

AF: From Vanessa Place and Rob Fitterman's book?

LS: I sense conceptual poetry in general hasn't done the best job theorizing itself, which seems fine. Not all art needs to provide the richest theoretical account of itself. But then I also sense a residual McLuhanism right now. Ten to 12 years ago, for instance, Marjorie Perloff begins to establish a canon of technologically oriented writers, including Darren Wershler-Henry, Christian Bök and Kenny

Goldsmith. They become "the new" because they work with the digital, according to this determinist idea of timeliness. Now I happen to like much of this writing. The problem is that the canon and underlying historical narrative of conceptual poetics, in its present iteration, essentially gets overlaid onto this prior "digital" moment, all of which makes it much harder to discuss alternate modes of "conceptualist" politics—like those associated with Kootenay, for instance. I think Lisa Robertson's work demands much more sophisticated rubrics. Again, its relationship to conceptual art becomes pressing. If we picture conceptualism playing out this late-'60s moment (when it's unclear whether language will approach the conditions of site-specific and institutionally critical art, or whether art will take a linguistic turn), then I want to hold onto these institution-critiquing/site-specific components, and not essentialize the mechanism of appropriation. I don't want to downsize this complex late-'60s legacy in which the disciplines came together. I see Lisa, and others not associated with conceptual poetry in its current figuration, as producing important parts of the actual legacy of conceptualism—which, again, includes site-specificity and institution critique.

AF: Do you feel that the discourse of relational aesthetics, as absorbed by the art world during the past couple decades, has not fully made its way yet to critical reflections on literature? Would that help to contextualize Lisa's work—her fields of engagement, her types of practice, the blend of institutionally sponsored and maverick projects in which she'll engage simultaneously?

LS: That's probably true. Many questions about the reception of minimalism anticipate this later relational conversation. But more generally I would say that poetry criticism desperately needs new perspectives and approaches. Language poets developed incredibly evocative theoretical models. They turn out to have been the best poetry critics across the board for the past 30 years. We still mostly operate under their interpretive paradigms. Yet these have performed the defamiliarizations that they're going to perform. We now need to shift the discourse. So here I have appealed to terms and concerns from outside, including some from art criticism. Still, art is ruthless… pardon me, art historians are ruthless when it comes to the maintenance of their field. They often steal from or caricature poetry. They'll just pluck up practices that happened in poetry—with little concern about poetry having its own history, you know? Carl Andre has a series of historians making sure to document every micro-event in his career, as if he invented concrete poetry. Or I just reviewed a book tracking Marcel Broodthaers' shift from poetry to art, which presents 1960s poetry as this completely moribund language. But the only poets this book actually mentions are Baudelaire and Mallarmé. The concept of "poetry" itself figures into art-historical discourse as this purportedly timeless, ahistorical, naïve form of personal expression from which art departs in favor of critical rigor. So I feel the need both to call out art historians on their ridiculous fantasy of "poetry," and to inject some new life into poetics discourse via art history.

AF: Yes, it does seem that, amid poetic criticism, points of art-historical reference have remained quite dated for 30 or 40 years, at least since Perloff's work comparing O'Hara to the Abstract Expressionists became a dominant paradigm—later picked up in accounts of how Language poetics pursue a discourse of surface. But if we could return to the specifics of *Fieldworks*: you carefully parse disparate conceptions of what a "generative field" might be. You distinguish, for instance, between a poetics of personal cosmology, which we might find in Olson, and a poetics that (in Foucault's formulation) founds a new discourse, such as Jerome Rothenberg's ethnopoetics or Gary Snyder's ecopoetics. Perversely perhaps, since it take up so little space in your ambitious book, I'm intrigued when you mention, in a passing aside, that Olson's seemingly more self-involved personal cosmology, rather than Rothenberg's or Snyder's discursive foundings, remains, for you, far more generative. What about Olson's field makes it so?

LS: Yeah, it's true. I've written this big chapter on Olson, yet still find myself working my way through him. But more generally, we might want to start with the fact that, in the '60s, the New Left presents this incredibly admirable desire to take massive fields of cultural knowledge and free them from their authorized, official, institutional trappings. Any object or event in an Olson poem consolidates his own position of authority—whereas in a discourse of ethnopoetics, or Amiri Baraka's early black nationalism, a wide range of references and critiques and idioms gets mobilized without prioritizing any author function. Yet Baraka here differs for me from the case of Rothenberg and Snyder. His actual poems excite and interest me, more than any broader discursive practice of assembling anthologies and delineating disciplines. Likewise, with Olson, I keep returning and trying to figure out what attracts and attaches me.

AF: Again, though it brings up a problematic distinction, something about Olson's poetry, more than his poetics, most captivates you?

LS: Well that weird component of Olson as a performance artist attracts me just as much. It must have been excruciating but also fascinating to witness that classic scene of Charles Olson in process at the 1965 Berkeley Poetry Conference. On the one hand, Olson's performance foregrounds gestures of connection—with its hey, Ed Sanders; hey, Allen Ginsberg; hey, Robert Duncan and Robert Creeley. Yet that same exhaustive love-in denies the very possibility of connection as it proceeds. Olson so rigorously, so continuously reaches out and withdraws at the same time. I can only think of something this bizarre in relation to performance art. But to return briefly to your question: I doubt any poetics from the '60s could have banished, simply and absolutely, all traces of a personal cosmology. I've grown up in enough of a Nietzschian environment to recognize how discourses relate to conditions of possibility shaped by particular artists' and audiences' needs. I sense an historical horizon, rather than an existential either/or.

AF: Here's another small, localized follow-up. Chapter 2, I think footnote 17, lists a series of travel journals poets produced during the '60s and '70s—including one of my all-time-favorite literary projects, Joe Brainard's *Bolinas Journal*. Could you outline the place of a personal/post-personal cosmology within these travelogues? Do all or some of these texts deserve renewed attention?

LS: You picked my favorite, Joe Brainard's brilliant *Bolinas Journal*. Joanne Kyger's *Strange Big Moon* contains a couple moments I love, such as her meeting the Dalai Lama with Allen Ginsberg and Gary Snyder. But I guess I wanted to argue that, in their historical moment, these projects took on a different cultural function than they might now. They didn't document personal soul-searching, so much as they engaged this culture-wide search for alternate genealogies and an expanded concept of North American or world literature. People actively pursued this gonzo style of research, which involved putting yourself into contingent situations.

AF: That leads into a broader question. Does it seem fair to say that, in the decades following site-specific art's emergence, the two most dramatic challenges to any fixed, ahistorical, timeless conception of physical place have been posed by human-made climate change (causing us to rethink any eternalizing, idealizing notion of ecopoetics) and by the internet's placeless polis (several steps further removed from the dream of an authentic community that you track in Amiri Baraka's Newark, or the collective be-in of '60s/'70s Bolinas)? From your own experience assembling this book, can you speak to how site-specific art and poetics have proved prophetic, prescient, oblivious and/or ill-equipped to meet the epistemic problems posed by these two new modes of contextualizing space or place?

LS: First, in terms of the foundational discourse for ecology, I only realized quite recently how math- and statistics-based its key components were. Early formulations of ecology overlap certain kinds of systems theory—with an a priori emphasis upon an input/output identity, a movement toward stabilization. Only since the late '70s have theorists argued that natural history does not work this way, but rather embodies the historical, with irrevocable changes all the time, climate change among them (although clearly we've made this much worse and need to address it). So here again, if we consider site specificity as dissolving easy distinctions between the local and the global, as prioritizing relationships of scale rather than of identity, then site-specific discourse seems quite useful for tracking those two historical developments you mentioned.

AF: Again, a does any such poetics of scale stand out from preceding generations? Does Whitman's complicated conflation of personal, social and textual bodies present one productive model?

LS: I absolutely adore Whitman, but find a somewhat fixed human core in his sense of scale. That scale radiates outward from the human body. That's fine. Though Robert Smithson, let's say, presents a series of different scales or frames or registers, only one of which we might identify as human—and not necessarily the central or stabilizing one. A model of scale that can move back and forth between the intergalactic and the subatomic most interests me. I don't mean to moralize about how humans have been in charge too long, and it's time to let the microbes have their say. But scale shifts allow us to encounter unsuspected questions. Their degree of abstraction precludes any simple identification of site specificity with rural locations, for instance. They don't privilege your particular hometown. They put into relation immediate, empirical scenes of encounter and potentially infinite frames of reference. So rather than Whitman, here I'd evoke somebody like Robert Hooke.

## INTERVIEW WITH DANIEL TIFFANY
Recorded on June 13, 2012
This interview focuses on Tiffany's book *Neptune Park* (Omnidawn).

ANDY FITCH: In *Neptune Park*'s epigraph, Strabo, the Roman geographer, declares, "I shrink from giving too many of the names, shunning the unpleasant task of writing them down—unless it comports with the pleasure of someone." I'm interested in the role preemptive or productive apology plays in your poetics. Who are some of your favorite apologizers? Robert Walser comes to mind, perhaps Joe Brainaird.

DANIEL TIFFANY: I haven't thought this through carefully, whether Strabo's statement suggests strategic calculation or an embarrassed admission. I like the way he doesn't just apologize for the obscurity of certain names and places, but acknowledges his hope of "comporting" with someone's pleasure. I appreciate an apologetics qualified by the hope that someone out there just might want to hear terribly dull things. I also love Strabo's way of cataloging obscure places, tribes, peoples he has heard or read about—almost as an obligation, from a sense of duty.

AF: That structure of thinking interests me, the clearing of space for a reader's potential pleasure. Your epigraph seems almost an invocation, or its opposite.

DT: Again this epigraph comes from a treatise on geography. And the book explores questions of place and placelessness, home and homelessness, what street kids call "housed thinking" (in contrast to ephemeral or abandoned spaces). Strabo's reference to remote places and tribes comes in his description of Lusitania, the Roman province corresponding to present-day Portugal, and my manuscript contains a poem ("Lost Liner") that alludes to another Lusitania—the British passenger liner sunk in 1915 by a German U-boat. Ezra Pound sailed from Venice to New York on the Lusitania in 1910. I also remember an obscure theoretical journal by that name from the 1980s, which lasted for only an issue or two.

AF: Your recent collection *Privado* adopts the "jody," cadences chanted by soldiers—or maybe dreams up this ballad form in its masterful self-mythology. What sorts of reading projects inform this new book's idiom? *Neptune Park* doesn't feel like the hard camp of David

Trinidad's *Plasticville*, let's say. It's not so explicit in its appropriations. Or it seems less schematic than Flarf's trollings.

DT: I'm not a constructivist in the sense that I don't have much interest in exposing appropriation or imposture (impostor, imposition, etcetera are related terms, so to "impose" means to swindle or cheat, to execute some kind of imposture). What we now call appropriation occurs as one particular variant of practices stretching back forever. Today this gesture typically suggests a constructivist practice, often used as a form of critique—a desire to expose the social context of certain vocabularies or discourses, to turn them inside out. As a pose, this could demystify and disenchant—functions that do not play much of a role in my poetry. Still, the way these practices can remain cloaked or veiled excites me, especially their relation to other veiling processes such as Sedgwick's notion of the epistemology of the closet, which provides a kind of halo of gossip and rumor that hovers around things, leaving their precise identity uncertain. Are such phenomena legitimate, stolen, queer? I prefer to raise these doubts and questions around concealed or borrowed texts, rather than exposing their procedures. Forms of social realism or pragmatism interest me less than the history of textual clouds and disguises and masks.

AF: The Gurlesque foregrounding of affect, the contemporary interest in fairy tales, come to mind when you describe processes of remystification—as does some less canonical John Ashbery, such as his Darger-esque *Girls on the Run*. Kitsch, of course, but again your own distinct conception of kitsch which still sounds somewhat private until it appears in your next critical book, *My Silver Planet*. *Neptune Park* seems to construct, quite deliberately, the supposedly unintended, un-selfconscious syntactic lilt of camp, kitsch, uncanniness.

DT: It's definitely not about camp—nor specifically related to kitsch. Audiences orient themselves quite differently to kitsch and to camp. Critics spend much time trying to sort through differences between objects of kitsch and objects of camp. To me that difference tells only part of the story. What does differ more consistently is how people orient themselves to such objects. As for the relation between a theoretical discourse about kitsch and the substance of these poems: it's a little like musing on different words for the same thing in separate languages (the difference between the words for "bread," say, in Italian versus German). Perhaps some correspondence exists between the terms, but I tend to approach each experience in discrete ways—as a poet, as a theorist. It spoils the relationship to press too hard.

AF: Could we consider a couple specific sequences, some of my favorite lines?

DT: Sure, making things concrete—so we don't float away too far.

AF: Well this might make us float away, given its title "How Many Days Can You Live on Vicodin and Frosty?" But could we look at the lines: "A lion is in the streets, / there is a lion in the way. // My niece, the little siren / taught her the slang: / mad married fiancée. // Dido has a quiver, / she wears a spotted lynx // skin and a belt. / My undefiled is not herself"?

DT: That picks up on the Virgilian Dido (queen of Carthage and lover of Aeneas, who kills herself after he abandons her). I saw a Wooster Group performance called *La Didone* a couple years back, which combined scenes from an early Cavalli opera about Dido with dialogue and décor from a '60s Italian sci-fi TV show. I found it stunning, thrilling, filled with lyrical moments against a crazy Pop background—yet all synthesized in some way, not simply a juxtaposition. I can't say these poems come out of that, though they try something similar, positing Virgil and Warhol as points of reference, veering between various shades of literary diction and Warhol's blasé descriptions of his superstars.

AF: I love the seamless synthesis or synthetic in your work, as different from the fake—as a deliberate diffusion of tonality. Placing oneself amid this tonal efflorescence felt liberating, for me at least, getting to experience so much at once. Could we talk a second more about Dido, queen of the classical grotesque? Dido seems terrifying both for the self-destructive, erotic pull she represents, and (as I read your book I thought) for the potential pomposity of that representation itself, which has sustained readers' interest throughout the ages. Dido endures, your poem "Neptune Fix" declares, because the "human torch" remains the "main attraction."

DT: I hadn't thought of her for that poem, actually. But Dido is certainly no figure of the grotesque in my book. She appears in various guises as the woman, or girl, whom Aeneas abandons in his journey toward the founding of Rome—an event which leaves an indelible stain on epic. That hitch in the narrative momentum opens up a world of feeling.

AF: It's just this reference to the "human torch."

DT: I'd thought of mass spectacle and contemporary forms of desensitizing, which *Neptune Park* seeks to embody—desensitized sensibility as an affect, listening to how desensitized people talk. It's a bit like Seidel in that way.

AF: Like what?

DT: Frederick Seidel—the flat register and diction he'll use to describe horrifying or troubling scenes. He has a great ear for transcribing certain dead registers of contemporary American English. And tone of course can get commodified. Particular registers of diction fascinate me because they present language's poetic dimensions receiving their widest circulation. Speech-writers or advertisers cultivate and exploit tone quite sensitively and knowingly. It hovers between pure music (similar to the poetic line's musicality) and meaning. Diction is a funny thing: not just music, and not just meaning, somewhere between. So this part of language always remains susceptible to commodification, to public enchantment. It gets a rise out of people. They want to use certain kinds of words, to adopt the features of a certain diction and identify with its sensibility. This can be regional, tribal, anachronistic—often an imaginary projection of class identity. Still, this powerful dimension of language has disappeared from the vocabulary of criticism for some time. Poets and critics speak exhaustively about form, or experimentation with form. When one wants to discuss the material qualities of poetic language, one frequently resorts to vocabulary involving aspects of form. Some writers want to address questions of tone or diction, but fall back on formalist vocabulary because the ways of talking about poetics have become so narrow, so clichéd. It's like trying to describe a vampire bat's physiology with terms developed for a tree or wrist watch. Crazy, crazy ferocious debates used to circulate concerning the types of language appropriate for poetry. Questions of tone get addressed best these days, usually inadvertently, in debates about sampling and appropriation.

AF: I've read different drafts of your manuscript, and noted the sudden appearance of "totally." This adverb's complicated tonal vectors make your work all the more pleasurable for me. As we address concepts of idiom, tone, I'm curious how these relate to gender—especially within the cramped/capacious confines of *Neptune Park*. If we could start with "girls," what's the place of, what's your place…this book mentions a "girls-only evening." Could you describe your place at a girls-only evening? Or could you describe the types of imitation, identification, affect at play in "Blow Pop"?

DT: That title "Blow Pop" has changed—now the poem's called "Neptune Society." I guess the adolescent, girlish voices produced by certain Japanese fairy or YA novels intrigue me. To place a simple, straightforward, declarative statement in that voice seemed to offer a powerful counterpoint. Its flavor has an immediate, dramatic effect on nearby tones and registers. It makes you pay attention. It makes somebody listen. It could cut through posturing, aggression, cleverness. It provides a verbal palate I can mix. I can accelerate a poem's movement by changing tones more quickly, or doing that more slowly.

AF: Does the function or impact of this girly diction differ when it comes from a man? Does the performance of authorship help to structure the tone?

DT: Yes, some kind of transvestite moment occurs at times in *Neptune Park*, which you can amplify or constrict, but toying with gender masks does not necessarily become a dominant impulse in the book.

AF: As we discuss aspects of performance, of obfuscation, could you describe your interest in Japanese lost-roof technique (which I know as roof-off technique, from Tale of Genji paintings, where we see an interior scene as if from above)? What desire does that concept hold for you? Do the vaguely pornographic vantages suggest analogous triangulations of a commodified tone? Does this mediated deployment of diction personalize the market processes of kitsch? What can lost-roof perspective reveal about such interplays among gender, idiom, identity, sexuality?

DT: I like that question. These poems each posit some predicament, which appears vaguely alarming, unresolved or incomplete. Exposure prompts a sort of voyeurism, a glimpse, pulling you in. And here I might note that, in terms of straight male sexuality, one doesn't find much of it, certainly nothing very sexy, in contemporary American poetry. The poets I could imagine responding to this aspect of my book (at least in terms of their public personae) are gay, or gay-identified. So the lost-roof technique comes from wanting to engage normative masculinity and heterosexuality, but to write new sexualities (forgeries really) across straight male identity, to construct something about sexual experience and sex that recommodifies the sweetness of the old ordeals, but under very different conditions—in the light of shipwreck, you might say. As that sexuality gets named and framed, the lost-roof vantage provides this peeping quality.

AF: Also, in terms of this lost-roof impulse, how about your characteristic italicization of faux lyrics and nursery rhymes? Do such formatting gestures likewise open up a lost-roof glimpse on a poetics of citation, transcription, imitation—what you've called modernist parasitism?

DT: Yes. I've been thinking recently about this Ben Jonson play called *The Poetaster*. I'd always thought the word was "poet-taster," when it's actually poet-aster—where the suffix functions as a diminutive. That suffix denotes a minor figure of one type or another: derivative, marginal, childish, stereotypical.

AF: "Aster" does?

DT: The play presents this poetaster and plagiarist in ancient Rome, who writes what Jonson calls "worded trash." But Jonson tracks what he calls "gnomic pointing"—the way texts identify borrowed material through italics, quotation marks, underline. A big part of my new critical book on kitsch considers poetic forgeries and all the fascination/anxiety with these practices in the mid-18th century. People wondered which documents were real. Ballad anthologies attempted to identify which parts of ballads were fabricated or original. Questions hovered around problems of exposure, ownership, possession, privacy, possible disclosures. But apart from denoting a phrase as borrowed, italics also can connote a private comment, an aside. The discourse suddenly can slip into a kind of private register, like a whisper. Some sort of secrecy can shroud the voice. So italics function many different ways. Some instances indicate the subjectivity of another character, speaker, commentary, confessional. Something doesn't belong to me, or seems different from everything else, or comes in a whisper not meant for public consumption. Format can help to structure a text's different voices. In *Neptune Park*, sometimes it felt necessary to set off this alternation between different voices, then sometimes it didn't.

AF: Again, for how formats create rhetorical texture, I very much enjoy what you've described as the feigning of flat affect. *Neptune Park* provides depth to the way this flatness gets picked through—sifted from any number of discrete vantages. Here I think of your peculiar-seeming constellation of section headings: "Correction," "Industry," "Haven," "Anniversary," "Nemesis," "Friends." That's a great magic circle of terms. It also could seem a forged blueprint for this book. *Neptune Park* can correspond to those section headings if one wants it to, but they also could provide a provocative false lead, a commentary on conventional modes of poetic demarcation, as performed by the multi-part poetic collection.

DT: Here again, a tonal impulse predominates. Language and circumstance within certain poems become heated. So I want the section titles to sound much flatter, more neutral, less remote. These titles function as space holders, while providing a kind of counterpoint. What would it mean to read the first section's poems through the concept of "Correction"? How does this filter alter the local affect? I wanted to introduce the poems through an indeterminate perspective, to alienate the text. Still I don't mean to provide a false or generic or arbitrary lead. I chose titles carefully for each section. They couldn't possibly be swapped.

AF: You mentioned a potential alienating effect, but it seems an elective alienation. The reader's mind has to decide whether he/she will read a discrete poem in relation to its global grouping around an abstract title. This reader could feel all the less or all the more alienated when faced with such decisions. I appreciated that.

DT: Yes you realize you can discard the affect associated with these titles, though that rejection of course prompts its own affect. Choreographing trajectories of affect perhaps most interested me.

AF: One affective register we haven't discussed: after admiring the song-like constructions in *The Dandelion Clock* and *Privado*, it pleased me to encounter here the occasional interruption of sonic outburst, incantation, unmoored chorus, abstracted nursery rhyme. Clipped utterances puncture this text. I'm thinking of sequences such as "then, too, then, too, then, too." Or "Bo Peeper / Nose dreeper / Chin chopper." Could you contextualize these passages amid your broader interest in toy media, riddles, argot, slumming, forgery, spying?

DT: For me as for many others, Mother Goose nursery rhymes sound at once cooked up (from some ancient English vernacular), pedagogical, yet somehow impenetrably strange, sinister. Terrible situations not only get described, but also illogically juxtaposed with scenes of happiness. Or descriptions offer details so obvious you can't understand why they've been included. Those "Nose dreeper / Chin chopper" lines evoke the milieu of a horserace track as well, so eventually these phrases became horses' names. Though I guess nursery rhymes often evoke punitive scenes—somebody punished or receiving their just desserts. Nursery rhymes coerce and instruct that way. This experience of scaring oneself provides an important pedagogical and poetic principle.

AF: The relationship between an innocent tone and a violent (potentially sexualized) scene seems crucial here, in lines like: "The 'bears' stopped at my house first, / done me all the harm they could." Some of my favorite passages offer this seamless amalgamation of a light, friendly idiom and then potentially disconcerting events: "To the south, to the south: / outlines of figures running for cover, orchards // aflame and conjurings in green ink." Or: "My sister threw a lit / candle at me for I had lingered // a moment too long." Have we sufficiently addressed these dramatizations of violence?

DT: *Neptune Park* contains an apocalyptic aspect, but more in a suburban than a futuristic sense, more banal than sublime. I guess I finally figured out a way to present this book as an allegory of dissolution, a descent narrative related, perhaps, to Alice Notley's framing of *The Descent of Alette.* You could describe *Neptune Park* as a graphic novel minus the pictures, an infidel pamphlet, a series of predicaments stirring up the kitsch of our own apocalypse. Its archive assembles a garbled voice, a verbal tranny—culled from a lost world of suburban squats, keyhole sex, teenage millionaires, queer idylls, and public shame. A space once occupied but now vacant.

AF: A space that your Strabo-esque pursuits serve to demarcate, or to excavate?

DT: Well, for me, fear or fright remain extremely receptive states. They also could become transformative. Scary scenes can place you in a different world. The world suddenly might reverse itself, which I find alluring. Although of course, as a reader, one remains sheltered (a key to the experience of the sublime). I don't offer a response to literal violence. I seek to investigate a specific state of poetic consciousness, related to aesthetic experience. Pushing beyond realist dramatizations, I'd point to a different notion of Pop—cult Pop, or subliminal Pop, or Pop without popularity, categories that embrace Pop's striking accessibility, yet directed toward some internalized investigation. The Hammer Museum in Los Angeles had a fabulous show of the Polish-Jewish sculptor Alina Szapocznikow, a post-war figure whose family died in a concentration camp. She did something I'd never seen an artist do, making reference to the Holocaust through Pop materials and affect. She produced these amazing lamps where she used transparent acrylics for lips and cheeks, very sexual, very erotic, in a Pop idiom, yet evoking the ordeal of the body in the death camps. I guess *Maus* brings together Pop and the Holocaust. Still Szapocznikow's embodied pieces seemed much more grave and elliptical—more corporeal, but also whimsical. I found that incredibly moving, the prospect that arcane Pop or deviant Pop could toy with Pop's lyric interiority.

### INTERVIEW WITH NICK TWEMLOW
Recorded on June 14, 2012
This interview focuses on Twemlow's book *Palm Trees* (Green Lantern).

ANDY FITCH: I found the title *Palm Trees* catchy and fun. The pun in Wallace Stevens' *The Palm at the End of the Mind* came back, or in Ashbery's *Some Trees*.

NICK TWEMLOW: Those both remain important books for me, though I didn't deliberately string them together. Perhaps someplace in my subconscious this was simmering. I've worked on this book for quite some time. It's gone through several titles and organizational structures. For a while I called it "Black Helicopter," after the book's second poem, as well as my obsession with the paranoiac. Then I visited Los Angeles for a few days on my return from a year in New Zealand, and the scenes that strike any visitor to L.A. struck me: the palm-tree-lined boulevards, the gorgeous sunsets (L.A. as a Patrick Nagel creation). I went to Griffith Park with a friend, and he showed me a patch of German Oaks—a gift from a sister city in Germany—and explained how city planners had considered replacing dying palms with trees more suited to L.A.'s climate. I balked. Given their prominence in my mental image of L.A., I had assumed palm trees were native to the city. Not so. Their iconic place in L.A. mythology represents a decaying monument to the tremendous social engineering that built this town in the early 20th century. Because of their natural expiration date, they'll need to get removed or replaced. That offered this perfect L.A. metaphor I kept thinking about, since I do lots of film as well.

AF: Please feel free to talk about film.

NT: The palms' transient nature connected not only to L.A. history, but also to my own family narrative. *Palm Trees* presents an indirect look at various aspects of my family. It avoids the straightforwardly confessional (whatever that might mean), but figures in this book do contain trace elements from specific family members. Our family immigrated to the States before my birth, from New Zealand, on a boat through the Panama Canal, to Miami. They then traveled by bus to Topeka, Kansas, where my father began his psychiatric residency at the Menninger Clinic. That migration, that combined sense of place and displacement, connects again to this notion of the palm tree. This disruptive move changed the face of my family. My parents divorced soon after. My brother and sisters, somewhat older than me, had had a life in New Zealand, whereas I grew up entirely in the States. They felt confused, bewildered, perhaps destroyed by the move. Though because they spoke English, albeit the Queen's English, they appeared to fit in. Which they did, sort of. Yet for this and other reasons, the palm tree became for me not an icon of paradise, but something gnarled and marginalized and sad. None of this directly addresses my own film and video works, but it provides some background for my filmmaking.

AF: I don't know if I've mentioned I'm in Melbourne, and went with a couple Kiwis just yesterday on a wildlife tour. But for your book's "Palm Trees" section, the L.A.-specific palms disappear quickly. Given the transient processes you wished to emphasize, was this inevitable? Does transience happen formally, even as it gets thematized? What forms or formal variations best capture the palm tree?

NT: Good question. I'll try to recall…at first I'd worked on short prose poems several years ago. I went to New Zealand on a Fulbright, and some of the poems I wrote there led to what become "Palm Trees." They sort of jump-started that series. But only later did I realize that something connected these pieces. I moved around a few other poems to see what else could fit. I noticed a motif of travel. The "Palm Trees" poems don't stay in L.A. very long. They wind up many different places: Vancouver, Paris, Wichita, Mexico. And consistent compression made most of these quite short (some a sentence or two). I just became comfortable with that form. I could sustain this particular type of energy for that particular amount of space. The poems move all over the place, so seem less about duration than continual attempts to gather everything I could imagine at a given moment. Eventually I decided I'd write a discrete series, a constellation, clustered around the title "Palm Trees." It never before had occurred to me to construct a composite series, organized by a governing conceit—which I know has become relatively common. I wanted to see if I could make all these small bits come together, and form a different type of global poem.

AF: On the thematics of ephemerality, transience, travel: your relationship to audience interests me as well. Your poems are often quite funny. Does writing a comedic poem construct a particular type of identification with your audience? Does no comedy exist without an intended audience?

NT: I actually don't imagine an audience. My audience remains pretty much a void. I just imagine talking into the void, receiving no response, which evokes an aspect of comedy. Stand-up, in particular, thrives on this tension between a void and a potentially responsive audience. Imagine all the bad jokes that get tossed out and the deadly silence that follows! But probably what motivates much of my anxiety, like anybody else's, are matters of death, or thoughts of my three-year-old son's well-being and safety. A lot of suppressed anxiety wells up, then manifests in my work. A dialogue happens, sort of with myself, with the part that reads my own book and other books, and contemplates how literature relates to my life and my place in the world. Another part of me, who docs the writing, offers commentary/interpretation/throwing hands up in the air at my own actions. So this internalized dialogue happens. I've seen poets described as comic poets, who seem quite aware of audience response. In some cases, their readings will include a beat where one expects the laugh. And most of the time they get it. Here watching Dane Cook comes to mind. Though even when I read aloud, I don't find my poems funny. Still, certain poems do get laughs. The best surprise comes when people laugh at moments nobody's laughed at before. I admire many comics, for different reasons. Richard Pryor's all about the body and performance. Louis C.K. seems more cerebral, much more deadpan. But I consider Samuel Beckett the greatest comedy writer of all (the end of his first novel, *Murphy*: the narrator, against his dying wish, witnesses his own ashes accidentally dumped on the floor of a bar and swept up with the trash. To me, this is the funniest moment in literature).

AF: Well part of what I find funny in your book is how repetition plays out. As you mention Richard Pryor's performative body, I wonder if repetition provides a means of steering readers through the deadpan tonality of your work. This gets dramatized in a poem like "Topeka, Topeka," even just that title. Can you sense why such repetitions might seem funny, might work well in a performance?

NT: Yeah, I can speak to that. For a quick digression: my next manuscript, which I've been slowly working on, provides, in its first half, a double crown of Shakespearean sonnets. They're not metrical, for the most part, but they rhyme. Early on when attempting to write poems, I'd written in strict form—just experimenting with poetry in general. Then I moved far away from that with *Palm Trees*, which probes what makes up a poetic line. Yet in either case, I keep coming back to repetition. Sometimes this provides a toehold, a place of familiarity, from which you can deform the familiar. You set up a lull, which the repetition turns into a surprise. There's a ruminative quality to this work. I ruminate a lot. And the generalized repetition in my interior life seems not exactly pleasant all the time, but rather this peculiar monologue that's continued since I was six. All of us have an interior monologue, but mine involves heavy repetition. My mind works that way, so it seemed helpful to get a handle on this in a poem. With "Topeka, Topeka" I thought of the song "New York, New York." I like refrains. I like music in simple forms, with much repetition. Pop music. For me Topeka presented a mix of different themes (among them a hellish place). But repetition helped me have an interior conversation about my sense of Topeka.

AF: You mentioned Pop refrains. "Topeka, Topeka" echoes "Corrina, Corrina," the Bob Dylan cover of Robert Johnson's song. That's always been one of my favorites.

NT: Sure, I definitely had that in my mind. This poem's probably the closest piece I have to a song. For a while I titled the manuscript "Topeka Verses." It contained even more poems addressing my birthplace—the hometown for an inordinate number of poets.

AF: Could you name some?

NT: Kevin Young comes from Topeka. Ben Lerner comes from Topeka. Ed Skoog. Eric McHenry. Anne Boyer was born but not raised there. She grew up an hour and a half west, in a town called Salina. Gary Jackson I've never met, but he recently published a book with Graywolf. My good friend Andy Carter, an amazing poet. Cyrus Console comes from Topeka. Gwendolyn Brooks was born in Topeka, while her mom visited a sister. Ronald Johnson spent the last bits of his life, I don't know how long, caring for his dying father in Topeka, then stayed and died also in Topeka. I can't remember the first poem I wrote about Topeka, but I know the process thrilled me. Topeka became the object onto which I could transfer everything. Even that word, "Topeka," now seems polemical, this Native American term that means "good ground for growing potatoes." For a while "Topeka" took on grand dimensions. A small, important literary subset of poems exists about Topeka. Perhaps someday someone can collect them. At one point I considered writing a so-called psychobiography, a study of this town's psychological history. Topeka even had a roadside sign naming it the "Psychiatric Capital of the World." That's why my family moved across the Pacific, so my father could study at the Menninger Institute, which has its own rich and strange history concerning the development of mental health treatment in this country. But I'll leave that for a better historian.

AF: Though the repetitions in a poem like "Topeka, Topeka" also have a nerdy boy quality to them (I mean this in the most complimentary fashion), suggesting someone obsessed with facts, with little sense how to convey these pressing concerns to others. Similar tonalities appear throughout the collection. Poems address "boy" themes like karate. Passages dwell on the eternal boy philosopher, Novalis. At one point *Palm Trees* posits 34 as "the new 12." Gurlesque poetics have galvanized many great projects in recent years. Could a Boyesque poetics add to, complement, develop out from the Gurlesque?

NT: We could start by calling the entire Western poetic canon "Boyesque." If the Gurlesque has galvanized, the Boyesque has necessitated this. Of course the very name "Gurlesque" reproduces the infantilization inherent in the male gaze. Girls don't write Gurlesque poems. And I think too much privilege exists in being a white, male, straight poet to necessitate a Boyesque—to carve out space the way the Gurlesque does. In the poems you cite, a "boyish" tone appears at times, but I would define this boyishness as a response to serious distress. Perhaps the comedy of a poem like "I Love Karate" derives from my view that politics resemble a cartoon, a cartoon with lots of visible (and, more dangerously, invisible) violence. I think many politically minded poets feel at a complete loss when considering how to reckon with this state of the world. I certainly feel reduced, at times, if addressing such concerns through a poem, to a quivering mess of nothingness. *Palm Trees*' anger and violence comes from that. Sometimes, when looking at my poems, I sense a little kid throwing tantrums all over the house.

AF: Sure I'm just formulating the Boyesque on the spot. But most male poets, even when addressing boyhood, tend to write from an adult voice looking back, or from some conventionally acceptable childhood idiom, whereas your work often foregrounds an unreconstructed tone that I appreciate. It veers toward the anti-social—less integrated into the normative ways that adults converse. "International Rate," for example, seems to thematize some formal tropes we've mentioned, especially in its claim that "anaphora's the disease of the stutterer." Here I think of John Cage, with Schoenberg telling him you'll always hit a wall if you try to become a composer. And Cage says I'll just make a career out of banging my head against this wall. And then Cage bangs his head against that anecdote itself, repeating it throughout his life. Do other unreconstructed, asocial, frustrated voices of repetition stand out for you, perhaps Thomas Bernhard, Stein, Robert Walser?

NT: Stein for sure. I like to read her work over and over again, because it warrants such repeated readings. Beckett I care about deeply. Repetition occurs especially in his plays. Someone will assert something then hear that same statement repeated back as a question. Or a question gets repeated as a statement. Beckett engaged Chaplin and other silent film comedians, such as Buster Keaton. If you watch Keaton or Chaplin, slapstick might allow for seemingly new situations, yet they'll encounter the same problem every time. They might fall through the front door then next time fall through a trap door, but that fall remains the same. Beckett picks up on this. In the trilogy whole situations get repeated, even as particulars change—providing something like a semantic rhyme, more than straightforward repetition. Or I started reading Fred Seidel 10 years ago, before everybody began talking about his work (I only mention that because a contemporary poet might find it hard to imagine this thirty-year period when no one read Seidel). Again repetition, here less intense than Stein's, attracted me. You'll find whole poems repeated with one or two tiny changes from book to book. He'll also repeat specific rhymes. I love these various small and large repetitions. Still, as a filmmaker and film viewer, I find myself less tolerant of cinematic repetition.

AF: We could consider a film like Hollis Frampton's *Zorn's Lemma*, where the main part begins by tracking alphabetical letters on street signs and labels, then gradually substitutes arbitrary/intuitive icons for letters, like "X" get replaced by burning logs. P becomes a meat grinder. Frampton runs through the alphabet 26 times. Does that type of structuralist cinematic repetition interest you? Or, more generally on how your filmmaking experience shapes your poetic practice: even the most straightforward, narrative-based film seems close to collage—splicing scenes, constructing rhythm through the repetition of establishing shots, tracking shots.

NT: I remember Hal Hartley saying in an interview that he hates the establishing shot, that it doesn't establish anything. I took from this the idea that you should jump right into your subject. And my film practice has become much more formalized in the past three years. I've wanted to make films since I was a kid, though didn't move in that direction until a video program started at my high school. I had a great teacher who gave us the fundamentals: how to use a camera, how to edit, basic techniques for working with actors. Then in 2001 a friend and I found ourselves in a dot-com boom-bust situation, got laid off, and received severance packages. She asked if I wanted to make a film, so I took a directing course at the New School, a four-week class. Afterwards we adapted a Denis Johnson monologue-like poem called "Talking Richard Wilson Blues, by Richard Clay Wilson." It played at some festivals. I wrote a script, but didn't do anything with it, then went back to writing poems. I didn't see any relationship between these two projects except in some surface way. Still, when my wife and I moved to Iowa City four years ago, I applied to the film program, because it emphasized experimental approaches to documentary and essayistic film. So during my first semester, as I started really to understand how video works, I began to see a relationship between my poems and my films, between my artistic and life practices—how I absorbed and retained, for example, my interactions with others, my internal dialogues. I sensed I could make visual sequences and create audio soundtracks that mirrored what happened in my poems: repetition, layering, erasure, found text. *Palm Trees* doesn't offer any endnotes, but a fair bit of found text appears in the book. Sometimes I use quotation marks with no attribution. Sometimes I just incorporate phrases. Similarly, most of my video work adopts found footage, combining loops and beats from multiple sources.

AF: Back to what you said about *Palm Trees* containing a discrete series, can we talk more about how sequence shapes this book's meaning? By the time I get to "Agony & X," I begin to wonder if *Palm Trees* contains some backstory that it tries to leave behind, or if that figment derives from me projecting significance onto the progress from one poem to the next. As you assembled this overall book, did you discover and/or construct new textures and resonances through these broader movements?

NT: Yeah, I really hope so. That's the challenge posed by a book which offers no obvious project. Projects seem easier for a critic to discuss, for an audience to grasp, for a press to push. And while I didn't worry about critical reception, here I began to think about the reader—really just my wife, the poet Robyn Schiff. I have other very fine readers who helped me finish this book. And I've begun to write for my family a bit, without consciously thinking about it. They all will read the book and want to discuss it. But Robyn helped me to shape the emotional narratives, to track the particular points and locators for them, the anecdotes or incidents or isolated words that construct a timeline from my earliest moments to now. I used to include more office poems for instance, having worked in various cubicles for a decade.

AF: I'd wanted to ask about some funny office lines, such as "DIY salad already / lost its luster."

NT: I wrote a lot on company time. For part of this I worked for the Poetry Foundation, so that seemed OK. I figured if I got busted they would know I was writing a poem. But too many office poems would push this book in a different direction. I really see it as a series of discrete sequences, a nod to the obliquely confessional (though from this boyish voice you mentioned), which speaks to family and my complicated relationships with them, especially with my brother, who's a great friend of mine—trying to address such topics while avoiding some kind of didactic or sentimental poem. There also might be a trajectory of anger in the book.

AF: Or the implication, if one wants to pick it up. You could find that pattern.

NT: Facing myself down, then coming back at that anger and those basic struggles provide the main trajectory. Though I hope this isn't an angry book. It isn't.

AF: The pattern I mentioned only pokes through gradually, provisionally.

NT: That's my goal. Perhaps you can take away lines from specific pieces, but that broader resonance remains my biggest aim—developing a larger mood or tone through the juxtaposition of these disparate poems.

### INTERVIEW WITH SOPHIA KARTSONIS AND CYNTHIA ARRIEU-KING
Recorded on June 14, 2012
This interview focuses on Kartsonis and King's chapbook *By Some Miracle a Year Lousy with Meteors* (Dream Horse).

ANDY FITCH: Collaborative books make me obsessed with process. We could start with the poem "Shoe-Tree," even just that phrase "shoe tree." I'll sense two different voices: one mimetic-tending, one more opaque. Of course both could come from a single author, but here I picture two people contributing, amid some primal scene, almost sexual. So where do these poems start for you?

SOPHIA KARTSONIS: Cindy, can you remember? I think that was your line.

CYNTHIA ARRIEU-KING: What's our first poem? The shoe tree poem?

SK: "Shoe-Tree."

CK: Let's try to remember that poem specifically. Didn't you…

SK: Oh god, that seems so long ago.

CK: One Christmas, over break, we started horsing around. We'd written ridiculous emails back and forth about Christmas cookies, then decided we should write a poem. No big discussion happened about how we'd go about this. We just alternated adding to existing lines, then soon gave up finishing whole sentences—leaving that as the other person's problem.

SK: We didn't plan to write a book, or even a poem that first time. One of us probably suffered a sugar low or nervous breakdown and the other kept kidding around. That's all we need for our collaborations.

AF: So you'd begin with some line-by-line exchange. I've got a specific question about opening lines. This chapbook offers great ones, which provide a sense of traction, clearing shared space in which to operate. Like for "Into the Celery Doors" I love: "Around the bodega its blunt black awning." From "Fox Shoots Hunter in Belarus": "Red weeds crinkling, a back taken up mountainous."

CK: For the first poem you mentioned I think I started, but honestly I can't remember who started that second poem. Once any amount of time passes we can't recall necessarily who did what. This work seems to have come from some other place. I'll sometimes think, that's definitely Sophia. But I'll often be wrong. Poems springboard out of conversations, or internet sites or whatever. We do this bird thing where we're like: look at this shiny object and can't we make something from it?

SK: Exactly right. And you did start "Into the Celery Doors." Initially I couldn't place myself. I loved that opening, since I so admire Cindy's syntactical mysteriousness. We work quite differently. I've collaborated with people where our voices instantaneously grate. With Cindy, this third voice takes hold and we've made the thing and now can't remember. Like for the "Fox" poem, we'll assume Cindy started since that responds to a news article she found. I too will spot something and think, that's a Cindy/Sophia idea, more than a me-alone idea. You can't hog all the best prompts for yourself. It's more as if oh, we could make that awesome.

AF: So had you collected and developed some material independently, before you started collaborating? Or does finding the material create a space that you two enter together?

SK: A different ludicrous-to-serious proportion occurs when I work with Cindy. I mean that in a loving way.

CK: Even with some aesthetic difference between us, we have this overlapping way to look at things. We'll agree that the more absurd and grandiose a story sounds, the more we can mine it for a poem. We see it; we know it. It's like shopping with a friend and saying that dress looks very you, or that dress looks very us.

AF: Nietzsche suggests that people formed corporations to start projects they'd never start on their own. They'd feel intimidated or ashamed or guilty by themselves. What have you tried here that you wouldn't try solo?

SK: Cindy's so brave and intuitive and trusts the reader in a way I don't always. I've sometimes offered what a friend calls "run-on imagery." I'd like to think I've tamed that. Cindy's work employs the minimal amount of words to make an idea come through. So we'll finish a poem with me not quite sure what we've said, and I'll sense it says something pretty cool, but won't know how we did it.

CK: I definitely feel the inverse. In grad school I called Sophia "The Maximalist," because she has this wonderful big vision. Wherever I get stumped she fills out the space with amazing leaps and swoops of thought. We complement each other, with our thinking moved ahead in the process.

AF: You attended school together?

CK: Tell the man, Sophia.

SK: The University of Cincinnati's PhD program.

AF: Do you want to describe how you met? Did it take a while before you started collaborating? Could that only begin once you lived far apart?

SK: Of course this sounds cheesy, but I remember the minute Cindy walked in. I was… a year ahead? Did it work that way?

CK: I think so.

SK: Yeah, OK. She joined us for lunch. I first saw her in the hall at Cincinnati, wearing this fabulous green t-shirt. I refer back to that as "the moment" since it stays so vivid, as if the little-girl portion of me wanted to grab her by the shoulders and say, "You will be my friend." It felt that instant. Then her poems, I loved her poems. But I couldn't imagine she'd want to write with me because we did such different things—which helps explain why it works, I think. Also, in terms of background, we have immigrant fathers, this work ethic we'd both learned and resisted. But the conversation started over lunch and opened into humorous exchanges, which later took the form of emails, which produced the kind of one-liners that led to this chapbook.

CK: Sophia's incredibly witty. Basically I'll just want to hear what Sophia ends up saying about some of these subjects. But I also find it interesting, Sophia, that you've mentioned work ethic because I remember sending these poems to places where we wouldn't have submitted on our own. Or places we previously did not get in. We'd be slightly begrudging the magazines for this. Still I'd send our poems and they started getting taken. Then we continued writing them sort of distractedly. We kept playing and didn't have this work ethic going where we tried to reinvent the wheel, or earn an A. We goofed around and ended up places we couldn't have reached consciously trying.

AF: Well, in terms of what's conscious and unconscious here, alliteration and assonance often seem to shape the poems' trajectories. Do these aspects provide some stabilizing structure or momentum—the way jazz improvisation happens amid a tightly woven structure? I can give a couple examples. Again, from "Into the Celery Doors": "Iron-scent / touches the ticket-edge before a run down stairs: / the dream of monotony gone, heads ascending / to some nightish-above." Or lines like: "I have pressed my liver between panes of glass like / a souvenir shop wild aster." I'll also note many "I"-driven assertions, anaphoric constructs. Do you deliberately and/or intuitively establish sound parameters in which multiple voices can bounce around?

CK: I've definitely had moments when I said to myself: I'm slightly overwhelmed here; I'll just repeat something to give it a direction, though I don't know what direction yet. As far as alliteration and assonance goes, I think we kind of overlap there. Or you know how you'll interject and take on the accent of the person you talk to a bit, just as this ball you pass back and forth.

sk: I like what Cindy said about how, work ethic aside, these poems came from the desire to play with a friend. I didn't know if they seemed good, whatever I might mean by that. And I certainly didn't think in terms of marketability. Sometimes I'd try to write a pretty line or one with strange sound repetitions because I wanted my friend to say oh, that's cool—or that I was "bringing it" to our poem. So we'll play, but playing at a level that includes respect and admiration for the other person as poet.

af: You're both polite. Everyone else I interview gives much longer answers, but I'll sense you leaving space for each other. And repetition, within this chapbook, occurs in less obvious ways as well—suggesting a call-and-response-based enterprise. This could take the form of list making, or repeated constructions. I remember: "A cool green gate to pass under, a cool green pill / and bliss." Or "A bamboo grove / of guesses: Should I be on this side, or the other?" I'll sense a seam where the poem got passed from one person to the next. But do such seams really track your collaborative process, or have you shaped them to hint at, to depict a polyvocal performance?

ck: I hope my students don't hear this, but I don't think we've consciously thought that through. How about you, Sophia?

sk: I didn't think so at the time, but am realizing, at least with some of those examples, that when I'd try to get my bearings with Cindy's lines but wasn't quite sure, or if I wanted to leave room for her to explore a thought, I might offer a restatement or make that list move—which allowed her either to expand the list or elaborate on what she'd wanted to say. I'd think, let's leave a couple doors open in case she hasn't finished exploring that, or in case she wants to riff for a minute on further possibilities.

af: That's great. In "Windshelf," we find: "Feeling buoyed up, in fall, the maple leaves a library / that dandelion spores pause against / before starrily descending // to where you are sitting." I'll think I hear one poet opening a description that the other extends, then the first takes someplace else, then the other does, all amid luxurious syntactical profusion.

CK: Most likely that happened. We write the poem then don't fiddle much after. Somebody sends an email that says, I think that's the end.

AF: Still, I couldn't help but assume this project required careful editing. In my own experience, editing often becomes the most difficult part to perform collaboratively. For some sense of stylistic unity, even a disparate unity, even an inconsistent tone, you'll need a coherent vibe to keep it all together.

CK: We'd maybe cut one word here and there. One poem about a girl in a closet got worked to death.

SK: I remember, early on, Cindy started going back and editing up to the current line, treating the whole poem as if editing on her own. This became kind of cool because I'd read through then go, no—I want to change that back. And by editing I mean tiny things. But enough to switch a word, or she might have caught a tense shift. Soon I got in a similar habit. So by the time somebody's email said "Done?" we probably were.

CK: Those edits I made without asking seem obnoxious. But Sophia would just restore things or say, how about this? Then she'd do what she wanted to do. More explanation, more debating might take all the energy and fun out of the process.

SK: I think it does. Here we both could have a loose grip. I can't collaborate with everyone and make that assumption, since people… even poets open to collaboration can get touchy in a way Cindy doesn't.

AF: Back to the question of what you got away with here: for your individual poems, could you edit this loosely and minimally?

SK: That's not how it goes with my work. I don't trust my first gaze enough to consider a piece finished or polished.

CK: I don't know. I haven't thought about it much. I do keep a pretty loose grip on my poems. I like that phrase of Sophia's. It makes sense with what we do. With my own work, I'll try something which resembles moving furniture around. But I wouldn't move a stanza with these poems.

AF: Did you feel a need to preserve the interpersonal exchange? Would more elaborate editing destroy that? Do you seek to provide some constructivist sense of how this finished project got put together?

CK: I want to keep a sense of fun. Sophia's able to sound lighthearted and grave at the same time, and this helps to show that we are playing. She brings that. Sometimes I feel like the guy tightening the screws. But I don't need readers to treat these poems as events or happenings, or footprints of what we've done. I'd like if our poems even could disguise themselves as poems by one person. What do you think, Sophia?

SK: First of all, Cindy's selling herself short, because there's absurd intelligence in the shorthand imagery she brings to our poems. She'll create the staccato that…in one of my own poems I might strive for fluidity, whereas here the music sounds harmoniously discordant—pleasing to my ear because it's not a pretty pretty bolt of shiny cloth. It's this crazy quilt that doesn't even limit itself to fabric, but includes tin cans, starfish and whatnot. That's Cindy. Those lists of…

CK: Can't we have it all? That would be me.

SK: Though then the poem breaks and moves to something else. And that break, that catch in the poem's throat—with my own poems I might ask, why this hiccup in the middle of the poem? But in our collaborations, poems punctuate themselves then move toward another plot in a way I find dynamic.

AF: Are there, for you both, collaborative duos you had seen, particular projects you read that gave a sense of license, of how this could operate?

SK: We should go on record as collaboration whores. We both have worked with a number of people, right? And I had seen the performance of Joshua…

AF: Matt Rohrer and Joshua Beckman?

SK: Yes. They came to Alabama. I found that much more courageous than I could be, because it happened on the spot. But with us, I didn't even think in the realm of poetry when we began. It felt more like chats, emails, keeping up a conversation in which we tried to stop each other from crying or made each other laugh or planned the next great food adventure.

CK: I definitely heard those collaborations back in 2000 something, at the Juniper Institute at UMASS. But also I loved not just the New York School poets, but hearing about New York School poets, about how much poetry became a part of their lives. Many people took inspiration from those ways of riffing off each other and competing in this funny way with each other. I've done challenges with Matt Hart and Hillary Gravendyk. And I've written some poems with Mathias Svalina. I'm sure there's many more. Then I always return to work with Sophia and it's just, you know, it doesn't feel like a trick. It seems something we do together, a pastime.

AF: One question about form. Until "Planet Plaint," near this chapbook's end, every poem seems to fit a relatively familiar shape of couplets or free verse stanzas. Did other types of spatial variety, of formal variety, just seem unnecessary? Could you describe your sense of the space in which a collaborative poetics resides?

SK: Well there's the joke about a poet's first book needing to work through all required forms, just to show us you can. Even within my own manuscripts I'll think, do the shapes and styles change enough? But again, the fun of assembling this chapbook was at first we didn't know we'd be gathering poems. I don't remember feeling very strategic about what their forms would be. If we decide to go with a larger book, we might try mixing that up a bit. We have 20 poems not included here. As many as that?

CK: At least 10 or 15.

SK: In part or in whole. Some seem quite different, presenting their own challenges.

CK: I think we maybe did one prose poem and felt funny not having line breaks.

AF: Here many phrases get hyphenated.

CK: That's Sophia. If I see a hyphenated phrase I'll think, there's Sophia. Sophia comes at life with all this joy and thinks if we can make something new out of what we know, then let's just do so and that will be our way. Sophia has this charming way of feeling like you're her person or something. She endears people to her by generating a common language or common set of terms. I'd assume most hyphens come from that.

SK: Thanks for pretending I didn't blow the whole thing.

AF: I'll sense concord or compromise (in the best possible sense—like "composition"). But back to Cindy detecting Sophia's presence: does an autobiographical "I" ever enter these poems, and what happens from there?

CK: I can't remember if "The Small Anything City" made it into this chapbook.

SK: We had to pull it.

CK: That's right. There we both use "I" and become each other as "I." We fluidly slip back and forth between separate autobiographical inspirations.

SK: Sometimes this "I" carries a wink-wink inside joke, with one of us knowing the other means it ironically. Interestingly, for the "Kathy Coles" poem, Kathy started off as Cindy King. Cindy found it incredibly—she's just too humble. She would not let it stand. I loved it.

CK: It seemed strange to have a poem called "Cindy Kings" with you one of the people writing this poem. You know, like when you watch a movie and want to know what's really real. I preferred it to show this weird way people become so tied together with their little name, which they didn't come up with. And the person we named the poem after, Kathy Cole—she lived a real-life nightmare where a person in town had the same name as her, the same birthday, and their fathers had the same name. It took them years to realize they had the same social security number. That all created a giant mess. I thought she deserved to have her name atop the poem.

AF: So Kathy Cole is two people, rather than one.

SK: Plus she's a delight.

AF: On the topic of how much you two get individuated in this book, how do you perform pieces live? Do they make for better embodied exchange or better reading?

sk: Here's a confession: we don't know yet how to read them. I'm thrilled to face that prospect, because it means I'll get to see Cindy.

ck: Did we maybe perform one at Publico, in Cincinnati? I think we read back and forth and did this weird thing where I tried to remember who'd wrote what, then it seemed ridiculous, so we just said screw that. But what you've done here, Andy, is to make us excited by that prospect.

sk: That's what we plan to do tomorrow.

af: Do you also appreciate the idea of an individual reader having to choreograph or orchestrate this whole scene in his or her head, without any bodily point of reference?

ck: These poems seem incredibly visual and compacted. So they do, I think, make good on-the-page poems. Especially for "By Some Miracle a Year Lousy with Meteors": I think that poem's ending really does something particular when you read it on the page. I almost wish we could run a scientific test, where certain participants know these poems are collaborative, but the control group thinks one person wrote them. I'd love to know how confused that control group gets.

sk: I kind of hope for readers to have the response Cindy and I feel when one of us says, "Done?" and we've got this incredible ending which takes you by surprise. I want a reader not to know where these voices begin and end, but just feel a cool chorus happening.

af: Should we stop there?

ck: I think I'm good. I did want to say I felt inspired to collaborate by seeing two male poets (who will remain nameless) read together, and they had tons of fun, and I had this little thought like, why do all the boy poets get to do this thing? Fuck that. I want to find a friend and write poems and eventually perform them, and have our own fun. That's something I thought of today as we went along.

af: Sophia?

sk: Oh no—that's a great way to end.

## INTERVIEW WITH GARY SULLIVAN
Recorded on June 16, 2012
This interview focuses on Sullivan's translations of Ernst Herbeck for the chapbook *Everyone Has a Mouth* (Ugly Duckling Presse).

ANDY FITCH: You've offered a compelling biography of Ernst Herbeck, both in this chapbook and your forthcoming *Tripwire* article. Though then you end the *Tripwire* piece by stating that you wish you could read Herbeck's work in the original. Haven't you, as the translator, done just that? Of course Herbeck's originals may exist in his notecards. And more generally, Herbeck seems to embody both this raw, naïve, authentic poet, and some sort of a literary figment—an institutionally contextualized curiosity for the Austrian public who first encounters him as the mental patient Alexander, in the clinical study *Schizophrenia and Language*. But what else might it mean to read this work in the original, especially given that, for contemporary readers, Herbeck's color poems perhaps recall Rimbaud and Trakl? Or that his short, elliptical lyrics with titles such as "The Panther" point to Blake at some moments, Celan at others? The typographical tics can seem similar to Saroyan, Zaum, Dickinson's fascicles. His schizophrenic Teutonic idiom sounds a bit like Robert Walser, or Adolf Wölfli. But so where would we find the original for Herbeck, and who reads it?

GARY SULLIVAN: Here we could start with the fact that Herbeck gets born the same year as Celan. Their lives of course look quite different. Celan grows up Jewish in Romania. Herbeck lives as an Austrian in Austria. But both remain cultural outsiders in terms of how they shape language. Their highly idiosyncratic idioms also share brevity. For Herbeck, this brevity comes as a consequence of format—with Leo Navratil, Herbeck's head clinician, handing him a three-by-five card and announcing a topic such as "red," "blue," "yellow." Herbeck's poems arise through that circumstance of someone asking him to write about a specific topic in a limited space. Navratil later gives Herbeck large pieces of paper, which produce longer responses that seem less focused. Some operate more as lists. Unfortunately I didn't have room here to include one of those fascinating list texts. But I love, for instance, his "Ten Pieces of Advice for Doctors," which includes the tips: don't institute childishness; don't denature the mouth. Then returning to your first question, I have no fluency in German. When I mention wanting to read this work in the original, I mean to understand Herbeck without first having to translate him.

AF: Well when I read a poem such as "Timeless Writing." ("The earth, the volcano and the hum- / ming of the bee are the timeless writing / also migratory birds. The vibration of / ants"), I love the piece, and admire the translation with its abrupt "also." Though if this poem appeared in some conventional nature-writing venue I don't know if I'd take it seriously. Or if we think of Herbeck as working for the Nazi cause, does that change our perception of the poem? Herbeck's bio seems an instant folk-art classic—so that even as his poems stun me, I wonder about the extent to which I project my own desires onto them. Could you discuss your personal relationship with Herbeck, past and present?

GS: I agree that the biography seems inescapable, with Herbeck as with anyone. I'll tell you how I found Herbeck's book. In 2003 in Paris, just down the hill from Sacré-Coeur, at the Musée d'Art Naïf, devoted to art brut, I spotted a squat volume titled *Ernst Herbeck: 100 Poems*, with en face French translation. Because I'd taken a bit of German and now had enjoyed this trip to France, I just thought, these look simple and short—maybe I can learn some French and reestablish some German. So when I returned to the States, I began buying dictionaries and word books and trying to regain some German. I learned more about Herbeck's biography. I found it easier to translate *100 Poems*'s introduction, because that had relatively normal syntax. Then I decided I'd basically do a Joseph Ceravolo version of the poems (Herbeck's pieces felt short and odd in a similar way). The short-lived online journal *Fascicle* published a dozen of them. People gave me positive feedback, so I continued with this idea of not precisely rendering the poems but rather privileging the literal situation Herbeck encountered when he wrote them, of receiving a topic and just getting it down quickly without revision. When I didn't understand a passage I'd make it up, playing on sound or other cues. I played around with Google's translator. It took about a year to translate 150 poems. Then one night Brandon Downing invited me to this Russian movie with a bunch of his friends, including Eugene Ostashevsky. Eugene's longtime partner, Oya Ataman, originally from Turkey though then living in Munich, happened to be visiting him. After the movie, I heard Oya say something in German. I had the Herbeck book with me because I'd been working on it before the film. I showed Oya the book and she read "The Dream." and then a couple more and couldn't believe it. She said they had this weird, gothic, haunted feeling with something slightly off—a bit naïve but also playful. So Oya and I started meeting, at first to discuss my translations, though we wound up collaborating on a huge swath of them. Oya works with the deaf. She's fluent in sign language and comfortable working among people who live with disabilities. And of course Herbeck had a severe cleft lip and palate for which he underwent several operations, never to complete satisfaction. This may have caused him great embarrassment or shame, given his difficulties with speech. Who knows how all of that related to his schizophrenia? But the only major piece of writing on Herbeck, in English, comes from a German academic and translator, Gregor Hens, at Ohio State. Hens published this long, not quite excoriation, but strongly critical analysis of Herbeck's work, "What drives Herbeck? Schizophrenia, immediacy, and the poetic process," addressing exactly what your first question...

AF: Herbeck reception or something?

GS: He presents Herbeck as more of a public spectacle than a poetic genius. He breaks down several poems line-by-line, attributing Herbeck's linguistic moves...

AF: He basically diagnoses Herbeck.

GS: Right. Oya pointed out that Hens completely misses Herbeck's humor. These dark, dissociative poems certainly have their sharp wit. We don't laugh at Herbeck's incomprehensibility. We sense a poignant editorial slant. Herbeck acknowledges, for example, Germany's involvement in the war. He worked for a while in a munitions factory. He saw Hitler when Hitler came. At least he remembered seeing him. Herbeck's poem "Adolf" begins "Adolf// is a werewolf-name name." Oya and I tried for a more direct translation of the poems than I'd been doing alone. I have no problem with that great American poetic tradition of false translations and fucking around, but with Herbeck I decided that accuracy seemed more worthwhile, given how unknown his work remains in this country. And new online possibilities have helped—such as *LEO*, a German-language dictionary and forum where you can ask questions, or this other site I used that focuses specifically on Austrian German. The amount of German-language material online has exploded since 2003. Eventually I could look up any phrase (or portion of a phrase) in Herbeck's poetry, and have a good sense if and how it deviated from normative German usage. Then when Oya visited Eugene for a second time, we began another round of translations. I think we did maybe 100-150 together. Including my solo efforts, I've worked on translating 300-400 poems now. I started a blog (since taken down) posting every piece from Herbeck's collected works, in order, and if I'd done a translation I would post that translation alongside the original German. I asked readers to point out problems in the translations. My friend Ekkehard Knörer, a film critic who runs a magazine called *Cargo* out of Berlin, jumped in a couple times and made significant enough suggestions that I credit him as co-translator for a couple poems. I hope to keep working with people on this.

AF: I note that even after you wrote an extensive record of translating "The Cigarette.," for example, you've gone back and made more changes to that piece. Could you discuss this ongoing revision process? Would you characterize it as orderly and intentional, chaotic and compulsive? And do the digital developments you've outlined suggest new types of translation projects to come? Do you sense other Herbecks waiting for the right translator and translating tools to find them?

GS: Definitely. In fact the next time I went to Paris, at the same museum, I bought another volume from this same series, *Triumph of the Shocked*, by an outsider poet named Edmund Mach. Many others must exist. And we've all had the experience of comparing multiple translations of a single poet's work and thinking, what the fuck happened? You really see then that translation is not an exact science.

AF: Here could you discuss your revising, restaging, republishing of these ongoing translations? Do you work on one poem at a time? Do multiple poems give you insights into each other?

GS: I have to work on several together. That does help someone with less fluency. And I did write deliberately about translating "The Cigarette.," because I knew that would remain an ongoing process. I sensed this would take numerous attempts, with pauses in between. But yes, the process might seem chaotic. I definitely wouldn't call it systematic. When I had the blog I did a good job, working on it every day—until I decided to try and get it published as a book. And in truth I've never considered Herbeck a primary project. I'll work on any number of things. I have too many projects. My multi-tasking day job as a managing editor seeps into my process of managing multiple poems, plays, comics, art reviews, album reviews, and now my music blog and these translations. I constantly need to engage something new and separate from myself to feel fully happy and alive.

AF: If we look at the poem "Language." ("a + b glow in the clover. / Flowers at the edge of the field. / Language. — / Language is fallen for the animal. / and strikes the a of sound. / the c merely zips around and / is also briefly its / rifle"), can you describe factors in the original that determined this particular translation? Did the symbols "a + b" appear in the original? Does the subsequent dash hint at a minus symbol? Do the italicized "a" and "c" somehow mirror the "a + b" phrase? Have you followed the poem's original lineation?

GS: Yes, I've formatted it to resemble the original. Herbeck uses a plus sign. He uses a dash after the minus sign. The later "a" and "c" do get italicized in print, although I suspect Herbeck underlined them in his handwritten piece. And the word "rifle" comes from the German word "Gewehr," which means gun, not rifle. Oya said I should use "gun." But "Gewehr" contains two syllables, and I wanted to keep that feeling and sound. I first translated this on my own, then worked with Oya. My original had "language is smitten by the animal" or something. We chose "fallen for," which sounds closer to the original German, "verfallen."

AF: Also a weird tense shift happens. "Is fallen" sounds confusing in a good way.

GS: It echoes the original's murkiness. Or if you turn to the end of "The Dream." ("the The Day is the dream / and the beam is the dream"), the original German says, "der Baum ist der Traum." "Baum," of course, means tree. The first translation I published used "tree." Then I changed it to "beam," because I realized Herbeck chose "baum" not to say "tree," but to add an "aum" sound. He basically just switched letters around. And of course, in terms of the English, wooden beams do come from trees. That similarity made my choices seem more faithful to the original—though either way I've felt the need to capture surface-level phenomena.

AF: One question also about this chapbook's overall arrangement. Given your introductory remarks on Herbeck's cleft lip and palate, your project's title, your interest in a previous translator's coinage of the verb "to demouth," the conspicuous length of the poem "The Mouth." becomes all the more conspicuous here. Have you positioned "The Mouth." as some sort of muted ars poetica for Herbeck?

GS: I did choose the title *Everyone Has a Mouth*, which gets taken from that poem, in part to foreground the original trauma of Herbeck being born with cleft lip and palate. Broader questions of course arise in terms of mental illness, of authorship and agency. Navratil helped pioneer the idea that institutionalized people have an aesthetic contribution to make. He remained sensitive enough and caring enough to see his patients as human beings with a perspective and point of view and something to say. I don't consider him a sensationalist by any stretch. And "The Mouth." does seem central, as well as emblematic of my translation process. "The Mouth." also demonstrates several characteristic Herbeck traits. He often uses reversals. Here he starts with "Not everyone has a mouth / some mouth is disqualified," though then adds "the doctor says everyone has / a mouth," then proceeds to describe the properties of this mouth—a descriptive mode common in these poems. He'll tell you something's purpose.

AF: Again as if completing an assignment.

GS: Exactly. Yet then he veers off toward this whole fanciful consideration of the lips and "phroat" (Herbeck writes "Nachen," which means "dinghy," but in context this suggests Nacken, or "neck"—so we came up with "phroat," which allowed us to hint at both "boat" and "throat"). The teeth, the jaws…though then also the nose might belong to this mouth. In Herbeck's case, of course, his mouth probably did extend up to his nose at first. But then also the earflaps. The index finger. All gets funneled into the mouth, into the voice. This poem creates its own whirlpool—with everything funneling down to one spot, one originary mouth and trauma.

AF: Along similar lines, how did you determine what went into this collection? Do you consider these Herbeck's greatest hits? Do they provide a representative sample, a slice of time or particular cluster of themes or tones? Do you plan to publish subsequent volumes? Does part of this chapbook's allure come from it seeming so small—echoing your own first fleeting glimpse of the poet?

GS: I sent Ugly Duckling a manuscript of about 100 poems. This project seemed very much up their alley. Katherine Bogden selected

26 poems, sent me the selection and said, what do you think? I liked it but added four more, for a round 30. Then I switched the first and second poems' order, because though "The Dream." appears first in every single book, with "Morning." appearing second, Navratil has written numerous times about "Morning." as Herbeck's first poem. So I put it first and "The Dream." second, and that was that. I wanted to include the original German poems so people could see what I'd done and make their own judgments. Ugly Duckling applied for a grant for these extra pages and I think wound up getting one. This chapbook appears in their "Lost Literature" series, "Lost Literature # 10."

AF: Since for Ugly Duckling this would be a legitimate question, how did the format get determined? Did you consider trying something like Herbeck's original notecards? UDP has published, for instance, Craig Foltz's *The States*. Or Susan Schultz's *Memory Cards* come to mind. Shouldn't notecards get more respect by this point in history—after Wittgenstein, Pessoa, Nabokov, and given what digital publication allows?

GS: That never occurred to me. I did think about reproducing some of the original handwritten work, as other editions have. But for this chapbook that seemed too much.

AF: Yeah I guess I mean, more generally, does no Herbeck poem exist independently of those initial notecards?

GS: You could say that. The cards contain Herbeck's expressive capitalization and punctuation. And the cards present their own mysteries, though obviously I can't go all Susan Howe on this project, since I just don't know German well enough. Herbeck's handwriting remains difficult to read even for a native speaker. For me it becomes impossible. I've had to rely on the collected poems, published in 1992—the year after his death.

AF: Did much work, for whatever reason, not make it into that collection?

GS: Yes. The Austrian National Library has over 1200 poems. The Collected Poems contains perhaps 500. A few stray pieces have appeared elsewhere. So we'll see what happens. Herbeck became very, very popular during his lifetime. A bigger book still might come out.

AF: Could we close with you discussing your own advocacy for people with disabilities, and if/how this factors into your appreciation of Herbeck?

GS: Well, my father was diagnosed with muscular dystrophy when I was a child, before my teens. He used a cane, then a wheelchair, and then a scooter. How my father responded to others, and his own self-image, shaped my awareness, while growing up, of people living with disabilities. And now I work for the National Multiple Sclerosis Society—a degenerative nerve disease (not muscular, though people consider these brother and sister diseases). So that's just been my life. Does it make me more attuned to Herbeck than I otherwise might have been? Perhaps. Also, a friend committed suicide in 2001. I didn't realize at first that psychiatrists had diagnosed him as either bi-polar or schizophrenic. He stayed lucid most of the time I hung out with him. Sometimes he suddenly would have to leave. In the middle of a dinner or coffee he'd abruptly say, I've got to go. So I sensed something. Then after he died, I attended the funeral and met his family and talked on the phone with his sister for a while, and realized the extent of what he had dealt with for much of his life. He heard voices. He kept notebooks in which he would write in order to keep these voices out. I just watched the Roky Erickson movie, if you've seen that. He sits in this room with all kinds of electronics turned on in part, it seems, to block the voices. To us it looks chaotic, but to him it probably feels relaxing (my guess, because he falls asleep).

AF: As I ask about disabilities, I think of Flarf—as a poetics that contests the solitary, self-reliant identity of the poet.

GS: I first thought of Flarf in relation to Tourette's, and doing or saying what you're not supposed to do or say. I pictured a person I knew in Minneapolis, a singer who, when speaking, often would bust out these long streams of clicking noises. To us this person's expression might seem to have no context, but to her it might. Right or wrong, I wanted to validate that. For me, Flarf became a way of validating language not valid within any poetics when we began.

## INTERVIEW WITH JEN HOFER
Recorded on June 17, 2012
This interview focuses on Hofer's book *Laws* (Dusie).

ANDY FITCH: Here and elsewhere you've referred to Lyn Hejinian's formulation of the person as "mobile (and mobilized) reference point." Could you describe how that notion has helped shape your manuscript—perhaps in terms of its sequences, sections, patterned units, and the repeated, redacted, rearranged language that accrues as the project progresses?

JEN HOFER: I'm not sure whether I'll decide to change my epigraphs, though I do feel quite attached to that *Language of Inquiry* quote, especially its final part: "there is a world and the person is in it." I feel a responsibility (sometimes excitement, sometimes dread, but always a responsibility) to respond directly or indirectly, abstractly or concretely (usually some combination) to the world, and to create writing that will enter this world. And to me Lyn's phrase about a mobile/mobilized reference point resembles Pierre Joris' conception of a nomad poetics—with both a physical and conceptual sense of the nomadic. Information now travels this way, as intellectual and physical boundaries become simultaneously porous and at times impermeable. So that epigraph says, in part "There is no self undefiled by experience, no self unmediated in the perceptual situation"—that is, no matter how much we might want to "get it right," we can't, and *Laws* can't, because the book both contemplates memory and presents a memory, and memory always fails. In my personal and poetic life, I tend to shut down when I get concerned about right and wrong, as if anyone could live in that dichotomy. Instead I mean for questions of mobility to raise questions of agency, autonomy, choice—who has these and who does not? Who gets moved around like an object? Or what does mobility mean for people who have never left their hometown? What does mobility become for someone incarcerated, someone forced to emigrate out of fear or intimidation, someone who simply can't afford (in all the different senses of that term) to become nomadic in the ways I've just posited?

AF: On these questions of agency and mobility, I love how your book not only complicates the autonomy of its first-person "I," but also foregrounds the active, evolving role of the reader. From your "Dear Reader" piece onwards, various overlapping forms of address appear: in terms of the poems' functions as letters sent to an ambiguous home, or from Mexico to New Mexico, or as personal and collective "reminders." Amid these kaleidoscopic possibilities, does the reader likewise become a mobile/mobilized reference point? Does the reader face questions of what it means to be a person in the world? Do you wish for your reader sometimes to feel like a whirling individual immersed in an overwhelming scene, sometimes like an all-encompassing world unto herself—in which these disparate narrative trajectories can cohere?

JH: To be honest, I have no specific wish for readers, except for the reader to do what she pleases. Though here my previous book *one* comes to mind. *one* uses epigraphs to signal my thoughts to the reader. When a long, dense, abstracted text contains at its top a concrete quote, saying, for instance, that we consider all Iraqis guilty until proven otherwise, then you know to think about the U.S. military presence as you read the poem. You can choose to ignore the quote but it still sits there, with you ignoring it. I don't provide those same pointers in this new manuscript. I feel less attached to what precisely the reader does, than to the simple fact that a reader does something. It interests me what that could be. Perhaps here I invite readers to think about repetition and mutation and ways that different experiences or forms of language fold in on themselves and become indistinguishable yet stay somehow distinct.

AF: In terms of what you've described as a nomadic poetics (again both for writer and reader) have particular projects shaped your interest here in paratactic phrasings, repeated lines and palimpsestic constructions? Hejinian's *My Life* captions came up for me. Ted Berrigan's *Sonnets* perhaps. I'm also curious what women authors shape your sense of how to write about a city. And we probably should cover J.W. Dunne.

JH: Right. I should add I've been working sporadically on this manuscript since late 1999. Thankfully I've completed other projects in the interim.

AF: You've done much.

JH: Never enough, I would say. But so I began this in 1999 and 2000. I added a bunch in 2003-2004. Then I worked on it, I promised myself for the final time, during the summer of 2008. And now here in

2012 I need to finish the proofs. I mention all this just to suggest that some writers who now influence me (on how to write about a city, about being a foreigner who also has come home) hadn't published their books when I started *Laws*. But the primary "text" I read at first, for the sequence "of deaths, days, futures, nations" (which started as 25 25-line poems, scattered throughout the manuscript), was Mexico City, with its enormous, cacophonous, language-saturated sense of simultaneity and inexhaustibility. I'd also read extensively for what became *Sin puertas visibles: An Anthology of Contemporary Poetry by Mexican Women,* which I translated and edited a couple of years later. Still, none of that work directly influenced my poetic practice in the way, say, that Lyn Hejinian, Leslie Scalapino, Harryette Mullen, Muriel Rukeyser or Myung Mi Kim do. I could add many names. But in some sense, what I perceived as a tendency toward direct speech, a lack of cacophony in what I read at that time, pushed me in an opposite direction. Much of the Mexican writing I was reading felt wonderfully foreign—and not just because Spanish is my step-mother tongue (to borrow a phrase from Cristina Rivera Garza). Rather than reflect on U.S. poetry, I spent almost all my reading time with journals and unpublished manuscripts by Mexican women writers.

AF: Looking back, what books did appear in the U.S. at this time, addressing questions similar to those raised in *Laws*?

JH: You could find some similarities in Bhanu Kapil's *Incubation* or *Humanimal*, or Renee Gladman's writing in *The Activist*, but also in her Ravicka series. I would say Kaia Sand's writing in *Remember to Wave*, or Craig Santos Perez's installments from *Unincorporated Territory,* or Allison Cobb's *Green-Wood,* and I could go on. I found certain examinations of place really powerful, such as C.S. Giscombe's books *Into and Out of Dislocation* and *Giscome Road.* More generally, I think of my work as existing in conversation with what we might call documentary poetics—and if *Laws* documents anything it documents my own life. Again *My Life* greatly influenced me by presenting a process-based work, by examining one's relationship to language as a primary aspect of being in the world, by suggesting that the first-person and a distanced, abstracted subjectivity can co-exist. But I would not choose now to write a book emphasizing my own experience this way. I would start with much more research. This manuscript's research consisted of many many hours walking through Mexico City. To me, *Laws* seems more of a historical document.

AF: Well I assume that by "research" you now mean something more like literary or historical or archival research. What makes such research seem more appealing or worthwhile than the immersive experience you've just described?

JH: Perhaps that it's external to me, and proposes an expansive engagement of the person with the world (as opposed to a more limited engagement with the person's experience of the world). Here I think of a text toward the end of *one*, which I've often performed as a live film narration piece, placed alongside collaged clips from the 1955 film *Kiss Me Deadly*. This text tracks various phenomena related to so-called "atomic veterans" in the U.S., who witnessed nuclear detonations at the Nevada nuclear test site, following the atomic bombs dropped on Hiroshima and Nagasaki. One section consists entirely of quotes from these military men. Another focuses on the names of bomb tests, which fascinate me for a number of reasons. These "found" languages, alongside other forms of research, mesh with my "own" language (if we can call language our own) of response to radioactive military practices, historically and presently. Here again I wanted, in part, to demonstrate that there is a world and the poet is a person in it. Poetry exists because I have a problem. We have a problem in this world, and need to talk about it. We need to use poetry or art-making as tools and as lenses, so we can understand the world differently and then act differently. Of course no one right way exists here, which takes me back to a more abstracted sense of personhood, since what's so special about my way to anyone but me and my mother?

AF: To get back to how working on *Sin puertas visibles* altered your approach to writing, can we consider Dolores Dorantes' claim that mainline Mexican poetry remains an officially sanctioned discourse largely limited to confessional verse? Did reading such work in some ways shape this particular book's quasi-biographical trajectory and testimonial or descriptive bent?

JH: Well, I'd keep in mind that many poems in *Laws* originally began as letters to someone I was in love with. I didn't expect to publish them. They had one single recipient/reader. I now can't remember what made me start publishing them, or when I decided to assemble a larger book. At first I hadn't been thinking about poetics, or how reading copious amounts of work that felt foreign to me (with me as the foreigner) might affect my own writing. I just thought: how can I share my experiences with this person who has never been to Mexico City? How can I give her an accurate glimpse?

AF: So the addresses to another become an additional form of self and/or social documentation. Do particular historical events then prompt this book's shift, let's say, from "Laws" to "Laws and Orders"—with "Laws and Orders" foregrounding its closed-captioned discourse of state violence? Also, about halfway through, the book's overall focus seems to veer from thematizations of a multivalent Mexico City, to something more like immigration. Amid the lengthy process of writing *Laws*, does some sort of historical/biographical timeline (however disjointed or collaged) remain present?

JH: Yeah, that sounds about right. I wrote the first 25 poems as letters sent home, not intended for further publication, though *Potes and Poets* did end up making a little chapbook, as part of their A.bacus series, called *Laws*, with drawings by the poems' original recipient, illustrating the effects of Newton's Laws on a sugar cube. I returned to the U.S. and came to Los Angeles in 2002. I bought a completely wrecked house and an Airstream trailer that my partner and I lived in behind the house. We ripped the house down to the studs and rebuilt it while I finished the translations and revisions for *Sin puertas visibles*. Around that time, Paul Vangelisti and Guy Bennett invited me to participate in a project called Lowghost. They asked people to send in-process work, which they would Xerox and send back out. You'd get a packet of everyone's projects, quite simply bound. So that became a wonderful impetus to help me write my way into, or toward, some of the ideas I'd brought back from Mexico City. And of course around 2003 I couldn't avoid addressing war—even more than immigration. Though you're on to something with your references to immigration. Again the book provides a trajectory of personal experience, but with all this horrific, really unimaginable and unimaginably distant violence accumulating and expanding. An air of both endless freedom and endless aggression fueled this book. That title *Laws* serves as a reminder to myself and perhaps readers that we never live separate from the workings of the state. Those delimitations created by structures seeking to define us, even when unperceived, remain forever present. In part I wanted (both by looking backwards and by looking forwards) to recognize those structures and write a new syntax for them.

AF: Well for me, as *Laws*'s repetitions accrue, that title sounds more and more like "loss." Laws attempt to establish and to maintain that which loss allows to seep beyond control.

JH: I like that. When I went to Mexico City, I moved in with a good friend whose partner had recently died of AIDS. I thought about myself as inhabiting this home of a person no longer there. Perhaps some readers will feel that.

AF: We haven't addressed J.W. Dunne. Pieces like "A Pigeon on the Bronze Head of History" provide inexhaustibly pleasurable lists, such as: people with no sense of privacy (border towns: "the worst of both worlds"), people shining shoes (unionized), people feeding pigeons (a tributary system), people selling christmas lights (a mafia system), people selling polyester sweaters (a false system), people squinting (a pigeon with its legs tied), people hobbling (bright metallic polluted sky), people on their way to work (Lucky Lady manufacturers of pants and outfits), people sweeping (a system of sticks without carrots), people praying (imperceptibly).

These lists suggest a drive toward indexical description, toward a cataloguing of all that is present. Yet even as you establish the solid, tangible existence of these figures, you acknowledge a sense of loss in trying to grasp them, a limit to literary representation. Soon the "Laws" sections start to posit an infinite regress of interpretation, a self recognizing itself. I think of your line about how the camera obscura helps us to see seeing, and wonder what role Dunne plays here: specifically in attempts to distinguish between the physical and the sensory, between an immersion in the world and our interpretation of it, between drifting through a city and reading, between tropes of unmediated experience and how these always get problematized by the act of writing.

JH: First, I find Dunne's prose completely amazing. I can't remember how I came across *An Experiment with Time*, but I thought of infinite regression as an echo, an echo that never ends—or the eternal half-life of an image. Those ideas felt so powerful and incredibly accurate in terms of how experience and memory and imagination commingle, forever. Dunne argues that all historical times are simultaneous. Partly I just use his prose as a pleasurable counterpoint to this perspective of an intensely self-conscious self aware of the self, which can continue ad infinitum. This links back to your questions about description and indexical cataloguing. *Laws* does resist any transparent lyric project that might seek to resolve the world's problems through the neat package of a poem. Still I don't think of description as verboten. To me the world seems in some sense made of descriptions. We rely on perception. Though when my descriptive pieces get detached from specific forms and redeployed in new contexts, then redeployed again in yet another context, a difficult type of mapping occurs. I wish I'd made, years ago, a neat and tidy infographic to map the book, if only to foreground further a sense of mobility.

AF: Some dense units of this text feel like material constructs themselves—recalling Anselm Kiefer sculptures of cement and pipes, and city-block stuff. Such sections seem relatively verbless, quite noun-heavy. I remember many Latinate constructions. One "of deaths, days, futures, nations" section contains a single tangible reference (to thumbs), but otherwise consists of "vengeance," "history," "dirge," "parade"—abstracted and/or affective nouns. Then amid these long, obdurate prose blocks will come evocative, elliptical, minimalist asides. Or short sections will follow long sections. Could you discuss such pairings? Do these modular, perspective-based, horizontal-tending oscillations somehow evoke what you describe as the "endless urban"? Or, if this question seems better: what role does the fragment play in your life and your poetics?

JH: Just as a quick aside, Spanish is a Latinate language, and even the English here comes from that world. And I do think of life as made of fragments. I consider disjunction and conjunction equally important. This particular poem you mention starts with the lines, "explanations do I need to need to make order / assimilate animosity invite / social control." Here I ask myself, my reader, the poetic universe, how much do I need to explain? That question has stayed with me my entire writing life. I feel a strong desire to participate in processes of discovery, in appreciations of mystery. But then I also want to teach you how to change the tube on your bicycle tire, or how to sew a book if you want to know. I don't want to seem impenetrable for impenetrability's sake. A place exists for impenetrability, and I certainly don't understand the world. I repeatedly don't understand the world. In writing I try to understand and try to accept (to embrace, even) not understanding. So as I re-read and re-wrote the 28 poems titled "of deaths, days, futures, nations," I experimented with adding a quatrain after each. I think of these as "translations" of the original pieces. Like many poets before me, I consider writing a type of translation. My work often rehearses the same idea a number of times in different words. Of course part of that comes from my returning to these poems much later and trying to understand them, trying to re-approach them and determine if I wish to be with them any more. The quatrains came from that. I didn't want this manuscript to feel like a huge wall of words. Or I meant for that wall to be textured and actually have places to grab onto, to move through. For me these fragments work that way. They create space, literally, physically on the page—but also provide for a more assimilable pause which refracts backwards or forwards, against or toward those more dense pieces, and helps to open little gaps.

AF: Here could you give a glancing account of some frequent motifs? We could start with mafiosos, unfinished train lines, the cold, bluebirds. How do such repetitions track your processes of composition and editing and reformulation?

JH: Well, *Laws* contains so much repetition. Each phrase from the quatrains appears at least twice. So I'm fascinated and delighted that those terms felt, to you, like the ones foregrounding repetition. That says more about you than about the book. And of course my own priorities also change. If I had just begun this project now, it would be entirely different. Though for me, two details always recur: the pressed yellow flowers around the Day of the Dead—that time of year in Mexico City, when I lived with a friend who had just lost a partner. These flowers (cempasúchil or Mexican marigold) and their color immediately call to mind both the material and abstract reality of death.

AF: I thought of *My Life*'s repeated line "A pause, a rose, something on paper."

JH: How funny. I hadn't thought of that but it makes perfect sense. The Mexican poet Tatiana Lipkes just translated *My Life* into Spanish with the title *Mi vida*, put out by this wonderful small press MaNgOs de HaChA. I looked over the manuscript, and we had long conversations about some phrases, and this was one. "A pause, a rose"…in English you have the echo of famous sonnets. You hear "arose" as in rising up (a verb). You have the sonic space between "pause" and "rose," and you also hear "a rose," the flower.

AF: And maybe "eros" as well, like Rrose Sélavy.

JH: You know, as we discuss questions of sound and idiom, I just want to make clear that when I refer to Mexico City, "la ciudad sin fin," as the "endless urban," that's not my phrase. That's like calling New York "The Big Apple."

AF: Yes, even the clichés I've read differently. Your saturated poetics, in Marjorie Perloff's formulation, produce endless difference. Each reader can have an irrevocably distinct experience of this book, and yet know that the book exists in the world, that it gets shared with others, like a city.

JH: Or like presence in general, and the ways memory folds in on itself—as language does. I look back on *Laws* and can't reconstruct my exact process, though I can see it wants to be a processual piece.

AF: I'd wanted to but couldn't formulate that question. I couldn't figure out the grammar for asking something like: is this past tense or present tense?

JH: Yes. Both and neither. I consider most (maybe all) writing constraint-based work, whether the constraints are chosen (through forms we invent, or through following someone else's thinking and vocabulary as we translate) or unchosen (since we are all wartime writers at this point, all subject to a language deployed in the service of institutionalized injustice). Sometimes process-based work can feel like a relief in this oppressive context of informational overwhelm and daily violence. For example, I'm just finishing a project with one year's worth of cut-up poems, titled *Front Page News*. Each day I made a poem using the front page of the newspaper from the place where I woke that morning. And I've just described that project to you in a few simple sentences. That doesn't mean you know all its content or whatever. Still, if I had to provide a similar description for *Laws*, I'd say this book takes the form of an untraceable process, with many digressions. It does fold back on itself, quite consciously using repetition, yet not in the constraint-based way I just described. You can't concisely articulate the form or shape of *Laws*. That seems like part of the project—not so much what I tried to do, but what the work did to me. And then the other point I should make (as a person translating, engaging in public practice, teaching, co-facilitating open conversations on radicalized pedagogy inside and outside of "school," as an artist who does language justice work as part of both social justice and literary work), is that I wanted at least to touch on experiences of discomfort, of being foreign, being away from home, yet not knowing if a home exists anywhere. Also the discomfort of seeing what gets perpetrated in our name here and around the world. Also sensing that what I can articulate in the face of those circumstances remains inadequate to the reality. That feeling permeates my whole relation to this book.

AF: I always feel that inadequacy when a book comes out.

JH: I know. People ask how I plan to celebrate and I'm like, celebrate what?

## INTERVIEW WITH FORREST GANDER AND JOHN KINSELLA
Recorded on June 17, 2012
This interview focuses on Gander and Kinsella's book *Redstart* (University of Iowa Press).

ANDY FITCH: I'm not much interested in classifications of genre or discipline, but given *Redstart*'s early consideration of the efficacy of ecopoetics, I would be curious to hear you two describe this book's primary functions, specifically its positioning of authorial agency. In an early essay Forrest outlines the possibility for a mediated, interactive, relational practice to construct an ongoing textual environment, one that might promote ecological-minded orientations among its audiences. John later provides a thornbill-inspired poetics of the passerine—a process which allows for cross-movement and cross-reference, even as the group internally migrates from place to place, thereby contesting categorical identities without abdicating collective agency. That all makes sense as a theory of this book. But I'm curious of the extent to which you wish for *Redstart*, in Forrest's words, to "make something happen." What would that something be? How does it depart from prevailing conventions in ecopoetics?

FORREST GANDER: That question of authorial stance is one we want to investigate. We hope to break down traditional notions of what authorial agency might mean. John, in writing about collaboration and using a word like "cross-hatched," challenges our assumptions about where authority comes from, challenges the very dialectic of subjectivity and objectivity. This book takes on such work without turning it into a logical exercise. It takes on a formal investigation and adventure.

JOHN KINSELLA: *Redstart* only could be completed collaboratively, for the very reasons Forrest outlined. The whole concept of so-called Western subjectivity gets imbued with concerns of ownership and possession. But here we've attempted to broaden the scale of our collective responsibility. Personally, I don't think there's much purpose to a poetry that doesn't try to make things happen. This world is damaged, and becoming rapidly more damaged. Though I've never felt that's irreversible. Individual components may be sadly irreversible. Still in a general sense, things always can get better. This book provides a blueprint for identifying problems—not only how they present themselves in ecologies, but how we actually talk about them. Because how we talk leads to how we change and rectify problems. Forrest's poetry always has offered an active textuality. The active world gets embodied in the words of his poems. These words aren't just representations of things. They almost become organic matter, be they rock or be they vegetable. This organicism extends across all existence. Ideas of the "I" or the self long have been challenged in poetry. That's nothing new. But the way we've described our relationship to place...I think we do need a new language. Not saying we've found that new language, but we've explored new parameters of representation.

FG: So saying collaborative writing can be redemptive, that's already an act. That makes something happen.

AF: I appreciate the premise that ecopoetics emerges from a critique, rather than a reaffirmation, of Western subjectivity. I like John's implication that *Redstart*'s dialogic structure prevents present global trajectories from seeming irreversible, since potential always remains for a shift in momentum. But before we get too far, can you give a brief sense of what you mean when referring to the big glossed lie of "experiencing nature." What makes this phrase a lie? Why does that equal the death of nature?

FG: That's John's phrase, and John also says in the preface that we have no landscape to speak of. He insists that as soon as we've identified a landscape, we have separated ourselves from it. Historically this leads to tragic consequences.

JK: Once again, we are not just this outside energy that can look and observe to gain leisure and pleasure. We are culpable and responsible and receptive to nature as well. The whole point to saying that one doesn't write nature, but actually is part of nature, is if you start fetishizing and objectifying and reifying, then readers can create a comfortable distance between themselves and what you've observed. One thing I love about working with Forrest is our shared sense that you don't have a debate without responsibility. Once you bring some sense of belonging and participation and inclusiveness to the so-called nature/landscape debate, that brings along responsibility. The exchange has a purpose. We write because we believe in the work. It's not just entertainment.

AF: One last question on *Redstart*'s dialogic structure. You cite Felix Guattari's work, which calls to mind the pairings of Deleuze and Guattari, Guattari and Negri, Negri and Hardt. And you've both collaborated in the past. Presumably this collaborative legacy contests largely unquestioned concerns in "nature writing"—its primary focus on individual experience as privileged mode of accessing the natural. Again along the lines of John's thornbill transcriptions, does this book implicitly argue that the natural resides in group behavior as much as in solitary epiphany? Does dialogue create its own ecosystem?

FG: John writes about this beautifully in "The Movements of the Yellow-Rumped Thornbills." He connects conceptions of property (as something an individual owns) to claims of authority and control. As opposed to property as something shared, communal, involved in endless process. Because no place exists free from event, from activity that impinges upon groups of people, upon everyone, all species.

JK: "Communal event" hits the nail on the head, Forrest. Even operating as so-called individuals, we actually have communal effect. Even if we live hermetically, on top of the mountain, the fact that we breath air and exhale and so on has its effect. The whole "butterfly flaps its wings" principle. We are not alone and can't be alone. I've increasingly felt, as time passes, that collaboration might be the only dynamic way of writing. For me at least. For others, not so. I've more and more lost interest in writing solo because ultimately I don't function alone, and don't think any of us does. Throughout this exchange, every time I'd get an email from Forrest, it made me rethink not only what I was doing, but the whole parameters of what poetry could and might do. That dialogue never seems static. I'm an anarchist, so I believe in mutual aid. I believe we assist and help each other and that this can have a positive environmental outcome. One problem for ecopoetics arises when it becomes exercises within the classroom, or within the text, without further reflection about cause and effect, including how a book gets printed, when and how it's read, how it gets discarded. All these practical concerns remain a part of writing, right down to issues of postage.

FG: Something else I find important: collaboration surprises the authority and stability of the self, and can make for a very productive discomfort. When John writes "I do self too, in self-same split / of bark," he connects the self to the landscape. Yet he'll constantly address the discomfort of that self. He doesn't deny subjective experience. In some ways this book seems very personal. John's wife, John's children become involved. Intimacy gets complicated through form and language in such a way as to provoke discomfort.

AF: Well a question did arise, following the…at least what seemed the dialogic preface (you both sign it). Why, after that, the consistent attribution of individual authorship for specific pieces? Especially since you long have embraced processes of collage, and there's John's "International Regionalism" project, and going back to what Forrest just said: do these discrete assertions somehow add to the book's polyphonic thrust, to the discomfort? Do you wish to foreground pluralities even of the individual's experience, as your points of reference, Nietzsche and Dickinson, do? Here the book's closing allusion to "male Noh actors in female masks, with beautifully feminine hand gestures" comes to mind. What types of rhetorical performances, solo and choral performances, does *Redstart* provide?

FG: I think both of us preferred not to attribute individual authorship when we'd handed the manuscript…

JK: Absolutely.

FG: We did not specify whose writing was whose. And anyway, the writing only happened because we'd worked together. We can't tell who even wrote some passages. But the editorial house's peer reviewers wanted that information. They thought it added something. We hadn't considered the book that way.

JK: We gradually had absorbed each other's registers. We'd approached a collaborative voice. If a liminal zone exists in poetry, I think we've neared this capacity. That's what excites me, not the initials at the bottom of the page or whatever. Of course there's a kind of geographizing in the sense that, oh, my parts came from this very specific point in Perth, West Australia. Forrest wrote his from particular places in the United States or North Africa. And those geographies shape the dialogue as much as anything else. But then parts of America flow into parts of Australia and vice versa, cross-hatching. That's an international regionalism if you like. These local integrities amid broader conversations hopefully energized the process. The author initials, which I think was our compromise—the editorial board has reasons for that, in terms of how this whole series works. From our point of view, neither of us owns any of the text.

AF: I love how, in the preface, all the sudden "me" starts appearing. As Forrest says, that "me" discomforts, because I've already attuned myself to reading multiple voices. I have to recognize that "me" could in fact be plural, or not.

FG: Right. Does this book have a "me"? Does it have an "I"? How singular is that "I"? We hope for those questions to stay unresolved, to problematize the assertion of a discrete logical argument.

JK: Yes, I think that's the nutshell of this book. You know the expression "sum of its parts"? I hope the parts aren't even parts. The book's about fluidity. It might provide a preface kind of section. It might hint at some sort of closure. But it remains open-ended, and these reflections only can be open-ended. The moment they close we blind ourselves to truly horrific ecological developments. Those developments demand a second-by-second proposition. This book has to get out there, has to stay open-ended, has to participate in something. Whether people love it or hate it, all I ask, and I'm pretty sure all Forrest would ask, is that it becomes part of the broader conversation. There is some kind of redemptive—that's the word Forrest used—some kind of redemptive gesture beyond just more paper scraps getting stolen from the world's forests.

AF: And this redemptive act involves provoking questions? Does redemption come through the momentum given to a reader to in some way respond?

JK: I hope so.

FG: One thing John says: "I and I: to implicate you" at some point of "Codex for Protest." That's exactly what takes place. It's a call-and-response not only within the self, but within the selves.

AF: Another question about *Redstart*'s overall arrangement arose near the end. The early presence of essays attributed to Forrest, followed by lyric pieces attributed to John, had seemed to suggest Forrest's status as initiator of the project, and the primacy of a critical vantage. Though then in *Redstart*'s final, email-based assemblage, I realized a reverse process probably had occurred. There John seems to initiate the dialogue with Forrest. So I'm curious, did you deliberately construct a convoluted presentation of this project's history? Did you wish to interrupt any seamless association we may make between the temporality of a bound book and the process of its making?

FG: This project's collaborative nature kept it in a kind of wonderful suspension. The book could have been ordered, and was ordered, many different ways. This particular possibility of an ordering came about by chance, really. But John's energy throughout, his incredible enthusiasm when I would go quiet or get wrapped up in something, kept us moving forward. I needed to draw on that.

JK: *Redstart* presents a moment in a broader, hopefully lifelong dialogue that started in the early 2000s when we first met. I had been familiar with Forrest's work, and he with mine. And not only through poems, but through critical discussions that happen around the poems, which we both see as vital and equally important. The way we'll possess a poem then break down that possession by sharing. Poems bleed together and become something greater. So this collaboration had started long before the first poem came through. Then even amid the silent intervals, the collaboration kept going. I'd read one of Forrest's books or essays. I think the main point with this particular project is that it's not a musty artifact. It's not a curatorial process of putting pieces on the museum or gallery wall and saying: there they are, go have your aesthetic relationship with that. These pieces, I hope, are morphologically out there, are part of the topography. They don't get closed off by the book. Forrest mentioned my energy—I am an enthusiast and probably get overexcited too much. But Forrest has incredible energy. It resonates in this work, geologically. It really echoes through the strata of rock.

FG: John writes that he remains doubtful of poetic practices as systems. Nietzsche has this lovely statement about the desire for a system being a failure of loyalty. For us, the loyalty of this book is to openness and to contingency.

AF: Though as somebody who often collaborates, I'm curious if you two have found that collaborative projects, which ostensibly contest concerns, models, projections of authorial identity…if collaboration often prompts those very habits in otherwise skeptical readers. I'm thinking of myself projecting onto your book: is this John talking? Is this Forrest? So what I mean is, does a demonstratively collaborative poetics perhaps unwittingly induce the type of projective identification that it seeks to dispel? Or perhaps a better way to put it—what's productive for the reader in undergoing this triangulated identification?

FG: I think both in our individual writing, and in the collaborative nature of the whole, we constantly invite the reader to participate in the conversation. So this triangulation doesn't make discrete particular voices and authorial identities. The triangulation allows for a passing back-and-forth. It invites a mode of meditation and consideration and experience that can be shared.

AF: Does the reader share as well?

FG: I hope that's the experience of this book. The question you asked interests me, but it's one the reader must answer.

JK: For me, a reader's never a passive entity. Readers are, first of all, never really alone. They may sit in a room reading on their own, but the reader remains a collaborative being. The desire to separate and identify individual authorship corresponds with the desire to individuate themselves as readers when, in fact, ultimately, they can't. The whole process of learning to read depends on other people. You don't learn to read very easily, and not very readily, on your own. The reader was collaborative from the start. But they want to become individual. They want to own or to possess—the very pursuits I personally would resist. And I think that offering a collaborative work and letting readers struggle (in the most positive sense of that word) raises a question they need to ask themselves, or that they might ask themselves. I'm not telling anyone to do anything. But it's the whole failure, if you like, of Western subjectivity for me. Western subjectivity never can resolve itself. Here we've played with those internal discomforts over what the self-reading self is.

AF: In terms of how encountering this collaboration can help to refine one's reading process (to sort through various projections onto and identifications with, possessions by and of, what one is reading), I'm wondering if you could talk a bit about the book's "Redstart" section. Does some sort of exquisite corpse happen here, perhaps along the axis of an epistolary exchange by mail, by email? And does the epistolary serve as useful model for the thickness of "perceptual experience on the page" that your preface demands? Even amid this dramatized call-and-response, did you edit each other's lines? Would somebody write lengthy sequences which only in retrospect resemble a dialogue?

FG: Yes, it's more complicated than simple dialogue. "Redstart" began with one person sending another some lines. But then these lines became malleable material. We felt we could edit each other's lines. I would incorporate John's words and phrases into what I wrote next. This call-and-response includes such transformations. The language kept changing across the borders of any one person's activity. That formal process matches the book's poetics—breaking down any easy or comfortable depictions of identity.

JK: Another component at play, another variable, is place itself. "Redstart" got written over a period of time. Topographical changes occurred. In the case where I live, watching large chunks of bush bulldozed over, that kind of thing. As the ecology itself became altered so our language changed.

FG: John's Jam *Tree Gully* project gets modeled on the movements of birds. Similarly, we wanted "Redstart" to reflect constant movement. Not to posit place or authorship as closed-off nouns, but to present constant transformations to which we could respond.

AF: You write across vast (but ultimately communicable) distances, and work within interrelated yet distinct idioms. For me, almost inevitably, Forrest's descriptions feel local. "Unsprung the / crab-spider rushes / (self returning to itself) / over the lip of hibiscus / (petal all detail / and anticipatory)." Somehow I hear Dickinson in that. John's descriptions compel me toward identification with "the local" for quite different reasons. It's their crystalline precision, their modest authorial vantage: "I have seen them almost 'gang up' on larger birds, but in general their energies seem spent on food collecting, communication, sentinel activity, and a vigorous display and response during courtship." I don't mean to affirm some nationalist identity for either of you, or your writing or reading habits, but did putting *Redstart* together heighten your sense of difference within the English language? Differences in idiomatic, cultural, historical, personal modes of poetic arrangement? What does is mean to meld present Australian and U.S. (and perhaps for John, U.K. as well) English, particularly in relation to John's postulation of a "center-edge effect," recognizing that there is "both no more weakness at the edge and no greater strength in the center"?

FG: That's one of the great pleasures in reading outside one's comfort zone of language, and why translation, for instance, remains so important to the life of a language, as other languages infect ours with different rhythms and image repertoires and syntactical possibilities. John's language, which of course isn't translated, still constantly refreshes my English with a vocabulary, with idiomatic and rhythmic particularities I find revelatory. It excites me as a thinker, as a feeler, as a writer.

JK: I feel the same way. I'm not saying this as a kind of "one says one thing so one says the other." That's not the way we operate. I say it because it's genuinely the case. But there's two or three important points for me. First, I'm anti-nationalist. I don't believe in nation as a mode of identity. I believe in region, locality, and community. And I take from Forrest's work a language of specificity mixed with a kind of ontological breadth, almost theory, where perspectives get shifted around and considered through the lives of other beings. That really interests me. Now his language and my language (our vernaculars) may sound quite different but we share, I feel, a vernacular of observation. Both of us right now are listening to birds. He's always sending emails about the bird songs. They're one of the great joys in my life. And I spend almost all my time outside with family and my work, actually in the bush, watching animals and plants, which have rhythms you can put into language. Hopkins does it. I think we all do in some way or another. I'll never forget one American editor 20 years ago saying about some of my poetry, "I don't understand these rhythms." And I wrote back, "I don't want you to understand the rhythms. They're just what I absorb around me and what I try and put into a poem." That's really where the model points, the Venn diagram of our collaboration—this harmonics of observation and experiential ecologies. That, to me, is the key. I lived in the U.S. five years and we had a son born there. I've spent a lot of time in Ohio. But that's not "Australia" or "America." These are immense places with many, many different environments amid the so-called sovereign nation.

FG: That word "harmonics" excites me. This book is also about the ethics of description. That in describing something, or trying to interpolate and to communicate rhythms and description, how do we keep from mastering, controlling it, owning it? John specifically says "I am not trying to ironize or diminish"—he's talking about the birds, their chests—"in describing this." And so, in that way, our whole book addresses a politics of observation and description.

AF: I'd asked about vernacular idiom, but your answers make me recall David Antin's concept of vernacular thinking, of the potential for a vernacular of observation, a vernacular of harmonics that *Redstart* explores. It's clearly not that you've just written this book because you like each other and admire each other's work, but because there is a more exemplary demonstration of international regionalism at play, a tracing of colonial histories, of environmental difference, of contemporary modes of commerce and exchange and their ecological consequences. This last question though…I'm somewhat dumb about birds, but the title, *Redstart*, could you say a bit about its significance?

FG: John, why don't you do that?

JK: Well, Forrest thinks I thought of it, and I think Forrest thought of it. I never will be convinced otherwise. I doubt he ever will be convinced otherwise. But that's the beauty. Obviously *Redstart* relates to a specific bird but also, in terms of physics, to red shifts and blue shifts and the variegating movements of light. Because something we hadn't mentioned while discussing sound is that the book's really, really concerned with light. I used to wake with joy when a piece would come in from Forrest. The first thing I'd clamor for was sound. But the second, and often simultaneously, was light. He has this great sense of the light where he's composing. For me, our title became an ecological identifier, but also became a marker of light and color in the text, and our thinking of—if I could mention Rimbaud, one of my favorite poets, his "Voyelles" and that movement between sound and light. I'll hand it over to Forrest now.

FG: One other of the multiple meanings comes from red zones on a map, designating critical areas. Those zones have been growing. That's where we start. That puts pressure on us all to do something about them.

## INTERVIEW WITH VANESSA PLACE
Recorded on June 18, 2012
This interview focuses on Place's book *Boycott* (Ugly Duckling Presse).

ANDY FITCH: I have questions about the book's origins. That might seem counter to conceptualist emphases upon reader reception, but could you give some background on your preceding engagements with (or provocations by, or responses to) these canonized feminist source texts? Do you see *Boycott* crystallizing tendencies latent within these texts? Did the decision to replace female-gendered terms with male-gendered terms simply start as an intuitive gesture that happened to work out well, or did you arrive at this plan over time? If I seem to be searching for an originary myth to a form of writing that precludes one: for me the pleasures of reading conceptual books often do involve this triangulated apprehension/projection of what a specific poet deliberately has done with a particular discourse or idiom or anterior project. So feel free to intervene in that triangulation however you see fit.

VANESSA PLACE: In terms of this specific manuscript, I don't know if you could call it intuitive, as much as I had absorbed Lee Lozano's fascinating *Boycott* Piece—executed at the same time as second-wave feminist texts were being promulgated right and left. Kate Millett, Shulamith Firestone and Angela Davis published celebrated books around that time, even as Lacan delivered his Seminar XX, where he says *la femme n'existe pas* (the Woman doesn't exist). To my mind, if you combine these contemporaneous claims, taking Lacan at his word while reading those iconic feminist texts, you can't help but understand their main topic was men. They don't address women. They address the male imaginary. So to literalize this operation…for her part, Lee Lozano literalized the operation by refusing to speak to women, refusing to recognize them, which produces its own revelations. Likewise, my first *Boycott* intervention, Valerie Solanas' *S.C.U.M. Manifesto*, seemed to reveal both more and less than the original text. That became fully clear when I started working with de Beauvoir. I felt thrown into some kind of ontological abyss by the easy essentialism, the easy gender constructs. As an undergraduate I had minored in gender studies, so I had read these books over and over, yet suddenly they became unfamiliar. I couldn't tell if I considered certain sentences true, even provisionally. When I would read, in de Beauvoir, for example, "it's the dream of every young girl to become a mother," I could accept some part of that sentence, at least historically. But when this sentence became "it's the dream of every young boy to become a father," suddenly the gendered aspect seemed thornier. Reading about puberty as a male trauma raised related questions. Of course, I still could default to the notion of pure constructivism you've described, throwing questions back onto the person encountering my *Boycott* text, such as: do I believe this assertion? Did it originally refer to a woman rather than a man? Why do I care about that? What part of ontology (everybody's biography) is simply the failure of symbolism, the failure of the Woman as such? *S.C.U.M. Manifesto* has this great line: "Women don't have penis envy, men have pussy envy." Through my *Boycott* that became: "Men don't have penis envy, men have dick envy," which sounds much more accurate. Latent intimations and revelations kept bubbling up, but these don't come from Solanas' text. They completely derive from my reception. They remain, like gender, interior to me. An older male poet has called this project a feminist screed, yet I consider it quite the opposite—not because it's anti-feminist, but because it reopens basic questions of gender.

AF: And how we define feminism.

VP: How feminism gets defined, and what are its stakes? Not just for "we" in the general, but "we" in the specific. What's my stake in this? What does it mean for me to become the author constructing gender all over again? Or for an audience to do so? People laugh when I read from *Boycott*, but why does it sound silly? If gender is a joke, it's an awful gag.

AF: One big surprise throughout your book is that this economical mode of defamiliarizing attention points towards any number of authoritarian discourses lurking within these liberatory classics. Gender, as you say, constantly gets reinforced by the source texts, even as they supposedly question its parameters. Then, at the same time, *Boycott* somehow humanizes these mythological figures, these authors I

*Interview with Vanessa Place*

too read in college. We see them as individuals trying to negotiate a difficult bind—resorting to rigid classifications, to a rapacious anthropocentric focus. Perhaps most obviously, Mary Wollstonecraft's professed desire to uphold the patriarchy, her primitivizing take on Islam and patronizing comparisons between refined women and crass military men stand out. Of course, such conflicted feminist assertion has produced a long history of divisive results regarding questions of race, class, sexuality. And the Firestone piece develops its own problematic relationship to "common people," while Solanas closes *Boycott* with a stirring genocidal appeal to "the elite of the elite." In each of these instances, your boycott practice hints at a Nietzschian approach to gendered categorization, less an earnest opposition to this polarizing rhetoric than a hollowing out of a priori distinctions, a revaluation of inherited terms. So how do you envision this conceptual treatment reshaping our reception of these texts? Would renewed critical attention to questionable rhetorical positions and connotations provide one appealing outcome? Would the construction of new idioms, new shapes of syntax, new argumentative strategies?

VP: That all sounds great, though here I'll revert to type and resist. Outcomes don't interest me. I maintain a Kantian disinterest, in the sense that I have no final preference. I believe I've succeeded in presenting a problem, puzzle, or proposition which can proceed in different ways, depending on who receives the text. I expect some readers would have the same response you had, where they critique these source texts in terms of counter-ideologies that bubble through once the main gender argument gets effaced. On the other hand *Boycott* does, I think, in the Nietzschian way you've described, also make such identity categories not irrelevant, but immaterial—or dematerialized. Here I wonder if part of the project may point to a post-structuralist hangover, as opposed to a holdover. That is to say: '80s French feminism as dutifully imported to the U.S. raised a difficult language issue, given we don't have a gendered language in the same way. This hindered the importation, I think, or should have exacted a tariff. With *Boycott*, English became much more gendered once I'd subtracted a second gender. For what remained gendered felt even more problematic, because gender itself became the sex that is one. And one, as Badiou maintains, is an operation. For example, I couldn't simply replace pronouns. After that first gesture, I still had to remove all exclusively female phenomena. Thus I had to conduct an internal debate about whether pregnancy remains distinctly female, whether breasts are sexed. I decided I could keep pregnancy and breasts. But I couldn't keep menstruation.

AF: I think abortion becomes castration.

VP: Right. Menstruation becomes ejaculation. *P-Queue* published two de Beauvoir chapters, "The Mother" and "Childhood," which became "The Father" and "Childhood." The "Childhood" chapter produced interesting formulations like "The first ejaculation is very traumatic for the young boy." Again I read this and wondered if it seemed accurate. But beyond questions of factuality, this sentence's medicalizing aspect became more apparent. Its Cartesian aspects get amplified. Similarly, I found it fascinating that even someone like Judith Butler, still considered quite contemporary, conducts a Cartesian way of thinking.

AF: Could you explain that?

VP: In order to position gender as entirely a construct, you have to imagine an entity called mind separate from an entity called body. But this construction of the body needs to include such rudimentary factors as hormones and spatial occupation, which should suggest a more cyclical or soupish engagement. Yet Butler maintains an old idea of physiognomy, of intellect, where I can step outside, I can apprehend my corporality and the corporality of others.

AF: While my grammar can stay stable enough to articulate this position to you.

VP: Exactly.

AF: But when you say you'd pause to consider whether a boycotted sentence sounds true, can you explain why that seemed significant? Did you just find it interesting that such a question came to mind?

VP: I don't care much about that specific question. As an attorney, by "true," I mean plausible. More accurately, I mean this as an example of various ontological trigger points. Over and over I'd reach points of resistance, oblivious of my preconceptions until confronted by their negation. Different readers will face different questions, and find other points of plausibility.

AF: Here could we turn back to the many male/female substitutions that arise, such as castration for abortion, and cocks for chicks? Or why the deliberately Borgesian bent to replacing the Medusa with the Minotaur? Does a systematic concept or theory dictate these substitutions? Did a more personal, pragmatic, experiential process play out?

VP: A sentence would pose a problem. Its solution would introduce a new constraint. Once I'd decided abortion represents an intervention specifically into feminine reproduction, I had to find an analogous procedure, a compromising of male fertility. Castration made sense because it could be voluntary or involuntary. Castration, like abortion, has picked up a charged political valence—various connotations of socialized, or criminalized, or state violence.

AF: So as with some theories of translation, one chooses between presenting a straightforward verbal equivalent, or producing a comparable function within the new language?

VP: Yes, for Medusa I wanted a combination of man and beast, like Minotaur. Also, the labyrinth of Medusa's hair, like the Minotaur's labyrinth, proves deadly, yet each monster is murdered by a hero.

AF: You also select another three-syllable word starting with "M." But more generally: Judith Butler and Donna Haraway, with their circumspect attempts to construct a non-totalizing discourse, came across as the most amenable to your project—in the sense that fluid pronominal substitutions seem to advance, to exemplify their claims, rather than to challenge them. I don't mean to suggest that these boycotts succeed more than others, though I'm curious if particular authors, for whatever reason, don't work as boycotts, or particular pieces by authors you did choose.

VP: Certain authors presented more difficult cases—Cixous, for example. "The Laugh of the Medusa," I think, ends up working reasonably well. But other texts by her did not. Haraway stayed difficult since she tries so hard to depart from gender. Still gender remains fundamental to the text, and "Simians, Cyborgs and Women" is my cosmic e.g., so I wanted to include that piece in particular. For Chandra Talpade Mohanty, from what I remember, the footnotes became the focal point. I omitted footnotes for a lot of these texts. Though for "Under Western Eyes" I wanted to foreground footnotes as literalizing and confounding the multiple, beneath a text that calls for multiplicity. De Beauvoir impressed me, given her historical context, for staying consistent in citing both male and female authority. Whereas "Under Western Eyes" posits much male authority.

AF: Sometimes footnotes did stand out—as a boycott's most expressive quality.

VP: The curatorial hand gets heavier. The difficulty becomes framing a pattern without providing an interpretive argument.

AF: With conceptual texts, I've long been intrigued by what happens once a reader "gets" a project, knows what's happening. What means of attention come after that? What space for critical reflection remains? If we take, by contrast, Stein's *The Making of Americans,* this book always does something new, producing an endless variety of tactile reading pleasures. And I'm not saying all conceptual texts lacking such shifts become problematic, but it interests me what follows once this sense of surprise and difference fades away. So I'm curious here if your construction of a quasi-anthology deliberately provides for greater variety of idiom, of localized intervention—allowing the project to proceed in divergent ways yet maintain a conceptual unity.

VP: Well, I do hope to complete a full boycott of *The Second Sex*. I've done four chapters already. But here I wanted a feminist history, a historiography actually. Too, second-wave feminism and most subsequent feminisms have foregrounded the anthological form. Still I didn't want this project just to seem some pointed critique of second-wave feminism. I sent my friend Susan Faludi the *Backlash* chapter, and she generously said that its *Boycott* version made the argument she'd been trying to make all along.

AF: Sure, many of these source texts position themselves as standing on the shoulders of preceding feminist arguments—absorbing, consolidating, rearticulating and redefining the terms of their predecessors in order to reinvigorate a broader tradition of thought.

VP: I've mentioned this too often, but I do believe that successful conceptual pieces present the allegorical. Here an obvious allegory about gender and feminism and history plays out. Or you could place this boycott anthology in relation to Eliot's somewhat thin "Tradition and the Individual Talent." How do later feminist texts, and even later boycotts, alter what came before?

AF: Could you also speak to how these separate boycott projects inform each other once placed side-by-side? They don't appear in chronological order, correct?

VP: They come in clusters, again throwing back onto readers evaluative questions, such as which do you like best? Which ones work for you? What fails? What fails worse? Ideally this provides for a self-critique. To me, the main point of interest isn't so much a critique of those texts themselves, but of our encounters with the texts, our preference for this one over that one. Here we don't interrogate gender so much as we track our affinities to different types of discourse. Still each of these feminist, egalitarian projects does become authoritative—by definition. And the problem remains that once you posit an epistemology of gender, then you're sunk. So the best option, to my mind, is to eliminate one of the terms. To change, in a word, the language game.

AF: On that elimination, could we address the erotics of this new idiom you've constructed? I thought of Roland Barthes's passage "The Goddess H," in *Pleasure of the Text*. The Goddess H stands for hashish and homosexuality. Barthes describes his principal pleasure of experiencing more and more and more of something. And of course *Boycott*'s male-saturated idiom can seem claustrophobia-inducing, as when Kate Millett's account of female-to-female rivalry gets re-gendered as Cain and Abel or Jacob and Esau—suddenly taking a more violent twist. But more often campy pleasures arise as the male monochrome abounds. I'll give one example, from Wollstonecraft: "Nowadays the King of England still considers it part of his royal male role to sport as much of the family jewelry as he can manage at any one time on all public occasions, although the male monarchs have escaped such showcase duty, which devolves exclusively upon their husbands." As this new male object-hood corresponds to historical projections of male power, your boycotts suggest that broader arenas of gender (defined by institutional discourse, by the binary of man and woman) long have showcased contests between men, by men, for men, ultimately about men. Here the proverbial, predatorial male gaze of feminist criticism aligns itself with Narcissus. Men gaze at men.

VP: Boycotts teach you everything about men. Men become brave and valorous, but also trivial and flirtatious. Men only care about money. Men only care about household objects. When Lacan says the Woman doesn't exist, he uncovers a foil for the Man, so that the male finally can recognize himself. This comes through clearly. And however campy these lists of male attributes, they again ring right, yes? Who doesn't know the flirtatious man? Who doesn't know the man obsessed with money? The boycott becomes a great leveler. On the one hand, you could make a somewhat easy Sedgwick-inspired argument about the epistemology of the closet and all that. On the other hand, in a stupidly reductive way, the boycotts trace this fundamental truth that what we really want are gender categories. That's the desire.

AF: You mean for all involved?

VP: For all involved: including the authors, the readers, the subjects, contexts and language of these texts. This categorical imperative seems quite different from what Kant had in mind. But then, after realizing that, what do you do? Here's my main question. Because no escape seems possible, which is why direct outcomes don't concern me. Each of these texts presents a philosophical trap, and when you sense such a trap you should walk into it.

AF: One last topic that might seem dumb. The Haraway piece contains elisions or compressions. I couldn't tell if all pieces do. But every time I searched online to compare one of your boycotts to a source text, Google took me to the Marxist Internet Archive. Did you want to explain your history with this site?

VP: The compression part sounds easier, and probably more humiliating. The fact is I want people to read these boycotts—unlike some conceptual projects. I don't need to revisit that discussion. But I mean for readers to finish these pieces. If you grasp the intervention, that's all well and good, but when you progress through the texts you really see how they work.

AF: And the serialized, comparative nature of these boycotts also requires that a reader finish each text efficiently, so that it can linger as a trace memory for subsequent chapters.

VP: For similar reasons I tried to find the most revealing passages. I would flip through *The Female Eunuch* for example, and sense no single chapter worked better than the rest. In fact, the basic point of this book depends upon approaching the book as a whole. So curatorial questions of selection arose. That's where the humiliation lies. Did I stack the deck? Did I thumb the scale? Probably.

AF: I don't think so, since your elisions break the apparent rule. They complicate the reading procedure. I get lulled into projecting a verbatim transcript with minimal interventions operating according to an explicit code. Then I have to rethink the ways in which this reading experience has been carefully shaped and constructed for and by me.

VP: Which again returns us to personal predilection. For example, with *S.C.U.M. Manifesto*, I wanted to include the "'Great Art'" section. But that particular text contains lots of repetition. I cut of a bunch of material. Then for that Marxist website: the dumb answer is I hoped to avoid retyping everything. That becomes physically grueling, in a way you wouldn't expect. So as a final gesture embedded in this piece, though I could have taken from other websites, I had more fun stealing from the Marxists. After all, who better to steal from than Marxists?

## INTERVIEW WITH JULIE CARR
Recorded on June 20, 2012
This interview focuses on Carr's book *Surface Tension: Ruptural Time and the Poetics of Desire in Late Victorian Poetry* (Dalkey Archive Press).

ANDY FITCH: Could we start with the concept of surface tension, as borrowed from physics and applied to Victorian-era poetry—specifically in terms of how a purported aesthetic of surface can be read for its participation in broader political discourses?

JULIE CARR: Surface tension explains why molecules at a liquid's surface bond with stronger energy. They do so because, with no molecules on top, fewer molecules surround them. This creates a horizontal surface density, which became a useful metaphor for describing what can happen in a poem when you read for (let's say, just using familiar terms) content. You'll try to understand a sonnet's argument, but various sound associations play out among the words, as do visual patterns. Surfaces also can become dense with invented languages, or borrowed languages, or pastiche, or collaged language. This density at the textual surface complicates our absorption of narrative or message. And of course these issue arise often in contemporary poetry, or in modernist poetry, but most readers of Victorian poetry don't understand the work that way. Specialists do. But for the average, semi-informed reader, if you ask about Victorian poetry they'll think of somebody like Robert Browning or Tennyson. They'll recall some long narrative poem or poem of deep feeling—one which doesn't seem to engage language's materiality. So reconsidering the Victorian-era interest in surface, especially amid a poetics engaged with ideals of transformation or sudden ruptural change, drives this book. Here I focus on three poets invested in the aesthetic surface as a redemptive space, but for different ends. They are not, all three of them, Marxist or revolutionary poets. William Morris does engage a Marxist discourse. But Gerard Manley Hopkins remains focused on some kind of conversion or Christian ontological...

AF: Apocalyptic?

JC: Rapture. And then I read Dante Rossetti as constantly trying to salvage the human—to have the individual subject reborn into some liberated space—because Rossetti recognizes contemporaneous culture, specifically market capitalism, destroying possibilities of freedom or transcendence. He tries to rebirth the subject, the self. So again I ask: how does a surface do that?

AF: For readers less familiar with Victorian poetics, this surface-tension metaphor, as you've said, could speak to a broad range of late-20th-century literary practices. New York School name-dropping, Language opacity, camp appropriations of corny content, conceptualist procedures, Gurlesque intensification of affect—do some of these models fit within your current scope, foregrounding a rhetoric of the surface while seeking to channel subterranean, transformational, ruptural change?

JC: Probably of what you've named, the Gurlesque most proactively probes surface tension as I try to define it, specifically in the Gurlesque anthology, which is filled with poems pressing language toward guttural, affective sets of expressions. This sense of the textual surface containing its own meaning (meanings directly tied to affect) returns me to Hopkins and Rossetti. But that doesn't happen with procedural or conceptual poetry at all. Those often don't pursue, along these lines of surface tension, an intensification of sound. They emphasize compositional processes as a means of interrogating the subject matter. And then you mentioned the New York School. You could make an argument for O'Hara as a poet of surface, since glitzy, shiny, fleeting, contemporary things interest him. But again: the poems don't emphasize a huge amount of orthographic or homophonic play. They just delight in representing surfaces and being quick and cool about it. Only with someone like Ashbery do you see different degrees of language density, foregrounding a kind of surface tension. You could think about this in terms of a discourse of "difficulty." When people say, "That poem is difficult," sometimes they mean it presents a philosophical argument the reader must struggle to understand, though often they mean that language play itself keeps distracting you from reading in other ways.

AF: Amid questions of language's density, of language's materiality, William Morris comes to mind. Do his poems provide a difficult surface, or not, or both? If Morris prioritizes the "lesser arts" of design, does he anticipate more recent emphases upon such "lesser arts" (compositional process, for example) in poetry? Here I'll think of John Cage's aesthetics of furniture, and where that places us in terms of surface tension, or Roland Barthes self-consciously embracing a "minor" key as its own distinct idiom. I'll wonder if such discursive interventions can produce their own forms of surface tension. But can we start with Morris?

JC: Morris presents a special case. It probably would have made more sense to substitute Swinburne. Morris' surface tensions foreground the visual. They don't emphasize sound, but the look of the page. And of course this only applies when you see his illustrated manuscripts, or his design work. If you look at, say, his wallpaper, you'll find intertwining, interrelated visual motifs. Vines and floral patterns recur, but not evenly repeated, not regular—complexly engaged with each other. So I try to think through Morris' interest in visual surface. His dense surfaces provide an important aesthetic for two reasons. First of all, Morris considers these beautiful surfaces, these beautiful patterns, the "motive cause" of revolution. If beauty surrounds you, and you engage beauty, especially as a worker, a proletarian, this will ignite a set of desires that teach you, in essence, to want. When you feel this want, you possess a motive. You can fight back. Society no longer has stripped you of desire. Beauty picks up a political charge. Still when Morris discusses the designs he prefers, he specifically talks about abstraction (but not full abstraction). Design cannot offer pure mimetic realism, since that gives nobody any hope, right? That's like sham flowers. Instead, we want something that embodies the aesthetic but remains recognizable, reaching toward a better world, directing us toward some idealized beauty. Such designs, in fact, might represent physical processes of change or growth. Flowers and vines become quite important. In his later projects, these begin rooted at the bottom of the page, but then climb out and up. And again, for Morris, this work must stay accessible in order to serve its political function. It shouldn't belong in a museum or aristocratic space. It has to indicate, to us, where we might go, how we should strive ("strive" is his word), what we might want. So Morris' surface tension has to do with the visual, yet underneath lies an elaborate political/aesthetic theory.

AF: We'd begun by discussing how such Victorian conceits continue to surface in recent poems. Your book argues that, for postwar North American poetics, specifically Language poetics, an emphasis on the semiotic or material surface often gets placed along a critical trajectory extending back to the Frankfurt School, or, in a literary context, back to Stein—but in both cases rarely further than that. Do you want to trace a trajectory here from the pre-Raphaelites to post-Language poetics? And then, the more pressing question becomes: how and why did that continuity get eclipsed?

JC: I don't consider this a continuity. It's more of a refraction. It's more a pairing I try to draw out, rather than a lineage that got erased. Because high modernists rejected the Victorians almost completely. Yeats became kind of this crossover figure. Hopkins was not totally rejected—grudgingly accepted, though never liked, by Pound, Eliot, Yeats. Then the New Critics loved him and brought him into the modernist canon. But my point is: it's not as though Language poets secretly read Rossetti and Swinburne and refused to acknowledge their debt. It would take a new book to trace this, but I find it fascinating how Victorian ideas about aestheticism and temporality reach back toward Kant and an even older eschatological Christian sense of time, and how related concepts filter through the Frankfurt School. In other words, the Frankfurt School (specifically the Jewish messianism that Benjamin picks up from Gershom Scholem) presents tropes about temporality and change and rupture similar to what we find in late Victorian Christian thinking. If we compare those two discourses, we can see how they parallel and differ from each other, but I don't mean to pretend that some successive lineage has been ignored.

AF: Can we briefly return to the New Critical embrace of Hopkins? Your Matthew Arnold chapter traces the gradual development of Arnold's position that the poem's primary purpose is to carry a moral message—often one borrowed from criticism. This reminded me of New Critical approaches in which the carefully trained, authoritative scholar extrapolates a latent message from the text. For Arnold, as for critics to come later, this ultimate message seems to require intermediaries, some kind of clergy interpreting the message. You've already outlined a parallel between poetics eras. Could you do the same for their corresponding models of criticism?

JC: Sure. Yes, similarities exist between Arnold's "Function of Criticism" and *The Well-Wrought Urn*. But what might be distinct and worth paying attention to are differences in reading practice. I found it fascinating, when reconsidering the New Critics and I.E. Richards and people like that, how reading difficult poetry, working hard at texts, gets framed as a kind of healing practice. They present their work itself as a kind of healing, a counterbalance to contemporaneous cultural ills. Right there I sense a stark difference from Arnold, who doesn't really theorize the reading practice, at least not in what I read. He theorizes the relationship between poetry and criticism as one where the poet waits on, relies on, a "critical free flow" of thought. The poet should not invent a knowledge, but should absorb and represent those new knowledges created through what Arnold calls criticism. Here "critic" remains a pretty vague term. And here one other thing I should say about why New Critics love Hopkins is that they admire how his language can represent complex feelings. Only this dense language seems adequate to the task of representing, say, a devout Catholic dealing with industrialization. The lyric grants us access and presses us toward a more complex set of responses to our world. So I think New Criticism in general has gotten short shrift. "Ambiguity" and "paradox," two of their favorite words, present a means of grasping language's fluidity, its complexity, its multiplicity, its contradictions (though of course this interested them, at least partially, because of their faith in language's ultimate effort to express a universal affect, or "truth," as they might say).

AF: Given your comments on this body of New Critical writing, I'm curious how your surface-tension concept plays out in texts by Arnold's critical contemporaries like Charles Baudelaire, Oscar Wilde, Walter Pater. Does a corresponding surface tension exist within their work?

JC: Do you mean a surface tension in their critical prose?

AF: Yeah. I'm wondering if syntactical convolutions in somebody like Walter Pater complement what you find in Victorian poets, and if paying attention to embodied critical language can counter the conventional sense of, say, New Criticism as a priesthood of privileged interpretations—pointing us, instead, to what you've described as its more ambiguous, eroticized means of communication.

JC: I hadn't considered that, but what you say makes me think of Lisa Robertson or Andrew Joron, the two poets I focus on for my final chapter. Both have written essays or critical prose that don't fully forego the surface-tension techniques you find in their poetry. So what work does this gesture accomplish? In a prose writer, let's say Walter Pater, a generative affect occurs in the writing, which strays far from purely utilitarian purposes. And I think that this generative affect is meant to be, in some sense, rhetorical or persuasive. And we could say the same for the two contemporary poets I just mentioned: to flatten out their language, to demand a more simple or less surfacey prose, would do an injustice to their thinking.

AF: You've sort of conjured a dream for me, that we could say the same for much New Critical writing—that it deserves a second read as a study of literature which becomes its own body of literature. Is this just a dream?

JC: You know, it depends who you talk about. I definitely would recommend Richards' *Science and Poetry*. The book has a kind of rhetorical beauty. It's short, condensed and very charged. In other cases, like *The Well-Wrought Urn*, for example, an authoritarian voice comes forward that kills any passion or vibrating affect.

AF: That New Critical tangent arose as we talked. But I'm also curious, given Hopkins' sense of his religious vocation, or Arnold's ultimate identification as a critic, if we could return to Victorian/contemporary comparisons. Here I think of Marjorie Perloff's "Language Poetry and the Lyric Subject" article, in which she distinguishes Language poets from a preceding generation by tracing how Ron Silliman, Charles Bernstein, Bruce Andrews all move from non-literary disciplines into poetry—how they arrive at this field from different methodological perspectives, with different models for how to function as poets. So this takes me back to Rossetti as painter, Morris as designer, Arnold as critic, Hopkins as priest. Could we consider surface tension's place amid this cultivation of a cross-disciplinary, multivalent discourse?

JC: Yeah. I'll withhold any sweeping statements, but what you point out interests me. Here Arnold seems the counter-example. He's not a poet of surface tension. He's primarily interested in content. He provides the model for an author who couldn't maintain multiple identities at once. Once he shifts to focus on criticism, he becomes much less of a poet, whereas others keep their dual vocations alive, with various amounts of suffering attached. Certainly for Rossetti and Morris, part of what makes their poetry their poetry is that they remain so deeply engaged in visual culture. So they'll paint, in some sense, or design a poem. For Hopkins, his two vocations go to war with each other. He quits writing for a while. He returns to it in a tortured way. He remains unable, I think, to justify his poetry to his religion. At the same time his poems provide an underlying theory that language, like all other surfaces in the natural world, presents a portal for accessing God. And the more complex that surface, the closer language can take us to God. So the vocations blend, but also a big conflict arises that goes deep into his theology and biography.

AF: Do you mind these broad questions? I like how you'll give more specific answers than my generalizing phrases could provide. Your reference to an underlying theory of Hopkins' poetics first let me to Romantic naturalism/supernaturalism, to the migration of the sacred, the retreat of the sacred into the secular. And throughout your book, I thought a lot about Rosalind Krauss's *The Originality of the Avant-Garde (and Other Myths)*. Her essay "Grids," for example, traces a migration from sacred iconic representations, to late-19th-century Symbolist motifs, to modernist surfaces—arguing that modern art becomes the final socially acceptable preserve for sacred yearnings. So if you look at the utopian rhetoric of Mondrian, you detect the lingering legacy of Christian spiritual aspirations. And Krauss literally grafts the late-19th-century Symbolist window (with its thematization of this displaced spiritual vantage) onto the 20th-century grid. The transparent, sacred vision becomes a periphrealized trope in a 19th-century atmospheric scene, then a 20th-century empiricist's exploration of the picture plane. Again, that's a quick, reductive summary. But can we trace analogous spiritual legacies playing out in Victorian and post-Victorian surface tensions?

JC: Let me enter that through a side door. Lately I've been thinking about Lyotard's essay, "The Sublime and the Avant-Garde," which makes a somewhat similar argument about Barnett Newman. Lyotard discusses Newman reaching towards the sublime (but defines the sublime coming more out of Burke than Kant). Lyotard describes this sublime as an experience of now-ness, of present time, so that the painting as pure surface, as pure abstraction, can become a moment, or represent a moment. Lyotard reads this kind of surface as the painter's desire, the painter's effort to access something that never can be accessed, which is present time itself. The painting attempts to present the viewer with what Lyotard calls an ontological dislocation—some kind of transcendent or transformative experience. So to come back to Hopkins: hmm, it all sort of hinges on this idea of "the now" or the present moment, on whether one truly experiences, or even tries to experience the present moment, which must mean experiencing sensation, experiencing the body. If you can reach that experience, if you can break through to divine access, then that's a redemptive moment.

AF: And the work's surface provides the point of contact with the body, which triggers this redemptive experience?

JC: Right. This is central. This helps us understand how Hopkins could stay so fascinated with cloud formations or light on water, or animal hides or the pattern of a leaf. Because he tried to (I keep wanting not to use the word "experience," which already implies some distance) truly touch, with his senses, those surfaces. He tries to remain truly in his senses. To me this resembles Lyotard's encounter with a Barnett Newman painting. No layers of mediation separate you from it. You stand there before the paint, and the paint never seeks to become anything other than itself.

AF: Could we bring this back to Rossetti for a second? If we think of a Newman painting as pointing toward transcendental experience, but also perhaps preventing us from considering the art market as a social institution which mediates and constructs our access to such experiences, that takes us back to what you say about Rossetti. He recognizes humanist individuality getting pulverized or destroyed by the broader contemporary culture, just as Abstract Expressionists do. But Rossetti, in your intriguing account, also has much more pointed things to say about the art market itself. He seems to verge on some form of institutional critique.

JC: You're right. Hopkins stands alone in that his relationship to writing does not get mediated by the market. He fails (or declines) to have his work enter a market. But Rossetti depends upon the art market for an income. And he also desires for his work, for art in general, to carry this transcendent force we've discussed. Still he remains entirely aware, in a kind of sardonic, funny, angry way, that any work he makes becomes a commodity. And he hopes for his works to become successful commodities. He wants to make money. So his writing gets laced with references to these contradictions. One reason he can seem the most relevant poet to read in this group comes from the tension between his concept of art as a kind of criticism (of the way capital empties out any hope for transformation or transcendence, and makes everything a servant of capital itself) and his continued resolve to transcend and rebirth the subject out of that bind. Of course no triumphant resolution occurs. But neither does utter failure or complete disgust. Rossetti's dense surfaces mark this struggle, this very difficulty of aesthetic labor—the only force to which one can cling and try to remain free in the face of institutional power.

AF: Well, a basic current running through your book, especially the Hopkins chapter, concerns the eschatological structure of the apocalyptic "new type." This "new type," which religious thinkers once had prophesied, continues to inform not only the paintings we've discussed, but also, as you've mentioned, Benjamin's or Adorno's emphasis upon a rhetoric of the difficult, an aesthetic geared toward an unforeseen future, to a utopian era for whose readers this work finally can reach its full potential. Much of your discussion of this "new type" follows the chapter on Matthew Arnold, who develops the trope of poetry as a perpetually pregnant discourse—one in which a moral message needs to be unpacked. So both this metaphor of the charged surface and of the pregnant poem seem future-oriented. You will do a better job than I explaining how these two future-oriented discourses both relate and differ. Does Arnold's pregnancy metaphor anticipate Hopkins' poetics of rupture? Does Rossetti's embodiment of aesthetic labor somehow harness (though, as you say, not reconcile) these countervailing movements?

JC: This book makes the basic argument that Arnold's perpetually pregnant poem metaphor provides a gradualist idea of change. So yes, poetry can carry us into the future, but it does so through a slow, developmental model. Pregnancy seems a good metaphor for that, for obvious reasons, but also because…Arnold emphasizes pregnancy, specifically, not birth. Pregnancy suggests development, but skips the suddenness of actual transformation, change, which birth provides. Birth is violent, right? Pregnancy just offers...

AF: An ongoing process.

JC: So my book argues that all three other poets model ideas of rupture and revolutionary upheaval, or birthing. Though you're right to point to Rossetti as maybe a bit closer to Arnold than I admit, because of this reliance on labor. You can't suddenly burst upon the world as an emerged being. You have to work towards that. You have to do what Rossetti calls "fundamental brain work." Again, analytical labor sinks into the aesthetic. This first interested me in Rossetti, as a poet who represents rupture through the image of birthing, which gets figured over and over in House of Life. Here he offers "Bridal Birth." He offers poems specifically about birth (or about a stillborn child so also about death). He'll use the metaphor of exodus and the Red Sea and people emerging through this break in the water. These rebirthing images drew me to Rossetti as a poet more interested in sudden transformation than some gradual development, some classic psychological growth of the ego. He rejects that. But he also doesn't. While he creates this epic poem *The House of Life,* a sonnet sequence focusing on amorous relationships, he doesn't design this poem in any kind of linear or developmental way. So people get confused when they read it. They'll ask: who is he talking about? Did a new woman arrive? Oh, two women are here. This sequence doesn't allow us to watch the subject develop and grow and mature. He never does. That presents a significant counter-model for how a person becomes him or herself.

AF: I'm picturing Rossetti as this institutional player for whom change remains important, but change within the existing order, through which he operates and on which he depends, versus Hopkins as this isolated, amateur (not that that's bad) poet for whom the dream of rupture, the fantasy of futurity, would have quite different significance. Here I'm especially interested in Hopkins' concept of the poetic "now." I wonder if poets get drawn toward a clean, shiny futurity in part because we feel haunted by delays not only in the production and reception of our work (that's the more obvious complaint) but also because poetry takes place in time, because communication and interpretation only can occur as temporal experiences—implicitly hinting at unending, unyielding delay and deferral. I guess that's what you said about Lyotard. But to formulate a question here: how does your study of the pre-Raphaelites shape your thinking about the poetic "now," about the now of any given moment?

JC: Well I'm currently co-editing a book called *Active Romanticism,* which presents a collection of essays about Romanticism's (here very broadly defined) continued life in contemporary poetics. Jeffrey Robinson and I make the argument that Romanticism describes a continuous mode, not a historical period.

AF: Something more like an impulse.

JC: An impulse or way of thinking about relationships between self and world, between language and world. So our book seeks to poke holes in periodization practice. I know that, for me, as a writer, I constantly lean on various 19th-century poets, Hopkins for sure. I think we all do that. We have our people or writers not from our moment but who feel present and contemporary with us. Didn't Jack Spicer say that poets have no history? Or poets stand outside history? We have to do that, in a way. That's how we keep poetry alive and continue to live as poets. We can't just read each other.

AF: One last question: if we accept the premise that the pre-Raphaelites construct charged aesthetic surfaces with pointed political implications at least some of the time, in some ways not unlike those of let's say Language poets, then what can we learn from the pre-Raphaelite legacy? Did this poetics of the surface become politically efficacious? I ask with some sense of an end-of-the-empire historical analogy between the Victorian era and our own. Within that context, returning to William Morris' poetics of desire, and more generally based on your overall study, do you sense unsuspected channels of desire to be tapped in our own particular present?

JC: Again, I think of Lisa Robertson as my book's final figure, based on how she offers utopia as a lived experience of the present, a lived experience of the body, of the erotic and of the relational, of proximity to the other and all this could imply. Of course this idea of utopia as a lived, sensorial present-time differs from Morris' Marxist/socialist vision of utopia. Though again, what makes Morris' socialism special is that it has to include desire. And it can't provide the satisfaction of all desires, because no life would remain. Existence would be flattened out by boredom.

AF: It can't foreclose future definitions and possibilities of desire.

JC: Exactly. So if I have some goal for this book, as far as its interaction with contemporary poetry, I wish to make the case for a poetics that doesn't give up on ornament, that doesn't give up on pleasure, that doesn't give up on pleasures of language itself, but also a poetry that doesn't forget the body, that doesn't reject desire, that doesn't preclude affect. Some of the contemporary rhetoric around poetry, especially around conceptual poetry, seems to ignore those arenas. But for me, and perhaps for these pre-Raphaelites embodying surface tension, to void or move away from what we might call subjective feeling, or emotional selfhood, only could bring a kind of death. And hopelessness. I'm not interested in that.

## INTERVIEW WITH BRANDON BROWN
Recorded on June 21, 2012
This interview focuses on Brown's book *Flowering Mall* (Roof).

ANDY FITCH: I'll want to discuss why the Baudelairean emphasis works so well, but could we start more broadly, perhaps with New Narrative? What about past or current New Narrative projects most informs this book? Does Kathy Acker provide an important point of historical reference? Do you consider *Flowering Mall* to be in conversation with recent poetry/prose, memoir-/research-based, lyric/anti-lyric projects by Rob Halpern, Dana Ward, Thom Donovan?

BRANDON BROWN: Absolutely. I'll start with Kathy Acker, who is extremely important for me, especially for the book's vampire piece. That piece, which I wrote first for this book, came out of a sustained reading through Acker's writing. I crib some forms of horror and violence and abjection from Acker. But then more broadly: I moved to the Bay Area at 19, in 1998, and have lived here since. And the work of New Narrative writers from this immediate milieu: Kevin Killian, Dodie Bellamy, Bob Glück, Bruce Boone, Camille Roy…nobody seems to me more relevant for a sense of politics, for a sense of the social as it intersects with politics, for a sense of experimental care. All of that shapes this book and the Catullus book I wrote just before it. As for Rob and Dana and Thom, besides being close friends, their work and influence and dozens of hours of conversation have meant more than I possibly could say.

*Interview with Brandon Brown*

AF: I've interviewed all three, and you come up in each of their books. But who else should we add as important figures in this exchange?

BB: Judith Goldman's work is critical to me, as is Julian Brolaski's, David Brazil's, Alli Warren's, Anne Boyer's, countless others'. A particular social milieu lurks behind the pain and glory of this writing.

AF: Baudelaire has his own specific milieu at a particular point in Parisian history. Did that offer one point of correspondence between your project and his?

BB: Yeah. I won't want to insist on it, though you've suggested an interesting parallel. Baudelaire's poetry emerges from a milieu of revolution, and his response to that revolution's failure fascinates me. Not just Baudelaire—the whole 1850s in France and what happened to poets, to visual artists and political figures and activists, deserves endless attention. But Baudelaire seems to offer an initiating point of modernity, as New Narrative does for post-modernity.

AF: Do particular studies of 1850s France appeal to you? T.J. Clark? David Harvey?

BB: Yes and yes. Of course Walter Benjamin. And then from a slightly later period, though harkening back, Kristin Ross's work on Rimbaud, which returns us to unresolvable strains of utopian hope and capitalist domination.

AF: Could you likewise introduce your broader translation practice? Which languages, which periods or texts or authors receive attention? Do your various projects propel each other? How does *Flowering Mall* sit beside your other recent translations? Did it offer a break from those projects? Did it extend them?

BB: *Flowering Mall* contains my third large-scale work of (I'll say, but won't want to say it fully) conceptual translations.

AF: Interesting phrase.

BB: I should be careful with the C word, because of our present, though it's finally an accurate description of these three books. But the first two projects engaged classics. I've studied Greek and Latin for 12 years. And both books (one translates Aeschylus' play *The Persians,* the other Catullus' oeuvre) cover quite different bodies of work and approaches to translation. Still all three record my dissent from the text.

AF: D-I-S-S-E-N-T.

BB: Right, though either spelling could work. Edward Said's *Orientalism* cites *The Persians* in its opening pages, as a starting point for the West's nightmarish perception, cultural appropriation, and misappropriation of the East. I'd worked on this in 2005, at the apex of the Iraq and Afghanistan wars, Guantanamo Bay, that whole disaster. So to find a Greek describing the Persians as effeminate, luxurious, weakened…the play dramatizes Persians learning their friends and family have been killed. That seemed impossible to translate in 2005. So I wanted to enter this impossibility and dwell there. Catullus presented a literary corpus much more beloved and better known. Though again, inside Catullus' work I found extremely violent, hateful responses to his social group and erotic relationships. I'd tried to dissent from all that. Anyway, that book tracks a failure to dissent enough. The climax of the book narrates my body-meld with Catullus, which produced all these unfortunate (real) social effects. That provided still another way to stage and maximalize my disgust with Catullus' forms of disgust. So after writing this Catullus book, the last thing I wanted to take on was another large-scale conceptual translation. Here I probably should mention that *Flowering Mall* doesn't deliver a full translation of *Fleurs du mal*. It takes a couple poems and elongates them, or, in the case of the vampire poems, slows them until they become unrecognizable. Of course Baudelaire gets threaded through the book, but more as a nauseating initiation moment for modernity, now viewed from inside its ruins—the contemporary. *Flowering Mall* tries to analyze everyday life from a Baudelairian perspective, which, by definition, sounds problematic, fraught. The book's integral social voice comes from this abject, self-hating, and hateful place.

AF: Whenever you translate, does your world pick up the palate of this translated author? Did that phenomenon seem specific to Baudelaire? To return us to New Narrative: I love how *Flowering Mall* tracks transformational processes taking place within the translator as much as the translated.

BB: Well I'd wanted to respond to the historical convention that erases the translator as a lived body. This reinforces a gigantic lie. All three books emphasize intense focus on the translator's life, at the level of what I eat or drink or what happened that day in Egypt. These events enter the translation process. Still I hope my world didn't take on Baudelairean hues. Almost everything I say in this book sounds the opposite of what I'd ever want to say out loud. It feels vile and horrible, and of course filled with lies, too. That becomes rather Baudelairean—this glorification of the grotesque both real and imagined, the grotesque of the real and the grotesque of fantasy. I didn't actually eat five bagels, you know?

AF: Can you here discuss how *Flowering Mall* came together? Did you start with the overall concept? It doesn't sound so from what you've said. Could you also keep disentangling ways in which you've embraced a Baudelairian spirit or sensibility, and ways you've departed from?

BB: The book's seven pieces got written separately, one at a time. Each originates from a different text. The vampire section borrows from Baudelaire's "Le Vampire," though it ultimately takes more from Nick Pittsinger's slowing down of Justin Bieber's work, from vampire cinema and TV. "Correspondences" obviously responds to Baudelaire's "Correspondances" then repeats it, a total of 15 times. "Fusees 22" comes from a late, dark, end-of-life prose piece which borders on all kinds of hysterical fantasy and frightening racist motifs. I imagine my overall project more as an encounter over a couple years reading Baudelaire, or reading about Baudelaire, thinking the spirit of *Fleurs du mal*. But *Fleurs du Mal* remains only one of many intertexts. In fact, the "Future Perfect" and "Pig Cupid" parts present less a direct engagement with Baudelaire than with texts about futurity. To me that seemed the critical question for 2011. But then when I'd return to Baudelaire, I'd find all this stuff about the future. So he stays contemporary, and so this peculiar act of translating through a quotidian life brought motifs from Baudelaire's own work into relief.

AF: I'm trying to grasp the relationship, if you think one exists, between futurity and translation. Does the curatorial nature of translation imply that the translator identifies some present void to be filled? Do translation's curatorial aspects foreground this basic element of any poetic practice—however unselfconscious we wish to remain regarding the intentionality of what we write, how we write, where we desire to place this work?

BB: Well, along those lines, I've always appreciated Benjamin's point (from "The Task of the Translator") that translation constitutes the afterlife of a text. This concept emerges in the vampire piece, which thematizes afterlife, an afterlife that feels kind of gaudy and horrible and endless. I sense we could say the same about our incessant reiteration of certain translations. So again, translation that prompts a powerful denial of the embodied text does not interest me. In some ways Zukofsy's Catullus offers a good counterexample, through how it self-consciously plays around with 1960s decadence. Then for futurity, although it remains hard to articulate what I want to say, I love Frederick Jameson's description of futurity as a trace from the other end of time. That trace, in a Deconstructivist sense, lingers from the past. This relates to translation. Because translation's first step of course involves reading. But as you read, you also live, and exist as a political subject, a social subject, which might seem the most banal story about reading, yet to me something remains mysterious and compelling about reading and life, like when you learn a new word then spot it 15 times that week. In a way, I want to take this lovely banal example from everyone's experience and sublimate that, or maximalize it to include: I stay home reading Baudelaire all day then head to the bar…how have I made my night different? How has the text inflected my experience? How does the syntax of social life get conditioned by my attentions? *Flowering Mall* raises such questions as much as possible.

AF: Your "Correspondences" embrace the metaphor of cannibalism, in relation to Benjamin. Than an inverse analogy throughout the book emphasizes constraint, almost as in constraint-based writing: not you ingesting/regurgitating Baudelaire, but you exerting yourself to produce fantastic formulations within a Baudelairian vein. So maybe Baudelaire ingesting you. Or you'll introduce the trope of the piñata, which again raises questions of inside and outside, of who's the consumer and who's consumed. And in case it becomes relevant, I had these thoughts while encountering some of my favorite lines: "In the rich, mealy, Burgundian / shadow of an ass that has never known paper, / look at me now." And I think I remember the phrase "whiff of an ass" from an earlier version. I'll try to outline a question. Can you sketch some ways in which cannibalism gets thematized here, in terms of appropriation, translation, capital, work, sex, consumerism, vampirism, "art" and "life?" But can you also situate the translating/poetic subject of this book (the "I") both as cannibalizer and cannibalized?

*Interview with Brandon Brown*

BB: How interesting. I have no recollection of a piñata.

AF: I could try a word search.

BB: I don't doubt you.

AF: "Recapitulated piñata interior."

BB: Sure, that seems to fit. It reminds me of a tremendous spectacle in Oakland around May Day, when people brought out what they'd called a "pigyata" full of fake money, then battered this into shreds surrounded by a ring of crazy cops.

AF: "Pigs" factor prominently into the book.

BB: The recapitualted interior may relate to cannibalism. Cannibalism became especially important because I'd wanted to foreground the body of the translator, which seems sort of porous at two ends, alimentary in a way.

AF: Did you want to develop that?

BB: The translator ingests, cannibalizes the material then recapitulates it, like shit. Still translation conventions remove precisely all arbiters of the body and intestines and the whiff of the ass. So I guess, in some simple sense I try to leave all that in, and more. I definitely maximize and exaggerate some hyperbolic drive to consumption. This starts with the vampire figure, for whom consumption becomes the totalizing urge of...Marx develops this through his great image in *Capital*, which provides an epigraph for my piece: "Capital is dead labor, which, vampire-like, lives only by sucking living labor, and lives the more, the more labor it sucks." You know someone (i.e., a book) told me that *Capital*, in translation, contains the first English reference to the real-life Count Dracula.

AF: It demystifies Dracula as some legendary, ahistorical monster.

BB: Right, with Bram Stoker's *Dracula* and *Capital* sort of written in the same London building. Anyway: those exaggerated urges and needs for consumption of course get intensified going to the mall. Such tropes get keyed throughout the text, just as they get keyed through our whole lives.

AF: Still in "Pig Cupid" you compare yourself to baloney. Or the "I" compares itself to the "erased birthplace" of baloney. Here I thought of Roland Barthes describing his prose as an act of corrected banality. Traces of corrected banality seem to recur throughout this book. Post-provincial identity, queer identity, the dandy come up—also the drunk, the flâneur, the vampire, the translator. Overall, de Certeau's concept of la perruque keeps getting echoed, as though you sat in an office writing this book.

BB: That's exactly where I wrote it, donning la perruque, wearing the wig, which depicts the translator's constant condition.

AF: Like the endless drag of Baudelaire's whole process.

BB: Exactly. Baudelaire glorifies this more than anything. "The Painter of Modern Life" celebrates cosmetics. What's most natural and authentic strikes Baudelaire as most evil, whereas the most artificial, the most costumed, most dissimulated—whatever joy he finds in life lies there. This conflux of the eternal and the transitory provides his definition of modernity. But this also hints at broader historical discussions about contemporaneity, right? If we adopt a Nietzschian and Agambenian sense of the contemporary as the untimely, then the contemporary always remains inarticulate, perched beyond the boundaries of discursivity. And amid our own particular contemporary, with technology we use, with how we've incorporated social networking as a literal prosthesis, we truly have no idea what's happened to our bodies and our social lives. We have no idea what kind of havoc we're wreaking—in the most glorious way. I don't mean that pejoratively. I want to think through this present's real unknowability, instead of avoiding or skirting it. So Facebook's social logic seemed integral to the book.

AF: Severed heads kept arising amid this undisclosed contemporaneity.

BB: Yes. Although I think more often this book tries to represent wild vacillations of affect implicated in that encounter.

AF: Well, when you mention the untimely, and in relation to your book, I'll think of punk—specifically how punk relates to Midwestern identity. Punk still can seem legitimate there, perhaps since the Midwest provides for untimely experience.

BB: Punk could not be born in the Midwest. Though I agree that now it probably lives more vividly there than anywhere.

AF: And just to explain: I'm from Milwaukee. But it interests me that several other books I've read for this project also consider Malcolm McLaren, or Joe Strummer. I can't remember if they both died.

BB: They did.

AF: Still, does punk provide a timely poetic topic because of parallel correspondences and/or tensions between artistic production and community engagement? Because of anxiety about how this community gets defined in fluid or static relation to other communities, particularly in an Occupy-inflected historical era? Anything about punk and the politics of this moment, specifically in relation to poetry?

BB: This whole talk could address that question, but I'll constrain myself to a few observations. One is personal. I'll often forget this about myself, but I moved to the Bay Area as a 19 year-old punk rocker much more than a poet. I came to do a zine and go to shows, not to fall in with swarthy poets. Have you seen Drew Barrymore's film *Whip It*?

AF: I don't think so.

BB: It presents this girl who lives outside Austin, and starts taking the bus into the city to play roller derby. I cried my eyes out watching because it portrayed exactly the misery of rural, provincial, white life—then getting to go to the city. I attended high school in Kansas City and stayed after classes and went to shows. I soaked up the enormous liberation of that community. Also from punk comes this tried and true message: if you want to have a show, you just have it. If you want to write a magazine, you write it. Again, I couldn't feel more grateful for having encountered that mode of autonomy and generosity, which informs everything about my life as a poet. And I also should say something, without getting too essentialist, about the contemporary Bay Area. It does seem, as I travel a bit and see other poetry worlds, pretty unique. That's not necessarily valorizing. It's not all good. An important Bay Area magazine over the past three years has been a bi-weekly, photocopied zine called *Try!* You could ask a lot of poets here, where do you read your friends' work? Where do you want to publish your poems? And they would say this magazine. Or the best readings really happen in people's living rooms. So again, that sort of punk training enabled me to feel at ease with being 22 and introducing myself to my heroes in art—feeling I could do that because, in fact, I'd been doing that since I was 14, and had found such generosity and grace.

AF: Does the assumption hold that if they deserve the punk heroism you've granted them, they should want to talk to you as much as you want to talk to them?

BB: Well, you often get heartbroken by divas. That's just being a bit snarky. But poetry offers a pleasant contrast to the visual-art world let's say, with its rigid and robust hierarchies—all tied to the object as a valuable commodity. Can I say one more thing about punk?

AF: Please do.

BB: For this book's final three sections, those focused on futurity, punk became central, partly because of that late-'70s historical moment, which is when I was born, and which we now see as the start of this radical Global West shift to the right, with Thatcher and Reagan. Of course The Ramones and Sex Pistols get caught up in that.

AF: "No future."

BB: Precisely. And finally I should say, in relation to Baudelaire: traditionally people describe Baudelaire as a "soft" thinker. His work remains full of paradox. He'll say something then take it back 10 lines later. But we also could call this process a dialectics, right? And for me, that's what hearing "God Save the Queen" feels like. This upset young person yells "No future"—but with such intense glee you immediately know, just by how your body responds, that that's not the full story.

AF: More generally, in terms of convoluted affect, I do hear more and more from people collecting, developing, writing about mistranslation. We didn't fully cover this. Do you want to suggest some poetic-critical-punk context from which that impulse comes?

BB: What do you mean by "mistranslation"?

AF: I'm thinking of projects like Christian Hawkey's *Ventrakl*, and a broader continuum of retrospective poetics on which your book could fit—especially in terms of modernist reference, from John Beer's *The Waste Land* to the appropriative rewritings in Vanessa Place's new *Boycott* series, then back to Acker in some ways.

BB: I'd paused on "mistranslation" because (and this is one of the first translation problems that got me hooked) translation's history gets dominated by two tropes: fealty and treason. This always fascinated me. Why adopt such an accusatory metaphor for something that seems pretty benign? And like you, I would emphasize the continuum. Strict rewriting seems as mimetic as one could get. My own work, especially this book, strays far from that. Only a little Baudelaire gets in.

AF: Am I right that Baudelaire often appears at the center of this treason/fidelity discourse?

BB: Well the trope has stayed in consistent use since ancient Rome.

AF: But aren't there very loose Robert Lowell translations, versus Roy Campbell, then Philip Larkin?

BB: You've got me on that. Still returning to Benjamin's "Task of the Translator": people forget that this essay serves as preface to Benjamin's own translations of Baudelaire. He didn't do these comprehensively, and they don't get remembered that much in the German, but for this Baudelairian project to provide the centerpiece of modernist translation theory becomes a fun trivia fact.

AF: Last question. Because it's one of my favorite endings to a book in many years, I'm just going to read your lines: "A laundry list of things in this book that beg me to cross them out. With glitter lipstick on, bragging at a mirror. But I'm going to leave all this error in the book. Smeared all over its pages, wet with Satanic fizzy water. All the monsters and lies and horny swans with booger-capped talons. Because I want to set an exact date to my ~~sadness~~ anger." Anything you want to say about that last sentence?

BB: I'll say two things. First, this actually replicates the historical text of *Fusées 22*, in Baudelaire's manuscripts, which gets written precisely as such.

AF: With the cross-out?

BB: "Tristesse," or whatever, crossed out with "colère" after it. But I also think this book affirms two operative extremes of emotional experience. Two affects get bound with how futurity administers our desires, or manages our desires. This optimistic attempt to consider futurity, if only to replicate one's sense of despair and outrage at present conditions...my own bodily experience offers a pretty wild vacillation between those affective extremes. And *Flowering Mall* amplifies or even lies about how extreme they are. Which is why it contains a lot of error, what makes it so disgusting, what makes me sick. To think of this book's contents horrifies me. But I also felt a countervailing urge to leave that all in.

## INTERVIEW WITH ZACHARY SCHOMBURG
Recorded on June 22, 2012
This interview focuses on Schomburg' book *Fjords Vol. 1* (Black Ocean).

ANDY FITCH: "Fjord" is one of the best words. But do you think of a fjord's sheer surface as somehow analogous to these compacted prose poems? Also, from what I remember, fjords now have disappeared in some places and popped up in others. Do you envision a Volume 2 following this one? Or does your title *Fjords Vol. 1* make just as much sense on its own? Should there be more room in life for Volumes 1, just Volume 1 of something?

ZACHARY SCHOMBURG: That title has little to do with literal fjords. I love the word's sound, and wanted to say this word for the rest of my life when I talk about my poems. A fjord emerged in one of the manuscript's earliest pieces. That poem appears first in the book. I wrote this poem knowing its first-person subject would experience death, but unsure where this death might come from. I think I wrote it late at night, and wanted to finish, and the phrase "from the fjords" sounded funny to me. It seemed such a strange place for this death to come from. So I first titled the book "From the Fjords." Then the concept of fjords became much more interesting—not for those fjords actually receding across the world, but as this word that means "from where the death comes." I listened to a lot of black metal at the time, and "fjord" seems like a part of the metal dictionary. It also sounded analogous to how poems, or prose poems, look and feel to me. I wanted to say, these poems are fjords. A chapbook came out called *From the Fjords,* and I liked already knowing that the full manuscript would get titled just *Fjords*, straight up. The idea of adding Vol. 1 came right before publication. I didn't want to stop writing fjords. I knew for my whole life I could write these kinds of poems. Unlike my first two books, *Fjords* offers a distinct formula. I wrote each poem in one sitting. I have several ways to plug in information to make these poems exist. They resemble each other. So when we added Vol. 1 I definitely thought I would write a Volume 2 and a 3 and 4. Or Volume 3 could come next or whatever. It interests me how books fit together and accumulate and fulfill their own role within a catalog. I have this fantasy of putting out books in volumes.

AF: Well for me the word "fjords" conjures scenes of vast landscapes stretching beyond the horizon. So I appreciate that you don't give us just one fjord. We pass through fjords into more fjords. Perhaps it makes most sense to start with the index. How does your inclusion of an index change this book's disciplinary or genre status? Did particular books or types of books prompt you to add an index—here and in your previous collections? For *Fjords*, did these short poetic sequences (clustered around overlapping topics) emerge before the index, in response to the index, in conjunction with the index? Would the name "Barbara" have repeated if you had skipped the index? Or did you find yourself recycling words like "Barbara" and think, I should keep an index?

ZS: All three of my books have an index. For *The Man Suit* I decided to add an index while assembling the manuscript. I used this as an exercise—to catalog which images repeated, so I could get rid of those that only happened once, and play with those that happened two or three times, allow them to appear five or six times, and create more themes. Originally this idea came from Joshua Clover's *The Totality for Kids*, though that book's index operates differently from mine, more like an independent poem. And I didn't know if a publisher would allow mine to stay, but needed to do an index just so I could know my book, know what it contained. I found I had many crutches. I'd used the word "cry" a lot in that first manuscript, for example, which I'd never noticed before. Then I didn't plan to add an index to *Scary, No Scary.* I thought, that's *The Man Suit*'s thing. But it seemed helpful as an exercise again, and I think the book became better for it. My books have turned into (though this wasn't a plan) projects that offer a few themes or images that recur throughout. With *Fjords*, I wanted the project to feel more like James Tate's *Memoir of the Hawk*, where the same formula, not the same image, moves through the book. I expected these poems just to share the same form. And most include death. Or many offer some kind of death which becomes synonymous with the word "fjord" in a way. I thought an index for *Fjords* would just have the word "death" and say, pages 1-60. But again, when it came time to publish, drafting an index provided a way of reading slowly, one word at a time. For the name "Barbara": I'd wanted to use it much more. I discussed this with my editor, Janaka Stucky. Originally many women's names appeared because these poems respond to dreams (both other people's and my own), and the names come from those dreams. But as I finished the book I wanted to change all names to one name in particular. I had at least four or five Barbaras. We ended up switching some to just the word "woman" or whatever. Still I like the idea of "Barbara" returning in part because an index exists.

AF: Of course *Fjords*' index points to the subjective, interpretive nature of all indices. The poem "Fjords of Deaths," for example, gets filed under neither "Fjords," nor "Death," but only under "Killing." Can you discuss the index as a perspectival, analytic project? And also, more generally, your indices help to clarify my thinking about your poetics. I sense that these poems could get translated relatively easily—without serious hang-ups concerning local details or idiomatic phrasings. They seem, as you've suggested, image- and theme-driven to a large extent. Does an index foreground this thematic nature of the project? Does it gesture toward the way that our encounter with (or projection of) themes constructs meaning?

ZS: Yeah. This index does remain functional, but not in the way it would in nonfiction or a science textbook. Because I don't necessarily want these poems read or understood for their images alone. I don't want to say, hey, you should turn to this particular poem since it contains blood, or sexual intercourse. Again, each index started with me trying to understand my poems, trying to understand their themes. I wrote *Fjords*' poems separately, without considering how they might add up thematically—other than the major tropes that we die and fall in love and have our hearts broken. But this time around, I'd wanted an index that traced how these poems do touch each other. Once again the index taught me a lot. Of course this index contains many flaws if one wants to read it that way. I arranged it in a couple sittings, and probably missed many images. And it does become, as you say, interpretive. The way "Fjords of Death" gets indexed suggests both a mistake on my part, and a fact about the nature of death and the nature of fjords and what this poem tries to do. Then you asked about translating these poems. Yes they can seem extremely simple in terms of language—still I think of them as emotionally complex. A third-grader probably could read and understand them, which does make them easy to translate. Some of my favorite poets work like this, and I try to carry on that stripped, limited and oversimplified relationship to language in a poem. Of course I also love to read linguistically complicated poems. But for my own poems I don't want language to get between (to present this artifice between) myself and a reader. I want to offer specific emotions and metaphors and themes without any static at all, in part so that sense of innocence can become abstract and complex and confusing.

AF: Last index-related question: given these themes of death and of fjords, this particular index surfaces like the afterlife of the poems, the burial of the poems, the debris at the bottom of a fjord or glacier which provides traction so its icy crust can move forward. Again this fjord metaphor plays out both topically and structurally. It hints at geological friction, at subterranean movements taking place—hard to isolate within any single instant or line or poem. But then another repeated trope, though I couldn't find it in the index, was "beach."

ZS: Huh?

AF: "Beach." When ice appears in movies or literature, I often think of beaches. Also I'd recently read Matvei Yankelevich's *Boris by the Sea*, which you published with Octopus Books, and which builds or beaches its themes in a similar fashion. Any thoughts on why "beach" doesn't make the index?

ZS: I want to answer that, but first I like what you said about an index resembling the debris beneath the fjord, which helps create friction between themes or concepts. In the index, when I say "FJORDS (see also Death)," this offers another way for readers to sense how these terms get built on top of each other. And then that's funny what you say about beaches. For whatever reason, I must not have underlined or circled "beach." "Beach" doesn't occur in my own visualization of these poems. To me, beaches suggest sun, freshness. I guess a fjord feels fresh of course. That makes sense now. But those poems that include the word "beach" I actually wrote on a beach. While sitting beneath the kitchen sink, with the door closed, in the dark among pipes, listening to metal, I never would consider the image of a beach. That's how I write most poems. I don't look out at the world or at parts of my day and try to discover actual images. I close my eyes and find them. "Beach" presents one exception.

AF: In terms of preexisting narratives that echo and resonate throughout the book, *Frankenstein*'s ice scenes come to mind, as do the Romantic poets. Somebody floats facedown in frigid water, as Satan does in *Paradise Lost*. Any number of entries start with a concise, definitional, Surrealist-inflected statement, like Kafka's short prose works (for example his piece "The Bridge"). When a poem mentions fucking a mountain I hear Bonnie Prince Billy. I even sensed a bit of *Free to Be… You and Me* in there. Yet more than all these others, the predominantly prim, anecdotal encounters with death evoke Emily Dickinson. Do you think of your work as rubbing up against some such referents? Does this type of intertextual expansion reflect your desire to write fjords on and on, into infinity?

ZS: I can't tell if this comes from living in the 21st century, but when I start an individual poem I've often just watched a movie or gone to a rock show and had a few ideas related to certain moods or feelings. And I wrote this book over a two-year period during which I read a decent catalog of books. I couldn't point to one particular thing, but they all swirl around in my head and my heart. I'd read a lot of Russell Edson. About halfway through these poems I picked up Anne Carson's "Short Talks." I don't know how she keeps it so simple, and I wanted to write like that and couldn't. I tried and tried. A few poems in *Fjords* don't make quite as much narrative sense as the rest. Those came from me trying to write like "Short Talks." Kafka, Frankenstein, Emily Dickinson, Satan, and Bonnie Prince Billy always will linger nearby. You can't write a poem that doesn't rub up against its referents, and I wouldn't care to. I write poems because just reading pieces I love sometimes feels not quite enough.

AF: In terms of "Short Talks," some fjord poems seem to present a quick series of absurd propositions. The whole of "Staring Problem," for instance, runs: "A woman walks into a room. I am in a different room. What has happened to your eyes? she asks." Then sometimes you'll trace elaborate symmetries. "Behind a Wall of Animals" opens: "You are behind a wall of animals tying your shoes in the blackness. I am in front of the wall of animals tying my shoes in the brightness." So some scenarios occur quite fast and make no sense. Others draw out a long series of logical movements. I thought both of your collaborations with Brandon Shimoda (the letter-by-letter stuff), and of the improvisatory collaborations by Joshua Beckman and Matt Rohrer. I wondered what role improvisation plays in *Fjords*. Do you consider each compact propositional sequence (each fjord) an experiment in some way? A scene experiment? An affect or emotion experiment?

ZS: Yeah, exactly. These structures immediately establish some sort of premise. In one line I need to set up the situation and setting and characters. That helped me think through how narrative works. Your reader has these expectations and only these expectations—since within the context of the book nothing else exists. In the same way, most of us probably can't remember the beginnings of our dreams. We just find ourselves in a situation. And then I try to develop that logic, to develop that narrative, to push how this new world works by adding a few more facts. Usually some turn appears. We'll learn that the world we came to expect contains a major problem or detour or surprise. Or the scope shrinks from really big to small. Some fundamental shift…

AF: The "I" might reveal itself as female.

ZS: Right. So a new set of expectations arises. And then an exit happens right after that. After the first line I immediately think, how can I get out of this situation? It becomes a puzzle and a fun game to play. Sometimes I only have to take a few steps in order to make the exit interesting. Other poems get more convoluted. The longer poems sometimes don't work. But the logical, repetitive back-and-forth you mentioned (in "Behind a Wall of Animals," or also "Someone Falls in Love with Someone") can sustain me and stay interesting for a while. I feel that, as a poet, the less I can explain to the reader, the more interesting the reader's experience. And I have learned a lot from collaborating. I've done collaborations with Brandon and Emily Kendal Frey and Mathias Svalina and Heather Christle, among others. This has taught me much about moving quickly through a poem—to reach a climactic place while constantly surprising myself at the same time. Heather says she likes to collaborate by herself and to try to surprise herself with every word. She'll write one word and stop and think about the millions of possibilities. I've started developing my own poems word-by-word more in new projects. But *Fjords* moves line-by-line. I'd write one line with its own logic, then move some distance away from that.

AF: You've mentioned the logic of dreams, which reminds me you've also developed an illustrated manuscript. Could you discuss your relationship to drawing? Contemporary drawing often can seem mathematically precise even as it renders the conceptually impossible. So when you talk about composing word-by-word, or sentence-by-sentence, I picture how drawing can trace that type of elemental decision-making process.

ZS: For this illustrated project, called *The Book of Joshua*, I've worked with the artist Ian Huebert. And it does offer dream-logic narratives. Except in our case the entire book could be one dream. Its first pieces look no different than poems from Fjords. But they track a timeline. So a subject gets born in the first poem. He dies in the last poem. Gradually he gets older, with each poem representing a single year in his life.

AF: So kind of with Lyn Hejinian's *My Life* in the background?

ZS: Yes. Ian illustrates this sequence. He has his own understanding of the ways dreams work, and how to illustrate these particular dreams. So now I get to watch my dreams reappear and how he illustrates them. When I wrote these poems, I had a vision of what Viking (the main character) looked like, and what his world looked like, and its color palette. I can't conjure that up anymore. It's completely changed. And I myself can't draw. That's probably why I write poems. They probably come from the same exact feeling. I'm teaching a group of 9th-graders in Taiwan right now. I also hung out with a few of the 5th-graders, and they wanted to play this scribble game. One boy would scribble on a piece of paper and then it was my job to make an image using that scribble. So if he drew a figure eight I might add a set of eyes and draw a face around it. I wasn't very good at it. I didn't know how to work with the premise he set up for me. So instead I would scribble for him. I'd draw this impossible scribble that didn't make any sense at all. And in one second this wonderful boy named Paganini would draw an entire landscape and these people over to the side. I try to be like Paganini with my poems.

AF: And again, just with this anecdote itself, we've got Surrealist exquisite corpses, Rorschach tests, Romantic music's histories of recycled variations (Paganini?) all combined into a single anecdote. How about a couple final questions concerning death's multifarious presence in this book? Does it offer an abstracted, emptied concept, like fjord, to be manipulated according to a particular poem's aesthetic or narrative logic? Does it build up resonance simply based on verbal or thematic repetition? Or does the concept of death permeate and underwrite this entire project's diverse flux of moods, situations, exchanges?

ZS: Death always offers something more. I'll write and talk and think about it for the rest of my life. It seems the one thing promised to me, and my only promise to others. It will unfold and reveal and complicate—in ways not so different from how death arrives and redirects these poems. We possess so much agency once we realize we're just writing a poem. And the same with love. Love and death interweave in these poems. They represent our only two promises.

AF: Hopefully we get both.

ZS: I think about this every day. I think about my real death—but not in any actual or specific sense (yet). I'm fascinated by death in a literary or abstract sense as much as by actual death. It's such a great word and, to me, an ultimate place where poems and fiction and movies go. We all share it. It scares us. We stare straight at it, and move quickly toward it—it remains such an incredible topic to think and talk about. So when I write poems, they often develop a narrative logic that progresses from beginning to end, moving through time. I've written like that for 15 years. I'll lay the narrative in some slight future from where the poem begins, and I'll often end this sequence with death. To exit a poem I'll think, how can I kill this character (even if I've only written three or four lines about the person)? Perhaps we all should ask ourselves this same question. Though I'll tell my students that if they don't know how to end a narrative, they should find an interesting way to kill their character. I often suggest getting mauled by a bear, especially if no bear has appeared yet in the poem. Hmm…have you tried bear mauling, I'll say. *The Man Suit* contains several endings in which the character just dies by being mauled by a bear. I've evolved from that, but only by using bears less. Characters still die at the end. They still must encounter their own deaths. In Fjords people keep dying throughout. The fjord poems seem less funny because they are less sudden. Hopefully they feel sad. And if I want to sadden the reader at a poem's end, death helps, or the loss of love, or some unrequited love—which amounts to the same feeling anyway.

AF: Sure, I like the French phrase "la petite mort" for an orgasm, and how your poems end both mortally and orgasmically. Here two visions of death stood out to me. There's "everything unravels back into blood and string," which seems to echo, in a deliberately grotesque way, preceding lyric conceptions of the ever-changing organic interrelation of all things. And then the line "Nothing happens next," which I think follows the description of a black scarf. I thought of how, in epic poetry, hateful darkness always descends over somebody's eyes. Does *Fjords* keep death as multiplicitous, again as intertextual, as it can?

ZS: Those lines you brought up were the two last lines written before the book got published. Neither appeared in the original poems. I'd wanted to change how each of these poems ended. I like your idea of how that last line about blood and string, from "Breath-Holding Championship," puts us all in common, all from the same sort of matter. So death presents a return back to the non-existence before we were born. And when I say "we," I mean not only the people currently alive, but even pre-humans or something.

AF: I thought of DNA.

ZS: Death for these poems provides an abstract feeling—not the death that occurs in war, or through disease, so much as this sense of inhabiting a place alone, lonely, with everything black and still and silent and without love, without the people we love. Nobody can love us back because we've squeezed beneath the kitchen sink and our mom isn't standing outside the door. Our mom has died. Nobody knows we're here. Death in *Fjords* feels like that. It might be peaceful. It's quiet. The poem "The Reckoner" used to end "Then she lifts up her dress." After some conversations I added "Nothing happens next." To me that line reads "nothing happens next." Something still is happening. Nothing is happening—even this.


## INTERVIEW WITH DOROTHEA LASKY
Recorded on June 22, 2012
This interview focuses on Lasky's book *Thunderbird* (Wave).

ANDY FITCH: Your title could seem goofy, but doesn't. That poise amid potential vulnerability makes it smart and charming. And you've never been shy about your admiration for Plath. So can we start with this title, *Thunderbird*? Do you enjoy picturing thunderbirds? I personally do.

DOROTHEA LASKY: A confluence of ideas made me decide on that title. First, I tend to write from the ground up. I finish individual poems without necessarily possessing some book-length idea. Then as I collected these poems, I noticed themes of airplanes, flight, large mechanical birds and different demonic forces—also death and the transference between life and death. My mom's a professor of Native American art, so I grew up around Native American imagery. The thunderbird of course connects to a Plath poem. But once I decided to call this book *Thunderbird*, many thunderbirds started popping up. A murder story happened at the Thunderbird Motel. My parents drove Thunderbird cars. There's the liquor. And some readers make comparisons to the search engine, though that seems less of an inspiration.

AF: With the continued reference to Plath across several books, did you feel pressure to expand or intensify or further elucidate her role in your poetics? Do you ever imagine a nasty review in which someone says, "She did that Plath thing again"? Do you see this ongoing immersion in Plath-infused ambiance as itself an interesting phenomenon readers could consider and appreciate? Or, overall, are you content just to live out the Plath years and let them lead where they may?

DL: I hope if somebody said, "She did that Plath thing again," I could take it as a compliment. And that otherwise I could just roll my eyes, as I do with many things people say. I started writing poems at around age seven. I stopped for one year, from 14 to 15. At 15 I took a poetry class and read Plath. I began writing again, so I think of Plath as coming at this pivotal time. And my deep love for her continues. I don't know if the Plath years could last forever, but I'm happy to ride that wave of influence however long and far it takes me. Of course, as I grew older, I started to notice snide jabs and various derogatory ideas circulating about Plath's work. So a kind of anger started brewing. At some point I decided to spend part of my life trying to get people to see how great Plath is, and move beyond the misperception of her as a whiny female. That misogynistic idea needed to get unveiled and cracked open. Scholars needed to take her work seriously. Because those critics with the negative opinion often hadn't read her poems. They'd read "Daddy" in an anthology, which I don't consider among her best. To really appreciate Plath, you should read the whole collection.

AF: Do you see changes in Plath reception? Here I think of figures like Frank O'Hara—deeply marginalized as a light, occasional, playful poet (at the expense of some all-important seriousness) for perhaps a generation, before a broader readership recognizes that subsequent New York School poets, Language poets, New Narrative poets all respond productively to O'Hara's precedent. With Plath, I wonder if developments such as the Gurlesque, with its foregrounding of affect, its strategic deployment of discourses conventionally gendered feminine or associated with youth, help point toward Plath's ongoing legacy.

DL: Well, I don't see this supposed youthful femininity dominating Plath's poems. But more generally: Gurlesque conversations provide one form of cracking open Plath's beauty. Still, scholars need to find more and better ways of discussing what happens in her work.

AF: As a potential pivot, how about the mournful tone in *Thunderbird*, which again has appeared before in your books? Is there an autobiographical context worth discussing? Or we could pick up the smart, careful staging of intimate exchanges between the "I" of the text and the "you" of the reader. How do you see constructions of identity and modes of address changing from book to book? Should we consider the "I" of *Thunderbird* the same (just a little older) as that encountered in *Black Life*?

DL: Again, autobiography gets associated with a non-gravitas, non-importance. That's another conversation. But I do think of *Thunderbird* as part of something like a trilogy. The "I" and "you" remain important throughout as characters, with poems resembling monologues from a play. So the "I" in these three books does keep developing, not necessarily growing older—more digging down to become a demonic element. *Thunderbird* provides the culmination of this descent into the demonic (which I mean in the best possible way, not as a scary devil). I mean a metaphysical "I" that can transfer and go beyond, that can turn the autobiographical into the universal, and allow readers to connect since it has fused elements of itself and from outside itself. So *Thunderbird*'s mournful tones suggest the culmination of this death, this becoming supernatural.

AF: Could you describe the demonic qualities of this particular "I"?

DL: Sure, and it's great you don't have to hear me repeat this every day, because I love to refer to *The Shining*. I wish I could find another movie to love as much. I think about Jack, who ends up becoming one with the hotel. And Delbert Grady says to him, in that red bathroom scene: "You are the caretaker. You've always been the caretaker. I should know, sir. I've always been here." Here a demonic "I" has split and shattered into so many parts that a stable center of identity becomes impossible. The terms "autobiography" or "confessionalism" can't begin to contain this process. So for *Thunderbird*, a father died and my father died. That's true. But the metaphysical "I" has descended and now can take on any costume—of its present identity, of the past, of language's endless possibilities.

AF: Do you conceive of this "I" changing from reader to reader? Do multiple readers access the same "I"? Does the fragmentary dissolution you described suggest that both an individual and a collective experience can happen?

DL: Yes, I don't mean this as a cop-out, but both processes take place. The reader always constructs meaning within a poem, which varies from reader to reader. Yet the reader too exists beyond or between past and present, self and other. I can't help thinking of this as a circular relationship—a radiating connection.

AF: The term "mythic" doesn't get used much anymore, but what you describe sounds related to how preceding generations applied this term to poetry.

DL: Definitely. I always wanted to become a mythology professor. That dream got dashed by practical reality. Though I did major in Classics in college. I've always been obsessed with the beauty of the old story.

AF: Do you like Pessoa's use of myth? *Thunderbird* claims to "say things / In the simplest way possible." Of course we could consider this a direct, straightforward statement—though announcing one's simplicity doesn't seem so simple, and echoes Pessoa's *Alberto Caeiro*. Or the boastful tone you'll adopt points back to Whitman's *Leaves of Grass*. Do Pessoa's or Whitman's poetics relate to what you've said about pushing beyond individual identity?

DL: Yes. Catullus stands out for similar reasons. And I love how hip hop can become quite boastful. In hip hop you argue that you've got the goods, more than somebody else. You set that up before you say anything at all. So I play with this crazy boastfulness—to balance the vulnerability and sadness and common human concerns. Whitman comes in here, embracing contradiction.

AF: I wonder if we should look at how these abstract principles play out in specific poems. "Baby of air" opens the book like this: "Baby of air / You rose into the mystical / Side of things / You could no longer live with us / We put you in a little home / Where they shut and locked the door / And at night / You blew out / And went wandering through the sea and sand / People cannot keep air in / I blow air in / I cannot keep it in / I read you a poem once." Basic tensions concerning the relationship between narrative and repetition, between argumentative assertion and a gurgling euphonia, seem to get foregrounded. A compulsive, palpable momentum carries with it a diffused, meditative logic. Plath remains one obvious reference point. But I do hear Gertrude Stein as well, specifically in terms of the relationship between repetition and narrative. Wendy Steiner, the scholar, argues that narrative requires a plausible, consistent character—one that repeats over time, yet also gradually changes. *Thunderbird*'s "I" often seems to emerge from a Steinian insistence, then to offer a Plath-like quick release.

DL: Gertrude Stein's an equal player in my poems. I love her. I don't love the words "incantatory" and "playful," but those parts of her genius I try to steal.

AF: How does your engagement with narrative change from the shorter poems to the longer sequences, such as "Ugly Feelings"? Do these different forms embody quite different goals?

DL: I don't know if they do different things. I love the idea of the monologue. I think of this book as a performance, each poem as a performance. "Ugly Feelings" provides more background information on a situation. "Baby of air" presents something more like song. Both help to push the narrative, I guess.

AF: And what we've called narrative (which seems an approximation) also gets carried over from book to book—through the continued exploration of why it's a black life, for example.

DL: I really enjoy doing that. I'll think of Bernadette Mayer's *A Bernadette Mayer Reader*, where she'll say something like, turn to page 121 to make love. Or one poem in *Black Life* references *AWE*. It's called "Ever Read a Book Called *AWE*?" That's my nerdy side laughing to itself. But I do think it's important to create this bigger cohesiveness. I don't know what will happen after *Thunderbird*, since I'm working on a book of plays.

AF: Plays by poets like Carla Harryman allow for further explorations of aesthetics, erotics, the hermeneutics of address. In your own poems, such as "I want to be dead" or "Death of the Polish empire," death or ghosts seem to serve as distancing mechanisms—prompting further explorations of poetic subjectivity, of poetic temporality, of what it means for us to encounter an "I." Sometimes in *Thunderbird* the pronoun "I" seems to get equated with death. When identity crystallizes around an "I," death often appears as well. Emily Dickinson poems about already being dead, or anticipating death (often as somehow analogous to literary identity) come to mind. Could you talk about death as a recurring motif in your work?

DL: Dickinson seems a great example. Or Alice Notley too. They help shape how death plays out in *Thunderbird*, because only through a close understanding of death does this "I" become a demon who can shed identity and take on any costume. That knowledge, a real knowledge of death, is important to *Thunderbird* and to my life in general. I think about death as the big equalizer. And poetry always exists between the realms of the living and the dead. These poems already have seen both.

AF: Do you sense that once identity flows into a poem, which gets shut in the book, then something has died? Does that help to describe how poetic life fuses with death?

DL: When you think of a reader, ideally stretching into the future (so far you can't even conceive of them, yet you speak to them), some sense of death always lurks in that. The poet has to die for her poem to become important. That intimacy only can happen when some person in the distant future reads it. Though I guess "the future" could mean the present, too. But the poet has to hand over that intimacy to the reader, which seems a type of death. That closeness can't truly happen in life. Even if somebody reads your work then you become friends or get married or whatever: as close as two people become in this lifetime, I don't think it equals the intimacy that occurs after death.

AF: The Borgesian poem "Time" seems relevant here. Does *Thunderbird*'s structure deliberately build up to "Time"? Does that piece provide some sort of minor culmination—either in your own trajectory with this "I" through three books, or across a broader tradition of literary meditations and reflections on time?

DL: Hopefully both of those happen. The "I" has to descend more and more, become something demonic, to confront time. Time seems even more abstract than death, since death (or death's approach) we can experience. For humans to consider time and how we construct it and what lies beyond that does seem a culminating idea. To think this way gives the "I" a kind of freedom, and increases her power. You said you like to picture thunderbirds. I do think of the "I" as this gigantic, beautiful, multi-colored thunderbird that has this freedom, these wings, yet through descent has grown even more beautiful, because she has gained a real knowledge of time and of death.

AF: I know you don't call this book's last poem "Hello," but I think of it as "Hello." I know it's "The changing of the seasons is life and death seen gently"—another great title. Could you describe why encountering the word "hello" in this poem becomes a form of life and death seen gently?

DL: "Hello" alerts the reader, almost as if a presence has entered the room. It could be animal, human, supernatural. How does it make its presence known? Our contemporary human way is to say "hello," to greet, to gently acknowledge another's presence even while announcing one's own existence. You don't say "Here I am!" or "Here's Johnny" or whatever. You acknowledge reciprocal presence.

AF: And does this relational acknowledgment also acknowledge death? Does the "life and death seen gently" in your title point to some broader reciprocity—suggested by the combined arrival/departure of the seasons?

DL: Here I think of Dickinson's "Because I could not stop for Death— / He kindly stopped for me—" and that idea of a gentle, tender, sweet way the death occurs, where it just is what is. It sees no reason to overdramatize itself. It just comes or occurs as a natural force.

Whether or not we believe death regenerates anything seems a separate conversation. But that mortal "hello" becomes entwined with an acknowledgment of presence. If you feel yourself getting sick and don't do anything about it, then you get really sick, and that's a kind of greeting. You acknowledge the illness's presence. There's a gentleness to that—though you don't feel it as the person sick. There's the message: this is how things work, you can't stop it, no idea ever will stop it, and this process will keep occurring right past you.

AF: Death as Dickinson's kindly, cordial suitor here comes back. Does this relation to death resemble being with someone who always will act appropriately, in any given situation, so you don't need to worry about making some huge gaff?

DL: I do think of death like that. Of course one could die in painful ways, and I personally hate death. But death will do the right thing. I do think death just lets you enter another space. It doesn't try to rip you from everything important, or erase your identity and cause you to split into a million pieces and turn to ashes or whatever we want to think. It's just doing what it does and your conception of certain experiences as so important, that's simply your misconception.

AF: Does that sound good as an ending for you?

DL: For sure: hats off to death.


## INTERVIEW WITH BRIAN KIM STEFANS
Recorded on June 25, 2012
This interview focuses on Kim Stefans' book *Viva Miscegenation* (Make Now).

ANDY FITCH: For readers most familiar with Brian Kim Stefans the practitioner of digital poetics, could you outline your early development as a poet—specifically in relation to this manuscript's playful, art-savvy, personal-without-the-person aesthetics reminiscent of the New York School? Reading *Viva Miscegenation* I thought I recalled the jocular tones of some John Ashbery, Frank O'Hara, Ron Padgett maybe; the sentence-based propositions of Lewis Warsh; the serial constructs of, in different ways, Kenneth Koch and Ted Berrigan; and then the subsequent, reconstructed lyricism of Eileen Myles,

John Yau, David Trinidad.

BRIAN KIM STEFANS: I've certainly read most of those poets. The younger poets you mentioned, such as John Yau or Eileen Myles, have interested me, yet none of them captivated me the way Ashbery and O'Hara did. Those two, like Ezra Pound for the modernists, presented this fantastic way to learn about an era's artists. Even just reading Ashbery's art criticism you discover a bunch of authors and painters and idealists you might not have come across. But I first began writing poetry very much under the sway of Pound and Arthur Rimbaud and Sylvia Plath. Prior to coming to New York I'd read anybody—both Robert Creeley and Robert Lowell. Language poetics didn't stand out until I'd moved to New York. Bruce Andrews and Charles Bernstein baffled me at first, but soon I was drawing quite a lot of ideas and inspiration from their work. When poets first got to know me that's the kind of writing I did. Nobody sensed how much I borrowed from Lowell or Philip Larkin or John Berryman. *Viva Miscegenation* does have one poem that I consider "after" Elizabeth Bishop. I try to remain open to all writers I've engaged with some seriousness in the past. And now that I've moved away from New York, I've started to see my poems as texts that circulate in a broader culture with no idea who I am or my friends are. Though part of why I took to Language poets was they seemed to follow through on what most interested Pound—innovation. Pound categorizes (I can't remember exactly) three or four classes of poets. After innovators come those that exploit the innovations, say Robert Browning.

AF: The consolidators or something.

BKS: The worst stage, the last, consists of the dilutors. Pound considered himself (correctly) an innovator. Of all the poets I came across in New York, certain Language poets seemed the strongest innovators. Of course you could argue that they exploit a broad range of projects picked up from modernists. But much of what they did no one had tried in English-language modernism. So at least from an American viewpoint, we can call them innovators. And then for me, in the '90s, I worked hard to absorb what felt like the forefront of poetry. That led into my digital stuff, by which people know me best (at least in other countries and the academy). I see *Viva Miscegenation* as my return to engaging with the lyric, with the…I don't want to say more conventional poetry, but I wanted to write poems that stand on their own, that can circulate in the culture the way a good pop song might.

"Accessible" doesn't seem the right word, since even what you and I consider a terribly accessible poem still would baffle most people. But I do want these poems to present many points of access—similar to a Radiohead song that sounds experimental yet somehow offers everything you need to know. You don't need any special awareness of Erik Satie or Ligeti or the hundreds of people I think Radiohead draws from. That's how I want the poems to feel.

AF: While we discuss your formative years, could you sketch your studies at the CUNY Graduate Center? When was that? Who was there? How did it shape your poetics?

BKS: As an undergrad at Bard, I got acclimated to the idea that an educated life meant to continue discovering new interests and integrating them into your mind. T.S. Eliot wrote that for John Donne an idea or thought was an experience. I still aspire to that. But after several years in New York I sensed myself missing a more intellectual climate. I'd read Milton in high school, though had no real grasp on the history of English poetry. In college I mostly took German and Latin, and then film and acting and other stuff. So I decided to enter a graduate program, but didn't realize people went to grad school essentially for training to become a professor. I just had no idea that to become an academic means to write a book that appeals exclusively to specialists (with wider appeal considered bad). I'd expected to continue my education in this weird, improvised way. So at the Grad Center I took classes in Old English and Chaucer. I took one Mary Ann Caws class, basically an art and literature course, which I loved because it seemed kind of crazy. Yet most students hated it because it didn't fit their professional trajectory. I took a great class on Blake and became obsessed with Blake for a short period. But when it came time to do my exams I just recoiled. I puttered around for a year then quit. Still I liked learning all this stuff nobody could call au courant in the New York literary world. When I went through my Blake period, for instance, I couldn't talk to friends about Blake.

AF: They didn't know Blake well enough, or just didn't care?

BKS: The latter, though some Language poets take pride in not knowing the history of English-language poetry—equating it with oppressive "tradition." Also, during this point in my mid-20s, I still lived in New Jersey. My life seemed divided between two worlds. Eventually I got into computer programming, so I tried a class on hypertext with this Victorianist, Gerhard…

AF: Joseph.

BKS: Then when I dropped out of grad school, I moved into computer programming and sensed I'd found my way to make a real contribution. I began writing programs and getting into graphics—all on this (by our standards) crappy Windows 2.0 computer my uncle gave me. I don't consider, let's say, my Microsoft Word-assisted translations from the Anglo-Saxon totally brilliant, but they did overcome some basic hang-ups in typical Anglo-Saxon translation, such as the attempt to reproduce sonic effects in verse form, which often seems artificial. Or on the other hand, translators will adopt straight prose, as if we only care about a poem's literal meaning. My translations rely on the number of characters and width of the letterforms, rather than on syllables, to determine the linebreaks and stanzaic shapes. They read fast like prose, yet contain a certain rhythm you associate with stanzas.

AF: And then, just completing this biographical trajectory, you seem, over the last several years, to have embraced life in Los Angeles—as evinced by your teaching topics and critical prose, or your investigations of L.A. poetics, punk, theatre. Your poem "Terrible Poetry Jokes" concludes with the line about Brian Kim Stefans entering a Los Angeles bar and ordering a Manhattan. Does it sound too optimistic to read this as you striking some satisfying balance between each city's supposed sensibility? Has settling in L.A prompted a return to perhaps less timely interests?

BKS: New York does like its own history. And a place like the Poetry Project started with this rich poetic community in the '70s, with so many fantastic poets. I've developed the theory that, in certain great literary periods, even the minor poets are quite good. If you read a good anthology of the Metaphysical poets, you'll of course encounter classics by John Donne or Ben Jonson, yet even a person like Herrick (still often considered minor) writes terrific poems. Traherne or one of the lesser visionary writers might be better examples, or even Edward Taylor in America. Similarly, 1970s New York includes figures such as Jim Brodey, who don't end up in the anthologies, but if you get a good Jim Brodey book you're reading great poetry. Now though, that whole New York or Lower East Side history offers both a blessing and a curse. You find many poets still under the sway of these projects from the past. L.A., on the other hand, doesn't care much about its history.

AF: About literary history, or history in general?

BKS: For instance I know a fellow professor writing the first sustained history of black culture in L.A., which seems weird, since African Americans have played an important role here for a long time. Will Alexander points out, in interviews, that people don't recognize L.A.'s working-class history, and how it remains a working-class city in many ways. Histories of L.A. music culture have just started coming out. Of course Stravinsky and Schoenberg lived here many years, so histories of German émigrés have begun appearing recently. We just had something called "Pacific Standard Time"—this huge, two-year project in which galleries and museums did shows focusing on L.A. artists, stretching back at least to the '40s. But less has happened in terms of literary culture, especially for poets. No historical anthology of L.A. poetry exists. Bill Mohr now has written a book centered around what he calls the Los Angeles Renaissance (basically a period from the late-'60s to '80s, that includes a lot of poets he engaged through his praiseworthy work on Momentum Press). Nobody else has tried to put that all together. Thomas McGrath, for example, lived here during the McCarthy era, circulating amid a group of lefty poets which produced a substantial body of work. A rich left-wing tradition exists. It surprises me most poets my age or younger just don't know about any of that stuff or don't care. I share with John Ashbery and a broader French tradition this desire to look at the past and find strange little moments that never got assimilated into the main narrative. You see that with Lautréamont, for instance. Everyone from Alfred Jarry to André Breton to the Situationists claims to have discovered Lautréamont (or at least to have rediscovered him for themselves). This obscure guy published one-and-a-half books, yet becomes the 19th century's most important poetic figure. I like that idea. I dove into Los Angeles poetry, trying to find those forgotten, quite intelligent individuals who just fell off the map. I found a few, not a huge number, enough to keep going. I've slowly begun an Ashberian "other traditions" account of American poetic history. L.A. seems hospitable to this embrace of minor, forgotten poets with weird life stories.

AF: Again in terms of L.A. poetics, and given your history of digital production, I would assume you often get placed among conceptual or proto-conceptual discourses. Yet with *Viva Miscegenation*'s first poem, "Daschle Denounces Bush Remarks on Iraq as Partisan," which comes from your *New York Times* project appropriating Raoul Vaneigem's *Revolution of Everyday Life,* I couldn't detect any obvious constraint or computer program splicing together the *Times* and Vaneigem passages. This text doesn't feel automatic, but rather painstakingly put together word-by-word. Presumably, any self-assured conceptualist would not face the same problem of sustaining reader interest, since no one would need to read the book anyway. Could you give some sense of the role readerly engagement plays in your work?

BKS: Initial ideas for the "Vaneigem Series" came from The Pornolizer, this program that replaced *New York Times* text with goofy old-fashioned porn language. The Shizzolator did the same with the idiom of Snoop Dogg. That algorithmic rewriting of text did intrigue me on a conceptual level. But I never got around to programming the Vaneigem project such that the quotes could be automatically inserted into the news articles. Basically, at my 9-to-5 job, I'd read some *New York Times* story about the second Iraq War, then open my *Revolution of Everyday Life* PDF, and combine these pieces. This happened back when you could just download a webpage—all the images and everything. So I began "Daschle Denounces Bush" more in the spirit of classic détournement. In terms of conceptual writing, I've never done one of those massive projects Kenny Goldsmith or Craig Dworkin do. I've never devoted six months of my life to some constraint-based enterprise. My conceptual works get quickly executed. And I do appreciate how computer programming removes or obscures the poet's hand. But I still remain an aesthetic polyglot. I like to explore a wide array of approaches. This may seem a huge contradiction (to write lyric poems while also putting out conceptual, computer-generated texts) but that's the challenge I would throw to anyone who cares about my work—somehow to resolve that.

AF: Well with *Viva Miscegenation* I'd wanted to ask about the manuscript's generous horizontal formatting, which seems the opposite of a boxy computer screen. Instead of quickly scrolling down, the reader encounters this lateral spread.

BKS: I've typeset all my books. Some, like *Fashionable Noise,* got retypeset, but according to my parameters. And strangely, as I did more digital work, my books began to look more bookish. Both *What Is*

*Said to the Poet Concerning Flowers* and *Kluge* foreground this quasi-Victorian feel, though not in some classic Book Arts way. Here I come back to my foundational definition of digital text as text vulnerable to an algorithm. Anything thrown on the web can get repurposed, screwed up, misdelivered through little tiny algorithms. A book, for me, even a poem, presents a work that resists these problems of the algorithm. For instance, if you ran an algorithm on a Shakespearean sonnet, the integrity of the lyric would seem to resist this entropic breakdown. In *Viva Miscegenation*, as I tried to construct poems resistant to algorithmic operations, I recognized the need, ironically, to provide something more like conventional lyrics (containing aphoristic lines or a close equivalent). With this overall manuscript I still might change the format. I really want to do a small book of poems you could carry in your pocket. Since these lyrics mostly contain short lines, I could try some trade-paperback dimensions. I would love to make something that feels durable and yet stays aware of the vicissitudes of our physical existence.

AF: You've mentioned the potential durability of poetic lines. Here, as in some of your Anglo-Saxon translations, I sensed more of an alliterative, syntactical thrust—privileging the grammatical sentence, rather than the discrete or autonomous poetic line, as the basic unit of composition. Feel free to differ with me on that. But have particular prose writers provided a good model?

BKS: Well, this actually ties into why lyrical writing interests me. In Charles Bernstein's "The Klupzy Girl," let's say, a single sentence can drip down 10 or 12 lines. Perfectly disjunctive verse doesn't allow for that particular pleasure. Then in terms of classic prose writers, I've thought much about Henry James. After one course on *The Ambassadors* I couldn't stop writing sentences filled with qualifiers—carrying this heft and sense of capaciousness. Ashbery sometimes works this way, again weaving a sentence over 10 or 12 lines, diffusing the syntax, which I just love. But both with Ashbery and a poet like Milton, even as they build these vertiginous sentences, each individual line still provides a plateau or distinct unit. I love to read them aloud because your voice gets challenged to make such a sentence hang together.

AF: We haven't yet discussed miscegenation. You've noted how non-literary enterprises informed your early writing. Here ekphrasis comes up in any number of contexts: related to visual art, TV, film, theatre. Do you consider this intermedia approach inevitable given your digital practice? Does it come more from your classical interests and education? And what about the unacknowledged citational motifs circulating throughout this manuscript? The phrase "six long years of my life" comes to mind. Your "Fairgrounds" piece seems to channel "Rusholme Ruffians." What makes Morrissey an avatar of miscegenation?

BKS: At Bard I got interested in dance and theatre. I'd watch everybody's senior projects and so forth. I really wanted to participate, but at first in New York mostly stuck with poetry. Right before I left however I did start getting involved in theatre. Actors and playwrights associated with, say, Richard Foreman and Mac Wellman, seemed more exciting than what I saw happening in poetry. And going back to Pound, I've always tried to integrate different sensory experiences and means of artistic perception into my poems. Though of course this can lead to problems—like why not just make a film? Why convert this vision into poetry? I still face that problem. I still write songs and do many different things.

AF: What makes this a problem?

BKS: Because you only have so much time to do any one thing. When you start dividing your attention you run the risk of making mediocre work in a variety of forms, rather than excellent work in one form. Yet I feel I'm always trying a thousand different things. I guess there's nothing wrong with that. I don't have to write poetry every day. And in fact I do not, by any means, write poems every day. Then to get to the whole Morrissey topic: as I said, I still write songs. At some point in the early 2000s I rediscovered Morrissey. I'd loved The Smiths in high school. I always considered Morrissey an influence on my poetics. He could craft this single line that contained such complexity: "I was looking for a job, and then I found a job and heaven knows I'm miserable now." That baffled me as a kid, and always stuck in the back of my mind. Then at some point I read an article about Morrissey, the 45-year-old singer. I couldn't believe it, and just started paying attention to him again, and became pretty obsessed. I listened just to The Smiths and Morrissey for half a year. I must have been depressed or something. Now I want to write a book on Los Angeles post-punk bands, which seems more useful.

AF: Again with that sequence "I was looking for a job, and then I found a job and Heaven knows I'm miserable now," we get both a sentence-based propulsion and these short, clipped lines. Here I wonder if Oscar Wilde lurks in the background for you, as he does for Morrissey—with "Oscillate Wildly," with that fluid alternation between elaborate, dandy-ish sentence constructs and lyric concision or brevity.

BKS: I didn't start reading Wilde until much later. *The Picture of Dorian Gray* is a marvel. I love the plays. His poetry never appealed to me, as much as I wanted English decadence to rival French decadence. But I do appreciate, both in Morrissey and Philip Larkin, this British aphoristic streak which combines negative and positive sentiments, which celebrates being abject.

AF: Well, your play *Being John Malkovich (aka, Gandhi's Groans)* thematizes what Screamin' Jay Hawkins refers to as the constipation blues. Your script reminds me of some Gertrude Steins plays, with their closet-drama embodiments of shit and orgasms—in the form of Alice's "cows." I also thought of Frank O'Hara's and Kenneth Koch's theatrical larks that end up producing quite engaging texts.

BKS: At Brown I took a playwriting class with Paula Vogel. I planned to complete a whole series of plays with the great Wooster Group actress Katie Valk as star. I only finished a few of those, yet one did get performed at St. Mark's with Kate Valk starring as Kate Valk. Tony Torn directed it. But the play you read came from constraints Paula had assigned in class. Le Pétomane, the farting Frenchman, actually did exist in history. All those historical characters displayed an interest in shit or farting, which doesn't necessarily interest me, though at least I (unlike most of my professional playwriting classmates) did utilize Le Pétomane farting aspect. And I do love Kenneth Koch's plays. At Brown the playwrights had this weird idea of avant-garde theatre, which they desperately tried to pursue. I actually knew avant-garde theatre, so I felt drawn to try conventional theatre. But here we return to the *Viva Miscegenation* title—which refers to Morrissey's first solo album, *Viva Hate*. Traditionally "miscegenation" has carried quite ugly connotations. Though given my own origins, I have to celebrate the fact that at some point in this world a Korean decided to bed with a German-American. Of course this also extends to the aesthetic realm. When you open Viva Miscegenation you find a mish-mash of styles beyond the somewhat stupid conversation about these two traditions in American poetry—the School of

Quietude and then everybody else. I've always read widely. I've tried to read every poet I could, mostly just to see what I can steal from them, but also to enjoy their work. That's how I've always felt any poet should read. So I feel a bit didactic when I publish my books. I hope for these poems to teach you something about poetry.

## INTERVIEW WITH CATHY PARK HONG
Recorded on June 26, 2012
This interview focuses on Hong's book *Engine Empire* (Norton).

ANDY FITCH: Could we start with the title, *Engine Empire*? Placed one on top of each other, those words look like a reflection. I pictured hood ornaments and vaguely assumed a book about cars or Detroit would follow. Instead we travel to the mythic/historic American West, to contemporary (yet industrial age) hybrid-city China, then finally to virtual, cybernetic spaces from a computer-driven future. Chronology contorts as places and times get combined and conflated. Though does your book trace something like the material genesis, evangelical spread, imminent internalizations of a rapacious capitalism?

CATHY PARK HONG: Yeah, I didn't want it to sound like an editorial on rapacious capitalism, but, of course, capitalism was on my mind. The title actually came much later. It riffs on John Crowley's *Engine Summer*, this beautiful sci-fi novel, and it definitely produces a mirroring effect—both words beginning and ending with "E." At first I'd thought of the title as "Engine West" but that felt so fixed, so located, overemphasizing the book's first section. "Empire" you can interpret any number of ways. And "Engine," yeah: you think of cars, Detroit, but it also fits with the final section's search engines and so forth. I should clarify that though I called capitalism one of this book's buzzwords, I never had that deliberate thought while writing. I didn't set out to provide some commentary on Western imperialist/neo-imperialist expansion. I tried to stay attentive to the present, beyond the interior self, tracking the individual's relation to community, to the city, to family, to one's civic duty. When you think about such topics you can't avoid the ramifications of corporate life. Likewise Manifest Destiny kept popping up. All three sections…well the first two happened accidentally. I'd lived in California. I started watching lots of Westerns and writing Western poems, then it spiraled into thinking

*Interview with Cathy Park Hong*

about the frontier, about expansion. I wondered where does expansion now occur, once we've completed our geographic mission? But I also want the book to feel intimate. It also explores individual lives.

AF: Before we go through the separate sections, can you talk a bit about serial production? *Engine Empire*'s architectural contours get clearly, deliberately delineated, shaping our overall experience of its three extended sequences, though each section contains concise lyric installments at the same time. Do you have any favorite literary or non-literary models for this type of modular narrative construction? You mentioned sci-fi books. And film comes to mind, but more like gallery-based film, in which the discrete composition of individual frames takes equal precedence to a gradual accrual of meaning.

CH: I'd wanted to push beyond classic poetic seriality, where you get one series then another and then another. I've described this book as a structural triptych. Movie series often come in triptychs, though perhaps made by multiple directors. I also thought a lot about Pessoa's heteronyms and trying to create different worlds with their own vernacular and characters and laws of being. Of course conceptual ties hold my three parts together. But I tried to construct a different self and then I ventriloquized as much as possible from section to section. You'll see this a lot more in fiction than in poetry. Poets tend to place themselves into specific aesthetic camps like Flarf or post-confessional poetry. But in *Engine Empire*, I wanted to assemble disparate lyric forms and genres to convey my concepts. I don't produce conceptual poetry in the way Vanessa Place and Kenny Goldsmith use that term, but some similarities do exist between their ideas and my ideas. I'm influenced by conceptual, post-studio-practice artists who first conceptualize their projects and then use whatever materials to implement their ideas (which seems quite different from what material-driven artists, like painters, do). *Engine Empire* presents that sort of conceptual approach to the triptych. The Western section introduces more traditional narrative elements, whereas the final section provides broken lyrics. Oulipian formal devices occur as well. And genres mutate in various ways, again more along the lines of fiction, someone like David Mitchell.

AF: Many poets work with genre, but I know few who combine so many different genres into a single text—actively inquiring into the nature of genre. And then as you discuss conceptual conceits in your work: when you develop a sequence, like "Ballad of Our Jim," do you design it subtractively, plotting in advance an overall story line, a narrative frame, subsequently split into a series of lyric instances? Or to what extent do you work additively, composing short, self-sufficient units which later combine into broader vectors of meaning?

CH: I like that question. I'd say I tend to work additively, though still within a loose framework. The forms actually come quite late. I have to get it all out there before deciding to write some loose iteration of a ballad. Or with "Ballad of Our Jim," I did want to write ballads and did have titles, yet didn't plot out the story or voices or what would happen. That story kept unspooling as I wrote it. So usually I start with some kind of framing structure, some canvas, but often just a vague sense of setting which I people with poems.

AF: "Ballad of Our Jim's" compressed poetic lines and phrases suggest a super immaculate process of elision. But I also assumed the vernacular dictions you adopt sound quite elliptical to begin with. Did you have to chisel this idiom out of some more sprawling draft? Or did working with the laconic faux-cowboy lingo bind you to quick, slangy references? You've mentioned film, but another art form that came to me—which I mean in the best possible way—is the musical. I hope "Ballad of Our Jim" gets made into one.

CH: That would be awesome.

AF: If I cite the sheer excessive musicality imbedded in certain lines, if I give an example, such as "Marshal's a marksman, maps Kansan's track, / calm as a shaman, sharp as a hawk," if I point to your playful embrace of an idiom not your own, though worked through familiar formal confines, can you relate to high-camp Stephen Sondheim or *Cat Ballou* or the Beastie Boys' "Paul Revere" or something?

CH: Thanks for mentioning that. I want to play up the camp. And I appreciate your reference to this section's musicality. "Ballad of Our Jim" contains serious elements, but I also hoped to emphasize the camp factor of appropriating a Western dialect—donning my cowboy boots and hat and affecting this bad Western accent. I tried to emphasize this performativity of the Western. Because the Western always has been a fake, a genre, coming from musicals and film and so forth. The Western is theatre, myth, fantasy. Here I convey that through the excess of language itself. And when you write any kind of poem, whether you use "plain" vernacular or not, you have to start with some kind of pulse, some musical pulse that drives the poems. So even for these Western poems, rhythm drives me more than anything else. If you can think of this propulsive beat as a clothesline, then I just adorned that clothesline with words accrued, collected from rancher novels, Sergio Leone films, cowboy dictionaries. When you read cowboy slang dictionaries, they sound so campy, filled with all these corny cowboy puns. I wanted that spirit in the poems. Still at first I feared not getting it right. I grew up in L.A., so in the West, but what did I have to do with the Old West really? Though because the Western constantly gets played and replayed, it seemed OK to write a Western with a bad accent.

AF: Well, when I began your book, Ed Dorn's *Gunslinger* came to mind, especially Marjorie Perloff's consideration of that project's idiomatic dexterity, its positioning of language itself as the epic subject. And of course we could think of Western texts as spare, solitary, with a macho white hero, perhaps a Native American or Latino sidekick or enemy or love interest. Yet your Western landscape seems much more diverse from the start, with its hero a "two-bit half-breed," its secondary characters slipping into scat, cross-dressing, always advancing that glam cowboy idiom we've discussed. Did you set out to re-envision a cultural as much as a physical landscape, to subvert purported hierarchies of race, gender, sexuality, ethnicity, language, anthropocentrism? Or did you find yourself tapping some underground Western tradition that already exists and deserves renewed attention? I vaguely remember Ralph Ellison essays about growing up in multicultural Oklahoma, a frontier different from the more orthodox "West." Or I think of Spaghetti Westerns—European, with Leone's first film itself based on Kurosawa's *Yojimbo*. Wasn't the West always this much more multiethnic, transnational, transgender phenomenon?

CH: The transgender part might come from me. I also want to mention that Joyelle McSweeney did a terrific hybridization of Annie Oakley and Hannah Weiner, called "Hannie Oakley." But you know, more generally, the Western gets fucked with so often and always has been predicated by our geopolitical policy at the time. The Western offered these triumphalist Cold War narratives, then during Vietnam became this dystopic myth about America's hubris, American failure. Somebody always revises and reinterprets and subverts (but also upholds) the spare West, the white masculine hero, the villain. Still as you say, some of these playful or politicized debunkings seem more historically accurate than that Western myth itself. Because the boomtowns, for example in San Francisco or all along California, stayed incredibly diverse. Depending on the era they might contain freed slaves, huge Chinese populations, Irish immigrants, of course Latinos, Native Americans, even French immigrants. I just recently read a lot of French people immigrated after the French Revolution.

AF: So, very late 1700s?

CH: I'll have to fact check this. They migrated to the boomtowns and became these lawless assholes. They weren't the revolutionaries, but the henchmen. All kinds of characters filled these boomtowns. So I didn't need to exaggerate or skew the facts.

AF: One last question about "Ballad of Our Jim." In terms of nomadic trajectories, I seemed to sense a narrative momentum progressing outbound, toward the frontier. Page 23 describes passing the last barricade. Page 24 moves "beyond the forts." But of course, as the plot progresses into supposedly open space, more violence ensues—conflict and unchecked exploitation of resident humans and resources. And here the sense of this mythic frontier as self-deceptive spatial construct (obscuring other cultures and species) seemed to get grafted onto a temporal, historical scale with your "Abecedarian Western." That poem reminds me of Juliana Spahr's "Unnamed Dragonfly Species," in which she addresses global warming and simultaneously lists, in alphabetical order, various animals going extinct. I just wondered if you see "Abecedarian Western's" alphabetical catalog providing some analogous scenario of ruthless eradication.

CH: I didn't consciously think of that, but I like that interpretation.

AF: Western narratives often get nostalgically hued, as if to preserve our glorious golden age, but as your catalog takes us from "A" to "Z" we begin to sense it all will end and won't be pretty.

CH: I did try to foreground an end-time tone. Though I hoped to avoid any specific apocalyptic thinking. Considering the frontier and the West can encourage a death drive. You sense no termination, no end, permanent continuity, so you travel to the frontier to defy your own mortality, to live again, to build a second Eden. Then of course life doesn't work out that way. We try to fend off Z for as long as possible. The frontier helps with this, its supposed condition of endlessness.

AF: And I guess your modular pacing presents its own implicit frontier space. You provide no single sweeping movement westward. You build up tiny settlements, hinting they'll all get stitched together in the end. So even your movement from A to Z never winds up offering some scary crescendo. Gradually the spaces starts to fill in, with little pockets that eventually might suffocate everything. I don't mean this in a bad way.

CH: Go ahead. I like it.

AF: Or when a character dies first off in a movie or book, though then remains an important figure throughout, that's my favorite kind of work. You know the ending, yet stay to see it play out anyway. You move beyond the stupidity of suspense. You can internalize regret and desire and appreciation for beauty about to disappear—like wishing a compressed lyric could continue a little longer, with linguistic constraint keeping you on the verge of total liberation. Here perhaps we should pivot to "Shangdu, My Artful Boomtown!" "Shangdu" the city seemed some hybrid of Shanghai and Chengdu. I love the choral choreography, the different voices that emerge simultaneously. I couldn't help picturing Robert Altman's *McCabe & Mrs. Miller,* with all its humble voices overlapping as you watch this town arise and eclipse the landscape. But also, am I right to hear in "Year of the Pig" a parodic response to Pound's take on "The River-Merchant's Wife"? There's the Kublai Khan inflected tête-à-tête. Do colonial parent texts appear throughout and I'm just too stupid to tell?

CH: They don't occur all the time, but definitely this second section tracks Western imaginings of the Orient, with some hopefully sly allusions.

AF: So *Engine Empire* first constructs the West, and only then constructs the East?

CH: Yeah. I didn't plan it that way. Now I can't…it seems so obvious a construct I should just say yes, I planned that all along: the Old West fading into the New East. Yet actually "Shangdu" comes from anecdotal inspiration. China now contains all these boomtowns. I spent time as a journalist in northeast China (in Yanji and Shenyang). These cities really had no regulation. Cars would drive in the wrong direction. But then new highrises kept opening—though not with Shanghai or Beijing's frenetic pace. It actually felt incredibly poor. It had a rag-tag Old West aesthetic. I made these intuitive sensory connections. Though maybe the other part of my brain thought, yes, now that I've written about the West, let's talk about the East.

AF: Could you discuss this section's choral staging or orchestration? Did you build that up as you thought through "Shangdu's" place in the overall triptych?

CH: For all three sections I wanted to fray the narrative. As you progress this narrative feels more fractured. The first section adopts the first-person plural and sustains that voice throughout. But the second section moves toward greater multiplicity. I wanted to address Shangdu as a city, a populous—to break away from the individual, or the romantic idea of Old West individuality. Chinese society focuses much less on the individual. This prompted my decision to jump from voice to voice. And also, going back to "Shangdu," the title: it definitely echoes Shanghai and Shenzhen, though actually comes from another text. Marco Polo's travels include a city called Shangdu. And Shangdu sounds like Xanadu. It's my fantasy of the occidental fantasy of China.

AF: Shangri-La's also there. But this section's prose-vignette style moves much faster than what came before. Like in that passage "Lucky Highrise Apartment 88," every condo has one wall missing amid the haste. Did you deliberately provide quick glimpses then move on? How does this speed and its corresponding points of access, its kaleidoscopic types of vantage, compare to the embodied duration of the "Our Jim" ballads?

CH: Well in this longer sequence, "Adventures in Shangdu," with the apartments all missing one wall, I wanted to dramatize a panoramic glimpse, or these different glimpses of city life. Here Calvino also became an inspiration, alongside Marco Polo's journals. The "Millennium Aquarium" title again riffs on Polo. So speed definitely serves as a formal device throughout this collection, though also as kind of a subject matter. One passage says "History intones catch up, catch up." Basically I hope to capture a desperate eager energy in different voices trying to catch up. But what are they catching up to?

The impressionistic quality of "Adventures in Shangdu" implicitly poses this question.

AF: That impressionistic quality, with its increased conflation/dispersion of localities, sets up the digitized space of the final section's World Cloud, in which one's imagination can link to any nation. Here a further reduction (to pixilated units) takes place.

CH: In "The World Cloud," globalization exists as a virtualization—which yes does get set up in the second section. Shangdu presents this imagined city, this fantasy of a global economy but with everything becoming further and further dematerialized. But I should say that Shangdu also situates itself in an industrialized age, again with its own idiom, though I never try to authenticate the experience of being Chinese, living in Shanghai, working at a belt factory or something. Instead I borrow from Victorian poetry, like Hopkins and Kipling.

AF: Then "The World Cloud" seems more comprised of short, declarative sentences. Do these again suggest a modulated, pointillist, pixilated consciousness?

CH: I hope so. No real formal constraint drove these poems. They seemed syntactic gestures more than anything else.

AF: In terms of the snow metaphor, which your epigraph from Joyce's "The Dead" introduces, did you write this book before the Fukushima meltdown? Does that event somehow haunt this?

CH: Oh no, this came way before. Of course the concept of nuclear winter resonates here, but I wanted to keep the snow a really loose image.

AF: It is, suggesting fractal space and all that. Then finally, with the "Fable of the Last Untouched Town" (a town which sounds a lot like North Korea—again conflating historical time and place, through this last Stalinist anachronism) your book's final line, "And this is what I saw," contains this conclusive, valedictory tone. Given the oppressed, administered poetic-subject that has come before, did you deliberately offer an optimistic ending here? Or one totally hollowed out of value? Or did you just want to end the book? That ending works well either way.

CH: I'm glad you think so. I don't want it to seem a hopeless book. I didn't want to end hopelessly. First this book had ended with "The Quattrocentro," on the phrase "swallowing it whole." That really smacked of closure, whereas "This is what I saw" sounded more hopeful, slightly more ongoing, even as it circles back to the start. So these three different sections get bound together, despite addressing three different time periods. That's why I wanted to end with this line.

AF: Which returns us to the present, facing the unknown.

CH: Right. That was my intention.

## INTERVIEW WITH JULIANA SPAHR
Recorded on June 28, 2012
This interview focuses on Spahr's book *Well Then There Now* (Black Sparrow).

ANDY FITCH: Could we first discuss this book's formation? Pieces have existed for more than a decade, sometimes in slightly different form. "Sonnets" started as "Blood Sonnets," right, with double columns braiding medical and lyric discourse? But more generally, does the span this book traces offer some sense of your writing process? Do multiple projects exist simultaneously under your consideration for a long time? Do some never get expanded to this scale? Does this diverse collection provide a coherent study or perspective or argument? The selection of timely, compelling content seems more important to you than to most experimental poets.

JULIANA SPAHR: This book has a long time frame. It contains a bunch of separate projects I did while developing full-length books. I self-published many of these pieces as chapbooks or PDFs, which I'd post on a now-gone website. Then at a certain point someone from Salt asked for a manuscript and I thought I'd gather up these various pieces because they'd had a really small distribution. And I thought of this as a collection about place. It moves through different geographies. Though eventually, things didn't work with Salt (no disrespect to them). Yet in the meantime, I had this typeset manuscript and no publisher and, because I'd worked on the design with a friend, I wanted to keep her design. But a typeset manuscript, I now know, can become a liability. Still Black Sparrow was nice enough to take it with the design. Or they let me talk them into it.

AF: Did each piece take a while? Do these discrete studies sit around and go through different iterations?

JS: I'll try to remember. I self-published them as parts of the Subpoetics, Self-Publish or Perish project. For that project, each of us on the email list (called "subpoetics" for some long-forgotten reason) would self-publish a book then send it to the others about once per year. So these chapbooks felt written for a quite small audience, persons that…I could picture the list to whom I'd send them. I might have edited these pieces after self-publishing them. But I might not have.

AF: On the topic of audience, of address (both for this book and much of your writing), can we discuss the discourse of complicity that appears? Colonial/neo-colonial complicity plays out. Class complicity. Complicity amid ecological disaster. Or in "The Incinerator," with its rethinking of Hannah Wiener's "Radcliffe and Guatemalan Women," you seem drawn to Wiener's status as not a "knowing…uninvolved witness," but potentially "a participant and part of the problem." How does your own book enact or engage a poetics of complicity? How could a complicit poetics prompt constructive thought or action, rather than the reader simply identifying with lyric self-laceration?

JS: I think about this a lot. I'm not sure what first prompted me to address such topics through poetry. That probably has to do with personal/educational narratives, with issues of access to various media and things like that. Another potentially less loaded term I might use alongside "complicity" is "embeddedness." With what do we coexist? What do we carry around? That image with which I end "Dole Street," walking up and down the road, thinking about the giant nest that Loren Madsen made, that's the kind of thinking that compels me as a human. Guilt also interests me, which I want to recuperate—to see as a possible place from where you start your thinking, rather than as an immobilizing shame. What might be guilt's usefulness?

AF: So guilt gets rethought as a collectivist call to action, rather than some cathartic confession?

JS: People argue against guilt that it makes one feel bad, which causes shame, which can become disabling. But guilt also could send you out into the streets. Or maybe I should say: I wonder if it could. Or, if it did, what would it make one do in those streets?

AF: Other poets also present fluid pronominal shifts between "I" and "we," but yours seem more deliberate—less some generalized defamiliarizing gesture than a sustained rhetorical strategy.

JS: That interest started with the beloved, the "you" of the lyric tradition—trying to embrace and manipulate it at the same time. "We" also appeals to me since it is such a bad pronoun. In the '90s, perhaps the '80s, academics wrote articles about the badness of the "we" (as falsely inclusive). When I went to Hawai'i "we" got super complicated. Can one use "we" if one is neither Hawaiian nor local? Or, to rephrase that: when one is neither local nor Hawaiian, what does it mean to use the "we"? What types of alliance remain possible? Can a "we" of variability exist? Could you acknowledge different relations to others within the "we"?

AF: Back to guilt or complicity as potentially productive forces in your work—does "Unnamed Dragonfly Species" present something of an exemplary tale? It offers no tortured confession, really. It probes an abstraction, an extraction from personal experience, pointing toward how we might represent, conceive of, think through endlessly complicated (though obvious) phenomena that occur right before us. The experiential complicity or guilt comes as the reader gets desensitized to your continued conceit of disrupting narrative progress by inserting names of endangered species, then reflects on his/her forgetfulness, then gets lost in this long poem's momentum again and again.

JS: As you spoke I pictured that endless list of endangered and at-risk species, that list's realism, and how we now go through life involved with this ever-evolving, never-ending story of more and more species disappearing. This list grows longer every day. And likewise, you hear every year about it being the hottest summer ever. We've heard this story since the '90s and might keep hearing it. That said, I always get nervous about being preachy. A million years ago I submitted a manuscript to Geoff Young, and he sent it back with a rejection note that basically said, "Not my cup of blood." But, to defend my anxiety—those issues you've mentioned remain part of how we now live life, and not to have them intrude would seem unrepresentative or insane or blindered.

AF: Well, I'd asked about experiential processes because it's not like you deliver some didactic lecture. You'll enact (or conjure) rather than impose a concern.

JS: Right, I guess I don't see poetry as very good at persuading people to act. It does though represent realities and can tell stories about this moment—a moment in which cataclysmic events keep happening, keep confusing us.

AF: You mentioned this book's different geographies. *Well Then There Now* provides not only the mailing address at which you apparently completed particular poems, but also precise, quasi-militaristic geographical coordinates. This suggests a conflation of the idealized, intimate local and the impersonal, digitized global—a poetic-subject somewhere between the letter-writer and the satellite signal. These fluid/convoluted conceptions of place reminded me of let's say Lisa Robertson's prose, or a publishing enterprise like *Tinfish*.

JS: Susan Schultz's *Tinfish* has been really important, and I compulsively read Lisa's books. Myung Mi Kim also comes to mind when you talk about locals and globals. I may not share the formal disjunction she adopts in much of her work, but I've learned much from how she thinks about globalization moving through her own life.

AF: Could we discuss Stein? Obviously Stein comes up in terms of repetition. But you also have explored ways that modernists such as Stein borrowed rhetorical elements from colonized cultures exporting their workers to imperial capitals. To me your own forms of repetition echo the call-and-response in some oral cultures—again constructing the reader as a complicit collaborator. Could the blues or gospel, for example, have made their way up through Appalachia into your poems? Or with your long anaphoric phrases like "As I write this other stories keep popping up," I'll think of mnemonic techniques associated with improvised and liturgical traditions. Of course the same could be said of your lists and litanies. So beyond the pure aesthetic pleasure (which remains strong for me, both in Stein's work and yours), does your use of repetition, anaphora and list-making seek to produce cognitive operations resembling reflection, dialogue, discursive exchange?

JS: I don't know. I like the question. But I can't tell if repetition does something special to the brain. Does it prompt reflection? Does it suggest dialogue? I have no idea. I'm not well-versed in cognitive studies. But the scope of oral poetries, of chant, etcetera, fascinates me. I often look at the patterning that happens in oral poetry. The *Kumulipo* might be the most interesting poem ever made. I guess I could say that poetry does something to the brain. But so do coffee and beer.

AF: What specific oral traditions do you look at? And when you say you "look at" them and what they do with repetition, can you describe this process of investigation? Do you intuitively absorb structural patternings? Do you note specific techniques to try?

JS: I just look at whatever I can find in the library. It all comes through books. Which seems probably the wrong way, eh? Which might be why I say "look." But studying oral traditions of Hawai'i , for example, also helped me learn what I saw when I walked down the street. It felt important to know that. And as I say this, I do remember in Hawai'i sometimes I would go to talks various halau hulu would do, where they would bring in someone to discuss a chant in great detail. I loved those talks.

AF: And when you learn about Hawai'i or how to walk down the street in Hawai'i , have you picked up historical context? Have you encountered a distinctive means of dialogic exchange—as a result of how the *Kumulipo* gets structured?

JS: Probably not a unique structure. But I did learn something.

AF: Could we briefly return to lists and repetition? Many of your gestures of repetition, of call-and-response, of parataxis, suggest something like an ongoing, generative, collaborative process between reader and writer. This reader has to stay attentive and dexterous and assimilate the unpredictable—as if attending a live performance. By contrast, your alphabetized lists, let's say again in "Unnamed Dragonfly Species," seem more ominous. A preordained sense of doom and death accrues as we make our way toward Z. Have you deliberately contrasted these trajectories or tones, with some lists inviting us into communal creation, and others dispatching predetermined ends?

JS: Lists become inclusive, because obviously you can stick anything into them. They offer endless possibility. And, of course, lists also contain a certain arbitrariness. I don't know if I've deliberately used lists in different ways, though. Like I'm not sure the list was the point. I wanted to write something that celebrates, or that emphasizes the ominous, and then a list would appear as one of the nervous tics I have, and so that gets used.

AF: That reminded me of Rosalind Krauss's essay "Grids." She'll talk about grids containing both centrifugal and centripetal tendencies— since a grid painting could be this boxed-off, framed, enclosed bit of art, or a grid can suggest an infinite set of coordinates expanding outward in every direction. Some of your lists seem to tap centrifugal pressures that could keep assimilating omnivorously and extend forever. Though then the A-to-Z lists offer a more centripetal pressure, bracketing off history, foreclosing experience.

JS: I like the distinction. I'll take a look at that Krauss piece.

AF: Or we have the conventional paradigm of a poet serving as a pacifying social conscious, and the more avant-garde paradigm of a poet prompting proactive forms of engagement, and your modes of address somewhere between. If we consider the role that critical discourse has played in Language poetics (in *L=A=N=G=U=A=G=E* magazine, let's say, which is all poetics), and then of the paratextual statements you'll attach to pieces in *Well Then There Now...* I know you're as critically minded as anybody, but your own paratexts seem much less polemical, much more pragmatic, practical, Oulipian or DIY. When you confess to taking lines from *A Guide to Ohio Streams*, I'll wonder what role does this gesture at poetic transparency serve. It feels quite playful. It's not as if this information furthers my comprehension of the poem.

JS: Once I read that poem and a guy approached me afterwards and said, you must do a lot of fishing. I don't do any fishing. So I felt I should admit I don't fish (instead I use the internet). But also I saw this poem as addressing the difference between information and memory. And it seemed important, given the historical pattern of unattributed appropriation, to show that I borrowed from "other" traditions. The phrase "gentle now" got stolen from Sufi poet Ibn Arabi, and I didn't want to claim it as my own lyric invocation. Once I'd added that detail, it made sense to treat the poor, unnamed writer of the *Guide to Ohio Streams* with as much respect as I could.

AF: Do you see your work as recalibrating the lyrical, the didactic and the procedural—restoring a sense of desire to an era after Language poetics? Do you sense that such desires never fully disappeared from Language in the first place?

JS: When I first started writing, people my age often felt the need to present themselves as antagonistic to Language work. The men in particular seemed to want to separate themselves. But I never really felt that. Barrett Watten's *Bad History* remains extremely important to me, as does Lyn Hejinian's *My Life,* as does much of Ron Silliman's work (despite my tension with how he talks about contemporary literature), as do Bob Perelman's essay-poems, etcetera. You could call me a child of Charles Bernstein, in the sense that I've absorbed so much from him that I can't even see it. Still I'll joke that I'm the disappointing child of Language poets. Eileen Myles has that line about desire and Language poets—something about how no desire exists in their work. But I feel a conflicted response to that line. I don't consider it entirely true (and the Language poets, when she said this, immediately began a list of work that contained desire—their list wasn't that long, though). At the same time, Eileen's line gets at something true. When I first started reading Language poetry, I appreciated their departure from this Western tradition that tends to focus on men's desires for women's bodies. I mean I'd read a lot of poems about women and desire. I liked reading poems about other stuff.

AF: Can you explain then what makes you the disappointing child of Language poetry? Because to me your books provide a smart response that such poets could respect. You'll integrate the atomized nature of their sentences or syntax, extending these to this whole new range of politicized subject matters and complex rhetorical structures that many so-called post-Language poets would never even try.

JS: I just remember this moment when Ron Silliman kept saying (he says many things, right?), about some anthology of poets who may or may not be "post-Language," that their work did nothing which hadn't already been done by Language writers. In terms of particular linguistic forms, I can agree with him. But we also could say that Language writing has offered no formal innovation that modernists didn't try, who themselves did nothing new that hadn't been done by…

AF: From what I remember, you've begun a new critical study. Could you give a brief sense of your thinking for that project, which emphasizes the heterodox blending of languages in '90s poetics? How does this relate to subsequent (or simultaneous) trends of appropriation in conceptual poetry, to digital and multi-media projects? Do points of continuity arise among such discourses—even when the work seems to have quite disparate origins and political valences?

JS: "Begun." Ha. I've "worked" on this project for the past 10 years. I started with funding from a "New Economy" grant. Remember that idiotic idea? Anyway, I began a book in the '90s examining contemporary literature. Now it has become a historical argument about the '90s. I argue that in the '90s many people start bringing into English-language literature other languages, and I look at this in relation to globalization, etcetera.

AF: Do appropriative and conceptualist poetics find their way into this paradigm—in the sense of integrating multiple tonalities and discursive registers and constraint-derived perspectives?

JS: No. That work interests me, but it doesn't fit. It does something else. It comes at a different moment.

AF: Your own work always impresses me for its willingness to contain more prosaic, hackneyed, outsourced language than one finds in most lyric-infused poems. But do you find such twinned discourses equally melodious in some way? If we go back to "Blood Sonnets," with all its medical notations, can that lab-report idiom, that mechanized pacing (at least when juxtaposed to other tonalities) provide as much aesthetic pleasure as any other? Do you feel drawn, aesthetically, to every language you embrace?

JS: I'm drawn to the aesthetics of their juxtaposition (as this plays out in poets like Olson). Such combinations always feel interesting or "nice." Aesthetics seem so weird anyway. They make so little sense to me. Yet complex information also interests me—some more straightforward lyric mode would fall flat.

## INTERVIEW WITH DANA WARD
Recorded on June 30, 2012
This interview focuses on Ward's book *This Can't Be Life* (Edge).

ANDY FITCH: Your book foregrounds tensions between "life" and "art." New Narrative seems an important influence. But could you catalog a broader range of work that informs this interest in the life/art threshold? Paul Blackburn's and Stevie Smith's journals come to mind. Of course Gertrude Stein's *Alice Toklas,* Creeley's *A Day Book,* Montaigne, Proust, Thoreau, poor overlooked Dorothy Wordsworth, Basho, Andy Warhol, Jonas Mekas, Chris Marker, Agnes Varda.

DANA WARD: You've named a wonderful list. And throughout the 20th century we find this basic, even axiomatic question about that boundary, about whether art could affect a dissolution of such distinctions, and then the ways that such a dissolution have been monetized or subsumed under an economic regime. So now that capital has totalized all related life processes, what does this question look like? Those precursors you mentioned fascinate me. I could name many more. But at the moment of this book's composition, certainly New Narrative writers (such as Dodie Bellamy, Kevin Killian, Robert Glück, Bruce Boone), and then authors associated with that impulse (Gail Scott, Chris Kraus) informed my work. Douglas Oliver's book *Whisper 'Louise'* became important. I read Bruce's *My Walk With Bob* and Douglas Oliver's *Whisper 'Louise'* in quick succession in 2008. I also began to realize that my email correspondences had initiated a laboratory of affect, prosody and thought—creating a tone and measure and sound which seemed more interesting than the lineated verse I wrote at the time. The impulse of desperately wanting to talk with specific people on a daily basis, from whom I felt separated, provided the initiating spark.

AF: Several of my recent interviews just skirted Bruce Boone, and you've brought up Douglas Oliver as well. Could you say more about what draws you to their work?

DW: Sure. Bruce's projects demonstrate an extraordinary ability to organize vast amounts of material (social, mythic, poetic, political, personal) through a charming, casual voice. I came later to his work than I might have. I knew Dodie's and Kevin's work, but not Bruce's. Of course Bruce's books have stayed a bit more fugitive. *Century of*

*Clouds* had gone out of print, and by 2008 only *My Walk With Bob* was readily available. But Bruce's ability to maintain this engaging, inviting tone (a tone he develops out of O'Hara and others) attracted me. Oliver's book seems similar in some ways. It's a book of incredible doubt and passion. It presents this dual biography/autobiography investigating the lives of Louise Michel (a French revolutionary) and of Oliver himself—offering this little diptych structure. Again that inspired me. I had all these topics I'd thought about forever. I hadn't found a formal way of addressing them that seemed suitable.

AF: *This Can't Be Life* could lend itself to the myth that this is who Dana Ward always has been (writing and living exuberantly, with both processes flowing out of each other, granting unchecked access to an unmediated poetic identity), yet here you've discussed rhetorical strategies and formal solutions you had to think through before the book's "I" could emerge. I also wonder about models from visual art, such as indexical composition—work that literally traces arrangements in the external world, the way photography might, as opposed to most painting. In your longer pieces, motifs seem to cycle through fortuitously, as though you've traced your present, you've recorded the grid of days and weeks, you've shaped your book the way life gets shaped. There is this dream of indexicality, though I know much else happens, too.

DW: I'm attracted to that description and my work does seem related, although I never think of it in reference to autobiography. I think expressly in terms of poetics, or a prosody. My own experiences may provide material or a means of access, but my primary point of departure is that I exist in history, that history contains economic and political dimensions, and that subjectivity and my being in the world derive from an intersection of all those dimensions. I pursue the musical arrangement of these parts toward some greater affect, It comes through an intersection of history and love and excitation and misery.

AF: When poets refer to musicality, they often mean localized linguistic phenomena. Your own arrangements emphasize broader juxtapositions of tone, idiom, discourse or interpretive register on a scene or event or an "I."

DW: That's right. Sonic difference creates certain localized or lyric effects. But as you suggest, discursive and tonal arrangements can play out across a broad range of thought or writing. Bruce's poetics for example produce this materialist church music, this harmony of grand symbols. You can sense this harmonic drive operating on a vertical as opposed to horizontal axis. Though of course I feel equally indebted to Alice Notley—who is deeply motivated by a set of musical effects inside language, inside its prosody.

AF: Do you think New Narrative innovations haven't received proper critical attention? I know scholars like Kaplan Harris are working on this right now. But do you sense systemic changes? Has New Narrative's rhetorical music grown more important to us in part due to the arrival of digital communication and its own layered discourse?

DW: The general lack of writing done around New Narrative is criminal. I can't tell how digital technology shapes our reception. Of course, the concept "New Narrative writing" also remains quite broad. You don't want to quarantine certain aspects at the expense of others.

AF: And just to take a step back: I do want to stress that *This Can't Be Life* displays meticulous editing on a local level. Again, I love how these broad, sweeping movements can feel so spontaneous and impulsive and fresh—like how "Imagine" seems to last just as long as smoking a cigarette. Still, in the Buffalo piece which opens this book, we encounter passages such as: "Tisa was utterly brilliant. She read from the work with the imaginary movie, then, from *Unexplained Presences*, her book, which attends the appearance of African-American faces & bodies in film, how they're figured, & all the different ways one might receive them. I read my own work, & settled into the typical ambivalence that comes after any performance of my own." Here we note pronounced stylistic touches, like the ampersands. Yet that "attends" stands out most. How did "attends" get in there? Could you describe the drafting, shaping, completing of such pieces?

DW: Sometimes this work comes rather quickly. Though often much reading and thinking and talking build up towards the moment of composition. I won't have any advance sense of how a poem will look. I'll begin to compile sentences, lines, ideas that might belong together in a piece of writing. From there I'll start to build something. But a piece like "Imagine" took weeks to write, and changed scale and got much shorter through tons of edits. None of these poems came in a single sitting. It's all "made." Again I take from Bruce this sense that casualness arrives as an affect—through careful construction, through artifice.

AF: When I'd asked about New Narrative's relation to digital media, I'd meant to ask more broadly about your own relationship to popular culture. "It's So Easy" appears in the book, as does a poem entitled "Michael Jackson." At the same time, your work demonstrates a fierce attention to the local, to what Dale Smith might call slow poetry. Could you parse that dual interest in purging and incorporating mass cultural discourse? Throughout this book, tensions between popular art and personal life can seem at times redemptive, at times corrosive. If I walk down the street with The Bangles in my head, does that represent a triumphant fusion of art and life? Or does that suggest some ugly underside?

DW: First I do not mean to purge at all. I only want to push deeper into these obsessions. My emotional/intellectual relationship to mass culture, to popular culture, remains excessive and probably quasi-religious. I hope to intensify that focus in my writing. I wish to construct a situation in which all the poisons can break through—to magnify or amplify their place, to chart these schizophrenic cultural instabilities for their unforeseeable personal valences, and to examine both sides with ever greater intensity.

AF: As a side note, my favorite Pop artists (Pop with a capital P, such as Warhol, Ed Ruscha, Joe Brainard) come from the middle of the country, from a world of pop-cultural consumers more than pop-cultural producers. Can you describe the impact pop culture had on you growing up in Kentucky? Could we find something essentially private and local in your obsessional attachment to this popular discourse? How does your experience of it differ as a function of region and class-based relations to cultural capital?

DW: Good question. As somebody who grew up right on the cusp of mass culture's global thrust, this gets a bit sticky. The local and global become entwined through processes hard to track. Class difference might be key here—degrees to which mass culture appears to offer the transcendental in a language everyone can speak.

AF: Then in terms of a more specific poetics discourse: a piece such as "After Post-Death Organizing Poem" offers a conceptual-seeming opening. Reading this, I wondered if you would provide supplementary details concerning your sources and/or process. When no such statement appeared, I wondered if you considered this a pointed omission. To some extent, this book seems even more inassimilable than most conceptual writing, which at least presents a digestible hook, a clarified concept framing the work.

DW: Brandon Brown's translation practice shows that when you appropriate a piece of writing, a body always must perform on some level. Even conceptualism's purest concepts occur in bodies situated amid a specific lived experience intersecting with history. So I wanted to chart these lived moments of appropriation. "Typing 'Wild Speech'" presents a type-up of handwritten work—by which I mean appropriation always had seemed ordinary to me. By the time I became culturally conscious, hip hop already had normalized appropriation as a means of making art. I never even thought about it. And then you encounter books like Berrigan's *The Sonnets*. Or I worked at the Capri Contemporary Art Center in Cincinnati, so appropriation always had seemed a part of art. For what has became codified in the past five years as conceptual writing practice, with quite specific features: a lot of that work attracted and enlightened me. At the same time, the discourse seems insufficient.

AF: Not necessarily the writing, but the critical discourse surrounding it?

DW: Yeah the discourse remains affecting and interesting, though not finally satisfying. This relates back to the question of where do we locate prosody. You can locate it in metrical effects and line-to-line relations, or through a broader juxtaposition of tones and discourses. You can take tensions between appropriation and autobiographical writing, and create a kind of music from that. And I do, for this particular book, feel a strong attraction to the look of long, unbroken pages, where you run into a wall of unbroken text.

AF: I loved running into that wall. For questions of where prosody resides, I here think of Whitman—how Whitman's rambling, long-lined take on death reminds me of a piece like "Dogs of Love." Death seems a constant organizing principle in your work. Could you somehow place length, inassimilability and death into a meaningful trinity? Or art and life and death? Or the natural and the artificial and death?

DW: Again, Douglas Oliver raises similar questions in *Whisper 'Louise'*:

how can we characterize the relationship between politics and mortality? Who is fungible and who is not, and why? Under what circumstances and what sorts of regimentation? Those topics animate my book for sure. The fact of our death, of our inevitable expiration and its relation to the act of writing, can't be overestimated. Perhaps this traces the connection between…what was the other part of the triangle?

AF: Let's say length and inassimilability and death, which takes us back to questions about purging mass culture. Death prompts us to urgency, yet pop life offers no clear answers on which to cling. That seems a generative principle for this book—pitched between endless desire and the constant confirmation that this desire can't be quenched, but with those two fueling each other rather than canceling each other out.

DW: That sounds about right. Though this book seems to suggest that were I to die thinking about "Manic Monday," that would be a moment of happiness. That moment would not lack syntax. In fact, quite the inverse. It would crystallize a former realization of almost unbelievable satisfaction. Both experiences would remain personal. I could connect to people I love through the thought of it. I could suffer a common infection, with "infectious" being the point. Like I said, when the poisons break through, they confirm our bodily link to others.

AF: The Bangles song for me is "Eternal Flame." I don't know if that makes it any worse.

DW: Even better—even more germane to the conversation.

AF: Sarah appears throughout this book. I'm curious how she feels about that. Is it indiscrete to ask?

DW: Not at all. Sarah has been absolutely integral in my life, and thus to making this work. She's a brilliant, well-read person who has encountered most of the same artworks I've encountered, and has been thrilled and enlivened by them. We've shared that. So I show her all the projects in which she appears and she's like, yeah. For her there always was a theoretical understanding of how experiences, lived intimate experiences, point themselves to art-making. That came before our life together. She's always known what's up.

## INTERVIEW WITH ROB HALPERN
Recorded on July 1, 2012
This interview focuses on Halpern's book *Music for Porn* (Nightboat).

ANDY FITCH: As I work through these interviews I've found myself tracking a resurgent interest in New Narrative—a sense that New Narrative poetics have not received their fair share of critical attention, have not been thought through sufficiently by a broad enough range of contemporary poets. You of course have helped to encourage this interest. Can you place *Music for Porn* in relation to several exemplary New Narrative poets, texts and/or concepts? Does it make sense to speak of a second-generation self-consciously consolidating inherited insights, experiments, practices? Or do New Narrative's deft evasions of conventional literary categorization preclude such distinctions in the first place?

ROB HALPERN: Where to begin with my relation to New Narrative? I'd been out of school seven years before I found myself in Dodie Bellamy's writing workshop in 1996. One crucial forum for nourishing young Bay Area writers is this network of writing workshops that take place in writers' homes. Finding myself in Dodie's workshop (with Kevin Killian participating) allowed me to realize that my writing actually might be legible. After the death of my first love, James, in 1995, I'd lived in a state of terrible doubt and uncertainty—not only about the readability of my work, but whether a writing community existed for me. Yet by then, forces of attraction already had taken over. In the late '80s, when I arrived in San Francisco, I'd looked up three writers who I knew lived here, and with whom I felt a sense of affinity and desire for apprenticeship. I actually looked up, in the phone book, Robert Glück, Aaron Shurin and Kathy Acker, and just by way of a cold call I sent them each a naive fan letter, together with what must have been a crappy piece of writing. I dropped these cold calls into the void of the U.S. postbox. After several months, I received generous, encouraging responses from both Aaron and Bob. Never heard from Kathy. Perhaps she'd already left San Francisco. But the fact that I received positive responses from Bob and Aaron was incredibly important. It offered a departure point of sorts, a permission-giver, though it would take five more years before I'd actually meet Bob through Dodie's workshop (I met Aaron sooner). Bob also ran a workshop out of his home, and I began to attend that in 1997. He became a crucial mentor, a teacher, and now he's a dear friend, as is Bruce Boone, who makes a cameo early in *Music for Porn*, in the first sentences of "Envoi," which serves as a kind of introduction to the book. Bruce's *Century of Clouds* and *My Walk with Bob* remain classic New Narrative works, and my "Envoi" invokes Bruce's writing, in part because I fear *Music for Porn* betrays New Narrative values. So "Envoi" rehearses a moment from a walk I took with Bruce, when he asked about my book's obsessively recurrent figure of the male soldier. For *Music for Porn* to pass as New Narrative, that soldier would need to be a person in my life with a nameable name. Instead, the soldier feels more like a negative imprint of all my social relations—a feeling I announce by citing this conversation with my friend Bruce. Of course the soldier, sadly, will never become my friend, which helps suggest the stakes in this book, and why friendship remains so crucial to its structure. In "Envoi" I write, "This would be the place in the story where Bruce asks me about the figure of the soldier in my book, and whether it has some bearing on my intimate life, or whether the soldier is merely an abstraction is the flesh real? and I'm struck by his manner of asking." Bruce's question contains serious implications for my writing, and I want to foreground this while simultaneously introducing the soldier as a cornerstone in the architecture of a fantasy. This departs from early New Narrative works such as *My Walk with Bob*, or Robert Glück's *Elements of a Coffee Service*, both of which were formative for me. I can't imagine myself as a writer without that work. At the same time, I feel as though I've departed from both texts' writerly values, insofar as *Music for Porn* privileges a critical fantasy over the narration of living relationships. That said, *Music for Porn*'s soldier fantasy seems inseparable from my lived social relations. And here I could point to a tension I feel I've inherited between New Narrative practice (developed among primarily gay writers in the early '80s) and a politics of form that one might say characterizes Bay Area Language writing, if not Language writing in general, whose rigorous critique of conventional narrative values also has shaped my poetics. I don't want to reproduce familiar generalizations, though. New Narrative shares an equal investment in form, yet proceeds from a different political stance, so probes distinct formal problems. In my own talks and essays such as "The Restoration of [Bob Perelman's] 'China,'" I've attempted to rethink this relationship between New Narrative and Language, for example by way of *Soup* magazine's second issue, edited by Steve Abbott, who christened the phrase "New Narrative." That prescient journal issue articulates and illustrates what this "New Narrative" project might look like. Most impressive about that issue of *Soup* is Steve's decision to include a wide range of writers representing divergent literary practices—creating conditions for what Jacques Rancière calls "dissensus," or the perceptible presence of two worlds in one. Steve's expansive editorial vision provides new possibilities for presenting tensions among various poetic approaches within a complicated early-'80s Bay Area writing ecology. Similarly, in early issues of *Poetics Journal*, Barrett Watten and Lyn Hejinian adopt practices of inclusion, again to make legible productive tensions and differences. Only in the afterlife of such projects, amid what often go by the name of the "poetry wars," do we think of these dynamic, syncretic, symbiotic writing communities as discrete, segregated, sectarian schools. So here I've offered a circuitous response to your question. I too find those historical tensions outlined above quite productive. I'd like to think that my work engages and complicates the relationship between both projects—through its movement toward narrative, certainly, but a narrative as indebted to Lyn Hejinian's and Carla Harryman's mode of distributive narrative (or non/narrative) as to forms of storytelling that I learned through my apprenticeship to Bruce's and Bob's work.

AF: Here could you clarify whether it makes sense, within this intimate poetic community, to distinguish between generations?

RH: I've thought about that question a lot recently—specifically the fact that we often need a so-called "third generation" to work through all the obstacles at play in a second generation's inadequate grasp of a specific cultural phenomenon (in this case New Narrative). One obstacle for me concerns the relative reticence of New Narrative, compared with the volubility of Language writing, when it came to theorizing and historicizing itself. Even while attending Bob's workshops, right there at the movement's hearth, so to speak, "New Narrative" felt like something of a rumor, a secret still waiting to be discovered. My generation—and here I think of writers with whom I formed important friendships while attending Bob's and Dodie's workshops, such as Jocelyn Saidenberg, David Buuck, Dana Teen Lomax, Yedda Morrison, Robin Tremblay-McGaw—had to work through what often seemed, to me at least, like illegible tensions and contradictions that we'd unwittingly inherited. Our work struggled to metabolize all this, though I suppose I only can speak for myself. At the level of affect, let's say, I could perceive the stakes attached to certain writing practices, but couldn't interpret those affective qualities, even as I worked to embody them as living feeling. So while I tried to stay faithful to New Narrative's apparent commitment to storytelling (where the narrative stakes hang on specific bodies, often abject and marginalized, in specific communities whose boundaries often get delimited by scandal and gossip), I also needed to make sense of Bay Area Language writing. I felt caught inside a set of aesthetic and social conflicts whose terms I hadn't quite grasped—in part because those terms still were shaking themselves out. Without consciously understanding it, my writing wanted to give form to these tensions, to resolve what remained unintelligible contradictions. While I've since done my best, through critical and editorial projects, to help make New Narrative legible for others, it will require a younger generation to achieve the distance necessary to see the terms, the histories and the stakes as if for the first time. And I think we find this now in the work of some younger writers who have conscientiously apprenticed themselves to New Narrative.

AF: As you outline your own "apprenticeship," could you give some concrete sense of how you and your workshop peers, whether intentionally or not, have revalued or repositioned characteristic gestures from both poetic communities? Does an initial New Narrative emphasis upon storytelling subsequently allow for unsuspected forms of syntactical and discursive intervention (of the type we expect Language to produce)? And in terms of the reductive scholarly take, the differential narrative in which Language and New Narrative define themselves oppositionally (all of which ignores a much stronger legacy of shared and overlapping commitments, exchanges—both interpersonal and poetic), what do you think of critical projects such as the CUNY "Lost & Found" series, which adopts archival research practices in order to return us to the lived social context for work often categorized entirely according to aesthetic or theoretical considerations?

RH: I think you've done a great job answering your first question by way of your second. And yes, I think we've grown accustomed to something like an official set of groupings based on recognized affinities, and lost the more nuanced, more complicated, more fraught and certainly more interesting engagements that many of these writers have had—across what we only now perceive as hardened boundaries. Granted, you read a book by Bruce Boone or Robert Glück or Dodie Bellamy, and it doesn't sound anything like work by Lyn Hejinian or Carla Harryman or Charles Bernstein. Still New Narrative and Language writers share a complex ecology of friendships and genealogies.

AF: I want to make sure we get back to your book as well. Can I steer us that way?

RH: Absolutely.

AF: Here could we start with porn? Could you characterize the various valences porn picks up? Of course one could conceive of porn as analogous to our safe, sanitized, solitary removal from the scene of contact or conflict—foregrounding exploitive dynamics between exposed and unexposed bodies. *Music for Porn* does speak of activating a "pornographic imagination." Yet it seeks to position this imagination "against the militarized common sense that has otherwise fully harnessed it and to unbind those affects otherwise sclerotically bound to the nation's ends." Subsequent passages suggest that this book's "I," its shifting poetic-subject, cannot determine precisely how/where such a threshold lies—what precisely it would mean to activate this pornographic imagination against militarized common sense. So to start, could you describe some liberatory implications or potentials for social engagement that get allegorized in your book's treatment of porn? What otherwise unspeakable intimacies can porn help us to realize? How and when does porn become abstract, avant-garde, utopian? If poetry can become a form of porn, can you describe porn's poetics?

RH: That huge set of questions might offer a nice segue from our discussion of New Narrative. Works by Bob Glück, Kevin Killian and Dodie Bellamy respond to porn. In many ways, porn is just another genre, and thus a way of codifying and policing the visible and the invisible, the sayable and the unsayable, the licit and the illicit. Market-driven pornography manifests a strict set of protocols, reinforcing predictable expectations that attend gender and sex roles. New Narrative often seeks to manipulate or explode such expectations. I've often referred to porn as a regime of representation in which one's most intimate relations—be they to one's own body, or to bodies of others—get mediated by the most impersonal images and discourses. As I write in the book, "Under current conditions, common sense itself becomes a kind of pornography (expropriation of my most intimate relations) just as pornography becomes a kind of common sense (everything bearing visible value, everything erasing the relations that produce it.)" But just as porn polices the divide between the licit and illicit, the perceptible and imperceptible, it also can challenge and reconfigure these division. My book aims to do this. I want the poems to make perceptible an otherwise imperceptible tension between my most intimate and most abstracted relations. And as I pursued it, this tension materialized in the figure of the soldier. So I return to Whitman's Civil War poems and explore my fraught relationship to them. Whitman's "Drum-Taps" sequence remains seductive and moving but also deeply problematic—as it transforms the soldier's historical body into the eroticized, sacrificial figure around which Whitman shapes his vision of post-Civil War democracy. The eros of Whitman's project fascinates me, an eros we can't separate from his ideological vision, from his own forms of militarized common sense. This eros has nothing liberatory about it. For Whitman, the soldier offers a kind of sap, a binding agent for a divided nation. Whitman gives us this metaphysical soldier, whose eros the poems arouse, to heal a damaged history. Is it too strong to characterize this as a militarized ideology inseparable from homosexual desire? Today we see an extension of that: homosexuality gets increasingly normalized while at the same time national borders get further militarized to protect us from other others. I don't consider such phenomena unrelated. So the broader question arises: if one's erotic life remains deeply implicated in precisely the social structures one seeks to resist, how can bodies and pleasures become scenes of resistance? My book's obsessive relationship to the soldier's body does not promise liberation, but rather further scenes of contradiction and obstruction. The soldier becomes an embodied location, a figural site where my own libidinal intensity emerges to block the realizations of my utopian social desire.

AF: Throughout *Music for Porn*, I wondered about the how these eroticizations of the soldier parallel Whitman's eroticizations of the slave's body. Did that potentially problematic precedent help prompt your own investigations? And in terms of a broader democratic discourse. How does Whitman's rhetoric of camaraderie (his embrace or construction of his era's affectionate male-male norms) correspond to the more fraught power dynamics implicit in his relation to the soldier's body?

RH: For Whitman, libidinal desire always contains the potential to activate what we might think of as real social agency. Yet Whitman's discourse around a democratizing camaraderie never adequately maps onto the social material the Civil War presents to him. And it interests me how Whitman's semantics of camaraderie transform from the period of "Calamus" to the period of "Drum-Taps." A profound shift occurs in the way eros functions. The pre-Civil War problem of democracy differs drastically from the post-Civil War horizon. On the eve of the Civil War, Whitman seems somewhat flummoxed. The democratic promise that *Leaves of Grass* elaborates as a vista of future possibility for this "great nation" has collapsed into a scene of profound failure. This amounts to a huge crisis for Whitman, both as citizen and as poet. He needs the fallen Civil War soldier to serve as a redemptive figure. Whereas the comrade represented the agent of a virile democracy, the soldier becomes a sacrificial figure for democracy's redemption. It's on this dead soldier's body that the obscure promise of post-war democracy hangs. But other equally important intertexts also shape my book's concerns, including George Oppen's "Of Being Numerous" and Jean Genet's *Funeral Rites* (Genet's baroque attempt to mourn the loss of his lover, a resistance fighter, without contributing to post-war nation building). As for Oppen, I take seriously the first lines of "Of Being Numerous": "There are things / We live among 'and to see them / Is to know ourselves'." Whitman factors prominently into Oppen's poem, too, but the broader problem that interests me, and this gets back to your questions concerning porn, is what happens when the things I need to see in order to know myself are bodies—fallen bodies in zones of militarized catastrophe halfway across the world, dead bodies from a conflict I can't witness but for which I bear some intense responsibility? Here perhaps I can unpack the pornography of that relation. Of course these dead bodies never become available to sensory perception. Our government has, until recently, forbidden photographs of these corpses. Even the language of the autopsy report remains taboo. Whatever representation might exist to denote those bodies gets banished from the public sphere, removed from circulation, as a matter of state suppression. A blackout occurs at every level of representation. Something at the very core of militarized common sense—a dead soldier—can't be assimilated except through forms of disembodied public mourning, which assist the reproduction of our militarization. *Music for Porn* tries to probe such contradictions by insinuating inassimilable bodies and pleasures into orders of invisibility and surveillance, even while transforming the sanctioned affects that typically attend those bodies (like sorrow and grief) into affects the system can't legitimately avow (like longing and arousal). So if we think of porn as a self-policing regime of representation, positing boundaries between the visible and the invisible, the licit and the illicit, then we move a bit closer to how I've attempted to activate porn in this book. Its final section, "Obscene Intimacies," for example, draws on the unavailable language of the soldier's autopsy report. I appropriate material from the relatively few citations of these reports that have found their way into media, yet the actual documents remain inaccessible and withdrawn from circulation. I don't seek to liberate myself from the shadow of wartime carnage by illuminating it, but rather to situate my body's affective life within that shadow.

AF: Could we then close with you placing, amid the broadest affective context, *Music for Porn*'s insistent liberatory/nonliberatory examination (again through the figure of the solider) of a conflicted yet conflated "Longing, shame, fear, tenderness, rage, sorrow"?

RH: Rather than lament that no liberatory politics seem possible, this book wants to make perceptible those structures that actively constrain utopian possibilities. Here I hope to have stayed faithful to a type of utopian negativity. For example, when you rehearse my list of affective responses (rage, tenderness, longing, shame, sorrow) my mind again returns to "Drum-Taps," to how Whitman arouses and stimulates all these same affects—homoerotic affects in which a whole contemporary history of queer liberation remains invested. He saturates those poems with affect, which the poems simultaneously lubricate and bind. As a result, the poems become incredibly manipulative as they mobilize a homoerotic network of stimulating (erotic) and constraining (ideological) impulses. Now, if Whitman's poems arouse all this affective material prosodically, while making it function in the interest of an ideological vision that, despite its "democratic vista," is nonetheless statist, expansionist, militarized, then what might it sound like at the level of song to unbind those affects, to make them useful again by making them useless for the state? Amid my attempts to hear that sound I encounter the depths of its unsoundability. The obsessive return to the soldier figure foregrounds a relentless desire to feel what I can't feel, the feeling of unbound affect. Or less abstractly, it's like I've beaten my body against the obstacle to whatever affective transformation I long for. And this obstacle—the soldier—is also the limit of my potential for embodied relation under current conditions, in other words, the limit of friendship. How far does *Music for Porn*'s language need to go in order to sense that limit? What place does fantasy hold in our militarized world? What might it mean to undo the terms of such fantasies? My book can't resolve these questions, but perhaps it allows us to feel the emotional architecture that haunts them.

### INTERVIEW WITH STEPHEN MOTIKA
Recorded on July 2, 2012
This interview focuses on Motika's book *Western Practice* (Alice James Books).

ANDY FITCH: If we could start just with the title. Can we say your title alludes to the retrospective, regionally-placed subject constructed by this book, to the conspicuous positioning of a self-conscious literary debut, and to the erotic undertones that triangulate the growth of a particular place and particular person or personhood, however loosely you want this "I" attached to you? Does that briefest synopsis work?

STEPHEN MOTIKA: I think that's all in play. The title came not from California but actually when I crossed the San Luis Valley of southern Colorado. The valley's bottom runs about 8,000 feet above sea level, along the Sangre de Christos into New Mexico. It abuts Taos, adjacent to the Rio Grande Valley. I was in this region thinking about art-making. D.H. Lawrence came to the mountains above Taos, and I went to visit where he's buried. Georgia O'Keeffe captured that famous tree against the night sky in her painting "The Lawrence Tree." I kept thinking about these two complicated figures in modernism. We have D.H. Lawrence who, for me, since I was a teenager, represented the body and sexuality. *Women in Love* was an important novel for me in high school. And then Georgia O'Keeffe's career seems more complicated, multitudinous, and more interesting the more you learn about and spend time with her. What we'd thought were just flower paintings that refer to the female orgasm become a really complicated story in the history of modernism. And both came to this place. So I was thinking about their Western practice—literally. Lawrence went to New Mexico then on to Mexico and then back to Europe. But he wrote a pretty over-the-top novella called *St. Mawr* there. Parts of it describe that landscape. My title came from this experience, very rooted in the West, and thinking about artists from elsewhere making art in the West. I wrote some notes while in New Mexico and the phrase "Western practice" was in my notebook. It was part of a poem I never finished, but I imported it when looking for a title. This made sense, given that I come from the West, California, and have thought about many different practices—the practice of life and practice of writing and reading, the practice of thinking about art, and having grown up in a family that privileged art. That includes all kinds of Southern California artists. We knew about Richard Diebenkorn's "Ocean Park" paintings. All those layers of art-making and practice. And other readers of my book have suggested the influence of Zen practice. That title, which originated as I traveled through New Mexico, became about a larger idea of the West. My father's family is from Colorado. My mother's came mostly from Utah, with Californians who went back and forth, traversing. So that in itself was a practice, a self-linking experience going from Los Angeles to Denver every year my entire childhood, back and forth.

AF: I like the resonance of "practice" as a rehearsal as well. I was just talking to Cathy Park Hong about her take on the Western idiom, and how our concept of the West always remains mythic and real at the same time. We're constantly practicing the West even as some of us live there. Then with appropriation and repurposing (like your title just appearing after it had another function), if we could move into that topic. The first poem, "Night, in the Oaks" raises any number of pertinent questions which run throughout the book. First, with its elliptical reference to intimate, decontextualized, details, it bears the trappings of autobiographical lyric. Yet a note at your book's end tells us this poem, in fact, borrows from David Bromige's *My Poetry*. Here I'm curious if you could touch on how biography and autobiography, constraint and appropriation, language-based surfaces and New Narrative-esque plot pivots, how these commingle in your work. There are gestures both toward and away from autobiography.

SM: Those four things you just mentioned are at the heart of this book. The tension between life-writing of the self and life-writing of others, between appropriation and generation of material—these I realize are problematic. As for the autobiographical: that's the great shadow of the project. Originally the manuscript moved from Southern California to Northern California. So Part II came first, then "City Set" and then the opening poem, "Night, in the Oaks," up through the Harry Partch poem, then it ended with the same poem. So I've re-ordered the geography. I say this only because readers responded strongly to the Northern California section, which has the most autobiographical poems. The lyric "I" gets embodied in a response to mid-century poetics. Or late 20th-century poetry and poetics that come from the Bay Area. David Bromige is important, Lyn Hejinian is important, Leslie Scalapino is important, Philip Whalen is important, Etel Adnan, Kathleen Fraser, among many others. The interesting part for me is that some of my poems fail. They fail as autobiography. They fail as lyric, their narrative "I." They don't quite work musically. There's awkwardness in that section I've come to like. This awkwardness of autobiographical writing interests me. Where it's like you're reading my life and you feel awkward. There's a surprise in every line of that work. "The Lakes" is an interesting poem because it has a lot of autobiographical details but, for me, is a poem about AIDS, an elegiac poem. I wanted that space present there. That's how it gets beyond the trap of the lyric "I." For me that's rocky ground. I see the poem as an attempt to produce this lush lyric that then falls apart. It becomes fragmented, or play-spaced, or sounds odd, or stutters. Or the poem leaves out so much it becomes abstracted.

AF: Well, that's why there's no sense of failure for me. I think of, for an art reference, Thomas Demand. Because it's all a constructed scene rather than an actual, natural one. I'll first think I'm looking at a photograph of a forest then only later note it's all made of paper. I certainly wouldn't consider that a failure on his part. I don't with your work either.

SM: I didn't mean failure as a judgment, but failure as possibility or opportunity. Failure as a way to create and invent in a space that's fraught, or exhausted. Autobiographical writing is exhausted. And yet there are ways to manipulate, or fail to achieve. I think of these as generative. As complex. But other texts since *My Life* have played with that. Like Susan Briante's *Utopia Minus*: I think that's an amazing exercise in autobiographical writing, in the sense that it fails to achieve certain expectations, but is not a failure in terms of a work of art. Her work in fact generates all these new spaces. But there's failure in meaning or a failure in reading or failure in form, too. That's important. I love poets who have such tight control of their work. Like Julian Brolaski comes to mind, a young poet who's just, like, whoa. Or even Cedar Sigo for different reasons. I was talking about Cedar's work with Brian Teare, who was teaching it. Kids in his class were like, these poems are hip and cool—what's the big deal? Brian put the poem up and scanned it with them. And they couldn't believe something was there. That its music was so sure; for me, in my own work, the poem's music never sounds that clean and neat. That's something I think about a lot right now. Has my resistance to poetry as a form been my resistance to that closure? Or feeling outside it? Or feeling an atonal, trebling note is integral to something I do?

AF: I'll want to get back to musicality, specifically in relation to biography. But while we're still on "Night, in the Oaks," one other question. You've mentioned local points of reference, authors whom your work is meant to evoke. I'm also interested in other ways that locality, or space, place, get figured here. Your emphasis on phrasal clusters as basic units. In this poem they'll be set off by commas. At other points they'll get framed by white space. I'm interested in how rhythmic properties relate to your representations of space or locality. When I first saw the spacious deployment of these compressed, minimalist verbal clusters, I pictured open California landscapes. I thought, this is like a big state with space. But as I began to read, that vision merged with Larry Eigner's Swampscott, Massachusetts. Lorine Niedecker's Lake Superior. I began to track overlapping depictions of geographical and textual place. I mean in terms of visual, syntactical, rhetorical, thematic space. Can you say a bit about if and how this vaguely Projectivist tradition appeals to you?

SM: Absolutely. Absolutely that space is part of what I was working through and thinking about. Reading the page, reading as visual and musical space. The landscape that they define makes a map. Those various intersections interest me. Of the people you've mentioned, Larry Eigner hits closest, because of the constraints he worked with and how much space had to do for him. You'll feel it in his every word choice. And that goes on, too, with work he made in Northern California, in the East Bay for a decade and a half. I really thought a lot about him, that monumental collection that came out at the time. I'm interested in this second generation falling away from Projectivism. What happens after the people at Black Mountain, literally at Black Mountain, are gone? What happens post-Duncan and post-Olson, and to younger people? I think Susan Gevirtz's last book, *Aerodrome Orion,* is amazingly complicated—politicized and historical. I love what she's doing. And this is something I'm still investigating, to go even further to think through typographical uncertainty and instability. Stuff that Philip Whalen has done. Or projects that appear cyclical or repetitive, like the poems of Leslie Scalapino. This form where things constantly circle about. The way her own muted music and textual notation create a space that's different yet again. So to hear her and to read her work on the page aren't two separate experiences. It's sort of a commingling of those two. Also Duncan ends up doing something with the self that's really important for me. Then those open-form poems of *Groundwork* are so, my god, that's what was happening those 15 years. And how they fall out of "Passages," and fall out of...I haven't thought about this and maybe this shouldn't be quoted, that some sort of pastoral element for him in the end is not possible. It happens to Ronald Johnson, too. He goes from...think of *Book of the Green Men* then he ends up at *ARK*. It's that same transition.

AF: Related question. On the minimalist phrasings that recur. What role did erasure play in your compositional process? What does erasure signify in terms of gaps, residue, amid the book's personal, cultural, historical retrospection?

SM: In terms of the creation of this work, there was little erasure. A few redactions, in a few places, but there are no erasure texts. I didn't take a piece and remove parts then put it back.

AF: I couldn't tell with the David Bromige if that's happening.

SM: I'd lifted then interspersed lines from his book, *My Poetry*. I was concerned when my book had been accepted for publication. Did I need to go back and track down all the lines I borrowed? But I'd lost track, Andy. I couldn't even remember all the places. And someone said, who cares? And this is really true for the Partch piece. What does it matter? That became freeing and wonderful. Everything was appropriated and nothing was appropriated. I wrote a ton. I appropriated a ton. No procedures were sacrosanct, or exact. I didn't follow the lead of any conceptual writers. There's a lot of translation. A lot of gesturing, especially in the Partch piece.

AF: Maybe we should move on to the Partch, to your more expansive sequences. Both "Delusion's Enclosure" and "City Set: Los Angeles Years." For "Delusion's Enclosure," just for context: who is Harry Partch, and how does the concept of the microtonal factor into your own poetics? What's microtonal about your work? Why that title for this poem? And this other question kept haunting my reading. Does Partch's trajectory as California-born, itinerant, instrument-inventing, Li Po-quoting, queer countercultural mid-century prototype composer…it seems so strangely to overlap with the myth of John Cage, or who John Cage was. Is that part of what you've constructed?

SM: Harry Partch, as you've said, was a California composer born in 1901. He died in 1974. He spent much of his life in California. He had two extended stints outside the state. In the second half of his life, he'd built these instruments. He was looking for a place where they could be housed, and where he could take care of them and produce music. Under those auspices he was at the University of Wisconsin for a while. Later the University of Illinois. Then California for the last two decades of his life. I think that's important. And the connection to John Cage. Cage is like—what do you do with Cage? Cage, whose centennial arrives in just a few weeks, is this huge figure. I discovered Cage when he died in 1992. I read a lot of the work. I know the music. I know the writing. He's sort of this impossible behemoth I didn't know what to do with. Harry Partch, on the other hand, was someone I was intrigued by. He was way quirkier.

AF: He'll seem, in your account, more Cageian than Cage.

SM: Cage stayed cloaked about who he was. I'm not sure we'll ever know how he really felt. And a lot of his practice was about nonresponse. Those famous talks at Harvard where audience questions became emotional and he stayed nonresponsive. What I love about Partch is that he was emotional and a drunk and indignant and restless. He was a visionary and more than a little off the wall. I love that messiness of him. I love that there's no way to fix him through a series of conversations or major pieces. That he doesn't have anything iconic. Nothing like *4'33"* identifies him. It's all rough. And it's a little hard to take. That's why the narrative becomes compelling. And I loved taking on that narrative and trying to break and play with it. The microtonal's important to pick up different registers from each part of the life. One could be Oedipal, mythic, or as you said like Li Po, in a sex scene, similar to an institutional meditation, to a coming-of-age narrative, to this traveling salesman. The microtones were about the whole range of his human voice. And Partch's story shows, in some ways, the whole range of human life. In many ways he did everything. That compelled me. I'd planned to write 43 parts, to match his microtonal system. But insisting on that structure seemed a bit silly because the poem happened organically. That's in the end what Partch is about. There's organic insistence. The music's about creating something ages old. For him this was sacrosanct.

AF: It seems, from your piece, that Partch somehow moves away from a notational system, from an abstract scale of notes as differentiated sounds, to using the human body as the basis of his tonal range. Can you explain a bit about that?

SM: He wrote a 450-page treatise. But part of what I also was doing was not worrying about that. I wasn't really responding to him altogether. I was listening to the work, and the work was in me. And I felt the instruments. Some of it's awfully hokey. It's perversely idealistic. When I saw *Delusion of the Fury* at the Japan Society in New York five or six years ago, some of that was hard to take. It felt racist. The colonial gaze seemed really at work. My poem's about his personal life, his thinking. And the thing that really shocked me—and this is true of Cage, of course—his whole queer identity is just buried in the literature.

AF: You're saying in responses to him, not in his own self-representation?

SM: He was born in 1901, so Stonewall happened when he was 68 and near the end of his life. So he was never in a culture that was terribly out. He wasn't closeted—he was amazingly open for somebody born in 1901, but didn't have the language or resources to be what we think of as a gay man. But what was amazing about the books I read, for the most part, was how straight they were and how they minimized that part of his life story. I wanted to reclaim that side of him. People who read the poem and came to me, and knew Partch, were shocked he was gay. They had no idea. This happens, too, with Cage. There's this cult of avant-garde music that's incredibly straight-identified. Now there's a major biography out. There's more known, and with Merce Cunningham dead, more will appear about Cage's sexuality. But it stayed buried and obfuscated for a very long time. Even the relationship with Merce is kind of grey in the '60s, '70s, and '80s. I think people were like, they're partners? Where was the sex? Where was the fucking? Where was the body-to-body contact? Where was the romantic spirit? Where the real engagement with that whole spectrum? It was absent. With Partch's work, it's rooted in the body. Yet this whole part of his experience gets elided.

AF: Along those lines, if we could talk about what you see as the potential for a poetics of the biographical. Again, I'm curious about your own microtonal performance here. This goes back to earlier, when you'd mentioned the sonic elements of your poems and talked about failure—how they deliberately fail in some ways. But the sonic thrust of your biography stands out clearly. Maybe it's related to the erotics of your telling Partch's story. Maybe the embodiment of the biographer gets denied in those straighter accounts you've mentioned. I guess I'm thinking of projects like William Carlos Williams' *In the American Grain*. For poets, for the historical/archival research poets do, the histories they provide, what roles can sound, can the bodily telling of the narrative play?

SM: I love that articulation. I'm not sure I have an answer. The poetics of biography: I've been asked about this. It's a really big question for me. For this project I felt compelled to engage a life. Then a poem happens, a text emerges. Part of me felt I could do that again. Then I was like, no, that's not what this is about. I'm not a biographer. But I did have the urge. I was like, oh my god, I could sit down and do this; I could do a whole book. I had a million ideas that just seemed crazy.

AF: I thought of Vasari's *Lives of the Artists* which, I think, too, come out of what he heard in bars or whatever, restaurants. Their oral nature.

SM: I'm working on a new project about elegy in a more exact and specific way. I wonder if that's one possibility for the body of the biographer to be more present, to be inculcated in the experience of telling the life, or grieving, mourning, tracing something that's passed. I really love the idea of people doing biographical projects that amount to volumes. *The life of Johnson*. People who are great diarists, etcetera, and there should be space for that. But I think for me, at this point, that's not where I wanted to go to next. Although part of my nature is to be obsessed with people's biography. I read obituaries religiously. I have this desire to know all the weird details: what's their birthday, what city were they born in, where did they really come from? All those things interest me intellectually and creatively and personally. So, for the microtonal, the very interesting question of the microtonal and how it relates to the telling and inscription of the writer? That's my sense of it. And maybe getting back to Vasari, it's questions of what defines a significant experience? How do you engage those things if it's posthumous and you're working with archival data? I don't know.

AF: And how do you represent them for the reader, further removed from the archival moment? How does that libidinal or erotic attachment transfer into poems deriving from archival research?

SM: That's really present for me. I've wondered, too, if being able to work both with music and film...I watched films of Partch and also heard the instruments—so it wasn't just looking at pieces archived somewhere. It became alive. There are diaries he kept in the '30s that are incredibly erotic. Those I repurposed. I sussed it out. I looked for it. It wasn't just lying on the surface. I went in and dug around. A music scholar would have written much more about the technicalities of what he did with instrumentation. In that sense this poem's very personal, very biographical. The inspiration's very much based on a living moment. And then there's Partch's obsession and complicated feelings about being visible, about fame, about being an inventor, about being original. In his mind he'd changed the course of human history.

AF: On that topic, perhaps we can proceed to "City Set: Los Angeles Years." Can we consider this timeline-based poem another biography of sorts? That comes up. And I'm curious what shaped decisions you made for how to represent this extremely heterogeneous city amid such tumultuous years. Of course, any reader would have conspicuous gaps for what she thought would be there. Like, for me, Duchamp's early-'60s presence is there but not Warhol at the Ferus Gallery and Pasadena Art Museum. Or for more conventional L.A. representations: Watts comes up, but Manson does not. So that's interesting—the personalization of this timeline. I'm also curious if art exhibitions you cite determine the precise span from 1955-77, or of other determining factors at play.

SM: The answer to the first question is that the poem started out longer, more detailed and denser. That was something people reacted strongly to. It was too much for them. Then the poem's shape suggested edits. Manson was there. Warhol was there. Some of that felt like overkill. I'd been trying to be encyclopedic, rather than registering different moments. It's also typographical. Chris Schmidt pointed this out, saying that while the Partch piece is notation, "City Set" seems defined by typographical and visual play. I wanted that to be true. I wanted a whole bunch of different registers. And I'd worked with lots of material and ended up with a poem shaped by the music and visual character of the times. That helped me figure out where to go. Some stuff seemed too obscure. There was a whole bunch nobody was going to get. And I'd decided I wasn't going to write extensive notes. So Warhol in L.A. was too confusing. People would go, Warhol was New York and Pop, what's it doing here? It was a red herring. Or with Manson I thought that was very sensational and not so interesting in a reflective way, in the way the Watts riots are interesting, especially as a creative space. The art-world's response is important to the poem, and the story of Noah Purifoy. I went to this Noah Purifoy sculpture set in Joshua Tree, and it was a revelation. I was reading Richard Candida Smith, his book on modernism in the West. Those two things sparked the poem. What happens when we think about West Coast art-making not as a laggard response to the East, or Europe, but as its own original space? And not just in some apologist way, but in a strong and defiant one? This was really important. I'd always believed that, but somehow the Noah Purifoy story and Smith's account, brought that into focus. The poem's set from '55 to the year I was born. There's a sort of pre-me thing, then I come into it. At the end there is this lyric "I," and it's like all of a sudden I show up. That's part, too. There's a visual filmic language and some of it I just thought, this is cool, and gave in. Or I liked some typographical modes that look a bit abstract. I like some architectural references. The notional. That was fun to work on.

AF: Brian Kim Stefans is sort of assembling a poetic history of L.A. which seems to have interesting overlap…

SM: We've talked about it.

AF: Going along with this "other traditions" principle. That it's not that L.A. work derives from something else. It just has been overlooked. One small question in terms of the art catalog: does the use of first names to refer to figures from the L.A. art world, does that suggest the intimacy of this particular community, and of the retrospective scholar reflecting on his or her biographical subjects? It seemed almost to transpose this classic New York School gesture, but as a means of comparing respective cultural histories.

SM: That's great. I love that you said that. I think that's totally at play. You know the James Schuyler poem about going out to dinner?

AF: With Doug and Frank?

SM: I love that move and love that intimacy, which seem both exclusive and exposed simultaneously. There's this experience they had that no one can be a part of, though still the art can touch it in an off-hand way. That was part of what's going on. Different textures and voices I played with were a response to the poetics of telling, the poetics of experiences I was appropriating. That inspired this whole project. I can become Jimmy Schuyler in the Chelsea Hotel. It's all OK.

AF: One thing we haven't fully gotten to. You just mentioned the textures available within the telling of a story. The poetics of the tableau, also foregrounded in this book, seem different. One example would be the last poem, "Near Los Osos." This seems to fuse the language to the landscape in a more visual/literal way. Another example would be the "Ocean Park" sequence. "Ocean Park" provides a network of details that depict a coherent, if abstracted, landscape not unlike those found in Richard Diebenkorn's own "Ocean Park" series. It's got these representational drives. But then opaque pictorial textures at the same time. One poem in "Ocean Park" provides this seamless assimilation of a transparent scene, though then ends with the enigmatic words "must call." Unlike the palpable presence which precedes it, that "must call" can be assimilated only by a much looser mode of conjecture. So does it deliberately disturb or leave unresolved the preceding sequence of descriptions? Does this apparent disruption of unified time and place, does it somehow break open the tableau you've been constructing?

SM: Yes. It's a breaking point, too, for the longer poem. It marks a shift. The third section's rooted in experience. It moves from abstracted descriptive language and free association to something very specific grounded in experience.

AF: The tableau gets traced and then we move—we enter the tableau we've looked at.

SM: Not that this answers your question, but it was written right after my grandmother died. It marks an important point in my own creative maturity. I felt I had to write to her and in response to her life. And Ocean Park is one of the iconic places in Los Angeles County—like for New Yorkers there's the Flatiron Building, the Empire State Building, Central Park. It's iconic in terms of place because of the ocean, but also the art Diebenkorn created. For me, it's the perfect... you know Oppen's whole thing about using general language words to make poetry? He said that eloquently, and I didn't. But Ocean Park to me, it's like perfection. So the poem's very quotidian, filled with daily details as it goes from an abstract to a specific location. But it's decidedly not Rococo or grand or flooded with color. I wanted it to exist the way it existed, though it does have this personal note of responding to someone who's passed, responding to a very important figure. Which doesn't answer your question about the tableau, but I wanted to speak about that poem, about why it's there, why I kept it in, why it's important. The larger question about tableau, that's big. I'm not done with that. "Near Los Osos" is a completely different interpretation of place. That poem is very hard to read aloud because of all the commas and stuttering and the vocabulary. There's a complexity of sounds that makes it difficult to annunciate. That's partially about having read a lot of, then edited a lot of, the Tiresias poems of Leland Hickman, as I was doing during this project. I don't know if you've worked on something where you've had an intellectual idea about it and you grow to feel more and more…in response to it. At the time I was a bit traumatized working on this because Hickman's poems are—I mean, talk about the full body: long lined, Whitmanesque, difficult, abject, sexual, overly-familial and obsessed by death. All the big things. It's attempting to be all this stuff. But I do think Hickman haunts my book in an interesting way. I think a part of me is realizing that and part is resisting his poetics. Like most American poets have. His poetics are untenable, really. But also it's like, ooh, there was this long-lined, messy, impossible, impassioned, brilliant California poet who's unknown. And his tableaus and landscapes and life lived and poetic spaces and incredible ability to create the six-, the eight-, the ten-page poem with repetition and incredible musicality. Incredible control. And talk about failure in his attempt to create this Olson-esque, Poundian, multi-volume epic. It was unwritable, unfinishable. I just don't think it was possible. And I love that. I love the whole thing. I love the starting and the failing. I love that it was necessary but proved to be unnecessary. It's all this one, two, three—it's like the Cantos; it's going to roll out. But the last one Hickman wrote in the Tiresias sequence was part "1:9b," It's a 70-page poem with 10 parts. That's where he ends. It spins out of control. I'm really interested in that. And they are tableaus, whatever that is. Whether it's theatrical or in the sense of visual arts. Or even Partch's pieces were tableaus, right? There were actors, a set and instruments. That's something. I'm still in the thick of that.

## SIXTY MORNING TALKS

### INTERVIEW WITH LISA ROBERTSON
Recorded on July 3, 2012
This interview focuses on Robertson's book *Nilling* (BookThug).

ANDY FITCH: Could we start with the acknowledgments, with the ongoing occasional nature of your prose projects? First, do these various professional alibis serve as a corrective prompt to some shyness on your part? Do they allow you to say things you otherwise wouldn't? Do they deliberately demonstrate your active engagement with specific traditions, discourses, audiences, communities? What continues to compel you to foreground the institutionally constructed nature of these investigations?

LISA ROBERTSON: Much of my critical prose remains occasional simply because I don't have much time. When I write a catalog essay (as in the case of some Soft Architecture pieces), or give a lecture (as with most of the Nilling projects), I try to make that occasion work toward my own current interests. Here I had the idea to construct a book of linked essays, loosely exploring a conceptual field, and used a series of lecture invitations to explore that concept. I never would have the time both to fulfill my institutional invitations and to write an unrelated book. I work slowly and just can't crank out six essays. Similarly, back when I started The Office for Soft Architecture's occasional works, I supported myself as a freelance writer, so had to find a means of bringing my economic life together with my research and creative interests. I suppose I foreground these contexts out of gratitude.

AF: Well could you discuss if/when such institutional engagements provide space for something like institutional critique—as that phrase gets used in visual art? In the case of exhibition writing, for the "Perspectors/ Melancholia" piece let's say, you seem to trace the epistemic confines of certain critical practices, rather than to provide some interpretive context that makes the artwork more legible. Your prose will stand alongside the art or text that it purportedly supplements. It becomes part of the exhibition.

LR: Canadian art writing includes a kind of minor tradition of the parallel critical text. My prose has developed in this context. I don't believe that practices of critique need to make art and its institutions more palatable for anybody. I don't think literary criticism inevitably should make texts easier to consume. Interpretation doesn't compel me, not as a reader or a writer. It interests me to elaborate upon a work's problems—in the most positive sense, to probe the problematics I discover (not to gloss over these problems, but to complicate them further, to make them juicier). Often that seems the most engaged and respectful stance. Hadley and Maxwell, the artists whose installation I responded to for "Perspectors/ Melancholia," don't want critics to turn their juicy, complex, problematic work into something easy. They want viewers to engage its difficulty, its layeredness, multiplicity, multi-textuality, openness. My job does not consist in creating closure, but rather exploring the openness I find present in a work.

AF: Again this layeredness and multiplicity you respect in fellow artists often finds its way into your prose. It interests me, for example, how *Nilling*'s discrete, occasional commentaries change when extracted from their oral context, from their relation to specific artworks or social spaces—as they get assembled into a collection. Did this book itself begin as a commissioned enterprise? How does its selection of pieces reflect *Nilling*'s overall function or form of inquiry? What particular theory of the book gets implied/inferred by projects such as "Time in the Codex"?

LR: BookThug did not commission *Nilling*, though we've worked together in the past. They published my book of poems *The Men*. And Jay MillAr, BookThug's publisher, has started a subseries focused on experimental critique, which includes projects by Sina Queyras and Phil Hall. Still I didn't develop this manuscript specifically to fit that series. I just followed what interested me, such as this notion of passivity or abjection as a form of agency. All the writers who publish in Jay's series have the opportunity to work quite closely with the series editor, accomplished poet and critical thinker Kate Eichhorn. Kate and I worked on shifting the register of these texts so they could come together as a book—also on sequence, which becomes crucial to the book's trajectory. *Nilling* begins with a history of materiality, and moves towards an immaterial poetics of politics.

AF: In terms of shaping a reader's experience, I've often considered your prose to be structured around the sentence as the basic unit of assertion, momentum, play, erotic pleasure. Yet these current pieces seem to showcase an ever-expanding range of modular practices. "Time in the Codex" complicates its own investigation of serial processes by adopting a numerical list form—one I associate with numbered maxims or manifestos by grid-friendly artists such as Sol LeWitt, Mel Bochner, Joe Brainard. I also think of John Coplans' *Serial Imagery* catalog, in which he discusses Gertrude Stein's uncanny practice of counting (one and one and one and one). Then later your piece "Lastingness," again derived from a delivered lecture, provides its own distinctive measure, suggesting some sort of projectivizing prose, sculpting its argumentative and associational pivots.

LR: For the "Codex" essay the shaping came later. I started with two separate pieces—a talk I gave and a catalog essay, both for the artist Marlene McCallum. Later I had this flash to splice those texts together and present one as subtext to the other, so that they could appear on the same page. Both went through major editing. And in terms of the numbering, which I have used before: I model my numbered texts less on conceptual art (although I love and certainly follow such discourses) than on philosophy (Wittgenstein, for example). I appreciate the slowed-down, serial nature of that numbering. It suggests a carefully constructed, fiercely logical, causal building of relationships—which my prose does and does not provide.

AF: So if we consider *Office for Soft Architecture* the template by which most readers know you best, could you discuss how the propulsive, descriptive prowess developed there plays out in *Nilling*'s more meditative, scholastic, philosophical projects? Does the description of complicated phenomenological, hermeneutic, interrelational processes call forth a different distribution of syntactical and rhetorical intensities than the flâneur-esque flair at play in Soft Architecture's seven walks?

LR: The *Soft Architecture* texts started with a simple problem—how can I construct a description, a document, that maintains an indexical relationship to this city I experience in my quotidian life? How can I develop a description that moves? Description long has interested me, partially due to its abjected place within the discourse coming out of modernism. For *Soft Architecture* I wanted to describe the tactile, temporal experience of urban change. Then *Nilling*, as you point out, seeks to map a much more contemplative, philosophical terrain. I couldn't just walk around and take notes. Instead I've tried to track the profound cognitive pleasure (one that approaches, for me, the intensity of a sensual pleasure) which I always have experienced as a reader of philosophy, in which I have no background or training. I read philosophy as a poet. I pursue this delicious process of getting lost and needing to slow down all my cognitive habits and backtrack—as if learning to read a new language. This thick meandering plays out stylistically, too. No rehearsed, subconscious structure helps situate me, and I hope never to lose in life this furthering, this unbound broadening I experience as a reader of philosophy. For example, as *Nilling* makes obvious, I have enjoyed a long and deepening and marveling relationship with Hannah Arendt's books. An undergrad course with Robin Blaser in the mid-'80s turned me on to *The Human Condition*. Robin also got me started reading Giorgio Agamben. I already had read, on my own, Nietzsche and Heidegger and some Roland Barthes. But Robin's class showed that a wider community shared these concerns—that they comprised a broader discourse. Of course this discourse also contains some of our most intensely gendered, authority-ridden constraints. As a woman with no authority in the field, it actually frightened me to admit I wanted to write these essays. This writing process did not produce the immediate glee the Soft Architecture book produced. In fact, in the future, I might aim more consciously to bring glee into philosophy. It took a long time to figure out what types of sentences could describe this nilling, this scooped-out negation I wanted to probe as a literary space. I don't consider these essays light or fun to read. They didn't feel light and fun to write. But I don't know…during the time I wrote *Nilling* all kinds of major events happened in my life and the lives of people I love. Serious illness and death and major changes informed this biological space I entered. As I finished writing the book I received treatment for breast cancer. One of my closest friends, Stacy Doris, suffered through a cancer that killed her. Although this writing never directly addresses the autobiographical, inevitably our corporeal condition shapes our work—and not just in terms of erotic pleasure. Sometimes it's terrifying.

AF: On this topic of corporeality (as well as on your discussion of trying to construct a description that moves, a philosophical register that foregrounds glee), *Nilling* announces the caesura as a regenerative point of reflection for the reader. Yet I appreciate how often this book, and your prose in general, gestures toward a pause, but provides no obvious space for it. Instead we keep moving on with this dream of the pause partially fulfilling us. Here the poetic line perhaps would pose a more dramatic break than the prose sentence does. Still do you think of these essays as providing room for a reflective pause? Or do they sketch a mode of reading philosophy that doesn't demand such ponderousness? Do they propel us forward rather than forcing us to stop and seek out answers?

LR: Many of my past prose-poetry and prose texts (already a false distinction) have foregrounded this declarative, manifesto-esque forward push. Always in my work I've tried to face something that I don't know. When, as a 30 year-old, I explored *XEclogue*'s splashy bravado, that felt new to me. I'd been a retiring, melancholic person in my 20s, then suddenly discovered a community. I encountered a series of discourses that opened fresh terrain, and I experienced wild joy in that. Then at 50 you just enter a different space, which again shapes the stylistic surfaces you want to pursue. I do feel that *Nilling*'s essays try to explore the conceptual space of the caesura. They ask, what goes on in this pause? What you've described as the dream of a pause sounds about right. The wild joy of writing now has to do with deepening my capacity to enter into and sustain an equivocation, a space of cognitive ambivalence where, rather than promoting and defending substantive positions, I explore the spaces between the substantives—the scary groundless middle before you make an argumentative leap.

AF: Since the concept of nilling itself embodies this fused appeal both to cognitive leaps and to interstitial stillness, perhaps we could discuss nilling.

LR: First off I should say I don't fully understand this concept.

AF: Perfect. Again we can engage a philosophical discourse with no fixed sense of our own place within that tradition. And here we might draw in your consideration of Pauline Réage's *Story of O,* with its frictive contest between a simultaneous willing and nilling. Your discussion of this conflicted or conflated or convoluted process recalled for me Nietzsche's treatment of the aesthetic priest in *Genealogy of Morals*—where Nietzsche internalizes Hegel's master/slave dialectic and places it within a single, multiplicitous self for whom any outward achievement demands its own obedience to impulse, to will (just as any external surrender implies a victorious passivity conquering within the submissive subject). Or Emily Dickinson's "Master Letters" seem to exemplify the erotics of nilling. Could you discuss how such models, or any others you wish to offer, relate to Arendt's concept?

LR: Sure. As far as I understand, Augustine's *Confessions* first directed Arendt to this concept. Her doctoral work addresses three formulations of love in Augustine. So to that extent, the profoundly ambivalent agency of this willing/nilling conundrum derives from a tradition of Christian thinking (somewhat ironically, given Arendt's Jewishness). That legacy of Christian thought of course conditions European subjectivity. Foucault situates the crystallizing Western subject in late-antique texts—the time of Augustine. I hadn't thought of Foucault and Arendt together until right now. But Augustine's work first dramatizes this doubledom, this negation/agency knot Arendt pulls. She says any act of the will gets founded on a simultaneous resistance to that propulsion. Likewise, some of my *Nilling* essays try, almost at an intuitive level, to frame these philosophical problems of the will and the counter-will historically, and vice versa. All of my work has swayed more or less between discourses and disciplinary regimes. With this particular book, history and philosophy seem to provide that axis.

AF: When you speak about graphing such structures of consciousness, and treating them both philosophically and historically, I remember how "Time in the Codex" ends with the line "She is free to not appear"—evoking the vanished face that concludes Foucault's *The Order of Things*. But I also think, more generally, of the nature of the aphorism. Do aphorisms provide a particularly pointed way of mapping or tracking mental movements and constructs? Can we say that some aphoristic projects (Wittgenstein again comes to mind) basically catalog structures of consciousness?

LR: Yes. I like that way of putting it. And in terms of the lack of time I've mentioned: there's always room for an aphorism!

AF: There's also a built-in caesura. An aphorism always implies a subsequent (and maybe a preceding) pause. And in terms of punctured texts, perhaps we could move to your piece "Disquiet." Does Pessoa also whisper in the background here as we discuss the aphorism? Does John Cage's *Silence* resonate? But first I should clarify that your book encourages us to read the "Disquiet" pieces with a specific sound accompaniment. These sound recordings serve to structure our temporal experience. That's where Cage came in—his "Indeterminacy" prose segments, for instance, each of which gets read in a 60-second interval. I wondered if I should read your individual "Disquiet" sections in precisely the amount of time each recording allotted.

LR: That sounds hilarious and fabulous.

AF: I tried it out. Of course I never finished most sections on time. But whenever a particular recording would end, I would seem to have reached a sudden, all-clarifying assertion such as "it distributes sound as non-identity." Silence would re-emerge and feel quite charged and disquieted. Then I would continue reading at my fast pace because I already had been reading fast—all until "Edge Dwellers," which finally allows for space to hear the endless sound of endlessly rejuvenating kids' voices. Could you describe the types of discrete and/or symphonic experiences that "Disquiet" shapes (auditory, textual time-bound or post-temporal)? And the recordings themselves all contain caesuras. They have pauses in them.

LR: Initially I gave the "Disquiet" piece as a lecture, using those recordings as interludes between the prose sections. But your pursuit of simultaneity delights me. And the recordings (made, in some cases, many years before my lecture) capture ambient urban sound discovered at the sites of early 20th-century photographs taken by Eugène Atget. I would travel to where he took the photos, try to stand exactly where he must have stood, then make a recording. At the time I wrote this lecture Stacy Doris and I worked together as a collaborative unit called *The Perfume Recordist,* collecting ambient everyday recordings which we remixed as 18th-century perfumes. We planned to compose a two-hour performance to give at a colloquium hosted by the Kootenay School of Writing. We learned together how to use GarageBand, and read tons and tons of theoretical and critical and historical work around sound. We read Cage, for sure. Then when I went back and tried to make some use of my 30-second Atget recordings, I finally hit on the idea to double them. As soon as I doubled these recordings, they had a shape. In order to mark that doubling I include a 10-second silence at each piece's midpoint—a direct citation of Cageian silence.

AF: As you describe how we can make meaning out of even the most abstracted sequence once we hear it twice, I wonder if philosophical discourse often develops similarly—introducing a concept then returning to it until we find it familiar, then redirecting it in new ways. But if I could get back to my masochistic, time-bound reading of "Disquiet": I loved, both here and throughout your book, how the encounter with dense philosophical reflection can resemble (and I mean this in a good way) skimming, walking, flâneuring a bit. Even as I rushed through, my attention would catch on and somehow arrange "Atget," "Haussmann," "margin," "radical politics." Do you think we could consider this quick, time-bound absorption a productive mode of reading? Does it, like many mystical and aestheticized departures (or partial departures) from philosophical speculation, grant distinctive access to what you call "our own bodily opacity"? Could you describe how *Nilling* hones and refines the reader's sense of one's own bodily opacity—perhaps by tracking kinetic operations of logic, thought, reasoning, or by providing a saturated text with too much to take in at once? Here I remember the over-stimulated audience-subject called forth by, let's say, Brecht's theatrics or Godard's cinematic simultaneities. That always has seemed to me the most civic, democratic subject that I can embody. Whom else do you consider prophets of this "prosody of noise"?

LR: Godard fits much more than Brecht. And I love that you've brought cinema into the conversation, because who I discovered cinematically, while writing these essays (it embarrasses me how late I came to him), was Robert Bresson. I watched all of Bresson's cinema and I also discovered the Portuguese filmmaker Pedro Costa. Costa often collaborates with communities living illegally on the outskirts of Lisbon. His film *In Vanda's Room* gets shot almost entirely inside a young woman's bedroom as she smokes heroin with her sister and has fabulous conversations with people who come to talk to her about their problems. In the background you hear wrecking balls because, in fact, Portuguese authorities are just then demolishing the shantylike structures these people inhabit. I find the way that Costa makes room in his shot for all of this information incredibly moving. He seems just to sit still, permitting our perception to dilate on the present in all its insane, senseless variousness. Pedro Costa's cinematic project currently shapes how I want to think about corporeality and politics—that goal of providing an unfathomable, minimally mediated density in which a reader, a viewer (and I) can receive glimpses of corporeality as a collective, shared experience (not corporeality as a demarcation of self, but corporeality as always a trans-corporeality, always interrupted, disturbed, layered, polyphonic, problematic, threatened, and terrifying and pleasurable at the same time).

AF: In terms of how corporeality negates and/or allows for philosophical reflection, you reference Rousseau's *Reveries of a Solitary Walker,* which has that mythic originary scene, traced by Roland Barthes in *The Neutral,* of Rousseau getting run over by the Great Dane—where he wakes up with this moment of bliss for which he can't account. All of his book's subsequent wanderings and writings seem centered around that pre-/post-verbal bliss. Something similar happens for me when my flâneur-esque reading of "Disquiet" reaches a sudden silence. In that repeated moment, I can't say whether the absorption of ambient urban sound has represented a relief from philosophical inquiry, or a further intensification of it. I seem to have been thinking with, rather than against, the vernacular. A utopian vantage emerges—as if philosophy could happen as fast as sound, as if profundity could come as easily and endlessly as background chatter does.

LR: That would be ideal.

AF: At the same time, after recently moving out of New York City, that utopian vantage of endless meaning spreading out in all directions seems to some extent a delusion that the city evokes. Not that some non-delusional place exists, but I do wonder if and how a city's intimations ever get realized. I liked giving myself up to New York's prosody of noise, but now I also appreciate turning my back on it. So here's the question: *Nilling*'s overall trajectory would feel quite different, perhaps more valedictory, if it ended with "Disquiet's" openness. That release into ambient city life would resemble the conclusion of John Ashbery's *Three Poems*—which propels us from the movie theater to walk the daylit city streets. Here, instead, you close with the fabulously dense "Untitled Essay."

LR: Well, "Untitled Essay" explores the relationship between civis and domus (between civic and domestic space), vis-à-vis the idea of the vernacular as a politicized, collective engagement. From there it proceeds into a poetics. And in a way "Untitled Essay" begins in the city, in the density that "Disquiet" has shaped—opening with a citation I found in Louis Mumford, from the Greek rhetorician Eubolus, who describes this noisy, insane density of the Greek agora (which contains everything from clocks to legal contracts to whatever…food). I wanted to end *Nilling* with a strong proposition about what a poem does and can do. And I decided to place that idea of the poem within the context of the city and of noise and disquiet and the caesura and density of corporeal experience. You could say the entire book gets set up in order to deliver this replete poem as a multi-corporeal vernacular space of potential and resistance.

AF: Your dog stretching at the end of that sentence added a nice touch.

LR: She's sitting here. She's talking to herself. She's been sitting, watching me for our entire conversation.


INTERVIEW WITH THOM DONOVAN
Recorded on July 5, 2012
This interview focuses on Donovan's book *The Hole* (Displaced Press).

ANDY FITCH: Could we start with a brief chronicle of this book's making, which doesn't describe necessarily its present function? Can we track how its structure and identity have changed over time? Of course *The Hole* presents its own narrative on both accounts, but I'd like to hear your own in case that's different.

THOM DONOVAN: The first hundred pages or so (the book runs about 160 pages) originally appeared as individual poems with titles, often dedications, on a weblog I've edited since 2005, called "Wild Horses of Fire." Many occasional poems directly engaged with some cultural phenomenon or particular group of people. An event often trigged the poems. Over time I assembled a manuscript, circulating various forms, less to find a publisher than to receive feedback from friends and peers. As far back as 2008 or 2009 Brian Whitener, who publishes Displaced Press, approached me about doing a book. But his commitment to publishing *The Hole* came gradually. I started to revise the poems, to think about design questions, still uncertain whether or not it would happen. Then in the summer of 2010 I drafted an email in order to address how these poems had emerged amid this very rich constellation of people and events, here inviting addressees of the poems to produce something, a response, to my manuscript. After lots of hesitation and conversations with Brian, finally in December 2010 I sent this letter. The published book presents about 40 pages of facsimiles from those solicited contributions. Again, after I'd received them, an intervening year occurred with this publishing project still up in the air. Scheduling issues arouse, further questions. During that period I began to write what I came to call the prefaces—essays about the state of the book, the status of a poetry book after social media, theorizing in some ways the manuscript, its conditions of production. That accounted for an additional 20 pages. The remaining material consists of email exchanges with Michael Cross as we designed the book last summer, and also an envoi which I composed at the tail end of this design process.

AF: The envoi, do both Rob Halpern's and Brandon Brown's new books contain an envoi? Certainly one does. Did you three write these in concert?

TD: I didn't have Rob's book in mind. Rob's definitely has one. I don't know about Brandon's.

AF: Even as you describing this chronology…a book's sequence often obscures its chronology, positing a manufactured progression. But here the poems did come first then the dialogic exchange and then the critical reformulations. Still your title seems to suggest a sense of rupture, harkening back to Romantic and modernist tropes (though with a homophonic W-H-O-L-E also tending in the opposite direction—toward totalizing structures). I'm curious how this gesture toward the interrupted text plays out here. Could we place your book on a continuum, with Coleridge's "Kubla Khan" dramatizing a break that stops the poetry, and Stein's *Making of the Americans* foregrounding a break that generates the poetry? Or yesterday Lisa Robertson discussed the caesura, which she finds so crucial to philosophical discourse, reflection, contemplation.

TD: At first I'd given this manuscript the provisional title *Nonsite Poems*—referring on one hand to the Earthworks movement and Robert Smithson. I can't remember when I started to call it *The Hole*, but the front cover reproduces a 1966 photo of Claes Oldenburg in Central Park, constructing a sculpture called *The Hole*. Oldenburg kneels before this hole, which resembles a grave, with another man in the hole/sculpture/grave actually laboring, digging it. A split appears between Oldenburg's cerebral or intellectual labor and the physical labor of this hired man. Then young boys stand around Oldenburg and his hole. The photo's uncanny. But of course you can't help hearing the homophonic W-H-O-L-E, which most of my email addressees played off, regarding our present moment of totality—of living through a system of governance and economy calibrated to be totalizing, to be without caesura or interruption. Poetry still can pick up use value by disrupting the stresses and rhythms of that totality. Poets do this in numerous ways. One way, one prosody, we traditionally have called lyric. The lyric's received a bad rap for some time, so I'll typically use the term prosody, siding with my good friend Robert Kocik's definition of prosody as a much more expansive linguistic form, where language functions not only through cognitive meaning but through non-discursive elements: sound, subtle vibrations, stress. From this perspective, poetry's disruptions or holes or caesurae represent a long history of language workers resisting that other "whole": totality.

AF: Oldenburg appears in the PDF I have of your book, but I didn't think of this as the cover. For me your book opened on the title page, a long letter crossed out except for the circled words "the hole." This title page seemed to reference erasure poetics. Can you track some structural affinities and differences between erasure poetry and hole poetry? Here a further discussion of non-sites might help. How does your working definition of the non-site manifest in your poetics? Lytle Shaw's forthcoming book considers Smithson's conception of non-site as a decisive trope for how art looks at landscape or space—versus how postwar poetry does.

TD: Well a long history of poets' engagement with Smithson does exist. I think of Lytle for sure. I'll also think of Barrett Watten, or any number of Language writers. Obviously Caroline Bergvall and others embrace the notion of a heap of language—of language as material, something that accumulates, that produces waste. I personally have come to focus more on political uses or values of non-site discourse. Smithson defines the site as a physical location in a supposed natural world or landscape, and the non-site as an abstraction or logical representation.

AF: And Lytle's book describes one form of non-site as something like a discursive intervention.

TD: For Smithson, a non-site could take the form of a text, of his essays and experimental writing, of a photograph, of a sculpture, of something placed in a gallery space, or of the gallery space itself. Various plastic forms can mediate the physical site. But I should say that my own social/political application of Smithson's work comes through my engagement with the Nonsite Collective. Though the Nonsite Collective really became active around the Bay Area, I remained in constant discussion from afar with the group (an evolving group with Rob Halpern, Taylor Brady, Tonya Hollis and a handful of others at its core). Working amid this collective I came to understand that what you've called a discursive intervention actually could happen through group process, through thinking differently about how one organizes, plans events, acts in social space. So whatever the writing or art it includes, the non-site can imply people gathering and interacting and intervening in a particular way. I've also come to understand the term "non-site" through a draft proposal many poets developed together, another kind of homophonic play, here on "non-sight"—suggesting that part of this discursive intervention involves making visible social processes that have become occluded, that have been withdrawn from our ability to see them. Both art and poetry can make such processes visible again, often producing an encounter with traumatic or tragic products of our culture.

AF: When I'd asked about erasure poetry...could we say that gestures of erasure both can outline a network of institutional power and direct our attention to alternate modes of engagement?

TD: Yedda Morrison's *Darkness* exemplifies how this notion of the non-site could be taken up by a work of erasure. Though when I think of erasure I'll think of *RADI OS* by Ronald Johnson or Tom Phillips' *A Humument*. I don't really consider...perhaps the Johnson, but I don't consider Phillips' project a discursive intervention, at least not how I've conceived of that term in relation to the Nonsite Collective. However Morrison does fit since she accomplishes something more abstract. If we consider Joseph Conrad's *Heart of Darkness* a kind of site, almost a landscape, then her erasure of all words unrelated to the natural landscape becomes an intervention or mediation foregrounding how the colonialism of Conrad's time operates in his text.

AF: Here could you sketch your working definition of cybernetics, as it applies to *The Hole*—given this book's uneven topography, its tracing of tectonic shifts in its own making, and since the book seems to track those totalizing structures that you described earlier? Of course your published book arrives, fortuitously it seems, at the beginning of the Occupy movement. I read it just as Occupy started in New York, so following dramatic developments in Tunisia, Egypt, Spain. Does *The Hole*'s cybernetic status not fully exist until it emerges at that particular moment? Or does this dramatic context for the book's emergence simply amplify rhetorical processes at play from the start?

TD: I completed a final draft, with the exception of the envoi, one year before Occupy began, during the summer of 2010. My envoi in some ways engages the Arab Spring, but more in terms of the global justice movement. That spring I heard a talk by Brain Holmes, a critical theorist who has written much about aesthetic politics and activism. He discussed how the global justice movement had gained momentum in the '90s, culminating for the United States around the WTO protests, then had been truncated and stayed kind of dormant. This sense of dormancy appears quite late in *The Hole*. But now, re-reading *The Hole*, its poems and the feedback from others, I can sense how the writing many poets have done has helped lay the groundwork for something like Occupy. Through my own engagement with Occupy, I've truly come to realize the importance of doing cultural work—how it undergirds social action. Writing these poems, having these conversations, prepares you in a way. On the other hand, I have a second manuscript and most of its poems also came before Occupy. These seem a continuation of *The Hole*, but also to develop something different, which has to do with a politics of community and what a discourse based on community might mean (versus, say, some broader acknowledgement of a public sphere). Still in terms of cybernetics: I mention that field rather naively. *The Hole*'s "Feedback" section presents a cybernetic metaphor. Though perhaps a more operative structural metaphor, one taken up by cybernetic theorists, comes from Dziga Vertov's *Man With the Movie Camera*—from its construction of a participatory cinema. Vertov's film foregrounds the cameramen (Vertov and his brother, Mikhail Kaufman) recording. You have images of them recording such images. You have images of them editing, producing this film. You also have images of people watching the film. Then you have images of people being watched as they watch the film. I had that matryoshka doll-like quality in mind when designing (again with Michael Cross) *The Hole*'s quasi-paranoid process of interrelation. You witness the production of my book. You anticipate its distribution. I'd hoped to construct a mobile discourse antithetical to books, or at least physical codices, as a fixed form.

AF: That's what I meant with cybernetics: the interrelation of this book's production, its reception, its theorizations of its own reception and of mental processes enacted by a reader who recognizes his/her role in the construction of meaning.

TD: Through this *Man with the Movie Camera* form, I also wanted to respond to social media's emergence, trying to demonstrate what a book becomes after social media. I consider that one of the main problems of our moment. Here I particularly admire Tan Lin's *Seven Controlled Vocabularies*. He gave me a lot to think about.

AF: In terms of questions about community, questions about literature in and after social media, you bring up models of agitprop, of proto-cinéma vérité, of participatory aesthetics. One obvious question about participatory aesthetics might address the role that coterie plays in your book. You yourself address this near its end. But do you believe that *The Hole*'s coterie qualities, that your friends' participation in its making, can function both literally (tracing a particular historical community) and analogically (speaking more generally to the communal production of poetic discourse among peers, among so-called writers and readers, among always unsettled elements of signification that comprise a text's meaning)?

TD: Coterie remains a super interesting topic. Of course I'd thought about it before I moved to New York, when I lived in Buffalo five plus years, developing strong friendships amid a spirit of collaboration. But I think in New York (as well as the Bay Area—more my spiritual home) that you have to contend with coterie, with the history of writing in New York and of New York poetry. That said, I don't consider *The Hole* a work of coterie. I want to distinguish between a coterie formation and a formation based on discourse. When I say "discourse" I mean a set of problems or issues that bring people together who may not assemble otherwise. Among *The Hole*'s addressees, I definitely would call them friends, but some I don't know that well. Writing a poem for them, or their writing a poem for me, perhaps established the friendship. This seems different than what happens with New York School poetry, which dramatizes forms of intimacy, presence, direct engagement.

AF: Well, does even this New York School coterie concept remain as static as it seems? From our own social media-driven vantage, can we think through preceding processes of coterie differently—as anticipating a broader range of dialogic exchanges, rather than simply tracing specific friendships?

TD: This semester I taught an SVA class called "Creative Speaking." We did two weeks on the New York School. We also looked at work by Steve Benson and Suzanne Stein together, but didn't really have time to look at New Narrative writing. Still I started to think about how much New Narrative takes from New York School poetry. Genealogical affinities arise, not only personal but through politicized sociality. And I feel that *The Hole* gestures toward this. Something anomalous in the book comes from its effacement of self and autobiography, gaps I never would associate with classic coterie writers, since coterie so often depends upon the person and on relationships—narrating that, using it both as material and as allegory.

AF: I'm still hung up on the allegorical part: coterie as metaphor for an implicit community that shapes any reading experience. I'm vaguely remembering a piece you wrote on the poetics of emergence. Of course disruptive emergence in poetic form quickly can become the most dated and thoroughly assimilated of phenomena, if everybody expects a disruption then just moves on. So the question of how a work could maintain this dynamic of emergent engagement becomes quite interesting. Don't you cite here Vertov's line about a participatory aesthetics being both of its time and untimely?

TD: One tradition of participatory cinema follows the Bolshevik Revolution, as all these aesthetic and social experiments address forms of communication, trying to sponsor dialogism, creating a more equal and democratic society. Vertov's work derives from this, but also Aleksandr Medvedkin's, who had a train that would cross the Soviet Union so he could record people having meetings, develop the film on the train and then screen the films. There's that tradition. Then a related tradition comes from figures like Jean Rouch—an anthropologist traveling to Africa, using film as a means of breaking down distinctions between observer and observed. And then participatory visual art has taken hold in the past decade or so. Though much of this so-called relational art produces a superficial intervention between perceived author and perceived audience, which encourages a quite limited participation.

AF: Superficial because circumscribed by the artist.

TD: Of course Claire Bishop comes to mind, who provides an extensive critique of relational aesthetics in terms of how politics and the public sphere can enter art. Social media reinforce a lot of these trappings. At its best social media can prompt engagement, keep people in touch, in some cases maintain a vigilant state of emergency as we've seen with Occupy. On the other hand it could become so numbing and pacifying and bound up with corporate power that it denies forms of action. So in terms of a history of coterie, but more a history of community, of small-scale writing communities, social media has been huge. It's changed the field and a lot of writing practices have had to respond to that (or have elected to respond to that).

AF: After everything we've discussed about *The Hole*'s constructivist, cybernetic, participatory nature, I feel we haven't given an adequate account of the lyric sections. I find it interesting, given what you've said, that you capitalize each line, that you provide neat and tidy quatrains, that you'll outline something like a sentence structure then close serialized sections with definitive periods. What draws you to this orderly local architecture? How has the significance of these lyric passages changed once placed amid the book's broader discontinuities? How would you describe the lyric's enduring status amid post-Language poetics or contemporary poetics? Here I can quote some lines if that helps: "What voice of lyric what / Voices would resist the doing / Should syntax still be a sacrifice / Like cutting off one's limbs / While still alive isn't that / How Mallarmé put it of Rimbaud's / Becoming an arms trader?"

TD: The term "lyric" seems inadequate. I tend to use it as a place holder. But often people will use this term as a foil—a negative way to define a retrograde poetics, an outmoded contrast to emergent constellations of writing. To me this all becomes quite problematic. I maintain a more or less daily (sometimes weekly) practice of writing poems that look lineated, that often deploy quatrains, that retain formal characteristics people associate with poetry. I value staying faithful to this practice, to its rhythmic possibilities, to certain compositional principles. But in terms of the dynamic you've drawn, between localized lyric details and globalized experimental structures, I'll sense how a literary form inflected with lyric potential can become much more interesting when you direct it someplace else, when you juxtapose more discursive elements, when you rethink design features. For example, I have a manuscript I've worked on for some time, with about 160 pages of mostly lineated poems. But I'll wonder what it would mean to distribute this manuscript, collect responses to it, then remove the poems. What if those withdrawn poems just served as the vehicle for inviting something else? Still I remain committed to poets working through more explicit rhythmic possibilities. One book I love that just came out (tragically, because published posthumously) is Stacy Doris' *Fledge*. Its intense prosody works through some of Celan's grammar. Much still can happen within existing forms.

AF: *The Hole* often mentions your hope for an alternate means of reception, distribution. Have you pursued such means? If so, in what form? How has that gone?

TD: We had a book launch...or not a book launch, an event this past February. But with *The Hole* I want not just to think of this text as something finite, but to extend the book in various directions through events, other actions, other objects. In February, no less than 12 poets gathered at St. Mark's Church to present work composed in response to *The Hole*. This substituted for a book launch, and allowed people to meet each other or read each other's work or hear it for the first time. So in that way, yeah, I think the book has allowed for different forms of exchange, if not reception. We also plan to publish documents from this St. Mark's event, producing a supplementary book. One can start to imagine an endless set of secondary materials until the original book almost disappears.

AF: This could be a loaded question that we skip. I did sense something more pointed you wanted to say about conceptual writing as it gets discussed in our present—how you would like to see the term more elastically or expansively defined.

TD: I have great conversations with Rob Fitterman who, more than almost anyone, gets identified with conceptualism. I teach a lot of work associated with conceptualism and find it really useful. I don't know if I had something pointed I'd wanted to say in *The Hole*, but I did witness during that time a kind of canonization and institutionalization of certain writing practices referred to as conceptualism. Of course this work excited many poets at first. But for the first time in my life I saw what I now consider to have been the framing, the consumption of a poetics by an academic machine. That part disturbed me. It reminds me of what Andrea Fraser says about this year's Whitney Biennial. She said, to paraphrase: the problem comes not so much from the art, not from the artists, but from critics and institutions and claims made about the work.

AF: Claims made for the work, rather than by the work? Is that a fair distinction?

TD: Well sometimes by the practitioners themselves, which constricts conceptualism's potential in a lot of cases. I wrote a piece recently about Rob Halpern's work in relation to uses of documentary materials and appropriative practices—processes which too often have come to be associated with a particular form of conceptual poetics. And one other phenomenon that has disturbed me comes from certain narratives or social histories, certain genealogies growing ossified so that you forget alternative genealogies. This problem directly relates to how so many divergent writers and artists historically have used appropriation to different ends, specifically in the throws of political and personal emergencies. Here I'll think of work Gregg Bordowitz and others did around ACT UP, which dramatically engaged appropriation techniques. These survival tactics get lost in amnesiac accounts of the social ties shaping contemporary conceptualism.

### INTERVIEW WITH DAN BEACHY-QUICK
Recorded on July 6, 2012
This interview focuses on Beachy-Quick's book *Wonderful Investigations* (Milkweed Editions).

ANDY FITCH: In your first essay's first sentence you identify yourself as a "nature poet." Could you give a condensed sense of what you mean by the term, both within *Wonderful Investigations* and within a broader ecopoetics context? In doing the reading for this interview project, I've been struck by the diverse range of contemporary poets who adopt that potentially fraught (because perpetually contested) self-definition.

DAN BEACHY-QUICK: That essay's initial draft came out of a panel talk on ecopoetics, for which I'd been invited to participate. I still don't feel particularly associated with ecopoetics, although I feel real sympathy toward it. The panel just provided an excuse to think about how my poetic concerns, and hopefully my poetic practice, address the world in a caring and protective manner. I had been reading much about initiation rights, early mythology, heroic cycles. I'd wondered how poetry might offer itself as an initiatory experience—not only to the poet, but to the reader, amid a kind of liminal space where assumed writer/reader relations get undermined. Initiatory processes move a person, from a profane relationship to the world, to one in which, through a symbolic death, they are reborn into a sense of the world as a sacred place. Similarly, to engage a poem risks a rewiring of one's nervous system, one's perceptive ability. This suggested to me a way of attending to the world on the world's terms, and undermining subjectivity in any normal sense.

AF: I like then how this first sentence serves as invocational gesture. You establish the space in which the book will operate.

DBQ: The first sentence also establishes that I don't think poetry abides kindly to pre-formed self-definitions. To consider oneself a nature poet could come at the cost of severing oneself from the actual object of concern, since to become a nature poet means to open oneself to certain forms of bewilderment which might, upon first glance, have little to do with nature. Here I'm very, very influenced by Wittgenstein—his sense that the only thing one has with which to imagine the world is the world, and his broader sense that any use of imagination confirms in the most radical way what it means to be a nature poet. Any honest and ambitious use of imagination requires a return back to the world.

AF: Lots of threads there I'll want to pick up. First, do you make distinctions between the writing and reading of poems and essays? Should we assume that these four essays enact a form of thinking, of questioning—coaxing forth an equivalent interrogative stance in the reader? If so, does it seem problematic for us to wrench particular concepts from the textual tapestry? Do anaphoric patternings, syntactical convolutions, verbal repetitions provide access to your prose's prompt as much as any extracted idea would?

DBQ: I do believe that attending to those rhetorical devices might be as productive as any thematic dissection. I've learned, as I've taught myself or apprenticed myself to essay writing as an artistic practice, that the essay offers this opportunity to slow down or mimic thinking's convoluted processes—to make thought available not as some fixed, static conclusion, but through a prose that follows the sinews and ligatures of how it feels to think. Those remain huge concerns for me. I often feel disappointed by more purely academic work when it doesn't invite readers into this drama of how it feels to be the person thinking. The essay's great promise, from Plutarch to Montaigne up through Emerson, presents this need to think as a basic human need, one that isn't simply rational, isn't simply ideational, or even wholly reasonable. So I wanted to write essays that trace a particular, peculiar labyrinth with no special agenda, taking every possible turn that seemed interesting, probing every avenue of approach in pursuit of a concern. I hoped to juxtapose perspectives that don't start in close proximity, and to use the essays to depict what that collision looks like.

AF: I'd asked about syntax, about form, because the performative implications of your prose intrigue me. This performance echoes the performance of philosophical poverty that Stanley Cavell detects in Emerson's writing. The "I" adopts a learned yet not scholarly, or at least non-professionalized tone. It appears as exemplary autodidact, less inclined to impart knowledge than to provide testimony of having learned from (rather than having learned about) particular books. You'll dramatize the effort required to recognize our own inherent ignorance, rather than obscuring that state behind a claim to critical authority. And even your unimpeachable-seeming mode of personal testimony can't help but undermine itself with the concluding reflection "I'm still not saying it right." That specific rhetorical gesture recalled Wittgenstein kicking the ladder away after climbing up his *Tractatus*. Or Proust's *On Reading Ruskin* comes to mind, as the reader ultimately gets cast back upon her or his own faculties, and, accordingly (hopefully), the world appears afresh. Is it fair to place your essays' implicit points along this experiential trajectory?

DBQ: Absolutely. I hope for *Wonderful Investigations* to provide the experience of needing knowledge, or moving towards knowledge, a knowledge that these essays realize they can't really offer. So the reader does get thrown back on his or her own faculties, hopefully with a renewed sense of those faculties, hopefully questioning ways in which we've been taught to say: this is how it feels to know something; this is how it feels when you've read a book correctly. When I've had significant reading experiences, I never felt any of that. To me it feels more like falling in love. It bears those same mysteries. And as naïve as it sounds, I want to write about things I love, to write honestly about love's complexities. I want to write so that readers of a certain bent of mind, or bent of sensibility, can be affected, can be reaffirmed (by their own strength) that this is why we turn to books—that the reading process doesn't divorce itself from analytic rigor, but also doesn't stand subservient to it.

AF: You seem to have described an erotics of reading.

DBQ: I love that phrase.

AF: Can we further discuss your own experience as a reader, perhaps in regard to Thoreau's and Emerson's dazzling performative styles, to the erotics of their books? Given your descriptions of Walden as in part a work of song (and your more general investment in philosophical definition as an initiatory, ritualized, ongoing process, rather than a set of static claims), I assume that stylistic/rhetorical concerns typically labeled aesthetic take on much broader depth and resonance in your reading of them. Your love for Thoreau's prose comes across in the lengthy quotations you provide. In Emerson's oratory training, his propulsive sentence-by-sentence thrust, I hear something of your own poetic lines. And again, Thoreau's ironic undertones, which apparently earned him (I don't know if you've read David Reynolds on this) a reputation as a hilarious, highly entertaining public speaker, creep into some of your later tales. But here's the question: can you explain why reflections on particular literary or rhetorical devices don't factor more explicitly into your current investigations? You don't examine Thoreau's and Emerson's prosody—at least not explicitly. Are there specific affinities, enthusiasms, insights into their prose styles you want to offer here?

DBQ: I'll start with a simple answer. I feel as if I've learned about paragraphs from Thoreau and sentences from Emerson. I love Emerson's ability to write a sentence in which you become so immersed that, by time you reach the end, you've forgotten how it started. This genuine philosophical bewilderment arises as if each sentence contained a kind of compass needle, and the next sentence's compass might point in a completely different direction. Then Thoreau provides a bodilyness to the paragraph. He'll write stunning sentences, but I fell in love with how Thoreau builds perception and thought across sentences, into the shapeliness of that paragraph. In some ways, each of my book's four main essays attempts to find a balance between the sentence as primary epistemological unit and the paragraph as primary epistemological unit. I'd become curious about the sentence as a source of knowledge, a source of encounter, and then how the paragraph's context forces each sentence to sharpen its point, or undoes it, undermines it, expands it, or alters it. Even now, several years after writing these essays, I still keep searching for a genuine balance. Balance isn't even the right word. But that motion from sentence to sentence as a paragraph builds fascinates me. I think long and hard about the beauty of a sentence, the beauty of a paragraph. I'll think about beauty more in prose I write than in poems I write. This takes me straight back to Keats's sense that beauty teases us out of thought, that beauty obliterates consideration. I love the essay as a model for this particular torment art always asks of itself—the way beauty might be a tumult inside the more rational effort to think. I want a sentence to become so beautiful that it threatens the thought it carries.

AF: On that great note, I'm still curious why the book doesn't foreground these formal concerns. You have described here the aesthetic, erotic, experiential, embodied nature of reading and writing. But your book never presents itself as a style or rhetoric manual. Is there a reason that it doesn't? Would that make for too self-conscious scrutiny?

DBQ: I do think that could become too self-conscious, too self-willed. I consider the erotic a kind of middle ground, a nexus where the energies of reading and writing can meet on equal and co-creative terms. To willfully design what a sentence looks like, to deliberately map the rhetoric in advance of the writing, removes you in some ways from the erotic compulsion, which must embed itself within the work. So in the midst of writing I don't feel thoughtful in any normal way. I feel curious about how the sentences themselves point toward what the next sentence might be, what the next concern has to be. Thought becomes less a reasoned, objective activity than a form of momentum. I'll feel devoted to tracking that momentum, to courting that momentum, to making it available to the reader—because I take the erotic quite seriously and sometimes quite literally in the work of writing. But the person who tries to seduce does not start from a good position. The one who would seduce already must be seduced. The writer has to experience what he or she desires a reader to experience.

AF: I've asked questions related to what we loosely could call style in part from curiosity about your choice of literary sources. There does seem to exist a lively line of scholars drawn to the erotics of Thoreau and Emerson. Your praise of Emerson's sentences and Thoreau's paragraphs echoes Perry Miller. But Sharon Cameron, Stanley Cavell, F. O. Matthiessen also come to mind—readers whose strong libidinal attachments depart from our typical conception of academic writing. Does it seem fair to say that scholarly reading need not preclude the modes of attention you just described?

DBQ: Definitely. Of those you've mentioned, Cavell has most seduced me. His book *The Senses of Walden* made me realize I needed to write about Thoreau, to have that experience.

AF: So the reading of Cavell, rather than of Thoreau, initially served as prompt?

DBQ: Or seeing that someone could write about Thoreau in the way

I desperately wanted to write about Thoreau. Cavell gave me a kind of license. I'd felt very nervous—perhaps because I don't have a PhD. I'd decided not to pursue this direction, because I worried it might complicate my relationship with work I love. Whenever I've written essays concerned with academic topics (be they Melville in A *Whaler's Dictionary,* or here Thoreau, Proust, Emerson, Keats and Eliot), I've felt this deep insecurity and shyness and audacity and arrogance at play, which for a long time stymied my willingness to take the risk of writing about literature in ways I wanted to write about it. But Stanley Cavell in particular, taking Thoreau and Emerson quite seriously as philosophers, made me feel OK enough to try it myself.

AF: Hopefully this sensation of insecurity, of feeling radically ill-equipped, eventually became productive. That sounds like Emerson's *American Scholar* approach.

DBQ: It is. And I take seriously Wittgenstein's notion that philosophical work picks apart the edifice of one's pride.

AF: Given the risks implicit in writing a collection of literary essays outside academia, I'd love to hear more about this particular book's origins. Did your Melville book prompt this one? And you mentioned completing *Wonderful Investigations* long ago. What happened in between?

DBQ: I started *Wonderful Investigations* after moving to Colorado from Chicago. After I'd finished *A Whaler's Dictionary*, a four-year gap occurred before I really started writing essays again, these essays, which took three to four years to write. I'd wanted to pay attention to literature in the way I thought it used to receive attention (I'm referring to the 19th century, to Thoreau and Emerson, how a public intellectual, whatever that meant, also could be a poet). I miss in contemporary poetic culture this space where poetry provokes something beyond the reflexive production of yet another poem. So I wanted to participate in this sense I had of the poet as thinker. I felt deeply connected to, and moved by, 19th-century American writers I loved, as well as by Keats, whose letters I consider as profound a document of soul-making (understanding the soul as something that thinks as well) as we have in the language.

AF: Again it interests me that the legacy of those mid-19th-century American writers has called forth such diverse poetic responses.

Here I'm thinking of D.H. Lawrence's *Classics in American Literature,* Charles Olson's writing on Melville, Susan Howe's *My Emily Dickinson.* But in your own case, you've mentioned anthropology as another source material. Can you discuss your reading into anthropology? Is it deliberative research? Random exposure? Part of an ongoing project or a piece of your past?

DBQ: That's all by bliss of interest, finding in one book the hint that another will speak to it in illuminating ways. The reading of Eliot and Frazer that appears so much in *Wonderful Investigations* came from living in Chicago and working for the Art Institute, wandering through parts of the museum less typically visited, looking at African art, looking at Mesoamerican art, at early Chinese art, and really wanting to gain some sense of what those objects meant—not as artifacts behind a case, but to find a literature that could open up their meanings in terms of use. My dearest hope for *Wonderful Investigations* is that these essays can put themselves into a theater of meaning that points beyond knowledge or knowing of fact, and become useful in quite unexpected ways.

AF: Useful in the way Cavell's book became useful for you?

DBQ: Yeah. This goes straight back to Emerson—to consider something useful because it liberates.

AF: Well with preceding topics still in mind, could we discuss the pairing of your essays with your tales? Do the tales enact something first thought through in the essays? Do they privilege doing over thinking? The increased irreverence as the tales progressed definitely made me reconsider, for example, what had seemed a more earnest, urgent tone that had come before. So could we address how these different book components function when placed in this particular sequence? And I wondered if the ostensibly archaic category of "tales" here…does that demonstrate an appreciation for broader narrative traditions, as well as for Borges, Barthelme, Robert Coover?

DBQ: Certainly Borges, but other sources for me include Hawthorne, the Brothers Grimm, the Scottish writer George MacDonald. Reading George MacDonald convinced me I had to learn how to write a fairly tale. I'd started writing these tales way back in Chicago. A couple of them predated the essays. Fairy tales present a literature devoted to wonder, to the difficulties of wonder and its trickersterish quality, or ironic qualities. So I began to attempt that in fiction, which for me felt nuts. Although I really don't think of fairy tales as fiction—I think of them as fairy tales, with a real distinction between those two. And again, fairy tales led me to reading about magic, initiation, ritual, about archaic art that remained present in the human imagination for countless ages (none of which appeared in my graduate education, which had prioritized learning to write a decent poem over cultivating an appetite for the wonderful). Of course, encountering the wonderful complicates what it means to think, to consider something. And so I got caught up in the writing of essays and continued to work on these fairy tales, until…actually my friend Srikanth Reddy suggested that these projects might belong together. So I began to place them in a kind of mirror relationship to each other, amid a form which tries to approach wonder, to conjure it, without triggering the immediate evanescence of that very thing it desires to speak about. In some ways, I feel that a great fairy tale writes itself, in order to create within itself a space of wonder, and shows absolutely no concern for the person reading it. The fairy tale can seem astonishingly selfish as a form. That feels quite different from the essay.

AF: As you describe the fairy tale's self-centered nature, I wonder how much of this comes from its murky origins in preceding tales, preceding modes of literature, which could be oral, or choral, or performative. When we access the fairy tale, do we access ancient ways of engaging story or narrative, far removed from contemporary notions of respectable literary expression, engagement, identification?

DBQ: I think that's true. There's a noble history of the fairy tale's relation to serfs, to the underdog. This destabilizing form of literature privileges the one without power always defeating the one with power. These stories, inherited through oral traditions, take pleasure in the downfall of the ones you'd love to see fall down, yet lack the power to attack. But your question points toward something equally important about fairy tales, which has to do with the nature of the symbol—not symbol as a literary trope, but symbol as Blake uses symbol, or encounters symbol. Symbols have this remarkable way (out of the myriad possibilities of their meaning, which nonetheless show one ostensible face) of providing an image that apparently can be understood, dearly loved, seared into the mind, yet also a source of trickery. The fairy tale gives us this moment of recognition, but also resists the possibility of a symbolic reading. The fairy tale lets itself fall into the labyrinthine difficulties of what a symbol might mean. That's what I meant when I described the form's selfishness. It attends to this internal life in ways that really stun me, to which I felt attracted, addicted, apprehensive.

AF: Your book's preface announces that the first tale most fully enters this wondrous realm, while the last tale does so the least. Given that statement, I expected greater disparities between the two. But short, clipped cadences give both pieces a similar pace. His- and he-driven constructions propel us each time toward an enigmatic conclusion. Beyond their attachment, as your preface scaffolds it, to different ages in human development, can you describe how these tales each enact differences (here I'm going back to your "Hut of Poetry" essay) in experiential "environments"? What types of environments or spaces of initiation does each create?

DBQ: I hadn't thought about the tales' similarities. I've always focused on their differences. The reader might sense less difference than I do. For me, it's really about the protagonists' relationship to these experiences, the ability to accept them versus a kind of questioning of them. The first tale never questions the nature of subjectivity or objectivity. A being just exists within this particular world—which gets accepted as a kind of fact. Then as the tales progress, especially to the last, a doubt that the world is as it seems somehow develops, pressing back on or against the first tale's initial wonder. It is this removal of the self from that self's experience which tracks each tale's gradation.

AF: And just to be clear, the tales do seem highly differentiated. But continuity appears, too. A Heideggerian idiom definitely emerges in the essays. Then this movement from essay to tale seemed very Nietzschian, in terms of a more stylized endeavor, perhaps with just as pointed a pedagogical thrust, but going about it through alternate means, as Zarathustra or Prince Vogelfrei does.

DBQ: Reading Heidegger was one of those eye-opening, world-shaking events, with his language that I wholly recognized and felt preformed in me, yet didn't understand at all. Just as I'd felt first reading Wittgenstein—that experience's uncanniness, in which the work of poetry seemed fundamental to the continuing functioning of the world as a world, became hugely moving and tied back to readings in Jewish mysticism and religion that remain important points of reference (ironically enough, in relation to Heidegger). With Nietzsche,

*The Birth of Tragedy* opened up a realm of influence I still feel deeply mired in, which treats the mythic world and the fairy tale as crucial to contemporary poetic practice. *Beyond Good and Evil* also challenged me, as he discussed what we consider when we tire of thinking. That felt similar to Heidegger's point in "What is Called Thinking?" when he says that if we ask, "are we thinking yet?" we are not thinking—just as, with poetry, the work never yet has begun. You do all this work then sense that it takes you to the beginning of some other kind of work, which feels both beautiful and absolutely maddening.

AF: To close, could we address your book's assertion that language is revelatory only when connected to the real? I'm curious how this corresponds to formalist criticism, someone like Viktor Shklovsky, his famous emphasis upon making the stone stony. Early in *Wonderful Investigations*, you say: "The semiotic crisis of modern poetics, the sense of a word's arbitrary connection to the object it names, the indefinite distance between signifier and signified that feels as if it threatens language's ability to name anything at all, is not a modern crisis at all." In terms of that statement, and in comparison to, let's say, Language poets' readings of Shklovsky or Saussure, is your point that such readers ought to broaden their historical scope? Or do you sense some fundamental incompatibility between their mode of inquiry and your own?

DBQ: I don't think they necessarily need to broaden their inquiry, nor do I think I'm necessarily involved in a process so different than what Language poets have done. To me, Shklovsky's emphasis upon making a stone stony reminds us that imagination as a tool remains invested in the actual. In the sentence you quoted, I mean to suggest that the difficulty of representing a world that is, already, in advance, real, always has produced epistemic difficulties—problems we too easily assume emerged only in the late 1890s or whatnot. This semiotic schism between word and the thing named doesn't feel new to me at all. It feels as old as names themselves. It feels biblical. You can find as much evidence of that crisis in Genesis as you can in Derrida.

## INTERVIEW WITH WAYNE KOESTENBAUM
Recorded on July 7, 2012
This interview focuses on Koestenbaum's book *The Anatomy of Harpo Marx* (University of California Press).

ANDY FITCH: If we could start with a quote from "Day by Day with Roland Barthes," written in 1979 for *Le Nouvel Observateur:* "The form sought for is a brief one, or, if you prefer, a soft form: neither the solemnity of the maxim nor the harshness of the epigram; something which, at least in tendency, might suggest the Japanese haiku, the Joycean epiphany, the fragment of the journal intime: a deliberately minor form, in short—recalling, with Borges, that the minor is not a lessening, but a genre like any other." Beside this Barthes quote I'd like to place your own assertion (this is deep into *Harpo*) of an incremental poetics: "Incremental poetics involves never finishing a point, never knowing my destination, rushing through culture's big store on sissy white roller skates, without a stunt double, and enjoying 'generalized chromaticism': every moment is an occasion to wave, point, bump, or stop, under the auspices of failing to speak properly. Why make such a big deal out of the 'proper?'" I'm curious how Barthes's soft style parallels your own compositional practice in a series of prose works, from *The Queen's Throat* to *Jackie* to pieces in *Cleavage* to *Hotel Theory* to *Harpo*. Do the soft style and your incremental poetics align perfectly, overlap yet diverge, exist in blissful ignorance of each other and often of themselves?

WAYNE KOESTENBAUM: That incremental poetics quote means a lot to me. When I gave a reading in L.A. recently, that was one of three or four passages from *Harpo* I chose, and I'm grateful we are clairvoyant about incremental poetics. Barthes obviously remains in blissful ignorance of my existence, so that's half the question right there. But I'd like to think that our styles, our soft styles, stand in perfect alignment minus obvious differentials imposed by decade, nationality, intellectual bent, the companies we keep, our forms of expertise and non-expertise. Maybe we align most in espousing the Schumannesque, which demands a preference for linked miniatures and retreat, forms of so-called public address that actually retreat from the public even as they try to sound seductive. Barthes' style has a tenderness that seems to wish to be heard, but given his addiction to amateurism, his preference for the at-home and the provisional, he always retreats from a public or from audibility. Similarly, I consider this

Harpo book a culmination of my soft style, perhaps the dead-end of it. "Culmination" makes it sound grandiose. I simply mean it's the last stop on the soft-style train. It travels as far as I could go, pushing a point as hard as possible toward inanity, though not pushing these points at length, just intensifying them stylistically. And then letting it drop. Dropping it. That's where the Schumann-esque appears—a preference for caesuras and pauses and interruptions and self-sabotage. Self-sabotage as a prosody.

AF: When you describe *Harpo* as the end of the line, does the soft style always seem to have reached its last stop?

WK: It's a decadent style, so if you believe in the rise and fall of civilizations or cultures, the soft style seems a late style. It's after-coherent, not before-coherent. It shares the relationship to tonality that early Schoenberg or Berg or Scriabin embody. I think of Scriabin's emphatic attenuation—rather than consolidation. That was only the first part of your question.

AF: While *Harpo* does emphasize attenuation, it also seems the most systematic of your books, in that it attempts, enacts, completes its totalizing inquiry. Did you deliberately push your incremental poetics toward the more thorough, more systematic, potentially more insane? Does an analogy to *Harpo*'s desire for seeking "stasis on the other side of mania" here emerge? Does this "other side" only exist once we've internalized what you describe as language's dirty secret, that it does not communicate?

WK: First: yes to that. That's a perfect reading of my intentions, if intentions matter. I certainly intended, from the get-go, for this book to provide the most ambitious and most thorough enactment of my soft style. Thorough because it all takes place within the totality of one body, Harpo's. For *Andy Warhol* and *Jackie*, neither book presented itself as a total statement. They are shorter and keep something like a respectful distance from their subjects' nearby monumentality (a.k.a. recently alive in New York, dominating the local scene). In Harpo's case, his long having been dead and being minor, not to mention his being speechless and, in a way, pointless, prompted the questions: what can I gain? What can anyone gain from an anatomization of Harpo? The project seemed unnecessary, which allowed me to feel situated and, in a way, grandiose (as if I had found my *Iliad* or *Odyssey*). I sensed a negative utopia, the enormous spaciousness of the tiny. Once I had this notion I decided simply to anatomize, rather than to synthesize, Harpo, to proceed chromatically, incrementally, and to take my embroidered style focused on pointless details to its logical conclusion. It became extremely pleasurable, if not a bit suicidal-feeling, to stay so thorough. *Harpo*'s as close to totality as I'll ever come. I mean that.

AF: I know. Still, on this question of totality, from the start you call this book an "experimental anatomization." Anatomizing gets presented as the opposite of synthesizing: "Anatomizing rather than synthesizing, I bed down with entropy and disarray." Yet it interests me that, in fact, you do seem to complete your task of analyzing every scene across Harpo's 13 films. Your book presents itself as *the* anatomy of Harpo Marx, not *an* anatomy. *Harpo* remains willfully caught between the status of an Oulipo masterwork, triumphantly fulfilling its impossible promise, and a self-doubting, fragmentary, asymptotic apologia. Tracking such apparent polarities of tone, scale, potentially dubious achievement, long has appealed to you—since, at least, the twinned essays "Logorrhea" and "The Poetics of Indifference." But within the Harpo book, does the film medium itself (with its conflation of the isolated camera still and the fluid cinematic sequence) somehow crystallize a variety of these concerns about the integral/modular nature of time, embodied experience, identity?

WK: I'm feeling waves of gratitude for being read this carefully. As *Harpo* says again and again: this book is my block of ice, an undeliverable message. Whatever I try to say, whatever it tries to do, that task remains uncompletable and cannot be delivered.

AF: Well there's Nietzsche's line "oh how you would love my ice!" Which sounds inviting in its own way. I think that's Prince Vogelfrei.

WK: To find my block of ice received rather than thrown out the window makes me love literature again—not because of any special claim of pathos I'm making, though the thoroughness of this project, in the sense that I tried to be as clear as I could, had, not just as a side-effect, but as its consequence, a growing depression, a sense of undeliverability. This conviction got embodied in *Harpo*'s physical size as the text grew more bloated. The book's current, published form provides a radical condensation of my original draft. I doubt that the initial version was any better, but if the book originally tracked an experience of flow and giddy overelaboration, it ultimately demanded a process of painful condensation. I sensed the limits of what I can do with a sentence. When I realized that each sentence probably would contain the words "Harpo" or "he," either as the sentence's subject or predicate or object, that became a claustrophobic enclosure I had to outwit. That's what felt Oulipian about the process. It became a syntactic adventure, sentence by sentence, to preserve variation. Then at some point I mention that the Marx Brothers, or Harpo in particular, is funny in motion but poignant in stills. The essential inaccuracy of this book, vis-à-vis Harpo's actual cultural contribution, is that I took the funniness away from him. Depriving Harpo of sound does not make him poignant. That increases his humor. But depriving Harpo of motion depletes the comedy.

AF: Theoretically at least, we have no temporal control over the film we watch. But that you only can speak when Harpo disappears, or that only forced film pauses allow you to say anything, means that only when Harpo's comedy ends can yours begin.

WK: The strongest way to put this is that I raped Harpo with poignance. I wouldn't say that's accurate. But just as there's always some sense of guilt writing about anybody, there's a huge sense of guilt and shame for me surrounding this act of commentary. First: the shame of producing something undeliverable or unhearable or indigestible. The shame (or what felt like aggression) of imposing on him not my sexual fantasies, because I think he could accommodate those, but of imposing mournfulness, this heady Romantic, post-Romantic mournfulness.

AF: So have you done something similar here not just to Harpo but to film itself? Does imposing this pause on cinema demonstrate that even a bad, time-based film can make for a pretty good collage? Did you deliberately interrupt all the seamless-seeming, interstitial segues that film provides?

WK: Two things. One: that I took down film's gaiety or festivity, film's sense of joy, with a kind of nerdy taste for stasis. This pushing of film's motility toward film's stasis still felt like failing to get the point of film, in the way that Roland Barthes's "The Third Meaning" essay (obviously the root of my whole book) talks about the poetics of the film still. Barthes's judicious choices provide only a few images for his overreading, for his search for obtuse meanings. His whimsical choice of images adds gaiety and frivolity to Eisenstein.

Here I attempt the opposite. I take a comic sense of motion and nerdily deepfreeze it. The other thing I realized was my own preference for painting over film, for poetry over novels, for contemplation over interaction (a kind of entropic poetics, or entropic temperament, saturnine), and that I wanted to make paintings or motionless, delectable compositions out of more frivolous, kinetic social events. I've been aware of that wish, teaching this year, when students, for good reason, resist Gertrude Stein's or John Cage's mandate to find meaning in everything, including random noises. More and more I find a need to defend the fact that anything you frame is beautiful and worth reading.

AF: Maybe we've already developed these ideas about motion and stillness enough. But I'll think of Warhol, the Saint Vitus Dance he suffered, his temporary paralysis. And Jackie, of course, keeps her photogenic silence, stunned by the paparazzi flash. Was the Warhol book prompted by your study of Jackie? Was *Harpo* prompted by the study of Warhol? When you mentioned your class, I had an auditory hallucination of you speaking about some Delmore Schwartz story where the protagonist sits before a film of his parents' early courting, and just keeps screaming "Stop stop," and then it ends (I remember you emphasized) on the curl of a lip of snow.

WK: How do you remember that? That's wild. The story's called "In Dreams Begin Responsibilities." For whatever reason I discovered it as a college freshman when my fiction teacher, my first writing teacher, said in response to the first story I ever wrote that it reminded her of Delmore Schwartz's story. So somehow that story, beloved by many people, not just me, sits at the root of my predicament. Schwartz's protagonist wakes on his 21st birthday and for some reason, that phrase…the windowsill holds this lip of snow. The whole story's momentum, at least what's important to me, is that the Oedipal or Philip Roth-like drama between a Jewish son and the disaster of his parents' marriage arrives at the destination of this poetic metaphor. That post-cinema, post-family crystallization, waking onto the phrase "lip of snow," seemed and seems important.

AF: I don't want to get tangential but there's Dickinson's poem that ends "Rafters of Satin and Roof of Snow." No, "Stone."

WK: That's my favorite poem in the world. And another version ends "Soundless as Dots on a Disc of Snow." I quote it in *Harpo*, actually.

AF: If we could contextualize these questions of motion and stillness in reference to Michael Fried's aesthetics of absorption: are there ways in which the silence of Warhol's screen test-takers, of Harpo's voiceless yet emphatic presence, come to stand in for the experience of the still, reflective, contemplative (and yet, according to most empirical measures, inactive) thinking subject? As I read and thought about Harpo's muteness, I, of course, became increasingly aware of my own muteness while reading—aware that much of my time as a reader, a thinker, must seem Harpo-esque to the rest of the world. If we imagined some specialized group to whom this Harpo book would most appeal, are they more Harpo-esque than they realize?

WK: That seems a distilled and accurate statement about the link between Harpo's silence (Harpo's absorption in being Harpo) and a reader, or any person who pursues this vocation of the contemplative or absorbed subject. I can't say Harpo dignifies that vocation, since he makes it seem foolish, but what I take from Fried's attention to 18th-century painting is the sense that these depictions of, say, the boy blowing a bubble, are touchstones or emblems we should imitate or emulate because they represent concentration having reached its fulfillment. If there's a polemic or even a wish in my book, it's to advocate experiences of absorption and concentration, to justify the mute life of the beholder, the meditator. I would even say, and perhaps this is a psychotic point, that I find in certain Harpo antics a physical literalization of the acts we undergo when we concentrate.

AF: Exactly.

WK: Harpo often squeezes his face or presses hard on something. His taste for forms of pressing, adhesion, coiling, self-consuming seem analogous to the kinds of silent, motionless theatre I undergo when I write. I don't mean just the motions of fingers on a computer keyboard, or my knee pressing against (I think I say this in *Harpo*) the table's underside. There's the sense that when I write I'm squeezing, pushing, espressing—in the sense of espresso. And now that I spend much time painting, I'm aware that writing and reading require inner ballets of cognition, stressful pliés and pas de deux. Particularly when reading difficult literature, whether Proust or Henry James or Nietzsche, Heidegger, poetry—anything that, through condensation or excess, demands concentrating—those inner ballets of cognition I undergo seem weirdly, masochistically, thrilling in the way isometric exercise can be.

AF: For this topic of the contemplative ballet, and my further curiosity about the extent to which you'll choreograph such sequences for the reader, I'd like to juxtapose a rhetorical question your book raises: "What's the point of a 'book' if it can't include scraps? Isn't inclusiveness the point of the big store, a warehouse of points, some insufficiently pointed?" Perhaps it's dumb for you to answer your own question, but what's the point of a book if it can't include scraps? Is it scraps, specifically, that prompt the inner ballet to happen?

WK: Honestly, I don't think a lot about a reader. I'm reading my own work when writing it and thinking about how I respond to the sentences I've written. If I respond with displeasure or boredom or dissatisfaction, I'll change them until they produce a pleasing reaction or at least one that doesn't embarrass me.

AF: So you'll try to stay aware of the affective value of sentences you're shaping.

WK: This has to do with musicality and the operations (as a pianist and listener to music) done to my body by music I love, operations which involve abstract issues of intensification and diminishment and energy.

AF: If we also could address your performance as a reader in this book: Dostoevsky, you're reading Dostoevsky?

WK: I definitely was. I'm reading Henry James now in the way I was reading Dostoevsky. Dostoevsky I'd approached simply because he wrote a book called *The Idiot,* and from what I had read, in the work of Avital Ronell and others…Dostoevsky formed part of an autodidactic program that preceded and accompanied the writing of Harpo, for which I felt I needed to make good on many unkept promises, included revisiting Dostoevsky, or *Don Quixote*. I just felt there were all these very major thinkers, great figures who had thought and written about pointlessness and idiocy, and I needed to spend time reading them. I wanted to avoid using my customary set of intellectual lenses on this project. I can't say I've succeeded in diversifying my portfolio, but I've earnestly tried.

AF: When *Harpo*'s citations cluster around a work by Dostoevsky, by Deleuze and Guattari, by Joyce Carol Oates, Paul Ricoeur, the book appears to offer a quotidian record of your reading life.

WK: That would be accurate.

AF: But it also kept bringing back—and this is where the autodidact's program appeals to me—Bertolt Brecht's formulation, which I only know from Barthes, that serious intellectual inquiry involves thinking in other people's heads and having them think in yours. Do you know that famous line?

WK: I forgot it if I ever knew it.

AF: Then relatively late into your book, you classify *Harpo* as an experiment in star immersion, a discourse you've deployed before. But how does Brecht's formulation of interpersonal, almost telepathic or identificatory activity, how does that align to your experience of star immersion? Or when you broach the topic of autodidacticism, I'll think of scholarship and star immersion, and wonder how *Harpo* triangulates these. How does Harpo's ventriloquizing through his brothers, his suffering identity eclipse at their proximity, how does that dramatize the subject characterized by thinking or by fandom?

WK: I'd never thought through the analogy between star immersion and...

AF: Scholarly research?

WK: Right. I can answer concretely by saying that, while writing this book, I taught for the second time a Graduate Center class called "Stars." This time around we read a philosophical text—the work had not much to do with movie stars—to accompany the theme of each week's film and discussion (Joan Crawford, Bette Davis). I remember, for example, that for Lana Turner we read Deleuze's *The Fold*. In fact I'll go get a paragraph to show you exactly what we did. I'm going to take arbitrarily a paragraph and make substitutions. Let's see: "Lana Turner has no windows, by which anything could come in or go out. Lana has neither openings nor doorways. We run the risk of understanding Lana Turner vaguely if we fail to determine the situation." You just add "Lana Turner" to any sentence and this book makes sense. And so if star immersion is the fact, then the question becomes how can the richest set of tools and intensifiers be brought to bear on that immersion. Star immersion isn't something one touristically decides to undergo, but comes closer to Benjamin and hashish—to the point of mania. So to extend the star immersion I already have, and have advertised myself having, why don't I steer it in a more baroque, intellectual direction by applying the lens of whatever I read to Harpo? Why not present one's own intellectual life as that of a scrap-keeper, scrap-hoarder, understanding scholarship as a process of poaching on others' interiority, dead and living writers? Your question speaks to the porousness of boundaries between the reader and what gets read.

AF: So scholarly practice taps and doesn't admit to tapping a similar mechanism of identification. Here Harpo's body serves as hinge between those two libidinous identifications that drive the work.

WK: Yes. I think both you and I can't ignore many experiences most scholarship refuses to acknowledge—its hidden agendas and pleasures. I've spent a lot of my life, for whatever reason, trying to admit those things.

AF: Not necessarily as a critique of scholarship, but more a rehabilitation, as if scholarship could finally come into its own.

WK: It's sort of a post-Perestroika acknowledgment of how I'm actually constituted. It's basically: am I going to interrupt and cancel the inner ballet of cognition, or am I going to televise it? I've chosen to televise.

AF: Well in terms of your own star immersion, I'm curious, when you watched Harpo's films, did you pay close attention to non-Harpo scenes? Do you expect their absence to intrigue your own audience? What I mean is: as you thread together this 13-film span, you'll discuss how Harpo threads together his siblings through a series of darting glances. And of course the camera does this too, right? A Hollywood film basically stitches scenes, stills, some ultimately invisible diegetic scenario together. So what's your relation to non-Harpo scenes is one question. And another is, do you envision us as needing to be threaded together, as problematically disconnected, either from ourselves or from each other?

WK: I have all sorts of investments and pleasures in the non-Harpo scenes. Right now I'm thinking of the actress Lillian Roth, who wrote the book *I'll Cry Tomorrow,* about being a drunk (which was later made into a film with Susan Hayworth). She appears as ingénue in one of Harpo's early films. Her entire subsequent career serves as an amplifier, a way of making Harpo's resonance resound with greater depth and unpredictability. What I'd decided, procedurally, is whenever I identified another non-Marx actor, I would give one or two weird details about their career, references to other films or to history.

AF: To the Holocaust.

WK: Yeah. My basic sense always, my working theory of stardom, is that a star intertext brings profundity and amplification of resonance (such as a cathedral brings to an organ) to the affects of cinema. To trace these folds of star intertext seems essential to plumbing the depth of conventional Hollywood films. So all the other scenes become important as part of the filaments and integuments—the stuff that makes Harpo sound. Also those scenes interest me in the way that sexual desire is, as everyone knows but Roland Barthes probably described best, a whole kaleidoscope of nuances and barriers and foreplays that don't have much to do with other people or sex organs. All the scenes we must wade through, waiting for Harpo to appear, keep Harpo exciting for me. And your second question was am I, like Harpo, threading together? Do I have a therapeutic or recuperative process?

AF: Or a drive, an unspeakable drive, to thread together.

WK: Maybe not now, but through most of my life, I was the family mediator, the go-between. That is constitutionally what I am. I have a drive to interpretation. I'm a wacky interpreter and usually get things wrong in some basic way. There's a lot of wish involved in my interpretations. But some part of my interpretation, I hope, contains a modicum of truth. I feel a drive to bring forward, to make audible, to explicate that one-third or one-fourth or fifth of rightness in something I see, as if correcting an imbalance in the universe. I find explication very exciting. I'll get physically and otherwise very excited when I discover what I feel and what I see. I'll sense immediately an infectious desire to communicate that discovery.

AF: Could we discuss a few specific images? Page 167, at the top. Here Harpo has a pallid, formless face. Do you know what's happening?

WK: If we're referring to the same picture, he essentially is doing skeptical duck-mouth. Barthes gives duck-mouth when he scolds doxa. Harpo scolds a policeman or whomever this guard is for his business-as-usual assumptions.

AF: OK, this should be the top of 174. You talk about Harpo's tie as his codpiece. But don't his pants also possess a conspicuous bulge?

WK: Oh my god, I hadn't noticed. Right in the pocket.

AF: It could be his horn.

WK: Something that happened writing this book is that I no longer consulted the picture once I'd started working seriously on the prose. And the second is that I'd originally worked from blurry images taken with my digital camera, from the computer. For the final draft I went back and made screengrabs that show more detail. This means some pictures I originally wrote about were close-ups within close-ups. I didn't see the still as a whole. I will even say, in some cases, because of the screen ratio I'd used…I'll often refer to Harpo's wide face. In digital pictures his face looks stretched out wide, but the screengrabs restored it to regular size. So I'm writing about a different set of images.

AF: That came through in the book—that the images weren't fully linked to their descriptions. That's interesting, again, beside questions of the still versus the fluid image, and parsing shots on your computer instead of the cinema screen. Of course page 118 provides the photo that seems "accidentally" to include your rough draft, and to expose the fact that all these photos come from your computer. What's the narrative behind that?

WK: You're right. That was the only instance in which I left the original picture.

AF: That's all perfectly communicated. There's something vaguely pornographic or obscene about this photo, because we'll see things that should be kept out of it. It's a perfectly executed composition. Or frame, as you said. And anything you want to say about the non-Harpo photo, da Vinci's "John the Baptist"?

WK: There are actually several. There's an Anna Moffo cover. There's also this picture of a woman with a frozen face. And then there's the final picture of the chestnut.

AF: I guess da Vinci seemed the most tangential.

WK: Yeah. I maybe feel a bit guilty da Vinci made it in, because I didn't really rationalize why I admitted that image. I had rules underlying this book's writing. I always have rules and procedures. The rule here was that all pictures should be of Harpo, in service to the project. I had to (like a finger in a dike) keep at bay the inundation of all the other things one could talk and think about. But John the Baptist came through. There are strange little exceptions throughout the book. And maybe, in general, I'll always let something break the rule.

AF: I liked how this photo echoes a scholar's gratuitous footnote that just couldn't be stopped. It has that quality. Returning to the chestnut: do you have an available explanation for why the book gets sequenced this way—acknowledging its chronological disruptions only in the final section, and ending with *A Day at the Races*? Was that film's triumphant final image the indisputable finale from the start? Here I thought of Nietzsche's claim that we only learn to respect the individual by first revering the monarch. Did we need to see Harpo (and ourselves perhaps) as king, so that we could fully appreciate the poignance of you dropping Harpo at the end, like a lumpy chestnut?

WK: I kept the chapters in the order I had written them because the book provides a diary of autodidacticism, and its style or tone suddenly change throughout. There's an arc of exuberance and depression I needed to keep intact. In terms of the sequence of films I chose, I'd started with *The Cocoanuts* because it was the first. I went with what I wanted to watch next. Then as I realized I was winding toward the end, I saved *Day at the Races*. One reason might be because it's the longest film, and it became an ordeal to complete the process of notetaking. I would annotate 15 minutes of film each day. That included 15 minutes even if Harpo wasn't in it. I always would be thrilled if Harpo wasn't in because I'd think, I don't have to write anything today. So I probably put off *A Day at the Races* because of its length, but also because I'm very fond of it, particularly its ending. The chestnut arrived as an addendum to the end of this writing process, after revision and revision, when I'd already begun mourning the book. At that point the chestnut appeared.

AF: You mentioned the lucky days that you and Harpo could take off. I'm curious about your reflective process then. Is there anything else you can say about the virtues of going blank, of seeing someone go blank, or of being seen wanting to go blank, which I guess all happen when we go to the movies?

WK: This could be where *The Idiot* enters. I'm aware of an uncanny and not necessarily joyful likeness between experiences of sublime attentiveness and pleasure on one hand, and experiences of traumatic deadness and catatonia. One precedes the other, or erases the other. An underground tunnel seems to connect them. So maybe the virtues of going blank come about because some of us get addicted to this sublime clarity, also because we're loners, and weird, and like to space out, and sense that some experiences of blankness most of the world wishes to avoid are the secret passageway to states of great intensity and pleasure. That's a working knowledge I've always had, which probably allows me to endure writing books, which is essentially a blank and painful process. Of course its sudden spikes of intensification are glorious. I have a tropism toward the volitionally psychotic. I've often courted experiences of…call them going blank. It's how I found Gertrude Stein, or why I like difficulty, why I like endurance tests, and why I work hard. My exertions contain blankness nested within them.

## INTERVIEW WITH SHANNA COMPTON
Recorded on July 7, 2012
This interview focuses on Compton's books *Brink* and *The Seam* (Bloof)

ANDY FITCH: I try to save potentially stupid questions for later, but have you seen Lars von Trier's film *Melancholia*? Did that shape this project in any way?

SHANNA COMPTON: I've seen some Lars von Trier. No, we haven't watched that one yet.

AF: I'd asked because as I progressed through your cataclysmic, asteroidal diptych, and underwent its proleptic process of meaning-making (like how the New Testament rewrites and recodes the Old Testament), I kept picturing…*Melancholia* ends with Earth destroyed by an asteroid. But mostly I'm just curious about a second half recoding the first.

SC: I think of my *Brink* section as a "before" and *The Seam* as an "after." Though it's not a perfect fit. In fact the editors have convinced me to separate those sequences a bit more by putting them in physically distinct volumes. I couldn't fully explain how they fit together. I wrote them at the same time, addressing interrelated themes, but they definitely differ in style and approach. *Brink* comes before *The Seam*'s disaster. *Brink* consists of shorter poems and linked sequences, whereas *The Seam* offers one long work. This asteroid, end-of-the-world apocalypse idea certainly did come from various films and science fictions.

AF: So if the manuscript pieces I saw won't be a single volume, could you describe their status now?

SC: I'd planned to publish these two sections as a single volume called *The Hazard Cycle*. But now we'll just do *Brink* as a volume and *The Seam* as a volume—available together, yet as two separate books. We'll design them somehow to fit together.

AF: I didn't reread *Brink* once I'd started *The Seam*. But I remember, during *Brink*'s last 15 pages, sensing the intimation of a break-up, perhaps Romantic intimations of mortality, though did I miss obvious indications of Earth's imminent demise? Or does *Brink* open various possible registers which only later get channeled into meteor showers? Did *Brink* ever exist as something else, other than a precursor to *The Seam*?

SC: *Brink* contains individual poems I'd gathered as a working manuscript, randomly putting pieces together. Then I started to notice repeated themes, and *The Seam* emerged from those. The poem "The Argument" probably came first, from several years back. I'd completely forgotten about it then found it on my hard drive and realized it fit. One of my readers said this poem sort of splits the two sections. Though what you've said about romantic dissolution and the second half's apocalypse…with poems like "Rare Vagrants," I purposefully mix all that stuff together. This makes the disaster scene both intimate and larger—shifting from a small fight to a big catastrophe involving world climate. I didn't want to produce something matchy matchy, but to play with registers and see what happened. *Brink* also has a different ending now, a long sequence called "The Deeps." Sorry about that.

AF: When I said "Romantic" I actually meant with a capital R. Still both could fit with general reflections on disaster and mortality and how, in our culture, the romantic love story allows more people to focus. I like how that all gets conflated as a general momentum takes us over the edge.

SC: Both romance and Romantic, even those words, appear. At *The Seam*'s end, Celo says "Good morning, Romantics," which I'd used as the title for an early chapbook.

AF: I probably should clarify, following my *Melancholia* question, that any number of literary affinities come to mind: the fluid, semi-opacities of vintage Lisa Robertson; the enigmatic equipoise of Susan Wheeler lyrics; the quant colloquialisms of James Schuyler; also Alice Notley's *Descent of Alette* and recent dystopic quasi-narratives by Danielle Pafunda and Cathy Park Hong; then epic evocations and archaic elocutions and campy newsprint, as well as the pop nonchalance of Brian Eno or "1999" or the Flaming Lips' "Yoshimi." Did any of those provide for generative thinking? Did you have compositional procedures you wanted to try, narrative and lyric forms you wished to fuse, refuse, split apart?

SC: Some of those came up while writing. Danielle's a good friend and we've shared work for years. I always admire Lisa Robertson's mythic narrative-making, and had been rereading *Debbie: An Epic*. Also a bunch of Alice Notley and *Engine Empire* by Cathy Park Hong. I didn't start *The Seam* thinking about those things, but basically just challenging myself to write something other than short, individual poems—something different than what I'd done before.

AF: I love the fractured sci-fi idiom here, though of course we don't need extraterrestrial interference to prompt the planet's demise anymore. Do you often imagine the world's end? For me, it can feel cleansing to adopt a retrospective, end-of-the-world vantage on certain parts of life. I love how your book describes "rumpled want-ads perpetually seeking / whatever." Perhaps some fascist part of me likes to purge. But can you discuss how this particular apocalyptic scenario plays out in relation to global warming, post-9/11 New York, discourses of girlhood, everyday fantasy?

SC: A few of the poems disappoint me for expressing irritation and constant frustration without necessarily going further. Still, a lot of this book grew out of such feelings, figuring out what to do about those feelings (and the situations that cause them). I think in one poem the speaker says, "I'm putting my hair up because I'm sick of this." She means the constant intrusion of the world and the news—everything being shit all the time. So in a fictional sense I wanted to exaggerate and move beyond that by making up some crazy story. Everything you've mentioned gets included. *Brink* contains a 9/11 poem and definitely lots of environmental topics. I cut some animal rights stuff because it sounded too…I get pissed. But pushing that all into a fictional setting through which one main character moves seemed somehow more positive than just bitching—letting her act, seeing what she creates of situations.

AF: Of course the fabular, the fairy tale, sci-fi all have undergone a rehabilitation in contemporary poetry. And I'll think of Freud's work on folk tales—how these get so gruesome in part because the deaths enacted allow adolescent audiences to work through their own growth and development and departure from the only world they know. Does it seem appropriate to place current interests in the fabular alongside some sense of ours being a "late" culture? Could we make a connection (as you seem to make) among fantasy and YA idioms and apocalyptic narrative scenes all tracking some broader developmental stage's end?

SC: *The Seam* definitely addresses parts of that. Celo enters the tunnels and makes her confessions and moves away from the broken town and so on. This narrative depicts young people and indulges in their characteristic gruesomeness. Especially after I'd begun the story, I started letting its pitch get highly emotional and a bit melodramatic—again, just to see what happened. Some passages emphasize this emotional content more than any narrative event. Those traits of contemporary poetry you mentioned appeal to me and I can't tell whether I've processed them consciously or not.

AF: I thought here, for example, about Gurlesque poetics re-valuing a mode of discourse often considered illegitimate, not serious, unworthy of attention—returning us to the repressed. From that a couple other models came to mind, such as John Ashbery's *Girls on the Run,* based on Henry Darger's *The Vivian Girls.* Does *The Seam* present something like the story of a solitary Vivian girl?

SC: I know that book. Those girls seem younger. Again I do read lots of science fiction and Grimm's fairy tales and John Ashbery. But I'd forgotten all about his book and how it might relate to my project.

AF: I can't remember why that came up. It had to do with colors you mentioned.

SC: I probably echo him and don't realize it. As for the Gurlesque: I know and love much work by poets classified under that description, a couple of whom we've mentioned. I don't know if I participate so much as I absorb something from their presence. My position when writing this felt quite open and receptive. So all sorts of material might have gotten in.

AF: Well I'll think of some of your early work as celebrating jumbled vernaculars, myriad forms of vernacular speech. *The Seam* embraces its own formal and informal idioms. Once you became apocalyptically focused, and began drafting *The Seam*, did you start to notice end-time discourses all around—in books, the news, overheard on the subway? Do intimations of apocalypse circulate through our daily lives without us recognizing it?

SC: I've always mixed different registers of language. I basically don't know how to stop. I'll get bored by a real steady tone in anything. You'd said something about the New and Old Testaments, and I definitely don't want to get biblical, though did want a more…something about those cadences and that language to feel ominous here. And this gets hard to articulate, but I attempted to make nothing seem causal—with the exception of some of Celo's speeches, where she starts to tell her back-story. Otherwise, bits and pieces come at you all the time in forms of atomized language. Then more generally: I think I've purposefully tuned into some menacing discourses because I felt I'd been a bit irresponsible and flippant. I sensed I hadn't reacted appropriately to everything I should react to. I still don't know that I have. But I've tried.

AF: That comes across clearly. And just to bring in your publishing efforts, can we talk about how this *Hazard Cycle* sequence fits amid your broader poetic practice? Could you describe the drafting/design/publishing process here, since that seems unique, given your admirably unapologetic decision to publish the book through your own press, Bloof? Had you decided on this publishing route from the start? Did it free up your writing to know that no (or so I had thought) editorial board, no commercial calculations, would impede your progress? We could even discuss little things—like in *Brink*'s manuscript form, many poems look exactly one page long, as though you'd already laid out the book.

sc: For this particular project, I knew early on we would do it with Bloof. Each book has an editorial board, and I do much of the editing myself of course. The decision to do these books with Bloof did free me from worries about making them suitable for someone else. I've gotten to where I prefer to work this way. I absolutely do conceive of the design and layout and even the typesetting and cover as I write. I automatically think about each poem as an object. I feel lucky to be in this position where I can ensure that the finished book represents what I'd wanted. Of course some drawbacks exist. Since nobody imposes deadlines and structure, some timelines get a bit loose. Because of the open way I preferred to work on these, I also wanted that uncertainty to be all mine. I didn't want to have to make it all OK or acceptable for someone else.

af: Again this especially interests me in terms of the book's proleptic process—how the second half changes our understanding of the first. Because who knows? If you sent this manuscripts to contests, to a publisher who'd only consider the first 10 pages, could you risk something like that?

sc: I can't imagine sending out 10 pages from this with a query letter. Again, to me, the writing, the design, the publication all become one project. Most sections of *The Seam* won't wind up in magazines. Excerpting felt too difficult. *Brink* seems more conventionally shaped, magazine shaped. But *The Seam* foregrounds an intention not to worry about such things.

af: I appreciate that you don't just skip certain stages of editorial evaluation—you do something you couldn't have done otherwise.

sc: I seek out lots of input. I'll have good friends who are great poets give honest feedback—not always the feedback I want, either. Bloof works like that. Even when I edit Jennifer L. Knox or Danielle Pafunda or Sandra Simonds, I'll give editorial suggestions. Still these always remain only suggestions. The idea is not for me (as editor) to make the book mine, but to assist the poet with its presentation. I'd hate for all the rough edges to get cleaned up. I've worked in publishing for a long time, and know how my favorite writing occurs. Other people have other approaches.

AF: You've mentioned before the long, illustrious tradition of DIY and micro-press publishing—however we want to define these historically. Could you give some specific examples, ancient or contemporary, that you find particularly inspiring?

SC: I can think of so many.

AF: How about an early personal influence?

SC: Well, I put my first chapbook together in third grade, for a class project. Then I did a zine in college, and other chapbooks. Then once I got to New York and started reading about the New York poets, their little pamphlets and chapbooks, that all became endlessly important. It felt like learning after the fact: yeah, this is OK to do. Also Buck Downs provided a great example—both as the first poet I saw read at St. Mark's, and for producing whatever the hell he wants. So I've always worked this way. Whenever I write something I want physically to make it. Those don't seem two separate processes.

AF: I'm talking to you from Sydney, Australia, where we've been eating tons of Thai food. My wife gets mad because, everywhere we go, I just talk about how we could make this same food at home. Your impulse sounds somewhat similar—with the making never separate from the receiving or appreciating. I do want to clarify for readers (since you've been quite modest) that your poems get published all over the place. Just as impressive as your self-publishing project is *Brink*'s long list of publications. But you've said you don't imagine many publishable excerpts from *The Seam*. Do you, as a reader, take particular pleasure in reading isolated fragments from larger, uncontextualized manuscripts? I'll love when short, inexplicable units sound like lyrics from outer space. And I ask because you've always impressed me by coming up with clipped, catchy phrases. Here, for example: "core rare" in *Brink*, "blisterhot tektites" in *The Seam*. But then I also love elaborate, elastic constructions of yours which seem to take pleasure in how they keep going. We could look at, from "Timetables & Humble Pie," this long question: "What do I need with cuspids, or limbs / to walk and fondle, a talent for speech, // as one typifying solace-less-ness, a wimpy biter / and squanderer of those trillion misplaced swans / in the reservoir by the highway, each curving // its legendary throat to query what dared I do, / and at such tizzy speed, hurtling as I was, flanked / by peeling fields, oblivious of the terminal stop long past?"

SC: For that I wanted to continue as long as possible. That happens a couple times in *Brink*, such as in "One More Favor." During a particular phase of writing I'd purposefully take a thought or question or sentence and wrap it around and around and around. This seemed to provide a productive contrast, an intensified sensation of maxing out the sentence. Though I like the short, punchy bits too. I don't think I answered your question—but yes, un- or recontextualized fragments attract me, here and in my previous book. They're why I've had so much fun with Flarf.

AF: "Various Natural Objects All Heaped Up Together" has these different "People who" constructions, then ends with a really long one: "People who believe / in weird things like uprisings and the potential / purity of sweat socks? People who believe / that Unseen Forces Control the World / from towers so realistically painted on the canvas / dropped flush with the horizon that they move / with the desert's breath, in and out, / modeling a living semblance for us, the people / who look so hard for the evidence in the crappiest fossil, / like the broken shell of an Oriental Hornet, / no longer converting the sun into its / lately discovered electrical buzz?" So here's my question: you seem drawn to and very good at both short, memorable phrases and longer associative trains. But did it seem harder to "get away with" such devices as this work veered toward fiction? Did you fear they might sound too tangential? Or does the narrative scaffolding call them forth from you? Do they just pop out?

SC: Again *The Seam* purposefully works against what I've done in other poems. *Brink* and *The Seam* push against each other. Also I don't know much about writing prose, and didn't want *The Seam* to become too prose-y. I prefer it to feel somewhat fragmentary, leaving space between sections instead of forcing them together—but all to let them spark. For the shorter space of *Brink*'s short poems, the maxing out and extended runs seemed OK since their end always stayed in sight.

AF: Well, could we discuss what gets left out of *The Seam*'s formal structure? I mean how it resembles trauma, for example, how it feels retrospective, and repetitively so. We keep returning to the start of this crisis, one that never gets processed emotionally or…a break occurs. And no build-up precedes the crisis. We hear vaguely about before the crisis, then experience in detail after the crisis. This whole time I keep wondering what you've left out. Why omit the asteroid scene then constantly recall it? Again, I love those parts of the book. I just hope to hear you discuss them.

SC: I deliberately don't provide anything beyond an archivist's introduction. Even that felt perhaps too much. Given this apocalyptic, dissolution-of-the-world-type story, an omniscient narrator didn't make sense. So whatever understanding Celo assembles of that scene only comes from scraps and pieces. The characters themselves don't quite know what hit them. Most remain passive observers, but Celo feels compelled to explain (to story-make) even without having all the answers.

AF: Could you describe the "Jacks" to close?

SC: The Jacks are mutant jackrabbits. I don't know what else to say about them. I can say they tried to take over the book and I had to wrestle with them. At a certain point they started to sound silly. The rest seemed more interesting. I still include them, but didn't want the focus to be, what the hell's going on with these mutant jackrabbits, you know? They serve as emblems or symbols of the ruptures and uncertainty and blendings throughout this book. They stay uncanny, strange, creaturely. I like them. I didn't want to abandon them completely.

## INTERVIEW WITH FRANCES RICHARD
Recorded on July 8, 2012
This interview focuses on Richard's book *The Phonemes* (Les Figues).

ANDY FITCH: If we could start with the "sounds" that would be great. I read your project in manuscript form, on double-sided paper, so didn't have before me the legend your printed book provides, with graphic symbols on one side and sound descriptions on the other. So for ^^º ^^º the sound, "Whir; small body in departure" et cetera—I didn't make that connection. But do you prefer to imagine the text presenting a prescripted experience of these sound units, which you then can sculpt into longer sequences? Or do you like the idea of these sounds retaining a negative capability? Do the synesthsesiac descriptions you provide seek to preserve some of that negative capability anyway?

FRANCES RICHARD: Negative capability: perhaps if one becomes a poet that's already an important concept. But it is a really important concept to me, so I'm happy you would choose those terms.

AF: I guess it's loaded. We could move away from that particular phrase.

FR: The sounds came from thinking about my experience of listening to the world in general, but also listening to poets read, what the voice and body can do. It's kind of like what you'd said about Skype. We can hear each other but not see each other. Even if we used the video function, we'd encounter that weird, pixilated delay. The live body delivering sound in real time does all this seamless, paralinguistic work. There must be a much more precise musical terminology, or perhaps a linguistics terminology, for what I want to say, but color and timbre and timing and accent and emotional valence shape what one expresses. Live performance allows for this. At the same time, poetry remains a solitary-feeling endeavor in our culture. It exists on the page largely for the page—or perhaps the screen, but printed. I'd started to imagine almost a sibling rivalry between sound in the air and print on the page. I've wondered what each mode does best. Sound in the air carries all this volume and personality. But the printed page can go where the body can't, and persists where the body won't. It can speak in your head and your voice instead of from my head and my voice. So *The Phonemes'* typography came out of… one thing that happens when you listen to the world: you might be at a poetry reading and a car alarm will start outside. Then the car alarm happens at the same time as the reading. That's one advantage sound has, this elasticity. I wanted the page to open itself to this intrusion of non-verbal sound, so I made up these sounds and a typography for them, but as we'd said before about the nature of the interview, it's not definitive. That's just the nature of language, right? Or the nature of representation. Part of me loves the idea somebody might jump back and forth in my book looking at the legend and thinking, OK, that's a whir sound. But I equally love that somebody could decide, I don't care what that sound says; I'm just looking at a visual design. Or could think, I know that's supposed to mean something but I forget what; I'm going to make up this sound. Or somebody could be like, oh, there's blank space for live sound—and then fill it with whatever he or she happened to hear at that moment. Each of these addresses the tension about how notation connects to meaning.

AF: You mentioned the car-alarm example. You've told me you're reading much about William Carlos Williams right now. There's one classic reading with him in a drafty room, where you hear cars pass the whole time. Have you listened to that particular recording?

FR: I'll try to find it.

AF: I can try too. For now I can't help imagining your reader internalizing some sort of Futurist sound-and-visual bombardment. But *The Phonemes* presents a calm, meditative presence perhaps familiar to focused readers. Here the bold move of calling these typographical elements "sounds" impressed me. The one thing that they're not is a sound. The auditory cues you do provide don't necessarily help much. I like that too. And of course John Cage on noise comes to mind. Your effort to open up the page as experiential environment echoes Cage's frequent compositional decision to include the external surrounds within his piece or performance.

FR: I've always assumed that Cage moved far beyond what I could hope for in terms of becoming a meditative master, because sound often disturbs me. I'm quite sound sensitive. I've lived in New York for 15 years and never gotten used to the assaultive street noise. I'll block my ears with my fingers on the subway. Cage's idea that all sound is music, all noise composition—that could not be farther from my experience. But I admire it. It suggests an equanimity and curiosity I wish I had. One Zen teacher says, "We disturb the sound." I'm sure my own sound project includes trying to befriend annoying noises. Though natural noises occur here too. Something annoying about annoying noises is that they have this mechanical, relentless, inhuman, juggernaut feel. I've tried to go against that, to reposition both sides, so that no difference exists between wind in the grass and a refrigerator's drone.

AF: Along those lines, as you edited this meticulous text, as you reread the sounds, how did you experience them? Was it auditory? Emotive? What experience do you have, do you imagine your reader having of, let's say, the parenthesis-covered page?

FR: That's a whole page of "car alarm."

AF: Then subsequent pages have parentheses, though not this same imposing phalanx.

FR: My own experience of that parenthesis page resembles a car alarm going off. I actually hear "wahwahwahwah, ah-ah-ah-ah-ah, weh-oo weh-oo." Just going on and on.

AF: Though the page presents a meditative, rhythmic, Agnes Martin-like layout.

FR: Well, if my car alarm can channel Agnes Martin, I'd…no higher aspiration could be fulfilled! But yeah, I experience this book both ways. When I read it, partly because I've practiced reading it aloud, and now have read it aloud a lot, even when I just cast my eye silently, I do hear it as such. Although I also see a series of symmetrical marks on the page. I guess, for the reader: if you see parenthesis and remember "car alarm," yet also picture meditative Agnes Martins, I couldn't be happier. And if somebody doesn't remember "car alarm," I don't really mind.

AF: So how do you perform it aloud?

FR: I do that noise I just did. I make the sound.

AF: For all these sounds?

FR: Yeah.

AF: Do you appreciate art and texts that train their audience in some way? When you'd mentioned hearing voices in your head, I remembered Bertolt Brecht's idea of true intellectual work involving thinking in others' heads, while having other people think in your head. Could you sense something constructive, rather than simply controlling or constrictive, in training the reader or getting trained yourself?

FR: Yes, I like that. This connects again to meditation, which feels wide open but not easy. It takes a lot of training, a lot of discipline, to enter that openness. And poetry's verbal artifacts demand attention, demand certain kinds of brightness in the reader's focus. You don't just loll back. I like this about poetry. I find it's good for the mind.

AF: It models to us that we are inherently trained beings, by language, already. It gives us a parallel structure to pursue, again with desire, but also a recognition that, yeah, this is what I am and what I do.

FR: Right. To understand, after a while, that a dotted line stands for a refrigerator humming—that's what all language-learning does. It applies to some symbol a concept and a sound and a feeling, until these conjunctions seem to make sense.

AF: In your notes you cite Anne Carson's Sappho translation which, from what I remember, foregrounds questions of how we read—by which I mean how we internally score, internally produce, not necessarily how we understand. How we should read a soundless notation signifying absence seems one of the basic problems animating Carson's book. Though to what extent did that inspire *The Phonemes*? Here you appear to present, in part, a deliberately different method. Because you do provide more guidance, however dubious or potentially misleading this discourse of guidance may be.

FR: The way Carson uses brackets visually in *If Not, Winter*—I don't think that ever entered my head while developing these sound symbols. Yet I do rely on Carson's book and always had valued Mary Barnard's translations, though when I first read Carson's translations, suddenly Barnard's fragmentary (but less so) versions…I felt their madness and claustrophobia, their closed-downness. I really appreciated the wild infusion coming from Carson's blank spaces. But I hadn't consciously thought about them as a typographic marking that is not verbal, yet stands for the failure or dissolution of the verbal.

AF: Just while you described the Barnard translations, which I too always admired, I sensed a paratext of Emily Dickinson and the way Dickinson gets normalized—how her dashes and constructions of poetic space and her history haunt my reading of Carson on Sappho.

FR: I recently heard Susan Howe give a brilliant short talk on Dickinson's manuscript scraps (not clean-copy fascicles), where Howe attended not only to dashes but to all kinds of stray markings on irregular pages. That talk was just heaven. It felt so satisfying, because the ghostliness of language pooled in these spots. They contain a libidinal charge.

AF: This brings up questions of how you designed your own symbols.

To me, they seem animated and subtle and playful. They'll suggest winking eyebrows or puckering lips. They made me think of English, of typeset, as more hieroglyphic, more anthropomorphic than I'd realized. I sensed more body behind both after looking at your sounds.

FR: Isn't it interesting that these symbols can go from evoking Agnes Martin, who seems so resolutely, sternly anti-figurative, anti-representational, and yet this bodily thing…it's there for me too. Perhaps not in an iconic way, not a tiny picture of the body, but closer to indexical mark-making, to a body making a mark or pressing a key to make its mark. Then also the whirs and nonverbal phrases push you back into the body.

AF: I always love, let's say how French people represent grunts, or dog barks. To realize printed characters have the bodily urgency of a grunt, yet even that grunt we hear gets socialized and coded through language.

FR: Even silence does, right? Carson shows this with her brackets. Dickinson does through her dashes. The Sappho/Carson silence that occurs in brackets (and in holes in the papyrus)—this silence sounds differently than Dickinson's dash.

AF: We've made a few art-world comparisons. But since you write so well about art, I'll try to formulate a more thorough question. Graphic designs tend to prompt an instantaneous, two-dimensional apprehension. They seem harder to read, if reading describes an activity that takes place in time. But sounds have temporal duration. Sounds, as you've said, can become intrusive and hard to avoid. Of course exceptions to this dichotomy exist. Mondrian's "Plus-Minus" paintings of the sea seem to ask to be read in time. Agnes Martin grids shimmer. You can't absorb them in an instant. Then, conversely, Ed Ruscha's word-paintings, or his blacked-out texts, give language an atmospheric hue, though not necessarily a syntactical directive. Does *The Phonemes* fit within any such constellation of artistic investigations? Or what would be a constellation in which this book fits?

FR: I have no constellations prepared, but it interests me when people propose them. Ronaldo V. Wilson, who wrote the book's introduction, talks about the car-alarm pages reminding him of William Pope.L's piece *Yard (To Harrow)*, 2009, which was a re-do of Allan

Kaprow's *Yard* (1961), a bunch of piled-up tires. Those pages with their black, semi-circular marks—and, I suppose, the car reference too—reminded Ronaldo of the Pope.L piece, and I was thrilled by that comparison, but never would have thought of it. I certainly didn't write this book thinking, oh, here's my mental gallery of artists that relate in some way. When you mention Ruscha, you're quite right that his word-paintings provide a different experiment in terms of probing how language functions as a disembodied sign in visual space. The word-paintings don't fully relate, but book-projects from the '60s like *Twentysix Gasoline Stations,* or *Every Building on the Sunset Strip,* do, because of their sort of syntactical...the way *Every Building on the Sunset Strip* resembles a sentence.

AF: Given the latter examples, can you contextualize *The Phonemes* in relation to seriality? I mean in terms of how sounds cycle through your book: how we apprehend them both as localized units, which carry literal correspondence, and as incremental notations of a broader composition?

FR: I see both of those aspects. But it's almost as though, the moment I formulate either impulse for myself, it breaks down. It breaks down into atomic particles, instantaneously. Conceptualist constraint, composing according to a single or rigorous set of rules attracts me, but I never can stick to it. The libidinal drive we mentioned surges back in and messes things up the very minute I establish the constraint.

AF: I'm curious about your broader relations to conceptual writing. My question about duration came from this. Conceptual writing raises for me these questions of, once we "get" what's happening in a piece, then which conceptual texts remain readable after that? There are any number of ways that all remain readable. But which continue to prompt a libidinal desire pushing forward in the way we're perhaps used to with reading? Here again the question arises, what does our body do with text? Especially in that moment after we've gotten the concept. Can emotional projection still happen? Can auditory and/or visual hallucination? Can we still pursue information in some utilitarian way? So again I'm wondering, do your own synesthsesiac symbols suggest similar interests in what a body does with text?

FR: An important difference, at least for me, exists between the gratification of desire for narrative submersion (to be sucked into a story and delivered into character and plot as with conventionally pleasurable reading) and the more diffuse, sort of stippled, oscillating, pulsing propulsion that you get when the means of communication or representation are foregrounded. But, that aside, as you asked your question I found myself recalling two performance experiences. One was Kenny Goldsmith several years ago, reading from his *New York Times* book.

AF: *Day*?

FR: Yeah. I had looked at the book, looked as opposed to read, but hearing him read from it was riveting. It was just an epic novel. I could have listened a lot longer. That case demonstrated what I've said about my listening and reading experiences being rivalrous relations—that they're obviously joined somewhere but often don't get along. Then the other example that popped into my head occurred at AWP last spring. I spoke on a panel about Les Figues' conceptualist anthology. Vanessa Place's piece provides this very simple conceit, where she substitutes the feminine pronoun for the masculine pronoun. This is with Simone de Beauvoir.

AF: She's got a book of those called *Boycott*.

FR: Yes. But for me it was different to hear it aloud. Once you get the joke, you get the joke, except it remains thoroughly pleasurable and exciting to hear, because every time you sense a pronoun coming down the pike you're like, it's going to happen again; it shouldn't happen again; it just happened again. The present female voice revisits the improper masculine pronoun. This little explosion of meaning and transgression and confusion between the written and the bodily present kept happening all over, though through a stupidly simple exchange which you could predict every time. That probably doesn't answer your question, but those are two examples where the experience of live performance and live listening became very rich, pleasing, yet also disruptive. If I could do that via rigorous constraint, I would enjoy it, but as a writer I'm too restless. If synesthesia includes not only the verbal or sonic or visual, but also the haptic, the sense of touch, then my sense of compositional touch isn't compulsive enough, or it's too infantile or something. I change too often.

AF: I think that's less infantile, if we use a Freudian model.

FR: By "infantile" I mean wanting gratification, wanting pleasure.

Being less charmed by a conceptual pleasure. Wanting a milky pleasure.

AF: You describe that well. And here's what interests me: the discourse that travels most widely about conceptual writing often explicitly states, even brags, that these texts will bore the reader. But as you say, I find both Vanessa's and Kenny's pieces totally compelling. So I wish, rather than having to bracket off the erotics of conceptual writing, that we could probe them more for what's at play. That's part of what your sounds do. That's great.

FR: The erotics of conceptual writing are important. The sense that there would be no erotics, that one would only find boredom or frustration—or that eros and frustration could separate—that reifies a mind/body split. Ultimately that says, this is an intellectual artifact, therefore not a physical artifact, nor a kinetic or energetic artifact. I think that's way too limiting. It's just not accurate to the minute-by-minute experience of listening, or reading, or writing. Or thinking.

AF: Well to broaden the scope a bit, could we discuss the thematics of your book? Meteorites appear often. Do meteorites somehow resemble phonemes? Are phonemes atomized units of matter bombarding atmospheric ecosystems?

FR: Yes, in some ways, a phoneme's a chip off the old block of language. It's a tiny shard of language. And a meteorite is a small piece of space-matter that runs around the universe by itself.

AF: I appreciated the solid clusters in which you'd often place language, with then this one phoneme breaking off to spark across the universe. But what about "Shaved Code"? "Shaved Code" stands out as quite different from the rest of the manuscript. You don't deploy the sounds. You focus more directly on ecological concerns. Yet this piece also fits well in the overall book.

FR: I want to ask how you think it fits well.

AF: Me? I sense a parallel between the environmental and the prosodic focus. "Shaved Code" seems to describe a body's situated place amid an ever-changing ecosystem, in the way that your sounds operate to suggest something similar.

FR: Right. That this book's in some fundamental way about landscape was not planned. That just emerged. The phonemic sections trace the topography of language. "Shaved Code" addresses an ecosystem, the coastal redwoods' ecosystem. It also foregrounds political systems in that it's about Judi Bari and the 1990 bombing of her car, in Oakland. A long string of discursive positions about these landscapes appear, in this poem, at cross-purposes, in conflict. I'd struggled with how to engage the heroic, because I do think she's heroic. She was taken down and yet survived her injuries; then died (of cancer); then triumphed posthumously. Thinking about heroism made me think in a more general way about assaults that are not definitively crushing, although still painful and disastrous—events which, because epic but not definitive, allow evolution. In Judi's case, some further chapters included the successful suit against the FBI and Oakland police, and the survival of her legacy of activism, but also the fact that old-growth logging and other violently invasive, wasteful, short-sighted land-use practices continue (think of fracking). When there's a disaster, some sequel chapters will be terrible and some will be amazing. That seemed a good ecological story to me—that a natural system's weave withstands huge destructive forces shot at it. It's not killed by those shots, but not unharmed or unaltered either. Judi was an activist, an orator, and then this attack happened that generated a lot of news coverage, and a famous trial. She wrote a book. These are multiple kinds of mark-making. She died, yet remains a powerful figure, speaking on posthumously without her body. Her story now exists in language, and in numbers. Numbers intrude, because the vindication of her case…in our culture, legalistic vindication comes with cash reward, measured by a number. That's another kind of notation brought in. To bomb a body, or to cut down a tree, is incommensurate with saying a word or counting a number. But you can't separate such things, either. This prompts further thinking about the difference between what happens when you confront a live body in real time, and what happens when you sit and read.

AF: I wondered about Bari's iconic place in your overall project. You'd mentioned the pixilated nature of our conversation earlier. There is this ambient, abstracted world in which your poems comfortably can reside, which I admire so much. I think of so-called Elliptical poets, who supposedly use Language elements to highlight lyric ends. But your work moves in the opposite direction, towards greater opacity, really thinking through how linguistic code and bodily operations parallel or diverge from each other. Yet at the same time, there is this sense of the pixilated scene swelling from ambient, localized details of sound and syntactical nuance to dramatized, heroic character represented on an epic scale. Your book picks up a sweeping gravitas.

FR: In an earlier iteration of *The Phonemes*, this idea about falling—the heroic act and the epic fall—played a bigger role. Social or political duty got traced like a meteor. The meteor appears as this dramatic being from another world. It comes from the beyond and enters flaming. For the meteor, to fall is not definitive. But back to Bari's specific story: I felt puzzled by that divide—which does and doesn't exist—between the violent touch of harm on the living body, and the power of words to galvanize change and record ideas. I hope I can have it both ways in terms of exploring the nature of representation, the discourse of sound, but still providing direct communication about this activist who did amazing work forging a radical ecological consciousness and analyzing labor practices in the logging industry. Bari got framed by the FBI and the courts vindicated her. That's enough of a story. Here I want to use language as an instrumental, communicative tool where I say the thing and you get the thing, a piece of information that is not totally pixilated, not falling to shreds.

AF: Again, you raise important questions about the purported purposelessness of some contemporary conceptual writing practices. What could a new mode of representation, one that gets worked through conceptual writing, look like? So finally, as an example of your representational processes, we've got "Blank Icarus." We've got "Blank Musée" which obviously calls to mind "Musée des Beaux Arts." Does the choral, fugue-like, collage-like construction of "Blank Musée" somehow echo the mosaical quality of the phonemes? Does Icarus' presence hint at some fall toward grounded meaning in your poetics?

FR: I always have kind of shamefacedly loved "Musée des Beaux Arts." So there's my really hip art reference, to Breugel. But "Blank Icarus" came about much more simply, through the last line, replacing "masters" with bastards." It kind of grew backwards from that little sonic accident. Icarus—of course, as you say, he's the meteor, the hero. Icarus and Daedalus are avatars, foils, and kind of blank each other out. "Blank Musée" continued to boil out of the coincidence between master and bastard and the idea of suffering, that you can, in this meditative way we've discussed, perhaps master suffering. That's an incredible aim. Or you can cause suffering and know a lot about its technical means, and be a violator. And maybe those positions, though opposite, can't be perfectly separated. The Auden poem got stuck in my head, and so did Shelley's "Mont Blanc." I was teaching it, and thinking about Shelley as one of these problematic visionary heroes who's not a very nice person, also probably a suicide. My mother is the other character in "Blank Musée." Part of the intrigue was simply to combine these three unlikely characters, to have Auden and Shelley and my mom work together. In terms of a conceptual proceduralism: the poem provides no words from me; only words from those three; and every word from a little phrase my mother wrote in her diary in the late '60s gets used in each stanza. That's my constraint. It's not a very rigorous one, but it was one I could carry through. I guess it represents another aspect of listening and inscription, in that their voices are encoded in my own mind and recycle themselves there.

## INTERVIEW WITH HEATHER CHRISTLE
Recorded on July 9, 2012
This interview focuses on Christle's book *What is Amazing* (Wesleyan University Press).

ANDY FITCH: Can we discuss the history of how this book came together, and how that history gets traced in the three separate sections? Some early pieces seem familiar, from *The Seaside!* Do all poems from the first section come from that same period of writing? Does that phase now feel far from you? I ask because this reads like a collected "Early Works."

HEATHER CHRISTLE: I didn't mean to arrange the book in chronological order, but that's what ended up happening. I wrote all sections fairly close together in time. The first section comes mostly from *The Seaside!*. I do feel quite far from that chapbook now, probably because I haven't written in that form for a while. From writing the poems of my first book, *The Difficult Farm*, to writing my second book, to this, I think form has propelled me to a certain extent. Other concerns do as well. But I'll invent some formal problem to investigate then write poems until I've reached, for myself, some kind of answer. I won't ever decide to stop writing in a particular way. Though once I've figured out how to do it, then I'll need to set up a new problem.

AF: I should clarify that when I'd asked if certain poems felt far, I don't mean they seem less developed or something, just that you show a great diversity within this single book, working with what feel separate phases almost.

HC: These phases do overlap somewhat. Once I get toward the end of something, I'll start to experiment with another form. So the second section's poems do overlap chronologically with some poems from the first.

AF: Did you conceive of the separate sections as stand-alone, self-sufficient units, or did you envision them placed side-by-side, perhaps to demonstrate your process of thinking through a poetic form, here by presenting three different takes?

HC: I hope that, even though the book does present these separate formal concerns, it also contains overlapping ideas about questioning where is the self and where is the world, and how does one differentiate between the two. Love appears throughout many of the sections.

AF: Could you start describing those different sections, so we can address how certain motifs circulate throughout?

HC: The first section's lines feel smashed together, with somewhat irregular capitalization and a lack of punctuation (other than exclamation points). This comes across as somewhat breathless or intense, energetic. It's kind of hard to describe one's own work.

AF: Yeah, for me section one gets characterized, as you say, by short, tightly sprung syntax, plus a lot of paratactic clauses. "And" keeps coming up, with few logic-steering conjunctions like "but" or "yet." It's more "and and and and and." Emphatic repetitions. Quick, clipped lines that turn like Frank O'Hara's. O'Hara's *Meditations in an Emergency* or *Lunch Poems* (I never can remember the title) opens with this poem "To the Harbor Master," which seemed maybe echoed in your opening poem, "The Seaside!" Then throughout the short, absurdist narratives feed on themselves. Again, somewhat O'Hara-esque, but with less of a documentarian bent than O'Hara. More playful, freely constructing scenarios. Lots of definitional poems about an "I" or an object, which produce plot-driven examinations almost like parables. You'll give the allegorical without the allegory. Dickinson's and

Kafka's fabular qualities come to mind, filtered through Mayakovsky and Walser.

HC: Well, Frank O'Hara's a poet I've thought about a lot. I tend to associate him with my first book, but perhaps he's stayed with me the way your parents remain always with you even if you think of friends more frequently. Though it's funny: I hadn't thought at all of him with that first poem, "The Seaside!," but that makes quite a bit of sense. For me, in terms of literary connections, I always imagined *Persuasion* and Jane Austen and that fall from the seawall there. Of course this poem doesn't literally engage Austen's narrative. It borrows some scenery. I've also realized another funny connection—my father is in the Merchant Marines, and soon will start sailing as captain, though that was not on my mind when I wrote this poem. When I worked on the poem, I really was writing through a rhythm, through rhythm and color and beauty and rage at being a human, the difficulty of being a person and trying to understand why one exists, why one sees the things one sees, or gets cast one's lot in life. Then, at this poem's end, Hans Christian Anderson's little mermaid seems to surface. She turns into foam at his fairy tale's conclusion. Here my speaker decides that's not her lot.

AF: In terms of fairy tale, this section appears to provide a copious, meticulous use of compression. Instead of plot development, disparate details end up side-by-side and the logic comes from that final ordering. The sleek, polished surface pushes us someplace unexpected.

HC: Actually, I'm not a very careful editor. I am, I hope, in selecting which poems I publish. But in terms of composing individual poems, I do a lot of preparing ahead of time, thinking about rhythm and language and linguistics and how sentences get formed, though when I sit down finally to work, I pretty much write without planning ahead. Preparation comes in strengthening the muscles and flexibility rather than in choosing content. I'll sit down and the content comes and I tend to revise fairly little. I do hope the poems' causality or logic seems tight, even if different from how causality tends to work in what we think of as "the physical world." I read some Marshall McLuhan today (I've been reading him a lot lately) and came across this passage quoting Ruskin, about the grotesque: "A fine grotesque is the expression, in a moment, by a series of symbols thrown together in bold and fearless connection, of truths which it would have taken a long time to express in any verbal way, and of which the connection is left for the beholder to work out for himself; the gaps left or overleaped by the haste of the imagination, forming the grotesque character." That made me really happy. It's always reassuring to find justification for something you've done.

AF: Your rhythms allow us to absorb events quickly. Repetition helps, also. The poem "Way out in the Country" ends, "It was painful I thought / I would be surrounded I thought I had thought." That's where Dickinson came to mind: "and then I could not see to see." Short, clipped anaphoric repetition or recycling of certain sentence-constructs provides some glue.

HC: Yeah, and to realize anaphora does not only repeat, but creates interiority within itself, so that there isn't a flatness of repetition (though that interests me as well). By gluing together repetitions you create between them a space of strangeness, a defamiliarization of an idiom that you thought you'd understood.

AF: Comedy also seems important here, as do opening and concluding lines. They sound very bold, very snappy. Room seems to be cleared for engaged audience responses. What's your relation to audience experience? Do you sculpt an experience for the audience which includes productive pauses, gaps, time to respond?

HC: I don't know if it includes time for them to respond, but it certainly encourages their responding. These poems perhaps move too fast to leave time for someone. But they believe whoever reads them is capable of keeping up and happy to do so. I've been thinking about this question: how does the poem position its reader? How does the reader then rise either to sit in the seat the poem has prepared, or to resist that seat? My poems tend to imagine decent, intelligent readers who won't mind if my lines seem smashed together to produce energy—rather than easily followable from one moment to the next. When I first began writing, I often would imagine my sister as my reader. She's a writer as well. She's absolutely fantastic. When we speak we'll get very involved in play, so even when we talk about death we know that we're using language to talk about death, that we can begin to turn sentences inside-out and throw them back-and-forth. That attitude extends to these poems I hope.

AF: When you mention how fast the poems move I think of aphorisms. Part of using language is using the pauses and gaps. Since we'll so quickly reach the end of one of your poems…that's where it feels there's room for the reader to respond, amid that rest which follows.

HC: That's not something I construct on purpose. You can consider the line as a unit of breath, but the poem also is a unit of breath. And I seem to have stunted lungs or something. I sometimes become uneasy about this and then try not to become too uneasy. I try to understand I'm still at the beginning of my writing, and perhaps these lungs will change as I get older.

AF: With this question of lungs still in mind, should we move to the second section?

HC: Sounds lovely.

AF: By section two (and like you say, it's not a seamless break, though section two does bring conspicuous changes in tone and form), gaps appear amid the solid, prose-like blocks. Less regular line breaks occur. Room opens for rhyme and rumination and reflection. We still find comedic, idiomatic usages of "go," "like," "which," but less Surrealist slapstick plot. Surprises that arise seem more linguistically inflected, rather than action-oriented. Repeated refrains such as "This always happens" seem to hint, then maybe don't, at more personal, less playful impulses. Is this all my projection? Did you explore different moods? Different authors?

HC: Certainly I explored different moods. I don't think it comes necessarily from reading different authors. My reading tends to be an ongoing process. I'll fall for someone and stick with them a while. There's a bit more Mayakovsky in the second section. "The Angry Faun" is very much indebted to Aleksandr Vvedensky. That poem grew out of an obsession with his "Rug/Hydrangea," which obsessively repeats whole groups of lines. It's crazy. I have, on various occasions, charted that Vvedensky poem, mapped its repetitions, made spatial representations. Once, I tried transcribing his form exactly into my own poem and it sounded so bad.

AF: So where some readers might scan a poem for rhythmic schemes, you tracked other types of patterning?

HC: I tracked A-type lines and B-type lines. Many lines begin with "I regret," but other phrases repeat as well. Variations occur. I developed this complicated system for charting it and substituting my own lines, which turned out awful. Then a week or two later I wrote "The Angry Faun" in Vvedensky's spirit but not his exact form. The Surrealist stuff does still happen here: "I bitch-slap the house / and my head falls apart."

AF: You're right. I'm not explaining well what seems different.

HC: I think there's much more of a recognizable world overlapping with Surrealist elements. The second section's opening poem presents this shark leaving phone messages, and that feels very much, I think, of the first section. But once you enter the next poem, "The Small Husband," section two transitions into not exactly a normal relationship, but there is a spouse, and a spouse stays there through the whole poem, and a series of actions suggest how one might talk to this spouse. Many poems move into that domestic sphere. There is "Journeying through our apartment." Someone attends a party. Someone else explores every part of our home. Then you climb up to the roof, which seems a less familiar space.

AF: Yet still the house as metaphor for a spatial continuity, an overall environment, with us exploring different components.

HC: That makes sense. I think ideally something stays stable in a poem, so that its changing parts become more apparent.

AF: I'm still drawn towards your Vvedensky experiment.

HC: I just recently tried a new visual representation of it, because I'm thinking about patterning this play I'm writing on it.

AF: On that same poem?

HC: Yeah. I'm really excited. I've never written a play before. But I saw tUnE-yArDs perform a couple weeks ago, which got me thinking about what you can do with looping, and how a domestic space has so much repetition, and that you say the same thing over and over to people you live with. So how could you condense and show that kind of absurdity of repetition? How could you keep a stable environment, within an apartment, even as things change and become unfamiliar?

AF: While we're discussing these expansive, elastic structures: "What

*Interview with Heather Christle*

is Amazing" is the first of this book's two longer poetic sequences. Given your brevity elsewhere, given the state of your stunted lungs, did any particular questions motivate these more modulated, tonally diverse sequences? What can you do here that you can't do elsewhere?

HC: "What is Amazing" actually is a much earlier poem. It almost went into *The Difficult Farm*. I'll have to go back very far to remember what it was like to write this. I know it came from my…I sometimes trick myself into writing long poems. I'll bait myself with the idea that I can write them in sections. The same thing happened with "Directly at the Sun." I just told myself, you've got to go longer—you've got to see what happens when you leave this space. And the numbers let me do it. They allow for slight turns. These very fast turns happen in the book's first section, even the second section. I like the energy of that. I like the dizziness. Though what can happen in these longer poems is that each part moves forward with some meandering, but mostly in the same direction. You get a chance to start again, yet moved slightly over. So there's a more gradual feel to this turning. Again it involves some repetition, some recycling of images. Still just a change of pace, I think, is useful. I take a lot of naps. They break up my day into not vastly different parts, but enough so that something has changed. Perhaps these poems work that way too.

AF: You'll take multiple naps in a single day? Or are you saying that many days you take a nap?

HC: Pretty much every day I take one nap. It's rare, but has happened that I've taken two naps in a single day. I feel so ashamed.

AF: I've never eaten two apples, nor taken two naps. Though in your longer poems, waking- and dream-life do tend to flip—shifting priority over each other.

HC: You know who would eat more than one apple each day is Agatha Christie.

AF: Weird.

HC: She sort of subsisted on apples.

AF: I think Justice David Souter…no, he ate the core. I won't put that in.

HC: Put that in. Put that in. Everybody should know as much as they can about apple consumption.

AF: I think he ate the seeds and core. This only came out after he retired.

HC: That's perfect in terms of Agatha Christie, because you know apple seeds contain cyanide.

AF: Interesting. Now just so we get to section three: it seems to provide another distinct tonality. Punctuation gets more complex. Openings sound more dense and ambiguous. Like "Go and Play Outside" opens: "The declaration of light as read by shadows / and the leaf the wind lifts in an elegant betrayal // of the stillness the morning'd arranged— / what caterwauls, what loops the world // gives us, gives us eagles!" It took us five lines to get there. That seems different. Also abstracted parenthetical phrasings appear. "Happy and Glorious" has a couple of these parenthesis, even, again, in its opening line. I'll sense a new type of meditative, rather than narrative, pacing. A frequent deployment of couplets hints at memory's eternal return, here triggered by rhyme. I'm curious—you've already said reading doesn't necessarily change your work, but were you reading couplets? Seeing what could be done with couplets? I've brought up all these male writers as influences, and don't mean to, but Creeley came to mind, in terms of the elided, suggestive syntax, or the rhetorical undercurrent summed up in: "What I can say represents what I cannot." Just these super-minimal formulations of what it means to write or speak at all.

HC: You're very much onto something with Creeley. I was reading *For Love* a lot. I also felt that this direction made sense to travel in, both for the book and for myself. Though I only began to understand why this made sense as I put the book together. This wasn't a book I wrote as a book. It become a book through its assembly over an extended period of time. Books feel somewhat arbitrary to me. I like books that exist as books, but still am more interested in writing a poem every day and living my life and seeing what comes of that. For me, these later poems came from a desire to slow down, to allow the gaps to seem less like space between events, and more like silence. Someone else often entering my brain during this time was Aram Saroyan. Probably I'm thinking of him because you used the word "minimal," but I wanted to give words space in a different way. This gets reflected in the hinged lines.

AF: That's what I'd meant when I mentioned the aphoristic tone—how a pause will end an early poem and remain implicit. But the third section frames and emphasizes those gaps or pauses.

HC: I hadn't thought of it that way but I like it.

AF: You had mentioned working on a play. Anything you want to say about the occasional Hamlet references? "The air I breathe in was once Caesar's" sounds like Hamlet to me. Also early in the book somewhere: "He is out / of whack with the world and it is like a crab / who walks out of its shell and that is not a metaphor / for X's emotional life." Does Hamlet just fit the meditative tone?

HC: Again, I hadn't thought of that, not even a little.

AF: Does it make sense or am I…

HC: No, it totally makes sense.

AF: I'm not just juiced on apple seeds?

HC: Hamlet's one of those apples you internalize, without even realizing why your skin turns that color, because of all the apples you're eating.

AF: What about math? Do you like math? I'm looking at one line again, "As a child X is too small for the furniture." That combination of math questions asked in words. Story problems, they were called.

HC: Word problems. I loved those! I saw someone on Facebook recently reinterpret word problems. It was, "What word problems looked like to me." It asked something like "If I have two bananas and you have three ice cream cones, which area should the circle occupy?" Then the answer was, like, "Nuns, because aliens don't believe in purple." I never had that problem. Word problems always made a lot of sense. So there is some resonance there. I'm curious about employing logical language as a form of mathematics that happens to be expressed through words, rather than symbols.

AF: Through grammatical structures, sentence structures, or rhythms or repetition. Because syntax seems part of this mathematics—how one word or sentence sits next to others.

HC: Absolutely. Diagramming sentences was my other great pastime as a child.

AF: That's one pastime I never got. Though one other spatialized trope throughout your book's various tonalities is its references to sky. "You" will look to the sky for answers, measure "yourself" according to the sky, appeal to the sky as primary source of communication. What other roles does the sky play here? Again, did Baudelaire, Mayakovsky, O'Hara, Eileen Myles, help direct your glance to the sky?

HC: Yes. Although I would say not only poets look in that direction for guidance. Not to be too universal about things, but it does seem fairly typical of humans to look to the sky for a sense of life's larger implications. It's very large and hangs over us constantly. And so I can't imagine not turning to it, over and over, in whichever mood occupies my body at the moment.

## INTERVIEW WITH MÓNICA DE LA TORRE
Recorded on July 10, 2012
This interview focuses on de la Torre's book *FOUR* (Switchback Books).

ANDY FITCH: When FOUR came I tried to slip a booklet from the pack, but couldn't do so without breaking the seal.

MÓNICA DE LA TORRE: Oh no. The seal broke?

AF: I liked that. Something irreversible had happened. Then flipping through the booklets, I soon lost their original order. This raised questions about the booklets' status. You had called them booklets, so that word stayed in my head. But how does a booklet differ from a pamphlet? How does it relate to, say, Renee Gladman's sense of a poetic "installation"? Does the booklets' serial formatting imply that all these parts should fit together? Or does it deliberately provide dissimilar doubles? Did *FOUR* ever exist as a single project, on a single computer file?

MT: I'd hoped for readers to slip each booklet out of the case. In fact, I worried about it breaking when discussing options with the designers. You've just redeemed the worst-case scenario. Thank you! *FOUR* gathers four projects I undertook separately—each occasional in its own way. One provides an elegy. One long piece I delivered for a festival of collaborations curated by Jen Bervin and Rob Fitterman at the Zinc Bar in 2011. "Photos While U Wait" takes its model from a photo album. Then "Lines to Undo Linearity" I wrote in response to the work of Gego, the German artist exiled in Venezuela who died during the '90s. Her penname combines the opening syllables in her first and last names: Gertrude Goldschmidt. Years ago Poet's House invited me to respond to an exhibit of hers at The Drawing Center, and I never knew what to do with the resulting piece. I find it productive to write in response to a particular occasion, because I'll have a goal and endpoint in mind. Yet even in these more directed instances, something accidental or chance-driven shapes the process. The occasions that gave rise to particular pieces occurred unexpectedly but also became meaningful. I wanted to avoid erasing those meanings by developing a streamlined book-length project. I didn't want to impose an overall structure on the works either. Even a partitioned, modular manuscript imparts its own structure. Still I didn't want to publish four separate chapbooks, because some conceptual content does tie the texts together. So I like that you could forget their initial order, since that confirms the integrity of this project. Once you've pulled out the booklets, you can re-assemble the whole any way you choose. The reader's ability to reformulate this collection interests me more than any fixed sequence. Similarly, for the title, I tried for the most descriptive, neutral thing I could find. I'd delayed going to press because we couldn't nail the title down. We at some point considered *Photos While U Wait,* then *Shift*, and then *Your Presence Is Requested,* which is a line in "Shift." Each of those overemphasized one section. But *FOUR* felt alright in part because Roberto Bolaño has a book called *Tres,* a triptych written in 1987, '93 and '94—put together much later as publishers tried to rescue the poetry for which his fiction brilliantly created a demand.

AF: Well *FOUR* also echoes F-O-R, each piece's dedicational nature, generated by and for the world in some way.

MT: Absolutely. I hadn't thought of that.

AF: I've recently talked to several poets about how a book's sequencing imposes its own logic, tone, hierarchies. I love your ability here to make that logic coherent but elastic. Because occasional pieces quickly could offer a chronology of your life. The overall project could become about you. Here a disrupted chronology keeps us more engaged with provisional social contexts than with the poet behind the pieces. And then the beautiful fonts produce this salad-bar effect, forcing us to pick and choose and blend the bright, vivid colors—foregrounding processes of desire that prompt us to read in the first place.

MT: Which did you pick first?

AF: "Shift" slid first out of my pack. "Shift" gets dedicated to Richard Maxwell. Could you briefly describe his *Theatre for Beginners,* so we can discuss elements of contemporary theatre that provide compelling overlap or provocation to contemporary poetry (or that should, if poets paid enough attention to theater)? I've been away a couple years, but along with Richard Maxwell, do Nature Theater of Oklahoma, ERS, Young Jean Lee, 53rd Street Press still produce good work? And what can poets learn from them?

MT: All those people come from the same generation, yet remain totally diverse in approach. Let's start with Nature Theater of Oklahoma. My work may not resemble what they do, but I'll think about one particular play I loved, *Romeo and Juliet,* which speaks so eloquently to appropriative and conceptual poetics. For that piece they called up relatives, friends (whom they had warned, not completely out of the blue), and asked them to retell, over the phone, *Romeo and Juliet*'s plot.

AF: They did something similar with *Rambo,* I think.

MT: For *Rambo Solo* this guy compares the film version of *Rambo* to the original novel. So these various participants actually write the plays. The people retelling *Romeo and Juliet* of course introduce wild variation. Nobody seems to have consulted Wikipedia and got their details straight. Then the transcriptions retain all their ums, ahs—all the signaling of giant memory voids traced by their retellings. Juliet's stories get delivered by Juliet, and all the Romeo stories by Romeo, both with dramatic hand gestures which perhaps come from Elizabethan theatre. Yet this total disconnect occurs between their diction, which sounds contemporary (like: "The Capulets— / And the—? / [And I can't remember the other guys]") and their faux Shakespearian delivery. This takes me to Rich Maxwell, who seeks to foreground, first and foremost, the text.

AF: I loved *Henry IV, Drummer Wanted, Good Samaritans, Joe*.

MT: People have this caricature of what a Richard Maxwell actor does, what a New York City Players actor does—presenting no display of emotions, no affectation, just a deadpan, machine-like delivery of text.

AF: Until each figure belts out some song, or does an abstract dance.

MT: Right. Critics focus less on that part of the work, though it's essential. But I especially take from him this idea that the text does it all. When you deliver a text, you don't need to emote it, or justify it, or believe it, even. That just gets in the way of the text and a listener's immediate reaction to it in a given moment. You can skip the story behind the poem. That takes you out of a text. But what does the language do? What experience does it elicit through this particular moment of delivery? What charge does it have there and then? So Rich's stagings become quite lyrical. Though the piece you asked about, Theater for Beginners, is not a play, but more a book-length manifesto. I had read the manuscript and offered some comments here and there. Then I got invited to produce something for this collaboration festival at the Zinc Bar, and thought Rich and I could work together. A lot of "Shift" responds to what he says in *Theatre for Beginners*. For instance, that the performer ought to stay in the present moment. I start with a daydream. I want to tackle this question: where are you when you write? You can inhabit many places at once. You can imagine delivering your piece at a distant time and place, yet still construct it in the present tense. I wanted to track discrepancies between these moments of composition, revision, delivery.

AF: Well your acknowledgements describe "Shift" as a site-specific poem, but don't fully specify its status as a performance text. So I thought of how "Shift" theatricalizes being, speaking, typing.

MT: That's key: the theatricalization of writing poetry and reading it in public.

AF: Alvin Lucier's "I am Sitting in a Room" came to mind, as one description built upon another. Then Vito Acconci and Kenny Goldsmith's weather-report transcripts got echoed in the repetition-heavy finale. So here's my question: let's say "Shift" investigates a particular downtown location, addressing itself to a collective, imminent audience. How do such constructions of conceptual theatre then get imported into *FOUR*'s elastic structure? How, if at all, does your writing change when pitched to the assembled audience, rather than the solitary, removed individual? What does the closet drama stand to learn from the live performance piece, and vice-versa?

MT: Everything. I think a lot about the reading situation. But I also know that, among my peers, I probably have more listeners than readers. Readings have become such a prevalent mode of disseminating work, that to disregard this mode of delivery means to miss an opportunity. So I care very much what poems do on the page, yet most of my projects end up being performative. I'll sense myself creating a persona in front of everybody. Here I very much relate to Rich Maxwell, since people expect poets to stand up and emote and reveal their interiority.

AF: When a reading only offers further mediation. Why attend a reading if you don't want that?

MT: Yeah. Just buy the book. But in any case, I've learned from performers, and absorbed the highly specific set of expectations that structure a poetry reading. And so I'll try to provide some form of institutional critique—not dismantling, just playing a bit with our idea of the poetry reading's conventions. Ultimately, for the actual performance of "Shift" (though I never say so in the printed text), I'd placed a Bose CD player onstage, with a recording of myself reading. The mic got angled toward the sound system.

AF: Probably creating some feedback and reverb.

MT: While I actually sat in the audience.

AF: So it did resemble a reading experience, where the poet disappears, like a waiter dropping off the dish then leaving. And "Shift's" pacing seems based on the sentence as much as the line. Again I wondered about your own auditory experience of contemporary theatrical productions, if that provides a pleasing or stimulating sonic environment as much as a visual one—not just in terms of rhythms, cadences of speech, but discursive social exchanges happening among multiple voices. So let's say you sit down to edit this piece, how does your mind replay the drafted material? Does it resemble hearing voices? Does it feel like talking? Do you see images or text?

MT: I'll hear myself delivering the text as I revise what I've already written and add new stuff. I hear a cacophony of past voices and voices projected into the future. Add to this cacophony thoughts bouncing back and forth from English to Spanish, or vice-versa, searching for the right words. As a writer I'll return to the very beginning of a piece before inserting anything new, so by the time I've finished I might have read it to myself a hundred times. Not only do I have an inner dialogue that I'll often make transparent in my poems—the poem's idiom always stays subject to the logics of a verbal exchange. Sometimes I'll wish I had the soaring lyricism some poets have. I'll wish I could free language from this dialogic structure.

AF: Like a projected narrative scene or something?

MT: My language can't get absolutely hermetic since the utterance serves as point of departure, perhaps more than the sentence. Instructions or adverts, all those rhetorical forms designed to convey specific information to the reader, fascinate me. Still the utterance need not remain regimented or instrumental. I want to deinstrumentalize, here by playing with forms of instrumentality, subverting them. Or to put it in more straightforward terms: to use language unconventionally within the frames of conventional exchanges.

AF: Sure, this goes back to Nature Theater's *Romeo and Juliet,* and how the ums and ahs perhaps tell their own love story, just about the body and bodies communicating—about parallel tracks of momentum. That brings me to "Lines to Undo Linearity," the second piece from *FOUR* I read. "Lines to Undo Linearity" points toward a quite different range of source material, such as Ed Ruscha's photographic books, Francis Ponge's lateral extensions (in a work like *Soap*), Gertrude Stein's or Nietzsche's or Wittgenstein's accumulative aesthetics, serialized prose installments such as Sol LeWitt's conceptual texts. Reading "Lines," and recalling your book *Public Domain*, I sensed how important an elegant synthesis of preceding interdisciplinary models becomes in your poetics. I'll miss many non-Anglo references here, but could you begin to describe how and why that assimilatory process takes place? Do you consciously make art- or literary-historical points by intertwining your predecessors' experimental modes? Does that combinatory process draw you?

MT: It does draw me. You brought up Ed Ruscha. At a recent New York Public Library talk, apropos of his process, he said, "It all goes into the Mixmaster...I guess, my brain." Same for me. Processing the strategies of others gets me going. In that sense, perhaps art especially stimulates me, because it tends to expose its strategies and the ways it handles its materials. So in "Lines," for example, I tried to match my utterances to Gego's artistic use of nuts, bolts, wires—all these found, instrumental scraps derived from engineering and architecture. She'd been an architect by training, but used these bits to compose lyrical drawings without paper. Light hits them and traces drawings on the wall. But the bolts and wires always float. The art comes from shadows they cast. She also wrote in her...as a German living in Venezuela her writing sounds a little stiff. Her syntax suggests someone who first mastered another language. The printed materials for the Drawing Center exhibition includes translations that retained some of this awkwardness. The following aphorism, for instance: "A line is an object to play with." I thought OK, if a line is an object to play with, what kind of lines should I use? That led to my list of idioms including credit lines, party lines, laugh lines.

AF: I love how "lines" could suggest appropriated, canned speech (similar to a pick-up line), but then you also address the line as a fundamental unit of drawing, or the line as historical lineage. So again, "Lines to Undo Linearity" foregrounds composition, tradition, even as it claims to undo linearity.

MT: Linearity gets undone since I don't believe in the teleologies that modernism and the avant-garde bequeathed us. Then back to your point about a combinatory process—I take from John Cage these ideas about paintings to be read and poems to be seen.

AF: To move on to "Mariposa Negra," with its postscript instructions that we should write the phrase "I am not here anymore," have you read Andy Warhol's *Popism*? Doesn't it end with Billy...the guy who's stayed in an alcove the last three years...

MT: Billy Name.

AF: Of course. Billy Name. Doesn't Warhol open up the curtain one day, because he's never known if Billy's still there, and the wall just says, "Andy--I am not here anymore"?

MT: Oh my god. I'll have to look that up. My own line came from a Latin adage: "nemo hic adest illius nominis" (There's no one here by that name). The word "nemo" means no one. Its reverse is "omen." "Mariposa negra" in Spanish means black butterfly, and at least in Mexico, where I grew up, a mariposa negra remains a harbinger of death. If you see a black butterfly you know someone close will die soon. But "I am not here" also echoes Heraclitus. Did I say that right? I struggle with Greeks because I learned them in Spanish.

AF: I can't pronounce. I can't speak English in English.

MT: Or "I'm not here" takes me back to Magritte's "This is not a pipe"—to language as absence, as index.

AF: In those terms, "Mariposa Negra's" aphoristic sequence works so well as an elegiac mode. But more generally, in your reading of aphoristic forms (perhaps the prose form most inclined toward silence, blank space): do aphorisms often prompt such meditations on prediction, loss, absence, haunting, fulfillment, residue? In "Mariposa Negra," does mortality get figured not just as death, but as our inability to avoid taking presence for granted—as a dramatization of the fact we soon will die and yet consistently fail to live up to this circumstance? Does the history of the aphorism, for you, provide one of our most compelling efforts to counter that tendency, to counter our forgetfulness about the present?

MT: Aphorisms almost seem predictions. A good aphorism, a memorable one, keeps unfolding. You think you got it the first time. You go: whoa, that's so true. But really it presents this retro-futurist device that activates meanings in the future more than the past. In that sense it counters mortality—a prescient utterance only gains full meaning later. Yet, strangely, this whole process relies on the workings of memory. You have to remember the aphorism to remake its relevance. And by doing so you change the aphorism.

AF: We always can see an aphorism's end. We sense the blank space coming soon. Everything feels more charged for that reason. But as you say, a lot of the meaning only occurs once you've reached that blank space. That's part of the aphorism.

MT: Definitely.

AF: So the aphorism, the elegy, stretch beyond corporeal limitations. Now could we move on to "Photos While U Wait"?

MT: Go for it.

AF: "Photos While U Wait" celebrates spare-time production. It also presents an apparently faulty second-language grasp on clichés as, in fact, a discrete, distinctive subject position worth pushing to the foreground.

MT: Yes. Sort of as we said with aphorisms, clichés provide endless potential for micro-alterations. And I loved how, with Flaubert's clichés, when you read blurbs from people commenting on his "Dictionary of Received Ideas," the standard, clichéd knowledge about them, what most surprises readers, is how they still hold true. 150 years later these clichés still circulate! That realization itself has become commonplace. But actually, when you look at Flaubert's clichés, many are not clichés.

AF: Interesting. Can you explain?

MT: For instance: "Our country's ills are due to our ignorance of them." I wish that was a cliché. Or "Domesticity: Never fail to speak of it with respect." People berate domesticity nowadays. We don't respect it. We consider it bland, pathetic, to be avoided. "Artists: Express surprise that they dress like everybody else." That's a beautiful notion. I grew up with that. Artistic people were supposed to enact artisticness by dressing poorly. Now hipsters dress like artists. It's the norm in Williamsburg, where I live. I find these clichés fascinating because despite their alleged inanity, they remain points of contention. So I've tried to construct a piece that takes its poetics from the cliché. Lines might seem obvious, but then you look again and they're not quite so…

AF: This recalls Emerson's description of language as fossil poetry—that to think we could escape clichés by refining our language might be the biggest cliché of all.

MT: Borges makes a similar point in "The Superstitious Ethics of the Reader." He describes all language as metaphor. No "metaphorical language" exists because everything is metaphor. That takes me back to "I am no longer here." "I" can't help becoming a metaphor. "I"

404

never was there in the first place.

AF: Well in terms of spatial presence, could you discuss "Photos While U Wait's" grid/box structures, placed opposite its modular prose units?

MT: Those boxes contain whatever you imagine them containing. If you go along with the conceit that this booklet provides poetic snapshots, or, perhaps, captions to photos you never get to see, then the boxes present a little prompt for you to wonder what each poem… what clichéd image they possibly could describe.

AF: The boxes foreground textual/material presence, just as your varied colors do. And your modular booklets seem like stackable boxes.

MT: They invite you to do whatever you want with them. So you end up seeing yourself reflected, just by giving these booklets a particular order, or projecting what images might fit in the boxes.

AF: That takes me back to cliché, to "Dial a Cliché," to Morrissey. Could you comment on his presence here?

MT: He endlessly fascinates me. I love his lyrics. They resemble great aphorisms.

AF: That's what I wondered.

MT: You remember them. You can apply them later. And they also serve as mirrors. They say so much about him, yet say just as much about the person who chooses to remember them.

AF: I'd forgotten until just now how Morrissey puts himself in a Wildean tradition. So you've got the mirror; you've got *Dorian Gray*; you've got the aphorism. Though are we talking about his new stuff, or old Smiths songs?

MT: I like some of that new stuff, but I stopped paying attention maybe two records ago.

AF: I feel bad. I think everyone stopped at the same time.

MT: He had a great solo album. What was it called?

AF: He had several. *Viva Hate* is one of my all-time favorite albums.

MT: Can you believe people categorize him as a mediocre lyricist? Some listeners I know (even my husband!) consider the songs too obvious.

AF: I never knew anyone had that thought.

MT: Really? It might be generational. Did you grow up in the '70s?

AF: No, no. Or did I?

INTERVIEW WITH TAN LIN
Recorded on July 10, 2012
This interview focuses on Lin's book *Heath Course Pak* (Counterpath).

ANDY FITCH: For people who haven't seen *Heath Course Pak*, could you catalog some reading platforms from which this book derives, as well as platforms on which it now exists? And we could consider the book a collection perhaps, as its front-cover list of contents seems to suggest. Or we could consider it an allover textual environment (in response, for instance, to its lack of page numbers). So could you sketch your current relation to bookmaking? What functions does a book now hold for you? Does it present a fixed culmination of several years' work? Does it provide a documentary trace of more expansive, ephemeral, performance-based projects? Does it offer one single, medium-specific component of what Marjorie Perloff calls a differential text—which exists in multiple, equally privileged media simultaneously?

TAN LIN: Let's see, for platforms: Tumblr, blogs *(Fuck Yeah Heath Ledger)*, PostIt, Index Card, press photo, mail-order catalog photos (J Crew), IM, SMS, RSS syndication feeds, eBay, Amazon Turk, e-mail, a course at the Asian American Writer's Workshop, Project Muse, disclaimers, warranties, press releases, art reviews, bibliographies, journalism such as *New York Magazine* online, sponsored ads, MS Word and its Track Changes function, legal contracts and the book, to name a few. *Heath* came about accidentally, as do all books. So new and old media (print and web-based) overlap and get laid out beside each other. I'd worked on a bunch of material that hadn't congealed, in book time or real time, and then Heath Ledger died, so he became the accidental catalyst. I wanted to present his death's coverage as a real-time mirror inside the text, and not merely something referenced outside it. The "publication," as such, hasn't finished. After the Zasterle book came out, Danny Snelson, a Penn grad student, produced an HTML version. Then David Jourdan's Vienna-based Westphalie Verlag did a bootleg. David didn't have image files, so he sampled new ads, providing a new set of web-based, photographic time-stamps within *Heath*'s various iterations. Also I've titled this latest edition *Heath Course Pak*, and added photographic reproductions of Post-It notes stuck onto the pages of my reading copy. Who is "Heath"? Probably a text corpora—mostly unparsed, or a set of CliffsNotes annotating previous live readings and a seminar. I keep trying to make the "course" more useful.

AF: You discuss the drop in retention when we read online. When a blog post gets printed, do we correspondingly gain new types of attention? What unanticipated textures of meaning have coalesced in *Heath Course Pak*? Which forms of meaning have not transferred as well from one medium to another?

TL: *Heath* doesn't prioritize that particular loss of content or a specific source medium. Instead, it establishes a loose parameter or grouping of materials, around which numerous meanings might be assigned. I wanted to foreground the moment before a book coalesces into a book, before meaning gets ascribed to a reading process. This amorphous state seems perceptual, less about a cognitive processing of information than a field of provisional perspectives. So the book constantly updates itself, resembling news and advertising. I've tried to assemble a text organized like mass media—to see if particular reading practices, executed in real time, might force dispersed data into becoming a (literary) book. We assume that literature repays re-reading and (academic) study, whereas the newspaper does not, and ditto for the blog. The blog in this case takes the form of an incipient bibliography, but a bibliography normally gets appended to something. To what, in this case? Perhaps a work of literature yet to be written.

AF: I've asked several poets now if they work according to what serial painters might call principles of additive construction—that you don't start necessarily with an overall meaning and then create the subdivided units of a book (incremental chapters and so forth), but that the broader meaning arises as discrete parts get placed side-by-side. In those terms, *Heath Course Pak* certainly merits book status, unless we conceive of books as only arising through a subtractive (top-down) mode of composition.

TL: Yeah. *Heath* has no fixed plan or meaning and its genres are not quite genres. It offers what Niklas Luhmann calls a loosely coupled medium in a stringently coupled form (i.e., a book). All sorts of quasi-literary genres, such as blog posts and faux-memoirs, Yelp reviews, etcetera, intersect with the discourse around Heath Ledger. Someone almost seems to write a novel inside this project.

AF: Well could you list some broader literary and artistic enterprises amid which you would place *Heath Course Pak*? Elsewhere you've pointed to legacies of modernist collage associated with Surrealism—and Dada and Cubism seem to have made their mark. But does *Heath* also engage pre-modern citational practices, such as those found in commonplace books? Does it adopt the futuristic/retrospective vantage of various book arts traditions? Does Derrida's *Glas* provide an implicit model for this distribution of content? Do the back-cover stains deliberately evoke Ed Ruscha? You can discuss appropriation, erasure. We could draw an infinitude of disparate lineages here, but which stand out most clearly for you in terms of affinities or equivalent propositions?

TL: *Glas*'s two-column collage effect is architectural. Spivak notes that the page presents an architectural device, one that invokes "capital, pyramid, pillar, belfry." *Heath*, by contrast, facilitates a vaguer, more allocentric, peripheral space. So where *Glas* deconstructs that building structure known as the book, *Heath* traces an environmental space or ecosystem of reading dispersed across various platforms. Still many books do influence it, such as Christopher Williams' projects featuring stock photographs—and addressing the procedures necessary to create those images. Arno Schmidt's elephant-folio book *Evening Edged with Gold* (which some critics consider the first hypertext work) also comes to mind, since its typographic elements seem to work their way in from so-called exteriorized data structures. Eliot's *Waste Land* remains quite influential for me—just in terms of combining disparate sources with no presiding mode of consciousness organizing the material. With *Heath*, I perhaps take this diffusive consciousness a bit further by asking, how does each discrete reading experience construct authorial identity or even phenomena such as character development?

AF: As you've said, this Heath Ledger project, with its reference to online posts, channels both biographical and autobiographical registers. Here I think of Wendy Steiner's formulation, in *Pictures of Romance,* that any biographical/autobiographical portrait posits an implicit narrative trajectory (of a person's birth and aging and death), and that this elastic yet legible outline allows audiences (especially audiences structured by narrative code) to assimilate more drastic temporal, logical, syntactical dislocations than they could otherwise. To me, this formulation speaks to the easy anecdotal content often lurking within experimental works by Gertrude Stein, John Cage, Andy Warhol. By analogy, how does the biographical/autobiographical content of *Heath* serve to expand your project's scope or potential for diversified reception? What does its idiom of accessibility allow you to accomplish that may not work otherwise?

TL: For me, *Heath* presents a drama of sorts, a staged piece. It also touches on acting, of course. It posits reading as a performative gesture in which one inhabits one's own text. Here the Heath Ledger material and the autobiographical material both help to allegorize this actor-driven process. The line between reading (or skimming) material and somehow acting through it or rehearsing it or practicing—all that stuff gets combined in the activity of reading. Once more this raises the question: where do we draw the boundary between a nonfictional event like Heath Ledger's death, and our desire-fueled projections of it?

AF: And what about your Samuel Pepys motif? Does Pepys appear as a figurehead of displaced, reconstructed, collaborative authorship? Why does Pepys feel so familiar to me? Does New York have a statue of him?

TL: Pepys's work interests me as a diary form that delivers a diurnal accounting of events. The time-stamping built into his project felt useful. Typically people expect a work of literature to obscure the passage of time, right? You get involved, get absorbed, and everything else drops away. You forget the dates, or particular contexts, of a piece's composition or distribution or reception. We normally don't think about literature as a time-specific delivery of text (in the way that I can track taking a phone call at 4:27 and receiving a voicemail at 4:29 and sending a text message at 5:22). Yet Pepys's narrative constantly foregrounds the time-frame of its composition. Likewise, I want to stamp such specific moments of creation, of distribution, redistribution and reception into *Heath*—so that in one sense *Heath* can function more as a communications medium than a literary medium. Again such time signatures get sucked into an amorphous reading environment. In that sense, reading doesn't seem much different from shopping.

AF: Also Pepys's diary possesses its own convoluted backstory—in that it never gets published during his lifetime. It gets discovered by somebody in a trunk much later.

TL: That I don't even know.

AF: Pepys's manuscript has many people's hands on it before it becomes a book. We can consider it an exemplary model of diaristic immediacy and/or as a highly mediated construction of identity and authorship.

TL: I'd argue that a similar degree of mediation takes place in most books. *Heath* tries to demonstrate this fact.

AF: Well clearly you embrace and accelerate the dilution of authorship as a privileged mode of discourse. Though does that goal itself get undercut through the design of a compelling, provocative, innovative project like *Heath*? What if, instead, an experimental poet decided to publish the most conventional love poems possible—as an alternate form of authorial critique?

TL: Dismantling the idea of authorship actually doesn't interest me. I'd rather probe the various circumstances in which authorship arises in the first place. That's why I titled this version *Heath Course Pak*—to dramatize the book's prior reception and its author's prior reception (however limited) within academia. Throughout an author is always emerging: on eBay, in a Yelp review, a text message. Interviews, bibliographic citations, magazine articles (in other words, manifestations of authorial identity) materialize in real-life architectural space, but also the information spaces that run through *Heath*.

AF: In terms of the fluff journalism you celebrate, such as Yelp reviews and tabloids, what most draws you? Do you have an acute appreciation for the actual idiom of this material? I loved, for instance, whenever the word "max" would appear as an adjective. Or, more generally, if we could place this book in relation to Warhol's "easy street" aesthetic, how do you negotiate the peculiar paradox that "easy" art of course doesn't feel easy when it first confounds audience expectations? "Easy" art only becomes easy over time—if and only if it gets assimilated and bastardized in the way Warhol's Pop project somehow did get absorbed by popular culture. Then it became easy. Part of Warhol's unspeakably abstract project involves making his work easy.

TL: Yelp combines advertising, news and entertainment. It does get authored, yet focuses less on individual authorship than on the reader's relation to an ongoing collective intelligence, what we used to call "public opinion." Likewise, Warhol examines subjectivity in relation to specific media: from perfume to piss to a tape recorder (the latter of which he called his "wife"). For Warhol subjectivity is specific to the medium. And Yelp, like Warhol or Heath Ledger (actor and book), remains preoccupied with matters of reputation, of "elite" status, which get tied to notions of subjectivity/authorship—here regarded as moments of dissemination.

AF: You align your own work with the ephemeral, with the short archive. But can't we hope for *Heath Course Pak* to undergo a Warholian fate? Couldn't it linger on, outlast the ephemeral, and eventually get assimilated into a broader tradition? Does any possible easy street exist for experimental poetry?

TL: For me "ephemeral" means a text that can get read quickly, processed quite rapidly, by almost anyone. Who can't read a blog entry on Heath Ledger's death? Who can't read an article about Jackie Chan? I've now tried to construct several books, such as *Seven Controlled Vocabularies* and *BlipSoak01*, that almost everybody can read. I don't know if any of them are in fact easy to read. Yet certainly I've aimed for a text that one easily could process (whether or not you read it in a more academic sense). I wanted to dismiss that exclusionary notion of close reading. Close academic reading almost always connects to other, more diffusive reading practices. *Heath* presents close reading as a socially networked, communal and collaborative environment.

AF: Still I often find that readers not trained in an academic context don't have liberated conceptions of literature or poetry, but in fact more conservative and/or constrictive expectations. That's what makes me wonder if any easy aesthetic (always a discursive intervention) ever comes across as easy. Do you wish for your easy-reading projects to challenge prevailing notions that poetry must be (and must seem) difficult?

TL: I do think that many such interventions occur within a fairly narrow reception-frame, emerging out of post-Language poetry. I've tried to address this. Really, who becomes my audience when I say that *BlipSoak* is supposed to resemble IDM or to provoke relaxation? These interventions get directed, quite specifically, at Language and post-Language movements, and often Language-affiliated poets themselves most appreciate that intervention. Poetry remains a highly specialized practice. I don't have any problem with that. The academic packaging of books, the blurbing of books, the reception of books, the teaching of books within seminars all interest me. How do we experience this institutionalized reading process as a temporal duration? What sorts of reading practices do we expect to adopt or to avoid within particular settings?

AF: How do people not trained as specialized poetry readers react to your books?

TL: I don't think they read them.

AF: Some early Language formulations characterized that work as a populist mode of discourse—yet its foregrounding of the textual surface ended up producing a voluminous critical apparatus rather than a popular readership. Though do you sense new ways (particularly through digital dissemination, through your engagement with visual art) of slipping out of this bind, so that more people could access and find significance in the aesthetic you've developed?

TL: That really was the aim here. And I've been told, oh, it's the simplest thing in the world to read this book. Then other people have said, no, it's an incredibly difficult project (though again they have trouble saying wherein the difficulty lies). Still many young people find *Heath* quite easy to read.

AF: Because they have more familiarity with such reading practices?

TL: I think so. They can translate more directly their habits of online reading and skimming. Yet I can't answer definitively even that question, which, to me, suggests that *Heath* provides an interesting test case for how one goes about reading a book.

AF: Elegant textual flourishes appear throughout *Heath Course Pak*, especially those that foreground editing processes and procedures—that produce extended (though always provisional) sequences. One line for instance just reads "HEATH." Then the following line offers "emitted a depth of field." Often this sutured, textured discourse, with its shifting distances or intimacies of exchange, enacts a push-and-pull that seems erotic, libidinous. Did you deliberately shape an elided, pleasurable, revelatory experience for the reader? Do aesthetic inclinations often guide your edits?

TL: Of course. And that specific passage focuses on being in love with Heath Ledger. It describes a sexual interlude with Heath or a Heath Ledger lookalike. For readers of the scene, an aesthetic rapture arises through vicarious participation. *Heath*'s author might even have imagined this scene. But then the problem becomes, who is the author? I can't now remember which parts of the project plagiarize blog content. Did I ever love Heath Ledger? Well, I'd say that the medium of love makes certain kinds of communication possible! A book cover announces a mood invoked by the things around it.

AF: Have you likewise shaped more expansive, durational experiences for the drifting reader? I think of Roland Barthes wanting "the novelesque without the novel." Does *Heath* offer various forms of narration without the narrative?

TL: I considered *Heath*'s whole opening section the most overtly autobiographical part. That's now the portion most posted over, though most of it gets "reprinted" in the "Outsource" section. So *Heath Course Pak* assembles a loop: it outsources itself. But your question about shaping interests me. I consider this book shapeless. It doesn't provide clear demarcations or boundaries. It traces and/or constructs an ecosystem of moods and reading practices and people and delivery systems that might pass through a book. *Heath* authors this material but so do many others.

AF: And do you consider *Heath*'s cultivation of the "least intense" moods a prompt to more abstract reflection on mood itself? Does that type of epistemic inquiry draw you? Here I vaguely recall Rosalind Krauss quoting Hegel on why one should paint "Nothing."

TL: Well, I didn't seek to deconstruct anything specific, such as contemporary notions of our fading attention and failure to retain material. I find those formulations uninteresting because they present attention as a single, homogenous thing. So yes, I did wish for the book to foreground a mood, if we think of "mood" as part of the apparatus of consciousness that moves through a temporal experience. It's hard to locate that consciousness specifically in the author or the person reading. It seems to inhere in their interaction, with the consequent production of minor affects. We could consider here Heidegger's model of a state of boredom or his idea of Stimmung, where you have a heightened attentiveness in flux, without any directed emotion—more of a receptive position than a harnessed mood, more of an affect than a feeling. A number of mental states and modes of affective processing remain bottoms-up, peripheral, grounded in ventral brain processes. Scientists have studied such phenomena in a neural Zen context. But you also see this with Daniel Stern and his work on mother-infant communications, which he describes as synesthetic and linked to amodal attunements and cross-modal experiences. Here we could say that "attention precedes processing," and point to diffuse, non-directed attentive states anticipating cognition or recognition. ERP (event-related potential) studies indicate bare awareness needs to construct a basic model of space (in order to detect, say, at about 200 milliseconds, a visual stimulus, or at 400 milliseconds to recognize a discrete object and identify its properties). *Heath* and its non-reading probably occur in advance of 200 milliseconds.

AF: I've got one final question, which engages more directly your own autobiography. What about middle-American childhoods (Warhol in western Pennsylvania, Ed Ruscha and Joe Brainard in Oklahoma, you in Ohio) inclines one toward Pop? Do you sense a different absorptive relation to mass-media culture, one that we could associate with regional experience—with growing up far from where such cultural forms get produced?

TL: Different degrees of mystique or desire or romanticization (both of high and popular culture) circulate in different places. In my own case, after I'd lived in New York 20 years, Heath Ledger moved to Brooklyn and became very much a part of the local environment. Still there's no doubt that the discourse connected to celebrity can produce specific types of longing which have to do with a separation from the sources of content-production. Jackie Chan makes a cameo here for such reasons (like an ad in a Heath Ledger movie). But I think everyone experiences some form of this longing in relation to actors or actresses they love—a phenomenon which again resembles many familiar forms of reading. Perhaps most writers, whether or not they come from the Midwest, deal with a related problematics of desire. Though yes, to answer your question's first part: both my sister and I watched inordinate amounts of television while drinking vast quantities of Coca-Cola.

## INTERVIEW WITH RONALDO WILSON
Recorded on July 19, 2012
This interview focuses on Wilson's book *Farther Traveler: Poetry, Prose, Other* (Counterpath Press).

ANDY FITCH: I wonder how you would place this book on a trajectory from *Narrative of the Life of the Brown Boy and the White Man*, to *Poems of the Black Object*, to *Farther Traveler*. Does "farther" in the current title imply an extension of preceding projects? Does this book's diverse compendium of forms derive from a deliberately hybrid construction? Does it collect divergent pieces? Does it theorize, in some way, the collection?

RONALDO WILSON: *Farther Traveler*'s definitely in conversation with the previous books, because doubling elements inform its creation. I wrote *Narrative of the Life of the Brown Boy* and *Poems of the Black Object* around the same time. In both, I'd worked through larger questions of form and daily practice. There were various interruptions, completing the poems while writing a dissertation, and living in New York, forces not necessarily in opposition to the poems, but distractions that fed them. So *Farther Traveler* provides the double to writing those books. Then doubling against *Farther Traveler* is a newer poetry project called *Lucy 72*, a series of persona poems in long-lined couplets that languish through ideas about race and representation. Lucy's body is sometimes white, black, male, skinny, fat, substance, landscape, texture. I'm interested in persona poems as embodied (sometimes disembodied) avatars, figures or configurations of the self. *Farther Traveler* presents a catalog of different experiences via assorted media, whether poems, paintings, essays, poetic statements, or figuring out my relationship to received and invented forms. And because I spent several years moving between New York, Massachusetts, and California, I wrote much of the work on trains, ferries, planes. This constant motion even found its way into my most productive and fertile arena, dream space. Plus I've been practicing Bikram yoga most every day for these same years, so focus, strength has influenced the book's scope through these doublings of content, event and activity. Right now, I'm not settled on its title, *Farther Traveler,* which I picked up at a family reunion. I'd travelled from Massachusetts to Oakland, where I received the "Farther Traveler" award.

AF: From the airline?

RW: From folks at the family reunion, people I can't recall ever meeting before that day. I won a Safeway gift certificate as reward for being the farther traveler, written on the envelope that held the card. It just kind of stuck. But the title stands for an entire process of traveling, through many manuscripts and many locations. Not always someplace fancy, sometimes just visiting my parents in Sacramento or staying with my partner on Long Island. I travel more professionally now, as a poet, which feels different, though the title has many separate offshoots. Still constant traveling informs the book's trajectories. I made videos while driving from MA to NY that have found their way into a small film project with the same title. I do sound recordings while jogging. I'm sure that this desire to create on the move came from living in New York so long, and feeling the endless need to finish work. My wheels were always spinning and with this book I tried to capture that.

AF: Just a bit more on the title. You present yourself as a traveler moving physically, conceptually, thematically through genre. And you've mentioned your relationship to received form, to expectations for what a poetic collection could be. But I'm curious, with *Farther Traveler* I do hear "Father Traveler," and "Fellow Traveler." You've got these filial relations, these love and companionable relationships. Does "farther" somehow bridge those, move in the wake of or beyond those?

RW: You're helping me get more behind that title, which has much to do with my father. I've been thinking about a poem in *Narrative,* "The Brown Boy's Black Father Loses It," which is based on a dream where my father goes crazy, strips, masturbates, and shits all over the place. This dream came to me well before doctors diagnosed him with dementia. Actually, at that family reunion he did his own kind of crazy. He'd just had his operation for prostate cancer and kept walking around the reunion with his catheter bag out. He wore his urine pouch on his thigh, and didn't even care. While trying to cope with all that embarrassment, I also wanted to track my love, and my curiosity about his sense of freedom (tied to loss). He'll now say, "Oh Ronaldo, it's like I'm walking through a new place…every day feels totally different, like I live in a dream." That's kind of how I want to live, despite loss, or because of it, with that sort of freedom that forms another undercurrent for this book. In a sense I try to theorize what freedom means, what it means to attain this mobility, which sometimes can feel dangerous. The more free, the more emotionally sound, the more under attack you are, especially as, say, a black person in the U.S., walking slowly through the airport, or deliberating, thoughtfully, about your order at a restaurant—there's still, in my experience, always an assault on your time, your body, your freedom. So here I've tried to map a space that contends with these forces through traveling, moving toward freedom, expectation, perhaps even fate.

AF: The book does provide parallels in terms of the pursuit of freedom, the drag of memory, perhaps the liberatory potential of memory loss and the idea of moving into an embodied present. I wonder if we could construct further parallels to your career. Because we both did our PhD at the CUNY Grad Center, for example, I have any number of localized questions about whether a "Pornographic Imagination" class of Wayne Koestenbaum's, a Proust class of Eve Sedgwick's, found their way into this volume. I'll stick to the broader topic which…

RW: Yeah, totally.

AF: We could discuss that, but I'd wanted to ask about this parallel between your father's situation and your own. *Farther Traveler* raises the question (it obviously does so deliberately) why, several years and volumes after graduate school, your dissertation process still compels extensive rumination. You cite Cathy Caruth on the relationship among trauma, repetition, narrative—the need for the traumatized subject continually to replay, retell, finally rewrite the traumatic experience as a digestible one. Did grad school prompt a similar trauma?

RW: That's really important, and makes me think about rituals, about what one returns to, invents, articulates, rearticulates. I'd entered the Grad Center to diversify my reading palate to become a better poet. I didn't think much about getting a job. My classmates' stellar presentations baffled me, because I still was focused on developing as a poet. It all felt so physical, that PhD. It involved much commuting, carrying many books, heavy ones, especially the artists' books and museum catalogs. I read a lot on trains. And I did my coursework at the Grace building, on 42nd Street, and loved walking around Bryant Park, the Public Library, Times Square, up through Grand Central Station, Penn Station. I would work, cruise, hang out. All the while I stuck with Eve, Wayne, and Meena Alexander, who eventually would advise my dissertation. I also studied with Michele Wallace. I took their courses obsessively and exclusively. Perhaps this helped to evade the trauma, because I felt so much openness and elasticity in their seminars. *Farther Traveler*'s drawings and watercolors came out of Eve's "How to Do Things with Words and Other Materials," which featured a studio workshop component. These works helped me to develop ideas about lynching and time and approximation to violence through visual art. I thought, let me just sit and meditate by drawing and painting for extended periods. I'd never before had the patience. Now I work on long conceptual sound recordings, sometimes an hour or more of non-stop freestyle rap, association, drift. I'll make them running, driving, walking, sitting in cafés, or even doing yoga. I suppose what I learned from my G.C. teachers was not to make the knowledge this sort of recognizable commodity, but to practice close study and attention (in part by negotiating its release). Maybe this relates to trauma and the need for repetition that Caruth describes, but it also has to do with ritual and discipline—a necessary tool when working through ideas, so that they can fly off into the unknown. This opens up and complicates the idea of one's expertise as say an African-Americanist, a cultural critic, which I have studied to become, but once you get named an expert it's like, oh my gosh. What pressure! Poetry helps to constantly spin out freely from under that, to let my work find its way into the world through various means and media.

AF: I'd asked about what seemed a traumatic cycle. But it sounds more as if, as with your yoga, this book traces a bodily practice of working through complicated motivations and choosing who you want to be going forward. Traumatic elements don't seem there as much.

RW: It's vexed, right? Recently I was talking about reiterative violence, which also stands basically at the center of my critical book project, examining how a writer like Gwendolyn Brooks or a visual artist like Ellen Gallagher contends with reiterative violence—through what modes or articulations, whether it be abstraction, modes of selfhood, self-representation? Of course there's the underlying or maybe ever-present traumatic relation to lived experience. But there's also a need to master trauma's form and to shape it. That's where the mediation and perhaps critical distancing comes in. Sure, it's traumatizing. Sure, it's embodied and horrific. Still how do I take this trauma and not necessarily make it beautiful, but at least patterned so I can test its sonic relationships and visual qualities as aesthetic form? Though even then trauma always remains and resonates, which makes the writing difficult, especially if the work makes one unrecognizable, because you're not the usual one lamenting, mourning. You're not producing this sorrowful song. You feel some kind of remove. That definitely came from working with folks like Wayne or Meena. There's real elegance amid the conversations they have with such very difficult and complicated realities.

AF: Well, I love *Farther Traveler*'s fluid citational practice. Your quasi-lyric musings point toward arguments raised by Samuel Delaney, Sonia Sanchez, Adrian Piper. Can you talk about critical, theoretical or scholarly potentialities that lurk amid lyric discourse? Who impresses you most by how they integrate intertextual, interdisciplinary inquiry into their poetics? Is there a pointed formal or theoretical agenda motivating your own casual-seeming quotes throughout this book?

RW: Thank you! I love that phrase "casual-seeming." Before the Grad Center I'd worked on my M.A. in NYU's Creative Writing Program, where I took Ngugi wa Thiong'o's "Prison Performance Narratives" course. My first grad school presentation, on the poet Dennis Brutus, was terrifying. I didn't even know how to approach the material or the process. I couldn't sleep at all the night before, because I kept re-reading the poems. I started writing about light, since I'd see these bright flashes when I tried to close my eyes. I thought I'd focus on moments of light, luminosity, flashing in Brutus' poems. But the next day I spoke for what seemed five or six minutes then stopped and said, "I can't go on. I'm exhausted. I haven't slept." Then Ngugi said, "Now I understand your secret!" And I just loved it because I'd reached a point of utter exhaustion, yet knew my ramblings had produced something valuable. I knew I had done all of this work. I just hadn't known how to track it. I couldn't adopt the language with which my classmates worked. These were American Studies and Performance Studies students who'd been accepted to the seminar. They had this densely theoretical manner in entering the text, but I'd always wondered, instinctively, what's the casual way into this material? How could I ease into argument in a tone most truthful to the poetic voice I'm developing? Similar stances still inform my work. I've grown to trust that my mind can become in sync from thinking things through a number of times. I've learned to ask, what's the freest way into the analysis? Because not to figure out your maximum, native potential with our work seems crazy-making and death-inducing.

AF: Just to illustrate how all of this relates to the book, how you'll ease your way into argument, could we discuss your use of the auto-biographical? *Farther Traveler* gives frequent reference, we've said, to academic job-market frustrations. It provides flitting testimony of an "I" wrecking its mom's Porsche, perhaps her Mercedes. Either of those tonalities risks seeming self-involved. But of course part can be read as documentary record, parts as staged scenes of confession, parts as camp fantasy. Do you expect readers to make such distinctions? Does it matter? In terms of easing into an argument here, you'll seem to present a polyvalent, polyvocal mode of subjecthood, yet never say so deliberately.

RW: You're right. Self-involvement seems crucial when trying to re-construct the self! Here multiple conversations happen in terms of class dynamics and thinking about my mother. She came to the U.S. from the Philippines when she married my father. The occupying Japanese government killed both of her parents. That vague sense I have comes from my dad, since she won't discuss any of it with us. I'm slowly gaining the courage to ask her myself, but the book offers what I knew thus far. She'd trained in the Philippines as a journalist. She also obtained a nursing degree, and for a time worked in a leper colony. But when my mom came to the U.S., she couldn't continue as a journalist or a nurse. No records. So she had to go back to school to re-train as a nurse's assistant. She did some other things, studied stenography, ceramics. I'm just thinking about class play within the Filipino community. Also in the Black community. What does it means to boast or show, to maneuver outside of one's class designation, something always in process and greatly contested? My brother, sister and I grew up to understand that we were poor. But we'd always had many things. My parents (and extended family) helped us finish college. My mother, later in life, drives these super fancy cars: Porsche, BMW, and Mercedes, all at the same time at some points! But still she works as a nurse's assistant at the same hospital since the '80s. Class identification appears more or less fixed within graduate school, or among faculty at most major universities. Most folks' lineages are legible within the same upper-class brackets. And it's pretty clear that most times people of color, or queer, have to perform this kind of elite drag in these contexts. We do usually look fabulous! That goes on in this book too. What is passing? How does passing function on a day-to-day level amidst class and race slippages, triangulations, whether they be real, performances, or dreams? Dreams both as in the subconscious and as aspiration. Also what to do with the gift of time? What does it mean to be able to ruminate? Everything in the book is somewhat autobiographical. Here's a hard fact: my brother bought the Porsche, used, when he got his first job, still living at home, then my mom bought it from him. The engine of this beautiful red vintage 1980 Porsche 928 just burst into flames one day, while I drove it.

AF: I've read somewhere you describing your mom's life. So in the book I assumed that was all made up.

RW: I like to make some of it up, especially in *Poems of the Black Object*, but often I'll take from the very real. That's what's so strange. I've often organized my life around fantasies, a kind of fantasy life. All I did that summer the car exploded was practice yoga, read, drive the Porsche around, and write. It really was this unreal life. I'm influenced by some conceptual artists, by what it means to make your life reflect and respond to the work. I'll often disengage from modes of normalcy which inhibit my relationship to daily life's extremes. I remember what Lorraine Hansberry discussed, the idea of being "poised for inclusion." Think of civil rights and pre-civil rights black people in the U.S., the whole decorum these folks had to present. There's perhaps in this…some tension in the notion of what "uppity" means, what it means to be poised, to have poise, which gets tied to a kind of elegance that often ends up under attack. I've tried to track that in my work. Fitness interests me. Fine things interest me. Low culture still interests me as I dip in and out of it. So what are new ways in which class gets marked? What does a black poet look like today? Or an Asian poet? Or queer poet? I'm not blind to the abundance of conventional readings that emphasize simple identity formations. But I embrace the uppity, even the realm of the narcissist—a title I've flirted with for an upcoming book. My identities always feel very fluid: black, gay, queer, yogi, teacher, runner, poet. This manifests in the work naturally, but also becomes a site for critical engagement, a site for pushing the self beyond what remains troubling, what remains hard to mark.

AF: In terms of being unapologetic, of assembling an identity that doesn't conform to reductive expectations, I hope that for contemporary readers, if this book raises taboos, it's not in terms of sexual scenes you'll describe. That what shocks is the diversity of autobiographical subject positions you'll take on simultaneously. That you don't have to be limited to any one. Still I'm curious how you envision those rhetorical vectors coming together, in terms of the reader's vantage on your book. I love the scenes of the "I" at the porn theater, descending towards this grey, hetero couple vicariously fucking on the cinema floor. I picture this cramped but capacious house of desire, that cinema, how it serves as a projection of this book's identity.

RW: I don't know if that particular scene projects the overall book's identity, but I see what you mean, since there's a sincere attempt to map the most truthful desire I could capture. At that moment (you hit it right on the head), I took the opportunity to witness that love from very much a "found" vantage point. How does one get so lucky? I've learned from Sam Delaney that these spaces (in porno theaters in particular) remain valuable because they'll engender possibility for an expression of human experience that doesn't need to be vilified, destroyed, canceled, removed, erased but instead, explored. I like being a visitor to that moment. That's what I most seek in my work. That kind of older, greying couple: it just was inspiring to see this level of protection happening amid all the other visitors, voyeurs, players. But also, I wanted to express an inability to trespass their desire for one another. All I could do was report it. The way one takes a photo of a beautiful flower, or an approaching bee. How do you bring that moment into representational discourse without upsetting the scene? Or maybe I was the bee! Because there's also, on the other hand, sadness and frustration at not being the object of desire. I'll never be that person, her. I'll never get what she has—though maybe that's part of the tension, that you can't invade every psychic experience. The other side of manifest destiny. This respect that maybe comes from knowing your own borders or limitations. What you said about a cramped but capacious space, that's the point where both "I" and the speaker can begin to analyze "us" and make some poetic sense of what's happening. And that, for me, is a turn on.

AF: On this point of how one brings certain reflections, tonalities, certain experiences into representational discourse, could we talk about the diptych format of "Forms"? What dialectics of a racial imaginary get depicted in this fusion of elided lyrics with expressionist, evocative scenes of lynching and more abstracted lacerations? What about the lyric/image combination for these particular topics interests you?

RW: Why the diptychs with the images? Well, they are tricky visual pieces/poems. It might help to know about the context for this work. I drew a lot of those paintings and did the watercolors at a residency at Djerassi, surrounded by giant redwoods, mist, in the Santa Cruz mountains. I don't know how, but I'd managed to get out of New York during spring, away from my fellowship at the CUNY School of Law. So there was this psychic split happening between my hectic New York work life and my leisured, bucolic life at the colony. Those drawings also helped me to negotiate writing the dissertation prospectus. The poems became important because they tried to make sense of all this weird stuff that happens at colonies as a black body in a white space (a common theme of mine). These various elements felt charged as I began to map out my focus on lynching photos, drawing, writing poems, exploring race, selfhood—all reminding me of Baldwin's "Stranger in the Village."

AF: The colony felt like Switzerland?

RW: I've never been to Switzerland, but take from Baldwin's essay his formulations of self-representation. I thought of how to map the differences between direct attacks and micro aggressions. At Djerassi, I'd run through redwoods just after examining the lynching photography. I'd immerse myself in this fantastic realm of color, mostly green. I had brought to the colony basic art supplies, inexpensive watercolors, simple black writing pens with which I like to illustrate. Nothing fancy. My room was small and rustic, and I had all this time to work with a limited but focused palate. Some mornings I would walk into the forest where I looked for geckos, listened to the rain, sat on a tree stump taking in the experience of reading (across the experience of letting images build). Perhaps these processes became the formative fields for the lyric/image space you mentioned. Later I tried to capture something of these dimensions in a talk at St. Mark's Poetry Project, a piece called "Hand-Eye Coordinates." I screened the watercolors and read the diptychs, between which I played tennis against a wall, describing the mechanics of my stroke. I even served a few balls into the audience. I was investigating what happens when muscle memory takes over the imagination. How are my fine motor skills connected to my poetic ear? Maybe the diptychs' two sides resemble those of a tennis court. One side, then the net, then the other. Tennis is a game of boxes, just figuring how to hit and move to this spot or that. At the colony I wrote for several hours each morning. Then I would draw in the afternoon. Each day just felt staggered in such a way that "Form" came together from what had been built and represented.

AF: Right. In terms of representational drive (which I understand gets complicated here), I'm curious about *Farther Traveler*'s "Poetics" pieces. In terms of a poet's occasional production, I'll think first of Frank O'Hara's occasional pieces—as willful rejection of performing some serious, solitary, self-contained personhood. And I love the playful constructions you provide, such as "Poetics Statement in The Great American Grille." At the same time, you do seem interested in communicating pointed ideas concerning race, gender, sexuality—more directly here than in your poems. Do you see the "Poetics" pieces as complementing, as categorically different from your poems? Do you make no such distinction?

RW: I see these "Poetics" pieces as part of the stride, like an adjustment in the pace of a long run, places where I open into an extended sprint. Or it's like coming up for air, between butterfly strokes. How does one negotiate being seen? What is the nature of visibility? How can you attack, via critique, in public space? How do you retreat? When do you listen? How should you speak about this process of writing? Over the past few years various people had requested my poetic statements for different publications and talks. I thought, why not use these as occasions to pursue questions about race, gender, and sexuality in a direct, essayistic manner, then publish them all together? Why not present a series of symmetrical excursions through all these different possibilities? In this sense, the pieces might suggest linked poems, but maybe more as conjoined essays that get linked. Again, I'm still as interested in play as in anything else. So how do you recognize and represent freedom in forms that expand beyond the poem, pushing further and further, but still wrestling with the same questions?

AF: Part of what I appreciate about the "Poetics" pieces is that there are, as you say, many of them. They seem statements about identity but none is the statement of identity. There's a propositional nature.

RW: Lately I've watched all this terrible reality television. I've considered how black people get cast and represented—just the levels of fierce, compelling rage and anger repeated with no outlet. I've wondered what does it mean to aspire to this as a primary, or maybe the only possible mode of being? So the poetics statements constantly shift, driven by such inquiries. But I suppose, given the nature of the form, and maybe the discourse of stereotype, the statements also stay constantly stable. Perhaps some tension gets released between the two states. The piece I wrote for Claudia Rankine's *Race and the Creative Imagination* got inspired after a performance with the Black Took Collective at Pomona College. Winding down after dinner, I pull out to pick up some pastries in Glendale, which results in police profiling and stopping me. I kept it together and more or less avoided physical harm, but wonder how I would have survived the event without all my friends (Tisa Bryant, Duriel E. Harris, Dawn Lundy Martin), who were at the house waiting for me, so that we actually could discuss what happened, sharing our overlapping experiences. Funny thing is the other day, as I drove back alone from a small retreat in the Berkshires attended by some of these same poets, I got pulled over for not making a lane change. Tisa stayed on the line while I spoke my way out of the jam. I kept my phone on in the car. I'm not sure I'd done this on purpose, but it's too difficult to bear that suffering alone, and I refuse to let it settle into my body. When these moments happen I think, OK, here's a performance in which I will engage. Perhaps this came from working with Meena and Eve, thinking about performativity, language, keeping very attentive to the way one moves, survives in the world, what's at stake, who's valuable. Those remain powerful lessons.

AF: In terms of performativity I've got one more question—about the cat poems. In the manuscript version these come last. And with this section's long, 18th-century title, borrowed from Erica Hunt, here seem to be distilled your Brechtian inclinations. He says true intellectual inquiry is to think in other's heads while others think in your head. That works great in these Ally poems, this camp-inflected elegy for a neighbor cat, which resonates with a wide array of related experiments. I thought of Dickinson's unidirectional master letters. Letters never going to get a response. Or if you've seen Chris Marker's epistolary tapestry *Sans Soleil*. Or interspecies interests of Christopher Smart, Virginia Woolf's *Flush*, David Trinidad's "Every Night,

Byron!" Those were just the first to come up. There's way too much to cover. Still what became most compelling for me (and this goes back to what you've said about the heavy burden not directly confronted in your work, though certainly there all the time): amid all the fun of the Ally section, there's this fantasy about talking to the dead. That dismal, prospectless prospect underwrites even this most fun project.

RW: These poems came from a need to get outside familiar modes which distanced myself from subjects directly at hand. This experience of losing a cat, and friend, felt moving, sad, strange, and I just wanted the poems to capture it. I remembered reading a Sharon Olds interview about poetry allowing her to be sentimental, totally sentimental. Here was one of those moments where this animal came into my life and became symbolic for so much beyond ours. So much began to surface dealing with sexual desire, cruising, addiction, the nature of love in my primary relationship—all these autobiographical aspects flooded into one signifier, a black cat, Ally. I'd had this very specific relationship of real mourning, moving so much between the dead and the living. The poems, of course, also provide projections of my mourning the great loss of the father I used to know.

AF: That's what I mean.

RW: Then they also track leaving the East Coast for California. Though the poems seem sentimental, overly so, they reveal a capacity for multiple ranges. Without them, the book feels informed mostly by its theoretical templates and its sense of the propositional that you named earlier, but the Ally poems become its tail, a cat's tail, swaying. Muscle, mind bone? Something happens I can't control in those poems. I don't even know how they occurred. They happened so quickly. In the middle of drafting this book's final version, Ally died. I had to catalog or experience that or else I'd carry this mourning in my body. There'd been something so powerful about spending time with her, long days alone writing, but she was there. I'd never been with an animal like that. And for some reason because I do believe, as an athlete (one who learned tennis by mastering fine motor skills), that over time muscle memory takes over. I just tried to write from this difficult experience of losing her, very loosely and naturally, letting the muscles take over through the letters. Cat feeling? Maybe. There was something so new, for me, trying to feel through the experience of that encounter.

## INTERVIEW WITH COLE SWENSEN
Recorded on June 25 and July 20, 2012
This interview focuses on Swensen's book *Gravesend* (University of California Press).

[June 25th]

ANDY FITCH: Could we first contextualize *Gravesend* amid a sequence of your research-based collections? *Ours*, for example, comes to mind. What draws you to book-length projects, and do you consider them serialized installments of some broader, intertextual inquiry? Does the significance of each text change when placed beside the others? Or do they seem discrete and self-contained?

COLE SWENSEN: They revolve around separate topics, yet address the same social questions: how do we constitute our view of the world (which of course in turn constitutes that world), and how does the world thus constituted impinge upon others? Ours examines an era in which science put pressure on definitions of nature. We cannot pinpoint when such pressures started, but 17th-century Baroque gardens give us a chance to focus on this pressure and question the accuracy and efficacy of making a distinction between science and nature in the first place.

[Skype glitch]

In short, both books question how we see, and how this shapes the world we perceive. *Ours* examines 16th- and 17th-century notions of perspective in relation to conceptions of scientific precision, knowledge, beauty, and possibility in Western Europe. *Gravesend* poses quite different questions, foregrounding that which we do not, or cannot, or will not see. Certain passages address this directly, such as "Ghosts appear in place of whatever a given people will not face." Communal guilt and communal grief remain difficult to acknowledge because our own lines of complicity often get obscured. Perhaps our inability to deal directly with such guilt and grief causes them to manifest in indirect forms. The English town of Gravesend offered a site through which to examine this because it can be read as emblematic of European imperialist expansion—a single port through which thousands of people emigrated, scattering across the world, creating ghosts by killing cultural practices, individuals, and in some cases, whole peoples. But the word "Gravesend" also hints at an after-life, a life that exceeds itself. The town of Gravesend stands at the mouth of the Thames. When people sailed out of it, they cut off one life and began another. So the concept of a grave as a swinging door seemed crystallized by the history and name of this town. And ironically, the first Native American to visit Europe, i.e., to have gone willingly (even before Columbus, many had been kidnapped and brought back to Europe, but), the first who seems to have regarded it as a "visit," died in Gravesend, as she waited for a ship to take her back to Virginia. The New World, the Western hemisphere, finally capitulates to Europe, and dies of it.

AF: For this trope of a swinging door: when I think through the book's distinct idiom (again in relation to your other projects), *Gravesend* seems to prioritize the gap, which I first had thought of as the false start, but which now sounds more like the second start. That brings to mind Roland Barthes' preference, in rhetorical terms, for anacoluthon—when an entirely new subject and predicate emerge mid-sentence.

CS: Yes, through this wonderfully slippery form, the direct object becomes the subject of the subsequent verb. Grammar creates a leap in subject matter that the subject matter can't make by itself.

AF: Exactly. Just as, in your book, the tales of Henry James and Edith Wharton appear first as appropriated texts, then veer toward vernacular testimony and/or stylized sonic variation. Syntactical pivots overlap with broader breaks in the narrative or discursive flow.

CS: Actually, the James and Wharton tales are not appropriated in the way we currently use that term. They are retold, which is different. When a tale (or any bit of language) gets retold, all sorts of distortions arise, allowing these tales, as communal constructs, to grow—to twist, to change, to evolve, or devolve—whereas appropriation (the verbatim incorporation of another text) freezes development, traps content within an individual history, ties it irremediably to a specific ego. That said: yes, the gap is less a false start than a second start. The stutter is not a stumble, but an insistence on endless beginning. In *Gravesend*, the gap provides the central formal principle, at times creating a gulf, abyss or blind spot, at times a bridge, and at times a re-ignition. What these different uses have in common is their suddenness, and it's that suddenness that links them, and thus the poems, with death, for no matter how prolonged an illness, no matter how foretold a death, it is always sudden. The poems' structural gaps point to the sudden absence that is death, but also to the presence of absence that is the ghost (when a ghost passes, it erases the air). The book's interviews operate differently. They track the differences between a ghost story as told by a person who has experienced it (which almost always contains no narrative arc, no character development, no moral, no point whatsoever), and literary ghost stories, which tend to follow a traditional narrative arc and deliver a strong moral message.

AF: In terms of how interviews inform this book, could we discuss the endnotes? You go out of your way to announce that interview sections do not quote people in their "exact words." Initially I wondered, why don't they? What has changed? Then as I began to think this through, a clear…

[Skype glitch]


[July 20th]

AF: Should we more or less start over? We could return to a general framing, to get warmed up. Or I could continue with questions about haunting and transcription.

CS: Why don't we just move on to haunting and transcription? As I wrote this book, I was thinking about writing as always haunted (à la Derrida, who touches on this often), always testifying to an absent voice. The fact that a voice and its transcription are not commensurate places us in the zone of the uncanny. Writing always echoes the uncanny. All writing gets lined with the ghostly.

AF: And in *Gravesend*, this haunting becomes further manifest when you engage other people. Your transcripts raise the broader questions: how does the historical event (you approaching, and interacting with and recording another) haunt the poetic text that later surfaces for readers? How does an interviewer's question haunt an interviewee's answer, and vice versa?

CS: Anecdotally, when I visited Gravesend and talked to residents, I started off by asking, how do you feel about your town's name? And I got absolutely nothing. First of all, I'd asked a bunch of English strangers, how do you feel? Stereotypically, that won't work. And it didn't. So I switched to something more factual: how did this town get its name? And they immediately could step out of themselves and tell a story. Similarly when I asked, have you ever seen a ghost, I noticed people using the "I" to step away from themselves, and tell a story that often had nothing to do with themselves (or featured themselves peripherally). So, to generalize, storytelling's power to transcend personal history through a marvelous self-estrangement, occasioned by the "I" as communal space, struck me. Since then, I've recognized the extent to which literary ghost stories use artifice and convention to bring such strangeness back into familiarity. This denies the personal ghost story's uncanniness, unfathomability and pointlessness. That pointlessness seemed the most important aspect of the stories I collected. They never describe someone seeking retribution. They never serve to warn anybody. Yet the literary genre demonstrates a deep unease with this type of story, to the point that we cannot write something (perhaps tell it, but not write it) without trying to make it "meaningful," even if our effort destroys the actual story, the actual "what happened in the world."

AF: You've mentioned that different questions call forth a different "I" to answer them. Could you describe how call-and-response gets structured both into the telling of a ghost story, and into this book? How do you envision your reader assimilating a ghost story Q-and-A?

CS: First, this book's overall framing brings up for everyone, I would imagine, their own thoughts on ghosts. And discussing ghosts can prompt people to unlock their entire worldview. We articulate who or, more importantly, what we think we are by answering the question: what is a ghost? Likewise, when we read such questions posed to others, we tend to answer them ourselves, and then ask more: does it matter whether something is "real" if that something has an effect in the world? Do we only classify something as "real" if we can perceive it with our five senses? In this regard, ghosts remain unsayable, and that's the part that haunts the writing—evoking all the other unseeable, untasteable, unfeelable, unhearable intimations pushing beyond the limited range of our senses. To some extent, both types of ghost story (the literary and the anecdotal) just try to tell us what a ghost is. I find that many of my projects simply try, above all, to define their principle term, whether it's "garden," "window," "hand," etcetera.

AF: As you describe the dim prospect for a definitional (or even a descriptive) book about ghosts, I think of Freud's take on the epidemiology of jokes—that if I hear a joke, if I undergo its shock, this produces surplus tension, which I only can relieve by telling the joke to someone else. Do ghost stories, however unsayable, get passed on for similar reasons? For you, as the interlocutor here, have you been haunted by stories you've heard? And if you can't deliver or define their ghosts, do you at least intend to show us how a ghost story spreads?

CS: Good questions. The reference to Freud is particularly apt. And of course, no definition ever becomes definitive. It remains bottomless, bound to another set of words, which again overflow themselves, creating new momentum. So yes, the stories overflowed and demanded retelling, and I retell them frequently. But back to Freud: you're getting at why I don't use people's "actual words." I don't use them because the story itself keeps turning over. As soon as someone tells it, it's no longer his or hers. You immediately pass it on. You share the anxiety, diffuse the confusion, negotiate the belief—all as a collaborative, communal process. Most important perhaps, a tale allows us to perform this communal activity even when the whole community can't be there.

AF: To bring this back to your writing, could we discuss the relationship between your in-depth research and your elided, elegant, erasure-tending textual surface?

CS: Actually, I never work with erasure. The fragments build up toward a surface, rather than starting with a "complete" surface and then removing pieces. The projects I work on constantly build toward something that never gets achieved. Each of them asks, what is a whole?

AF: And how do these syntactical vectors correspond to your archival or intertextual research? How does your engagement with scholarly content get refracted or traced through surface dynamics?

CS: Through that engagement, I hope to transpose a given body of knowledge into a different mode—to see how content changes though a shift in textual devices. If we think of poetic language as that which disrupts the one-to-one (the ideal, impossible) relationship between the word and the thing, then the higher the degree of poeticity, the more disruption present. I try to use such disruptions to create fissures in a subject that offer new points of access.

AF: So a project like *Ours* does not just introduce some new idiolect into poetry. It introduces poetic rhetoric into the investigation of gardening.

CS: Right. I feel it's very much that way and not the other. It interests me how poetic language (how non-referential aspects of language, such as sound, juxtaposition, ambiguity, ellipsis) can augment the referential—particularly with subject-matter not typically addressed by poetry.

AF: Well your description of gaps as generative got me thinking about additive composition in visual art, that some pieces don't start from a basic global structure, but get assembled as the local details get put together. Here could you discuss your sense of how poetic collections operate, again in relation to haunting? Can we think of *Gravesend*'s incremental or interrupted pacing as haunted by some broader (though additive—not originary or teleological) progress binding it all together?

CS: I do hope for some weird doubling or echoing, with the poems acting both as component parts and as self-sufficient units. The model of fractal geometry comes to mind—in which a given figure repeats across widely differing scales, so that a given structure such as a book can get broken down into smaller and smaller yet equivalent structures.

AF: Once more *Gravesend* traces the basic principle that words and meanings always haunt each other, with…

CS: Or we could say they overflow each other, to return to that term. I think of haunting in terms of overflow, a kind of intangible overflow for which we can't account, paralleling art as a form of excess—a lavish uselessness that a society only can indulge in once it has met its basic needs. Art celebrates this available excess, as, in some ways, do ghosts. Ghosts flaunt an excess of life by living beyond their deaths. That same defiance marks all art.

AF: Have we left out other types of haunting? Certainly Dickinson's death-as-chivalrous-suitor trope comes to mind.

CS: And her dashes. She can put such presence into the absences indicated by those underdetermined/overdetermined slices. But though death may seem a chivalrous suitor, does this have anything to do with ghosts? Do ghosts, after all, have anything to do with death? I found while writing *Gravesend* that the ghosts people told me about were not necessarily connected to death, nor did they evoke a threatening presence. Instead, they had more to do with time. It has always fascinated me that we can move through space, but not through time. We get pinned on a continuum, trapped in a single time, while all the dimensions of space stretch out freely before us. Yet ghosts possess a different relationship to time. To describe or define a ghost becomes tantamount to describing the relationship between space and time. A ghost is the articulation of the incommensurability of time and space. In short, I think ghosts do exist, and that they are not at all supernatural. Ghosts are completely normal entities that just happen to exist beyond our conceptual abilities because we cannot conceive/perceive time with the fluidity that we do space.

AF: At one point *Gravesend* opens onto a genetic history, as we encounter the familiarity of a face—of all faces. So the past haunts the present in any number of ways. Does the future haunt as well? You've already cited the line "Ghosts appear in place of whatever a given people will not face." This gets followed by the passage: "There are days / the entire sky is a ghost    though again    it's not necessarily what you'd think / bright sun    full of birds    you're in a park    and everything in sight is alive." That sequence evoked for me (if you don't mind an overliteralization) a sense of daily premonitions—let's say about apocalyptic climate change, about the constrictive horizon shadowing today's bright sky.

CS: Right, and also about our contemporary expansionist activities. *Gravesend* only queries Occidental ghosts because I wanted to address the Occident's effort to haunt its way into everybody else's culture—and not just historically, but now more than ever. We've created a situation (politically, ecologically, et cetera) in which the future inevitably haunts us. What should be open questions have become much less so. We have predetermined, preoccupied, our political spaces and closed many doors prematurely.

AF: I guess we always haunt our descendants as much as our ancestors haunt us.

CS: And as you said, we also haunt our own futures. We think of haunting as coming from the past, but haunting actually pulls us forward. It eliminates choices. And it is we, it's always we, who haunt ourselves. But again, I'm not sure this has anything to do with ghosts, and the more I worked on the project, the more I saw them as separate.

AF: *Gravesend* provides cumulative references to the photograph, to the gramophone. These objects offer eerie, fin-de-siècle affects. But they also point to a present haunted by media narratives, which, like ghost stories, reflect, embody, ameliorate and exacerbate our loneliness.

CS: I'm so glad you brought loneliness into the equation. Loneliness is an emanation of the empty body. The poem "The Ghost Dance" addresses the emergence of the "gramophone voice," which constituted an invention (or re-invention) of disembodiedness. So the poem asks how that disembodied voice differs from the voice-of-the-other-within that Tolstoy discusses in *The Kingdom of God is Within You*, in which he attributes the internalized voice to God. And in terms of Occidental culture's imperial reach, we have a strange confluence of dates, a single recurring year, 1894, that saw the publication of Tolstoy's book, the beginning of the gramophone's commercialization, and the recording/filming of the *Ghost Dance*, which likewise sought to access internalized voices and visions. The fusion of this internal voice with the radically externalized machine voice created a fundamental shift in subjectivity—and as you point out, we've multiplied and become increasingly occupied by such voices ever since.

AF: Somewhere you've described the historical development of the ghost—moving from being an intimate to being a stranger, which again seems to trace the trajectory of us becoming strangers to ourselves.

CS: Yes, we empty ourselves by projecting our lives onto the recipe lives we watch in film, television, and advertising. Contemporary media offers myriad ways to externalize ourselves through a variety of self-emptying processes. The idea of a society whose ghosts don't even want to know them—it's because we're not there to be known. To ghosts, we must look like empty shells.

AF: Well, for me, just envisioning you walking through an English town asking people questions…it's sort of like you did what we all want to do with ghosts (or strangers), which is ask them questions. And the ideal outcome would be some collaborative construct in which our voices could comingle.

cs: Precisely. That's why I'd wanted to present the interviews the way I did—to have a communal voice, with no distinction between where one ghost story ends and another begins, or whose ghost story is whose. We participate in the tellings, but no individual creates them. We inherit them.

AF: I have one last, slightly biographical question. I loved the early line characterizing death as "endless endlessness    that replaces us." How does this concept of an endless endlessness relate to your own propulsive, itinerant, project-oriented approach to poetry? Do you feel haunted by previous and/or future projects? Do you just complete one and move onto the next?

cs: I always miss a book once it gets finished, because (of course) I select topics I love. I could have happily kept on writing poems about medieval paintings, or ghosts, or gardens for years, but I impose limits and structures from a desire for communication. There's a limit to the number of ghost poems any sane person will want to read. I try to keep this in mind, which means that sooner or later I have to end each book. But I'm always sorry. Certain projects stay with me longer. Gardens remain especially important. I did a book in 1991 on the Luxembourg Gardens, then did *Ours* in 2008. I've done that with paintings also—come back to them. I figure that as long as you leave 10 or 15 years between projects, people don't realize that you're repeating yourself. So in that case, no, they don't haunt me as much as I would like them to.

## INTERVIEW WITH TRAVIS ORTIZ
Recorded on July 21, 2012
This interview focuses on Ortiz's book *Variously, Not Then* (Tuumba).

ANDY FITCH: Your acknowledgements state that a recording of "When the Nation was Sound" launched this whole project. Could you discuss the book's origins both within and beyond that recording?

TRAVIS ORTIZ: I've been a ROVA fan for a while. ROVA's *The Works*—

*Volume 1* came out back in '97. I just had gotten it that week. I sat in my living room listening to the first track, "When the Nation was Sound," then started leafing through the liner notes, and read that Larry Ochs wrote this piece on the night the U.S. began bombing Baghdad in the first Gulf War. That got me thinking about my own situation at the time, finishing high school in San Diego, feeling isolated as a voice questioning this run-up to war—this whole tying a yellow ribbon around the old oak tree. I didn't have any allies voicing their opposition to war, but started listening to the musical composition through that filter. After a couple listens I began writing responses to this music. First I just wrote the prose pieces, which took much longer than expected. I carefully would edit and put a piece together. I wanted to produce a confining, somewhat alienating experience. They all have a boxy feel, similar in length, quite uniform. I'd pick up this project then put it down again. It took many years to write. After 39 prose pieces it seemed done. I started shopping around the manuscript either as a chapbook or a small, perfect-bound book. Feedback I received described the project as too constrictive. One editor actually broke a few prose sections into poetic lines. At first I thought this would ruin the concept, but that idea of poking air into the prose began to appeal to me. A friend had said, about a chapbook of mine, that he thought its writing resembled how a DJ might sample and remix and break down language. For that chapbook, *Geography of Parts*, I had taken various quotes, snippets, then reconfigured these decontextualized phrases. So I thought, well, why not do that to my own text and remix each prose piece—especially since this writing emerged in response to music? So the companion pieces come from that. Here I only applied one rule: their language had to borrow entirely from the prose sections. Also the height of each prose section determines the limit…

AF: I wondered.

TO: Only one page-spread breaks that rule. Pages 16 and 17 break that plane. For complicated reasons based on wording I use, page 16 follows the height of page 13.

AF: I'm curious about your work as a designer, as a DJ. From the start, even without any biographical information, this book's design seemed integral to the text. How did you first envision it—as a visual, sonic, conceptual medium? How did it finally assemble itself in your head?

TO: Visual elements provide a key component. Even the prose blocks present this standardized aesthetic. But I used their companion pieces to blow that open. You can just jump in and find little thought clusters, as opposed to this giant, oppressive prose block that makes you feel blocked in.

AF: Those graphic elements help to construct a physically layered text, pushing beyond the flat fields of, let's say, Mallarmé's compositions. Your representation of space seems more closely aligned to the apparent depths of digital space, as displayed on a multitasking computer screen. And this third dimension of depth prompted my awareness of a fourth dimension of time. Do you have a desired sequence for how the reader encounters or assimilates any given page?

TO: I want that to remain open, especially with the remix sections. Sometimes language gets cut off, presenting only slices of words. Some individual letters resemble abstract patterns. So these remixes break up the prose linearity. For my book launch I placed all the remixes in a looped slideshow appearing on a screen beside me. Before long the remixes got totally out of sync with my reading. Those repeated words and phrases offered a new type of layering effect.

AF: I like picturing this audience experience not just structured by the perceiving body, not just contained on the page or screen, but circulating amid various planes. Again musical metaphors arise, echoing your co-publisher Lyn Hejinian's refrain that "the obvious analogy is with music." Or Rosalind Krauss, the art historian, discusses texture in relation to collage, painting, sculpture. At a time when theorists defined painting as an interrogation of the flat, two-dimensional picture plane, collage's three-dimensionality pushed painting closer to sculpture. Similarly, in terms of how texture plays out in your book, does the layered, discursive delivery move it closer to music than to prose assertion? Do tonal dynamics and rhetorical shifts, rather than what you've described as prose's linear processes, take precedence?

TO: I like that idea. From talking with friends, I've realized how much more acceptable it remains to engage a super abstract painting, rather than an equally abstract poem. So I've tried to use language in a similar mode—to make my abstractions, if not accessible, at least more understandable, easier to grasp. With music or cinematic or painterly abstraction, people don't stop and say, wait, what's this all about? Here I allow abstraction to take a front seat, but without obscuring the musicality.

AF: Certain motifs function like familiarizing hooks. Repeated terms or constructions stand out. Then broader themes gradually arrive. When I say "theme" I just mean a tone or topic that by accumulation picks up greater meaning. You've mentioned distance, isolation, solitariness. But the theme of repetition (as structural conceit as much as a verbal trope) both reinforces and counteracts those tendencies.

TO: Talking about repetition even while laying out repetitive phrases seemed interesting. I love poems, in some cases sound poems, that repeat a word or phrase over and over and over again. That word never takes on the same nuance twice. Just in repeating something you change it. I wanted to explore those tonal and syntactical and semantic changes here, while discussing repetition in this same context.

AF: Other motifs seem to cluster around a poetics of improvisation, of collaboration, of variations amid the same—also breath and narrative. Gertrude Stein, Black Mountain, David Antin came up for me. Do some of their diverse yet overlapping concerns interest you?

TO: Definitely, especially Stein's uses of repetition. But you also mentioned breath and poetic improvisation. In that "When the Nation was Sound" recording, and then two other ROVA pieces…I also would listen to this old ROVA piece "Knife in the Times," and a ROVA plus four additional saxophones performance called, I think, "Triceratops." I tried using 20-30 minute tracks so I didn't have to change the music too fast. But so especially with "Triceratops," you'll encounter these little moments when you hear the saxophonists gasping for air. Glenn Spearman does this incredible solo and you hear these crazy gasps. That led me to new forms of repetition. Let's see if I can hear the actual human behind the saxophone. Let's trace how those repeated breaths play out differently for each different person, at different points in the piece.

AF: Given your title's "variously," your project's emphasis upon variation, it seems worth returning to the specific circumstances in which this book began—the post-Gulf War I era, and how the book's ongoing process then gets pulled into the Gulf War II era. Here "various" and "variation" become broader topics or tropes, both in terms of public discourse and in terms of autobiographical retrospection.

Could you discuss how the delayed, repeated, sampled temporality of this book relates to individual, collective, media-saturated historical experience?

TO: I wanted the title to point to my own autobiography, and also to throw that subject into question. Perhaps it all happened like this, or maybe like that, or it never happened. I also want it to remain murky what time periods I refer to, with Gulf Wars I and II overlapping—along with material all the way from childhood up to the present moment of writing this piece. Overheard news phrases appear without any specific time reference. Autobiographical patterns arise, but contexts and interpretations always change.

AF: In some ways your initial ROVA experience, your quasi-autobiographical approach, seem not so different from collective improvisation, since jazz solos typically don't present an individual abandoning all restraint, giving him or herself up to unchecked internal drives, but rather situating each note in response to others'. And your polyphonic autobiographical perspectives only enhance that. Does it make sense to read these layered physical pages as something like a choral or group performance with different voices, different tonalities, different rhythms and instrumentalizations happening simultaneously?

TO: That seems a great way to think about it. I wish readers could encounter all the different phrases at once.

AF: Maybe they can though.

TO: Maybe they can. But definitely a group could read these overlapping texts aloud. I've considered trying that. As I continued to work on this piece after those initial improvisations, the repeated phrases and concepts all began to blend and get orchestrated. I'd love to explore that through live performance.

AF: When I suggest that we could read like how we'd listen to a live quartet…when I edit a piece, I'll suddenly sense I should use a particular word (let's say the word "between") and then I'll realize, as I look, that this word appears five lines down. I must physically have seen "between" before my mind thought it had read that sentence. I can't help but see a whole page at once. Somehow your book made that broader perceptive field concrete, crystallizing my layered attention to any page.

TO: Well sometimes while writing I'd listen to pop tracks with vocals (Kate Bush's "Running Up that Hill" comes to mind) and encounter these unconscious overlaps of selecting a word just when it appeared in a song. I wanted visually to translate that.

AF: In terms of the prose blocks themselves, their syntax echoes Ron Silliman's "new sentence," just as the arrangement of motifs recalls Lyn Hejinian's *My Life*. Again, in what ways does your career as a digital designer shape your approach to early '80s Language writing?

TO: Language work changed my whole approach to writing, back when I attended UC Berkeley. I took a contemporary poetry class with Charles Altieri and he had us read Ron Silliman and Lyn Hejinian and Charles Bernstein. That just blew away my whole concept of poetry, informed by '60s and '70s confessionalism. All the sudden I could address more complicated concepts in an abstract way. I'd been reading folks like Heidegger and thinking about tropes of revealing and concealing—of how whenever you reveal something you can't help but conceal something else. Now I could present those ideas in a form that didn't feel too revealing, yet which also opened other possibilities. Here repetition became compelling. But you'd asked how I see myself in relation to these poets.

AF: I wondered if, through your work in digital design, you've developed a more visually minded attunement to them, which might differ from how most poets read them.

TO: I can't tell if this will answer that question, but after I finished school I didn't want to get a copywriting job where I just would sit for eight hours polishing somebody else's projects. If I gave my employer all that creative energy, I wouldn't have any left for myself. So I got into visual design by learning how to typeset books. Lyn and I started developing Atelos. We couldn't afford to hire someone to lay out the books, so I took that on and began studying design principles and book layout. It turned into a career without me knowing it, one that allows me to be creative. And it has in some ways changed how I write. I don't necessarily approach all Language poets visually, but do have a greater sensitivity to material properties of language.

AF: Could we consider some specific lines and passages? Of course, based on what you've said, extracting significance from isolated bits becomes problematic. Still certain moments stood out, such as "the loss of pronouns requires a different register." First am I right no proper nouns or pronouns appear in this book?

TO: You are correct. I wanted never to use the word "I," because the book already was that "I," an autobiography—without representing itself this way. There might…I may use "you" or "we" a couple times, but more in relation to quoting somebody.

AF: Not positing a "you" that is the reader. "You" and "we" remain objects, not subjects.

TO: You need to take a different tack to approach this book's personhood. "I" or "you" or "we" or pronouns or proper nouns can't get there.

AF: Page 70 also stood out, those big gray lines. I should have mentioned, when we discussed spatial depths, how a chiaroscuro shading appears—here with the text "topo- / graph-."

TO: This particular example provides pieces of words. They could come from "topography," but also might offer discrete parts or bits more suggestive than syntactical meanings. The text might get cut off or bleed into the gutter. Yet these visual disruptions provide their own form of verbal communication.

AF: "Graph" could begin or comprise or end a word. "Topo" suggests surface as well as topic. "Topo- / graph-" makes concrete the shifting topography that this book traces. Those associative elements shimmer in the background. Then page 77 offers the line, "The desire to remain various." Does that desire in part compel this book?

TO: I like this idea of constantly changing—not pinned down to a certain identity, not constricted to being the grammatical subject of an "I." Variation, as opposed to fixed identity, allows my work the freedom to contradict itself.

AF: Will it continue to do so going forward?

TO: For now, I have several projects that do not emphasize writing, though in my mind they relate. I love photography and painters such as Gerhard Richter who do blurry portraits, again pushing the boundaries of representation—here by softening the focus.

AF: Like his Baader-Meinhof series.

TO: Exactly. I've started to work with similar principles. I've got this lens I fit over my phone, this macro lens, so that I can get close up and take photographs. But if I pull back and try to point the camera, anything not super close becomes blurred. Just by accident I discovered this and started taking video, shots of people moving. I went to a modern dance performance that incorporated classic ballet-type moves. That all became just light and motion—this really amazing kinetic painting. So I've started to compose blurry portraits of certain events, commuting to work, for example, capturing movement without representing it.


## INTERVIEW WITH EVELYN REILLY
Recorded on July 22, 2012
This interview focuses on Reilly's book *Apocalypso* (Roof).

ANDY FITCH: Could we start with the apocalypse then get to the calypso—hopefully the Trinidadian historical context for calypso? First, to what extent do this book's fraught references to climate memory, to finding oneself awash in premonition, to wholesale legislative abandonment, provide explicit reference to the present moment?

EVELYN REILLY: I do consider these explicit references to our historical and cultural moment. I've tried to convey a communal mental landscape I think we all inhabit. The apocalyptic imagination has become such a part of us, as people alive right now, although the language we use to describe it necessarily draws from inherited models. So I wanted to play with some of those models and probe what uses this kind of imagination and idiom can have in the present.

AF: Your opening quote from *The Material Sciences Division* states, in part: "Materials that we cannot now imagine will form the basis of devices and applications in a future about which we can now only dream." Here the apocalypse could seem less literally apocalyptic—positioning epistemic limits along a historical trajectory of progressive paradigmatic shifts. Though later we find references to the Book of Revelations, to end times, to Bruegel. And then the conflation of "Childe Roland to the Dark Tower Came" with *Harold and the Purple Crayon* demonstrates your virtuoso ability to move between alternate subject positions on an impending crisis. Again, to what extent do you seek to advance an ambiguous, abstracted concept of apocalypse, as inherited, let's say, from the Romantics? To what extent do you wish to enhance our efforts at imagining this specific environmental collapse before it exists as a full-blown material reality?

ER: I doubt I can claim so grand an ambition. I wish I could. That *Material Sciences Division* quote, from the Lawrence Berkeley National Laboratory, struck me because it still appears on their website and sounds so undilutedly optimistic. I'm not anti-technology or anti-science (positions which seem a waste of time), but do believe that our status as animals harnessing potent technologies presents huge problems. And of course, through feedback loops, technology structures our brains, and our brains structure it. I wanted to explore that process. But the relation between apocalypse and calypso became important—because for whatever crazy reasons we continue writing this stuff. I think we still need to embed ourselves in the joy of art, even when that art addresses potential disaster. So I hoped even for this grief-stricken book to stay tethered to that notion of music, of joy. I don't have any deep knowledge of calypso music or Caribbean culture. I wish I did, but can't pretend to. I did attempt to signal, from an ecopoetic point of view, that somehow human work, human art, still has to emerge from our animal joy in being alive.

AF: You mentioned the desire to convey or address a communal mental landscape. Does that mental landscape itself provide a technology you wish to harness? Could we develop more constructive forms of envisioning futuristic scenarios, rather than overcoming ourselves with a constrictive, worrisome passivity?

ER: I consider language one of our basic human technologies, one means by which we engage our environment. Our shaping of language has a strong impact on how we live with others (in the largest, trans-species notion of others). And I retain some…I couldn't call it optimism, but I wish to inhabit this space of not knowing how things will turn out—of developing language as much as all our other technologies to see where they can take us.

AF: From what I understand, calypso initially functioned as a highly politicized form of lyric, even a respected news source. By comparison, how do the light, effortless-seeming sequences throughout your book correspond to the heaviness of that "real emergency / beneath the emergencies"? Do you deliberately deploy elided structures for more argumentative ends?

ER: Interesting. I think those structures came from that desire to stay tethered to pleasure, even while presenting an ominous landscape. And in the long poem "Apocalypso" I let myself do something I hadn't in the past—embrace some traditional poetic rhythms and a more lyric sound. That poem's quite easy to read aloud, though much of my work has not been. Depictions of animal life and even beauty flowed into my apocalypse, which helps explain why I gave that concluding poem the full title "Apocalypso: A Comedy." I don't know if I could have finished this book, quite honestly, without allowing in these positive elements.

AF: In terms of the forms you adopt, the broader rhythmic patterns, I also appreciate the occasional aphoristic brevity, those passages possessing the air of the non-sequitur. "Powdery Flowers" makes compact, elegant use of the page with entries such as "So many bodies setting off detectors // this is the meek and the lame." I wondered if such concision…can a line-break, an aphorism, construct its own mini-apocalypse? Do the localized disruptions throughout anticipate, emulate, contemplate apocalypse?

ER: When I wrote the "Powdery Flowers" section, from the long poem "Nature Futurism," I hadn't yet written "Apocalypso: A Comedy," which doesn't invalidate your point at all. But because I've tended to write quite densely, with "Nature Futurism" I wanted to explore a more minimalist form—to see what would happen. Like I've said this book addresses grief, but not so much personal grief, as communal grief. Here I wanted to ask, what would it mean for me to channel such grief through a kind of radical minimalism, as many fellow poets have done?

AF: With their elegies for instance?

ER: Some elegies (although I don't consider that a form marked by minimalism), but also other examples of grief-stricken poetry. I didn't plan to assemble a personal project. Yet regarding that specific "Powdery Flowers" section: one of my brothers is a Vietnam veteran and an amputee, and when you walk through airport security with him, he has to step off to the side or he'll set off the detectors. And so, for me, that little page you quoted acknowledges him, which doesn't matter for the reader, really.

AF: One last question related to minimalist depictions of grief: do you distinguish here between grief for what already has happened and grief for things to come? Does this book position itself more forcefully in either direction, and does the minimalism help shape that trajectory?

ER: Again, I think it helped me to go minimalist for a while but then let myself return to the maximal. And in terms of past grief, I think that the more you live, the more that you absorb of history, the more you understand how easy it is for terrible events to happen. So that awareness of the past shapes my sense of our future.

AF: I'm dumb on Walter Benjamin, but his conception of history as the wreckage from all past exploitations, from all these desperate utopian efforts that failed, seems to provide a related form of extra-weary optimism.

ER: Well I make my living in the museum world, working mostly on history exhibitions. And most of these exhibits depict some staggering catastrophe. I don't need Walter Benjamin for my sense of that. But I recently read some Benjamin after Angela Hume wrote about my work in relation to his notion of emergency. "Apocalypso" quotes one line she pointed out to me, about "the real state of emergency."

AF: Your work experience makes me think of you as coming to poetry from a broader scientific/curatorial context—bringing with it a multi-faceted perspective on political, historical, environmental concerns. Could you describe how these professional endeavors inform your poetics?

ER: Sure. I first got a degree in zoology and planned to become a scientist. But I just couldn't give up my broader interests. Still I worked as a research assistant for many years to support my start as a writer. Just by accident I fell into a position at this design firm that creates exhibits for museums. For a long time now I've worked with curators, helping them write for the public, and have found myself placed in between the worlds of curation, architecture and design. I've never received an academic literary education. I'm self-taught in that way—which has plusses and minuses. Now I mainly work on history and cultural-historical exhibits. I soon will finish a project on

Russian Jewish history in Moscow. Again this probably sharpens my tragic sense of history. You just can't get away from it.

AF: Does curation attune you to proactive modes of engaging your reader? Independent of developing individual scenes, does it shape your approach to providing broader contexts or sites of engagement? Does it present a productive vantage for designing a book that probes our limited abilities to imagine ecological disaster?

ER: I have no idea. Because when I write these books I feel a bit like a crazy person. I think, who in the world would want to read this stuff? It always amazes me if I have readers. And of course the museum world demands clear, concise presentations for the public—whereas poetry often calls for the opposite, which I do find a relief. Still this life around design and architecture has given me a preference for finding basic compositional structures into which I then let a lot of variation enter.

AF: "Dreamquest Malware" deliberately integrates faux-architectural language into its idiom. Can you discuss the role that François Blançiak's work plays in this piece's composition? More generally: could you describe your methods of appropriating discourse from architecture and other disciplines (fiction as well)?

ER: I've learned much from poets who productively adopt alternative vocabularies. Judith Goldman and Kristin Prevallet and Lisa Robertson, for example, often generate work from non-poetic sources. The Blançiak offered a more fleeting source, though I felt obliged to credit him. He produced this fey, wonderful little book called *Siteless: 1001 Building Forms*, presenting impossible structures nobody could build. For each, he provides this charming little drawing and a wonderful title. That helped me get going. But *Battlestar Galactica* had a much bigger impact on the *Dreamquest* series. I suddenly thought I could channel the experience of an engineer off on a distant planet. The whole genre of dystopic sci-fi colors this book—that shift from a 1960s *Star Trek* optimism ("to boldly go where no man has gone before") to a sense of ourselves as exiles from a destroyed Earth, searching for some kind of home.

AF: What about the parts of "Apocalypso: A Comedy" that you describe as "events"? From what circumstances do these pieces derive? They almost feel like field work.

ER: I guess this book's long, elastic poems just allowed for the insertion of various materials. So twice I thought, I'll share here one of my favorite poems, from *Technicians of the Sacred*, that early Rothenberg ethnopoetics anthology. I've hung these two on my wall forever. And he calls them "events," so I wanted to honor that. Again this didn't shape my poems so much as fit in with them—not that I believe in originality anyway. We all just channel each other.

AF: We tend to think of events as emergent phenomena, so it interested me here to consider Rothenberg's "event" as a re-emergent phenomenon, one that comes back—posing questions of whether its recurrence becomes a different type of event, whether anything ever really could return.

ER: That sounds appropriate, because for these particular "events" I think Rothenberg transcribed an Australian Aboriginal ritual and one from Papua New Guinea, both of which seem to emphasize recurrence rather than occurrence.

AF: Well this brings back questions about the temporality of your own book. Do you think of it as future-oriented? As retrospective? Does it take place on a personal timeline, or according to some broader global/human/ecological measure?

ER: I've thought about this. I don't think I've ever achieved it, by the way, but I've explicitly thought, what would it look like to write from the vantage point of geologic time, or astronomical space? Perhaps the science person in me always wants to frame things within these largest natural structures. I bothered to get a science degree because evolutionary theory seemed so amazingly liberating. So how in poetry can one suddenly telescope out to a totally different timeframe? The idea of attempting that does give me some pleasure. Christopher Dewdney wrote a book which describes a kind of erotics of geological time and place, as one model.

AF: In terms of the design work you do, again questions of scale seem quite important. That's why I'd asked about your minimalist structures and syntax. How can we scale a book to direct its reader towards broader, more historically-oriented, more future-oriented thoughts? *Apocalypso* creates space for this type of readerly reflection, and scale seems to help with that.

ER: Those minimalist pieces do seem less controlled, presenting an ambiguous space, whereas "Apocalypso's" quasi-narrative flow feels shaped more by the writer. Then Browning's "Childe Roland to the Dark Tower Came" offered another alternative—especially its vision of a very, very contemporary devastated landscape. That poem engages doubt about everything. Roland arrives at this tower, and the tower's just a wreck too. He doesn't do anything with it. So one poem in my book, titled "The Whatever Epic," picks up on Browning's language. *Apocalypso* as a whole is something of an anti-epic.

AF: Anti-epic because no sweeping trajectory could tie it all together? Or given the triumphalist tone of most epics?

ER: I guess the end to the notion of "progress" has been with us 125 or 150 years by now—the end of this human hubris about our cosmic quest as the chosen species. I hope to keep constructing some new sense of shared humanity (and animality), of common goals, common trajectories. I don't understand anything about allegory, but Eileen Myles wrote about allegory for *Apocalypso*'s back cover, and when I read that I thought, really? Still she felt strongly about it and that made me reconsider this form that might seem dated to us.

AF: Eileen's Bush-era opera *Hell* works well that way.

ER: She also mentions Tarkovsky. She and I both became obsessed with Tarkovsky, who directed some very dystopic anti-epic films like *Stalker*, in which his characters tramp through this amazing polluted landscape, in 1972 or something. Or *Solaris*. And I think Hollywood, too, keeps making dystopic futuristic films because most of us inhabit that imaginative space. Perhaps they speak to the fearful part of us that we try hard to repress. But we need to show it, to see it, because we still face it.

## INTERVIEW WITH ELENI SIKELIANOS
Recorded on August 5, 2012
This interview focuses on Sikelianos' book *The Loving Detail of the Living & the Dead* (Coffee House Press).

ANDY FITCH: I've enjoyed reading this collection in manuscript form, with the relative lack of paratextual information, like a table of contents or section breaks. Yet given your history of producing book-length poems and expansive projects, I've projected a good deal of continuity here. Could you talk a bit about the book's experiential contours—its spatial and temporal shapes, as you envision those coming together? For example, one-line pages will repeat or anticipate phrases found elsewhere. Do these serve to establish a multi-directional, refractive text, one that incorporates Aymara conceptions of time, situating both past and future before/behind us?

ELENI SIKELIANOS: I first tried to resist developing a project here, feeling somewhat exhausted from…almost every book of poetry now, by myself or others, seems some sort of project. For a while I've wondered what has happened to the discrete poem, especially in experimental poetics. I keep gesturing toward that though then can't help stitching together some fabric, thinking of the book as a fabric, I guess. I'd also thought of this as an installation, with those one-line pieces both puncturing the density of individual poems, and weaving a thread through so that all becomes connected at the same time. I pictured the one-line passages as breathing holes, where a seal might poke through ice, gasping for air, and so yes, in that sense, occurring more spatially then temporally. My last three books contained visual elements, whereas this one barely does, with those occasional moments that seem not non-languaged but less-languaged—like little pooling places, little eddies.

AF: That model of installation art seems to hold for your previous books as well.

ES: Right, I feel it strongly in *The California Poem,* where different parts function almost as different rooms you wander through—with visual data set alongside language data, echoing Olson's conception of the page as a field, but incorporating images as much as text. Robert Smithson's ideas about sites and non-sites also play out here.

AF: Then in this new book, figures passing between life and death become points of reference. The assertion that "peas in the garden show time's shadow" recalls Persephone. Orpheus appears. Charon, the ferryman…is it pure coincidence that Charon shares his name with your serialized Charlene?

ES: That is an awesome pure coincidence. I love that.

AF: Could you characterize Charlene's function throughout the book?

ES: I've wondered about this myself. Charlene provides one of these threads, or waves that wash through the book, creating the sense of a dissolute whole. She first appeared in a dream, which happens fairly frequently for my poems. She had been my best friend in fifth grade. We felt like outsiders in this wealthy, conformist small California town, and both came from poor, single-parent families, living in apartments rather than suburban homes. Her first appearance in the book coincided with my first dream about her. Curiously, about 10 days later, the real Charlene contacted me for the first time since we were 12 or something. But in the poem, Charlene seems kind of my double. I think she represents the past, this bifurcated past. The real Charlene now lives on a small farm in Oregon, working some kind of manual job, while I do this other thing. In the poem she becomes this goddess figure or savant or oracle. I found in my journal from a year ago a note about Charlene: "a body that appeared in a dream with hair like a Hollywood moon, a living ghost (as in memory), connecting my words to the dead and the living."

AF: Again the name Charlene, with its "Ch," made me sense she was a child.

ES: How interesting. I don't think I give her that characteristic, but something both quite childlike and quite evolved stands out. I describe her with a childlike language, presenting simple statements: "Of course she is a goddess. / She has some chickens. / She's my friend."

AF: Other motifs cycle through this manuscript that I've seen before in your work. Atoms, shadows and worlds circulate. At the same time, the book's title and dedication page do suggest a distinctly elegiac text. But could we start with the versatile conception of "world" that gets deployed here, along with its homophonic associates "word" and "whirled"? Your opening page announces that "a bit of fire from the world pools in the ear / & burns there." Then the book's second poem places a variety of worlds side-by-side: "world the black—world the blank / —margin." Later this concept of world gets externalized through scientific, political, philosophical discourse. Yet it also gets internalized amid intimate, idiosyncratic processes of language. I mean in lines such as: "Each human carries her own in- / side feeling of of." And I'm curious, amid this mathematical expansiveness of potential worlds, how your meditations on death have been informed by Roubaud's *Plurality of Worlds,* which also appears.

ES: Although I remain a huge Roubaud fan, and that's probably my favorite of his books, I haven't read it in 15 years. But raising a child has made me particularly sensitive to this shuttling between public and private worlds. I've perhaps become more aware of the private way we experience language (poets in particular, but probably everyone). I've wanted to reclaim this private language experience and not leave everything to the public sphere. So my last book shuttled between those two worlds. And here that opening line you quoted, about a bit of the world pooling in the ear, definitely refers to outside media, political or news information we absorb which burns inside the individual—needing to get reprocessed some way. That theme recurs throughout this book. And then the next line you quoted, "world the black—world the blank / —margin," plays at providing an entire world history in a three-page poem. I'd even played with making this whole book just pieces of world history from time's beginning until now, then into the future, with, as you've said, past and present overlapping. Of course we could call that an old poetic trope, given Pound's notion that all of time is contemporaneous in the mind, or H.D.'s sensibility, especially in *Trilogy,* where you can feel all times present at once. Quite a few deaths of people close to me occurred during the period when I wrote this book. Bearing a child curiously puts a finite term on one's own life, as well as the child's you've brought into the world. Then I sense that for so many of us the world seems to keep moving closer and closer to cataclysmic disaster. I've wondered, while editing, if this book feels extremely pessimistic. I don't know if you thought that.

AF: Elegiac, yes. But pessimistic? I'd call it apprehensive in reasonable ways. I only feel truly pessimistic and freaked when a person can talk endlessly without worrying about the world. For me, frank acknowledgment doesn't cause pessimism. It produces relief.

ES: I'm glad to hear that.

AF: In terms of reflections on mortality, and of tropes that shuttle between worlds, shadows likewise take on significance. Shadows appear as relational, rather than as substantial entities: "'that's when the child realized that the shadow is not a substance…driven away by light, / and learns where a shadow will fall.'" Shadows open us to broader perceptual cognitions. Shadows serve as hinges, doors down to the dead or enigmatic aerial shadows. There are shadows of smell and shadows of sound, and there are shedus. So we could discuss how shadows play out. Or, again, it interests me how elemental topics such as worlds, shadows, atoms, atomized language circulate through this book and your work more broadly.

ES: Experiencing those recent deaths made it hard not to engage the shadow world, which seems by nature (in all its forms) relational. And Charlene remains a kind of shadow figure—not quite present, not completely real, a partial projection of myself or my hopes and fears. But also the reading I did influenced these thoughts about shadows. That quote comes from Piaget, where he detects a cognitive shift when the child recognizes a shadow as not an object, but a phenomenon caused by the human body. Also some specific moments of watching my own shadow as I walk prompted this image of stepping down to the dead—seeing that spot where the living foot and shadow foot meet, the real and the projected body, projected either toward the future or past. I also read a fascinating book on when shadows first appear in painting. Egyptian reliefs, let's say, depict no shadows. Even the early Greeks don't.

AF: I think shadows don't enter Japanese work until the late 1800s.

ES: Amazing. Or just think about shadows say in Renaissance paintings, where a shadow could depict the spirit of an angel, or the spirit of God touching you, impregnating you, or hold quite negative connotations. This trope has haunted artists for a long time. And the other person I read concerning shadows of course was Plato, whom I've never studied formally, so I get to misinterpret to my heart's content. Still one quite real experience of a substantive shadow came with the death of my uncle Poppy, to whom "Essay: The Living Leave the Dead" gets dedicated. It was as if I could feel my organs being replaced by this shadow version.

AF: Your own organs, you're saying?

ES: You know it felt as if a familial, collective organ had been replaced with…it wasn't a negative feeling, or negative shadow, but as if parts of this living person had gone, so your own organs had to get replaced with a shadow organ. I don't know what else to say, but consider this a real, quite visceral experience beyond any intellectual process of thinking about shadows.

AF: When motifs cycle through your various books, a shaded or shadow text seems to appear. Do you envision the books being read intertextually?

ES: I just appreciate that somebody has read them. I don't consciously think, oh, I wrote about shadows last time, so make sure they enter this book too. I sort of just can't help it. And the atom as well goes back for me…I briefly studied biology and loved microbiology and the cell's inner workings and the macroscape of how bodies or elements interact.

AF: Well, I found especially compelling here the interstitial swim through nothing, as it gets described in your poem "On the Bus." I wondered, if we consider this book as constructing a cosmology amid its ever-shifting worlds, where would this nothing "Right in the middle of the equipment" fit? I guess part of what intrigues me is the role that your elegant, hyper-compressed, yet never abrupt syntax plays throughout the manuscript. Does this conspicuous/inconspicuous foregrounding of elision, compression, point toward a generative potential in nothing? You'll mention, for example, the darkest substance ever known, blackout fabric—which again, like shadows, provides a non-space where meanings proliferate.

ES: I think I do experience syntax atomically. Linguistic compression allows for a breaking apart and reconfiguring, similar to a chemical process, to hydrogen splitting from oxygen then recombining. So I don't know how that relates to nothing. But that line you quoted does conflate nothing and everything—each a part of experience, and of the world too. Blackout fabric, or dark matter, as I envision it, gets so tightly packed that it resembles nothing, yet in a lovely way. Poetry (life) plays in that juncture between the possibility and impossibility of speech (a kind of pregnant emptiness). Cage asks us how to make a representation of nothing, and I suppose language constantly does point at something and nothing simultaneously. Syntax allows us to break it all down and build it up again. Some poets' primary genius lies in that process.

AF: You've mentioned biology, chemistry, physics. You'll quote the *Science Times*. Could we discuss your reading, allusive and citational practices? Do the Simone Weil and Rachel Bespaloff *Iliad* essays, for example, appear as pure historical coincidence, since the *New York Review of Books* put out that title as the U.S. engaged in a war of choice? Do you wish to trace a specific historical moment? Or does Weil's broader argument about the need to be humbled by mortal limitations in order to become human—does that more generally shape your approach to death, loss, aging in this book? Also the endnotes pointing to *Doctor Atomic*, to knockout mice, to Goya's black paintings...to what extent do these suggest an individual's passive exposure to persistent media? To what extent do they suggest a more pointed, personalized, directed mode of inquiry?

ES: It's probably a combination of those two. Certainly the atom picks up an ominous presence—in terms of the cracked atom and generalized sense of DNA being messed with and about to go haywire, like with genetically modified animals and plants. Then I happened to see the opera *Doctor Atomic* after having these thoughts. So you could call that whole sequence curated, even as it tracks what just happens to come into the curatorial sphere. I'd started these poems about three years ago, when I was 43 or 44. I thought a lot about Dante waking in the middle of a dark wood at exactly the midpoint of his life. Almost every morning death was my first thought.

AF: That was specific to this book?

ES: It was specific to my life I'd say, just waking and thinking, oh, I'm going to die who knows when. Then for the Simone Weil part: out of complete madness I taught *The Iliad* to my graduate workshop. Along with the book we read those essays. And I just find Weil's essay so moving—partly in its parallel to our own war of choice (which parallels the insane disregard for human life taking place when Weil wrote in 1939), but also in terms of the finite bodies we inhabit.

AF: When you refer to waking with thoughts of death, I'll recall moments of conspicuous mortification that occur amid the graceful delivery of your work. Sometimes these get patiently recorded, through lines such as "my ankle is breaking but my thumb is not / breaking / around my thought," then "my stomach is starting to break / around my mouth." Some episodes seem potentially self-induced. Charlene contemplates ripping out the organs from her own body. But then sometimes these mortifications seem socialized. A man gets called "Dad" and turns with his face "a moving / wreck of skin...a fruit ripped in two." And one other trope present throughout the book is meat: as an index of our carnivorous, cannibalistic means of preserving ourselves; or preserving our ancestors and descendants by internalizing them; or meat as threshold between death and life, as corporeal extension, excision, incorporation. Again, in terms of multi-directionality, of references to mortality, to family, organs, ghosts, a child's "live animal ghost" soon to fade—does this state of being meat (a meat that contemplates, savors, sings to, loves meat) seem a gross but somehow accurate metaphor for your book's poetics?

ES: Yes. Though it interests me that you used the word "mortification." I've recently returned to this manuscript, and felt a bit uncomfortable with certain quasi-religious implications. Of course some sense of mortification does take place. But this book also celebrates great joy in the meat body.

AF: Sorry, we should have discussed that more.

ES: Oh no. That's OK. The project totters between...two tropes always come back for me, the meat body's joy and its predictable putrefaction. Or perhaps the facility with which the meat body could get torn apart, versus the beautiful shapes that the mind can create (which include the mathematic or scientific worlds, the types of mortifying and horrendous bodily shapes that these have made).

AF: So structures of historical consciousness remain part of this meat body?

ES: I think so.

## INTERVIEW WITH EVIE SHOCKLEY
Recorded on August 6, 2012
This interview focuses on Shockley's book *Renegade Poetics: Black Aesthetics and Formal Innovation in African American Poetry* (University of Iowa Press).

ANDY FITCH: *Renegade Poetics* outlines what "black aesthetics" might mean amid the ongoing legacy of the Black Arts Movement. I notice a basic tension in your book between wanting to confirm that the BAM's reductive tendencies have had a constrictive impact on both creative and scholarly production, and wanting to assert that our own conception of the BAM itself is a reductive one—that this movement remained much more multifarious, complex, diverse than subsequent critics have assumed. Could you provide a brief summary of current critical approaches to the BAM? Then could you point to common limitations in our conception of the BAM's ideological or aesthetic range?

EVIE SHOCKLEY: You've given a good sense of two of this book's main goals. I guess they might seem in tension with each other, though I'd like to think of them as complementary.

AF: Sure, I meant it as a productive tension.

ES: That sounds accurate. My book points to problems that have emerged from the Black Arts Movement, its reifications of a certain black aesthetic. But I try to address both audiences with a complex understanding of the BAM and audiences less familiar with it. I'd hate to perpetuate a narrow view of what the BAM accomplished. Perhaps the most influential people setting the ground for how we (in the academy, in African-American literary circles, in related circles) think about the BAM have been Houston Baker and Henry Louis Gates. They came to writing about the BAM from quite different places. Baker did not participate directly, but became a BAM enthusiast in his younger years, then slowly moved away, first towards a poststructural approach. Gates cut his eyeteeth dissecting problems with BAM ideology, especially the racial essentialism he'd detected in its rhetoric. His book *Figures in Black* presents a scholarly conception of the BAM that has become conventional—as a movement which placed politics before aesthetics, a criticism which emphasized political consequences over any analytic description of what literature does. Gates distrusted both tendencies. And alongside such theoretical constructs appeared popular notions associating the BAM with positive messages, such as "Black is beautiful"; the idea that Africa offers a source of rich cultural heritage; or the belief that African-American ways of being and speaking and musical forms should be celebrated. Those broader cultural assumptions provided the BAM's privileged terms and sites of inquiry. So the confluence of scholarly assessment and popular conceptions come together in a perfect storm to produce our current, rigid definitions of the BAM, focusing on how much profanity or "non-standard English" appears in the poetry, how many references to revolution occur in a poem, how "angry" or African the poem sounds, rather than any number of the literature's equally or more interesting aspects.

AF: As we discuss the dominant, yet constrictive, vision of the BAM, can you point to neglected individuals, particular readings or texts, polyvalent concepts that do not receive the attention they deserve, which could offer a rounder, fuller sense of the movement? What can we learn, for example, from the visual arts, where this type of semiotic play (in which emergent institutional discourse suddenly becomes ironized) seems to happen faster?

ES: Let's start with the first question. This question prompts us to think through how the BAM gets associated with its most vocal or visible core activists, writers, and theorists. But for a movement to become a movement it must involve hundreds of people. It most likely spreads beyond Harlem, beyond New York. James Smethurst's *The Black Arts Movement* presents the BAM as a movement that occurs nationally by way of local clusters: West Coast clusters around Watts and so forth; Southern clusters that include New Orleans as a center point; Midwest clusters in Chicago, Detroit, other places; then on the East Coast, not just Harlem but Newark, Philly, etcetera. Still scholars begin to canonize a handful of figures, to generalize from specific individual definitions of black aesthetics, or particular personal accounts of the movement—an interpretive process that excludes folks exploring different questions in distinct local contexts, who didn't feel the need or attain the platform to assert their vision as the representative vision of the BAM. Many such debates, divergent practices and heterogeneous conversations never made their way into print. So the definitions derived from the BAM's most famous texts (by Larry Neal, Amiri Baraka and a few others) end up overshadowing parallel events or arguments or concerns. Jayne Cortez works with the Watts Writers group then moves to New York because she becomes politicized through activities we associate with the BAM, yet produces a different type of work and, for a time, gets written out of the histories. Or if you look at Ed Roberson interviews, he says he took part in the BAM, and not just as an onlooker: engaging in conversations, attending readings, learning from Baraka and Sanchez and so forth. He worked through BAM ideas in different ways, which doesn't mean he didn't participate. I discussed this very point with Aldon Nielsen not long ago, who emphasized that people we tend to focus on participated not just as writers and theorists, but as activists who also wrote and theorized. Yet the movement took place not just among those at the forefront pushing their agendas in the most public contexts. Countless events occurred off-stage, so to speak. I look forward to future critical studies focused on figures who have been marginalized, as well as studies that reassess the central figures. For example, my Rutgers colleague Carter Mathes writes about Larry Neal (by all accounts, a key figure and dominant voice) further expanding the scope of his thought following, let's say, his iconic essay "The Black Arts Movement." Carter's research demonstrates the breadth in Neal's work which didn't get published, which doesn't get remembered, yet contains this striking range of ideas that keep growing more refined and complicated over the years. Or, as a segue into your question about art, we could consider another recent study, *Spectacular Blackness*, by Amy Ongiri. Ongiri looks at how the Black Panther Party in particular, but also a broader group of '60s and '70s artists associated with Black Power, used the visual, the spectacle, to capture the attention of the so-called black masses. Spectacular Blackness critiques accounts of the BAM that privilege the literary, with occasional reference to music, while excluding art and popular visual media.

AF: I began with metacritical questions about the BAM because *Renegade Poetics* seems to provide a revaluative process—rethinking certain types of work, bringing forth new rhetorical questions or problems. A second set of reductive principles that this book contests, for example, concerns conventional assumptions that African-American poetry as a whole attaches itself to urban experience, emphasizes political struggle, prioritizes a vernacular-based rhetoric in order to address a black mass audience. By contrast, the authors you examine (Anne Spencer, Ed Roberson, Harryette Mullen, Will Alexander, among others) construct poetic texts with unmistakable affinities to the "natural," and/or emphasize meditative, writerly strategies of textual production. They do so, as you argue, not in a departure from blackness, but as a dynamic embodiment of blackness. So here's my question: to what extent do you provide the individual cases of Spencer, of Roberson, in order to suggest that scholarly accounts have reinforced an artificial, inaccurate, stereotypical conception of black experience—one that overshadows many of the 20th century's most compelling achievements? To what extent do you seek a broad revisioning of the field? To what extent do you mean to say, here are some exceptional cases, outliers perhaps, but which ought to add nuance and detail to current scholarship?

ES: My take probably tacks between those two alternatives, but moves more toward the latter. I'd encourage a broad relooking at the tradition, since this questioning of inherited assumptions keeps scholarship healthy. However, my book attempts to provide an open-ended assessment, not to suggest that preceding versions got it wrong and...

AF: That you can give us the right version.

ES: Exactly. I want to point towards a much more nuanced and detailed picture. So *Renegade Poetics* focuses on texts which foreground the dilemma that produces black aesthetics—the dilemma of writing black subjectivity in a racist society. The authors I consider use this dilemma to push their poetics in particularly innovative directions. Of course any number of compelling African-American writers do this, people we don't think of always as innovative or writerly, but who could benefit from a broader conception of black aesthetics. Rita Dove's work would benefit from this broader definition. At least in her early career, Dove gets framed as somebody not writing "black" poetry, almost along the lines of Anne Spencer. And again this raises questions with which I often struggle. What do I mean when I call a piece "innovative"? How can I adopt this word without denigrating poems that remain excellent though not exactly path-breaking (at least to my eyes)? Whether or not I've succeeded at articulating such a difference, I've tried. Take someone like Lucille Clifton, who writes fabulous books but doesn't necessarily push the envelope as Sonia Sanchez does with *Does Your House Have Lions?*—in terms of new formal ground, new territory, the coming together of craft and idea in unanticipated ways.

AF: Could we further address your point that African-Americans can leave behind confining stereotypes of black identity without obscuring their racial subjectivity, their historical experience? Late in the book, this argument takes the form of a "freedom from/freedom to" distinction. Since they make for a coherent triptych, could you explain how this distinction plays out among Gwendolyn Brooks, Sonia Sanchez and Harryette Mullen, three poets you identify...I think you present them as the only African-American women to publish long poems in lyric stanzas. Could you describe the "freedom to" in the case of these authors? Here maybe we can get to a poetics of excess—what it means for an African-American female poet to appear "excessive," given this term's positive connotations in poetry, though negative connotations elsewhere in the world.

ES: I raise the distinction between "freedom from" and "freedom to" in my chapter on Will Alexander, though he might have a different sense of this binary than I do. But let's just say, from my perspective: I think "freedom from" and "freedom to" operate in all three female poets. The freedom from oppressive life conditions, from stifling expectations for what black poetry does, from limitations readers might associate with race and gender and sexuality—those concerns remain extremely important for all three women. Inevitable generational differences arise, but each poet, like most epic poets, seeks to use all available tools, to speak to a broad range of audiences and avoid being read in really narrow ways. If you take Brooks as someone who evades certain expectations about a working-class black woman's life (supposedly cut off from those exciting adventures we associate with men's activities), that's her gaining a "freedom from." But her excessiveness in "The Anniad" also stands out, for example through the types of intricate rhyme schemes she uses. She takes Chaucer's standard rhyme royal stanza and, instead of deploying the same ababbcc pattern, winds those rhymes any number of ways—a different way for almost each stanza. She uses super tight meter and a diction that she must have dropped into the dictionary to get, which certainly sends her reader back to the dictionary to unpack it. But again this performance of excess, this "freedom to" approach form so aggressively, never abandons the historical realities she hopes to push beyond. Part of why she has to out-Chaucer Chaucer in the first place is just so her use of form can register. Readers projecting a less sophisticated black poetics upon her work might overlook anything more subtle.

AF: Of course as we look at any individual, it seems hard fully to parse "freedom from" and "freedom to." And your book engages the broader premise that scholars need to consider historically specific conditions, rather than just generalize about African-American letters or something. Can we consider how this historicist approach plays out with one particular concept? Let's take polyvocality, and how this manifests in Brooks, Sanchez and Mullen. For me, polyvocality suggests communal modes of production. Call-and-response in gospel or blues, or collaborative improvisation in jazz, provide obvious points of reference. But Brooks's case at least (and this goes back to a poetics of excess) suggests something different. Here polyvocality refers to a single, albeit quite complex poetic-subject hitting multiple registers of discourse. Polyvocality seems to occur through a collage of tonalities, through audience reception.

ES: I pick up this use of the term from Mae Gwendolyn Henderson's study "Speaking in Tongues." She analyzes a number of texts (focusing on novels) to consider ways in which black women writers use language. It's not quite as simple as calling this language coded, not equivalent to Gates's concept of "signifyin(g)," but nonetheless describes a language use that encourages the reader or listener who is also black, also female, to hear one current of thought, while allowing other audiences to hear other meanings. So here emerges the idea of how polyvocality takes place through audience reception—through how a speech act gets heard, rather than solely how it gets made.

AF: That's great, because Brooks offers this inferred model of polyvocality, and then for *Does Your House Have Lions?* Sanchez builds polyvocality into the book's basic structure. Then Mullen's *Muse & Drudge* presents a palimpsestic, appropriation-based approach—perhaps a more post-humanist form of polyvocality. But again, what strikes me most is how you track various polyvocal projects fulfilling quite different intentions or functions, framed by the discrete historical circumstances in which each writer participates. So polyvocality remains consistent throughout African-American literature, yet demands nuanced accounts of how this concept gets embodied by any particular poet.

ES: That's exactly what I hope readers take from the book. That's my modulated approach to redefining black aesthetics. Again, if we consider how the BAM introduces black aesthetics, as a particular response to writing black subjectivity in a racist society, this response privileges particular types of politics. This response, coming immediately out of a Black Power context, draws heavily (and, to the extent possible, exclusively) on black culture producing art intended to change black people's way of seeing themselves in the world—both in terms of valuing their past and considering themselves as political agents in the present. That set of political goals I do not wish to set aside, but simply to place in its historical moment, so to open up other possibilities for a black aesthetics. These alternate approaches might seem equally political, though in different ways, or could take a depoliticized turn in a specific author's context. Their politics might become unrecognizable from our own particular vantage point, but if we focus on the time and place of each writer, we can begin to see her politics more clearly. And so to circle back to questions about polyvocality in Brooks, Sanchez, Mullen: my chapters on these poets do not seek to codify a specific set of strategies as an authentic black aesthetics, but to unearth each poet's approach to negotiating broader historical dynamics. Polyvocality means one thing when you work in the 1940s, hoping for attention from a literary establishment that treats black writing as inherently inferior. It means something else when you write, as Sonia Sanchez does in the late 20th century, speaking to an audience you'd helped create in the 1960s, though now rethinking the politics of that earlier moment, especially the gender and sexual politics embedded in various black nationalisms. Then polyvocality again means something new when Harryette Mullen deliberately constructs a book speaking to (at least) two divergent communities or audiences. Each poet mentioned above faced different circumstances, and their responses differ accordingly, so our use of critical terminology likewise should differ.

AF: Well, when you argue for increased individuation, as scholars, in our critical approach to African-American authors, do you see that as contradicting and/or as fulfilling the broader impulse behind categorizing authors according to race, gender, sexuality? Do you encounter frustration from critics who say we need a unified understanding of what it means to be African-American—to be a black writer? Does that tendency still circulate in the field?

ES: You've put your finger on one of this book's underlying motivations, one problem that inspired me to write this way. But here again, I need to historicize my response. The BAM ushers an African-American literary tradition into the academy. Sonia Sanchez and Amiri Baraka become some of the first people to teach black literary courses at the college level.

AF: With Larry Neal?

ES: Right. African-American literature becomes a recognized scholarly field about 40 years ago. Its founders have to assemble it, canonize it, map it out. It has to be fought for, then and at every moment. Scholars in the early years have no choice but to assert what makes these texts black, why we need to study them as a singular tradition—the same concerns that animated advocates for American literature (as opposed to British literature). American Studies scholars now confront similar questions, though without the same threat of American literature disappearing from view in the academy. So my book never means to dismiss productive work people did to constitute the field, but means to provide a counterbalance, so this swing of the pendulum, a very necessary swing, doesn't linger too long on the far side of that spectrum. Of course we could apply an analogous argument to studies of women's literature, of Jewish literature and so forth. Once we articulate that common historical backgrounds, common lived experiences shape these fields, then our job becomes to find further nuance, further differentiation. At some point we've got to permit ourselves to pose the opposite question: what if we consider these writers as individuals identified by our society as African-American? What if we decide to treat some texts less on the grounds of their engagement with common threads of a collective tradition, and more in terms of their rhetorical or formal coherence? How could we construct a critical tradition that doesn't exclude aberrant figures to save its own life? So here I offer a kind of push-back, but not a dismissive push-back, fully recognizing that sometimes the pendulum needs to swing toward commonalities.

AF: We do see explicit threats to Chicano Studies right now, in Arizona. The need for some sort of defensive posture remains perfectly clear. But also, in terms of urgent historical realities, we haven't really discussed ecopoetics, which your book's second half addresses. From your perspective as a scholar attuned both to the positive and negative legacy of the BAM, what advice do you have for ecopoetics? Let's say advocates for ecopoetics, like advocates for the BAM, made the case that pressing political conditions demand a honed activist agenda, rather than an introspective appeal to further inclusivity—how would you respond to that? And then, conversely, does considering the pointed vantage of present ecopoetics make you more forgiving, more understanding of the BAM's own legacy?

ES: You want to know whether I see analogies between ecopoetics and the BAM, as aesthetic movements articulated around or organized by political urgencies?

AF: We could turn to page 151 in your book if that helps, the sentence: "From this angle, these proponents of 'ecopoetics' are ironically reminiscent of those participants in the BAM who similarly advocated a particular, politicized, potentially transformative aesthetics as the grounds for inclusion in a category of poetry—in that case 'black poetry.'"

ES: Got it. That's actually the sentence that popped into my head.

You've pointed to this moment when I mention that the discourses organized around Jonathan Skinner's ecopoetics journal and Brenda Iijima's eco language reader remain exclusively interested in innovative writing. This provides an ironic counterpoint to how the BAM drew its aesthetic lines based on political ideology. Of course, ecopoetics foregrounds innovative writing because this can help to question a reductive nature/culture binary, a romanticization of nature embedded in the aptly-named Romantic tradition. I understand that and sympathize, as I sympathize with the BAM's intense focus on looking beyond a Eurocentric tradition and high modernism for models—on turning toward more politically empowering precedents. But I do think that ecopoetics could learn from the BAM's mistakes in this instance. One shudders to think of offering Jonathan Skinner advice on ecopoetics, since he's such an intelligent person and formidable thinker, but I would ask whether reserving the term "ecopoetics" for innovative writing (especially an exclusionary sense of experimental writing, one that marginalizes many people I consider in this book) really will help to reach the vast number of readers required to promote serious environmental change. Conversely, what happens when you use your own particular ideology not as a wedge, but as a bridge?

AF: Well along similar lines, it interests me that the phrase "double consciousness" never makes a real appearance in your book.

ES: Not so much.

AF: Though you clearly describe analogous binaries between avant-garde and black aesthetics, between experimental and activist agendas. We could consider that. Or I have another approach to this question, which focuses on your scholarly writing style. I love your generous use of dashes, colons, semicolons. Roland Barthes's praise for anacoluthon comes to mind: a sentence that starts one way, then pivots and becomes something entirely different. That happens a lot here. So we could discuss double consciousness in terms of a scholar/poet duality—how you see your own deft syntactical moves shaping this text's argument.

ES: Your first question deserves an answer, but your second question fascinates me, since nobody's framed my writing style the way you just did. I'm very conscious of writing sentences that try to hold the nuance in place. I live for dashes. You should have seen how many I had! I also get policed on my use of parentheses by most copy editors.

So I don't know if I would have said this spontaneously, but yes, I think my syntax becomes part of the argument. I hope to remain both readable and complex. You don't need a PhD to parse this book. It tries to address audiences outside the academy proper, but also to create sentences that almost can't be quoted out of context. They bear their context within them. I want to bring that complexity to these traditions: to studies of African-American poetry, of innovative poetry, of nature poetry and ecopoetics. One way of remaining responsible to complexity in the larger sense is to stay responsible at the smallest level.

### INTERVIEW WITH TYRONE WILLIAMS
Recorded on August 21, 2012
This interview focuses on Williams' book *Howell* (Atelos).

ANDY FITCH: Normally I'd start with more general questions, but I last interviewed Evie Shockley, and we discussed the complicated legacy of Black Arts Movement poetics—how the BAM seems quite generative yet also quite constrictive in its impact upon subsequent writers. And I remember, in the past, you citing the BAM's personal importance. As a poet suspicious of stable identity formations, of instrumental language, your career could seem antithetical to what the BAM advocates. But have you found space for your work under the BAM umbrella, and can you describe this space? Can you trace a perhaps convoluted trajectory in which the BAM's liberatory struggles help to produce your own liberatory aesthetic practice?

TYRONE WILLIAMS: Absolutely. I began taking myself seriously as a poet during high school, the early '70s, in the middle of the BAM (depending how you cite the movement's historical trajectory). Again, this is high school, so I thought of myself primarily as writing love poetry, occasionally some political poetry. I remember trying to address what seemed an absence in both fields. I admired what I saw from the BAM, to the extent that I knew about it, but conceived of myself as trying to complete this other project, defined by traditional love poetry. Then as I went to college and beyond, reading and thinking more about the BAM, I began to sense its contradictions, its gaps, how I could contribute in my own way. I didn't have to restrict myself to one tiny sector of romantic poetry, based on the faulty premise that the BAM already took care of all social and political and economic issues. Some of these same problems needed to be addressed from a different angle. And I still see myself as operating (though you're right that much of my work could seem antithetical to certain reductive formations around identity politics and so forth), as following in the wake of the BAM and with the BAM's spirit—trying to create new spaces for African-American culture and people, not just in terms of a popularized embrace of African-American music or whatever, but every aspect of what it means to be black in this country.

AF: When you mention the spirit of the BAM, and say you detected absences within what the BAM produced, it sounds as though you also sensed an invitation to engage and address those absences, rather than an imperative to deny them.

TW: Well I never felt directly encouraged nor excluded, because I wasn't involved. I was so out of the loop. I read much but didn't know anyone. Certainly my most supportive teachers did not recommend that I follow the BAM's example. Nonetheless, I felt included. Though never personally addressed, I sensed that this movement spoke to me.

AF: Perhaps the BAM's emphasis upon community engagement, its thematizations of place and urban space, can lead us into *Howell*. If we take *Howell* literally as a place, a distressed community, do you see yourself somehow speaking of/for/to/with that community? Alternately, we could explore how you here have abstracted the BAM's modes of public address.

TW: In terms of that particular community, and also one of *Howell*'s central figures, Timothy McVeigh, I tried to enter, to a certain degree, what you could call a sympathetic space. I didn't want to write from some point of pure critique, pure abjection, whatever those might mean in terms of slamming McVeigh or adopting a supportive point of view. Rather, I wished to enter a sympathetic relationship with broader events that lead to the Oklahoma City bombing. So this book begins, in part, by describing relationships between the colonists and their surroundings, their environments—in terms of Native Americans already present, but also in terms of immediate flora and fauna (here the book's first part pays homage to Susan Howe's work). Though of course it remains impossible really to enter another historical period, or another person's consciousness, so points for critique do soon arise.

AF: Along those lines, your endnotes, like many endnotes from the poetic past, could be said to obscure more than they reveal. The first note opens by telling us that three online histories of a small Michigan city inspired *Howell*. This doesn't explain why you or anyone else ever would read those histories. The subsequent sentence asserts that media reports mistakenly claimed Timothy McVeigh came from Howell. Here parallels start to appear between the faulty logic of our political discourse and of McVeigh's own quixotic project. At the same time, McVeigh's inscrutability seems to stand in for your own, or for your language's, or for all language's inscrutability.

TW: You definitely sound on the right track there. I understood why Atelos wanted to include these notes. But I didn't go into more detail because I preferred to foreground questions of mistakes, questions of error, of misreading or inscrutability—both in relation to language and to history. It turns out that Decker, not Howell, is where Terry Nichols, not McVeigh, came from. Still as you said, these mistakes show how misreadings actually constitute our sense of history, yet remain references to real events which occurred. That provides the motive for including such figures but also explains, from my point of view, the necessity of trying to enter a sympathetic relationship, rather than presenting a cold critique. We all…I'm not immune to misreadings or misinterpretations or inscrutable tendencies. So when people call this book quite inscrutable I say, that's the point.

AF: Though a couple preceding books stand out as clear points of reference. Paterson seeks to embody both a gritty, post-industrial city and its anthropomorphized poetic-subject. Ginsberg's Howl of course resonates, along with Whitman's line "what howls restrained by decorum." And here we could draw some contrasts as well, between, let's say, the active embodiment that Paterson or Ginsberg's incantatory delivery of *Howl* presents, and the disembodied howls your book produces. I'm thinking of McVeigh's displaced explosive howl, of Malachi Ritscher's implosive suicidal howl. Or this may veer off topic, but given the historical span in which you developed this book, I couldn't help re-hearing Howard Dean's so-called "howl" following the 2004 Iowa primary—that supposed end to progressive dreams. Do any number of disembodied or multi-bodied howls play out here?

TW: Yes. For example, in one section, each of five poems starts with the word "how." One refers to the aftermath of the Six-Day War. One line presents all those symbols from a computer keyboard that traditionally indicate swearing or cursing. But I also took this, as you say, to stand in for a silent howl. Malachi serves as something of an alter ego to McVeigh, since rather than kill other people, he chose to kill himself. His howl gets counterposed to McVeigh's.

AF: Just as you refer to contrapuntal howls—I brought home a puppy two days ago, and suddenly a howl seems a form of call-and-response, rather than an expression of solitary grievance. Howls I guess should be answered.

TW: That sounds like American history to me, in terms of the catastrophes that punctuate our history. One howl produces or elicits another, and so on and so on.

AF: Here could you describe a bit *Howell*'s structure, in whatever way you see fit? Do you conceive of it as primarily organized around the book-length concept, the section, the poem, the line, the word, syllable, letter? And what role does the integral/arbitrary numerical scaffolding (like "Part 1," "Part 1+") play in binding together or dispersing various scales of meaning?

TW: When I began to think about *Howell* as a book, I wondered how to organize the various ideas I had. I didn't write these poems sequentially. Separate parts arrived at different points. So I thought in terms of assemblage, then came across 19th-century etchings by William Hogarth, in particular his series sometimes called *The Descent of Man*. Hogarth produced these parables in woodblock form that take you from one scene to another, illustrating moral lessons. One four-part sequence concerns a young boy who starts out abusing animals, then kills a horse, then winds up in the third frame killing a woman. He gets arrested, and in the fourth frame undergoes vivisection—live autopsy. Looking at Hogarth I thought, this is it, this is how I'll organize the book. So my book's first half, if you will, raises problems related to the treatment of animals (horses specifically) and the abuse of women. The last section, "Xenopsy," celebrates Malachi, and this celebration allows for the vivisection of McVeigh. "Xenopsy" plays on "autopsy" and so forth. Of course, amid the book's four basic sections, I include many smaller frames. You mentioned the "Part 1" and "Part 1+" division, which derives from the fact that the second online history I found for Howell actually attempts to refute the first. So questions of where Part 1 ends, where Part 2 begins, get confounded.

AF: I guess Paterson seems quite empirical by comparison, in terms of assembling scientific data. But for *Howell* I think of Jewish scholarship's midrash tradition, of endless commentary, unceasing argumentation.

TW: That writing has fascinated me for a long time, which may explain why I've just started teaching (last night, to the horror of some students) Mark Z. Danielewski's *House of Leaves*—this 670-page tome containing every postmodern quirk you can imagine, all organized around a guy who receives a manuscript from his friend, which someone who died in this friend's house wrote. This manuscript presents the story of a movie that never got made, so the narrative keeps getting framed and framed, with footnotes to the footnotes. Do you remember *Pale Fire* by Nabokov?

AF: Sure.

TW: The students didn't know that last night. And I pointed out how we think of all this as quite postmodern, yet it also revives the 18th/19th-century frame novel, where a character finds a manuscript, say in Poe—or how *Wuthering Heights* gets told in flashback, partly in letters.

AF: In terms of such dynamics between architectural frames and mimetic scenes, *Howell*'s "Biographical Sketches" come to mind. Do you conceive of these as having representational ends? If so, what gets represented? An actual, embodied historical figure? Something closer to the abstracted/erroneous historical and mnemonic processes you've mentioned? Or if we look at "Two Days in Chicago," this poem seems to track a continuity in the Chicago Sun Times' canned, tickertape idiom—both before and after Malachi Ritscher's November 3 suicide. This hints at interesting affinities between the indexical and the elegiac. Does the piece's depersonalized-seeming procedure offer a distinct means of evoking or imagining Malachi's lived historical presence?

TW: That particular piece does get counterposed to the "Biographical Sketches." The sketches do provide, albeit in lineated form, snapshots of particular historical figures. But with "Two Days in Chicago" I wanted to say, alright, here's someone largely insignificant according to the media record. His dramatic act of committing suicide just provides another statistic, another plain fact rolling across the tickertape as you watch television. The event only acquires significance in retrospect. So I mixed up this two-day set of divergent stories, with passing reference to a man who immolates himself on the Kennedy Expressway. I didn't want to ignore the sense of desperation behind Malachi's act, which had to seem futile except perhaps to people who knew him. It lacked the kind of impact…I can't remember the mother's name who travelled around a few years ago protesting the Iraq war.

AF: I can't remember either, though of course I knew it quite well then.

TW: Exactly. She had her fifteen minutes. But Malachi Ritscher emerges as just a statistic counterposed to the "great men of history"—an ordinary, unknown man, who commits what he sees as a heroic gesture, protesting the Iraq War's injustice. Of course McVeigh himself had served in the first Gulf War, which provides another connection, both in terms of the futility of fighting that first war, and in protesting the second.

AF: I love how your work often adopts procedural constraints, but for pieces that project something like the elliptical, ephemeral tonalities of the lyric, rather than the monumental scope and glacial pace associated with much contemporary conceptual writing. You seem to prefer these short units, not the tomes that you have praised. "Walk, Stop, Look and Walk (Live)" stands out for prompting such questions about the fleeting concept's place amid the disparate catalog. Could you follow up on the many procedural "hows" that comprise this apparently gray, uniform, monolithic "Howell"?

TW: I didn't want to foreground one procedure, one method. I hoped to draw from as many poetic forms as I could. To back up a bit more generally: I saw Language writing as an attempt not to erase what had come before, but (again, as with my own relationship to the BAM) to complement that—to say, here's what's missing, here's what we haven't yet done, here's one part of the larger picture. This suggests that narrative and the lyric still can possess a certain validity, even when co-opted by the market or some ideological or institutional apparatus, such as the academy, the workshops, the prizes and so forth.

To me, *Howell*'s narrative and lyric pieces echo, even as they depart from, Walter Benjamin's fragments or feiulletons, like little particles that cohere in nuclear physics, which only exist for a nanosecond. To me this reflects how we experience life, experience history, through fleeting moments of clarity. I don't think we could exist as human beings without those moments, however quickly they collapse. That helps to explain why my procedural poems tend to cohere around specific (ordinary) people. Then other poems address more celebrated figures, such as Joe Strummer from The Clash, because we do have bodies that get swept up in broader historical currents, over which we have little control.

AF: Several Joe Strummer references appeared in the 60 books I read this spring. So his death had its impact.

TW: It did on me. I loved the band, but especially what he did after The Clash, which embodied the boldest hopes for this whole era of music—that you don't just fade and play Las Vegas, you keep pushing forward.

AF: Back to the ephemeral, to capturing the nanosecond, could we talk about your Aunt Sally poems? Some seem to respatialize source texts—presenting structures halfway between comics and sentence diagrams, both reifying and reconfiguring cognitive sense as it passes from one medium to another.

TW: The Aunt Sally pieces return us to Hogarth's third frame, to that woman who gets killed. I had came across this Aunt Sally dream book, a book used by people playing the numbers. I don't know if your readers will know what that means.

AF: They should.

TW: So I began researching the phrase "Aunt Sally," which I hadn't realized once served as a nickname for the British game skittles. Skittles anticipates bowling, billiards, horseshoes. You set up a wooden doll called an Aunt Sally, with a pipe, and try to knock the pipe from her mouth. People also called this game quoits, which I use in the book. But that term "Aunt Sally" seemed to suggest some racist detail from the British past, though apparently scholars do not consider this a racist toy or game. One just happened to throw things at this Aunt Jemima-type figure. So here I decided to use Aunt Sally within the context of game theory, which circulates throughout the book—to treat this character as completely innocent in terms of racist overtones. Nonetheless, in terms of race, to say nothing of gender overtones…you don't see a man standing there with a pipe in his mouth.

AF: A white middle-class British guy.

TW: Right.

AF: And then what function does Aunt Sally serve in U.S. slave narratives?

TW: It provides a supposedly kinder, gentler term for describing the nanny figure. Dream books then appropriate this image, since the grandmother stands for the wisest member of the house—however problematic that might seem in terms of stereotypes and so forth.

AF: Again those translational, transnational, transformational trajectories for Aunt Sally somehow parallel the status of your English pit ponies. A book about Howell produces associations with Detroit and the auto industry and forms of labor that make themselves obsolete. Here could we talk more generally about processes of doubling that occur throughout the book—how these might relate to questions of double consciousness, of an experimental poet addressing broader social concerns?

TW: *Howell*'s pit pony part comes through more research. I went to find out about these horses used in the mines, obviously thinking, as you said, about labor's economic value in present-day Detroit. But also, as problems of violence and violent suppression arise, these relate not only to labor struggles, but back to the BAM. When one horse accuses another of betraying the horse community, I had in mind this *Invisible Man* passage, where the protagonist mistakenly enters a union meeting and they start calling him a fink. He must be a fink because he's associated with finkism and so forth. This ridiculous send-up of politicized paranoia unfortunately anticipates certain aspects of BAM. But the pit ponies don't just present an allegory for human labor. They represent animal labor, too. That was real experience. People more versed in ecopoetics, such as Brenda Iijima, can address this better than I can, but I wanted to present these oppressed animals not just as a metaphor for human suffering, but as a sentient part of our lives, of history.

## INTERVIEW WITH ROD SMITH AND COLE SWENSEN
Recorded on August 27, 2012
This interview focuses on Smith and Swensen's translation of Emmanuel Hocquard's *The Invention of Glass* (Canarium).

ANDY FITCH: I'll ask about Hocquard's translation workshops from the '80s and '90s. But could we start with the curatorial implications of this particular translation project? Why this Hocquard text? As publishers of La Presse (devoted to translations from the French) and Edge Books (with its post-Language, Flarf, experimental inflections), do you see *The Invention of Glass* making a pointed intervention into English-language poetry?

ROD SMITH: I don't see it necessarily as an intervention. I do see *The Invention of Glass* as important within Hocquard's body of work. He's collected glass for a long time, and this particular approach, this serial poem with a set number of lines and pieces, seems especially ambitious. In parts it resembles Language poetry, and certainly fits within the serial-poem aesthetic of many New Americans. It's Spicerian though also feels European.

COLE SWENSEN: Hocquard often works out a formal problem, yet does so informally. He deploys a set form but affirms the inability to contain language in any such form. This book provides a pointed example, foregrounding issues of transparency, transparency in language and transparency in glass. Still Hocquard never works metaphorically. He's written quite a bit about refusing figurative language, and about the imperative of orality. So glass never becomes a strict metaphor. The word "glass" demands its own reality separate from that of any actual glass in the outside world to which it may refer. But back to your original question: perhaps in a sense it does intervene into American poetry. Hocquard himself has made this point many times—that translations intervene in the target language, inflecting it with something unavailable within its own system. This book definitely offers that.

AF: Rod said Hocquard has collected glass a long time. Did you mean that literally? Or did you mean he gradually collected this book, these forms?

CS: He does collect Depression glass, particularly the green Depression glass.

RS: Peter Gizzi has great stories of going glass hunting with Hocquard when he'd visit the States. But in terms of Cole's comments about literality and transparency: Wittgensteinian questions arise, such as can language point? What does it point at?

AF: So does Depression glass filter even as you see through it? Does it cast the world in a particular hue?

CS: That sounds too interpretive for Hocquard. "Glass" is "glass," period. Much of his work insists on that materiality, which language ends up disrupting by creating some symbolic structure you can't fully abandon. Hocquard plays with this tension. He more or less coined the term "negative modernity," further pursuing the modernist project, which by this stage involves removing figurative layers, trimming down language, insisting upon a horizontal axis and its flat absolute.

RS: I often think of Clark Coolidge's *The Crystal Text* in relation to this manuscript—that kind of material meditation.

AF: I'd wanted to ask specifically about that Coolidge book. But first, can you describe the group-translation seminars Hocquard ran in the '80s and '90s: how these worked, their methodological rationale, their legacy? Does your own collaborative process, for instance, interrupt any reductive analogic model—not just presenting an English equivalent for the purported French content, but further complicating any gesture towards unmediated authorial transparency?

CS: We both took part in Hocquard's seminars. These started in the mid- to late-'80s, and included poets working in many different languages. Emmanuel considered it important that poetry be translated by poets, not scholars or critics, and so he invited some 15 to 20 poets to participate in his seminars. As each seminar focused on two poets, participants would split into groups arranged around two big tables, one for each translated poet. These groups felt quite pragmatic, designed to get language moving, to put it out "on the table" as an object of discussion, negotiation and argumentation. One person would suggest how to translate a line. Someone else would respond, how about this? And the group as a whole would work through an entire draft within a few days. Then, after the seminar ended, one person would take charge of the text to make it cohesive and ready for publication, which followed in a year or so.

AF: This took place at an apartment? Or with an institutional affiliation?

CS: It happened in a marvelous 13th-century abbey called Royaumont.

RS: The building has a terrific history. Its once large church got disassembled during the revolution, to construct new houses. You still can see where that church stood. But they left the abbey. There's documentary footage of Chomsky and Foucault teaching in the same library where Emmanuel and company produced translations.

CS: It was part of a network of abbeys throughout France. Each of the perhaps 10 abbeys covered two arts. Royaumont emphasized classical music (particularly voice) and translation. Another in Normandy, for instance, did dance and theatre. The Ministry of Culture fully supported them. I don't know to what degree that network still exists. The Royaumont translation center was really the masterwork of Rémy Hourcade, who extended it to several other countries—mostly in Europe. Emmanuel worked with him intensively on French-American exchange, focusing on his own area of expertise, particularly in relation to the legacy of Objectivism.

RS: Emmanuel also has been involved in several similar seminars in Marseilles.

AF: Several books I've read for this project offer some sort of self-consciously constructivist translation process. Brandon Brown's *Flowering Mall*, for example, thematizes, theatricalizes, theorizes translation itself—departing from any pretense of a neutral, objective rendering. So I'm still curious about the collaborative nature of Hocquard's translation seminars, and of your own working relationship, how these might relate to concerns of negative modernity, of interrupting the analogical.

RS: Well, we've actually tried to translate what Emmanuel said.

CS: Or we could use the term "reenactment." I think our translation assumes no direct verbal equivalence. Here Emmanuel's thoughts and writings on the blank spot, or blind spot, come to mind—which suggest that a translation points toward an otherwise unthinkable spot in the translated language (or literature). He often will say, of American poetry translated into French, for instance, that no French person could have written this. That kind of uncanny off-ness, that enacted incongruency, foregrounds a refusal of the analogic, and an assertion of the sovereignty of every language act (and could, in turn, be claimed to be rooted in a negative modernity, a modernity of skepticism, arguing against any notion of progress). But it also could suggest a positive assertion (an emphatic insistence on presence as absolute). Though Emmanuel himself remains a highly skeptical person, I think his sense of poetry's power, through its radical deformations of language, reaches a state of optimism at times.

RS: Emmanuel, we should note, dislikes facing-page translation. He wants the translated poem to stand on its own. Cole and I gave a reading from *The Invention of Glass* when Emmanuel came to the States in 2008, and he seemed pleased. I think he said, this moves correctly.

AF: Something in the book's idiom suggests a step beyond literality, beyond the straightforward translation of an opaque French text.

CS: The translation becomes its own absolute, not pointing to the absent French book, but instead offering, as Emmanuel would say, a contribution to American letters.

AF: So while working through this multi-part project, did you note characteristic syntactical, rhetorical, sonic, referential gestures undergirding Hocquard's fluid constructions of dubious sense? What did his texts allow you to try in English?

RS: Right, we haven't really answered how we went about this. We met at a coffee shop with the idea of completing at least one section from "Poem." I don't know if we ever finished more than one on a single occasion.

CS: I don't think so.

RS: We met more than 20 times. Certain types of repetition taught us what we wanted as we went along. Cole did most of the work on the prose sections. Things had come up in my life so I couldn't be as involved, but we stayed in contact and kept looking at the poem. It was great to share a project over time in that way—not simply the examination, but the re-examination.

CS: Rod's description of learning how certain passages worked, often in relation to others, confirms something that seems true of most translations—that the process does not proceed linearly, but always loops back, creating a figure-eight of progress. *The Invention of Glass* offers multiple articulations, not just a chain, but also a structure of reflecting facets that complicate each other.

AF: Cole had mentioned early on Hocquard's combination of procedural elements and an informal idiom, an emphasis upon form amid an air of the informal.

CS: For instance, as Rod suggested, each part of the long poem contains the same number of lines, positioned the same way. Each begins with italicized words. But these formal principles also seem arbitrary. No apparent reason emerges for why first words get italicized. Then a kind of looseness unfolds. Hocquard is not counting syllables. He doesn't emphasize sound principles.

RS: We could use the term "gestural," which bounces back and forth between French and American poetry. You think of Reverdy, you think of O'Hara, et cetera—here amid this mixture of abstract, reflective (talking about glass) considerations, combined with, not the mundane, exactly, but the everyday.

CS: This book's basic form recalls the Möbius strip. It doesn't really begin anywhere. The play with footnotes reinforces that. We get sent backwards and forwards amid these different registers: the register of quotation, the register of footnote, the register of sectioned poems. Which discourse has primacy? Which came first? Of course you can't say.

AF: Here could we return to the various valences glass takes on—specifically amid the intersection of French/English literary traditions? Of course Derrida's *Glas* comes to mind, as does Paul Auster's *City of Glass*, which Hocquard translates. Rod mentioned Clark Coolidge's *Crystal Text*. I thought of Francis Ponge's object-specific works, such as *Soap*, and from that Stein's "Tender Buttons"—where glass figures prominently. Did you feel the need to foreground these fluid valences or connotations or cross-cultural reference points?

RS: Emmanuel certainly knows the texts you've mentioned, but he doesn't necessarily build those into his work. Ponge might inform this choice of projects. Auster I believe translated some of his poems.

I would just emphasize that he's deeply embedded in both traditions.

CS: I'm thinking, too, that the French word for glass, "verre," goes in such different directions than the English "glass." And Emmanuel works a lot with association and allusion. The French word "verre" is famous for having more meanings than any other phoneme in the language. Few words could seem more overdetermined, and Emmanuel plays with this potential for overdetermination, on the one hand, and the distinctions that writing can make that speech cannot, on the other. Here we return to Derrida's suggestion that every word contains within it many other words, so that you never can reach the bottom of any single word. I haven't talked to Emmanuel about these particular pressures put on language, but I've always assumed they must be quite important to him. And of course, the phoneme "vers" evokes the poetic line. Hocquard also explores all the material associations glass has to transparency, fragility, danger, et cetera.

AF: Then in "Poem's" Section 15 we encounter this sentence: "Once / detail gets distracted, / landscape becomes / a stabilized event / entirely fluid, / since expression comes / from the surface." That got me thinking of Stein on landscape, on how glass embodies both fluidity and stasis—not as separate, autonomous states but as parts of a process-oriented continuum.

CS: Stein's "Tender Buttons" pushes language toward unthinkability, or a prethinkability. A statement, once begun, gets distracted. The shifting landscape becomes a stabilized event—now phrased as an authoritative, declarative statement. "Tender Buttons" celebrates this process of creating the sense even while the statement gets made. No pre-established sense exists. Hocquard picks up on this productive process of Stein's, but he's less interested in the absurdism. He tries to find precisely that point where language creates rather than echoes.

RS: When you come across "Once detail gets distracted," it's almost an end stop. It has no real referent. It causes meaning.

CS: Exactly. It doesn't point to anything. And the word "event" keeps appearing. Hocquard's carefully chosen phrases lead us back to "event." This work seems all an event on the page. The word "surface" reinforces that, since the action here stays on the surface. What happens happens in the language, and nowhere else.

*Interview with Rod Smith and Cole Swensen*

AF: The book's surface-oriented nature gets foregrounded further by its "Story" and "Notes" sections. Annotations placed at this book's end don't link to any specific points in the text. Or at least we didn't know they did. Or some annotations seem to appear out of sequence.

RS: Again I think of Spicer, in terms of something like Josh Ware's *Homage to Homage to Homage to Creeley*, a book that offers ongoing commentary on itself, on a poem by myself, and on Spicer—who of course commented on Creeley.

CS: Emmanuel relies also on fragmentation. I rode down to Bordeaux once and spent the afternoon with him. I'd point to a certain phrase and say, oh, what an interesting blah blah blah. And he then would tell a long story for which that initial phrase served simply as the starting point. But taken out of context and put in a poem, this phrase would achieve a different type of materiality, deprived of any layered resonance. Though sometimes he'll choose to flush this out. So, for instance, on page 36, you find: "There is means something / rather than nothing: the bison's / trail still visible / beneath Broadway. Here is / the sea." Whether or not realistic, this "bison's trail" beneath Broadway offers a concrete particularity. We can picture it. Though then, in the "Story" section, we read: "P. 36. 'Roads in the United States often follow old Indian paths, but this is also true of certain city streets. Broadway is the best known example.'[5]" So two things happen here. First, we can anchor this fragment in U.S. history and span time with it. All of a sudden the "Story" sequence seems to insist on a certain historical sweep. But through the additional reference to a footnote, we also span the temporality of this "Story" experience. Subsequently, reaching footnote 5 in the "Notes" section adds an unexpected, completely different articulation. Footnote 5 cites a Gilles Tiberghien text. Gilles Tiberghien is a French philosopher and critic who often writes about land art. Here we've gone from France to America then back to France. This cross-referenced articulation doesn't seem transcultural, so much as it annihilates cultural boundaries and cuts the pie quite differently.

RS: *The Waste Land* of course has had a huge impact across many traditions. Hocquard's final section takes this someplace else, suggesting the possibility for footnotes on footnotes on footnotes—grounding the poem in history, then ungrounding it, then regrounding it over and over.

AF: Similarly, I wondered how Hocquard's translations of North American poets had shaped his idiom. I'd sense a familiar phrase, or diction, passing back into English first through Hocquard's French, then through your translation.

RS: I know Emmanuel had a sustained poetic conversation with Michael Palmer. Still, we didn't say, oh, this line should sound like Palmer, or something. At times I remember wanting the translation to sound like English versions of Wittgenstein. Emmanuel seemed to have thought of that, or even consciously pulled from him, or slightly misquoted him.

CS: Yes, exactly, Wittgenstein and Deleuze. He'll want that echo or unannounced voice in there.

AF: How about, from Section 6, the part: "If we suppose / that the world exists / as more than / a picture book, then the subject / has no reason / to be and so the world / is now no more / than a habit." Of course we hear Wittgenstein, but this sounds like an argument one could find in North American Language poetics, yet it also seems structurally different in ways I have trouble delineating.

RS: That could come from a Carla Harryman text.

AF: Right. Or I remember an early Steve McCaffery essay on language's false transparency, and how we've got to see this referential window pane itself, rather than look through it for some representation beyond. I know it's problematic to extract lines from this book, or any other, then treat them as straightforward statements of poetic principles, but could you characterize just a bit more how Hocquard's lines both do resemble, and do depart from, or differ from, models familiar from Language poetry?

CS: Hocquard seems much more engaged with specific philosophic questions. With that passage from Section 6, I certainly hear Wittgenstein. Also, even more than Language writers, I think Hocquard directly engages contemporary French thinkers, and aims toward a fusion of philosophy and poetry.

RS: I hadn't thought about it until this conversation, but the film *Deleuze from A to Z* contains a series of interviews organized as an abecedarium. And at one point Deleuze presents Wittgenstein as the enemy of philosophy, an influence to be guarded against. That moment reveals an interesting tension. I don't know that Emmanuel was aware of Deleuze's distrust of Wittgenstein—which certainly didn't circulate much in public. Deleuze had asked that these interviews not get released until after his death, but if you consider Deleuze's expansive and even optimistic philosophy, versus Wittgenstein's skepticism regarding possibilities of and for description, then the tales of Wittgenstein talking a gifted student into becoming a motorcycle repairman rather than a philosopher…

cs: Wow, I want to watch that interview. Though perhaps to be called the enemy of philosophy isn't such a negative thing.

AF: And I appreciated Rod's reference to Carla Harryman, because I'll sense here something like a critique of the lyric subject, yet without a departure from the idiomatic. The idiomatic somehow says it all, both in Carla's work and your Hocquard translation.

RS: Like Carla's poetics, this book appears to offer a constructivist approach, quite consciously not a deconstructionist one. Though the inclusion of Deleuze complicates this.

cs: Deleuze puts the emphasis on language as a constantly transient, community-based construct, emptying specificity from subjectivity, which simply passes on: there's a glass-like fluidity.

## INTERVIEW WITH ANDREW FELD
Recorded on June 19, 2012; revisited on August 29, 2012
This interview focuses on Feld's book *Raptor* (U. Chicago Press)

ANDY FITCH: Just to clarify, in falconry, does the falconer first spot the prey, then slip (if I've used that verb correctly) the falcon? Do their desires stay that close?

ANDREW FELD: The art of falconry consists in making the bird work with you. If you see the game before the bird does, then you signal to it, so that it follows your signal in pursuit of the game. Though they have such better sight than we do, and much faster reactions. Often you don't spot any game until you hear the jingling of bells, with your bird in full dive. With rabbits, you can't hear the rabbit until they've caught it. But so first you train the bird to go where you want it to go, perch where you want it to perch. You stand, say, on the far side of a brush pile and beat the brush and anything in it runs away from you and toward the bird and then the bird dives down and grabs it.

AF: I'll hope to return to some of these topics, and how they relate both to the discourses of ecopoetics and disabilities studies—how our contact with nature never presents an unmediated, isolated, self-reliant experience, but a collective, codependent enterprise (here with the bird seeing for us, knowing what we seek).

AFe: Yes, we could consider falconry an artificial art. You train the bird to go against its instincts—which otherwise compel it to avoid humankind and hunt on its own. Raptors are not social species. You have to work hard with them to change this. Here ecopoetics does help in its departure from Romanticism, and from a religious evaluation of nature. We might feel estranged from nature, but also remain a part of it, even as we threaten its existence. Our impact on the planet has become so complete that, as Jameson says, when the work of post-modernism has finished there will be no more wilderness. In fact that moment seems to have arrived a long time ago. So falconry provides a metaphor for our present, as we wholly control this species threatened by us.

AF: Still as I read *Raptor*, I kept thinking falcons come up, or should come up, in Sappho. Later I remembered Yeats' *Second Coming*. Does this brief, imaginary lineage provide some sense of the expansive parameters within which you apply metaphors of falconry? From Sappho (again, perhaps a false lead), I would take an intimate and/or triangulated erotic lyric. From Yeats, esoteric visions of the apocalypse. Between such polarities of scale, *Raptor* presents metaphors of falconry as birth, parenthood, interpersonal struggle, poetic production, as science, as emblem of Renaissance rationality and restraint, as subjugation to desire or to death. You reposition this idiom quite dexterously, however archaic its terms might seem. Had you sensed such varied resonance before visiting the Cascade Raptor Center in Oregon?

AFe: I've always loved falcons. I've had a lifelong fascination with them. So when the opportunity to work at the Cascade Raptor

Center appeared (because I lived in Oregon and was unemployed and the place needed volunteers), I jumped. And it became a full education. You do a lot of veterinary care, since only injured birds arrive. You learn about our disastrous impact on each distinct species—which ones have managed to adapt to humans and which keep getting further endangered. I don't know of any Sappho reference. I know Homer in the *Iliad* describes a hawk, I think in relation to Achilles pouncing on his prey. After that, the Holy Roman Emperor Frederick II of Hohenstaufen wrote this book *The Art of Falconry*, which had a huge impact on me. It's really the first work of taxonomy (and of observed, replicable science) in Western literature. Frederick worked with Arab and Persian falconers, basing all his observations on phenomena that one could replicate. He also patronized the arts, and his court in Sicily invented the sonnet. So the arts of falconry and of the sonnet overlap from the start with certain scientific methods. Then following the dissemination of Frederick's book, falconry became a noble pastime, practiced by some English poets. Wyatt practiced falconry. A long tradition of falconry poems and metaphors exists. Shakespeare adopts this, of course. *The Taming of the Shrew* contains a long metaphorical passage, and other references occur throughout his work. Later, during various stages of English poetry, further treatments of the sport become a prism through which to view political change. By the 19th century, amid attempts to revive (say by starting the Boy Scouts) notions of manliness that remained so important to colonialism, a resurgence in falconry and falconry poems begins. Depictions of English boys out with their birds get used for this purpose. Robinson Jeffers subsequently writes "Hurt Hawks" and various pieces in which the bird becomes something better than us. So this bird, both as living being and as poetic metaphor, shifts its significance throughout history in all these ways I found fascinating. Still, Yeats' apocalyptic scene kind of bothers me. Most poets writing about falcons really know falcons. Yeats does not. They don't actually hear you. They see you and hear whistles. If the falcon leaves you, that's because you haven't done a good job. Though Yeats' poem blames the bird for something. This all may sound pedantic, but I love science too intensely to ignore such details. And concrete knowledge, which I hope *Raptor* provides, changes the way you see these birds and yourself and your relationship to them. Yet the book also positions so-called common sense as an enemy of actual knowledge. The more you learn about the birds, the more you notice common misperceptions.

AF: Frederick II comes across as part Mengele, part Empress Wu (who chopped off her female rival's limbs then drowned her in a vat of wine), part Chomsky-ite, part proto-scientist, part proto-Wallace Stevens seeing things "'as they are.'" Your treatment of Frederick offers yet another example in which the elasticity of metaphor itself seems to resemble a poetic bating-on-the-glove—a consistent straining to break free and hunt down new meanings, then return to settle into overall, book-length coherence. Could we characterize the rhythms of scholarship, of knowledge acquisition, as falcon-like?

AFe: Again, the more you know, the more you realize your preceding (and ongoing) ignorance. I first worked in the Cascade Raptor Center taking care of birds, but only when I became a falconer did I become more aware of how their minds operate, the distinctiveness of their personalities, the characteristic traits both of each individual and each species. And my activity as a falconer changed how I experience the world, how I see the world. Driving by a field does not convey the sensation of hunting in that field. There is a line in Field Guide where Hass observes the fish and discusses the dangers of romanticizing this taking of another's life, and that intensity only increases when you hunt and have to stay aware of so many interrelated phenomena. Still of course, on a personal level, I hate guns. I can't stand guns. But I love hunting. Falconry satisfies this urge. I know many vegetarian and even a vegan falconer. But back to your question: I remain just as attracted to the fact that falconry has shaped so much of our vocabulary. All of these strange yet common words, like "gorge" and "boozer" (or obscure terms such as "bowse," which means for a bird to drink a lot of water), redirect my interests to the linguistic sphere—though always with a sense of purpose. A raptor is not a pet. You don't keep one in your yard because it looks nice. You train one in order to hunt, which forces you into an unknown world, from which you must gain new types of knowledge. Again, this proactive exploration of new perspectives seems analogous to various modes of poetic thinking.

AF: When you describe the psychological possession that takes place, the focus brought by hunting with falcons, for some reason I picture the strapping on of the glove as this transformative experience. It seems theatrical or cinematic. Then as you discuss (both here and in the book) your hatred of guns, I can't help recalling Emily Dickinson's poem "My Life had stood—A Loaded Gun—," here as an apparent analogy to falconry. Her "Master Letters," with their oscillating imperative to master and be mastered, also come to mind.

AFe: I'll have to think about that. I no longer can separate Dickinson's poem from Susan Howe's response in *My Emily Dickinson*, which emphasizes all its gender-shifting. But I would say the danger of falconry, especially for someone who starts out, as most people do, just absolutely smitten with these creatures, is that you view them through a kind of awe. You capture a bird. You put the jesses on it. You position it on your hand, holding it by the leashes. You can't believe that you possess this thing. But then you have to work with them—teach them, train them over aggravating stretches. You have to overcome that awe, that sense of their majestic difference, in order to see them as they are. This demands a vast amount of behavioral science and knowledge of how raptor brains differ from ours (for instance, you can't force a raptor to act through threat of punishment: that makes them fly away). And we do have a lineage, from Horace to the Eclogues, imparting related fields of knowledge—all of which shaped my language and the forms I wanted to pursue. In English poetry we have Ben Jonson and that tradition (including Wyatt of course) valuing submerged meanings. That became quite important to how I approached this subject. Because when you place the raptor in a more straightforward lyric context, it quickly becomes a metaphor for the sacred or the Romantic. I wanted to avoid that trap. Then whereas Dickinson's poem contains a gun and a hunter and this sense of waiting to be carried off and put to use, *Raptor* never claims to speak for the falcon, or from the falcon's point of view. A great deal of human subjectivity circumscribes our dealings with them, even as it brings us closer to the ways their brains function. Flat-brained animals process images and information quite differently than we do. This presents a big wall. The whole pathetic fallacy of entering bird consciousness became a threshold I hoped never to cross.

AF: Well, as you describe these complicated relational negotiations that take place between falconer and falcon, my mind returns to the model of the epic, in which mastery becomes crucial—mastery of countless idiolects, countless different vocabularies and paradigms. Of course in *Raptor* the falcon gets mastered in any number of ways. It gets starved like Kafka's hunger artist, reined in by jesses, sung back by lullabies at feeding time. Yet within the broader context of interspecies relations, you demonstrate quite clearly that the falconer him- or herself likewise gets mastered—by an ancient desire perhaps, by a hard-won relationship to the falcon, by an all-consuming, multifarious pedagogical pursuit. Here, could you develop further your distinction between offering a short, discrete poem and an ongoing (book-length) investigation, and how all of this relates to your concerns with avoiding certain types of lyric identification?

AFe: Well, as you would know, I'm sure, when you become involved in a book-length project, at some point you start thinking of the book as the unit. And in this particular case, because falconry metaphors remain so prevalent in so many distinct cultures, foregrounding such divergent aspects of the bird, I would finish one poem then start another as a corrective to the first. I wrote a love poem to my wife (we got married later in life) about this whole notion of the "haggard" as a hawk quite difficult to train. But I also had to address the less playful conceit of the falcon's accrued military significance. We have deployed the iconography of the falcon quite brutally. The hawk, the eagle became an essential part of Nazi regalia. And the falcon does in fact kill to eat. But human hawkishness of course remains much more lethal. So one poem concerns the Republican candidate who dressed up in SS regalia. Once I'd gained traction with the overall project, such scenarios seemed to arrive unbidden. They would fit into the whole by expanding it, correcting it. Suddenly I would discover that Dante Rossetti did this beautiful translation of a 14th-century Italian sonnet, in which the lady laments her lost love by adopting the figure of the falcon. That figure could become the pursuit of a lifetime.

AF: I also appreciate that, amid this great diversity of cultural and historical vantages, the looming threat of ecological disaster stays clear throughout—again not only the threat of disaster, but its imminent reality. As you already have said, the obvious raptors here, the agents of rapacity, are more or less exclusively human. And within that context, your own omnivorous scope quickly will shift from the testimonial to the macrocosmic. You'll refer to "the auto-da-fé we're making of our / Planet," yet remain wary of "the chthonic thrill / Of apocalyptic porn." So could we say that your virtuoso deployment of poetic forms and metaphors suggests (in part) an attempt to redirect our communal consciousness toward envisioning this present moment's mobile, amorphous threats? Here, could you situate *Raptor* (in terms of tone, structure, investigatory intent) amid a broader field of ecopoetics?

AFe: Yes. Falcons, all raptors, are enormously sophisticated machines, finely calibrated in the amount of energy they expend. This may seem slightly beside the point, but you exercise a hawk by practicing vertical jumps. You'll place the hawk on the ground before you, then hold food high above to train it to fly straight up. You do this because for a hawk to take off demands a great deal of energy, whereas soaring with outstretched wings expends little. Hawks only can take off so many times before they start starving. Deep-woods hawks, such as goshawks and accipiters, have almost no margin for error. Every little move must make sense. And these poems, with their formal symmetry, emulate that usage. I don't mean to imply that the so-called free verse poem lacks precision. I don't prioritize one mode over the other. But when I do write in form I strive for this type of balance and unification, in which the poem's intricacies parallel the raptor's place in the natural world—showcasing that bird's efficient magnificence. So certain forms seemed integral to the book. My first book had offered much free verse. After finishing it I knew I didn't want to write something similar. Still, at first, for *Raptor*, poems would come to me and seem like poems from *Citizen*. The Johnny Carson poem, with its declarative public-speaking voice, sounds like it could fit in *Citizen*. That stopped me for a while. Then gradually the qualities of this distinct bird and its coloration and how every part fits into place seemed to call forth formal poems presenting a clear, transparent structure on the page. I planned to adopt a three-part structure always unfolding and repeating itself. The book would work inward and sculpt its own bird-like shape. Later this seemed a less good idea, though I did retain remnants of that organization.

AF: I've got one last question concerning the light, idiomatic touches that continually aerate this text. References to "the Badlands' Brazil-waxed hills," or the self-implicating portrait of a socks-and-sandals fellowship of "nerdy birders," get thematized in your response to Johnny Carson's final jokes—his aphoristic elegies to/about genocide, or so they seem. Do comedy and elegy come together naturally for you?

AFe: Berryman and his comedy of horrors, and then some post-Berryman poets have had a huge impact on me. Also Frederick Seidel to some extent—another poet who emerges out of an Eliotic tradition in which the speaker is not precisely you, yet represents a zone of consciousness presumably shared by others. The comedy stays pretty black, I hope. It comes out of the grotesque. It might suggest a kind of cowardice, I suppose. We live in a time of mass extinction. Or when I wrote this book my father just had died, and I'd just had a son, yet I have to admit that this enterprise of bringing children into the world seemed of dubious morality. One does it because one really really wants to, even on a planet facing Malthusian problems. But more generally: faced with our contemporary horrors, it seemed helpful to filter the subjectivity through a speaker who remains at least somewhat aware of his own ridiculousness. Of course most poets shy away from a Carolyn Forché-like taking on of the world's sins, because who are we to do so? How could my care for individual birds compensate for the sheer fact of my being an American consumer? Any ecopoet, anybody aware…the poor, overburdened world still would be better off without you, no matter how pure your motives. So I try to depict a comedy of good intentions. That drive across the Badlands became this consumerist nightmare, this capitalist myth run amok. Still, I don't mean to suggest that poetry offers no redemptive qualities. It remains a vital act of communication. One points to the threat of even more massive extinctions, and hopes to increase awareness about the alternatives. So "redemption" might be the wrong word, but other worlds do remain possible.

### INTERVIEW WITH BHANU KAPIL
Recorded on November 1, 2012
This interview focuses on Kapil's book *Schizophrene* (Nightboat).

ANDY FITCH: You've described this edition of *Schizophrene* as a mutation of its predecessor. Could you discuss what has changed, and the motivations or circumstances behind those changes? What only can be arrived at through mutation? How does mutation-based composition facilitate and/or complicate your ongoing efforts to develop a book or sentence or narrative that "never arrives"?

BHANU KAPIL: Before you called I tried to find a copy of Schizophrene. Fittingly, I found one that is neither the first nor second edition, but a literal mutation that Lucas de Lima sent to me with a letter. Hang on. I shall open it. It says: "Enclosed is an occult copy of *Schizophrene*. Hope you don't mind me saying that I love both versions of the book. So did most students, who thought the repeated pages were intentional, as did I." Around page 19 this version repeats. Following the line "'Reverse migration...' Is psychotic," the book just starts again. But not only does it restart. It condenses and excludes some sections. Perhaps 100 similar copies have circulated. Lucas has written about it on the Montevidayo blog. Though my own emphasis upon mutation comes from the thinking of Elizabeth Grosz, as communicated to me by her protégé Andrea Spain. Andrea and I will teach a workshop on this topic next summer at Naropa. From Grosz I take the notion of non-reproductive productivity. The larger the number of generative acts that do not result in "progeny," the faster a species' outer boundaries evolve. Mating need not involve childbirth. The mutations always occur in another place, a place not visible as a boundary, but which precedes a boundary. This pre-space or activity vibrates with the limit of what that space will become. *Schizophrene*, in its notebook form, presents both an installation and a staging ground. In fact the bulk of this project does not reside in the finished book, but in many notebooks and documents that contain my research on psychosis, immigrant experience, touch.

AF: Trauma circulates throughout *Schizophrene*. How does the aesthetic or logic or working-process of mutation relate to traumatic structures of thought—those that endlessly delay, defer, yet never fully depart from overwhelming memories or experiences or scenes?

BK: I can answer your question in one word: Pakistan. This word contains within it images never seen by me, but which persisted in stories told to me. At some point I understood that the bloody fairytales my mother told at night derived from this other scene—the primal scene that opens *Schizophrene*, of the women tied to the trees. This scene did not happen at the border, though here we encounter a problem: how do you write into the space preceding conjugation, that mixture or rupture of vital forms? Because this image of the women, of their evisceration, continues to appear in a context devoid of all markers of place. The image itself repeats, in an attempt, I sometimes think, to break down, to become a part of history. In addition, this image (less an image, perhaps, than a scene) always will remain a partial one. Why? Because a family member (my mother) observed it through a hole in a cart. My family member hid beneath straw and hay, and looked through the hole. Curation here amplifies a glimpse of the body, organ life, sacrifice, to the max. The viewer cannot look away. A breach keeps happening—whether life gets given, taken, or returned to that observed body. So this circumstance evokes the trauma vortex, to read "breach" through Peter Levine's Somatic Experiencing model. To exit, one must build the counter-vortex: a capacity for pendulation, titration (the way a fragment starts to oscillate, or shake). In Schizophrene's final minutes, an ochre shard, held up to the sky, begins to stream a fire/water mixture (energy). For me, this registers an anti-clockwise movement, an initiating gesture of a new structure.

AF: Both the process-oriented nature of your mutational writing, and your reflections on the legacies of colonialism, partition, racism, track some sort of multi-generational echo, or silence. "Information," you say somewhere, can become "a grave." But as your cannibalizing of previous versions suggests, a grave need not mean the end of affect. Have you, for example, in your psychological studies, encountered the concept of trans-generational haunting, as developed by Nicolas Abraham and Mária Török? Could you describe how such haunting informs not only the content of your work, but the specific forms that it takes? And you've already suggested how mutation might accelerate and intensify processes of decay. But Schizophrene also seems to track those moments when traumatic mutation becomes a future-oriented source of growth, of life—for the individual or culture or species.

BK: Just now, in Vancouver, I met Gail Scott, and she spoke about Abraham and Török's project, about the broader exchange between experimental prose and cross-cultural psychiatry, which has happened for me through the work of Dinesh Bhugra and Kam Bhui, who consider the same (non-white European) clinical subject (the schizophrenic) as I do. Yet rather than recall Abraham and Török's structure of the crypt, Schizophrene sets a trap. I wanted to create the conditions under which I could write a subsequent book, an anti-colonial novel, *Ban*. In Schizophrene's next iteration, Ban (the figure) emerges from that vertical, triplicate space of the notebook— expelled, I sometimes think, by the force of this notebook hitting the earth. Ban embodies an orbital of soot and ash moving at high speeds around London, a body perennially orbiting, not yet born and never born and dying off before given an existence. In a way Ban already has vanished. I recently returned to some sites that appear in *Schizophrene*, to a post-social architecture, an architecture that did not retain the specific cultural memory I associate with it (as if someone had taken a spoon and scooped out bits of it and poured concrete and planted ivy in the background). The alleys I recall have been boarded up and surveilled. New immigrants have arrived: Croatian,

Romanian, Polish. This all seems normal enough. But how can you trap something no longer visible, traced as "Asian"? That world of the race riot, that place depicted in *Schizophrene*, has disappeared—overwritten by further narratives of arrival and destruction, though the question of species life remains. To return, for example, to *Schizophrene*'s emphasis on the "monster body": what if you get born in a country, yet never considered a native of that place? I needed to document this monstrous individual before she too has gone, before I have gone—the person who could write her. Already it felt strange to write the history of a surface. I wanted to write a surface that deflected a content. So I did.

AF: Well in terms of questions of the body, questions of arrival, can we pivot from mutation to questions of touch? Touch factors strongly into your own description of how this book operates. Your acknowledgments suggest the intent to create a therapeutic discourse of touch (specifically "light touch"). We can get to the mechanics of how this text touches. But less benign forms of touch also appear throughout the book. *Schizophrene* opens by suggesting that chronic, quotidian stresses of racial oppression most commonly trigger schizophrenic breakdowns—that this apparently lighter, daily contact in fact becomes the most corrosive. Then later you describe schizophrenia itself as a much more active process: "touching something lightly many times." Could you parse the conceptual reversals at play here?

BK: Yes, I feel I could have written something much more comprehensive, but wished to sustain the rhythm and value of not being touched, along with its corollary—a very light, repeated touch. I didn't want to exaggerate or appropriate modes of psychosis, yet did want to enact schizophrenia's negative symptom, anhedonia (signaled, in part, by a pulling away from touch). In addition, when considering what re-establishes the rhythm and cadence of a functional nervous system, I drew upon my own training as a bodyworker. My practice combines integrative and structural processes, with a particular focus on supporting clients as they progress through long-held traumas caught in the body as patterns of movement, breath and color (energy). As a writer working on contraction and crisis, on the history, let's say, of a particular society, I attempt to loosen something interred in the body as memory, as an image, an intensity that cannot be borne. As a bodyworker, you create a spiral that deepens a limb into the body. You amplify the site of contraction. Then through shaking, vibration, tonifying actions, you bring the limb out of its socket. You take, for example, the arm and spiral it in, all the way to the gestural root, then wait for the person to make a brief internal study of colors, images, information. Finally, after spiraling this limb back out, you lightly realign the structure or posture, pressing on the bones or stretching the fascia along a diagonal plane. Similarly, *Schizophrene*'s small patches of intensity get worked through—to an ultimate softness with a lot of space. And given trauma's chronic rhythms, I try to touch not only this reenacted originary scene, but whatever else in the body connects to it. I hope to mimic, to elicit and create something new from that rhythm, all without retraumatizing the subject, the body, the historical figure that I describe.

AF: How does this all play out for the reader? The discourse of touch I know best comes from Roland Barthes, from his reflections on the punctum—this unintended/unaccounted for prick of recognition, this coproduction of an elusive, unmotivated affect. But when your acknowledgements announced a spatiality of psychosis (again I think borrowed from Elizabeth Grosz), I began to envision, or to feel, that you deliberately had constructed a poetics of touch through choreographed shifts in perspective, syntax, idiom, sound, formatting. Those all seemed important to this poetics of touch—even font. Do these various fronts suggest where touch happens for a reader?

BK: Well when I gathered up the original discarded manuscript from my garden, with no intention to write but simply to retrieve it, I sensed too much space. I sensed too much space in the garden and in the notebook—which, eroded, had become a dirty white blocked-out smear with a few sentences here and there still visible. Those charred, stripped, oily sentences had survived a winter treatment. Something about taking each of these singular sentences (reading them, transcribing them into the next notebook) resembled the successive, calibrating touch I spoke of earlier. I recall also the left-to-right (yet rotational) eye movements that happened as I copied out the sentences, a vagal orientation or settling that happened there. One form of bodywork I have received, and received during the writing of *Schizophrene*, called "brainspotting," provokes a discharge of post-traumatic states through eye-movement therapy. The therapist's "wand" pauses at the place where your eye movements "glitch," then spirals in. Through this brain spot you let the images come, without describing these to your therapist, until you can't see them any more, until they dissipate. So this seems less a punctum, perhaps, than a glitch—a discharging of memory that does not rely upon "disclosure," as the disability activist and poet Petra Kuppers has put it.

AF: I'd love to get to individual sentences. But first I also love the garden-based creation myth that surrounds *Schizophrene*, which you've cultivated in this compelling way. In that garden, when re-confronted by the abandoned text, you describe it as a screen "repelling the ink or the touch." Later in this originary scene, you refer to a "curiously rigid" page. Again this raised questions about different types of touch that happen. As you constructed *Schizophrene*, did you conceive of the individual page as a basic unit of meaning, a point of contact for the reader? How does this instantaneous visual touch relate to the sentence's or aphorism's or prose block's durational touch? Do distinct temporalities of touch deliberately get interwoven?

BK: Perhaps some sentences do embody impact—that other kind of touch that moves closer to violence. Yet I don't think I set out to construct prose blocks from this soft-tissue language or philosophy. To put it as simply as possible: I wrote from the sentences that had persisted. These became a frame for the opening sections. Also I kept some sentences available for when a terrible pause or blanking-out occurred in my writing process. Again such sentences stayed legible and the larger work got built around them. In this sense, each fragment generated its own environment, its own span of time.

AF: Here could you discuss a bit more broadly the types of inquiry, the types of research, in which *Schizophrene*'s narrative "I" engages? I especially mean the descriptions of interstitial institutional spaces—as you cross an endless hall let's say, on your way to interview a scientist or something. You won't yet have arrived. You'll describe this state of being on your way. Do even those passages offer some abstracted form of haptic investigation, touch, contact?

BK: I have been "on my way" since early childhood, with the endless journeys from London, the layovers in the Middle East or Russia, that other kind of existence a person had in 1970s airports. Sometimes we'd visit my uncle, a civil engineer from Delhi, who worked in Baghdad. Because of a delayed flight we would camp in an airport for days. I can picture Moscow's pale blue, slanted rain through the airport glass. Or my family lived near Heathrow Airport and, as a teenager, I'd go to the airport with an empty suitcase and hang out near the flickering flight board in Terminal 4, pretending to check my flight time—glancing up, now and then, from the poetry of John Donne or Ezra Pound. Though I can say, returning to your question about chronic elements and the rhythms of these sentences: such parallels (to the lags or architectures in *Schizophrene*) did not arrive deliberately. Nor do those processes finally complement each other. They resemble each other, but not toward any fixed point.

AF: Here should we look at some individual sentences? I have the manuscript you sent a while back.

BK: I have my mutated copy of *Schizophrene*.

AF: I don't know how our pagination will differ. I've opened to page 5.

BK: I should have a page 5 in this copy. Yes.

AF: You know I think our pages can't be the same. But I can read the sentence: "And the line the book makes is an axis, a hunk of electromagnetic fur torn from the side of something still living and thrown, like a wire, threaded, a spark towards the grass." What types of touch or touches does such a sentence offer, impede, redirect? How do dynamics of touch play out here?

BK: Extracted, this sentence provides a representation of dismemberment. I had not intended it that way. Though out of context it describes a body still alive, but with its boundary membranes devastated, perhaps the image of someone being eaten. Everything I write contains this cardinal image of a woman tied to a tree with her viscera hanging out, yet still alive. This image repeats without variation, not just in the cultural war I discuss but in other wars. But you also have asked about touch. Here the sentence's commas become quite important to me. They suggest a witnessing touch. Does my own body touch them? No. I don't think so. I touch the gelatin membrane that bounds this livid scene, this scene I myself did not live through. I sense myself outside that sentence, as if I didn't write it, yet those commas allow me to maintain contact with the scene's inassimilable content.

AF: Here's a passage that likewise enacts and/or records the most fleeting of cognitive/experiential phenomena: "I walk the long way to the Tate from the Pimlico tube, a fact more intense each time I repeat it in my mind. An erotics. A mad progression that exceeds a central frame, like seeing something then falling down."

BK: Yes. How strange. I just returned to the Tate, from a different direction, reversing that walk, two weeks ago.

AF: I loved that lacuna in "seeing something then falling down"—like Rousseau as the Great Dane hits him, in his *Reveries of a Solitary Walker*. Your phrase catches this quickest of moments, yet also contains a delay. Maybe that's too vague.

BK: Returning to this sentence, or part of this sentence, I can remember what I had read at that time, Marguerite Duras' *The Ravishing of Lol Stein*, with its idea that you might collapse in the middle of a walk, like Sebald's narrator in *The Rings of Saturn*. That scene of potential collapse also hints at madness, at the rupture of a cognitive node. And I don't know how to put this in words, but I picture myself as a child, lying beside the fountain and letting it rain on me for a very, very, very long time. Or now in *Ban*, my novel, a girl lies down on the pavement during the opening minutes of a race riot. Why? Because I like to analyze the slow-motion gesture/posture/event that brings a body to the world's floor. The body's capacity to stop time's forward movement or progression interests me. When reading a narrative that deals with traumatic events, we know what time will bring. We can't stop it. Yet, as a writer, one can enact a form of social (and/or neural) delay. Perhaps, in such a moment, something else can arrive, something that could not, and did not, arrive back then.

AF: In terms of porous borders, of migrations, I appreciate how one text of yours will trace its origins back to another—for example in how you've described the anti-colonial novel *Ban* arising from the act of preparing *Schizophrene* for publication. Amid these intertextual emergences, do you wish for all of your books to touch in some way?

BK: Yes, I think so, though I also wish to write works that feel more sustained. An orange-red sunrise opens Schizophrene, as the ferry approaches the coast of Great Britain. These colors introduce gametes. Re-combined, they will become the butterfly at the close of the book, or the orange spot on the butterfly, but also the flame at the end (emitted by the clay shard). That recirculation of materials depends upon a visual, sensory decay. And this takes us back to touch. I wish to write beyond fragmentation. I wish to create an embodied work of art, with sentences resembling nerves—throbbing on the riverbank. I want to take those nerves and build a nervous system that's both visceral and vital, capable of receiving and giving touch in turn. *Schizophrene* emerges at the borderline of human and monstrous aims.

AF: Though amid its mutational composition, I do note interpersonal or relational processes shaping the book. You describe Melissa Buzzeo's *The Devastation,* for example, as "accompanying" *Schizophrene*. Can you elaborate on this mode of accompaniment? And given your generous engagement with any number of peers (in terms of blog posts, interviews, etcetera), could you provide some sense of how your work accompanies which contemporaries?

BK: Melissa works on abiogenesis, the notion of life arising from inorganic matter. She asks what it means to track such phenomena through narrative, through what happens in a sentence. Or following a society's devastation, how can it begin to love again, to touch again? How do you form a community with always at its center this kind of creaturely life? With Melissa I can discuss such topics all the time, and also with Andrea Spain, who works on anti-colonial literatures—on racism and its chronic effects. I also find broader communities quite important, such as the Bay Area community. I've learned much from their Marxist/performance art aptitudes, as well as from Amber DiPietra and the disability community, from Eleni Stecopolous and the curations connected to her Poetics of Healing. The Politics and Poetics cluster at Santa Cruz, led by Andrea Quaid (with its own connections to the avant-garde Los Angeles communities of CalArts and Les Figues) also has helped very much. The cross-conversations between queer or trans communities and disability communities have been the best conversations, because we discuss what obstructs movement, what compels it, and what allows us, again in Petra Kuppers' words, to proceed from discourse to discharge. We talk about the body, in other words. And with my own learning community at Naropa and Goddard, with my students, I incubate the books to come.

AF: Could we close with the final "'o'" that ends Schizophrene, which again seems to come from outside this project, binding it to other texts and to the world?

BK: Yes, that "'o'" comes from a scene in *Humanimal*. I became obsessed with the mouth—the moment at which the wolf-girl's hair, as she flees, gets caught by a dominating hand, and her mouth (its soft tissue, lips and teeth) opens to an "o." That's what I hear and see at the end of *Schizophrene*. I hear a wolf's howl.

## INTERVIEW WITH RACHEL BLAU DUPLESSIS
Recorded on November 9, 2012
This interview focuses on Blau DuPlessis' book *Purple Passages: Pound, Eliot, Zukofsky, Olson, Creeley, and the Ends of Patriarchal Poetry* (University of Iowa Press).

ANDY FITCH: The phrase "patriarchal poetics" makes me picture an exclusionary male coterie, perhaps with Charles Olson calling out "There it is, brothers." And I can infer how analogous group-formation dynamics arise in relation to racist, heterosexist or anti-Semitic constructs. But your examination of patriarchal poetics suggests that even those individuals who try to escape this constrictive model often end up demonstrating just how elastic, amorphous, almost irresistible its discourse is—say in the "imperial" rhetorical gestures that you describe certain liberatory poets making. Could you start to sketch the parameters of a patriarchal poetics by contextualizing these imperial deployments of multiple gender identity?

RACHEL BLAU DUPLESSIS: Here's the issue: when you first read Stein's little essay-poem "Patriarchal Poetry," you sense she has a conflicted (though that sounds too negative) attitude toward this topic. Noting this, I found it satisfying to observe that I, too, have a conflicted attitude. The word "patriarchal" picked up entirely negative connotations during second-wave feminism. It evoked, as you've described, an exclusive male coterie saturated with sexism and misogyny. Yet a more generalized usage of "patriarchy" remains quite tempting to Stein, since it suggests a type of totalizing discourse. Its "imperial" manifestation demonstrates that some poets' subjectivity can reach any position in the sex-gender system. This provides an effective rhetorical strategy many men have deployed. They often possess the social capacity to shift among a variety of gender stances, all under a general rubric of maleness. Of course certain stances do get coded as queer, as fem, aggressive, then passive aggressive. But more generally I argue that because of male social power, male poets have had this capacity for an imperial appropriation and accumulation of wide-ranging subject-positions. The corresponding fact of women's diminished social power precludes them, in general, from acquiring this capacity to deploy and inhabit and grab whatever subject-position they desire. And yes, women do have their own great range of female-oriented subject-positions. Though as soon as a woman reaches for male subject-positions, she often gets slapped down. Again yes, there always have been transgressive women who dress in tuxedos and so forth. But in general, male figures have the capacity to range and appropriate many more subject-positions, including those that contradict each other. This gesture I call "patriarchal," and men often get praised for it. Critics consider it a positive. Male poets struggle to retain such possibilities. You see that in the relationship between Pound and Zukofsky. Both want imperial authority, and Pound keeps slapping down Zukofsky because Pound thinks only one poet at a time can have it. Here we return to the more rigid feminist definition of patriarchy as a problematic form of dominance and exclusion. Yet my book adopts an ambivalent approach to patriarchy—noting both its oppressive and its liberatory capacities.

AF: Contradiction here seems essential in several ways. The privilege to inhabit (on an aesthetic level) these myriad subject-positions often depends upon not facing the real-life social/historical constraints and suffering that such positions bring with them.

RBD: Correct. Men might inhabit these positions in their image repertoire, in their poetic work, perhaps to some degree in their social relations. But the privilege of adopting such roles with glee and getting praised for it remains the exclusive property of select male figures. Because even the most adventuresome, avant-garde women historically have encountered strict social limits, both in their literary and lived experience. I should make a teeny star and footnote gay male experience, insofar as that it has, over the period I discuss, remained less acceptable, more maligned—though fascinating to straight men. Of course as the social positions of gay people change, so does this dynamic.

AF: Could we discuss the limitations specific female poets have faced when assembling an equivalent imperial project? Here I think of Stein's *The Making of Americans,* and its attempt at representing totality through a sweeping syntax as much as any cumulative plot or character; or of Eileen Myles adopting novelistic forms, probing queer desire as a means of accessing a more expansive first-person subjectivity; or Alice Notley developing an epic scope and scale in works like *The Descent of Alette*.

RBD: Anne Waldman also fits well on your list. But Stein still seems the exception. Stein did not identify as a woman exactly. She considered herself a genius. Genius became her chosen sexual and gender subject-position. But I agree that, apart from Stein, most female poets attempting to access this positive patriarchal power have done so in our contemporary period. This comes directly from the benefits of the woman's movement I would say, along with changes in gay status, lesbian status. Though that argument does make me a bit queasy, since one always can produce exceptions. H.D. comes to mind (again for trying to inhabit all available perspectives), but Woolf not really, Moore not really, Loy not really. Even H.D. generally does not inhabit the male subject-position, whereas Stein clearly does. Here I'm mostly not referring to sexuality or sexual practices. In many ways, one never really knows other people's sexuality, even a contemporary's, so that doesn't motivate my project. But H.D. idealized certain male figures, perhaps because they provided that part of her she did not seek to inhabit.

AF: We've discussed the imperial gesture as an imaginative act on the part of male poets who don't face certain social constraints. But beyond that imaginative act, do the material and relational conditions of literary production (which disciplines or idioms you can access, what types of books you can put out, how a given culture might receive them based on how it perceives you) likewise amplify or reinforce one's authorial identity within a patriarchal discourse?

RBD: It does demand an imaginative act, yet one, as you say, that takes place and produces consequences in the real world. And women writers still do face a somewhat marginalized position in terms of literary production, reception, dissemination. That specific social difference still remains. Women don't necessarily write any differently. Anybody can adopt his or her own particular style, his or her particular vantage on inherited conventions. But the conditions of literary production move at a different pace. We could develop many explanations, for example, why John Wieners ends up writing the Olsonic "Curriculum of the Soul" pamphlet called *Woman* (or *Women*, depending on the version). Perhaps the publishers found this juxtaposition intriguing. Perhaps no woman wanted that ghettoizing assignment—ghettoizing at the time. Perhaps it just didn't occur to anyone to ask a woman. And here Wieners' own qualifications depend upon his interest in drag. So yet again, in multiple respects, one encounters the familiar canard that the best woman for the job is always a man.

AF: Pound and Olson stand out as the most problematic cases in your book, since both articulate their desire for a liberated gender regime, then directly marginalize the poetic contributions and social status of their female peers. Yet here, as elsewhere, you adopt a neutral, descriptive tone. *Purple Passages* doesn't seek to examine why such contradictions took place, so much as to assert that they did take place, that they didn't have to, and that we now live with their legacy. Still many "why" questions came up for me. First, could you begin to describe Pound's situation—how he mostly gets it right in his editing of *The Waste Land,* though then so clearly gets it wrong with Mina Loy?

RBD: For me, the most fascinating discovery writing the book came from this notion of choice, of existential and social choice amid constrictive gender norms. A regime of absolute gender binaries provides little freedom of choice. But modernity suggested this all could change. People could choose among a wide array of perspectives—unless one considers men hardwired to be sexist, which I do not and never have believed, not even in 1968 or whatever. People made choices: intellectual, relational, emotional, aesthetic and so on, continuously. So I propose that both Pound and Olson drive toward a choice that would proclaim, make women coequal with men. Then they turn the car. They just veer right off and you can see it happening. You see Pound kind of wobble. Pound remains quite opportunistic straight through his embrace of Italian fascism. He tries to play all the angles. And of course some men sense a great benefit in women's sexual liberation (you can see this in the 1960s also). Still Pound places himself among a cohort of brilliant women. He takes great interest in them. He gives them some credit, some airtime. Yet he never quite acknowledges their originality. This pattern gets epitomized by the disparities between Pound's editing of *The Waste Land* and his editing of Mina Loy's "The Effectual Marriage," which happens during the exact same period. Here Pound could help construct a gender-wavering *Waste Land*—a kind of androgynous, messy, queer, everybody-not-quite-real ghostly sexuality, and could claim it as a masculine subject-position. Cutting out the poem's most raunchy or jolly parts, as Pound does, allows for that to happen. Though then with Loy's poem Pound basically operates as a gleaner. He was a quick study, Pound was. He saw it and knew it was new. Then he used the elements (authorial persona doubling as narrator, serial form, framing structure), I would say, to even better effect than Loy. Yet he gave her no credit for this. Again the problem doesn't derive from him deploying her strategies (steal away—that's my position). But she doesn't have the right to get credited, and lacks the equal right to steal back. She wrote "The Effectual Marriage" while making lampshades. She led a different life than the person determined to become a great poet. You could say she let the ball drop, if you were so inclined. Or, to cite O'Hara: "oh Lana Turner we love you get up."

AF: Though this goes back to conditions of production, too.

RBD: Right. But so Pound edits, apparently with absolute authority, Eliot, who then trumps him by inserting the Notes section—which adds this authoritative presence really to the body of the poem. This unexpected insertion establishes a new power position between Eliot and Pound, one that never again will change. At the same time, Pound appropriates somebody's whole mechanism for a self-conscious poetics yet never, never says, I got all of this (or even some of this) from Mina Loy.

AF: Here I'd love to address some similarities in Olson's relation to Frances Boldereff, but I also have a more general question. I hope we can get to the parallels you see between the growth of an individual, the choices an individual makes, and then broader social developments—how we have in our heads this (perhaps reductive, as your own examples suggest) model for a neat trajectory of personal growth, then often apply this model to the conflictual, back-and-forth, hesitant nature of discursive social change. I'll want to ask about your use of individual scenes or narratives to dramatize these bigger historical contexts.

RBD: Well all of these poets struggle to make their work. That remains clear throughout. They undergo immense struggles to complete certain poems, to explore territories that fascinate them. So I don't mean to scold Olson. What's done is done. But the broader implications, as you say, still demand attention—how a sex/gender system comes into view and gets articulated by the choices these individuals make around literary productivity. And almost every project I discuss becomes a powerful and important text for the rest of the 20th century, producing consequential perspectives on sex, gender, society, poetry. Yet here I sense a strong contrast between my position and that of, say, Sandra Gilbert and Susan Gubar. You can see this through our different treatments of Fresca in *The Waste Land*. They make a tremendous amount out of the fact that Eliot wrote this somewhat nasty, amused and amusing satire of a bluestocking woman. Eliot deliberately dispenses corny clichés and remains invested in them at the same time. Eliot's opinions do "suck," as the kids might say, but his piece offers some fantastic writing. Then Pound cuts it, and Eliot concurs. No evidence suggests that Eliot went back on Pound's cuts. He famously expresses his gratitude for them. Yet Gilbert and Gubar assess *The Waste Land* as if it still contained the Fresca material. They act as if the published, canonized poem retains these tonalities—and suggest that we should consider this scandalous. Whereas I, after acknowledging the importance of examining Eliot's manuscript, treat it more as a shadow text. You can't ignore it once you've read it. It does color your opinions. You sense in Eliot's satiric mode that awe and fear of women from his early poetry, which does carry over into *After Strange Gods* and which he tries to ease by his career's end. Still my point is you have to read the evidence, yet this doesn't place you inevitably in the position of deploring. *Purple Passages* makes clear that I dislike or disagree with certain choices made in certain instances. Though there they are. We should study them, but not repeat them.

AF: Here perhaps we could discuss your own polyvalent relation to some of this work. In regard to Beat poetry, for example, you state that a conflicted or reactionary gender discourse still can inspire feminist responses. You assert that "tropes are never transhistorical," that even the most misogynistic text will encounter an autonomous audience, one who can read it in unpredictable, non-determinist, potentially liberating ways. Along these lines, could you characterize your own personal relationship to the poets addressed in this book? Have they to some extent prompted this particular response—in spite of their sexist, hypocritical, opportunistic tendencies and decisions? Have you recognized a fraught, yet liberatory potential in their poetics, and tried to redirect this to more constructive ends? Does such a revaluative critical approach allow for its own imperial project?

RBD: Yes, indeed. It goes something like this, to speak just personally about a few texts from the book. Certainly Eliot remains crucial. *The Waste Land* never has gone out of fashion for me. Pound too has been extremely important, and later, in a parallel way, Zukofsky. Their long poems could epitomize the imperial gesture, though women stay off the screen for the most part. You'll encounter a name here and there, but no co-equal gender norms appear in these poems, period. That's a big lacuna. Still both fascinating poets present projects of great obscurity, here producing an implicit, exigent demand to study and to saturate yourself as reader in their world (which thereby becomes magnetic and quite hard to abandon). And then to get to the Olson parallel: very few women appear in *The Maximus Poems*, which seems astonishing, considering his historical claim to reconstruct Gloucester. If you decide to celebrate ship-building and fishing's dangers and the brilliant navigational skills of these men, you also might want to describe the back country—the farms and small businesses women ran while the men stayed at sea for a year at a time. Both realms had economic necessity, but Olson couldn't care less. I find it almost comical. I've said before that in Olson's corpus women are mythic, whereas men are historical and mythic. Women receive no such historical credibility. They get shifted into the mythic register almost instantly. By contrast Creeley stands out as a very, very important figure for me, because of his (late, certainly uneven) attempt to think complex relational thoughts through poetry, through line and diction and a vernacular voice. Here I refer to his texts, not his life. Of course Loy remains quite important also, even in what we would have to call a somewhat aborted career. She's a savvy, acidic poet who goes for the jugular. I appreciate that model.

AF: So again, one central purpose of *Purple Passages* seems to involve foregoing a dismissive account of these patriarchal figures, and claiming your own ambivalent engagement with them as a productive one.

RBD: Absolutely. And beyond my personal experience, I mean to construct a quite polemical book in some ways, emphasizing the fundamental point that women want to be coequal and coeval. By coeval, I really mean cotemporal. We don't inhabit some other, ahistorical, mythic time. We shape real time, real society, real history. This book basically articulates a form of liberal feminism. It says, coequality and cotemporality are what I require of a culture for women and for men.

AF: You occasionally cite the gender critiques posed by a subsequent generation of male poets—figures such as Bob Perelman, Michael Davidson, Barrett Watten, Charles Bernstein. Have these poet-critics addressed analogous gender dynamics in a more competent, proactive, inclusive fashion?

RBD: In certain works, definitely. And again, I'm not here to judge their personal affects and attitudes. Bob Perelman stays quite aware of these gender conflicts throughout his book on Pound, even if his scholarly focus often lies elsewhere. But with Davidson, Watten, Bernstein—these poets have taken clear critical stances, regarding gendered discourse, that I cite and praise (I also praise women who write on maleness, including Libbie Rifkin, Colleen Lamos). This book does not address what those particular male poets have done in their own poetry. That would make for a very different project. Barrett Watten has offered his own critique of *Legend*, presenting it as an amazing work from the point of view of male bonding and male jouissance, which seems about right. Women have no place in it, and that big lack does produce a question mark. Barrett sees this and states it quite clearly.

AF: And more generally: after sifting through numerous ways in which self-described progressive poetic communities continually have reinforced certain retrograde tendencies, can you share any insights regarding forms of self-oblivion among progressive poetic practices in our own present?

RBD: Self-oblivion does remain quite tricky. It's hard to enact the attitudes you espouse. The seductions of male privilege do remain quite strong. And this book does ask something of male figures, which is to understand this sexual mechanism, to recognize more positive depictions of women, to help produce these both on a personal and social level. No one act, one poem, one critical article, one book can do the job. We need a much broader shift—with all its unspecified, unintended consequences to our literary culture. We have not gone the whole distance, even if certain men have done a good job articulating alternative positions.

AF: Along similar lines, what does this book ask of contemporary scholarship—especially, again, in terms of your self-consciously "analytic, invested, affectual" methods?

RBD: Well, it does ask the critic to wear her heart on her sleeve a bit more. It does ask, what are the stakes for the writer (poet and/or scholar) in any particular literary act? Right now, as I write on Duncan's *H.D. Book*, his notion of criticism seems quite drastic, and probably not for everybody. It deprofessionalizes the scholarly by transforming literary criticism into the personally invested, high-toned, all-encompassing essay. I doubt that the professional field of literary criticism can or would move this way. But it does suggest that critics should show their investments more, just as poet-critics continually need to refine their scholarly sense. Back in the days when I wrote *The Pink Guitar* people would say, oh I wish I could write this way; I'm going to start writing this way. And I'd think, uh-oh. Because you have to know what you're talking about and not fuck up the evidence. You can't distort as you see fit. You need to embrace the ethics of the scholar (in fact, *The Pink Guitar* underestimates what Dora Marsden ventured in shifting from *Freewoman/New Freewoman* to *The Egoist*—I didn't understand her investment in what we now might call "post-feminism.") And here, with *Purple Passages*, I only wish I'd written a longer book. The way presses operate these days, your book has to stay so focused. That why, when people come to me for advice I say, a book is about something; it's not about everything. And this particular book is about something, not everything. People will ask, did you include Oppen? No. How about Duncan? Only as a little codicil. Did you treat gay male poets? Should Ashbery factor into the book, etcetera. But many, many concerns did not make it into this book. That's too bad, let's say. Yet a kind of unity exists in the network of topics I do address. And the tonal shifts from *The Pink Guitar* to *Blue Studios* to *Purple Passages* do suggest a series for me. I hope to have made clear that *The Pink Guitar* operates most like an essay, *Blue Studios* inhabits a (tonal) middle space, then *Purple Passages* required more concentrated scholarly correlations—such as comparing Pound's "revisions" both of Eliot and Loy, treating them in the same essay like that. This book doesn't present a free-form collage sensibility, aside from the codas I put in. I don't insert mini-poems into the text. So it seems a bit different along my color spectrum. That's just the way it happened, so to speak. It turned out that way. That's what I would say.

# AFTERWORD BY AMARANTH BORSUK

ANDY FITCH: Can we start with ~~you characterizing~~
 your personal trajectory , which, ~~as far as I under=
stand~~, begins in poetry before moving to hybrid
 prose— leads into ~~more~~ expansive

fiction? Does a return to
 phrase-making and/or breath-taking
 project from an earlier, "po-
etic" phase ? Also, if
I'm wrong ,
please save me. And also:
 bird-flu

AF: I couldn't tell, the
 work,
 "through which I push
and can't get through" , seemed coded
 what I'm saying is:
 perpendicular pivots ~~can~~
get traced by prose's precisely demarcated punctuation.
 to allow for a foggier drift
~~across~~ through places and times?

AF: So is drifting away the experiment of
 loosening
up to what's not ~~necessarily~~ ur-
gent—like domestic life
 ?

A : You seem concerned with
 this book's hyper-elliptical
 structure? If it is help-
ful ~~to get more specific,~~ "iron...
in air " offers perhaps the most wide-open space in the book.
Even in prose, blank space
 types ( thinking, experience)
 into the
 interstitial undertext ?

---
507

# SIXTY MORNING TALKS

AF: ~~I'm curious, but~~ feel no need to know, what processes of compression shaped this text. But I especially love "came out the ground wet," reminiscent of ~~maybe~~ magic. So, did you know you wanted to start extensive excavation? And great blank Cassavetes films with silent opening credits?

A : Short, deft lines often fuse shifting and contradictory perspectives , "I" exchanges roles on the threshold of sleep. On the next page, Ought we to stall or fail Or, given your interest in mutually-exclusive propositions , at least, ? Is this how math departs from draft? Do questions demarcate difference? clipped idiom and syntax al- low divergent strands ?

AF: Two motifs ~~that~~ come up in your book: shredding and mess. these tropes hint at ~~processes of~~ collage, stitchery, assemblage employed both by poet and bird a nest of scraps I pictured a bird thinking: "Damn. Another mess." Is unraveling a strength ~~or threat~~ in your work ?

A : Again, embodiment seems important your reductive tracking ~~of~~ ~~ten~~ involves

508

*Afterword by Amaranth Borsuk*

attention to "the problem of edge," and ~~any number of~~ modes of interface: the glance, the nap. Near book's end, this current shades into intimation, perhaps more lyric to move a plot along?

AF: And yet
 I'm thinking of the lines "unreadable light of a reading light ." What can we see, ~~what~~ can we learn, by unreading ?

A : Sorry, but I'm curious
how you could redefine nonfiction on your own terms, allowing ~~for~~ dramatic compression, collage, impersonation, rumination, blankness, embellishment, contradiction, ~~all~~ amid meticulous attention to ~~the~~ line — Perhaps it makes most sense to question : what prompts your ongoing allegiance to ~~this~~ form?

# INDEX OF INTERVIEWEES

Cynthia Arrieu-King, 196
Eric Baus, 29
Dan Beachy-Quick, 346
Rachel Blau DuPlessis, 497
Amaranth Borsuk, 11
Brandon Brown, 252
Julie Carr, 241
Heather Christle, 387
Shanna Compton, 368
Joel Craig, 97
Thom Donovan, 337
Andrew Feld, 481
Forrest Gander, 223
Rob Halpern, 308
Jen Hofer, 214
Cathy Park Hong, 286
Bhanu Kapil, 488
Sophia Kartsonis, 196
John Kinsella, 223
Wayne Koestenbaum, 356
Dorothea Lasky, 270
Tan Lin, 406
Stephen Motika, 316
Amanda Nadelberg, 154
Hoa Nguyen, 114
Travis Ortiz, 435
Danielle Pafunda, 38
Caryl Pagel, 146
Emily Pettit, 140
Vanessa Place, 233
Srikanth Reddy, 132
Evelyn Reilly, 442
Andrea Rexilius, 58
Frances Richard, 376

Lisa Robertson, 328
Chris Schmidt, 19
Zachary Schomburg, 262
Leonard Schwartz, 161
Lytle Shaw, 169
Brandon Shimoda, 104
Evie Shockley, 455
Eleni Sikelianos, 448
Dale Smith, 122
Rod Smith, 473
Juliana Spahr, 294
Brian Kim Stefans, 277
Gary Sullivan, 206
Cole Swensen, 427, 473
Catherine Taylor, 49
Daniel Tiffany, 180
Mónica de la Torre, 396
Nick Twemlow, 188
Chris Vitiello, 87
Dana Ward, 302
Laura Wetherington, 73
Tyrone Williams, 465
Ronaldo Wilson, 415
Matvei Yankelevich, 64
Jenny Zhang, 80